THE COMPLETE GUIDE TO
CAPITAL MARKETS
FOR QUANTITATIVE
PROFESSIONALS

The Complete Arbitrage Deskbook by Stephane Reverre

Quantitative Business Valuation by Jay Abrams

Applied Equity Analysis by James English

Exchange Rate Determination by Michael Rosenberg

Dynamic Portfolio Theory and Management by Richard Oberuc

Building Financial Models by John Tjia

Modeling Financial Markets by Benjamin Van Vliet and Robert Hendry

The Handbook of Business Valuation and Intellectual Property Analysis by Robert Reilly and Robert Schweihs

Hedging Instruments and Risk Management by Patrick Cusatis and Martin Thomas

Pricing Derivatives by Ambar Sengupta

The Treasury Bond Basis, 3/e, by Galen Burghardt, Terry Belton, Morton Lane, and John Papa

Stock Valuation by Scott Hoover

Quantitative Equity Portfolio Management by Ludwig Chincarini and Daehwan Kim

THE COMPLETE GUIDE TO
CAPITAL MARKETS
for QUANTITATIVE
PROFESSIONALS

ALEX KUZNETSOV

McGraw-Hill

New York Chicago San Francisco Lisbon London Madrid
Mexico City Milan New Delhi San Juan Seoul
Singapore Sydney Toronto

4 5 6 7 8 9 0   DOC/DOC   1 5 4 3 2 1

ISBN-13: 978-0-07-146829-9
ISBN-10:   0-07-146829-3

McGraw-Hill books are available at special quantity discounts to use as premiums and sales promotions, or for use in corporate training programs. For more information, please write to the Director of Special Sales, Professional Publishing, McGraw-Hill, Two Penn Plaza, New York, NY 10121-2298. Or contact your local bookstore.

Library of Congress Cataloging-in-Publication Data

Kuznetsov, Alex.
    The complete guide to capital markets for quantitative professionals / by Alex
    Kuznetsov.
        p.   cm.
    Includes index.
    ISBN 0-07-146829-3 (hardcover : alk. paper) 1. Capital market.   2. Investment
    analysis.   I. Title.
    HG4523.k89   2006
    332'.041—dc22

                                                                                    2006015514

To my father

CONTENTS

ACKNOWLEDGMENTS   xi

INTRODUCTION   xiii

PART 1

THE FINANCIAL INDUSTRY

Chapter 1
Financial Markets 3

Chapter 2
Market Participants 23

Chapter 3
Financial Firms and Their People 43

PART 2

MARKETS

Chapter 4
Markets and the Economy 67

Chapter 5
The U.S. Treasury Market 97

Chapter 6
Equity Markets 151

Chapter 7
Financial Futures 193

Chapter 8
Interest-Rate Swaps 235

Chapter 9
Options Markets 263

Chapter 10
Mortgages and Agencies 293

Chapter 11
Credit Markets 321

PART 3
TECHNOLOGY AREAS

Chapter 12
Reference Data 341

Chapter 13
Financial Analytics and Modeling 353

Chapter 14
Market Data 375

Chapter 15
Trading Systems 395

Chapter 16
Risk Management 423

Chapter 17
Research and Strategy 441

PART 4
TECHNOLOGY PRACTICES

Chapter 18
Production Cycle 463

Chapter 19
Development Cycle 481

Chapter 20
Production Support and Problem Management 495

Conclusions 513

Recommended Reading 521

Index 543

ACKNOWLEDGMENTS

Many people have contributed to the creation of this book, and first I want to acknowledge the role of my wife, Olga, who (despite a healthy skepticism about this project) graciously put up with the inconvenience of having a writer around the house and provided that writer with invaluable moral support and much else besides. I had been vaguely thinking about writing a book like this one for quite some time, and it was Carl Carrie who tricked me into assuming that it would not be that hard to actually go ahead and do it—now that all this work is behind me, I can be properly grateful to him. At a very early stage of this project, Andrew Gelsey provided some much-needed encouragement.

This work would never have been completed without support and understanding from the people who were my managers in my daytime jobs, Min Gao and Vlad Shpilsky. People who attended my "Business Knowledge" seminars at Barclays have helped me greatly in understanding the needs of my target audience; I am grateful to all of them, but especially to Sonia Saldanha and Xuan Pan, who were always there for me. Jesse Goodman, Dave Puchyr, and Victor Zhurakhinsky reviewed the early drafts of this book and had some interesting ideas that I tried to incorporate.

Among the people who have seen and commented on the manuscript as it evolved toward completion, I want to acknowledge Nick Young, Alex Popelyukhin, Min Gao, Jesse Goodman, Marlene Green, Jon Jonsson, Sergei Shmulyian, and Lev Selector. Last but not least, I am grateful to Lisa O'Connor and Stephen Isaacs, my editors at McGraw-Hill, who were instrumental in shaping the book and provided an important steadying influence throughout the publication process.

Wall Street is always in the news—open a newspaper and you will read about bankers, deal makers, traders, CEOs, and other business folk who define the financial industry in the popular mind. The following Wall Street statistics, however, you will never hear on CNBC: between one-quarter and one-third of the total headcount at a typical Wall Street firm today are computer programmers, engineers, physicists, and other "hard scientists"— the group to which I proudly belong. Our quantitative skills and technical expertise are major drivers of Wall Street's success, but few people outside the industry (and, frankly, not many of those inside) have a clear idea of what kind of work we do so far away from our academic home. This book offers an inside perspective on this subject; it describes what technical professionals do on Wall Street, and it attempts to address the common educational and cultural challenges that we face. Any book about Wall Street almost has to be about making money, and I can claim that this book is no different: it describes how people with technical backgrounds make money on Wall Street the old-fashioned way—by working there.

Over the last two decades, Wall Street has become one of the most technologically intensive industries on the planet. It now spends tens of billions of dollars on technology every year, much of it on compensation for its technical workforce. This technological revolution was both accompanied and driven by a great migration of technical professionals from more traditional occupations in academia, research, the defense and aerospace sector, and the like to the greener pastures of the securities industry. I made this journey in the 1990s, together with a great many of my physicist colleagues. It has been quite a ride: challenging, fascinating, rewarding, and frustrating all at the same time. Looking back, I realize how similar our experiences have been, and how much stress and frustration we would have avoided if we could have, back then, read the book that you are now holding in your hands.

The paradox of quants on Wall Street is that while most of us are doing pretty well and enjoy intellectually (and otherwise) rewarding careers here, on a deeper level we as a group continue to have a hard time adapting to financial industry realities. Almost nothing in the typical educational path of a hard sciences major prepares you for the decidedly nonacademic environment of a Wall Street firm. Usually it takes years for new arrivals from the groves of academe to figure out how the business they are working with is organized, how it makes money, and what role it plays in the larger industrywide scheme of things, not to mention lesser but still important things such as terminology.

When I started thinking of writing this book, I often recalled an episode back in early 2000 when I first found myself sitting at a computer terminal at the Treasury desk at Goldman Sachs, where I was supposed to be monitoring our electronic market-making program. Almost immediately, I was confronted by a very agitated trader who blurted out something like: "We are showing May 07s at buck plus but they are two and a quarter bid in Garban swap box and I got lifted twice for five; we have to do something about it now!" I don't remember exactly what he said, but I will never forget the feeling that no matter how I parsed that sentence, it did not make the slightest bit of sense to me. To cut through the Treasury market jargon (which, a week later, I was easily able to do, and so will you be when you are about halfway through this book), he was losing $10,000 every time someone took advantage of a malfunction in our program, and he understandably wanted this to stop. Little did he know that for me at the time, the only useful information content in his speech was his tone of voice.

The problem was resolved 10 very stressful minutes and some $30,000 later, but I still wonder why for heaven's sake someone had not explained these (very simple) things to me ahead of time. Over the years I had dozens of similar encounters, perhaps less frustrating but sharing the same central feature: the people around you, who often critically depend on your ability to do your job, assume that you know certain basic things about what is going on, while in fact you have no idea of those basic things until they literally hit you in the face.

For a long time I wondered why no effort is made to provide some alternatives to these painful experiences, such as actually training me and my colleagues for the jobs we are called upon to perform. Ultimately, I realized that this is part of the Wall Street culture: we are expected to either be born with the knowledge of whatever is required to do our job here, or be smart enough to figure it out quickly. People who survive here are smart enough, but the learning curve is steep and often downright exasperating. I strongly feel that it does not have to be that way. If Wall Street will not train us for our jobs here, we have to do it ourselves. Hence this book.

THE BOOK'S TARGET AUDIENCE

The purpose of this book is to help people with scientific and technical backgrounds make sense of the financial industry as a workplace. The main target audience for the book is the community of technical professionals that are already working in the financial industry. The book aims to give these

people the kind of practical road map to industry realities that they need to
have if they are to do their jobs, but that is almost never provided by their
employers. Most people in this group have a good grasp of one or more business and technology areas in which they are directly involved, and usually
know bits and pieces about other areas, but very few feel that they have
a comprehensive view of what is going on around them. This book offers a
realistic and perhaps even entertaining way to change that.

The book is also addressed to those who are considering joining the
financial industry in a technical role. This group includes college graduates
majoring in computer science, engineering (including financial engineering), and the hard sciences, as well as technical professionals working in
other industries and academia. One of the main ambitions of this book is to
be able to transform a member of this second group (let us say a bright MIT
graduate) into a useful member of the financial technology community by
teaching her the ropes of this occupation in a way that respects her intelligence but recognizes her lack of business knowledge. If you belong to this
group, you will find here a useful guide to financial industry institutions,
practices, and job roles; a reasonably detailed description of various financial markets; and an overview of the main technology areas in a typical
Wall Street firm. Aside from this practical information, the book should
give you a fairly realistic idea of what it would be like to work here.

Last but not the least, I believe this book can be very useful for traders,
salespeople, and business unit managers who want to improve the quality
of their interaction with the technology areas. This interaction is often fraught
with frustration stemming from a large and growing communication gap
between the "business side" and the "technology side" of most Wall Street
institutions. Communication gap is a charitable way of describing the all-
too-common situation in which the technical people do not understand what
the business is trying to do with technology, while the businesspeople have
no idea of what the technology people have to go through to implement their
requests. The overview of technical areas, problems, solutions, and challenges contained in this book will help businesspeople understand the complexity of the technical issues faced by financial industry firms and will make
them more educated consumers of technology.

Before proceeding further, I want to state up front what this book is
not. It is not a book about pricing options or about interest-rate models.
There is a vast literature on these subjects, much of it directed at the same
target audience. I read many of these often excellent books when I was in
the process of switching from academia to Wall Street, and so did many

of my current colleagues. As a result, we all came here worrying about how
we would have to divide our time between pricing options and building term
structure models. These worries were misplaced: Wall Street offers plenty
of other intellectually challenging areas for the quantitatively inclined.

I was never able to fully understand why derivatives pricing receives
such a disproportionate amount of attention in the trade literature, but I
do understand that the world does not need yet another book about options
pricing. I will discuss options and derivatives, as well as term structure
models, in the appropriate places in the book; however, I will not delve into
the quantitative details. The workplace reality is that you will almost never
have to derive or even know the details of financial analytics; most of the
time you will simply call a function from a library or an Excel add-in. The
book will give you enough information to get a qualitative feel for how and
why, say, option prices depend on volatility or bond yields depend on coupon,
but for all further details, you will be referred to other books. I expect my
readers to be fairly proficient in math and computer science, so the presentation of quantitative and technical issues will be at a correspondingly high
level. The book does not require prior knowledge of financial analytics
(although it clearly would not hurt), but neither does it offer much in the
way of such knowledge. Instead, it aims to cover practical issues that are
left out of most financial analytics books.

ORGANIZATION OF THE BOOK

The book is organized into four parts. Of these, the first two can be seen
as a remedial course on the business side of Wall Street, specifically designed
for people whose educational background is in science or technology. Part
1, "The Financial Industry," provides a practical overview of financial markets and their institutions and explains what people inside Wall Street firms
actually do. The first chapter is a brief introduction to the role of the financial markets in society, different types of markets, their purpose, and their
history. The second chapter describes the main institutional players in the
financial markets and their business models, while the third and final chapter of this part of the book is devoted to the internal organization of these
various financial institutions from both a business perspective and a technology perspective, with particular emphasis on the different job roles that
technical professionals can perform within those institutions.

Part 2, "Markets," is intended to provide some hands-on understanding of how the main financial markets operate. Its opening chapter describes

how capital markets are related to the larger economy and discusses their main economic drivers, the role of the Fed and inflation in shaping the yield curves, and the market response to economic news announcements. The next chapter uses the U.S. Treasury market as a platform for introducing and explaining a number of issues that are in fact common to many other financial markets: issuance of securities, trading in the secondary market, market making and proprietary trading, and the concepts of risk and profit-and-loss measures. These concepts are then reinforced in the next chapter, on the equities markets. The chapter after that explains the futures markets in preparation for a discussion of interest-rate derivatives, which is presented next. After this we discuss options markets, and the last two chapters in this part of the book cover the remainder of the fixed-income universe by focusing on mortgages and then credit markets. Money markets, foreign exchange markets, and commodity markets were left out for lack of space (and author's knowledge), for which I apologize.

I also apologize for the fact that this part of the book turned out to be much more U.S.-centric than I had originally planned, again partly because my experience has mostly been in the United States, and partly because of the already considerable heft of the book as it stands right now. I can only hope that this book may inspire some of my European or Asian colleagues to write something similar, but focused on their part of the world. Despite this lack of geographical balance, I believe that the book will still be very useful to those in other countries who have an interest in financial technology, since so much of it is completely global in nature.

The goal of these first two parts of the book is to give technically inclined readers enough knowledge of the business issues faced by Wall Street to be able to see the related technological challenges. In fact, almost every chapter in the first half of the book concludes with a section outlining the technological problems and issues raised by the business needs of the market or markets discussed in that chapter. However, we start tackling these technical issues in earnest only in Part 3, which is called "Technology Areas." This part emphasizes the commonality between the technology organizations of every Wall Street firm—they are trying to solve the same business problems, and therefore they come up with very similar organizational solutions. So regardless of what they are called internally, every bank will have organizational units dealing with product databases, market data, financial analytics, and firmwide risk. There is typically more variability in the trading systems area, which is often subdivided into systems dealing with pricing, execution, and risk, but that does not change the big picture.

The chapters in this part of the book deal with each of these areas by describing their *raisons d'être*, common technical and quantitative issues, and their role in the business organization, while pointing out the links to various market realities described in the first half of the book. Many of you will notice that this section is somewhat biased toward the front office, reflecting my personal experience. Also, I should mention that most of the technology is described from the perspective of a dealer firm. There is really no other way to do it, as the technology organizations of other market players are in almost all cases either scaled-down versions or subsets of those of the broker-dealers.

The final part of the book, "Technology Practices," complements the preceding part by focusing on how these technology units operate. We discuss the production cycle, the development cycle, software quality issues and approaches to quality assurance, the challenges of global technology systems, and, very importantly, production support and problem management. In my experience, many new arrivals in financial technology, as well as people outside the industry, tend to underestimate the complexity and importance of these seemingly mundane issues. In practice, developing, maintaining, and supporting software is what the majority of technology people on Wall Street do every day, and most of us would benefit from an improved understanding of the best industry practices in this area.

The book ends with a brief concluding chapter. For those with little or no prior knowledge of the securities industry, I recommend reading this book from cover to cover; much effort has been put into organizing the material in a logically consistent way, with all concepts used in one chapter having been defined in the previous text. However, I realize that is not how most people read books, so I also tried to make the book readable for those who jump from place to place. Throughout the book, technical discussions refer to business chapters and vice versa, so that it is possible to skim one business chapter and immediately see which technology sections are relevant for that area so you that can read about only those.

Regardless of their reading style, I believe that most readers will appreciate the fact that there is a Recommended Reading section guiding them through the available literature for every chapter and giving Web resources related to that chapter. A disclaimer: this section is not intended as a comprehensive bibliography; I simply list the books and resources that I have found useful in my daily work or that have impressed me otherwise.

Throughout the book, I tried to maintain an informal conversational style. You will not find a single formula here (there are a few inline scribblings here and there that a pedant may call formulas, but I will not), nor will you find the proliferation of section headings and subheadings and subsubheadings that take up half the space in most technical books (those that you do see were all added by my editors). One of my friends who saw an early draft of this book was almost offended by this latter feature; he told me that marketing science has proven that breaking information into bite-size chunks is essential for marketing success and that people will not read anything that does not follow this model. To that I modestly replied that Dostoyevsky wrote without subheadings and people read him just fine—I do not kid myself about my writing abilities as compared to Dostoyevsky's, but I do believe in uninterrupted narrative, and I did my best to follow this belief here.

One of the main purposes of the book is to make you comfortable with market terminology, and I tried to speak the language that you may actually hear on the trading floor, while taking care to define every new term. To make this terminological onslaught a bit more obvious, I italicize new terms when they first appear. My final stylistic comment concerns the use of "he" and "she," which has always baffled me (my native Russian has a much more elegant way of dealing with personal pronouns). Wall Street is no longer the male bastion it once was, and some of the best people I've met here in all lines of work are women. So when I have a choice of using "he" or "she," I will frequently pick "she"; I believe this not only ensures equality of the sexes, but also tends to wake you up.

Before I decided to write this book, I tried out some of these ideas on a smaller scale. At Goldman Sachs, I organized and ran a series of seminars called "How Things Work," where people from various technology areas presented and discussed their work. What I learned at those seminars formed the basis for a large part of this book. Later, at Barclays Capital, I created another series of seminars called "Business Knowledge" seminars, which were really lectures for information technology staff about various markets and their interaction with technology. Both programs met with a very enthusiastic reception, and the feedback from the attendees was invaluable for the creation of this book (as were my lecture notes). These experiences convinced me that there is a great need for this kind of knowledge, and prompted me to take the leap of writing this book.

I often talked with the participants in those sessions about what they wanted to gain by attending. Many of them gave obvious but very valid reasons, such as that they hoped to become more productive by learning more about the industry. But many others were driven by something deeper, something that I would summarize as a fundamental human need to make sense of the world around you. I hope this book does not simply provide information, but on some level satisfies that need for my current and prospective colleagues. Furthermore, I also hope that this book will make you realize what an interesting place Wall Street is; I did try to share my sense of fascination and pride at being a part of what I believe is the most complex, dynamic, challenging, and successful industry in the world today.

Having said that, I am happy to let the reader proceed to the main text. May you have as much fun reading it as I had working on it.

PART 1

The Financial Industry

CHAPTER 1

Financial Markets

Over the last few years, I have had the opportunity to interview many bright young people who were applying for quantitative Wall Street positions. Overall, I have been very impressed with their intelligence, drive, and technical skills, but all of them had one glaring gap in their knowledge: they had no idea of how the financial industry works. The pattern was repeated with such predictability that I stopped asking them whether they knew anything about how Wall Street works and instead started asking them to explain why they—a very smart group if I ever saw one—were going to interviews on Wall Street without bothering to find out what it was that they were getting into. According to what they told me, it is very difficult to get a clear idea of what the financial industry does and how it is put together just by reading books and going to economics classes—these sources left them with the vague notion that Wall Street is the place where lots of money is being made, plus perhaps a couple of canned definitions, but no real understanding of the issues. One of my interviewees asked me if I could answer the questions I was asking him when I started working on Wall Street, and I had to admit that I could not. I felt guilty about this at first, but then I realized that I am still right to ask the questions about industry organization because life itself will ask them once they start working on Wall Street in almost any role—and if they know the answers, much of what is going on around them at work will begin to make sense. I am therefore starting this book with an attempt to explain how the financial industry works. This is what Part 1 of the book is about.

Before we can examine the way the financial industry operates today, however, it is important to discuss why it exists in the first place, and how and why it took its present form. Therefore, in this opening chapter, we discuss the "why" questions about the financial industry and financial markets, while the next chapter will focus on the "how." Finally, the last chapter of Part 1 will take a look inside one of the industry players to see how it is put together. That's the plan, and let us now delve into the first part of it: figuring out why Wall Street is there.

The short answer to the question of why the financial markets exist is that, given that capital is the lifeblood of capitalism, there needs to be some type of "cardiovascular system" that carries it around the capitalist economy. At any given time, there are people and organizations (companies, governments, and individuals) that want money—to invest in a new factory, to build a highway, to pay for prescription drugs for seniors, to buy a house, and so on. At the same time, there are people and organizations that have money to invest—a family saving for college, an insurance company sitting on a pool of premiums, a social security trust fund. The first group is willing and able to pay the second group for the use of its capital; the question is, how do they find each other? This is exactly where the financial markets come in.

Note that these two groups of people have existed in every society from the beginning of history. Suppose that in medieval Europe, a king wanted to wage another costly war, and city merchants had money. They would ultimately find each other, and the king would be off to his war, and the merchants (if they and the king were lucky) would grow somewhat richer from its spoils. A society does not have to be capitalist to have capital and the need to invest it. However, back then, "ultimately" could be a long time, and the amounts of money that kings could raise by arranging loans from individual merchants were minuscule by modern standards, so the process of raising money for projects was quite inefficient (as it still is in much of today's world). So both groups kept trying different ways of putting capital to work, and that effort went on for many centuries and continues today. The modern financial system is the result of that long effort.

Interestingly, despite this long and varied history, humanity has been able to come up with only three logically distinct ways of moving money and other forms of capital from those who have it to those who want to use it. These are, in order of historical appearance, theft, debt, and equity. We do not discuss theft in this book, as it is covered extensively elsewhere and is not (supposed to be) part of the financial system whose workings we are trying to understand, so we proceed with the briefest of overviews of the evolution of the other two modes of capital transfer: debt and equity.

THE HISTORY OF DEBT MARKETS

The concept of debt predates recorded history. People would borrow a tool from a neighbor in prehistoric societies, just as they do today. They also borrowed living things that could multiply, such as seed or farm animals, and it is only natural that when people borrowed such things, they could return, say at harvest time, something more than they originally took, which gave rise to lending with interest. The earliest recorded laws—those of Hammurabi, dating from about 1800 BC—not only recognized but attempted to regulate such loans by imposing a 33⅓ percent per annum[1] limit on interest on loans of grain. By that time, it had already become common to lend money (rather than seed and livestock) for interest.

The individually negotiated loan described in the laws of Hammurabi—effectively a binding agreement between two specific parties outlining when the *principal* (the borrowed amount) was to be returned and how much interest was to be paid—has remained the most common legal form of debt ever since. This is the arrangement we enter into when we take out a personal loan at a bank today. Of course, the banks themselves went through a lot of changes before they took their present form, but the essence of the bank-lending business has not changed much in the last 3,800 years. While banks are the mainstay of personal finance in most of the developed world today, corporate entities and institutional investors, especially in the United States, the United Kingdom, and the rest of the Anglo-Saxon world, usually rely on a newer branch of finance, the *capital markets*, that has developed over the last 800 years. Wall Street is an offshoot from that branch, and therefore in what follows we focus on this relative novelty.

Strictly speaking, one can argue that financial markets existed much earlier than we claim here. In ancient Rome, the government of the republic outsourced tasks such as tax collection and some municipal services to semi-private entities that raised their operating capital by selling shares to the public, and people traded these shares (known as *particulae*, or particles) in the Roman Forum as early as the second century BC (Cicero inveighed against trading of *particulae*, calling it gambling). However, it is a sad fact of Western history that this Roman invention, together with a great many others, was completely forgotten after the fall of Rome and had very little effect on the formation of the modern capital markets.

---

1. This is the last time I say "per annum" in this book. All interest rates are annual percentages unless explicitly stated otherwise.

The roots of modern capital markets are not in this Roman practice, but rather in the medieval *trade fairs,* which began to appear all over Western Europe as early as the eleventh century AD. The fairs brought together buyers and sellers of agricultural and manufactured goods from far afield by offering the merchants two advantages. The first was physical proximity. In those days, there were no payment systems that would allow you to buy, say, spices in Venice and pay for them in Lyons; the business had to be done face-to-face, and the fairs offered an opportunity to do exactly that. Second, the fairs usually negotiated exemptions from the onerous taxes and duties that crippled commerce done outside the fairs. The fairs were held periodically, typically twice a year, but by the late medieval period, some of them, most notably the Antwerp fairs, had become permanent, causing many merchants to relocate to these free-trade zones and making Antwerp one of the first true financial centers. Some merchants at the fairs traded not in goods, but rather in money—they offered loans to other merchants, as well as what we now would call foreign exchange services. These money dealers at the fairs were the first members of what has grown into the modern financial industry. There were, however, other sources driving the development of finance in those early years, and in this chapter we review two of them.

A new form of debt, called *census,* or *rente* in French, had become widespread in early medieval Europe. Census was akin to a modern mortgage—the owner of a property granted a borrower the right to use it in exchange for periodic payments. This was a convenient way for owners of land and other property (those notorious feudal barons, and very often the Church) to convert their illiquid wealth into money as the economy began to shift away from the self-sufficient feudal manor system. In fact the very word *mortgage* originated in those times. There was a *live-gage* census, where the borrower in fact repaid the loan after some (usually long) period of time and took possession of the census property, and a *dead-gage,* or "mort-gage," where the payments continued forever. (Of course, today's mortgage is eventually paid off and is therefore the live-gage of old; also, *gage* is a valid, if archaic, word that means "pledge."[2]) The innovation here was that this form of borrowing or lending exchanged a sum of money today for income in the future; the return of the principal, if it happened at all, was a secondary issue. This is when "fixed-income" investments first began to play a noticeable role in society. The whole class of *rentiers* living off

---

2. We will review a competing explanation for these terms in Chapter 10.

these *rentes* sprang up as the Middle Ages turned into the Renaissance. This kind of borrowing "in perpetuity" became standard procedure during this period and remained so until the early twentieth century.

These census and, in the later medieval period, annuity contracts (where payments continued for as long as the contract holder remained alive—in the United States today, this is viewed as a hot new financial product) were agreements between two parties and could not be easily transferred to another owner. The first significant change in this regard came in Venice in the thirteenth century. The government of the Venetian Republic was always hard-pressed to raise money for wars, and (as was fairly common at the time) imposed so-called forced loans on its more prominent citizens in proportion to their wealth. Today we would recognize this as taxes, for which we accept government services in return, but in those days, these *prestiti* were viewed as loans, with the government simply paying interest on the amount it took away (the word *prestiti* means "loans" in Italian). In 1262 many earlier such loans were consolidated into a single loan called *monte vecchio* that promised to pay 5 percent interest forever in two semiannual installments of 2½ percent each. The government retained the right to pay back some or all of the borrowed amount at its discretion, as well as the right to assess more money as part of this, in today's parlance, issuance program.

The novelty of *prestiti* (and similar forced loans by other Italian cities) was the relative ease with which citizens could buy and sell these loans. They traded at the then newly built Rialto bridge. A buyer of *prestiti* acquired the promised stream of income in return for a lump payment to the seller. The new owner was recorded in a registry maintained by city officials, and interest payments were made based on these records. The price of this transaction was negotiated between the buyer and the seller, and the government (the ultimate borrower) had no say in it. Thus, for the first time, the concept of tradable and negotiable debt was introduced, and the first modern financial market was born. The city of Venice continued making interest payments on these obligations through thick and thin during the fourteenth century, which made the *prestiti* a very desirable investment throughout Europe. This investor interest made it much easier for Venice to raise money. However, people from outside Venice needed special permission to invest in the *prestiti* market, and it was hard to get, or, as we say today, *prestigious*.

This early example of tradable debt gives us an opportunity to introduce the modern concept of *yield*, or rate of return. The 5 percent rate on

the *monte vecchio* is *nominal yield* in today's terminology—this is the rate
of return that the original lenders would get on their initial investment
(called the *par amount*). However, these loans could often be bought for
far less than the par amount because of the ever-present doubts about the
ability of Venice to maintain the interest payments. If you bought these
loans at 50 percent of par value (or simply at 50; all bond price quotes
are expressed as percentages of the par amount), then the return on your
investment would be 10 percent. The ratio of nominal rate to price is called
the *current yield*. When the price drops, the yield increases, as you are getting the same interest payments on a smaller principal investment, and vice
versa. The current yield on these perpetual loans was in fact the going
interest rate for lending money to the Venetian government, and in this
early market it was already set by supply and demand and not by government decree. As it happened, the *prestiti* often traded way below par in
the early fourteenth century, then rose close to par and, for a brief period,
even traded above it (therefore yielding less than 5 percent) as their reputation grew.

The success of the *prestiti* was due not so much to their marketable
nature as to the steadfastness of the Venetian government in maintaining
payments. This was definitely not typical of the vast majority of other governments at the time. For the next 300 years, in most of Europe, "government" simply meant the king, and kings very often played fast and loose
with their credit, frequently defaulting on their debts, jailing or banishing
their creditors, and doing other unsavory things. Well-documented examples
of this include the 1648 default by Louis XIV of France that ruined many
of his Italian bankers, as well as the "Stop of the Exchequer" by Charles II
of England in 1672 that famously did in the London goldsmiths who had
financed his exploits. As a result of this unfortunate practice, lenders were
forced to charge exorbitant interest on loans to kings and princes—50 to 80
percent was not uncommon, and in one instance Charles VIII of France paid
100 percent to his Genovese bankers at the end of the fifteenth century.

A decisive break from that tradition occurred in the second half of the
seventeenth century in the newly formed Dutch Republic. A combination
of a popular and stable government, a relatively peaceful international situation, and the frugality of the Dutch people led to a remarkable flourish-
ing of government finance. This was perhaps the first example of a society
that managed to channel the savings of its people into productive projects,
either private or government-led, on a truly large scale. The debt instrument
(*instrument* is an often-used synonym for *security*) of choice was the

perpetual annuity, issued by provinces and municipalities. These municipal obligations were an attractive way for the prosperous Dutch population to invest its savings, given that none of these entities ever defaulted on its debt, and the amounts of money that were raised in this way were enormous by contemporary standards. This also led to a steady decline in the interest rates that government borrowers had to pay. By the end of the seventeenth century, the rate on those annuities had dropped to around 3 percent. This happy state of affairs came to be known as "Dutch finance" and was the envy of the rest of Europe.

England in particular tried hard to emulate the success of the Dutch. In 1693, William III (who was a Dutch prince himself before becoming the king of England) and his Whig government had to borrow at 14 percent to finance a war with France; they found this rate onerous and were very keen to bring it down. In the process of doing so, the English government came up with another financial innovation[3] that endures to this day: a *central bank*. The Bank of England was established in 1694 and quickly took over all matters of government finance, becoming the manager and issuer of government debt as well as the manager and issuer of bank money (bank notes), which, in today's terminology, means that it was responsible for *monetary policy*. It also started acting as the lender of last resort that could stabilize the financial system during crises. The turbulent history of British banking, which was undergoing tremendous growth during the eighteenth and nineteenth centuries, gave the Bank of England plenty of opportunity to practice its crisis management skills, and many of the tools for managing liquidity used by today's central bankers are the product of that period. Other European nations followed suit, establishing their own central banks and otherwise stabilizing their financial systems.

Despite these advances in banking, the predominant form of debt remained essentially the same as in the seventeenth-century Dutch Republic, perpetual bonds, although they had become more easily tradable, and an active and open market in government debt and other forms of debt had sprung up. By the second half of the nineteenth century, the British finally reached the level of interest rates they had set out to achieve 200 years earlier: in 1888, almost all outstanding debt of the British government was consolidated into 2½ percent perpetual bonds called *consols*. They are still traded and pay interest today (the British take their perpetuity seriously).

---

3. RiskBank in Sweden was established in 1668, but many people do not consider it a true central bank in the modern sense. Its main impact on modern finance is that the celebration of its tercentennial in 1968 was the occasion for establishing the Nobel Prize in Economics.

By the late nineteenth century, investors' preferences had shifted away from perpetual bonds toward bonds where the principal was expected to be returned at a specified future date. Return of the principal was always a right of the issuer of perpetual bonds—if interest rates were to fall, the issuer could pay off the investors (*redeem* the bond) and issue another bond at a lower interest rate. This was inconvenient for investors, as they had to start looking for another place to put their money, so they sought to restrict the ability of issuers to redeem their debt at will.

In the early nineteenth century, the U.S. Treasury started issuing bonds on which the redemption was guaranteed to take place during a specified period of time in the future. During that period of time, the Treasury could *call* the bonds if it was to its advantage (that is, if interest rates had fallen by then); however, at the end of that period, it was obligated to pay back the principal. The latest date on which it could do so was called the *maturity date* of the bond. Most other issuers started following this model, so that today nobody issues perpetual bonds. In fact, the trend has been to further simplify the redemption options: since 1984, the U.S. Treasury no longer issues such *callable* bonds, and the predominant structure has become the *bullet bond,* where the principal is returned at a well-defined maturity date.

Aside from this variation on the maturity theme, most of the essential trappings of today's capital market for debt instruments were in place in London circa 1750. A variety of issuers (national and local governments and their agencies, and also public and private corporations) could come to this market and issue, or *float*, bonds in order to borrow capital from investors seeking a return on their funds. In the eighteenth century, these investors would overwhelmingly be wealthy individuals, whereas today the debt markets are dominated by institutional investors.

The essential features of the typical deal that borrowers and investors enter into are shown in Figure 1–1. At the inception (the *issue date*) of the deal, the borrowed amount of money is transferred from the investors to the issuer. In return, each investor gets a promise (which would most often have been a paper certificate in the eighteenth century and increasingly is just an electronic record in the twenty-first) that the borrower will make periodic interest payments on specified future dates, and at some point in the future (between the first call date and the maturity, or due date) will also repay the principal. The original investor can hold this contract to its maturity, or can at some point sell it to someone else in the open market; if it is sold, the new owner will have all the rights of the original owner. The

FIGURE 1–1

How bonds work: the borrowed amount of money is transferred from the investor to the issuer of the bond at the issue date. The issuer then pays periodic interest (coupon) payments to the investor, and (usually) returns the borrowed amount at the maturity date.

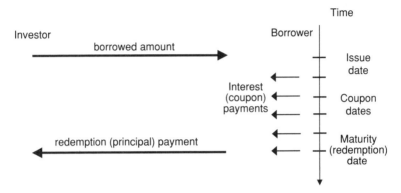

structure shown in Figure 1–1 has financed much of the remarkable growth of the industrialized nations and continues to do so to the present day.

The interest payments are usually called *coupon payments*, again for historical reasons—when bonds were issued as paper certificates, they had a set of cutoffs, or coupons, one for each future interest payment, as illustrated in Figure 1–2. When a payment came due, the holder of the bond would cut off (clip) the corresponding coupon and present it to the issuer (or its representative, known as a trustee) for payment. Posters depicting a coupon-clipping capitalist in a top hat, often with a cigar, looking, in Kipling's words, most excruciatingly idle, adorned many a classroom wall in Soviet secondary schools as an illustration of the inequities of capitalism (this was my first exposure to capital markets concepts). Their propaganda value was somewhat reduced by the fact that I, like all of my schoolmates and most of the teachers, had no idea what a coupon was. Now, however, I have to admit that the main point of these posters was essentially accurate: investments in debt instruments have allowed people, from the medieval *rentiers* to the nineteenth-century top-hatted capitalists to today's retirees, to live off the stream of income that such instruments generate, and that stream of income was and is the primary purpose of these "fixed-income" instruments. Their prices can rise and fall, but that is a secondary issue.

FIGURE 1-2

A bond certificate with coupons attached. This bond was issued by the U.S. Treasury in September 1918 to finance the First World War effort. This Fourth Liberty issue raised $6 billion, a huge sum at the time. It had 20 years to maturity, could be called after 15 years, and carried a 4.25 percent coupon. Note that each coupon has a number and a date (April 15 or October 15), and the amount of interest due ($2.12 or $2.13); the text on the coupons instructs the bearer to present it at the Treasury or a designated agency to receive payment. Reproduced by permission from Scripophily.com—The Gift of History (www.scripophily.com).

THE HISTORY OF EQUITY MARKETS

The opposite is true of *equity* investments. The main point of buying an ownership stake in a corporation (which is what equity investment means) is the hope of price appreciation, or *capital gain* (which is what happens when we sell something that has gone up in price). The idea of breaking up a commercial venture into shares can be traced to medieval partnerships that organized overseas voyages. The cost of outfitting and manning a ship that would sail to faraway places and bring back exotic goods was so high that it was beyond the reach of an individual merchant, so the merchants learned to pool their financial resources and then divide the profits from the voyage in proportion to their investment. In one form of such venture, known as a *commenda*, the partners were of two types: voyagers (who actually went with the ship) and investors (who stayed on land). The voyagers risked their lives and received one-fourth of the profits; the investors risked their capital and received three-fourths of the profits (I'm not sure if this was a fair division, but that's how it was).

These ventures were originally one-off deals formed for a single voyage, but in 1609 one such partnership, called the Dutch East India Company (formed, as the name implies, for trading with what is now southeast Asia), received a permanent charter from the Dutch government, which allowed it to outfit a whole fleet of trading ships (known as VOC ships, from the Dutch name of the company: Vereenigde Oostindische Compagnie) and operate it on a permanent basis. This required a much larger ownership base, and the newly formed company had to come up with a new arrangement, which, in retrospect, appears to be the most important financial innovation of the last 500 years: equity finance.

The formation of the Dutch East India Company can be seen as the birth of the equity markets. It was the first joint-stock company—individuals could buy its shares, or "stock," which entitled them to a proportional share of the profit from the company's operations. The original investors could sell their shares freely, and a lively market for those shares bubbled up almost immediately. The Amsterdam Stock Exchange was organized in 1613, more joint-stock companies were formed, and the newly born stock market went through a series of speculative bubbles almost immediately. Most of the stock trading techniques in use today were developed on the Amsterdam Stock Exchange during the first half of the seventeenth century (we will discuss some of them in Chapter 6).

By the early nineteenth century, joint-stock companies had become indistinguishable from today's corporations, and the market for their shares continued to expand. Note, however, that in those days, the "stock" exchanges also traded government bonds (the British still call their government bonds "government stock"). Of the four securities traded on the newly formed New York Stock Exchange in 1792, three were Treasury bonds, and it was not until the 1880s that the volume of shares traded on the New York Stock Exchange exceeded the volume of bond trading. Most readers are surely familiar with the stock market bubble of the late 1990s and could be forgiven for thinking that equities are the only investment vehicle out there. In reality, although stocks were always pitched more to the unsophisticated individual investor, the institutional players have divided their trading and issuance more or less equally between equities and debt for most of the twentieth century, and this pattern is likely to continue.

How does an equity investment work? As seen in Figure 1–3, at the issue date, the issuer sells shares of the company to the investor. The company can now use the proceeds from the sale for whatever purpose it wanted the funds for—it never has to pay back the amount raised. The only payments the shareholder is likely to see are *dividend* payments, which represent her share of the company's profits. The dividends will vary from quarter to quarter—they are paid at the discretion of the company and can sometimes disappear entirely (many technology companies pay no dividends at all).

FIGURE 1–3

How stocks work: money is transferred from the investors to the issuer on the issue date. The issuer never has to return the money, but (usually) pays periodic dividends to the investors.

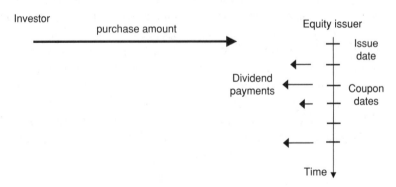

While in theory the value of a share is the net present value of the dividends it will pay, in practice a company share is worth however much people are willing to pay for it. An equity investor expects that his company will do well, and that people will recognize its greatness and be willing to pay more for its shares. This potential for price appreciation is the main rationale for equity investments; dividends, if they exist at all, are a secondary issue.

From the point of view of an investor, the choice between fixed-income and equity investments is largely a choice between safe income and potential capital gains, with the safety of fixed income being further enhanced by the fact that, in the event of the bankruptcy of an issuer, creditors are ahead of stockholders in their claims to the issuer's assets. From the point of view of the issuer, the choice between debt and equity issuance is determined by several considerations. Issuing new shares in the company dilutes the value of existing shares but does not commit future revenue. Also, equity is forever, although a company can buy back its shares at some later point. Debt does not dilute ownership, but it is temporary (at least in this day and age), and it has to be repaid out of future revenues. Note that many entities cannot issue equity because they don't have any (governments are perhaps the best example of this). To be able to issue debt, it is necesssary to have a claim to future revenues, which is exactly what governments have through their powers of taxation. Interestingly, even individuals with claims to future income can now issue bonds—there are "celebrity bonds," where people like David Bowie trade their future income for money now.

OTHER FINANCIAL MARKETS

So far, we have emphasized the differences between the equity and debt markets, but they both serve the same economic function: allowing entities that need capital for long-term projects to obtain such capital. For this reason, both equity and fixed-income markets are called *capital markets*. What else is out there?

First, there are *money markets*. One can argue that these are in fact markets for short-term debt instruments, but historically they have served completely different needs: the needs of everyday commerce, both domestic and international. When a merchant must pay money today for goods to be delivered in a few days, weeks, or months (or the other way around), the necessary short-term financing is provided by the money market. The financial instrument enabling these transactions is called a *discount bill,* a contract representing a promise by the issuer of a single payment in the (usually near) future. The merchant in the previous example would write such a bill and sell it to money market dealers, thereby obtaining money today and paying off the holders of the bill at a later date.

Of course, the price of such a bill is always less than its par value (the amount of the single future payment). The percentage difference between the par value of a bill and its price today is called its *discount*. A discount is a fee for the privilege of using the money until the maturity of the bill and can be expressed as an interest rate. The *discount rate* is the discount divided by the time period to the bill's maturity, expressed in years. For example, for a bill maturing six months from today with a price of 99, the discount is 1 percent and the discount rate is 2 percent per year. Note that the discount rate is not the rate of return—in this example, we will get $1 in six months (or $2 in a year) on our investment of $99, so our return, or yield, is $2/99 = 2.02$ percent. The rate of return is obviously always greater than the discount rate.

The business model of the money markets has changed little since the second half of the nineteenth century, when Markus Goldman, an immigrant from Germany, could be seen walking around Lower Manhattan carrying such handwritten discount bills, or promissory notes, under his hat (to protect them from the wind). The bills were written by small local merchants; Goldman would advance them money for a few days or weeks to tide them over until their goods arrived by sea (Manhattan was still a thriving seaport in those days), and later sell these bills to local banks at a small profit. The legendary Wall Street firm that he founded still does what he did then, only on a much grander scale (along with a lot more).

The instruments that Goldman traded would be called *commercial paper* today—short-term bills written by corporate entities (short-term means less than nine months for commercial paper in the United States). Governments are also major players in the money markets. Treasury bills (typically with one year or less to maturity) are important money management tools for many national governments. Although in effect these money market instruments are a means of short-term borrowing, the societal function they serve is more akin to a lubricant for business and commerce, allowing the participants to change the timing of future cash flows and smooth out short-term fluctuations in their cash positions. Businesses use the money market on an almost daily basis, whereas they go to the capital markets fairly infrequently.

The amounts of money flowing through the money market exceed those in the capital markets by an order of magnitude. The conditions in the money market therefore affect business and commerce in a very direct way: if money is hard to get, the discount rate on money market instruments rises, whereas if the supply of money in the economy is plentiful, money market rates fall and it becomes easier and cheaper for businesses to borrow for the short term. Because of this direct link between money markets and business activity, the central banks use money markets to manage the economy by controlling short-term discount rates.

Foreign exchange, or *FX,* markets are close cousins of the money markets. They were born together in the late Middle Ages in the form of the *bill of exchange,* which for many subsequent centuries was the workhorse of international commerce. A bill of exchange was a contract covering the common situation in which money was borrowed, say, in Antwerp on Monday in Dutch guilders and repaid in London on Friday in pounds sterling, matching the physical flow of goods between the two places. Today we would view this as a combination of two contracts: a short-term bill covering the borrowing from Monday to Friday, and an FX *forward* contract for exchanging guilders into pounds sterling on the same future date (FX *spot* is a contract for changing one currency into another on the *spot date,* or two business days from today).

An FX contract specifies the exchange rate from the base currency into the countercurrency and the amount of base currency to be converted; for example, a 100M EUR/USD trade at 1.220 means that on the spot date, the buyer of the contract exchanges 100 million euro (EUR) for 122 million dollars (USD). EUR is the base currency, USD is the countercurrency, and 1.220 is the exchange rate in this example. Today this market is dominated by foreign exchange dealers linked together by electronic networks. Every day they execute trillions of dollars worth of FX transactions on behalf of their institutional customers—global corporations, governments, importers and exporters, and investment companies—giving them the ability to move huge amounts of money across currency boundaries at a very low cost and at a moment's notice.

FX and money markets went their separate ways after the seventeenth century with the gradual disappearance of bills of exchange, but they remain closely linked. FX forward contracts are in fact combinations of currency exchange and short-term borrowing; and in order to illustrate how this introduces the dependence between the two markets, let us consider the following stylized example of a forward FX transaction. Assume that the spot exchange rate between EUR and USD is 1.200, that the interest rate for borrowing or lending for a year is 2 percent in the EUR money market and 1 percent in the USD money market, and that we are a trader who has been asked to provide a quote for a one-year forward EUR/USD exchange rate. If we take 1 euro and invest it in the money market at 2 percent for a year, we will get 1.02 euro a year from now, whereas if we first convert this euro into dollars at the spot exchange rate and then invest the dollars for a year, we will get 1.2 (the spot FX rate) times $1.01 = 1.212$ dollars a year from now.

If we quote a rate that is sufficiently different from $1.212/1.02 = 1.188$, people can *arbitrage* us. Let us say we decided to ignore these complexities and quoted a forward exchange rate of 1.2, the same as the spot rate. Another trader could then enter into a forward trade with us at 1.2 for €101 million and simultaneously do the following: (1) borrow $120 million in the money market at 1 percent, so that in a year she would owe $121.2 million; (2) convert this $120 million into €100 million at the spot exchange rate of 1.2; and (3) lend these euro in the EUR money market at 2 percent, so that she will be owed €102 million a year from now. At the end of the year, she converts €101 million back into dollars using our forward exchange rate of 1.2, which exactly pays off the $121.2M loan she obtained in step 1 and leaves her with a riskless profit of €1 million (less the transaction costs). We are paying too much for forward euro; as this example shows, the euro can be obtained more cheaply using the chain of transactions described, so we are in fact giving money away.

People will actually go to the trouble of arranging these three-leg transactions and keep hitting us for forward euro at 1.2 until we (or our bosses) realize that something is not right and we start reducing our bid. When we get it down to 1.19 or so, the amount of money we are giving away will become comparable to the transaction costs of these chained transactions, and people will stop taking advantage of us. Such arbitrage opportunities are extremely rare in today's markets, but the mere threat of them will keep us on our toes and will force us to watch not only the FX market but the money markets very closely. Today both markets operate together as a very efficient mechanism enabling the short-term movement of money through the global economy.

Another major market we need to mention is that for *commodity futures*, which is a more liquid part of the larger *commodities* market that ensures the smooth flow of industrial and agricultural commodities across the world. Oil futures are perhaps the most visible example of such markets: an oil futures contract entitles the holder to take possession (*take delivery* is the proper term) of a barrel of oil of a well-defined type (say, West Texas Intermediate, or WTI) at a specified date in the future. Buying an oil futures contract is not quite the same thing as buying a barrel of oil, but it is reasonably close, as it can be converted into that barrel (or rather 1,000 barrels, the size of a typical contract). But the futures are much easier to trade, so the "oil prices" we hear about in the news are in fact the prices of such futures contracts. We can buy these contracts as well as sell them—when we sell, we collect the selling price of the contract, and in return we are undertaking to deliver the barrel of oil. Because of the need to specify the conditions of such contracts in great detail (delivery dates, locations, and the quality and quantity of the commodity to be delivered), futures contracts trade on organized exchanges that guarantee the performance of the parties under the contract. The first futures exchanges were formed in the United States in the mid-nineteenth century in order to support the grain and cotton trade. Many of the most important futures exchanges are still located in Chicago, the grain hub of the American Midwest.

Most futures contracts in fact never end with actual delivery—the buyers and sellers can cancel out each other's obligations. For example, imagine that one trader buys a WTI oil futures contract from another trader at $40. If they both hold their positions until the delivery date, the second trader will have to find a barrel of oil and deliver it to the first (there are well-defined procedures for how that should be done). However, in most cases, the first trader would simply sell his contract before delivery date, say at $41, and someone else, perhaps the same second trader, would buy it from him, *closing out* their positions. This way, they both have no delivery obligations; the first trader made $1 and the second lost $1 without ever touching crude oil.

This may sound like unvarnished speculation, and much of futures trading is indeed that, but it plays the important societal role of *price discovery*—the process by which buyers and sellers determine how much people are willing to pay for their wares. Even though the overwhelming majority of actual deliveries of oil are negotiated outside the futures exchanges, the prices in the physical market cannot deviate too much from the futures prices (the differences are usually due to transportation and storage costs). There are futures contracts on just about any tangible commodity—oil, gas, pork bellies, grain, metals, and electricity—as well as on many intangibles, such as stock indices and interest rates. We will discuss futures in much greater detail in Chapter 7.

The futures market is our first example of a *derivatives* market, where the value of the products that are actually traded is derived from the value of some other quantity, called the *underlying* (for oil futures, crude oil of the contract grade is the underlying). Aside from futures, the best-known examples of financial derivatives are *options,* which, in their simplest form, entitle the contract holder to buy or sell the underlying (say, the stock of a public company) at a certain price (the *strike* price) at some point in the future. For example, one can buy a call option on IBM stock struck at 100 that can be exercised any time within the next three months. The option is valuable if there is a chance that the stock will rise above the strike price during the exercise period. If IBM stock trades above 100, say at 110, one can exercise this option—buy IBM stock at 100 from the option seller (*writer*) and resell it on the stock exchange for 110, for a $10 gain. If the stock never goes above 100, the option expires worthless. Very simplistically, the value of an option is determined by how likely the underlying is to rise above the strike price, which in turn is a function of two main factors: how close the current price is to the strike price, and how much the stock price is likely to change during the exercise period, that is, the variability, or *volatility*, of the price of the underlying. We devote Chapter 9 to options markets.

While futures and options have been around for at least two centuries, the role of derivatives markets in the financial system has changed dramatically in the last three decades. One watershed event in the history of derivatives markets was the development of quantitative models for option pricing in the 1970s. The famous Black-Scholes formula was published in 1973, but the underlying theoretical work by Merton was even more important than the formula itself—it opened a systematic way of valuing almost any derivatives contract. The Nobel Prize in Economics that these researchers[4] were awarded in 1997 recognized the fact that few twentieth-century discoveries had a comparable societal impact.

The financial industry players got very busy applying their theoretical insights—trading options and other derivatives proved much more profitable than plain old stock and bond trading, and the profits often accrued to those who had better pricing models. Derivatives trading volumes exploded, and Wall Street started hiring "rocket scientists" from academia and other industries to build and maintain the derivatives models.

Another milestone in the recent history of the derivatives markets, perhaps less well known than Black-Scholes but equally paradigm-changing for the industry, was the development of interest-rate futures and swaps in the early 1980s. The success of these financial products defies description—

---

4. Robert Merton and Myron Scholes; Fischer Black died two years earlier.

at the time of this writing, there was about $140 trillion (more than 10 times the GDP of the United States) of outstanding interest-rate swaps, measured by the notional amount. The advent of these products has allowed market participants to slice and dice interest rates in heretofore unknown ways (we discuss swaps in Chapter 8). As with equity options, this required the development of complex models for describing the dynamics of interest rates, leading to further inflow of quantitative talent into Wall Street trading floors.

These developments coincided with the technological revolution in computing, which transformed all aspects of how the financial industry does business. Computerization of books and records, front-office systems that automate trade entry, live market data displays, real-time pricing and risking systems, derivatives pricing systems utilizing whole farms of powerful servers, electronic trading networks—these modern trading floor realities would be as baffling to a New York bond trader of the 1960s as they would be to a London bond trader of the 1750s. So would the army of technical people creating and supporting all these technological innovations, which has become an integral part of Wall Street.

This phenomenal growth was (and is) driven by the changing role of the financial industry. It is moving from its traditional role of capital markets facilitator to a new identity as risk manager to the world. With the expertise it has gained over the last two decades, the industry now stands ready to provide a financial derivative for every risk its customers are facing. However, despite the tremendous changes of the last two decades, in many ways the basic organization of the financial marketplace is still similar to what it was centuries ago: there are those who seek capital, those who have excess capital, and the financial intermediaries in between. The financial industry has been phenomenally successful at avoiding the fate of middlemen in many other areas of human endeavor; instead, it has dramatically extended and strengthened its position and power in the economy and society at large. The following statistics are really thought-provoking: over the last five years, financial companies employed less than 3 percent of the workforce in the United States, but earned about 40 percent of all corporate profits—a feat no other industry can even aspire to match. This is one of the reasons why it is such an interesting place to work.

In the next two chapters, we take a much closer look at how the financial industry operates today.

CHAPTER 2

Market Participants

The structure of the financial industry today reflects the long and tumultuous history that we touched upon briefly in the previous chapter. To serve its societal purpose, the industry has developed a bewildering variety of institutions, and it is often difficult for the outsider to make sense of all these names, like NYSE, CBOT, Morgan Stanley, Fidelity, the Fed, and so on. Unfortunately, getting a job on Wall Street in and of itself does nothing to improve one's understanding of the industry structure. I started my Wall Street career at an interdealer broker firm, and for the first year or so I kept calling our brokers "traders," which did not improve either the quality of my interactions with them or the quality of my work. I had no idea how the company I worked for made money, and nobody bothered to explain it to me. This sad state of affairs is very common, and I hope to remedy it somewhat with this chapter.

Here we will discuss the types of institutional players in today's financial industry, their business models, and their interactions. If, after reading this chapter, some of you can place the firm you are working for (or interviewing with, or thinking of working for) on one of the industry diagrams presented here (which should be enough to explain to you how that firm makes money), I will have achieved my goal. This is an example of setting the bar low, since many of you are undoubtedly able to do that before reading this chapter. To those advanced readers, I say, what if you change jobs? Would you be able to place your new employer on one of the diagrams? The answer to that may depend on whether that new employer even makes it to one of our diagrams—our discussion here will be focused on the types of institutions that are likely to employ a sizable quantitative and technology workforce. That leaves out a very large part of the financial industry (in particular, retail banks and real estate agencies), which to most of my readers should be no great loss.

The original purpose of the financial industry was to arrange the transfer of capital from its suppliers (the investors) to its consumers, and we begin by discussing how this process is currently organized. The "consumers" of capital are by and large outside of the financial industry—they are mostly corporations, governments and government agencies, and supranational entities like the World Bank that need money for their own reasons. When these organizations turn to the financial markets to raise funds, they *issue* securities and sell them to investors (which is why this group of players is often referred to as the *issuers*). The role of the financial industry in this process is quite straightforward: it takes care of the actual selling of the newly issued securities. The investors (one of my early mentors taught me to picture them as a group of widows and orphans clutching their crumpled dollar bills and looking for safe but profitable ways to put those dollars to work) do not generally go to the issuers directly, nor do the issuers have much expertise in finding all the people who would be willing to buy their securities. Instead, the financial industry steps in between these two groups and arranges the sale of securities in a process known as *investment banking*.

A typical procedure would be for an issuer such as Ford Motor Company to hire an investment bank like Goldman Sachs to help it design the securities it is going to issue and take care of the many legal and regulatory requirements related to the issuance process. Once the securities are ready to go, Ford effectively sells these securities to Goldman and gets its capital right away, and it becomes Goldman's problem to distribute the securities to actual investors and collect back the (huge amounts of) money it just paid Ford for the securities. Luckily, Goldman Sachs and its peers are in an excellent position to do this. They have a large base of investor customers, a highly skilled sales force that tends to those customers, and, most importantly, a wealth of experience in distributing securities to those customers, so that typically the process is over within hours—Ford gets the money, investors get securities, and Goldman gets a fee (as high as 7 percent of the amount raised) for its services. We summarize this process in Figure 2–1.

We are not going to discuss investment banking beyond this vastly oversimplified description; while this is an interesting and extremely lucrative

FIGURE 2–1

Organization of the primary financial markets in which securities are issued. The securities flow downward on this chart, from issuers through the investment banks to the end-user investors. Money flows the other way.

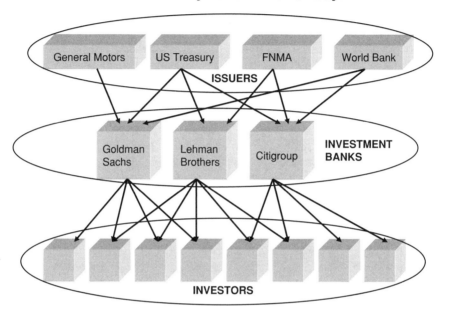

business, it does not require much technology of any kind, as it has changed little over the last two centuries, and therefore very few of my readers are likely to be working in the investment banking area. However, this process, as depicted in Figure 2–1, is important for our further discussions because it is responsible for the creation of securities. It is often and rightly called the *primary market,* where securities originate, as opposed to the *secondary market,* where securities trade after they have been issued. An automotive analogy may help clarify this distinction: the primary market for cars is the new-car market, where dealers sell brand-new cars to customers, whereas the secondary market is when (the same or different) dealers buy and sell used cars. It is this secondary market that we are mostly concerned with because of its technological complexity. Its basic structure is depicted in Figure 2–2. To make sense of this diagram, let us go through each group of boxes there and discuss what each of them really represents.

FIGURE 2-2

Organization of the secondary financial markets where trading of securities takes place. Arrows represent trading flows. The investors, as buy-side companies, can trade with dealer firms or on exchanges through broker intermediaries.

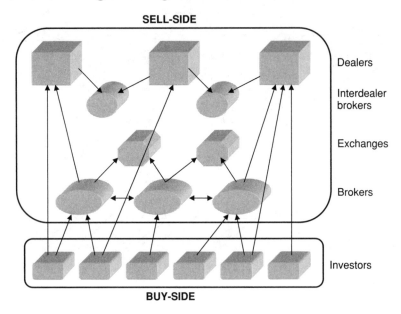

THE STRUCTURE OF FINANCIAL MARKETS

The boxes on top of the *sell-side* entities in the diagram are the equivalents of used-car dealers in our automotive analogy—they stand ready to buy securities when someone wants to sell, and to sell when someone wants to buy. These *dealer firms* make money by buying low and selling high, just like the used-car dealer does. The act of being ready at all times to buy a security at a (lower) *bid price* and/or sell it at a (higher) *offer price* (also known as an *ask price*) is called *making a market* in that security, as indeed it makes it possible for anyone to buy or sell that security at any time, which is what a market is all about.

When a market maker buys a security, it becomes that security's legal owner until it sells the security to someone else, and during that time the market maker assumes the *price risk* (the risk that the security will drop in price and the market maker will lose money on the trade). The bid-offer *spread* (the difference between the offer price and the bid price) that market makers appear to collect from their trading customers is intended to compensate them for assuming that price risk. Almost all investment banks that participate in bringing securities to life through the primary market also act as market makers in those securities in the secondary market. This tells their investor base that if they sell some new security, they will always stand ready to buy it back should the investor not like it, which is not only a very important assurance of the integrity of the financial markets, but, in many markets, a legal requirement. Because of this, the terms *investment bank* and *dealer bank* are largely synonymous—a typical dealer bank is a huge organization with an investment banking division and one or more trading divisions. We will take a closer look at the internal organization of the dealer banks in the next chapter.

These big sell-side firms like Morgan Stanley, Goldman Sachs, and Lehman Brothers now compete with their brethren that have merged with even bigger commercial banks—firms like Citigroup (which is the former Citibank plus the former Salomon Brothers), JPMorgan Chase, Deutsche Bank, Barclays, and UBS. These banks (together with perhaps a dozen or so smaller players like Greenwich Capital) have come to dominate both the primary and the secondary securities markets. Most of what we discuss in this book will be presented from the point of view of such a dealer bank because that is where an overwhelming majority of my potential readers will be working. There are several reasons why these firms are called the sell side of Wall Street; one of them is that these firms make money both from the initial sale of securities and from secondary market trading of those securities. We will introduce other reasons once we have looked at the opposite side of Wall Street, which is, you guessed it, called the buy side.

The *buy side* of Wall Street is depicted in Figure 2–2 as a group of entities at the bottom. Its function is to buy what the sell-side firms sell (we just need to clarify exactly what that is). This group includes individual investors—people like you and me who may dabble in trading stocks and who, because of their large numbers, play a significant role in some (mostly equity) markets. In almost all markets, however, this group is dominated by *institutional investors*, which are organizations that, by the nature of their business, constantly face the problem of investing money in assets that can bring in income and/or appreciate in price. Think of an insurance company like State Farm that collects huge sums of money as premiums. It does not and cannot spend this money as fast as it comes in, and it needs to put it somewhere where it will be reasonably safe but also earn some return. A pension fund like CALPERS collects retirement contributions from a large group of people, thus continuing to produce cash that it has to put somewhere.

These entities can either invest this money by themselves or turn to a professional *asset management* company to do it for them. An asset management company such as Fidelity collects money from its customers for the purpose of investing it in various assets, usually securities, that it thinks show promise of earning a good return for its customers. Whether these buy-side organizations act on their own behalf or are investing for someone else, they have real money to invest and generally *buy* massive amounts of securities (which is another reason why they are called buy-side companies) from the sell-side dealer firms. A salesperson at Morgan Stanley would therefore admiringly call Fidelity a "real-money" account.

In addition to these "real-money" investors, there are also speculators, who generally borrow money to buy some securities and to sell others in order to benefit from expected price movements. While this group does as much selling as buying, it is still classified as being on the buy side, since it is ultimately trying to do the same thing as the firms we have already discussed: achieve good investment returns. The hedge funds make up the majority of such "leveraged-money" buy-side speculative entities. Typically, speculators have a much shorter investment horizon than real-money investors and therefore are often also called "fast-money" accounts.

Asset management companies (both real-money and fast-money) earn their living mostly from the *asset management fees* that they charge their clients; these are generally a percentage (usually around 1 percent) of assets under management. Note that asset managers get paid whether or not their investment strategies are successful. However, if an asset manager consistently loses money for its clients, the clients will give their assets to someone else, so there is an indirect link between pay and performance. Many hedge funds also charge a *performance fee,* which is a fraction (often as high as 20 percent) of the investment returns, so they have a powerful incentive to be successful in their trading efforts. Note also that for many buy-side entities (such as insurance companies), their investment performance is secondary to their other business activities and is not their main (or even major) source of income.

While most of these buy-side companies are interested in buying securities rather than selling them, the real commonality among them is that they always *initiate* the investment transactions, that is, they decide what to buy (or sell) and when. In this, they differ from the sell-side market makers, who offer their quotes at any time and cannot control the timing of the trades. A useful concept here is *liquidity*: the sell-side companies provide liquidity by making it possible for others to trade at any time, whereas the buy-side companies consume liquidity by trading with the liquidity sellers at a time of their choice and paying the dealers' bid-offer spread for the privilege. From this point of view, the distinction between buy-side and sell-side companies is that buy-side firms *buy liquidity* and sell-side firms *sell liquidity*. Yet another way of saying the same thing is to call the buy-side companies the *market takers*, whereas the sell-side companies are market makers.

BROKERS AND EXCHANGES

In some markets (such as bond markets and FX markets), all trading is indeed done through dealers as described here. If Customer A wants to buy something and Customer B wants to sell the same thing, they both have to go to a dealer, who will buy the thing from Customer B and sell it to Customer A at a slightly higher price. In dealer markets, there is always a dealer on one side (or both sides) of every trade. Markets do not have to work this way, and in other markets (most notably equities, futures, and options markets), many trades are done directly between end customers, without dealers being involved (much like "for sale by owner" transactions in the automotive world, where people avoid paying the dealers by trading directly with each other). Just as in the automotive world, the main problem with such direct trading is finding a counterparty that wants to buy the exact same thing that another person wants to sell, and the financial industry has developed facilities that help solve this problem. The organizations that make a living by matching buyers with sellers are generally of two kinds: *brokers* and *exchanges*. They are shown in Figure 2–2 as belonging to the sell side, but in reality they can and do serve both groups.

A broker finds buyers for those who want to sell, and vice versa, and whenever she successfully arranges a trade, she charges one of the parties a *commission*. An *interdealer broker* helps dealers trade with one another anonymously. These brokers embody the idea of brokerage in its purest form, as they simply match dealers that want to buy with dealers that want to sell and do nothing else. A *retail broker* (who mostly serves individual investors) and a *prime broker* (who serves small institutional clients such as hedge funds) may also provide other services, such as maintaining accounts for their customers, but they rarely charge for those services—commissions are their main source of income. The big sell-side firms also provide brokerage services for their institutional customers—when a customer wants to trade, these firms can either find a suitable counterparty somewhere else (acting as a broker, or agent of the customer) or take the other side of the trade themselves (thereby acting as a dealer). Therefore the broker ovals and the dealer boxes on our diagram very often refer to the same institution. This is also why these firms are often called *broker-dealers*.

How exactly do brokers find people who are willing to take the opposite side of every trade? It is possible that a broker will have two customers at the same time whose orders match exactly, in which case the trade can be arranged right away (this is how interdealer brokers operate). However, if all brokers could somehow get together and share the orders of all their customers, the chances of finding matching orders would be exponentially greater, and the financial industry has come up with institutions that do exactly that; these are called *exchanges*.

An exchange is a place (physical or, increasingly, electronic) where brokers send their customers' orders in the hope of finding a match. Imagine hundreds of brokers who collect their little trickles of customer orders and pour them all into one big pot (the exchange), where the orders find their opposites and get *executed*. The exchange can operate purely as an *order-crossing* facility, where incoming orders are executed by crossing them with offsetting orders from the incoming order stream, or it can have internal market makers (sometimes called *specialists* or *floor traders*) who fill customer orders by buying or selling for their own account if an offsetting customer order cannot be found. For brokers who route their orders to the exchange, these details generally do not matter—all that happens from their point of view is that the exchange acts as an execution machine that takes in customer orders and *fills* them one way or another.

To operate efficiently, exchanges have to impose some structure on their trading process, which is typically codified in the exchange *rulebook*. First, the exchanges undertake to trade a limited set of securities, which are said to be *listed* on the exchange. They also agree on a discrete set of prices at which trades can happen (for example, stocks used to trade in ⅛ increments and now trade in 0.01 increments; price has to be rounded to the nearest increment) and define the trading hours. The exchanges also impose some constraints on the brokers who use their services, such as some minimum credit requirements and, more generally, adherence to some code of conduct.

As a matter of fact, most exchanges were created by brokers who got together and formed a sort of club, where, as in any club, there were some membership standards, and the main membership privilege was that the members could trade with one another. Initially, such exchanges covered their expenses by charging their members a membership fee, but gradually their business model evolved away from that and toward charging trading and execution fees on every trade. Note that it is the member brokers and not their customers who pay the exchange fees. The exchanges that are membership organizations are technically nonprofit entities, but in recent years almost all major exchanges have switched to the for-profit corporate model through the process known as *demutualization*.

Note carefully that neither exchanges nor brokers ever own the securities they process, and therefore they do not care much whether the market goes up or down—they make a little bit of money on every order that passes through them no matter what happens to the prices. Dealers, in contrast, buy and sell for their own account and end up having an *inventory* of securities that they have to manage (just as used-car dealers do). Securities dealers (again just like used-car dealers) would love not to have an inventory but instead immediately sell whatever they just bought and make a little profit on the bid-offer spread—if this happened, they also would not care which way the market goes.

However, this is not what happens in practice. The flows that the dealers get never match exactly, so as they keep buying and selling their securities (note that, unlike car dealers, securities dealers can sell securities that they do not own); they accumulate both long and short positions in those securities. As the markets move, the value of those positions changes, but the dealers are generally not trying to profit from those market moves. Instead, their game is to try to keep their inventories market-neutral so that the profits on their long positions balance the losses on their short positions and vice versa. This way, on average, they do not care where the market goes and can focus on earning their bid-offer spread, but they have to work at keeping it this way; this is what is meant by inventory (or risk) management. The need to keep track of and manage these inventories makes a dealer's business vastly more complex technologically than that of a broker or an exchange, which is one of the main reasons why the dealer banks employ so many quantitative and technology professionals.

THE EFFECTS OF TECHNOLOGY ON SECURITIES TRADING

The world of brokers and exchanges has undergone wrenching changes over the last two decades, mostly driven by developments in technology. Much

of what brokers and exchanges do is fairly easy to automate, so their traditional business model, based on the idea of charging high commissions for
doing simple things, is not sustainable in a world where computers can
match buy and sell orders very quickly and at negligible cost.

The changes have been the most dramatic in the brokerage world.
The retail brokerages, which numbered in the hundreds just 10 years ago,
are now dominated by perhaps a dozen low-cost online brokers. The interdealer brokers have consolidated to an even higher degree—there are now
two major brokers (ICAP and Cantor Fitzgerald), where there were dozens
10 years ago. The established exchanges such as the NYSE are also struggling in the face of competition from all-electronic rivals, but so far the
technological changes have actually increased the number of exchanges and
electronic crossing networks available in the equities markets, while the
futures exchanges have largely held their ground by developing their own
electronic trading technology.

Technology is now such an important part of Wall Street that some
companies providing technology services have become vitally important
to its smooth operation, even though these companies are not themselves
trading with anyone (and are therefore left out of Figure 2–2). The two
giants in this field are Reuters and Bloomberg. Both do a great many things,
but the main and most visible part of what they do can be called information services. Both Reuters and Bloomberg provide software (which is
installed on the desktops of *every* Wall Street trader and salesperson) that
allows the user to see live market data for all the securities he cares about,
browse and search through market news, perform all kinds of analysis on
securities he selects, and communicate with his trading partners at other
institutions through electronic mail and instant messaging.

For these services, both companies charge each user a sizable monthly
fee (from $1,000 up, depending on the exact services used), which is their
main source of revenue, and with an installed user base of around 300,000
people, the revenues of these companies easily exceed those of all but the
largest of the financial firms they serve. Both Reuters and Bloomberg have
been remarkably successful in making these services absolutely indispensable to everyone involved in securities trading, to the point where people
simply would not be able to trade without having one or (usually) both of
these applications in front of them. As one Bloomberg ad puts it, "You are
either in front of a Bloomberg or behind," and there is a lot of truth to that.

Several other large companies used to make a living in the same space,
but they gradually either lost their independence (Reuters bought Bridge

Information Systems in 2003 and is acquiring another major service, Telerate, at the time of this writing) or became providers of various types of financial information to Reuters and Bloomberg (an example is Thomson Financial, which ended up acquiring many smaller information providers). Reuters also owns, directly or indirectly, most of the leading technologies for market data distribution (TIBCO and Talarian are the two important names in this group). And, of course, Reuters is also a world-leading news agency, with reporters all around the globe (it actually started as a news service).

While these two giants basically own the information delivery space, there are many smaller technology companies that cater to other needs of the financial industry: financial analytics packages, trading and (especially) back-office and risk management systems, and the like. As we will explain in greater detail later in the book, these software companies compete not so much with Reuters and Bloomberg as with the technology organizations of their Wall Street customers, which develop similar software in-house. Because of this "insider" competition, the penetration of these third-party software vendors into Wall Street trading rooms is somewhat limited at present, but it is growing, and I personally think that a lot of these companies have a bright future, and that many of my readers may end up working there.

CLEARING AND SETTLEMENT SERVICES

Another group of entities that did not make it into Figure 2–2 but is crucial to the industry's day-to-day functioning is providers of clearing and settlement services. Let us first try to demystify the terms *clearing* and *settlement*. When a trade occurs anywhere in Figure 2–2, ultimately Party A has to deliver securities to Party B, while Party B has to pay Party A money for those securities. The trade *settles* when securities are delivered and money is paid, after which Parties A and B have no further obligations to each other and can get on with their lives.

The settlement process work roughly as follows. Each institution keeps its money in a bank, just as we do. The bank is called a clearing bank, and the money is kept in a *cash account* for that institution, while the securities that each institution owns are kept in its *securities account*. To settle a trade, the securities have to be taken out of Party A's securities account at its clearing bank and deposited into Party B's securities account at its clearing bank, while the cash account of Party A has to be credited for the appropriate amount taken out of the cash account of Party B.

Not so long ago, these transfers were done by sending a messenger across town to deliver security certificates, while another messenger delivered a check for the payment. By the end of the 1960s, this system had become completely unworkable—thousands of messengers were crisscrossing Manhattan carrying bags of checks and securities, and yet some trades were going unsettled. The situation got so bad that the New York Stock Exchange had to close every Wednesday to reduce the trading volume.

The financial industry came up with two basic approaches to alleviate this problem. One was the creation of the Depository Trust Company (DTC), which took charge of the securities delivery problem. All trading parties have agreed to maintain their securities at the DTC (which plays the role of a *custodian* for those securities, keeping these valuables in custody on behalf of other parties), so that when they traded with each other, the securities remained *immobilized* at the DTC, which just had to update its records of who owned what. Following the same principle, some markets gradually switched away from issuing paper security certificates at all (after all, why bother if these certificates spent their life in a custodian's vaults and the average owner of securities never got to see them?). Instead, these markets started to rely completely on the records of their custodians instead of delivering securities—for example, all U.S. government securities have been issued in such *book-entry* form since early 1980s, and the Federal Reserve maintains records of who owns how much of what security.

The other approach was the expansion of *clearing services*. A clearing agent makes sure that for every trade, both parties have the same understanding of the trade terms, so that if Party A says that it bought 1,000 shares of IBM from Party B at a price of 95, then Party B should say that it sold 1,000 shares of IBM to Party A at 95. Those messengers that were carrying checks and securities that we mentioned in the previous paragraphs were also carrying *trade confirmation* slips that contained each party's records of a trade, and clearing agents had to compare these records before settlement could occur. The clearing process makes much more sense if both parties use the same clearing agent, and over the last 30 years the clearing agents have consolidated to the point where in the United States there is a single company called NSCC (National Securities Clearing Corporation) that clears all equity trades, and another company called FICC (Fixed Income Clearing Corporation) that clears all trades in fixed-income products (and both of them plus the DTC are subsidiaries of the same parent company: Depository Trust and Clearing Corporation).

An immense benefit of this centralization of clearing arrangements is the possibility of *netting*. If two institutions trade the same security between each other several times during the same day, it is very likely that some of these trades will *net out*, meaning that if A sold B 100 shares of something and later bought the 100 shares back (perhaps at a different price), and if both use the same clearing agent, which knows about all such trades, then the clearing agent can recognize that there is no need to deliver any securities whatsoever and that all that needs to happen is that A should pay B the price difference.

Since the number of big trading institutions is relatively small, the likelihood of some of their trading flows netting out in this way is surprisingly high, and the introduction of netting systems has cut down dramatically on actual payments and security deliveries. For example, NSCC claims that its Continuous Net Settlement system reduces the total volume of payments by up to 95 percent. And, of course, we should mention the other major factor that has allowed this sector of the financial industry to keep up with exploding trading volumes: technology. An overwhelming majority of the trades done today are handled in a completely automated fashion from origination to settlement (this is called *straight-through processing,* or STP).

REGULATORS

The last major group of players in today's financial industry that we have not yet discussed is *regulators*. Although they do not trade, regulators set the rules of the trading game. First we should mention the government agencies that oversee and regulate financial markets and the banking system. Every country has a central bank (the Federal Reserve, or the Fed, in the United States) that is ultimately responsible for the health of that country's banking system, and to that end, central banks subject the other, normal banks to a variety of regulations, mostly designed to make sure that the banks have adequate capital on hand, do not take too much investment risk, and therefore are financially stable (the smooth functioning of the interbank payments systems is also under the Fed's purview). Regulation is just one of the many things that central banks do (we will explain some of these other things in Chapter 4), but there is a multitude of other government agencies whose primary job is to tell banks what to do, most notably the Office of the Comptroller of the Currency (which mostly deals with nonfinancial regulations, like fairness in lending, on the federal level); in addition, every state has its own regulatory body that oversees that state's "local" banks.

Another regulatory agency in the United States that deals primarily with financial markets and investment banks is the Securities and Exchange

Commission, or SEC. This organization was established in the 1930s to restore investors' confidence in the financial markets, which had been badly damaged in the wake of the 1929 stock market crash and the Great Depression that followed. The SEC focuses mostly on ensuring the integrity of the primary markets and tightly regulates the process of issuing securities. Basically it requires issuers to provide truthful disclosure of their financial condition and business prospects, which the investment banks working on the issue must put in a prospectus and distribute to investors before the new issue can be sold.

Over the years, the SEC has acquired many other regulatory powers, and it is now deeply involved in almost every aspect of secondary-market operation (in the futures and derivatives markets, however, the Commodity Futures Trading Commission, or CFTC, created by Congress in 1974, is the main government regulator). However, the secondary markets are mainly regulated by the NASD (National Association of Securities Dealers). The NASD is not a government agency; this is an example of a *self-regulatory organization* that imposes rules on its members. Every dealer and broker in the United States is a member of the NASD (it is not required by law, but as a practical matter it is impossible to do securities business without being a member). There are several other similar self-regulatory organizations, such as the NFA (National Futures Association), the Bond Markets Association (BMA), and the like, which also play a role in their respective market segments.

The NASD is the regulatory agency that people are most likely to have direct contact with in their professional life if they work in the financial industry in any capacity that involves trading, sales of securities, or giving financial advice and trading recommendations to customers. Everyone in those lines of work has to be registered with the NASD, a process that requires fingerprinting, full disclosure of personal and credit history, and, most importantly, taking a set of examinations that attempt to make sure that they know the markets and all the regulations that go with them.

Series 7 is the NASD exam that is the most widely known; it is called the General Securities Registered Representative examination, and it involves some 250+ multiple-choice questions about various financial products and the rules governing the behavior of brokers, traders, and salespeople. Series 63 is the New York State extension of Series 7, and it is necessary to take it along with Series 7 in order to work in New York City. The exams are often preceded by a few weeks of mandatory training, so taking these exams requires a significant investment in terms of time.

Generally, technical people have little trouble passing the exams because the securities section is fairly low-tech (a calculator is not necessary), and the regulations section amounts to endless variations on the "thou shalt not steal" commandment applied to typical securities markets situations (e.g., John takes funds out of a client's account and buys 1,000 shares of IBM for himself; is he allowed to do that?). However, for many people, these exams are the main barrier separating them from the good life of a Wall Street broker, and we should all be grateful for that.

Last but not least, exchanges such as the NYSE and the London Stock Exchange act as regulators in their markets. Exchanges can impose their rules not only on their broker and dealer members, but also on the companies that list their securities on those exchanges. Some of the more stringent corporate disclosure rules are actually imposed by exchanges rather than the government. Generally the exchanges are highly visible in their regulatory and educational capacity (the Series 7 exam is actually developed by the NYSE).

If we put together the central banks, various government agencies, self-regulatory entities, and the exchanges, we find that a typical securities industry firm has to deal with a couple of dozen organizations that regulate what it can and cannot do, and the sheer number and complexity of the rules is such that no single person can possibly know them all. To cope with this regulatory burden, every firm has a *compliance division* whose job it is to make sure that the firm's activities do not violate anything in the sea of regulations. Compliance officers working in those divisions oversee the operations of existing business lines and play an important restraining role in the development of any new business processes (as one of my trader colleagues used to tell me, compliance's job was to say that anything I wanted to try was not a good idea). Since technology is often part of new business ideas, you are quite likely to deal with compliance if you work on Wall Street in a technical role.

AN INSTITUTIONAL PERSPECTIVE

This discussion of the market players has been functional—focused on what the different types of players do and how they make money. In the remainder of the chapter, I will attempt to summarize this information from a slightly different, institutional angle. This is useful because many institutions do many things at once, and it also will serve to reinforce what we have already learned. Let us begin this process at the bottom of the market organization chart in Figure 2–2, with a summary of the buy-side institutions.

A common trait of all buy-side institutions is that they take money and buy and sell securities in the hope of producing more money. While you and I would probably qualify as buy-side institutions based on this definition alone, in this discussion we are mostly interested in organizations that are engaged in such investment activities, and there are many different kinds of those. There are institutions that invest (or, in industry parlance, manage) their own money (insurance companies and pension funds are the most common here), but most such institutional investors give their money to professional asset management companies such as Blackrock, PIMCO, BGI, Deutsche Asset Management, and many others. Some of these companies do nothing but invest their clients' money, but many of them also have other related lines of business. For example, companies like Vanguard and Fidelity started out as pure mutual fund companies, collecting pools of money from small investors and investing those pools (called mutual funds) in different ways, but then started offering brokerage services for their small-investor clients, allowing the clients to trade other products, such as stocks and bonds, along with their own mutual funds (and they are also not above managing the portfolios of institutional investors).

Some of the business lines that these companies have are in reality quite removed from their core competency of asset management. For example, Fidelity is also a dominant force in the benefits management business—it takes employee pension plan contributions and invests them in various products based on each employee's preferences. Here Fidelity makes no investment decisions whatsoever, but rather leverages its vast experience in maintaining millions of individual trading accounts. Fidelity also opens checking accounts and sells life insurance. As a result of this diversification, the distinction between buy-side, sell-side, and nonfinancial companies is much less clear-cut now than it used to be.

This observation applies even more to the flagship sell-side companies like Goldman Sachs, Morgan Stanley, Lehman Brothers, Bear Stearns, and their peers. Each of them has an investment bank that brings new securities to market, which places them firmly in Figure 2–1 (in fact, most people would refer to these companies as investment banks). But they also have trading operations that are active in the secondary markets for almost all financial products. In their secondary-market capacity, these firms can act as dealers (in fixed-income and foreign exchange markets), as brokers (in futures and equity markets), or as broker-dealers, where they either fill customer orders themselves or send them to other places for execution (this mostly happens in equity and derivatives markets). All of these are typical sell-side activities, so these firms are all over the top part of our secondary-market diagram in Figure 2–2. In recent years, however, most of these firms have diversified into the buy-side companies' turf by building or (usually) acquiring asset management subsidiaries, which essentially do the exact same thing as traditional buy-side firms (except that they tend to cater more to wealthy individuals rather than to institutions). To muddle the picture even further, many of these firms engage in proprietary trading, and their units that do this act very much like hedge funds, which firmly belong to the buy side.

And the muddle does not stop there. There is now in fact little difference between a "normal" bank (the proper term is *commercial bank*), which lends money to people and businesses, and an "investment" bank, which is a securities business. In the 1930s, the U.S. financial regulations prohibited the combination of commercial banking with most types of securities business, and many great financial firms of the time had to split in two to comply with these regulations (Morgan Stanley and J. P. Morgan are good examples). By the late 1990s, however, these regulations were largely out of date as a result of globalization (major U.S. commercial banks were happily trading securities through their overseas subsidiaries) and market developments (the derivatives markets, which had become huge in the 1990s, were never covered by the Glass-Steagal Act that imposed the split).

In 1999, the U.S. Congress finally repealed the provisions of the Glass-Steagal Act that prohibited commercial banks from combining with securities firms, and within a couple of years some prominent investment banks were swallowed by the much larger commercial banks—Citibank bought Salomon Brothers, Chase bought J. P. Morgan—and, perhaps more importantly, large overseas banks like UBS, HSBC, Deutsche Bank, Credit Suisse, and Barclays (which always combined commercial and investment banking in their home markets) have become much more active in the U.S. securities business. Such conglomerates have a significant (and, many of their pure investment bank competitors say, unfair) advantage in that they are able to extend bank credit to their investment banking clients on favorable terms in order to get their investment banking business. As a result, these conglomerates are rapidly climbing in the investment banking league tables and are generally seen as the wave of the future.

From the perspective of this book, this presents us with a difficulty: although these conglomerates are beginning to dominate the industry, most of the people working for them are in the relatively low-tech commercial banking business, while our discussion applies mostly to those who are part of their much smaller but technology-intensive securities subsidiaries. To keep us focused, therefore, we will pretend that these security subsidiaries are still stand-alone companies, like their "independent" investment bank competitors. This approach makes all the more sense given that in practice there is little meaningful day-to-day interaction between the commercial banking and securities trading parts of such companies.

Generally, I think it is more important that you understand the functional role of the business you are working in rather than its position within the corporate hierarchy of the company. A brokerage business, for example, can be a stand-alone company like Ameritrade, part of a broker-dealer like Morgan Stanley, or embedded within a buy-side company like Vanguard, but in all cases, it will make money by collecting trading orders from its customers, finding the best ways to execute those orders, and charging commissions for the completed trades. At the end of the day, there are only a few distinct ways to make money in the securities business: (1) investment banking fees, (2) asset management fees, (3) brokerage commissions and exchange fees for executing other people's trades (and for trade facilitation services such as securities lending and financing), (4) market-making revenues from providing liquidity to other people, and (5) proprietary trading revenues from successful investment of one's own capital. The business you work for may combine some of those—for example, hedge funds combine 2 and 5, and most dealers combine 4 and 5—or it may embody one of those ways in its pure form. In any case, one of the most important things you can do to advance on Wall Street is to quickly figure out the sources of income of the business you work for. In most cases, this is not very hard to do if you understand these basic business models.

GEOGRAPHY OF THE FINANCIAL MARKETS

To conclude this chapter, let us take a look at the financial industry players from yet another point of view: their geography. Few other industries are as concentrated in just a couple of business centers, and in the case of the financial industry, this concentration can be easily understood from a historical perspective—until very recently, trading activities required the trading partners to be in physical proximity to each other so that securities and payments could be transferred between them within a reasonably short time.

In the early 1700s, the securities business was concentrated almost exclusively in London, with satellites in Amsterdam, Paris, and a few other European cities such as Antwerp. As the United States began to turn into a major economic power by the mid-1800s, New York emerged as America's financial center, building on its prominence as a hub for international and domestic trade. In the twentieth century, while London and Europe in general went through two world wars, New York continued to grow, and by the 1950s it had achieved "sole superpower" status in the financial world. However, the financial turmoil of the 1970s and the restrictive regulations that the U.S. government imposed on the financial industry caused much of it to migrate back to London, and as of the late 1980s London had regained its historic status as a major financial center, equal to New York in every respect. The economic rise of Japan and other Asian countries led to the emergence of Tokyo and, later, Hong Kong and Singapore as financial centers by the late 1980s. At present, the relative importance of these major centers can be roughly described as 40 percent New York, 40 percent London, 10 percent Tokyo, and the remaining 10 percent spread across the rest of Asia.

Exactly what is located in these centers that makes them so important for the financial industry? First and foremost, all investment (and a great many commercial) banks have their major offices in both London and New York, with smaller but still sizable offices in Tokyo and sometimes in other cities in Asia. London and New York also host major stock and commodity exchanges (although in the United States the dominant commodity exchanges are actually in Chicago, for reasons that we explain in Chapter 7). These exchanges acted as a nucleus, around which modern financial industry institutions gradually developed. Investment banks in their dealer capacity plus the exchanges make sure that an overwhelming majority of all securities trades are *executed* in New York and London, even if they originate all over the world. This clustering of execution venues used to be dictated by the need for the physical delivery of securities and payments. This historical factor no longer plays a direct role, but it has a lasting legacy nonetheless: most of the technological facilities of the financial industry that replaced the outdated procedures of yesteryear are still located around these execution venues, since this is where they were first built.

This partly explains why financial industry technology is concentrated in New York and London to an even greater degree than the industry itself. Yes, there are many financial institutions outside the two metropolitan areas, but those tend to be fairly low-tech affairs. All major investment banks, for example, maintain sales offices in many U.S. cities and most world capitals, which house salespeople who serve clients in each region. The combined number of people working in such offices can be as high as 5 percent of the bank's total headcount, but the number of technology people working there would be 0.5 percent of the total—a couple of people per office at most, and those people would invariably be focusing on support (making sure that everything in the office works) rather than development.

On the buy side, there is much greater geographical diversity—many major asset managers, such as PIMCO and BGI, are located on the West Coast of the United States. The hedge fund industry, being relatively new and unshackled by historical demands, is spread all over the world, with the emphasis being on nicer locations such as Florida, California, the Caribbean, the French Riviera, and the like, but even the hedge funds are overwhelmingly located in the New York and London metropolitan areas. They do not technically have to be there, but since most hedge fund people come from the sell-side institutions located in these centers, the funds locate where these people live. The retail brokerages and exchanges are also more spread out geographically. Almost all European capitals have at least a stock exchange, with Frankfurt and Paris being important centers far beyond their home markets. The American Midwest has a long tradition in this area, with futures exchanges and large brokerages being located in the region in Chicago and beyond (did you know that Kansas City and Minneapolis have important futures exchanges?). And, of course, the commercial banks are scattered all over the map.

Despite this geographical variety, the fact remains that with regard to quantitative and technical jobs, the industry is overwhelmingly concentrated in New York and London, with Tokyo holding a strong third place. To the extent that technical jobs exist in the industry outside these centers, they are typically filled by people transplanted from those centers. The upshot of this excursion into geography is this: to work in a technical role in the financial industry, be prepared to move to either the New York or the London metropolitan area.

Speaking of technical roles, it is now time for us to ask an important question: what exactly are the technical roles of which we are speaking here? What do technical people actually do in the financial industry? To answer these questions, we need to take a deeper look at what is going on inside these financial industry players. The next chapter attempts to do exactly that.

CHAPTER 3

Financial Firms
and Their People

As we discussed in the previous chapter, Wall Street is a community of many different types of institutional players, and we have just spent some time talking about the business relationships among different boxes in the industry organization diagrams. However, I do not expect you to play with these boxes much in the course of your professional life (unless you become a CEO or other captain of the industry). That professional life is likely to take place inside one (or perhaps several) of these boxes, and on a practical level it is quite important to understand what the boxes look like on the inside. In this chapter, we will attempt to look inside some of the different types of financial firms and try to get a feel for how they are put together and what it is like to work there in a technical role.

This plan immediately presents us with a difficulty: there are quite a number of different types of securities firms, so we have many different boxes to look into. Where should we start? I think the best place to start is with the big sell-side firms—the Goldman Sachses and Morgan Stanleys— because (1) they do so many different things that many other smaller players resemble parts of these big broker-dealers, and (2) they employ so many people that my average reader either is working in one of these firms or will be at some point. As we mentioned in the last chapter, these broker-dealers do a wide variety of things, and their internal structure reflects this diversity. Before we plunge into a discussion of the internal workings of these firms, however, a disclaimer is in order: there is great variability among the different firms in terms of organizational structure. While it is possible to generalize, as we do here, there will always be firms whose structure does not fit some or all of our generic scheme. However, comparing the structure of your specific firm with our generic blueprint would be a very useful exercise, despite these differences.

STRUCTURE OF A SELL-SIDE FIRM

Figure 3–1 shows a generic organizational chart of a broker-dealer. The boxes on this chart represent *divisions* of the company—organizational units that are broadly responsible for various types of business activities. Some of these divisions are revenue-producing; the investment banking, asset management, and trading divisions are the most typical in this group. But there are also divisions that do not generate any revenue, such as legal/compliance, building and facilities management, financial risk management, and, of course, technology. The total number of people working for a company like this is usually in the low tens of thousand, and each division will have between a few hundred and a couple of thousand employees. The divisions are usually separated in terms of location (sometimes being on different floors of a building and sometimes in different buildings). There is typically little meaningful interaction between the revenue-producing divisions, but many nonrevenue-producing units, such as compliance and especially technology, are designed to work with all divisions at once (and therefore are sometimes called *firmwide* divisions, as in firmwide risk).

Let us first examine the revenue-producing divisions. In this book we really care only about places where a technically inclined reader can find interesting work, and this fortunately eliminates many of these divisions. For example, an investment banking division (which is responsible for bringing

FIGURE 3–1

Internal organization of a broker-dealer.

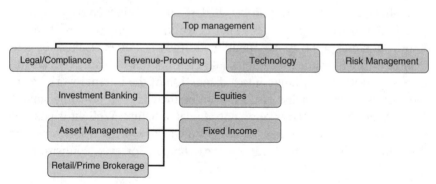

new securities to market, advising companies on mergers, and other such activities), despite its popular-culture glamour and the very significant revenues it generates, is a decidedly low-tech business—the most complex piece of technology in an investment banking world is a PowerPoint presentation with animated pie charts. The same largely goes for a retail brokerage division (which maintains accounts for individual investors), while an asset management division is really a captive buy-side firm, which we will discuss elsewhere. That leaves *trading divisions*—what exactly do they do?

A trading division makes money by trading securities with the firm's clients in the secondary market. Usually such a division will be focused on one type of market (equities, FX, or fixed income), although sometimes a single division will trade all types of products. Inside a trading division, there are broad *business lines*—for example, rates and credit in a fixed-income division—and each business line is further subdivided into trading desks that trade different products, as illustrated in Figure 3–2. There are also salespeople (that's why it is called a sell-side firm). The sales force (sometimes euphemistically called *distribution*) is usually organized not by product area but rather by type of customer (hedge funds, banks, asset managers, corporations, and so on).

Each trading desk has anywhere between 5 and 25 traders (who are sometimes spread across several geographic locations, such as New York, London, and Tokyo), plus trading assistants, interns, secretaries, and other support people. These people are physically located in an area on a *trading floor,* a huge open space where people sit at long benchlike desks in front of their monitors (usually several flat-panel monitors per trader) and phone systems, where nothing separates them from their neighbors sitting

F I G U R E   3–2

Organization of a trading division in a broker-dealer firm.

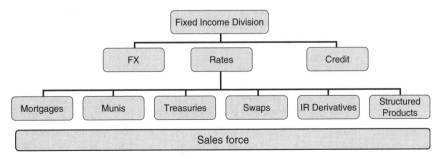

three feet away on each side of them so that they can communicate with them instantly. A trading desk is like a mini-solar system on the trading floor: the traders sit at the center, in one row within easy earshot of one another; the next layer of seats around them will be occupied by their assistants; in the next layer will be salespeople who work closely with this particular desk; then perhaps there will be some quants and technology folks who support the desk; and beyond that there will be other solar systems (if it sounds like the distance from the central trading area reflects some sort of pecking order, that's because it does).

To understand how life on the trading floor works, let us begin with salespeople. Each salesperson is responsible for several *accounts* (customers). Every day, the salesperson calls up each of those accounts and conducts some relationship-building small talk about the weather, golf, and the latest football game, into which she then slips something like, "And by the way, we have this interesting trade idea for you—you should sell X and buy Y instead." This is called *trade solicitation*, and to do it well, a salesperson should not only be able to build rapport, but also (1) understand the business needs of the clients and (2) understand the products that the firm can sell to those clients.

Let us say that the solicitation works and a customer actually wants to do this trade. The salesperson will then pass this *trade request* on to the traders on the appropriate desk—either by shouting across the trading floor something like, "Peter, show a hundred tens for Blackrock," or by calling the traders on the phone. The traders now have to *price* the proposed transaction. They look at where the market is trading, look at their positions, factor in the importance of the customer, and quote a price that is sufficiently competitive for the customer to accept it but that also contains a markup that will allow the desk to make a profit. The salesperson relays the quote back to the customer, and if the customer accepts it, a new trade is born.

At this point, the salesperson has done her job and earns a *sales credit* (which is basically an imaginary sum of money that will accumulate during the year and then be used at the end of the year to determine her compensation), but the trader's job has just begun. The new trade will be entered into his *trading books* and contribute to the trader's positions, and the trader will have to *manage* those positions in such a way as to make money over time. The result of the trader's work is his *profit and loss*, usually known as *PnL*, which (unlike sales credits) is a tangible sum of money that contributes directly to the firm's revenues (and is the defining factor that affects the trader's compensation at the end of the year). We will discuss all of that in much greater detail in the next few chapters; for our present purposes, it is enough to remember that the salespeople bring in trades and that the traders turn them into profit.

Actually, the statement that it is traders who turn trades into profit is only partially true. The trades become money only when they *settle*—when the securities are delivered and the money is paid—and this happens outside the trading floor in another area called the *back office* (or, less dismissively, *operations*). The back office processes all trades done by the *front office* (this term encompasses all customer-facing activities and largely coincides with the concept of a trading floor), checks them for consistency (*reconciliation/clearing*), nets out trades done with the same counterparties to reduce the number of payments and deliveries that need to be made (*netting*), and finally *settles* the trades by making the payments and delivering the securities as specified by the terms of each trade. It is a big job—a typical broker-dealer firm does hundreds of thousands of trades a day—that obviously invites automation. In particular, the movement of trades from the front office to the back office (which used to be done by messengers) is now handled by multiple layers of software plumbing, which, together with the people who support these pipes, is called the *middle office* (while the software pipes themselves are often called *middleware*).

THE USE OF TECHNOLOGY ON WALL STREET

If there is anything more removed from the academic ideal of the abstract pursuit of knowledge than the money-making machine I just briefly described, I do not know what it is—what can a theoretical physics Ph.D. possibly do in a crassly commercial environment like that? To understand the role of technology and technical people in the trading world today, we need some historical perspective, and in the next few paragraphs I offer a brief history of Wall Street technology. That history begins in the late 1960s, when the first mainframe computers were installed at Wall Street firms. They went into the back-office areas, which were creaking under the strain of processing rapidly increasing trade volumes, and by and large made further volume growth possible. The people looking after those mainframes formed the core of the firmwide information technology organization, which serves the firm as a whole rather than specific desks or even specific trading divisions.

The front-office areas saw little technology in the early 1970s aside from an occasional pocket calculator, but that began to change as the decade unfolded with the introduction of terminal services such as Nasdaq terminals, Reuters VideoMaster, and Reuters Monitor, which provided screen displays of stock, futures, and foreign exchange quotes. By the end of the decade, the trading floor was filled with CRT displays and keyboards. Again, the people hired by the banks to maintain all that new equipment and infrastructure became part of firmwide information technology.

By the end of the 1970s, some of the terminals on the trading floor were actually connected not to Reuters but to the firm's mainframes (and newer "minicomputers," such as the VAX and PDP-10), allowing the traders to run simple computing jobs. These terminals were quickly joined by the latest novelties, such as Apple and IBM personal computers, which were followed by Sun Unix workstations by the mid-1980s. This was long before Internet browsing, e-mail, and word processing—these computers were actually used, believe it or not, for computing.

The need to compute things on the trading floor was primarily driven by market developments of the time, mainly by the rapid growth of derivatives trading—the traders needed to be able to price derivatives trades, and even the most pedestrian options trade still requires running the Black-Scholes formula or one of its adaptations for specific markets. While many options traders were (and still are) quite proficient in math, making these early computers do what the traders actually wanted them to do (and they wanted increasingly complex things, especially in the interest-rate markets) presented both a challenge and an opportunity. The challenge was that the traders did not have the time (and very often the skills) to either improve upon the pricing models they used or actually write some working code that would implement these new models. The opportunity was that those who managed to do this anyway reaped an instant competitive advantage in the derivatives markets.

As with many other similar quandaries in life, the solution that many traders chose was to hire a professional, and that professional was more often than not a physics Ph.D. who could (1) understand the existing pricing models and improve upon them, and (2) develop programs that traders could run on their computers to make use of the new models. Thus the first *quantitative analysts*, or *quants*, appeared on Wall Street in the mid-1980s and went to work building models and software for the specific trading desks that hired them. They were not part of the information technology divisions, which at the time were busy organizing the firm's infrastructure and adding newfangled things like networks and databases.

The number of quants hired by the trading businesses grew rapidly, and by the end of the 1980s it had become clear that their work could be organized more effectively. The all-too-common situation where five desks would hire five quants to do exactly the same thing five times called for a better organizational structure, and such structures began to coalesce around 1990. They were based on the idea that quants and programmers should be a resource for the trading division as a whole. Many of them therefore migrated from their trading desks into new divisional-level "research" units, where they worked with one another and the traders from the whole division to develop models and products that could be used by everyone in the division.

These research departments quickly developed a dual identity. On the one hand, there were quasi-academic groups of quants who dreamed up new pricing models, wrote papers for quantitative finance journals, went to conferences, and generally were charged with thinking big thoughts. On the other hand, Wall Street finally recognized that what many of the quants were doing was software development, and so some of the new divisional-level groups were organized more or less as professional software development shops, with a shared code base and source control systems and other standard software development infrastructure.

While almost all early quants did both modeling and programming, the new division of labor separated front-office technology people into "pure quants" and "software developers," and for a while the pure quants appeared to have gotten a better deal than their software developer colleagues. It is not coincidental that most of the standard financial models of today were developed in the early 1990s in or around the academic parts of the divisional research groups on Wall Street, and initially Wall Street was happy to pay for the upkeep of these research establishments, as the new models helped the traders and enhanced the firm's credibility with its clients. However, by 1997 or so, the allure of pure research on Wall Street began to dim, as it became increasingly clear that every firm ended up using the same models, so there was little competitive advantage in maintaining such research groups.

While the research groups began to stagnate in the mid-1990s, the software development arm of Wall Street technology grew at a frenetic pace. The first factor driving this growth was the continuing advance of computing technology, which made it possible to computerize more and more of the routine trading activities, such as position keeping and trade entry. The new *trading systems* that were created by these in-house development groups allowed the traders not only to book trades using specially designed *trade blotters,* but also to see their positions, PnLs, and risk in a timely manner through a computer application, which simplified traders' lives enormously.

While many such applications used financial analytics libraries created by the pure quants, their main point was not so much the analytics per se, but rather integrating analytics into other useful things. In fact, the development of financial analytics proper was at this time segregated into special "core" development groups, which went through mountains of disparate code left behind by early quants, salvaged what they could, added the more modern stuff, and packaged all of it into well-designed common libraries that everyone (not only in the division, but across the whole firm) could use.

By the mid-1990s, a new wave of technology hit Wall Street with the widespread deployment of modern *market data platforms*—while the platforms themselves remained the purview of firmwide information technology, the divisional-level development groups started integrating live market data into their systems. This gave a second wind to trading systems development, as different parts of the trading systems could now communicate with one another via the real-time messaging platforms. For the first time, it became possible to integrate many disjointed first-generation systems into a coherent whole.

The second major factor behind the explosive growth of in-house software development was (of course) the Internet boom of the late 1990s, especially that part of it that promised swift and certain death to any business that did not immediately begin to spend lots of money on e-commerce. Wall Street did exactly that, on a truly massive scale (it helped that the late 1990s were a period of record profits for Wall Street, fueled largely by that same Internet boom)—the number of software developers working on Wall Street easily doubled between 1996 and 1999. These newly hired people started building all kinds of e-commerce portals and other such applications, most of which are now long defunct, but there were areas where their efforts proved very useful for their employers: most notably, electronic trading systems and connectivity to trading partners, both of which today are critical for any firm's ability to stay in business.

Interestingly, much of this Internet-inspired work took place not on the divisional level, where all software development had been done until then, but rather within the information technology divisions, which heretofore had focused on maintaining the infrastructure. These divisions, having grown large and important, demanded and got a piece of the Internet action and have stayed in the software development business ever since. In fact, the latest trend has been to either move software development groups from trading divisions to information technology, or create groups within information technology that are assigned to specific trading divisions, which boils down to the same thing: reporting to information technology bosses but actually working for the traders.

One lasting legacy of the Wall Street research groups of the early 1990s was the development of *quantitative risk management*. Prior to that time, Wall Street firms had looked at their risks more or less the way a bank would: based on their balance-sheet assets and liabilities (i.e., if someone bought a $100 million par amount of some bond, he would think that he had an asset worth $100 million). However, every trading unit within these firms gradually started looking at its assets and liabilities not based on their book value, but rather based on their mark-to-market value (if the bond we mentioned trades in the market for 95, it had to be treated as only a $95 million asset). This kind of mark-to-market valuation is easier said than done for more complex instruments, but the derivatives models that had been built by the early 1990s were doing a credible job of it for most products on the level of individual desks, and the quants were arguing that the same kind of analysis had to be applied to the firm as a whole.

This line of reasoning received a major boost in 1994, when many Wall Street firms lost hundreds of millions of dollars because of an unexpected rapid rise in interest rates and had to resort to mass layoffs and other belt-tightening measures, but the first firmwide risk divisions had in fact been created a few years before that. The "research" quants not only created the concept, but also provided much of the workforce for the newly formed risk management units—many people who had previously worked in the quasi-academic divisional research groups found a new home in firmwide risk management.

After a few years, these risk management units also stratified into risk management proper (which is done by *risk managers*) and risk management technology (which takes care of all the mundane tasks of getting all necessary information together and processing it); taken together, these units now constitute a significant (about 20 percent) fraction of the technical and quantitative population at Wall Street sell-side firms. They are doing a good job, too: when rates unexpectedly shot up in 2003, none of the big banks had significant trading losses, which was in stark contrast to the 1994 experience and was attributed to the improvements in the risk management process since that time.

OTHER MARKET PLAYERS

It is time for us to move on beyond the dealer banks to other market players. Let us begin with the asset managers (the "real-money" clients of the dealer banks). These companies are typically somewhat smaller than the sell-side firms, with total headcount ranging from a few hundred to a few thousand people (although the biggest of them, such as Fidelity, have almost 30,000 employees). Many of these companies have other lines of business that are totally unrelated to our narrative (from life insurance to human resources services), which we will ignore and instead focus on the basic asset management business model, which at its core is quite straightforward.

An asset management company collects pools of money from its clients (retail or institutional investors) and invests these pools on those clients' behalf. Its sales force focuses on bringing in "assets under management," which are then given to *portfolio managers* who decide how to invest them. These investment decisions are then implemented by traders, whose job is to provide the best possible execution of the portfolio manager's instructions. Unlike the sell-side traders, the traders at asset management firms initiate the trades and pay transaction costs. They also perform day-to-day management of the portfolios—for example, making sure that allocation percentages stay within the limits prescribed by the portfolio managers.

The relationship between the trading and portfolio management prowess of asset management firms and their actual revenues is actually quite indirect; the firms earn a management fee proportional to assets under management (usually around 1 percent a year) almost regardless of what happens to those assets. If the investment performance is bad, then the investors are likely to withdraw the assets and give them to somebody else, so good performance does matter in the end, but there is none of the immediacy that is typical of sell-side trading (where if you screw up today, your PnL gets hit today).

The distribution of power in the asset management firms is also different from what we observed at the sell-side institutions. Generally the portfolio managers get to run things and are either rewarded or penalized for their investment decisions, while the traders play a supporting role. This is reflected in the technology needs of these companies, which are tilted heavily toward *portfolio management* software that is supposed to help the portfolio managers make their investment decisions by showing them how various assets have performed in the past, how they are correlated, and other such information (which are essentially *data mining* tasks). There are also tools that resemble the risk management applications used in sell-side firms that analyze what would happen to a given portfolio if the markets moved in a certain way. The traders also get pieces of technology—trade blotters and position management systems that simplify their day-to-day trading activities (and, of course, there is back-office technology). This software is developed in-house at larger firms and often purchased from third parties at the smaller ones. Overall, compared to the sell-side banks, the technological organization as a whole and its software development branch in particular are significantly smaller at these firms (although there are interesting exceptions at some companies that are trying to turn technology and modeling into their competitive edge).

Hedge funds are similar in function to asset management companies (they also, technically, manage their investors' assets), but they have a very different feel. These are much smaller operations (from just a couple of people to perhaps a couple of hundred for the larger ones), and they are focused on making trading profits rather than on following a portfolio management strategy (in fact, there are no portfolio managers there at all). The traders who work at hedge funds are overwhelmingly former sell-side traders who wanted to strike out on their own. Unlike their brethren at real-money asset managers, these traders care very much about the success of their trading strategies, because they get to keep something like 20 percent of their trading profits as an incentive fee. Again unlike their asset management counterparts (and like sell-side proprietary traders), they have very few restrictions on what kind of trades they can do and are free to go long or short on pretty much anything (in particular, they can borrow in the money markets using their investors' capital as collateral, which allows them to establish positions far in excess of the assets they have).

Because of their smaller size, hedge funds usually have no technology organization to speak of—the back-office work and position keeping are usually done by the broker-dealers with which the hedge fund maintains accounts, and there is little need for standard trading systems for booking trades and other such functions because the number of trades the fund does is usually low (although there are some funds doing high-frequency trading where the situation is different in this regard). What they do have a great need for are proprietary trading models that analyze the relative value of securities in different markets and ultimately tell the traders what to buy and sell. Unlike standard financial analytics, which the hedge funds usually buy as a package from software vendors, the proprietary trading models are often viewed as a source of competitive advantage and are therefore developed internally either by the traders themselves or by quants hired for that purpose (often these quants end up trading as well). This is a rapidly growing segment of the industry (and it's clear why—what's not to like about these arrangements?).

For completeness, let us take a brief look at various financial intermediaries, such as interdealer brokers and exchanges. As we explained in the previous chapter, these companies do not take positions and therefore do not incur market risk (which eliminates the need for most of the technology that is so widespread at dealer firms)—their job is to simply match buyers with sellers, and this dictates their internal structure. Traditionally, this matching up has been done by human brokers (either on an exchange floor or inside an interdealer broker firm), but this model is being rather brutally displaced by electronic trading platforms, which in this case are built around a *matching engine* that (you guessed it) matches buy orders with sell orders.

These establishments are now rapidly consolidating and getting rid of their traditional broker workforce, but those that are left standing (mostly in the derivatives area, which has not gone completely electronic yet) actually have fairly sophisticated pricing needs and do employ quants and developers to build and maintain their pricing models. Of course, all these electronic trading platforms do not just happen—the brokers are being replaced by developers who write those systems. But overall the importance of brokers and exchanges as places of employment is now declining.

Last but definitely not least, we need to mention the financial software industry. While many people would maintain that this is not a genuine part of Wall Street, from the technology perspective it definitely is—should something (heaven forbid) happen to Bloomberg or Reuters, Wall Street would stop in its tracks much faster and stay in that state much longer than if something happened to a major bank. Again, many people (including some at both of these companies) would object to calling Bloomberg and Reuters software companies, but from the product perspective they are, and most other financial software companies are trying to emulate their business model: not just selling software, but delivering services through it.

The sizes of financial software companies vary enormously, from single-person operations to huge global companies with tens of thousands of employees (again Bloomberg comes to mind), but from an employment perspective, they all offer essentially two job roles: (1) sales and (2) software development (sometimes blended into a single person at smaller shops). If we leave sales aside, the total number of developers working in that segment is relatively small (I estimate fewer than 10,000 worldwide), but it is growing rapidly and is likely to continue doing so.

WALL STREET JOBS FOR TECHNICAL PEOPLE

To help make sense of the various financial industry job roles that have been described, in the remainder of this chapter I will simply list them for easy reference, with brief comments about their relative advantages and disadvantages. I will list only jobs that are of interest to people with technical backgrounds, which leaves out lots of roles, such as corporate lawyer, human resources professional, portfolio manager, and, unfortunately, investment banker (although there are some technical people who go into investment banking simply because of the pay). I will focus on jobs that are directly or indirectly related to trading (and risk management as its consequence), and the organizing theme will be the imaginary yet sharply drawn line that separates the "business side" of Wall Street from the "technology side." On the business side, the goal is to make money; on the technology side, it is to build technology that helps the business side make money; and there is rarely much ambiguity as to which side you are on. While the two sides often work together very closely, there are profound differences in their day-to-day priorities, career goals, and performance benchmarks, as the following description of the job roles will make clear.

We begin our list on the business side, with the job role that is the furthest away from the business-technology interface: that of a *salesperson* in a dealer firm. A salesperson's job is to bring in trades, which is done by maintaining good relationships with her accounts and supplying them with trade ideas that match their business needs. This job role is very people-oriented (a salesperson will spend most of her day talking to people), and also often involves extensive travel to visit clients in far-off places—both of these features can be advantages or disadvantages, depending on one's preferences.

Salespeople need a fairly deep understanding of the financial products they sell, as well as of the business models of their customers. Therefore most salespeople have business degrees, such as an MBA, and very few of them come from a technical background. However, their use of various pieces of technology is rapidly growing—they are now increasingly able to analyze historical data in order to produce trade ideas, and there are special applications built for the sales force that allow them to keep track of the trades they bring in (and the corresponding sales credits). Their interactions with technology are often confrontational for two reasons: (1) very few salespeople are technologically literate, and (2) some technologies (such as electronic distribution channels that allow clients to trade with the firm directly) present a threat to their livelihood. In general, most salespeople are so removed from the technological frontier that I would have lumped them together with investment bankers and portfolio managers and left them off my list entirely were it not for the fact that *sales technology* is a growing area, and people who work there need to understand their business counterparts.

The *traders* in dealer banks are much closer to the business-technology divide. While many of them come from a business background, many others (especially younger ones) have a technical education (and many of the ones who do not are quite tech-savvy anyway). They as a group have been exposed to (and benefited from) technology for about two decades, so even the most senior traders today do not remember how it was before they had all these trading systems, market data displays, and one-click execution ability. The other side of this observation is that most of the technology that exists on the trading floor today was built at traders' behest and with their active participation (at least in setting the requirements).

While many traders are quite capable technically (some of the most complex and clever spreadsheets I have ever seen were built by traders), they rarely have the time to do anything technical themselves; the reality is that flow trading is a grueling full-time occupation that requires 120 percent concentration as well as an extraordinary ability to multitask. However, proprietary traders at dealer banks and especially at hedge funds have more time and motivation to engage in quantitative modeling, to the point that many of them call themselves *quant-traders* (although their work rarely goes beyond spreadsheets). Of course, the importance of technical skills for traders depends decisively on the products that they trade, with fixed income and derivatives traders being by far the most technically sophisticated.

The advantages of being a trader are many. Traders are perhaps the most powerful and prestigious group in dealer banks, the work itself is very interesting and challenging, and there is a clear performance measure (PnL), which tends to reduce the bureaucratic clutter. Another advantage that is important to our discussion of the business-technology interface is that generally the traders get to tell the technology people what to do. There are, of course, disadvantages as well: the work may be interesting, but it is also very stressful and demanding, as well as somewhat repetitive. Trading is often likened to either a video game or a poker game, but neither of those would be much fun if you had to play them for 10 hours every day. The gaming analogy also extends to the results of the trader's work—spending a life trying to achieve a high PnL is on some level not much different from devoting a life trying to beat a previous high gaming score.[1] Overall, though, there is much to be said for a trading career.

Going across the business-technology boundary, the first job role we consider is that of a *desk quant*. The desk quant works with the traders on a trading desk and does what the traders themselves would like to do if they had the time and/or the skills: he creates and maintains quantitative models that are used in day-to-day trading activities. This role originated back in the 1980s and is becoming increasingly rare these days, as most of these tasks are handled by units of the technology organization. Even where desk quants still exist, the content of their work today is much different from what it was originally: in the early days, quants were building both models and the software that made it possible for the traders to use those models, while today the software part is almost always handled by divisional-level software development technology units. In fact, one of the most important job functions of a desk quant today is to act as an intermediary between traders and technology units. The desk quants often are the trader's mouthpieces in formulating systems requirements and in making sure that those systems actually work as promised.

The advantages to being a desk quant are interesting work, with a relatively low percentage of mundane tasks; deep involvement in trading activities (often without the drawback of being responsible for the PnL); and generally a pleasant feeling of being in the center of things. The disadvantages are (as usual) the flip side of the advantages. Being a rarity means that this is a lonely job, with very few opportunities to work with peers. Many desk quants really want to be traders and dislike the fact that they have no PnL to call their own. They also feel an almost daily need to justify their existence, as the technology units that are doing the programming for them are in fact hungry to take over whatever interesting work they are doing. In the long run, the technology organization will probably succeed

---

1. Those to whom these musings do not make any sense actually make the best traders.

in taking over the desk quants' tasks everywhere (whereas now this has happened almost everywhere), but while it lasts, this is one of the more desirable jobs for quantitative people. Another feature of being a desk quant (which can be an advantage or a disadvantage, depending on the person) is that from that position it is relatively easy to defect to the business side and become a trader.

Another area for technical and quantitative people that is right on the business-technology boundary is *sales research* (also known as *market research*). Wall Street research has gotten a bad name recently as a result of highly publicized scandals involving stock analysts, but this area is in fact much broader than it seems from the news coverage. The goal of the research organization is to give the salespeople some intellectual ammunition with which they can go out and bring in trades; this often is reduced to pitching individual stocks and companies, but just as often it includes a broader analysis of the economic, political, and technical issues driving the markets.

A research unit produces a whole array of daily, weekly, and monthly reports on these and other market-related matters often involving significant number-crunching, so many people working in this area (especially in fixed income and derivatives) come from a technical rather than a business background. This is almost the only role a technical person can fill where she will have extensive interactions with the firm's clients and get to visit them all over the world (in most other job roles, business travel is limited to major centers: New York, London, and Tokyo, and maybe Hong Kong, Chicago, and Singapore).

The advantages of working in sales research are many: the work itself is often quite interesting and involves interaction with a large number of people from both inside and outside the firm, there are ample opportunities to learn how real market participants think about their markets and what drives their decisions (something that is almost impossible to learn from books), and the hours are some of the least demanding in the industry. The main disadvantage is, in a way, contained in the very term *sales* research— this role has much more to do with sales than with research. At the end of the day, this is a sales job. A person doing sales research is not just sitting there creating market models; he is selling his models, his firm, and himself to the clients, and his success is measured by how well this sales process is going rather than by the quality and content of his creative output. This is why many people who want to go from that position over to the business side end up as salespeople rather than traders. Another disadvantage is that the research organization is often fairly big and bureaucratic, and in the absence of a clear performance measure, this can lead to some ugly office politics.

Desk quants and sales research are a small minority of the quantitative and technical workforce in Wall Street firms (under 5 percent of the total). Most technical people should properly be called *software developers* because this is what they do (although many would object to this classification and call themselves quants or other fancy names). They work in software development groups and typically perform both programming and modeling tasks, but their primary output is software rather than abstract models.

These groups exist at different levels in the firm's organizational structure. First, there are groups organized on the divisional level to serve the needs of specific businesses within the division; these are usually called front-office technology or something similar. People working in front-office technology usually interact with the desks quite extensively—in fact, many people who used to work as desk quants now work in (or at least formally report to) such front-office groups. Front-office technology is often critical to the business unit's ability to function, which means that whatever problems these systems develop have to be resolved within minutes, which, in turn, means that developers in these groups are almost always on call and generally spend a significant amount of time on supporting their systems.

There are also software development teams that belong to firmwide IT; they typically are responsible for *middleware* systems such as market data, exchange connectivity, trade and position management systems, and the like that are used throughout the firm. While these groups usually have few direct interactions with the business areas (and are usually located away from trading areas), they still have an unmistakable Wall Street feel that distinguishes them from their software industry counterparts. They work with financial objects and (ideally) need to understand what those objects are and what the impact would be if this or that were to break, and the requirements for speed of development and dealing with problems are not that different from those in front-office technology areas. Developers working in professional financial software shops outside the banks operate in a different environment in this regard; their focus is usually on the software itself rather than on the business case for it (this is handled by the software sales team).

Despite these differences, financial software developers have a lot in common almost regardless of what they do. They all have to deal with a fast-changing market landscape that often necessitates quick adjustments to development plans; this often wreaks havoc with testing and deployment procedures and makes the support burden higher than the software industry average. Because of this fluidity of design requirements, this profession is in dire need of more people who understand the underlying business issues better (the problem that this book aims to address). Very few software developers these days have the immediacy of access to the traders that early quants enjoyed 20 years ago, and therefore it is difficult for them to acquire the necessary understanding of the business just by working in a software development group, even at a top Wall Street firm.

Another commonality among financial developers is that what they actually develop is almost never a stand-alone product—it is always something that will use services provided by some existing systems in the bank and perhaps provide some services to other such systems (this is true even of the software companies outside Wall Street proper; their products still have to be integrated into the client firm's systems). Because of this, it is unusually important to know what other systems are out there, what they can and cannot do, and who are the people that can make things happen with those other systems.

What are the advantages and disadvantages of a financial software developer role? The list of advantages should include the opportunity to do interesting work that often requires high levels of professionalism in both computer science and quantitative areas, and the fact that this work is performed some distance away from the hustle and bustle of the trading floor, which means a quieter work environment and a more predictable paycheck. Another thing that I consider an advantage is that software development is a group activity that involves a fair amount of interaction with immediate colleagues and perhaps other areas.

As for the disadvantages, the mix of programming and modeling that this group does varies greatly, but more often than not it is tilted toward programming and away from modeling, which many people with advanced hard sciences degrees working in this field find regrettable. There are also no objective performance measures, which leads to bureaucratization—a growing problem as the technology organizations of the big banks grow larger and more powerful. But a far more important negative consequence of this rapid growth is that the opportunities for learning about business issues that people in this role used to have are rapidly disappearing. In a typical bank today, the developers outnumber traders 5 to 1, so for any given developer, the frequency and quality of his communication with his business-side clients have both suffered as a result of this growth.

COMMON ISSUES

Let us review some common issues that apply to both the business side and the technology side of Wall Street. Many people will be surprised to learn that in practice there is little real difference between the business and technology sides in such vital areas as the hiring and firing process, career development, and (believe it or not) compensation.

There are generally two distinct ways in which people join Wall Street firms: either straight out of a four-year college through a *graduate program*, or from another firm or even another industry or academia through a *lateral hiring* program. When people go in straight from college, they start in an *analyst* position, where, perhaps after going through a training program, they will spend the next two to five years. At this stage they may have an opportunity to rotate through several different areas of the firm and hopefully find the one they like the most. They will play a very junior role at first, but as their responsibilities grow, they will eventually be promoted to the next level, which is usually called an *associate*.

The next level after that (most people make it in five to eight years) is variously known as *vice president* (VP) in some firms or *director* in others (and in some others this layer is further subdivided into associate directors and "real" directors). At this stage, people will often have some small-scale management responsibilities, with maybe a couple of individuals reporting to them directly. The next step above that is *managing director* (MD), who will typically be responsible for some well-defined area (perhaps a trading desk or some decent-sized chunk of the technology organization), with 10 to 50 direct reports. Beyond that, we enter the stratospheric levels of management, of which I thankfully know very little. When people join the firm as lateral hires, they go directly to one of the higher levels commensurate with what they had at their previous place of employment (for recent Ph.D.s coming from academia, this usually means an associate-level position, while a tenured professor may become a VP).

The Wall Street compensation process also works the same way on both sides. Compensation consists of a *base salary,* which comes every month, and a *bonus,* which comes once a year (the timing depends on when the financial year ends for the firm and ranges from December to February). The sum of the two is called total compensation, or *total comp*. When a person starts out as an analyst, her compensation is almost all salary and very little bonus, while at the managing director level and above, it is almost all bonus. The base salary tops out in the low six figures even at the highest levels, so in practice, after someone has been in the industry for several years, the bonus becomes a central feature of compensation. The annual awarding of bonuses, therefore, is the main event of the year for most experienced people. It is preceded by a couple of months of "comp meetings," where the management fights for chunks of the bonus pool and haggles over who gets how much.

In theory, your bonus depends on individual performance, the financial performance of your division, and the financial performance of your particular business unit within the division. Measuring individual performance is notoriously difficult, however, and most firms run internal employee evaluation programs whereby people submit their opinions of one another and of their management, which are taken into account by management in determining your performance score. In practice, the most important factor affecting your bonus is your total comp for the previous year—what does depend on individual performance is by how much one's bonus will increase. While the total comp for people at the same administrative level is comparable regardless of whether they are on the business side or the technology side (at least at the lower rungs of the administrative ladder), the business side offers more chances to rise through the ranks faster if you make a lot of money for the firm—it is not uncommon to see a 29-year-old MD on the trading floor, while this is almost unheard of on the technology side.

The fact that people get much of their annual compensation once a year has the side effect of distorting the normal turnover process—if people want to leave, they tend to wait until they get their bonuses before going. Because of this, within a couple of months after the bonuses are delivered, there is often a noticeable changing of the guard, with some people resigning and going to other firms and people from other firms coming in to take their places.

The standard Wall Street employment contract states that it can be terminated by either the employer or the employee at any time for any reason or no reason at all, and both sides generally act accordingly. When the employer terminates the contract, it is called either a firing (if it is limited to one person) or a layoff (if a whole group of people is let go); in both cases, the person let go may actually get a severance package worth a few months of salary even for fairly low-level positions. The person will also get no advance warning; his manager will take him to a conference room and announce the decision, and security will escort him out of the building right away (sometimes he will not even be able to pick up his stuff). This seems more than a bit inhumane on the face of it, but it does make business sense—many people, especially on the business side, have the ability to inflict huge amounts of damage on the firm if they act maliciously (and being fired can put you in that state of mind), so the policy of immediately stripping the person of all forms of physical access to the firm's property (buildings and computer systems) is, unfortunately, born of necessity.

When an employee terminates the contract, the process is a bit more drawn out: she submits her resignation to her managers, they usually try to talk her into staying, and there is a custom of giving the employer two weeks' notice (this is often skipped on the business side, especially for traders, who usually have to give up their trading privileges right away). People who switch firms usually do so with the help of *headhunters* (who get paid by the employers and collect something like 30 percent of the total comp of every person they place) or through their personal contacts—it is almost impossible to find jobs on Wall Street in the help wanted section of a newspaper.

The other side of the excellent compensation is that you generally have to work a lot—on both the business side and the technology side, the hours are pretty tough. The traders and salespeople usually get in around 7 a.m. and get out maybe at 6 p.m.; the technology folks usually come in later and stay later, although there is more variability here. There is no concept of overtime pay, and there are generally no compunctions about requiring someone to work on weekends or about calling someone at 3 a.m. to help resolve some crisis in another time zone—to a large extent, the firm owns your whole life. In fairness to Wall Street employers, it must be said that many of them try to introduce work-family balance programs or perhaps some work-at-home arrangements to ease the pain of commuting, offer unusually generous maternity (and even paternity) leaves, and so on, but for the overwhelming majority of the Wall Street population, their work continues to take up most of their waking hours.

I want to end this chapter on a personal note. I came to Wall Street from academia, and so did many of my current colleagues, and we as a group never looked back. Life is very different here, and, as everywhere, it has its frustrations (commercialism, bureaucracy, too little free time, and so on), but there is also dynamism, challenging work, interesting people, and the fact that those around us do care very much if we do a good job (even if for purely commercial reasons). It is a great place to work if you are up to it.

This chapter concludes the first part of the book, and I expect most of my readers to feel at this point that I have been long on generalities and short on specifics. "This is all very noble," you may say, "but what do all these people actually *do*?" Read on—the rest of this book is an attempt to answer this question.

PART 2

Markets

CHAPTER 4

Markets and
the Economy

If there is one area where the wall between the business side and the technology side of Wall Street is the highest, it is probably the understanding of the macroeconomic context of trading. Technical people working on Wall Street tend to view the markets in static terms—as collections of facts and rules that they need to know in order to be able to do their jobs. The software and models that they create have to be flexible enough to accommodate anything that can happen in the market, so the specifics of where the markets are today usually matter very little. The view of the traders, salespeople, and brokers is almost diametrically opposite: they care a great deal about what the markets are doing today and why they are doing it, and therefore they spend much of their time and energy thinking about the reasons for market behavior. Again, an automotive analogy comes to mind here: the technical people are like car mechanics, who know how the car is put together and worry about keeping it in good running order, while the traders are like drivers, who know how to operate the car, but mostly focus on figuring out where they want to go.

I think it is important for Wall Street technologists to understand how their business-side colleagues think and talk about the markets, and therefore we begin our journey through the world of capital markets by taking the trader's point of view and discussing the fundamental drivers of market behavior. These drivers will be somewhat different depending on the specific market; in particular, in the interest-rate markets, the drivers are almost exclusively macroeconomic in nature. This is because, unlike stocks, interest rates are usually not sensitive to events affecting a single company or even a single industry sector. Instead, interest-rate markets are a pure play on the state of the economy as a whole and give us a good starting point for discussing the relationship between the economy and market behavior.

Most of my readers are probably not very strong on economic fundamentals—economics is rarely part of the hard sciences curriculum. Therefore, we will begin with a brief explanation of the necessary economic concepts, one of which is monetary policy and the role of central banks—we will spend most of our economic education effort on that single topic. We will then explain why "interest-rate markets" are really markets in which interest rates are bought and sold, using the U.S. Treasury yield curve as an example. We will then put it all together and show how monetary policy and inflation affect the yield curves, and how economic news translates into shifts in interest rates. In the process, we will introduce much of the terminology heard on a trading floor when these subjects are discussed, which they almost always are.

BUSINESS CYCLES

Here's our three-paragraph summary of macroeconomics: a market economy develops through a series of *business cycles,* which can be discerned by tracking the three main economic statistics: the *gross domestic product* (GDP), *inflation*, and the *unemployment* rate. GDP is the value of all goods and services produced inside a country within a period of time, such as a year. Most people care less about the GDP itself than about its rate of growth minus the rate of inflation; this shows how fast the economy is growing in real terms. Inflation is usually measured by the value of an imaginary basket of consumer goods (in the United States, the most commonly used measure is called the Consumer Price Index, or CPI). The value of the index itself is expressed as a percentage of its price in some base year (January 1980 = 100, which had grown to 198.3 by January 2006), and its year-over-year percentage change is called the inflation rate [inflation rate = (CPI today – CPI year ago)/CPI year ago]. Finally, the unemployment rate is the percentage of people in the country's workforce who want but are unable to find a job. In Figure 4–1, we show the history of these three quantities for the United States over the last 50 years.

In theory, business cycles are expected to work in the following way. Let us say we start at the *expansion* stage, where the rate of GDP growth is high and inflation and unemployment are low. As unemployment drops, labor becomes more expensive and inflation begins to increase; this eventually

FIGURE 4–1

Performance of the U.S. economy, as measured by real GDP growth, inflation rate, and unemployment rate. (Data from Bureau of Labor Statistics and Bureau of Economic Analysis, www.bls.gov and www.bea.gov.)

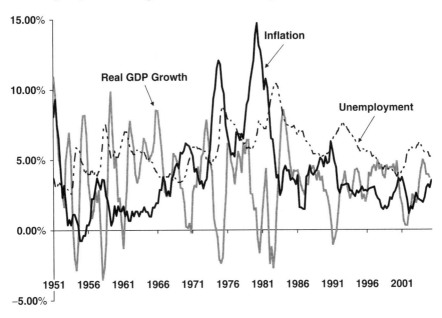

stifles economic growth, so that we move into the next stage, called *contraction*, or *recession*, in which output growth drops and unemployment rises. At this stage, there are too many goods produced and too few people wanting to buy them (in the eighteenth century, Malthus called recessions "gluts"), and so prices (inflation) begin to come down and production aligns with demand. After a while the growth begins to pick up and we enter the *recovery* stage, which eventually grows into a full-blown expansion, and the whole cycle begins again.

As is clear from Figure 4–1, economic growth does indeed exhibit an oscillatory "boom-and-bust" pattern, although it is much less clear-cut than economic theory would lead us to expect. Also, it is hard not to notice that the oscillations have become a lot less violent since the mid-1980s— both the amplitude of the swings in economic growth and the frequency of recessions appear to have gone down dramatically (this is true also of the major European economies). There are many reasons for this (remember all that talk about "the new economy" and "the death of the business cycle" that we heard so much of in the late 1990s?), and one of those reasons is that the central banks in the developed world have become much more successful in using interest-rate markets to manage the economy.

THE ROLE OF CENTRAL BANKS

What are central banks, and what exactly do they do to manage the economy? To answer these questions, let us start in the United States. Its central bank is called the Federal Reserve System and was not established until 1913, much later than central banks in most other developed countries. In the United States, there was much opposition to the European concept of a central bank, which was viewed as government encroachment on the rights of the private banking industry, and two earlier attempts to establish a central bank in the United States in the early 1800s had failed. To understand what a central bank does, it is instructive to consider what happens when there is no central bank, and the United States at the beginning of the twentieth century provides an illuminating example.

Prior to the formation of the Federal Reserve, whenever a financial crisis occurred in the United States (and there was no shortage of those in the late nineteenth century; they occurred in 1873, 1884, 1890, and 1893, to name just the major ones), the big bankers of the day got together and provided funds to rescue at least some of the institutions that were failing. These crises, more appropriately called *panics*, typically started with the collapse of some speculative scheme in which prominent people were involved. Then the population found out that these prominent citizens were also directors of depository banks and trusts, and in many cases had treated those institutions as their private piggybanks, so a natural reaction on the part of small depositors was to try to get what remained of their money out of those banks.

These "bank runs" usually obliterated the affected banks, often within hours—the banks kept only a relatively small percentage of their deposits as ready reserves, so when all depositors showed up at once, they paid off those who came first until their reserves ran out, after which the bank had little choice but to close its doors. The sorry example of those whose savings were lost in this way prompted other people to start a run on their banks, often with similar results, and this kept on until the major bankers decided that enough was enough and stepped in to rescue the troubled banks by, as we say today, "providing liquidity." The big boys deposited significant sums in the affected banks, giving them enough money to survive a run. After the funds were made available, the bank failures eventually stopped, the panic subsided, and once things went back to business as usual, the rescuers were handsomely paid for their timely services. Everyone (except perhaps the small depositors) was happy about these arrangements, and all attempts to bring some sanity to this system were methodically thwarted by the bankers.

The panic of 1907 initially followed this well-worn scenario. In October 1907, a gentleman named Augustus Heinz tried to corner the market in United Copper Company stock. He spent enormous amounts of money pushing the stock up to $62, but then in three days the stock collapsed to $15, wiping out Heinz and his associates, some of whom controlled several banks and trust companies in New York and had provided him with the funds for his failed corner scheme. People rightly concluded that the banks associated with Heinz must be in bad shape and began a run on them. Within a couple of days, Knickerbocker Trust, the third largest bank in New York, collapsed after paying out $8 million in deposits, and other banks and trusts came under severe strain. Enterprising New Yorkers took it all in stride—people were offering to hold the queuing depositors' place in line for $10, restaurants served "panic specials," newspapers tried to predict which bank would go down next—everything was going as in previous such episodes, and, as before, a group of bankers led by J. P. Morgan stepped in to handle the mess.

However, this time around, it soon became clear that the banking system had grown too large for the private bankers to rescue. Despite their best efforts, the runs continued, and the huge sums they poured in, such as $10 million provided by John D. Rockefeller, increasingly looked like drops in the proverbial bucket. For the first time in the history of bank panics, the federal government had to intervene. The U.S. Treasury provided an immediate infusion of $25 million into the troubled New York banks, later followed by other assistance. It struck many observers as ridiculous that the government effectively had to give money to private bankers to handle the crisis because there was no mechanism by which it could intervene in the banking system directly.

The Treasury intervention, Morgan's able management of the crisis, and some creative steps taken by the New York Clearinghouse (which started substituting its own loan certificates for cash when settling transactions between banks, providing an effective if unlawful way to expand the amount of money available for depositors) eventually succeeded in stopping the panic, but the banking establishment finally realized how close the system had come to a complete collapse. One interesting number illustrates this point well: at one time during the panic, the working capital of the U.S. Treasury reached a low of a mere $5 million (or about 6 cents per capita, given the population at the time—it was like letting your checking account balance drop to $0.24 for a family of four).

The experience of 1907 convinced many important players in business as well as in government circles that this was no way to run a major country, and six years later the Federal Reserve System was born. One of its main functions was to act as a *lender of last resort* during financial crises, taking over the role that had previously been played by J. P. Morgan and his colleagues—a bank that was in trouble could go to the Federal Reserve and borrow money there instead of relying on the largesse of the private banker groups.

The problem in financial crises was that (1) banks did not maintain enough reserves, and (2) there was no easy (or even legal) way to extend the supply of money during the crisis. The Federal Reserve was charged with solving both problems; it was given the power to set and enforce *reserve requirements* (i.e., the percentage of total deposits that has to be kept on hand), and it was also given a monopoly on issuing bank notes, which previously had been issued by large "national" banks (look at a dollar bill—it says "Federal Reserve Note"). The Federal Reserve could not arbitrarily print money, as money was still backed by gold at the time, but it could inject its reserve holdings into the banking system, easing the money supply situation. It is from this latter function that its current power over the economy has gradually developed, so let us look at it in more detail.

The functions of the Federal Reserve are similar to those that the Bank of England has been performing since at least the 1750s, but it is organized somewhat differently, partly because the United States is a much larger country. The United States is divided into 12 Federal Reserve *Districts*, each with its own Federal Reserve Bank (with the New York Fed being, of course, the largest by far), which plays the role of a banker's bank within that district—the banks located in that district maintain accounts in their Federal Reserve Bank and transact with one another through these accounts. Some of those accounts are called *reserve accounts*; this is where the banks keep the required percentage of the two-week average of their "transaction" (checking account) deposits. The percentage (the *reserve ratio*) is also set by the Fed. It was gradually reduced from 20 percent in the 1930s to 10 percent in 1992. So each district Fed bank is really just a bank that serves other banks and has some regulatory power over them.

The systemwide decisions such as setting the reserve requirements, however, are made by a central body called the *Board of Governors* of the Federal Reserve, located in Washington, D.C. There are seven governors, one of whom is the chairman of the board (Ben Bernanke at the time of this writing), but the board is much larger than that—it employs almost 2,000 people, whose job it is to ensure the smooth functioning of the country's financial system; they supervise banks and payment systems, and collect and analyze all kinds of economic data. This structure—a set of regional Federal Reserve Banks plus a governing board at the center—was designed to balance the federal government and regional banking interests.

The most visible function of the Federal Reserve today is the conduct of *monetary policy,* which means that it gets to control how much money is available for the U.S. economy. The main way in which the Fed influences the amount of money circulating in the economy is called *open-market operations.* The "market" here means the money market, and the operations are simply trading high-quality debt securities with the securities dealers. When the Fed wants to increase the amount of money in the economy, it buys securities from dealers. The money it pays for securities becomes part of the outstanding monetary mass because the dealers will put it in their bank accounts, increasing the amount of reserves in the banking system and allowing the banks to make more loans against them. Conversely, when the Fed wants to tighten the money supply, it sells securities to the dealers, and the money the dealers pay for the securities is taken out of their banks' reserve accounts, reducing their reserves and therefore the banks' ability to make loans.

The open-market operations are conducted by the trading desk of the New York Fed on behalf of the whole Federal Reserve System (meaning that other regional Fed banks never do this on their own) and are relatively straightforward. Every day in the morning, the desk decides how much securities it wants to buy or sell (or, most of the time, borrow or lend for a short period of time) and invites bids from the dealers, which are submitted and filled by late morning. A far more interesting, trillion-dollar question is: how does the Fed decide which way it wants to move the money supply?

This decision, like many others, is made by a committee. This particular one is called the *Federal Open Markets Committee* (FOMC), and it is made up of the seven governors of the Fed plus five of the twelve regional Fed presidents. One of the five is always from the New York Fed, and the four others are elected on a rotating basis from the other Fed banks (in fact, all Fed banks are represented in the committee meetings, but only the five that are on the committee get to vote). The committee meets eight times a year (these are the Fed meetings you read about in the news), looks at all available data about the economy, and issues a *monetary policy directive* to the open-markets trading desk specifying what it wants to do.

The thought process behind this directive is very complex, but it can be simplistically summarized as follows: if the economic data (such as GDP, unemployment, and inflation, but the committee also looks at a host of other data, much of it collected by the Federal Reserve System itself) indicate that the economy is slowing down, the Fed wants to increase the amount of money available for the economy in order to stimulate growth, whereas if the economy looks as if it is growing too quickly, so that inflationary pressures are beginning to build up, the Fed wants to tighten the money supply. The way in which the Fed expresses its decision is crucial for our discussion: in the directive, it specifies a *target level* for an interest rate called the *federal funds* rate. Why is that, and what does this rate have to do with the money supply?

As we mentioned before, the banks are required to maintain reserves in their Fed accounts; the money residing in those accounts is called *federal funds*. The Fed does not pay interest on those accounts (the reserves at the Fed are treated the same way as cash in a bank's vault), so the banks are strongly motivated to keep their reserve balances as low as possible. The required amount of reserves is a percentage of the bank's deposits, and those fluctuate from day to day. So on any given day, Bank A may end up having slightly more reserves than it needs, while Bank B may end up having less. In this situation, Bank A can loan its excess reserves to Bank B overnight, and the interest rate charged for this overnight loan is called the federal funds rate.

Note that the overnight loan rate is negotiated directly between banks (or sometimes through a broker); the Fed does not have any direct say in it. The prevailing rate for fed funds loans is therefore set by supply and demand, and it is here that the Fed can exert its influence because it can control the supply. If the Fed takes money out of the banking system by selling securities during its open-market operations, the total amount of reserves in the system will decrease and more banks will want to borrow them, which will cause the fed funds rate to go up. Conversely, when the Fed buys securities and pays for them by crediting the reserve accounts, there will be less demand for overnight fed funds and the rate will go down.

Before the mid-1980s, the Fed tried to control the amount of reserves directly, but it found that it could do this much more efficiently by trying to maintain a target level of the fed funds rate—if the fed funds market trades at a higher rate, the Fed injects enough liquidity to bring the fed funds market back to the target rate, and vice versa. Figure 4–2 illustrates how well this has worked in practice over the last two decades—the Fed clearly does not hit the target every day, but the average of the daily rates follows the target very closely.

Note that the fed funds target rate shown in Figure 4–2 for periods prior to 1995 is an estimate—the Fed did not announce its policy target until early 1995, and the market had to guess what the target was by looking at what the Fed was doing during its open-market operations. In early

FIGURE   4–2

Actual and target fed funds rate, together with inflation rate and GDP growth data from Figure 4–1. When growth falters, the Fed lowers its target; when inflation rises, it raises the target. The actual fed funds rate can exhibit significant daily fluctuations, but overall it closely follows the target. Note that the fluctuations used to be much larger in the past. (Data on the fed funds rate from Federal Reserve Board Web site, www.federalreserve.gov.)

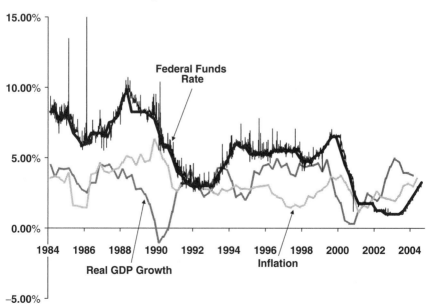

1994 it started raising its target, but the market missed the beginning of this, resulting in large dislocations in short-term rates. After that, the Fed started announcing *changes* in its policy, and in 1995 it began explicitly stating what the new target rate was in its meeting announcement. It continued this trend toward more disclosure by adding a "balance of risks" statement in 2000, which now gets parsed by the market participants for clues to what the Fed will do next.

Figure 4–2 also overlays the charts of inflation and GDP growth on the fed funds target history. The target rate clearly correlates with the larger economic picture—when GDP growth falters, the Fed gradually cuts rates; when growth is strong but inflation is beginning to rise, it raises rates, with the intention of dampening the violent swings in output and inflation that were prevalent in the earlier era. Thus we see that the Fed, by manipulating very short-term interest rates, is able to bring about significant and largely beneficial changes in the larger economy.

Before we describe how this short-term rate manipulation affects the interest-rate markets for all debt instruments, let us briefly look at the central banks of other countries. We have mentioned one of them several times already: the Bank of England, which predates the Fed by more than two centuries. Its organization, however, is very similar to that of the U.S. central bank (and recently became more so when the Bank of England became independent)—it is a banker's bank through which banks settle their transactions and where they maintain their reserves, led by a governor and two deputy governors, whose role is similar to the Fed Board of Governors. There is a Monetary Policy Committee analogous to the FOMC that determines monetary policy at its regular monthly meetings, and the policy is also expressed as a short-term interest rate called the bank repo rate. Unlike the U.S. fed funds rate, this is a nonnegotiable rate at which banks can borrow from the Bank of England. The BOE holds large quantities of debt securities of other banks, some of which mature every day, so these institutions have to pay significant sums to the BOE as the holder of those securities. The banks borrow these sums from the Bank of England at the official repo rate, which therefore plays the role of a price for short-term money and is largely equivalent to the U.S. fed funds rate in its economic effects.

In 1999, the central banks of the 11 European countries that had adopted the euro at that time (the twelfth, Greece, joined in 2001) merged into the *Eurosystem,* with the European Central Bank (ECB) at the center (it is located in Frankfurt in a swanky new skyscraper, but it is already looking for a bigger building). The central banks of the individual countries in the Eurosystem, many of them centuries old, retain their identity as national central banks (NCBs) and play a role very similar to that of the regional Fed banks in the United States, while the ECB is analogous to the Fed Board of Governors in that it makes systemwide decisions and conducts monetary policy common to all Eurozone countries. The monetary policy is set by the ECB Governing Council, which is made up of the ECB executives and the presidents of all the NCBs. This body holds a rate-setting meeting each month and announces its official rate for its open-market operations, which, as in the United Kingdom, is nonnegotiable. The ECB uses what it calls "decentralized implementation" of its monetary targets, with open-market operations being conducted by all NCBs simultaneously, unlike the U.S. system, where only one regional bank (the New York Fed) does this.

This pattern is followed, with minor variations, by central banks in the rest of the developed world—they all conduct monetary policy mostly by controlling a short-term interest rate, which they change in response to economic data. If the economic news is good, the monetary policy is tightened by increasing the short-term rate (a *rate hike* is a common term for that); if it is bad, the monetary policy is eased and the rate goes down (a *rate cut* is the proper term). Even though the rate controlled for monetary policy purposes applies only to very short-term borrowing, it indirectly affects the interest rates for all longer-term loans through a mechanism that we illustrate using a stylized example.

HOW INTEREST RATES ARE SET

Let us say that we want to invest money for a year. Let us further assume that the fed funds rate is currently 2 percent, and we do not expect it to change during the next year. One possibility we have is to invest it in the fed funds market overnight and keep reinvesting it every day for a year—if we ignore subtleties such as compounding, this will get us a rate of return very close to 2 percent over the next year. Now consider another interest-rate scenario: the Fed will raise the fed funds rate to 3 percent six months from now. In this scenario, rolling over our overnight investment for a year will get us a rate of return close to 2.5 percent. If we restrict the universe of possible interest-rate scenarios to these two, and further assume that the one-year rate of return can be traded in the market (we will show how that works in a few paragraphs), then the market value of the one-year rate will be a function of the relative number of people believing in each of these scenarios—if all market participants believed that the short rate was not going to change, the market one-year rate would be 2 percent; if everybody believed in the second scenario, it would be 2.5 percent.

If there are differences of opinion among the market players about the likelihood of the two scenarios, the market rate will find a level between these two extremes at which the buyers and sellers (borrowers and lenders) balance each other out. We can think of this market level as reflecting the probabilities that the market assigns to each of the two possible outcomes. Any event that increases the likelihood of the Fed's raising rates will cause the market to reassess these probabilities in favor of that scenario and push the market rate up, closer to 2.5 percent. That event can be a piece of positive economic news, a statement by Fed officials, or perhaps a research report—the market will digest all such information and reassess the probabilities of all possible short-rate paths, which will lead to changes in the market level of the one-year rate.

This general pattern that we see in this example—the market setting the rate of return based on its assessment of the various possible short-rate scenarios—is independent of the details used in that example. In particular, the pattern holds for rates of any maturity. If we had a market for interest rates of various maturities, and if we plotted the market rates as a function of maturity, we could see graphically what the market thinks the Fed is likely to do in the future based on the current understanding of the economic situation. Luckily, such a market does in fact exist; it is called the U.S. Treasury market, and such a plot of rates versus maturity is called the *yield curve*. Figure 4–3 shows an example.[1]

Before we take a closer look at Figure 4–3, we clearly have some explaining to do—what are U.S. Treasuries, what are yields, and how exactly are they traded? We will take a much closer look at the U.S. Treasury market in the next chapter, but we can introduce its basic concepts here. The U.S. government borrows money from investors mainly by issuing *Treasury notes*. The Treasury is a department of the federal government whose job it is to see that the government does not run out

---

1. There are no publicly available sources for Treasury prices, unlike stock prices, and I was unable to obtain permission to use internal closing data from a dealer bank, so I had to use a simple simulation to produce this and other figures related to U.S. Treasuries. The U.S. Treasury publishes daily values for constant-maturity Treasury yields, as well as the list of all outstanding Treasury securities (as part of its monthly public debt statement); these can be combined to produce an approximate value for the yield of each security on any given date, which is good enough for illustrative purposes.

FIGURE 4–3

U.S. Treasury yield curve as of August 5, 2004 (simulated as described in the text). The curve is simply a plot of the yields of all outstanding Treasuries as a function of their maturity date. The yields can be thought of as the borrowing or lending rates for different future horizons, as discussed in the text, and their value is constantly changing, driven by market forces. This figure reflects what the market thought of different interest-rate scenarios as of the close of business on August 5, 2004.

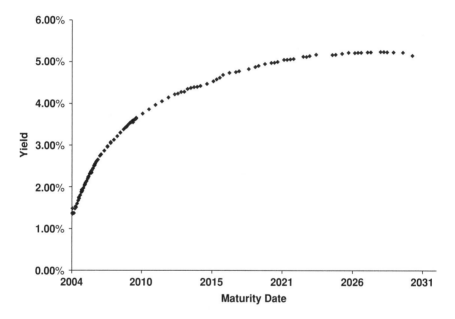

of money. Treasury notes are in fact bonds as we defined them in Chapter 1 (securities that pay periodic interest and return the borrowed principal on the maturity date), except the Treasury calls them *notes* if their original maturity is less than 10 years, while anything issued with more than 10 years to maturity is called a bond.

These notes are issued during periodic auctions. When they are issued, their maturity is a nice round number, like 2 years or 10 years, and their price is 100 (remember, all bond prices are percentages of the borrowed amount); but as time goes by, these bonds age (so that a 10-year note issued three months ago now has the maturity of 9 years and nine months), and their prices move up and down from 100 as market conditions change. The Treasury has been doing this for many years, and as a result we now have about 150 outstanding Treasury bonds and notes with different maturities, coupon rates, and current prices. Each data point in Figure 4–3 corresponds to one such bond or note, and the horizontal axis shows their maturity.

What is shown in the vertical axis in Figure 4–3 is called *yield*, and it is time for us to explain what it is. Yield is always a measure of the *rate of return* that an investor gets on her investment in a bond. Another useful way to think of yield is to interpret it as a *lending rate*—the rate of interest an investor earns when she lends money by buying a bond. There are several different ways of calculating yield (we talked about *current yield* in Chapter 1 in connection with perpetual bonds), but in most bond markets today, yield almost universally means *yield to maturity*—the rate of return an investor would get if she bought a bond on a given date (called the settlement date) and held it to maturity.

There are two sources of return on a bond investment; one is the periodic coupon payments, and the other results from changes in the bond price between the settlement date and the maturity date. Suppose that we bought a bond with 10 years remaining to maturity and a coupon of 5 percent at its current market price of 90. For the next 10 years, we are going to be paid 5 percent of the par amount, which would give us a return of $5/0.9 = 5.55$ percent—this is the current yield of this bond, which depends on price, but not on the maturity of the bond. Over the next 10 years, however, the price of the bond will go from 90 to 100 because at the maturity date, the Treasury will pay off the bondholders in full. This will give us an additional 1.11 percent return (10 percent of par over 10 years on a 0.9 investment). Note that this component of return depends on both price and the time to maturity. Overall, our rate of return, or yield to maturity, is about 6.66 percent. For a purchase price of 100, the yield will be exactly 5 percent; for a price of 110, the yield will be 4.64 percent—the higher the price, the lower the yield. The actual formula for computing the yield as a function of coupon rate, time to maturity, and price is somewhat more complicated than the simple reasoning here [which can be expressed as yield = coupon rate/price + $(100 - \text{price})/(\text{price} \times \text{time to maturity})$], but it gives qualitatively similar results.

Figure 4–4 shows the price-to-yield relationships for two Treasury bonds with different maturities and coupons. To get a qualitative feel for these relationships, it is helpful to get two "anchor points" right: when price is equal to 100, yield should be equal to the coupon rate, and when yield is zero, the price should be equal to the sum of all coupon payments plus

FIGURE 4–4

Price-yield conversion example for two Treasury securities, one with 5 years to maturity, and the other with 26 years to maturity.

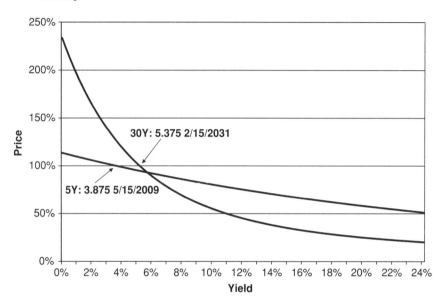

100 (zero return means that we pay exactly as much today as we will receive in the future). The two bonds in Figure 4–4 have very different times to maturity (5 and 26 years) but comparable coupons, so that for the one with a longer time to maturity, the sum of all the coupon payments is a lot higher than for the other. This explains why its price graph drops off much faster with increasing yield than the one for the shorter-maturity bond.

This slope itself is a very important quantity that is often referred to as *duration*; it is a measure of how sensitive the price is to changes in yield. Duration is usually defined as a logarithmic derivative of price with respect to yield (the "straight" derivative divided by the price). This quantity has the dimensionality of time and in fact represents the lifetime, or "duration," of the average payment we get from a bond: if a bond has a zero coupon rate, its duration is equal to its time to maturity, and with a nonzero coupon rate, the duration becomes less than the time to maturity because we receive some of the payments earlier. The straight derivative of price versus yield also has a name; it is called the "dollar value of a basis point," or *DV01* (a *basis point* is 0.01 percent), and it is used extensively when we need to know how much the value of our bond will change if the yield moves. It is important to keep in mind that both duration and DV01 increase linearly with time to maturity.

Another important feature of the price-to-yield curves in Figure 4–4 is that these curves are *convex*. For a mathematician, this means that they have a positive second derivative, but the financial markets infuse this simple fact with a deeper meaning. For traders, *convexity* means asymmetric risk—they stand to gain more in price if the yield goes down than they would lose if the yield went up by the same amount. This makes investments with larger convexity more valuable in volatile markets—if a trader anticipates a wide distribution of future yields, convexity makes the expected value of the price larger than the price corresponding to the expected value of the yield (the difference between the two is often called *gain from convexity*). We will discuss convexity effects in more detail later; here we just note that convexity is quadratic in time to maturity.

Now we are ready to take a closer look at the yield curve in Figure 4–3. Its most important feature is that it does look like a curve—yields of outstanding Treasuries do in fact form a relatively smooth curve when plotted against their times to maturity. The market prices of Treasuries with similar maturities but different coupons can be very different and would be all over this chart, but the yields are quite close. This tells us that yields make more economic sense than prices—they represent the market values of borrowing rates to different future dates, just as we discussed in our example, and different bonds can offer different ways of achieving the same rate of return. And the economic meaning of yields is just what we saw in our fed funds scenarios example—they represent the market's way of averaging all possible short-rate scenarios according to their perceived probabilities. Figure 4–3 is a snapshot of the Treasury yield curve at a particular point in time, but it is important to realize that Treasury yields are constantly changing—trades occur in the Treasury market almost every second, so the yield curve is always moving in response to the latest information. Let us take a closer look at the main factors that determine its shape.

The curve shown in Figure 4–3 is for August 2004, when the fed funds target rate stood at 1.25 percent (and the yields for very short maturities were very close to that level), but the economic data were strongly suggesting that the economy had begun to grow rapidly, so that most market participants were expecting the Fed to keep raising rates for the foreseeable future. The fact that the yields at the short end of the curve were rising rapidly with maturity simply reflects these market *expectations* of the Fed's behavior—the slope of the yield curve represents the market's forecast of how soon and by how much the Fed would raise the rates based on what was known about the economy on that particular day. We can look at the short end of the Treasury yield curve at different points in the past (Figure 4–5) and see the same pattern: the current fed funds rate is the anchor for the shortest-maturity yields, and the curve slopes up or down depending on what people expect the Fed to do given the current understanding of the economic situation.

The curve for May 1, 2003, in that figure exhibits a common feature of yield curves that complicates their interpretation as the expected path of short rates. This curve is for a period in which it was considered nearly certain that the short rate was not going to change for a long time, but it

F I G U R E   4–5

The short end of the Treasury curve at different times in the past: (1) on December 29, 2000, when the Fed was expected to keep lowering rates; (2) on August 5, 2004, when rate hikes were expected; and (3) on May 1, 2003, when rates were expected to stay constant at 1 percent for a long time.

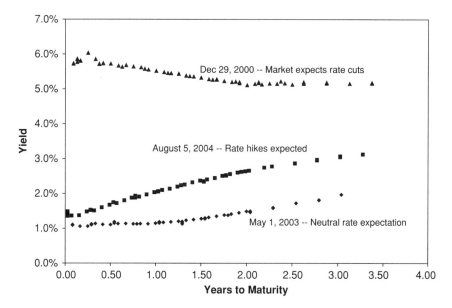

still begins to slope upward after a few months. This tendency for yield curves to slope upward no matter what is often described as the *risk premium* effect—investors are believed to demand higher rates of return for holding longer-maturity (and therefore riskier) bonds.

A simple explanation of the nature of the risk premium is offered by the following game example: suppose I have a desk with two drawers, and I put $1,000 into one and nothing into the other. How much would you pay to play a game in which you get to open one drawer and keep what is in it? If you say $500, you are risk-neutral, but most people would prefer a certain $500 to a 50 percent chance to win $1,000, so if you would play this game for $400, your risk premium is $100.

Risk premium is a staple of theoretical finance and is a parameter in many models of interest-rate behavior, but it is very difficult to estimate in practice—it is almost impossible to say what part of the slope of the yield curves in Figure 4–5 is due to "genuine" rate expectations and what part is due to the risk premium effect. In fact, the curve corresponding to May 1, 2003 in Figure 4–5 that we offered as illustration of the risk premium effect tracks the subsequent evolution of rates pretty well—the Fed did start raising rates about a year after that date.

As we move further out on the yield curve to longer maturities, it becomes progressively more difficult to make believable predictions about the possible fed funds rate scenarios. Indeed, think about a Treasury bond issued 20 years ago and maturing today. Its lifetime spanned the second Reagan presidency, when short rates were still at times touching 10 percent; the recession of 1991–1993, when rates went down to 3 percent; the boom times of the second half of the 1990s, with short rates reaching 6.5 percent; the recession of the early 2000s, with the fed funds rate at 1 percent (see Figure 4–2)—who could possibly have predicted all of that when this bond was issued in the late 1980s? When we look today at a Treasury bond maturing in 2025 and ask ourselves what will be the average of short rates over the next 20 years to determine what its yield should be, we are equally unlikely to foresee the exact path that short rates will take over the next two decades. Fortunately, this kind of clairvoyance is not strictly necessary to value this 20-year bond—we only need to estimate the average short rate over this period, and this can be done by looking at past experience.

Over long periods of time, the overwhelming force that affects all fixed-income investments is *inflation*. Generally, we hope that the return on our investments will beat inflation. The difference between the actual rate of return and the inflation rate is called the *real* rate of return, and that quantity has been remarkably stable over time. In periods with high inflation, the interest rates also rise, as the Fed is trying to bring the inflation down, while during low-inflation periods, the interest rates also come down. If we compare the long-term averages of interest rates with long-term inflation averages, the resulting long-term real rates turn out to be positive and range between 1 and 2 percent. Therefore, if we need to estimate a rate of return on a 20-year bond, the best we can do is try to estimate what inflation will be over that 20-year period and add 1.5 percent to that.

Estimating future inflation, of course, seems just as difficult as estimating the rates directly, but that does not stop people from trying. There are a number of economic surveys that attempt to measure *inflation expectations*, and they can be summarized by saying that people seem to estimate future inflation by looking at the recent past—the best predictor of the measured inflation expectations is a moving average of inflation over the last few years. Any current information indicating that inflation is heading up today will shift the long-term inflation expectations up, while anything that suggests that inflation is heading down today will shift them down. What is important for our discussion here is the fact that there is no real time structure to these long-term expectations—it would be very difficult to justify a difference between, say, 10-year and 30-year inflation expectations, as both are vaguely "long term."

From the perspective of inflation expectations, the long-term interest rates should not really depend on the time to maturity—they should be equal to these long-term inflation expectations plus some constant representing a long-term real rate of return. If we look at Figure 4–6, where we show examples of the long end of the Treasury curve at different times in the past, we see that this not quite true; the long-end yields are more constant than the short-end yields, but there is clearly a tendency for these yield curves to slope upward initially and then decline for very long maturities, so something else is clearly affecting the shape of these curves.

One of these extra factors we have discussed already: it is the risk premium effect, which, other things being equal, tends to increase the rates as the time to maturity increases. Note that risk premium is a convenient way of including supply-and-demand forces into our thinking: increased demand for Treasuries can be thought of as a reduction in risk premium that decreases the slope of this linear component of the curve shape and pushes down the yields, and vice versa.

Finally, the tendency of yields to decline for very long maturities is usually attributed to convexity. Bonds with high convexity are more valuable

FIGURE 4–6

The long end of the Treasury curve at different times in the past. The shape of the long-end curves is formed by three main factors: (1) long-term inflation expectations, which give a maturity-independent baseline, (2) the risk premium, which increases linearly with time to maturity, and (3) the convexity correction, which leads to a drop-off in yields at the longest maturities.

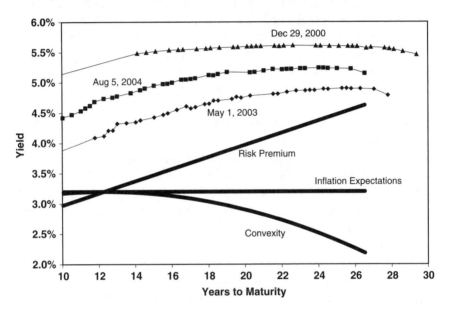

in volatile markets than they would be if their price-to-yield relationship were linear. This extra convexity adjustment should push the prices of all bonds up and their yields down from the values established on the basis of rate expectations. However, because of the fact that convexity increases as a square of time to maturity, such convexity adjustments are extremely small for short-maturity bonds and become significant only for the longest available bonds, where they gradually overcome the risk premium and become sufficient to tip the long end downward. At any given time, the market blends together these three factors—inflation expectations, risk premium, and convexity—to produce the different shapes seen in Figure 4–6.

To summarize our understanding of the forces shaping the yield curves, let us recap the arguments of the last few pages. The yield curve begins at a level very close to the current value of the central bank target rate and slopes upward or downward depending on what people think the central bank will be doing in the foreseeable future (the next couple of years). Beyond the first few years, the yield curve usually levels off around a value corresponding to a long-term equilibrium rate that mostly depends on what people think about future inflation. There is an overall tendency for the curves to be upward-sloping because of the risk premium effect, which typically increases in volatile times, and for very long maturities convexity tends to further complicate this picture by pushing the yields downward.

A physicist may ask at this point, "If we understand these main drivers of the yield curve behavior, can we have a quantitative model that would put them all together so that we could explain why, say, the 10-year yield is 4.251 percent at some point in time?" We will return to this question later in this chapter, as well as in Chapter 17, but the short answer is no—the driving factors are all very subjective and difficult to quantify. However, even a qualitative understanding of these forces becomes very useful when we consider the practical issue of how and why the yield curve moves.

HOW MACROECONOMIC FACTORS AFFECT THE YIELD CURVE

Since all our drivers are macroeconomic in nature, the yield curve should move only when the macroeconomic picture changes as a result of new information about the economy becoming available to market participants. The process by which such new economic information comes out is very interesting and complex. Economic data are usually released in big chunks called *economic reports*, or, more informally, economic *numbers*. Collecting and analyzing data about the economy is a very large and expensive under-taking, the bulk of which is handled by several government agencies. In the United States, there is the Bureau of Labor Statistics (BLS), which collects data about unemployment and inflation; the Bureau of Economic Analysis, which collects data about the components of the GDP (both are part of the federal government); and a number of private entities, such as the Institute for Supply Management and the Conference Board, that do their own widely followed economic surveys. All these entities produce periodic reports about their findings, which are released according to a strictly followed schedule, and the markets digest each such report within seconds of its release. To illustrate this process, let us walk through the release of one such economic report.

The number we are going to follow in this example is called the Employment Situation report, also known as the payrolls report. The report is compiled by the Bureau of Labor Statistics each month and is released at 8:30 a.m. on the first Friday of the next month. We are going to look at the report for July 2004, which was released on Friday, August 6, 2004. The employment report contains the new figure for the unemployment rate and, more importantly, an estimate of the actual change in nonfarm payrolls, which is a proxy for how many new jobs the economy has created during the survey month. The latter number is one of the most important measures of the current health of the economy (note that, unlike many other economic indicators, it is released with very little lag after the survey was taken), and it can significantly change the market's perceptions of what the Fed will do, which this particular July 2004 report did quite spectacularly.

Because of this market-moving potential, all the bigger players in the market prepare for the release of these reports by having their economic research team do its own analysis of the employment situation and come up with an estimate of what this number will be. The big information providers such as Bloomberg and Reuters poll the economists from leading Wall Street firms ahead of each major economic news release and distribute the so-called consensus estimate for the most important components of every report. So, the morning before the release, each market participant has the following information: the consensus estimate for the payroll number (up 192,000 in our case), the estimate by his bank's own economics team (which rarely differs much from the consensus number), and of course the past history plus whatever rumors and innuendo he has heard from his clients and colleagues. This set of information remains unchanged until 08:29:59 a.m. Trading activity grinds to a halt in the minutes before the release.

At 08:30:00 (sometimes a few seconds later, but never earlier), the report hits the Reuters and Bloomberg pages (for most reports, it also becomes available at the releasing agency's Web site). Usually the economists at every bank are standing by to provide some immediate guidance on the report—their comments are broadcast across the trading floor through the "hoot and holler" system built into every trading turret. The trading floors across Wall Street erupt in a frenzy of activity, which is usually proportional to how far away from the consensus the actual number is.

For our July 2004 employment report, this element of surprise was unusually large—the payrolls increased only by 32,000, versus a consensus estimate of 192,000—and caused a very large market move. In Figure 4–7, we show the change in yields on the Treasury curve between the closing

FIGURE 4–7

The yield curve move after the employment report of
August 6, 2004–a textbook example of a steepening rally.

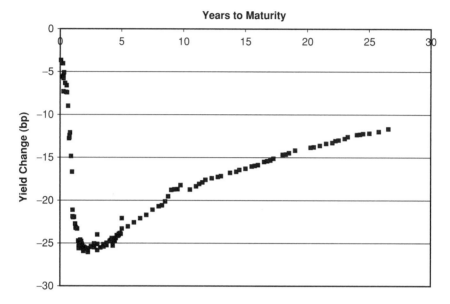

values before the report (on Thursday, August 5—that is our yield curve
from Figure 4–3) and the closing yields at 3 p.m. on Friday August 6,
after the report. Most of these changes occurred within a few seconds of
the employment report release. The 10-year Treasury note jumped 19 basis
points in yield, or more than 2 percentage points in price, right after the
release, and then traded around this new level for the rest of the day.

With these kinds of response times, traders have very little opportunity to appreciate the subtleties of the actual report (which runs about 10
pages with charts and tables) and have to focus on a single most representative *headline* number. Interesting scenarios are possible here: sometimes
the number differs greatly from consensus and the market jumps, but within
a couple of minutes the economists discover some details inside the report
that make the headline number less significant (for example, that the
change in employment was the result of some seasonal factors, or involved
revisions of previously reported data), and the market quickly moves back
to where it had been. In any case, the market usually finds the new equilibrium level within a couple of minutes of the release.

We should mention the obvious precondition for this system: nobody in the market should know what the number is before the official release time, or they could make almost unlimited amounts of money. This is achieved by *embargoing* the news. It is a criminal offence punishable by many years in prison to disclose the contents of an economic report prior to its release time. The only people who are notified ahead of time about upcoming releases that are likely to have large market impact are the president of the United States and the chairman of the Federal Reserve—they are told the night before so that they can prepare to respond to any resulting market disruptions. The news media representatives attend a press briefing about half an hour before the official release time so that they can prepare their reports and analysis, which are released right after the report itself. Despite the fact that hundreds of people participate in the preparation of economic reports, and that the potential for illicit gains is very high, the embargo process seems to work remarkably well—prerelease leaks are almost unheard of, and any hints thereof are vigorously investigated by market regulators.

If we take away the theatrics accompanying the release of the July 2004 employment report, can we understand why the market reacted to it as shown in Figure 4–7? The main economic significance of that report was to show that the economy was much farther away from a full-blown recovery than everybody had thought, and that was expected to have a direct impact on the Fed's interest-rate policy—the report made it much less likely that the Fed would increase its target rate anytime soon. The new information should have caused the market participants to reassess their favorite short-rate scenarios by making the anticipated rate increases smaller and/or by pushing them farther out into the future; either way, the likelihood of lower-rate scenarios had just gone up drastically. Therefore, the main effect of the report was to push yields down and prices up, leading to a frantic wave of buying across the maturity spectrum. A market move in which prices go up and yields go down is called a *rally* in interest-rate markets, and the opposite of this is called a *sell-off*, so now we understand why a dismal employment report should cause a rally in the Treasury market.

What is shown in Figure 4–7 is an example of a *steepening* rally, where the curve not only shifts down, but also becomes steeper; in this situation, shorter-maturity debt outperforms longer-maturity debt. This can also be understood from the rate expectations point of view: a bad employment report in a single month can very well push off the timing of rate increases but is unlikely to change the long-term average of rates. This change in timing can have a major impact on a 2-year yield but will not affect a 30-year yield to the same extent. As a result, "bad" reports that are likely to affect the immediate outlook for the Fed's behavior lead to steepening rallies, and "good" reports (e.g., payroll numbers or GDP growth exceeding expectations) lead to the opposite—flattening sell-offs. In either case, the short-term yields move much more than yields at the long end.

At the other end of the economic news spectrum are events that do not necessarily affect the outlook for Fed behavior in the immediate future, but have an impact on the long-term level of rates. Events like this are quite rare; the release of an inflation expectations survey may fall into this category, but the market rarely pays much attention to those surveys. However, when such events do occur, the market reacts with either a flattening rally, where the long-end debt outperforms shorter maturities, or a steepening sell-off, where yields at the long end go up by more than the short-end yields.

Almost any economic release lies somewhere between these two extremes—there is usually some impact on both long-term and short-term rate expectations, and the market will try to decompose the new data into these long-term and short-term components. Consider the CPI report, which also comes from the BLS in the middle of every month. If it reveals that the CPI increased faster than consensus last month, it should cause reasonable people to increase their long-term inflation expectations, pushing the long-end yields upward; but inflation is also one of the main things the Fed looks at when deciding its rate policy, so an uptick in inflation rate also increases the likelihood of a fed funds rate hike in the short term.

OTHER INFLUENCES ON THE YIELD CURVE

While most economic information comes to the interest-rate markets in the form of these numbers releases, one should not think that the yield curve just sits there waiting for the next economic report. There are a variety of other sources of information that the market pays attention to. Statements, both scheduled and unscheduled, by Federal Reserve and government officials are parsed by the market for their macroeconomic significance and can cause large market moves. The market correctly assumes that a Fed governor or the U.S. Secretary of the Treasury has access to a much deeper pool of information than the average Wall Street economist and can intentionally or inadvertently reflect that pool when speaking.

Other financial markets also provide valuable inputs: a spike in oil prices or a decline of the dollar is usually seen as increasing inflationary pressures, and vice versa. Equity markets are a particularly important influence that deserves a closer look. The effects of economic news on the equity markets are usually the opposite of what we just described for interest-rate markets: "bad" economic news leads to declines in stock prices because of the worsening outlook for corporate profits but causes rallies in the bond markets because of the lowering of rate expectations, so it is often said that stocks and bonds tend to move in the opposite direction.

However, unlike the rate markets, stocks are also susceptible to news about single companies, such as announcements of mergers, changes in business strategy, major new products, and so on. These types of unscheduled news releases cause traders to instantly reprice the stocks of the affected companies (and often the stocks of their competitors as well) and are responsible for much of the daily movement in the equity markets. There are also scheduled news releases, of which the most ubiquitous are quarterly earnings reports. At the end of every quarter, all public companies are required to report their financial results, earnings and profits in particular, and these have the potential to cause large swings in the stock price. Typically Wall Street analysts produce an estimate of earnings per share, and if a company reports results that fall short of that estimate (this is called an *earnings miss*), the stock can suffer out of all proportion to the significance of the miss. Note that it is a tradition in the stock markets not to report anything important while the market is open (most economic announcements also happen at 8:30 a.m., while the equity markets are still closed), so these announcements are made either before the open (at 9 a.m.) or right after the close at 4 p.m., and people generally have some time to analyze the reports and make their trading decisions before the markets open.

Generally, some companies will report good earnings and some will report bad earnings, and their stocks will move in opposite directions, so the overall stock market may not be affected much. However, if a large percentage of companies report earnings that are below what people expect, the stock market may move down as a whole, and the bond market may interpret this as a macroeconomic signal (the economy is doing worse than expected) and rally in response. This behavior often reflects a deeper reality: both markets are competing for the same pool of investment money. Depending on the economic situation, investors can sell stocks in order to buy bonds, and vice versa. When one of these two markets sells off, the money taken off the table has to go somewhere, and very often it quickly ends up in the "other" market. Empirically, there are periods in which the correlation between daily moves in stock indices and interest rates exceeds 90 percent and periods where it almost entirely disappears, but overall the equity and interest-rate markets always watch each other very closely.

The last example brings us to the subject of supply-and-demand forces, which we have largely avoided up to now. A core part of the mythology of capitalism is the belief that all markets are driven by supply and demand—are interest-rate markets any different? One frustrating thing about economics is that almost anything can be explained in many different ways, and the subject of supply-and-demand forces in interest-rate markets offers a prime example of that. Consider an empirical fact: bad news about the economy causes Treasury yields to decrease and prices to rise. A few paragraphs ago, we explained this fact by changes in Fed rate expectations. However, we can equally well say that bad economic news leads to increased demand for Treasuries, as they perform better during bad economic times. It is almost impossible to prove either of these explanations wrong, so the question is, which is more useful? Most participants in the fixed-income market prefer to think in terms of rate expectations and inflation expectations. In fact, one of the curve-shaping factors we discussed earlier, the risk premium, offers a way to include broad supply-and-demand considerations in our analysis of the rate markets: increased demand for Treasuries can be seen as a result of a decrease in risk premium.

However, sometimes supply-and-demand effects are undeniable. Consider the yield curve from early 2000 shown in Figure 4–8. During this period, the U.S. government had a budget surplus, and the Treasury started reducing the issuance of new debt; it even initiated a buyback program that began eliminating some of the outstanding long-end issues. The market viewed this as a drastic reduction in the *supply* of Treasuries; the perception was that there were not going to be any more long-end Treasury securities, and people were paying almost any price to get what was left of them. This led to a huge run-up in prices of the longer-maturity Treasuries that caused their yields to drop so much that the curve became *inverted*: long-end yields dropped below short-end yields, even though, as is clear from the short-end shape of the curve, the Fed kept raising the short rates.

Supply-and-demand effects also work on a micro level. Often there is particular demand for a specific bond or note, pushing its price up and causing its yield to drop relative to that of its neighbors on the curve. This

FIGURE 4–8

The yield curve in early 2000 shows the effects of a supply shortage at the long end.

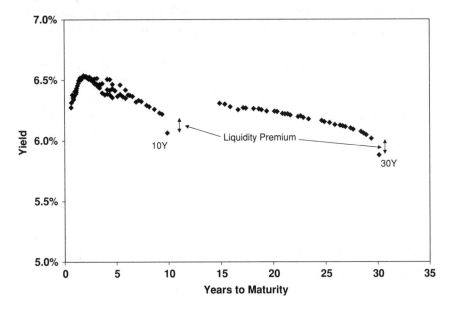

is also clearly visible in Figure 4–8; the two points way below the "main" curve here correspond to the most recently issued 10-year note and 30-year bond. The most recent issues, also known as *on-the-run* issues, are often seen as being more valuable than older securities, and market participants are therefore willing to pay a premium for them; in Figure 4–8, this demand-driven *benchmark premium* exceeds 10 bp for both the 10-year and the 30-year on-the-runs, which is much larger than usual. Because of such supply-and-demand factors, Treasury yields in fact depend not only on time to maturity, but also on the specific issue, so that the yield curve looks smooth only "from a distance," if we neglect these 1- or 2-bp differences. As we will discuss in the next chapter, exploiting these differences is the source of livelihood for many traders.

To conclude our discussion of economic forces affecting the interest-rate markets, let us note a certain one-sidedness to our arguments: we assume that the economy is the cause and the yield curve the effect, but in reality interest rates are powerful economic factors in their own right because they determine the cost of long-term capital. The borrowing costs for the federal government, represented by Treasury yields, determine all other interest rates in the economy—mortgage rates, corporate loan rates, and so on—so that changes in Treasury yields cause all these other rates to change in the same direction.

Because of this, interest-rate markets act as a powerful countercyclical force in the economy: good economic news leads to a rise in interest rates; this increases the cost of capital for everyone, which slows down investment and growth, which after a while causes the economic indicators to turn bad, which then decreases the rates and encourages growth, and on and on. In fact, this feedback mechanism is one of the reasons that some people question the wisdom of central bank intervention in the economy; according to this argument, the economy may be perfectly capable of taking care of business cycles all on its own. Discussing the merits of this "abolish-the-Fed" view is far beyond the scope of this book, but any discussion of interest-rate markets would be incomplete without mentioning their capacity to act as shock absorbers for the economy.

In this chapter, we discussed the macroeconomic context of financial markets. The concepts we introduced here—macroeconomic indicators of business cycles, central banks, monetary policy, short-rate and inflation expectations, risk premium, convexity, and supply-and-demand forces—govern much of the daily life in these markets, and market participants think and talk in these terms. Hopefully the reader will now be able to understand such market talk and appreciate the interesting issues behind it. I realize, however, that this brief overview glossed over many important details and may have created more questions than it answered. I suggest two ways of dealing with these questions. One is to read the rest of this book—some of the answers may be in the subsequent chapters that describe individual markets in much more detail. The other is to turn to the books and Web resources mentioned in the Recommended Reading section. Either way, I hope this chapter has provided a good start.

A quantitatively minded reader will no doubt see some interesting technical challenges in this area. How can we predict the market response to economic news? Can we move beyond the qualitative arguments outlined here and build a quantitative model that explains the shape of the yield curve as a function of economic fundamentals? Such a model, if it in fact worked, clearly would have enormous value to its user, which partially explains the fact that there is no such universally accepted model even though every investment bank and many hedge funds keep trying to build their own. In Chapter 17, we will discuss the main features of such empirical econometric models, while here we just note that modeling the relationships between markets and the economy provides many quantitative people with interesting and creative things to do on Wall Street.

A related area of economic forecasting and research also employs significant quantitative talent, but, unlike building market models, it typically requires a degree in economics. This chapter also contained our first encounter with *financial analytics*—calculating yields, durations, and other measures of return and risk for fixed-income products is an important business need that requires quantitative skill. This area, however, offers little room for creativity; these *bond math* calculations are completely standardized across the industry. If two banks were asked to convert a given yield into price, each would use its own software, but the resulting prices have to agree to a very high degree of accuracy or people could not trade based on yield. While there are few unresolved mathematical issues in this area, the design and development of software that performs such standard computations in an efficient and flexible way is a nontrivial pursuit that keeps many technical people busy. We will review financial analytics in more detail in Chapter 13.

We are now ready for the next chapter, which takes a much closer look at the U.S. Treasury market.

CHAPTER 5

The U.S. Treasury Market

This chapter is really two chapters in one (which is why it is so large). The first half of it describes the U.S. Treasury market, and the second half uses the realities of this market to introduce and discuss some common trading concepts that we will encounter over and over again as we look at other markets. Why did I decide to discuss the Treasury market first instead of, say, the stock market, which everyone is already familiar with? I will offer several arguments in my defense: (1) we have already used examples from this market, and by now we know that it plays a fundamental role in all interest-rate markets, (2) I think that a passing familiarity with the stock market is more of a hindrance than an asset when it comes to understanding institutional trading businesses, and by beginning with the Treasury market, I can be sure that what I say does not collide with some preconceived notions, and (3) I just like this market, OK? Besides, on some level, it is not that important what market we start with (you can jump to the next chapter, which covers equities, and then return here if you want to), as long as we ask the right kind of questions, and the questions we will ask in this chapter should give you a template for studying other markets as well.

THE STRUCTURE OF U.S. GOVERNMENT DEBT

As with any other market, the first question we need to address in relation to the U.S. Treasury market is: why does it exist in the first place? The answer to that question is provided by Figure 5–1, which shows the

FIGURE 5-1

History of the public debt of the U.S. federal government. The United States first took on a noticeable amount of debt during the Second World War. The level of debt stayed constant until mid-1970s and then started growing exponentially; this process was briefly interrupted in the late 1990s, but as of now continues unabated. (Data from U.S. Bureau of Public Debt, www.publicdebt.treas.gov.)

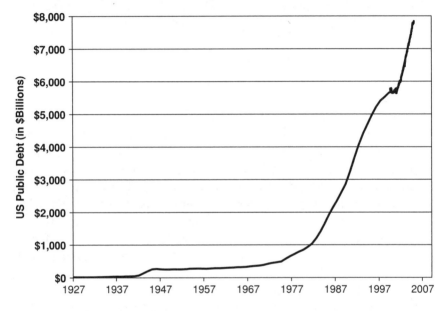

historical chart of the public debt of the U.S. federal government. The U.S. Treasury is a cabinet-level department of the federal government that manages government finances. Managing government finances is not dissimilar to managing your personal checking account: the government has income and expenses (called *receipts* and *outlays* in budgetary language), and when the inflows of money into government accounts are not sufficient to pay its expenses, the government has to borrow to cover the shortfall. In the case of the U.S. government, the shortfall is called the *budget deficit*; at the time of this writing, it amounts to well over $400 billion a year. This kind of money is impossible to borrow from banks, so the U.S. Treasury raises funds in the securities market by selling various debt securities—bonds, notes, and bills—to the investing public.

The U.S. Treasury has been doing this for many years (since 1790), but, as Figure 5–1 suggests, it started raising funds on a truly massive scale only in the late 1970s. In Figure 5–2, we show the history of the Treasury *issuance programs* since that time. An issuance program consists of the periodic sale of securities with a certain number of years to maturity— for example, the 2-year program issues a Treasury note with a maturity of 2 years every month, while the 10-year program issues a 10-year note every quarter. As can be seen in Figure 5–2, the Treasury at various times has issued bonds and notes with the following maturities: 2, 3, 4, 5, 7,

FIGURE 5–2

History of Treasury issuance programs—original maturity of Treasury bonds and notes as a function of the issue date. At various times in the past, the Treasury has issued 2-year, 3-year, 4-year, 5-year, 7-year, 10-year, 15-year, 20-year, and 30-year securities, and both the composition and the frequency of issues have varied widely (note how the dots become much sparser in 1999 to 2001, when the government was briefly running a surplus and did not need to borrow as much). Some series, such as the 4-year, 7-year, 15-year, and 20-year, have long been discontinued; others, such as the 3-year and 30-year, were discontinued and then brought back.

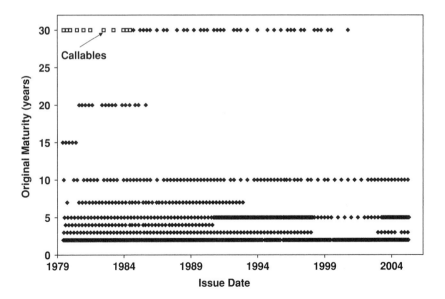

10, 15, 20, and 30 years. Those issued with over 10 years to maturity are called bonds, while those with 10 years and less are called notes; they are identical in all other ways, and we will frequently use the more generic term *bond* to cover both types. All Treasury bonds and notes have semi-annual coupon payments. As we explain in more detail later in this chapter, at the time of issuance, the coupon rate is close to the prevailing market yield for the appropriate maturity. The Treasury also issues discount bills with 4, 13, and 26 weeks (1, 3, and 6 months) to maturity. The pattern of Treasury bill issuance was last changed in 2001, when the 1-year bill program was discontinued and replaced with the 1-month program. Finally, since 1997, the U.S. Treasury issues inflation-linked securities called TIPS, which unfortunately we do not have room to discuss.[1]

We see in Figure 5–2 that the mix of issuance programs and the frequency of issuance have changed many times in the past and are likely to do so in the future. How does the Treasury (or rather its Office of Debt Management) decide which maturities to issue (and also how often and how much)? The problem it is trying to solve is actually quite complex. First, it needs to estimate how much money it will have to raise in the next period (usually a quarter). This is an unknown quantity; the Treasury's estimates are usually based on budget forecasts and known seasonal patterns in government receipts and outlays, such as the April tax season. The expected amount of new issuance will then be the expected budgetary shortfall plus the amount needed to pay off outstanding securities maturing during this period. This second number is known beforehand and usually greatly exceeds the first.

To understand why, let us consider a hypothetical example in which we are just starting out as the U.S. Treasury. We have only one maturity series, the two-year program, and our financing need is $10 billion every month. Initially, we can cover that by issuing, say, $11 billion every month (we need a little extra to cover the expected interest payments). For the first two years this works like a charm, but two years after our first two-year note was issued, we have to pay it off while still raising $11 billion of new cash. This forces us to switch to issuing $22 billion of new two-year notes every month. Two years later, when the first of the $22 billion

---

1. TIPS are perhaps the most interesting Treasury products, and are a matter of long-standing interest for me personally, but they are still a very small part of the Treasury market, and it is hard to justify spending a few pages discussing them while not discussing the FX and commodities markets. If the inflation-linked market keeps growing, maybe we will have a chapter about inflation trading in a future edition of this book.

issues comes due, we have to bump the size of each new issue up again, to $33 billion, and so on.

This cannot go on forever, as there is a limit to how much demand there is in the market for two-year government debt, so at some point we will be tempted to introduce another maturity series, say the five-year. For the first five years after that, the five-year program will be our cash cow, as we do not have to pay off anything in that series (we may even decide to use some of the proceeds from the five-year program to reduce the size of the new issues in the two-year program). Of course, in five years, the sizes of new issues in the five-year series will have to be increased as well, and we may be tempted to consider yet another maturity series. After doing this for several decades, we will find that the sizes of new issues in all series are steadily growing, and that most of the proceeds from selling new securities (currently about 90 percent) goes toward paying off maturing debt.

Keeping the sizes of new issues manageable for all maturity series is therefore one important concern that the Treasury needs to address. Another factor that determines how it structures the issuance programs is the desire to minimize the interest payments on the outstanding securities (which at the time of this writing total over $300 billion a year and are the third largest item in the federal budget, behind defense and Medicare/Medicaid spending). As we saw in the previous chapter, during recessionary periods, the yields on short-term debt are usually much lower than for longer maturities, so issuing more short-term debt during such periods leads to lower interest expenses. This was the primary factor in the Treasury's decision to suspend the issuance of 30-year bonds in 2001—the interest on the 30-year debt at the time was around 4.5 percent, while 2-year debt could be issued at about 1.5 percent. However, the danger of shifting the debt issuance toward lower maturities is that it has to be refinanced more often, and by the time this short-term debt is up for refinancing, the rates may have gone up.

A useful concept in this area is the average maturity of Treasury debt, which, as the name suggests, is an average of the maturities of all outstanding Treasuries weighted by the issued amount. Figure 5–3 is a chart of the average maturity that the Treasury releases every quarter. The inverse of average maturity tells us what percentage of all Treasury debt has to be refinanced every year. As can be seen in Figure 5–3, historically the average maturity has been kept above 5 years, which means that less than 20 percent of all debt had to be reissued every year at new interest rates. After the recession of the early 2000s and the decision to suspend the 30-year program, the average maturity has dropped drastically and is now below

FIGURE 5-3

Average maturity of Treasury debt. (From the Q2 2005 quarterly refunding statement of the U.S. Treasury Bureau of Domestic Finance.)

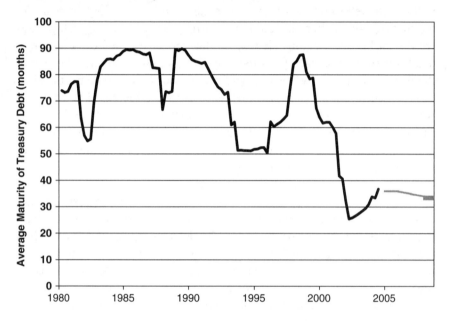

3 years and falling, so that the percentage of all debt exposed to the risk that rates will rise is now over 30 percent and rising. The decisions taken to minimize the interest expense in the short term may eventually end up costing the Treasury dearly in the long term.

The history of Treasury issuance programs shown in Figure 5–2 explains the current composition of Treasury debt. In Figure 5–4 we plot the original maturity of all outstanding Treasury bonds and notes against their time to maturity in an attempt to understand where all the points on the current yield curve come from. As can be seen in Figure 5–4, the Treasury curve naturally separates into *sectors* with different mixes of securities. The *long end* of the Treasury curve (securities with 10 or more years to maturity) is formed exclusively by old 30-year bonds. Some of them, issued about 20 years ago during the period of very high interest rates, are called *high coupons.*

Prior to 1985, the Treasury issued 30-year bonds in callable form— they could be redeemed 5 years before their nominal maturity if doing so

FIGURE 5–4

What the Treasury securities universe is made of–the original maturity of currently outstanding Treasuries (as of August 2004). The hollow squares show the callables.

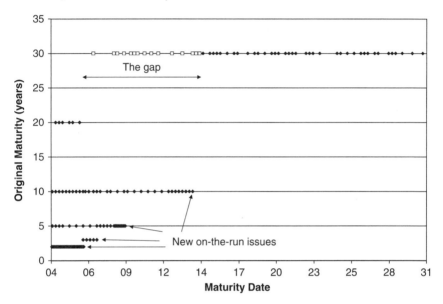

was to the Treasury's advantage (i.e., if by then the interest rates had dropped below their coupon rate). A few of those are still outstanding and are also shown in Figure 5–4; however, since today's interest rates are much lower than the coupon rate on the callables, all these bonds are certain to be called, so their "real" maturities are 5 years shorter than those shown in Figure 5–4. The first noncallable 30-year bond is 11.25 percent of 2/15. In 1986 the Treasury stopped issuing 20-year bonds, and the last 20-year bond is 9.125 percent of 2/06; as seen in Figure 5–4, this created a 9-year-wide *gap* in the Treasury maturity spectrum. The gap started closing in 1996 when the newly issued 10-year notes started having maturities later than 2/06, and it closed completely in February 2005, when the newly issued 10-year note reached the 2/15 maturity (the gap is clearly visible in Figure 4–8 in the previous chapter, which shows a yield curve from the year 2000).

Therefore, up until February 2005, all securities in the *10-year sector* (between 5 and 10 years to maturity) were issued as 10-year notes and were quite similar in terms of coupon rates, whereas after that time, the

10-year vintage has to coexist with 20-year-old 30-year bonds with coupon rates almost three times as high. Similarly, in the 5-year sector (between 3 and 5 years to maturity), 5-year-old 10-year notes coexist with recently issued 5-year notes; in the 3-year sector (between 2 and 3 years), there are old *tens, fives, and threes,* all maturing on the same set of dates but having different coupon rates and outstanding amounts. Below the 2-year point, it's a mix of all series. As we see, each of these sectors has its own unique composition; trading businesses usually organize their Treasury desks around these sectors, with each trader specializing in one sector so that she can know its peculiarities well.

With each passing day, all the dots in Figure 5–4 move one day to the left. Those that touch the vertical axis mature and have to be paid off. To do that (and raise new cash), the Treasury issues new securities that become the rightmost points in each series on this chart, as marked by the arrows. This can be viewed as the reproductive cycle for the Treasury market: old securities mature and disappear on the left side of the chart, while new securities are added on the right and begin their leftward journey toward maturity.

The most recently issued securities in each series are called *on-the-run* issues. As we will see, most secondary-market trading is focused on these *benchmark* issues. There are five of them at the time of this writing— 2-, 3-, 5-, 10-, and 30-year on-the-runs (the latter is also often called the *long bond,* while the rest are referred to as *twos, threes, fives, and tens*). An *old ten* is the 10-year note that was on-the-run before the current on-the-run was issued (in Figure 5–4, the point immediately to the left of the current rightmost point in each series); there are also *double-old* (or *old-old*) issues, and so on. The importance of the on-the-run issues in the Treasury market is unique among the major bond markets and deserves a closer look. Let us first consider the process by which these on-the-runs are created.

ISSUANCE OF NEW TREASURY SECURITIES

Since the late 1970s, all new Treasury securities are issued through periodic *auctions* conducted jointly by the U.S. Treasury and the Federal Reserve Banks. It is useful to think of such an auction not as a single event, but rather as a series of consecutive steps that make up an *auction cycle*. The cycle begins with the auction *announcement,* followed by a few days of *when-issued trading,* after which there is the auction proper, followed a few days later by the *issue date.*

The auctions follow a rigid schedule that is changed fairly infrequently. Currently, the 2-year auctions are conducted monthly, with the issue date and the maturity date at the end of the month (this has not changed since the late 1970s). Three- and 10-year auctions are conducted quarterly, with issue and maturity dates on the fifteenth of February, May, August, and November. The 5-year auction used to be on that quarterly cycle as well, but it was changed to monthly issuance in 2002 (with the issue and maturity dates remaining on the fifteenth of each month until February 2006, when they were switched to the end of the month). The 30-year program also followed the quarterly cycle until its suspension in 2001. The long bond was brought back in February 2006 and, as of this writing, is expected to be issued once a year. Let us go through the steps in the auction cycle for a particular security: a 2-year note issued in August 2004.

The auction cycle begins with the Treasury releasing, at a predetermined time (usually 11 a.m.), a document called the *auction announcement*, which we reproduce here as Figure 5–5. It is distributed by the news services and also becomes available at the Treasury's Web site. As is seen in Figure 5–5, it is just what its name implies: the Treasury announces that a few days later it will sell $24 billion of a new security. Note that the announcement also mentions how much money the Treasury needs in order to pay off the maturing notes (the August 2004 notes issued two years before)—in this particular case, the auction will actually set the Treasury back $2.7 billion.

The announcement also mentions the Fed holdings. The Federal Reserve holds significant amounts of short-maturity Treasuries in its own accounts (it uses these securities during its open-market operations, as described in the last chapter). When its holdings mature, it usually requests that the Treasury replace the matured holdings with freshly issued securities. Since this transaction is between two government agencies, no money really changes hands here. However, some of these Fed holdings may end up in the public domain if they are sold during open-market operations (which is also why the maturing amount mentioned in the announcement is not a round number: it is made up of the original issue amount of the August 2004 note—$27 billion, as you can read in its own auction announcement—less the amount the Fed bought during its open-market operations).

The announcement of the quarterly auctions, released a couple of weeks before the fifteenth of the quarterly cycle months, has a special name—it is called the *quarterly refunding statement*. It is somewhat more elaborate than the document in Figure 5–5, as it announces several upcoming auctions (currently, the 3-, 5-, and 10-year) at the same time, and,

FIGURE 5-5

Auction announcement for the August 2006 two-year note. (From www.publicdebt.treas.gov.)

DEPARTMENT OF THE TREASURY

TREASURY  N E W S

OFFICE OF PUBLIC AFFAIRS ● 1500 PENNSYLVANIA AVENUE, N.W. ● WASHINGTON, D.C ● 20220 ● (202) 622-2960

EMBARGOED UNTIL 11 : 00 A.M.   CONTACT: Office of Financing
August 23, 2004   202/504 – 3550
TREASURY OFFERS 2-YEAR NOTES

The Treasury will auction $24,000 million of 2-year notes to refund $26,734 million of publicly held notes maturing August 31, 2004, and to pay down approximately $2,734 million.

In addition to the public holdings, Federal Reserve Banks hold $7,807 million of the maturing notes for their own accounts, which may be refunded by issuing an additional amount of the new security.

Up to $1,000 million in noncompetitive bids from Foreign and International Monetary Authority (FIMA) accounts bidding through the Federal Reserve Bank of New York will be included within the offering amount of the auction. These noncompetitive bids will have a limit of $100 million per account and will be accepted in the order of smallest to largest, up to the aggregate award limit of $1,000 million.

TreasuryDirect customers requested that we reinvest their maturing holdings of approximately $631 million into the 2-year note.

The auction will be conducted in the single-price auction format. All competitive and noncompetitive awards will be at the highest yield of accepted competitive tenders. The allocation percentage applied to bids awarded at the highest yield will be rounded up to the next hundredth of a whole percentage point, e.g., 17.13%.

The notes being offered today are eligible for the STRIPS program.

This offering of Treasury securities is governed by the terms and conditions set forth in the Uniform Offering Circular for the Sale and Issue of Marketable Book-Entry Treasury Bills, Notes, and Bonds (31 CFR Part 356, as amended).

Details about the new security are given in the attached offering highlights.

more importantly, discusses the changes in the issuance pattern and the auction process in general that the Treasury proposes to introduce. Because of this discussion of future plans, the refunding announcement is required reading for anyone involved with U.S. interest-rate markets (we explain how to find it in the Recommended Readings for this chapter). Up until December 2004, the auction announcement also contained a unique identifier for the new security called the *CUSIP number*: most settlement systems require a CUSIP number to settle bond trades, so until the CUSIP number is known, the security cannot be traded (see Chapter 12 for more detail about CUSIP). Since December 2004, the CUSIP numbers are released the week before the auction announcement.

The auction announcement contains enough information to allow the market participants to start trading the new security even before it is actually issued. This kind of trading is called *when-issued* or *WI* trading, and it begins within seconds of the auction announcement. Since the coupon rate on the new note is not yet known, the trades are done in terms of yield and settle on the issue date. When-issued trading serves an important purpose: it allows the dealers to establish how much demand there is for the new issue so that they can decide how aggressive they want to be when bidding for it at the auction.

This is probably a good time to remind the reader who the main market participants are (those who need a more detailed discussion should go back to Chapter 2). Institutional investors who ultimately buy Treasury securities do so through the dealer firms, as do more speculative financial companies such as hedge funds. The dealers trade with their customers as well as with each other (the latter type of trading is facilitated by the interdealer brokers), and when-issued trading occurs in both dealer-to-customer and interdealer markets. For customers, the primary motivation for when-issued trading is to roll their positions in the current on-the-run that is about to lose its on-the-run status into the new issue. The dealers buy the current on-the-run from customers and sell them the new issue, thus accumulating a short position in the new issue that they hope to cover during the auction.

The dealers can bid in the auction for their own account (*direct* bids) or on behalf of their customers who want to purchase the new security (*indirect* bids). The New York Fed maintains a list of primary dealers (currently there are 22 firms in that group) who are allowed (actually more like required) to submit so-called *competitive* bids at Treasury auctions. A competitive bid specifies how much of the new issue we want and how much (in terms of yield) we are willing to pay for it, while a noncompetitive bid (which everybody, including individual investors, can submit) specifies only how much we will purchase.

The traders at the dealer firms (the responsibility for submitting auction bids lies with those traders in the primary dealer firm who trade the corresponding sector in the secondary market, so in our example it would be the two-year trader) submit bids either electronically or over the phone. The bidding yields they specify are usually based on where the new issue is trading in the when-issued market, as well as on the positions the dealer has in the new issue—if a dealer has a lot of orders for the new issue, it may want to bid a shade more aggressively than the yields at which the security can be bought in the when-issued market. Since the market keeps moving, the traders prefer to submit these bids as late as possible—minutes if not seconds before the 1 p.m. deadline. At 1 p.m. the auction closes, the bids are processed, and each bidder is told how much it has been allocated within a couple of minutes (a public announcement of the auction results is also made at this time).

Since 1998, all Treasury auctions are conducted in what is called the *single-price format*. To explain how single-price (also called *Dutch*) auctions work, let us consider the following hypothetical example. We assume that the Treasury wants to sell $20 billion of two-year notes, and that it has received the following bids: a total of $1 billion of noncompetitive bids, one $10 billion bid at a 2.49 percent yield, two bids at 2.50 percent, for $5 billion and $10 billion, respectively, and one other bid for $10 billion at 2.51 percent. First, $1 billion of the new issue is set aside for the noncompetitive bidders, which leaves $19 billion to allocate. Then we go through the bids, beginning with the most competitive (lowest yield), and allocate as much as we can until we run out of securities to allocate. In our example, we begin by allocating the whole $10 billion to the bidder at 2.49 percent, which leaves us with $9 billion, which we will give to the two 2.5 percent bidders. Since we cannot fill their orders completely, they will be filled in proportion to what they want: the first will get $3 billion and the second $6 billion. The least competitive bidder, at 2.51 percent, will get nothing.

The *clearing yield* is the level at which the last dollar was allocated—2.5 percent in our example. In a single-price auction, all winning bidders, including the noncompetitive bidders, pay the clearing yield regardless of what their bidding level was. This is in contrast to the discriminatory-price auctions used before 1998, where each bidder paid its own bidding yield. There is an interesting branch of theoretical finance called auction theory that considers the advantages and disadvantages of different ways of conducting auctions. Its main result consists of empirical proof that auction rules actually matter—"good" rules should encourage people to bid aggressively while ensuring some basic fairness so that winning bidders do not overpay, and the Treasury has moved to single-price auctions in order to bring its rules closer to the theoretical ideal.

One of the main reasons the dealers participate in the auctions is to cover the short positions they accumulate during when-issued trading with their customers. If for some reason a dealer is unable to buy enough of the new issue at the auction, it has to go and buy the rest from other dealers at whatever price the other dealers charge. This opens the possibility of a *short squeeze*, where one dealer accumulates most of the new issue and

forces others to pay exorbitant prices in order to cover their short positions. In 1991, Salomon Brothers famously cornered at least four Treasury
auctions, causing much aggravation to other market players (some smaller
firms were forced out of business, and overall losses are estimated to have
been more than $200 million). To prevent this from happening again,
another auction rule states that no single bidder can accumulate more than
35 percent of the auction amount—this rule was in place at the time of
the Salomon debacle, but it has since been enforced more vigorously (note
that our auction example would violate it).

   In its announcement of the auction results (reproduced here as Figure
5–6), the Treasury does not disclose the distribution of individual bids,
but specifies the total amount tendered (the total of all bids) and the clearing yield. It also sets the coupon rate on the new issue. The coupon rate
is set in increments of $\frac{1}{8}$, so it is not necessarily equal to the clearing yield.
Note carefully how the auction process makes sure that the coupon rate
(a property of the newly issued security) is very close to the when-issued
yield at the time of the auction (which is set by the market). In the August
2004 two-year note auction, the clearing yield was a touch short of 2.5
percent, but the coupon (called the interest rate in the announcement;
see Figure 5–6) was set at $2\frac{3}{8}$ percent. The coupon is always set at or
below the clearing yield, so that when the issue price is calculated from
the clearing yield using this coupon value, the resulting price comes out
slightly below par. This is done to accommodate small noncompetitive
bidders who send their payments ahead of the auction—if someone sends
in a check for $1,000, he expects to get at least a $1,000 par amount of
the new issue, which would not be possible if the new issue was priced
above par.

   The market participants scrutinize the auction results announcement
for signs of how successful the auction was. The main measure of this is
the bid/cover ratio, shown at the end of the announcement; it is simply a
ratio of the total amount of submitted bids to the amount auctioned, and
the higher it is, the more interest there was in the new issue. The recent
average for that number is around 2, so any auction with a bid/cover ratio
above that is seen as successful. Another, more sophisticated measure of
auction success is called the *auction tail*; there are many definitions of it,
but all of them attempt to measure the width of the bid distribution. For
single-price auctions, it is often defined as the difference between the lowest
bid and the clearing yield. In our example (see Figure 5–6), it is a rather
large 6.4 bp (the difference between the clearing yield of 2.494 percent
and the *low yield* of 2.43 percent, as stated at the end of the announcement).

FIGURE 5-6

Auction results for the August 25, 2004, two-year note auction.
(From www.publicdebt.treas.gov.)

PUBLIC DEBT NEWS

Department of the Treasury • Bureau of the Public Debt • Washington, DC 20239

TREASURY SECURITY AUCTION RESULTS
BUREAU OF THE PUBLIC DEBT - WASHINGTON DC

FOR IMMEDIATE RELEASE   CONTACT: Office of Financing
August 25, 2004   202-504-3550

RESULTS OF TREASURY'S AUCTION OF 2-YEAR NOTES

Interest Rate:	2 3/8%	Issue Date:	August 31, 2004
Series:	S-2006	Dated Date:	August 31, 2004
CUSIP No:	912828CU2	Maturity Date:	August 31, 2004

High Yield: 2.494%   Price: 99.769

All noncompetitive and successful competitive bidders were awarded
securities at the high yield. Tenders at the high yield were
allotted 32.34%. All tenders at lower yields were accepted in full.

AMOUNT TENDERED AND ACCEPTED (in thousands)

Tender Type	Tendered	Accepted
Competitive	$ 51,580,904	$ 23,005,209
Noncompetitive	994,798	994,798
FIMA (noncompetitive)	0	0
SUBTOTAL	52,575,702	24,000,007 1/
Federal Reserve	7,806,533	7,806,533
TOTAL	$ 60,382,235	$ 31,806,540

Median yield 2.465%: 50% of the amount of accepted competitive tenders
was tendered at or below that rate. Low yield 2.430%: 5% of the amount
of accepted competitive tenders was tendered at or below that rate.

Bid-to-Cover Ratio = 52,575,702 / 24,000,007 = 2.19

1/ Awards to TREASURY DIRECT = $791,719,000

A wide distribution of bids, as measured by a large tail, indicates that some dealers did not really want to win any of the new issue and therefore casts some doubt on the true market demand for it.

Although the auction sets the coupon rate on the new issue, it continues to trade in yield for the rest of the auction day, just as it did prior to the auction. This is mostly a systems issue; most Wall Street software systems cannot switch from using one set of on-the-runs to another intraday (we discuss some of the reasons why in Part 3 of this book). The new issue becomes the new on-the-run (and begins to trade in price, like all other Treasuries) only on the morning after the auction date. We illustrate the timeline of the auction cycle and the timing of the on-the-run status change in Figure 5–7. Note that even after the new issue has become the new on-the-run, it is still somewhat unusual in that the trades done in it cannot settle before the issue date, which is still a few days ahead (whereas

F I G U R E   5–7

The auction cycle timeline for the August 2004 two-year auction. The cycle begins on August 23 with the auction announcement at 11 a.m., which creates a new security that immediately begins when-issued trading. At 1 p.m. on Aug 25, the auction is conducted, and the coupon on the new issue is set (2⅜). The next morning, the new issue becomes the two-year on-the-run, while the old issue becomes an old two-year. The new issue trades with a nonregular settlement (8/31/04) until the day before the issue date. At the end of the next month this cycle repeats with the September 2006 two-year auction, and so on.

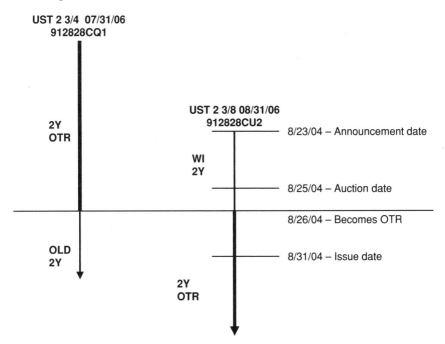

normal Treasury trades settle on the next business day). The issue date marks the true end of the auction cycle and is a very important day from the Treasury's perspective, as it is the day when it receives money from those who bought the new security (and also the day when money finally changes hands to settle all trades done during when-issued trading), but it has little significance in the secondary market, to which we now turn our attention.

SECONDARY-MARKET TRADING OF TREASURY BONDS AND NOTES

Who are the players in the secondary market, and how exactly do they trade Treasuries with each other? As we discussed in Chapter 2, the participants in the secondary market are the same characters that we have already met in our discussion of the primary markets—the dealer firms and their institutional clients—except that the Treasury itself is out and interdealer brokers are in. There is no centralized exchange for Treasuries (or for bonds in general), so at least one end of each Treasury trade is done by a dealer firm. When a customer (such as a mutual fund company or a hedge fund) wants to do a trade in the Treasury market, it approaches one or several dealers and asks for price quotes; usually the dealer offering the best price wins the trade, although there could be other factors such as quality of service.

Very often, when a dealer sells a Treasury product to a customer, it turns to the interdealer market to cover the sale by buying the same product from another dealer. It could in theory trade with the other dealer directly, but in practice this rarely happens, as the interdealer brokers provide a convenient and anonymous alternative. Therefore, we can say that there are only two types of trades done in the secondary Treasury market: dealer-to-customer trades and interdealer trades. Dealer-to-customer trades are invisible to other market participants, but all dealers see trades done in the interdealer market. So this is where *price discovery* occurs, which means that this is where the dealers turn to find out how much they can buy or sell a given Treasury for. To discuss this process in more detail, let us consider interdealer trading of the on-the-run issues.

Back in the olden days (before 1998 or so), the interdealer Treasury market was a low-tech affair. There were about 10 broker firms, and each operated along the same lines: the brokers sat at their desks talking on the phone to traders at dealer firms. When the traders wanted to buy or sell something, the brokers would enter the order into a simple program that updated a *broker page* distributed across Wall Street by Reuters or some other market data provider. The Treasury traders at all dealer firms were watching these pages constantly, and when they saw a price they liked, they called the broker and did the trade (there are direct lines on traders' phone turrets that are constantly connected to all relevant brokers). The trade would be reported on the broker page, so everyone else would see it. Today these brokers would be called *voice brokers* despite the electronic distribution of the pages.

One of these broker firms, Cantor Fitzgerald, came to dominate the area of on-the-run trading. The traditional role of a human broker who endeavors to find the other side of a trade is reduced to mere data entry for on-the-run trading, as these are among the most liquid and frequently traded securities in the world, so Cantor Fitzgerald became the first to introduce an electronic system for order entry. That system, called *eSpeed*, was first deployed internally within Cantor, but in early 1999 it was rolled out to Cantor's customers. Each trader got a small desktop application (a screen shot is shown in Figure 5–8) that connected to eSpeed servers at Cantor's data center. Traders from different firms could enter their orders, and their counterparts at other dealer firms could see and trade on them without much human intervention.

The emergence of eSpeed took the Treasury market to the bleeding edge of electronic trading almost overnight. The dealers, however, were concerned about the fact that eSpeed quickly forced other nonelectronic brokers out of the on-the-run trading business. To counter eSpeed's growing clout, the dealer firms formed a consortium called *BrokerTec* that went into the same business of electronic interdealer trading. BrokerTec went live about a year after eSpeed and created some much-needed competition in the area of on-the-run trading. For the first few years of their coexistence, eSpeed heavily dominated, but in 2004 BrokerTec pulled ahead, and as of this writing has a slightly higher market share.

Figure 5–9 shows a mock-up of a Treasury trading application that is similar to the GUIs used by both eSpeed and BrokerTec—it is somewhat simpler than the eSpeed screen, but it has all the essentials that we need in order to understand how these things work. Let us make sure we understand everything we see on that screen before discussing what we can do with it. First, we see a row for every on-the-run security. In this row, from left to right, we see the following fields: bid price, ask price, bid size, and ask size (the sizes are separated by an "×"); let us ignore the last column,

FIGURE 5–8

A screen shot of the eSpeed GUI. (© 2006 eSpeed, Inc. All rights reserved. Reprinted by permission.)

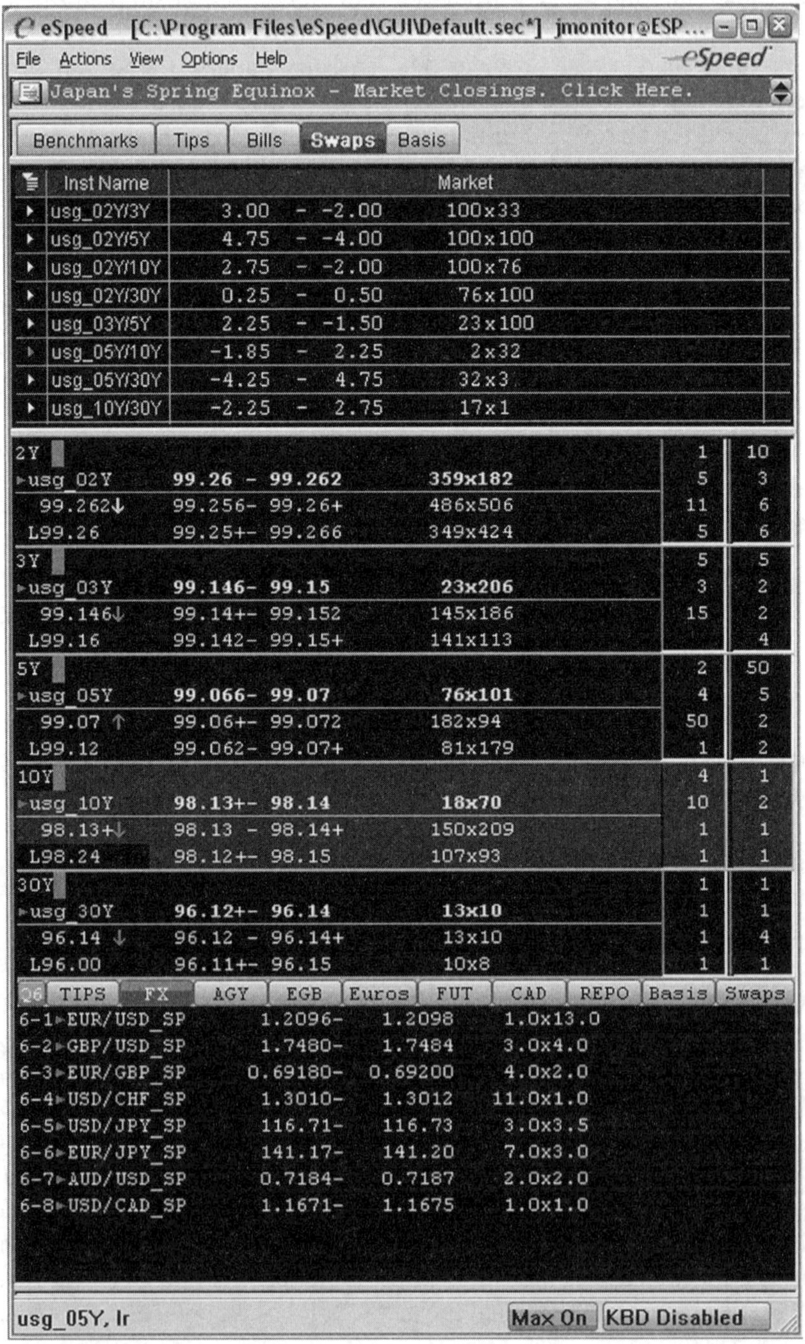

FIGURE 5–9

A mock-up of a screen for electronic trading of Treasury on-the-runs.

Security	Bid	Offer	BSize	⨯	OSize	LastSize
2_YEAR	TAKE	99.21+		⨯ 44		40
3_YEAR	99.26	99.26+		11 ⨯ 17		1
5_YEAR	100.096	100.096		22 ⨯ 15		4
10_YEAR	101.22+	HIT		⨯		3
30_YEAR	108.04+	108.07		9 ⨯ 6		1
2_YEAR ROLL	4.00	–3.75		500 ⨯ 20		90

which shows the last trade size. The *bid price* is the price at which we can sell this security, and how much we can sell is indicated by the bid size (all sizes are in million-dollar par amounts), while the *ask* (or *offer*) price is the price at which we can buy (up to the ask size). The ask price should always be higher than the bid; otherwise we could buy at the ask and immediately sell at the bid and make a profit.

The prices look a little funny; this is because they are expressed in thirty-seconds, not in decimals. Let us take 108.04+ as an example. 108 is the *handle*, and the first two characters to the right of the dot separator indicate the number of thirty-seconds, or *ticks*—04 means $\frac{4}{32}$, or 0.125. The third character, if present, indicates the number of *eighths* ($\frac{1}{8}$ of a thirty-second); this can range from 1 to 7, with 4 (half a tick) being replaced by the "+" sign. The table in Figure 5–10 is a conversion (and pronunciation) guide intended to make you comfortable with thirty-second pricing. Interestingly, this strange practice goes back to the early financial markets of the sixteenth and seventeenth centuries. In those days, money was coins, and if a person wanted to buy something that was worth less

FIGURE 5—10

Thirty-seconds pronunciation guide.

Price quote	Pronounced	Conversion	Decimal value
100-23	twenty three	=100 + 23/32	100.71875000
101-011	one and an eight	=101 + 1.125/32	101.03515625
99-232	twenty three and a quarter	=99 + 23.25/32	99.72656250
101-10+	ten plus	=101 + 10.5/32	101.32812500
99-116	eleven and three quarters	=99 + 11.75/32	99.36718750
100-055	five and five eights	=100 + 5.625/32	100.17578125
101-00+	buck plus	=101 + 0.5/32	101.01562500

than a full coin, he simply cut the coin in pieces. It is easy to cut a coin in half (and then in half again, and on and on), but difficult to cut it into 10 pieces, so all pricing was in powers of 2 fractions rather than in decimals. Decimal pricing took off when paper money came on the scene, but in many financial markets the powers of 2 pricing persisted until the end of the twentieth century. The U.S. and Canadian bond markets are the last two holdouts at this time.

A trader using this screen can do two main things with it. The first of them is to initiate a trade by *hitting* a bid or *lifting* (or *taking*) an offer shown on the screen (that is done by using one of the hot keys on the keyboard; BrokerTec distributes a keyboard decal to traders so that they can remember which key means what, and so do other electronic trading platforms, so many keyboards on a fixed-income trading desk look like a sticker project of a young child). The resulting trade does not happen instantly, but rather a trade cycle begins: the price the trader acted on begins to flash on the screens all over Wall Street, while the other side of the market is replaced by a flashing "HIT" or "TAKE" (we see that in Figure 5–9 in the 2-year and 10-year rows). The flashing goes on for a few seconds, during which other traders can join either side of the trade in a process known as *workup.*

Let us say that our trader wants to sell $10 million of the 10-year note. When she hits the bid of 101-22+, she sells $1 million instantly (the amount shown as bid size), after which the screen begins to flash, inviting others to join the ongoing trade. Someone may come in and buy the rest of what she wanted to sell, and even try to buy more, say $20 million. If this happens, our trader will have the first shot at selling more to the new buyer. If she passes (or sells less than the buyer wants to buy), someone else can join on the sell side and sell more 10-year notes. Eventually there will be no one willing to take the other side—the screen will flash for a couple more seconds and then stop. If at that stage there is still more for sale at the trade price, but nobody wants to buy just now, the sell order becomes an offer at the trade price; if the opposite happens, the buy order becomes a bid at the trade price. If before the trade the market was 101-22+/23 and the 22+ bid was hit, after the trade the market will either go down to 101-22/22+ (the trade price becomes the offer) or remain the same (the trade price remains the bid).

There are two important consequences of this workup procedure: (1) the trade can last a significant amount of time (often a minute or more), and (2) during this time, there is *only one trade price*. This is very different from the more common exchange-style execution (which we will discuss in the next chapter). The main reason for it is the desire of the brokers to enhance their revenues: the brokers are paid commissions based on the amount traded, so they naturally want to encourage their clients to trade more, and turning each trade into a big festive event that everyone can join is an effective way to do that. However, this procedure also has the beneficial side effect of making the prices "sticky" and dampening market volatility.

The second main thing a trader can do with the eSpeed or BrokerTec screen is to submit a bid or an offer and let someone else initiate the trade. So if a trader wanted to sell the 10-year note when the market was 22+/23, he could either hit the 22+ bid or *join* the 23 offer. If someone else then decides to buy and lifts the offer, he will sell at half a tick higher than if he had initiated the trade himself, but this is not guaranteed. So active, or *aggressive*, trading (hitting the bid) results in a worse price but more certain execution, whereas passive trading (submitting an offer) gives a better price but much less certain execution. This illustrates one of the main principles of all trading: the aggressor pays the transaction costs (we will discuss other principles at the end of this chapter). The costs are not only the difference between the bid and offer prices (the *bid-ask spread*), but also the broker's commission, which is paid by whoever initiates the trade. However, the commission is almost irrelevant compared to the bid-ask spread—half a tick on a $1 million trade is $156.25 (½ of ½₂ of 1 percent of the par amount), whereas the commission is usually just a couple of dollars per million traded.

When we submit an offer, we choose the price and the size. The size is entirely up to us, but the price is somewhat constrained: we can join an existing offer, we can submit a higher (worse) price (which will not even be shown on the screen), or we can submit a lower (better) price. Note that each on-the-run has a finite trading increment (half a tick for the 10-year) by which we can move the price, so if we want to submit a better offer in a 22+/23 market, we'll have to go down to 22+. Again unlike with exchange execution, the brokers will *not* automatically cross a bid of 22+ with a 22+ offer, so the market will be *locked* at 22+ (we see this situation in Figure 5–9 for the 5-year note).

When we join an existing bid or offer, our order is put on a *stack* behind those that are already in the system. If we are second in the offer stack at 23, and there is one order for $10 million ahead of us, and someone lifts the offer for less than $10 million, the first person in the stack gets partially filled and remains ahead of us in the stack. If someone then comes and lifts the offer for $50 million, the orders in the stack up to this size get completely filled, after which the first person in the stack gets an option to sell more within the next couple of seconds. If that person either passes or sells less than the remaining amount on the buy side, the workup process moves on to our order and we get an option to sell more. Because of this workup option that everyone has, stack position is very important for successful execution.

Paradoxically, the workup process makes the prices move more slowly than they would in an exchange market, but makes being fast with order submission extremely important. Let us consider what happens when the market is falling fast and everyone wants to sell. We see a bid that we and 15 other people want to hit and we submit our sell order, but if we are not the first in the stack, it is likely that the first one there will get the whole bid amount, and the next bid will come in lower; again, everyone will try to hit it, and only the fastest will succeed—the market can move a lot before a slow submitter gets its order filled. The eSpeed GUI shown in Figure 5–8 displays the composition of the order stack for all bids and offers, as well as during trades (they are shown on the left; of course the BrokerTec GUI can be configured to show the stack as well).

To illustrate the dynamics of the on-the-run trading in the interdealer market, Figure 5–11 displays a history of 10-year note trading on eSpeed for a 20-minute period on a day when an important piece of economic data was announced. Before an economic number release at 8:30, the 10-year note traded up and down around the same level. At the time of the number announcement, it jumps (or, as a trader would say, *gaps*) up almost a whole point—it misses many price levels on the way up, leaving gaps in the sequence of prices. Then it goes down, briefly stabilizes about 24

ticks above its preannouncement level, and (apparently as the market decides
that the announcement was not that important after all) resumes its downward march in a directional trade, where every bid that appears is hit
immediately; once the trade is over, a new bid comes in a plus lower and
is also hit right away, and on and on. In this 20-minute period, more than
$3 billion worth of the 10-year note changed hands in about 200 trades.

The daily trading volume in the 10-year on eSpeed is usually upward
of $30 billion—the same order of magnitude as the NYSE volume for *all*
stocks on a typical trading day. To tie this discussion to the topics of the
previous chapter, let us emphasize that when we say that interest rates are
set in the market, we mean this interdealer market—the screens in Figures
5–8 and 5–9 are exactly where it happens. Our description of the 10-year
trading has been somewhat mechanistic, but we should always remember
that every time the price changes in the interdealer screen, the new value
of the 10-year yield is the 10-year interest rate that the whole economy
now has to live with—all other interest rates are derived from that number.

F I G U R E   5–11

Trading in the 10-year on eSpeed on December 3, 2004.
Bids are shown as hollow boxes, offers as solid horizontal
lines, and trades as solid dots. (© 2006 eSpeed, Inc. All
rights reserved. Reprinted by permission.)

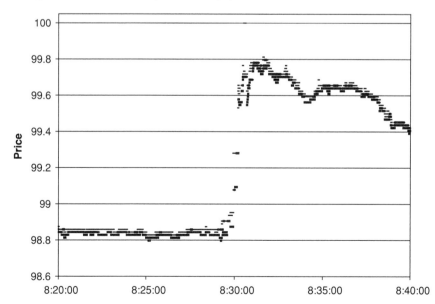

Each Treasury trader who buys and sells the 10-year cares mostly about whether his trades make money or not, but the traders' collective behavior has economic consequences—the price jump we see in Figure 5–11 translates into a 10-bp drop in the 10-year yield, which has a nontrivial impact on everyday things like mortgage and car loan rates.

While the five on-the-run issues are easily among the most liquid securities in the world, many old off-the-run issues have just a couple of trades a day, and the trading mechanics for the rest of the Treasury universe are quite different from what we have just described. Although off-the-run issues are much less liquid that the on-the-runs, an interesting (some would say defining) feature of the interest-rate markets is that the value of such less liquid products is closely linked to that of the actively traded on-the-runs. This is because on a fundamental level, all Treasury issues are very similar securities—they all represent a stream of future cash flows that is not that different for, say, a current on-the-run that trades every couple of seconds and a more seasoned issue with six months less to maturity (in this example, the timing of all coupon payments is the same, so the main difference is that in one case we get the principal back six months earlier). Therefore, the value of this off-the-run *relative* to a similar on-the-run issue should not change very much, even if the absolute value (price) of the on-the-run goes up and down every few seconds. Most off-the-run trading is based on this relative value concept; usually these issues are traded as a *bond switch*, where we buy an off-the-run issue and simultaneously sell an on-the-run (or vice versa), so the economics of the trade depends only on their relative valuation.

Let us consider how a typical bond switch works. Assume that we want to buy $10 million of an off-the-run issue (say May 14; at the time of this writing, there was only one Treasury note with that maturity, so this uniquely identifies it) and sell a certain quantity X of the on-the-run 10-year note. We will transport ourselves into early November 2004 for this and a few other examples, so the on-the-run 10-year at that time was the August (or Aug, pronounced "augie") 14. If the yields on both issues were to go up by 1 bp (a parallel move in the yield curve), we would lose $10 million times the price drop on the off-the-run issue on our off-the-run position, and make X times the price change on the on-the-run.

The price change for a 1-bp change in yield is called the dollar value of a basis point (DV01); as we discussed in the previous chapter, it is a quantity that is roughly proportional to the maturity of the issue. The

DV01 of the May 14 will thus be slightly less than that of the Aug 14, so a 1-bp change in yield will cause the price of the Aug 14 to drop slightly more than that of the May 14. If we sell proportionally less of the Aug 14 (i.e., if X = $10 million times the ratio of DV01s for the two issues), we can structure the trade so that the overall price of the portfolio will not change at all for a parallel move in yields. In this case, our trade is not sensitive to the parallel shift in yields but is sensitive to changes in the difference between the two yields, which is called the *yield spread.* Such a *spread trade* is a way to capture the relative value differential of the two securities. If we want to do a spread trade, within certain limits of our linearized approach, we do not care what price (or yield) we pay for each leg of the trade as long as we get the yield spread right. Most off-the-run trading is organized around this spread trade idea.

The dominant interdealer brokers that trade off-the-run Treasuries are, at the time of this writing, Garban (now part of a larger brokerage called InterCapital, or ICAP) and Liberty; unlike Cantor, they never really went electronic, so most trades are still done by phone. The brokers show their prices for the off-the-runs on pages that the traders look at through their market data system; Figure 5–12 shows an example of what we can see on such Treasury broker pages. Let us ignore the right-hand half of that page for now (we will return to it in Chapter 7) and focus on the left. The topmost line on the left reads 215/10Y +3.6/−3.3 10 × 5; let us decipher this. The 215 is Feb 15—the Treasury note maturing in February 2015 (as we discussed before, there was only one such note at the time of our example)—and /10Y means "against the 10-year note." The two numbers indicate the bid and ask yield spreads—the broker stands ready to buy $10 million of Feb 15 and sell the DV01-weighted amount of the on-the-run 10-year note at a yield spread of +3.6 bp (a trader would pronounce that as "pick 3.6 over tens"—the broker is *picking up* yield by switching into the Feb 15 from the 10-year note), and sell $5 million of it at a yield spread of 3.3 bp ("give 3.3"—the broker would be *giving up* yield on the opposite trade) against buying the same amount of the 10-year note.

If we call the broker and take this offer, we will get two trades done; one is a sell of the current 10-year note at something close to its current market price (in the amount of $5 million times the DV01 ratio), and a buy of $5 million of Feb 15 at a price calculated by taking the yield on the 10-year leg, adding 3.3 bp, and converting to price. You are invited to work through this example and convince yourself that the total amount of

FIGURE 5-12

Interdealer brokers publish quotes for off-the-run Treasuries on pages such as this one, which are distributed by market data services.

```
215/10Y   +3.6/-3.3      10  X 5
815/10Y  +10.0/           5  X
N15/10Y  +14.7/-12.5      5  X 5           3YR ROLL      PK 7.5 (150) GV 7.25 (175)
216/10Y  +17.4/-17.0      5  X 5           5YR ROLL      PK 3.0 (140) GV 2.75 (450)
516/10Y  +24.6/-23.8      5  X 5          10Y ROLL      PK 2.0 (160) GV 1.75 (385)
N16/10Y  +29.5/-29.2     15  X 5
517/10Y         -32.0          X 35
817/10Y  +36.4/              5 X
518/10Y  +40.3/              5 X          =========== DEC BASIS =================
N18/10Y  +47.4/              5 X          Z4 5      8/11   15.2(10)   15.+(110)
219/10Y  +48.4/              5 X          Z4 4 7/8 2/12   24. (10)   26.+(10)
============ 10YR SWAPS ==================  Z4 4 3/8 8/12   35. (10)   36.2(15)
  5       2/11|107.12+-13     10x20       Z4 4     N/12
  5       8/11|107.11+-116    30x70       Z4 4 1/4 8/13
  4 7/8 2/12|106.152-162 10x10            Z4 4 1/4 N/13
  4 3/8 8/12|103.01+-02  10x20            Z4 4 3/4 5/14
  4      N/12|100.13 -15      10x10       Z4 4 1/4 8/14
  3 7/8 2/13| 99.10 -11   10x10           =========== MAR BASIS =================
  3 5/8 5/13| 97.16 -176  10x10           H5 4 7/8 2/12    - - (--)   38.6(10)
  4 1/4 8/13|101.156-162  10x10           H5 4 3/8 8/12
  4 1/4 N/13|101.096-10   10x10           ====================================
  4      2/14| 99.09 -092  10x10
  4 3/4 5/14|104.312-31+  10x10
10Y 4 1/4 8/14|101.00 - 00  10x10
```

money that you have to pay for this combination of trades does not depend on the individual prices, but depends only on the yield spread as long as the price changes are small, so that the DV01s do not change much.

However, many people find it unsettling that they do not know the prices at which the two legs of a spread trade will be executed, so a more widespread practice is to fix both prices instead of fixing the yield spread. This type of quoting is shown in the lower left corner of Figure 5–12, in the area under the heading "10YR SWAPS," which is commonly called the *10-year swapbox*. The second line from the bottom is a quote for May 14 and shows bid and offer prices. These, however, are *swapbox prices*—we can buy May 14 at 104-31+ and sell (the DV01-weighted amount of) the current 10-year (Aug 14) at the *lock price* of 101-00, as indicated on the last line.

The economics of this *bond swap* are identical to that for the previous example except that there is no uncertainty about the prices for each of the two legs. Everything still depends only on the yield spread between them; this quoting convention simply expresses the yield spread differently—it specifies the two prices instead of a single yield spread between them. In the previous example, the price of each leg of the swap will fluctuate as the on-the-run trades up and down, while in a swapbox trade both prices are independent of the current market price of the on-the-run. Again, everything depends only on the yield spread as long as prices do not change by too much; the brokers reflect that fact by making sure that the swapbox lock price for the on-the-run is reasonably close to where it is currently trading. The lock price will stay at 101-00 as long as the 10-year is trading within a few ticks of that level, but if it moves up to 101-08 (a quarter of a point), the broker will change the lock price to 101-08 (and recalculate all swapbox prices to keep the yield spreads the same). Either way, the swapbox prices or the yield spreads on the page will be updated fairly infrequently (only when the *relative* valuation changes), which clearly makes them easier to maintain.

Another area of the screen in Figure 5–12 illustrates the concept of when-issued trading, which we discussed earlier in relation to the auction cycle. The screen shot was taken in early November 2004, after the November auctions for the 3-year, 5-year, and 10-year notes were announced, so these new issues had started when-issued trading. The upper right of the screen shows three lines for the WI rolls; a roll is a trade in which we sell the existing on-the-run (Aug 14 for the 10-year note) and buy the new Nov 14 issue (thus *rolling* our on-the-run position from the old to the new on-the-run). The roll trades are a natural way to value the new issue relative to the current on-the-run, and the screen shows these relative values in terms of the yield spread; for example, the 3Y roll line says "pick 7.5/give 7.25 bp." Note the huge sizes on these roll quotes.

These relative trades dominate the interdealer market for Treasury off-the-runs except at the very short end of the curve (with maturities of one year or less). In this sector, prices do not move much (they all approach par as the issues approach their maturity date); besides, there is no convenient benchmark to do relative trades against (the two-year note is too far away in maturity), so these short-end Treasuries are quoted and traded *outright* (the same as on-the-runs).

TREASURY BILLS

Treasury bills are also an important part of the short-end Treasury market. These bills are non-interest-bearing securities that trade on a discount yield basis. They are issued at a discount to par—for example, if a six-month bill is sold at the auction at 99, the discount would be 1 and the discount yield (discount divided by time to maturity) would be 2 percent. Figure 5–13 shows a broker page where interdealer bill trading is done. The

FIGURE 5–13

A mock-up of an interdealer broker T-bills page. The on-the-run 1-month, 3-month, and 6-month bills are identified on the upper left, and in the upper right there are quotes for the when-issued bills. The discount yields for the rest of the T-bill universe are shown at the bottom (each bill is identified by its maturity; for example, D/30 means December 30).

```
                              ------- US TREASURY BILLS ---------------
===================================================
        1MO    O/14   1.515(25)-51 (05)
        3MO    D/16   1.635(05)-63 (35)      3WI   D/23   1.69 (05)-66 (10)
        6MO    3/17   1.835(05)-83 (55)      6WI   3/24   1.865(05)-85 (05)
===================================================================================
      3MO ROLL    PK 6.0 (25) GV 3.0 (25)          D/09   1.63 (05)-62 (05)
      6MO ROLL    PK 3.0 (125)GV 2.0 (25)          D/02   1.62 (05)-61 (05)
=====================================                N/26   1.615(05)-605(15)
               3/10    1.825(15)-815(05)            N/18   1.585(05)-58 (05)
               3/03    1.815(05)-81 (05)            N/12   1.575(05)-56 (05)
               2/24    1.795(05)- - (--)            N/04   1.55 (05)-54 (05)
               2/17    1.80 (05)- - (--)            O/28   1.545(05)-535(05)
               2/10    1.785(05)-785(50)            O/21   1.51 (05)-50 (05)
               2/03    1.78 (05)-77 (126)           O/07   1.515(05)-49 (05)
               1/27    1.77 (05)-765(05)            9/30   1.475(05)-47 (05)
               1/20    1.75 (05)-745(05)            9/23   1.40 (05)-385(05)
               1/13    1.73 (05)-72 (10)   =========================================
               1/06    1.705(05)-70 (05)
               D/30    - - - - 1.66 (05)
               D/23    1.67 (05)-655(05)
===================================================================================
```

quotes are all in terms of discount yield instead of price, and the bills are identified by their maturity date (the year is not specified, though).

To understand the structure of the T-bill market, we need to review the bill issuance process. There are three on-the-run T-bills: six-month, three-month, and one-month bills. They are all auctioned every week and mature on Thursdays. This creates an interesting situation: suppose the Treasury wants to issue a three-month bill maturing on a Thursday in three months. But such a bill exists already—it is the six-month bill issued three months ago. Since it does not make sense to create two identical securities, the Treasury *reopens* the existing three-month-old six-month bill, which simply means that it sells more of those bills at the auction instead of creating a new security. The one-month bill is issued through a similar *reopening* (as there always is an existing bill with exactly the right maturity). Reopenings also happen for Treasury coupon issues—for example, every 10-year note is issued once a quarter and then reopened one month later (which means, as with bills, that the Treasury simply sells more of it). Reopenings of this type are sometimes referred to as *taps* (which I always visualize as a tap out of which money flows) and are much more common in European bond markets.

STRIPS

To complete our tour of the Treasury product universe,[2] we need to discuss STRIPS. All Treasury issues can be seen as collections of future payments: many smaller coupon payments, and a single principal payment. Up until 1983, Treasury notes and bonds were issued in paper form and looked similar to Figure 1–2—a "body" representing the principal payment and a set of coupons attached to it, each representing a single coupon payment. In the 1970s, the Treasury dealers started "stripping" the Treasuries of their coupons and trading each coupon and principal payment separately. The resulting securities were called *zero-coupon bonds* because a bond issued with a zero coupon rate would have the same single cash flow.

   The main reason for the sudden popularity of these *zeros* was tax avoidance. The tax rates in the 1970s were very high, but under the tax laws of that period, the discount on a bond purchase was treated as a capital loss, and all these stripped products were sold at a deep discount to par; for example, the price for a zero maturing in 30 years was around $5 (I will explain why shortly). Therefore, an investor purchasing a $100 par amount of such a zero instrument from a dealer could pay $5, deduct $95 from his taxable income, and be sure that in 30 years he would get the full $100 back—obviously a very good deal.

   In 1982 this tax loophole was closed, and the next year the Treasury stopped issuing bonds in paper form, making physical stripping impossible (ever since then, all Treasuries have been issued in *book-entry form*—they exist only as account entries at Federal Reserve Banks). However, by that time, many investors had come to recognize that zeros had many desirable properties beyond tax avoidance; in particular, they make it possible for us to tailor our investments to very specific future funding needs. Therefore, there was still significant demand for zero-coupon products, and at first the dealers tried to satisfy it by creating such instruments synthetically—for example, by putting a bond in a custodial account and selling the rights to each payment to different investors. The investors were thus confronted with an array of such dealer-specific zero instruments with catchy names like CATS, TIGRS, and the like that were not directly exchangeable into one another and thus were much less liquid.

   The Treasury recognized that it would be in its best interest to capture this demand, and in 1984 it introduced its own STRIPS program (Separate Trading of Interest and Principal Securities). Under this program, a dealer

---

2. I apologize again for leaving out the TIPS.

who owned a Treasury bond or note could ask the Federal Reserve Bank where the bond was held to replace it with an equivalent set of STRIPS representing each payment as a separate security. For example, someone holding $100 million of a 10-year note with a 10 percent coupon could get this security position converted (*stripped*) into a set of 21 securities: a $5 million position in each of the 20 coupon STRIPS, or C-STRIPS, and a $100 million position in the principal STRIPS (P-STRIPS), representing the principal payment. Each of those 21 securities could be then traded independently of the others.

Since most Treasury bonds and notes are issued on a rigid schedule, most coupon and principal payments fall on the same set of dates (for anything longer than five years, the set is made up of the fifteenth of February, May, August, and November), so a lot of different bonds would have coupon payments on, say, May 15, 2008. All these interest payments would be converted into the same security, regardless of which bond they were stripped from—coupon payments are said to be *fungible*. Principal payments from different issues falling on the same date are not fungible and are represented by P-STRIPS with different CUSIPs that are not directly exchangeable into one another. The program was (and continues to be) a spectacular success with dealers and investors alike, and its introduction has played a major role in the Treasury's decision to stop issuing callable Treasury bonds (stripping callable bonds is highly problematic—it is difficult to explain to investors what would happen to a STRIPS they purchased if the bond were to be called prior to its maturity date).

In 1987, the Treasury also started to allow dealers to reverse the stripping process, using a procedure called STRIPS *reconstitution*: if a dealer owns STRIPS representing all the coupon and principal payments of a particular bond, the Fed can upon request convert these holdings into a single position in the corresponding *whole bond*. The existence of the reconstitution process imposes an interesting constraint on the prices of the whole bonds and the STRIPS they are made of: although they all trade in the market independently of one another, the price of the whole bond should at all times be reasonably close to the sum of the prices of its constituent STRIPS. If this constraint is violated—for example, if the sum of the STRIPS prices is appreciably larger than the market price of the whole bond—the dealers will start buying the bond, stripping it, and selling the resulting STRIPS for an instant profit. The dealers monitor the STRIPS market and constantly compute *recon* prices (the prices they would get if they bought the STRIPS and reconstituted them into a bond) for all bonds and notes. Most of the time the recon price and the market price are within a tick of each other, but when they occasionally get further apart, the dealers execute stripping or recon transactions, which quickly brings them back in line.

The STRIPS, and zero-coupon bonds in general, are the darlings of the financial theorists because they appear to be a pure representation of the concept of the *present value* of future cash flows. Indeed, the price of a STRIPS is a measure of how much the market is willing to pay today for a promise of a single future cash flow and thus represents the present value of such a cash flow.

To understand how STRIPS prices depend on interest rates and maturity, it is convenient to think in terms of the complementary concept of the *future value* of today's money. Suppose we have $1 today, and we invest it for six months at interest rate r and keep reinvesting it every six months (we use six months because this is the coupon period for Treasuries). In six months it will grow to $(1 + r/2)$, and after n six-month periods (at time $T = n/2$ years) it will become $(1 + r/2)^n = (1 + r/2)^{2T}$ and will keep growing exponentially thereafter. If $1 grows to a future value of X at time T, so that X dollars at time T are equivalent to $1 today, it follows that $1 at time T is equivalent to $1/X$ dollars today—the present value is the inverse of the future value. Therefore we can say that under the constant-interest-rate assumption, the present value (or price) of a STRIPS maturing at time T is $1/(1 + r/2)^{2T}$ and decreases exponentially with time to maturity (incidentally, this is exactly the formula used to calculate the price of STRIPS given their yield).

For a 30-year STRIPS and an interest rate of 10 percent (typical for the 1970s), we would get a price of about $5.30, as we stated in the beginning of our discussion of STRIPS, while using today's interest rates of under 5 percent, its price would be around $25. STRIPS prices as a function of maturity represent the *discount function* for all Treasury securities; this function shows what each cash flow of a Treasury security should be multiplied by to get its present value. To calculate the price of a bond (which is nothing but a bundle of cash flows), we take each cash flow, multiply it by the discount factor corresponding to the time of that cash flow, and sum the resulting present values over all cash flows; this exactly corresponds to the recon price calculation described earlier. Note that the only moving part in this calculation is the discount function (all cash flows are fixed), so it is constantly changing to reflect the movements in market prices.

The discount function, often called the *discount curve* (almost any function of maturity is usually called a curve in finance; witness the yield curve) is something that should be determined empirically. The pure exponential function just described is an abstraction that holds only if yields for all maturities are exactly the same. It is often said that the STRIPS market prices directly represent the discount function for the Treasury market. Unfortunately, these prices are generally *not* directly observable in the interdealer market. While some more liquid STRIPS trade there as a yield spread to the on-the-runs, just like other off-the-run Treasuries, and also as *pairwise swaps*, where one STRIPS is swapped for another or (in the case of P-STRIPS) for the corresponding whole bond, most STRIPS transactions are done between dealers and customers and are therefore mostly invisible to outsiders. However, the STRIPS prices are related to the bond prices through the recon price calculation, and the bond prices are much easier to collect from the interdealer market. The whole idea of the discount function is therefore usually turned on its head: one starts with the market prices for whole bonds and deduces what STRIPS prices (or a more general discount curve for all dates) should be to give the observable bond prices. We will discuss this process (often called *bootstrapping*) in Chapter 8.

Let us summarize what we have learned about the Treasury market so far. We know *what* is being traded in that market (Treasury bonds and notes, bills, and STRIPS), and we understand how these products are created. We also discussed *how* they are being traded—the interdealer market is organized as a hub-and-spoke system, where on-the-runs are very liquid "hubs" and off-the-runs are "spokes" that in most cases can be traded only relative to an on-the-run issue. The question that we are now ready to address is, *why* do people trade these products? Obviously, all market participants are simply trying to make money trading Treasuries, but there are different ways of doing so that translate into different trading patterns and different types of trades. We will spend the rest of this chapter looking at the Treasury market from this money-making point of view, and in the process we will introduce many trading concepts and terms that are equally applicable to any other market.

THE MECHANICS OF BOND TRADING

First we need to get a clearer picture of what actually happens when bonds are traded. Let us consider the following example: on Monday, November 8, 2004, a trader at ABC Capital, a dealer bank, buys $10 million of the then-current 10-year note (T 4.25 8/15/14) from XYZ Partners, a hedge fund, at a price of 101-01. The first step in the life cycle of this trade is that it has to be *booked* at both institutions. A *trading book* is effectively an account that can hold securities, and it is a way of grouping trades and positions logically (it really used to be a paper book in the precomputer age). The books usually are referred to by name rather than by account number, so at ABC Capital the trader may decide to book this trade into a book called BOOK1.

ABC Capital maintains a *trade database* that holds the records of every trade, and the act of booking a trade consists of adding a record to this database. Typically the ABC trader (or a trading assistant) would enter the trade details in a front-end application that would do some validation of the inputs and then commit the trade record to the trade database (we will discuss the details of this in Chapter 15). The trade record should contain the following pieces of information: the uniquely identified security (T 4.25 8/15/14), the trade amount ($10 million), the trade type (buy), the trade price (101-01), the book where the trade goes (BOOK1), the counterparty (XYZ Partners), and the *settlement date* (the date when the securities should be delivered and payments made). For Treasuries, the *default* settlement date is the next business day (it is said that Treasuries settle T + 1), unless a different settlement date is negotiated at the time of the trade; in our example, the settlement date is November 9, 2004. The trader at XYZ Partners will also book this trade (which is, of course, a sell from her perspective) into one of the books in XYZ's trade database. On settlement date, the *back offices* of the two institutions will settle the trade—XYZ Partners will deliver the securities into ABC Capital's securities account at its clearing bank, and ABC Capital will pay for it by crediting the cash account of XYZ Partners.

One important feature of bond trading is that the amount of money paid for the bond is generally *not* the trade price, but rather the trade price plus something called *accrued interest*. Accrued interest is a reflection of the fact that bonds are interest-bearing instruments. Normally interest is paid only on coupon dates (August 15 and February 15 in our example), but the trading convention is to pretend that interest is paid daily, so if we sell a bond between coupon dates, the buyer will compensate us for the interest we earned while we were holding the bond. Our 10-year note pays its next coupon on February 15, 2005 in the amount of $4.25/2 = 2.125$. This amount is divided by the number of days in the current coupon period (there are 184 days between August 15, 2004 and February 15, 2005), which gives daily interest of about 1.155 cents.

When this note is sold for November 9, 2004 settlement, the buyer will be required to pay this daily interest times the number of days in the accrual period (86 days since August 15, 2004), or $0.993207, over the trade price, so the actual payment, or *dirty price*, will be 101-01 (101.03125) + 0.993207 = 102.024456. The purpose of this convention is to make sure that we earn daily interest for every day we hold the bond—for example, if we were to sell this 10-year note one day later, the buyer would pay us accrued interest for 87 days while we paid it for 86 days, so we would effectively earn one day's worth of interest. The dirty price represents the true economic value of the bond, while the *clean price* quoted in the market eliminates this deterministic part of the bond's value.

ABC Capital has just committed to pay $10,244,560 for the 10-year note on the next business day—where will it get the money? In all likelihood, this sum will be borrowed in the money markets through an arrangement known as a *repurchase agreement*, or, more colloquially, a *repo*. In a repurchase agreement, ABC Capital borrows the dirty price of this Treasury note from a repo dealer and transfers the legal ownership of the security to the dealer for a period of time (usually overnight), at the end of which time it repurchases the securities for the *same dirty price* plus an interest charge.

Note that even though the repo dealer is the legal owner, it is still ABC Capital that retains the risk that the market price of the security can change, since the repurchase price is set beforehand—we will get our security back tomorrow, and we can then sell it in the market for whatever it is worth tomorrow. Often the arrangement is automatically renewed every day, with the borrowed amount being adjusted for the daily changes in the price of the collateral securities. For ABC Capital and other securities dealers, the repo market is a convenient way of financing their transactions. For repo lenders, it is one of the safest ways of investing money short-term. This is an example of secured lending, where, should something happen to the borrower, the lender can immediately sell the collateral securities to get its money back.

When the purchase of a bond is financed through a repo transaction, the economics of holding a long position in that bond works out like this: every day the dealer bank has to pay the repo charge (the original dirty price times the repo rate times one day), but it gets to keep the accrued interest earned for the day (because the repurchase price is kept constant, so we do not pay for extra accrued interest). Since, as we saw in the previous chapter, short-term rates such as repo rates are usually lower than long-term rates such as coupon rates, the coupon income is usually greater than the repo charge, so every day we hold a long position, we come out ahead. This fact is usually expressed by saying that bonds have positive *carry* (or negative *cost of carry*—there is some terminological confusion here). The presence of carry introduces dependence between the price and the settlement date. Suppose the customer wanted to settle the trade next Tuesday (November 16, 2004) instead of on the regular settlement date (November 9, 2004). The customer (the seller) could then buy the 10-year note for regular settlement at the *spot price* of 101-01, repo it out for a week and earn carry for seven days, and then deliver the bond to the buyer. The price charged to the buyer for such *forward settlement* is called the *forward price* and is equal to the spot price plus the *cost of carry* between the spot and forward dates (this is true generally for other products as well, such as commodities, as we discuss in Chapter 7, and represents the total cost to the seller of delivering the goods on the forward settlement date). For bonds, the cost of carry is usually negative, so forward prices are lower than spot prices.

Let us calculate the forward price and its components for our example, assuming a 2 percent repo rate. The spot dirty price is 102.024456, the repo charge is that times the 2 percent repo rate times the *year fraction* for our period, which would be the actual number of days in the holding period (which is 7) over 360 (we will discuss year fraction calculations in Chapter 13); this gives us the repo charge of 3.9676 cents. The coupon income over this seven-day period is calculated on a different *basis*—as described previously, we use the actual number of days in the coupon period times 2 instead of 360 for the number of days in a year—and comes out to be 8.0842 cents. The difference between these two amounts is the total carry of 4.1166 cents; it has to be subtracted from the spot price of 101-01 to arrive at the forward price of 100.9901 = 100-315.

For those who wonder why anyone cares about these penny-sized adjustments, the total weekly carry on our modest $10 million trade is $4,116.60. The difference between the spot and forward price is also often called the *price drop*; the name itself implies that carry is usually positive. The price drop is almost independent of the market price, so a trader would typically figure out what it should be for one extra day and then, when asked to quote for a nonregular settlement, simply multiply this daily drop by the required number of days. In the Treasury market, the regular settlement is T + 1, but a customer can ask to do a trade for *Cash* (T + 0), *Skip* (T + 2), or *Corp* (T + 3) settlement, or generally for any good (nonholiday) settlement date.

What the price drop most significantly depends on is the repo rate—how is that determined? When a repo lender just wants to invest money and does not much care what particular Treasury he receives as collateral, the rate quoted is called a *general collateral* (or *GC*) repo; it is typically very close to the fed funds rate and is set mostly on the basis of the macroeconomic factors discussed in the previous chapter. Sometimes, however, a repo lender may want to specify that he needs a particular security as collateral, in which case he should be prepared to receive a lower rate to compensate for his pickiness; this rate is called a *special repo* for that particular security.

Consider what happens when a dealer sells a bond it does not own (establishing a short position): it has to get this bond somewhere to deliver it to the customer. The standard procedure for this is for the dealer to do a *reverse repo* transaction, where it lends the price of the bond in the repo market and requests that particular security as collateral so that it can deliver that security to the customer (the legal ownership of the collateral passes to the lender in a repo transaction, so the dealer can do whatever it wants with it). If that particular bond is in short supply, the dealer has to entice people to give it up by offering a lower (special) repo rate. This situation is typical for the on-the-runs, where special repo rates are often significantly lower than the general collateral repo and sometimes drop to zero (and have even gone negative on a few occasions). When a security gets into this tight supply situation in the repo market, it is said to have *gone special*; this usually leads to people being willing to pay higher spot prices for it, since they can finance the purchase at a below-market rate, so going special often causes *richening* of the security.

Let us dispel a frequent misconception here: the forward price has nothing whatsoever to do with what the market price will be a week from now (nobody knows that); it is merely a way to account for the carrying costs. The only relationship between a forward price and the market price a week from now is as follows: if we buy the bond today for the spot price, hold it for a week, and then sell it at the forward price, our total profit is zero. This is why the forward price is sometimes called the *breakeven* price: if the market goes higher and we manage to sell the bond above that breakeven price, we have made money, and vice versa.

PROFIT AND LOSS

This finally brings us to a concept that is central to all trading—that of *profit and loss*, or *P&L*, or *PnL* (pronounced "peenEL"). This is the number that measures the economic outcome of trading, makes or breaks trading careers, and generally is the main organizing theme for most trading-related activities. Let us now turn to explaining this powerful concept.

PnL is measured in dollars (or other currencies). Every trading book has a PnL, as does every trader (it is the sum of the PnLs for all books the trader is responsible for), as does every trading desk (the sum of the PnLs for each trader). We will consider book-level PnL, since it is the foundation for everything else. To simplify our discussion, let us assume that we are a new trader at ABC Capital, that the trade with XYZ partners just discussed was our first trade ever, and that we were given a brand-new BOOK1 in which to record our trading exploits. It begins with zero positions in all securities and zero PnL, and then we buy $10 million of the 10-year note at 101-01. A few minutes later, noticing that the market has gone up a bit, we sell our whole $10 million position at 101-02. What happened in terms of PnL?

Our PnL in BOOK1 at this point is $3,125.00; it is the difference between what we have to pay for the first trade and what we are going to receive from the second. Note that since both trades are done for the same settlement date, PnL is simply the difference in clean prices times the size of the trade (accrued interest drops out, since it is the same for both trades). Also note that we have achieved this remarkable result without ever really owning the 10-year note, as the trades will not settle until tomorrow, but we do have a nice positive PnL already, and it is the best kind of PnL, called *realized* PnL. Realized PnL is money in the bank, and nothing can happen to it (short of default by one of the counterparties, but this is not something that an individual trader has to worry about; this falls into the *operational risk* category and is dealt with by the back office). Since we have zero position in the 10-year note, the market can go up and down and we still will have the $3,125 PnL until the next trade.

Suppose we want to expand on our early success by repeating the trade; the market has gone back down, and we buy $10 million of the same 10-year note at the original price of 101-01. This time, however, we decide to be more disciplined and wait for the market to go up significantly before we sell. The market does indeed keep going up, and by the end of the day the 10-year note can be sold in the interdealer market for 102-01. But we believe the market will keep going up and do not want to sell just yet. What is our PnL at the end of the day? We clearly made a profit, but we cannot be 100 percent sure as to exactly what it is—if we *assume* that we can sell at the current market level of 102-01, our PnL will be $103,125; it is composed of the realized PnL of our first two trades and the *unrealized* PnL of $100,000 on our current position. Unrealized PnL is just what the term implies: our profit or loss based on what we think the current value of our position is.

From the trading management perspective, however, it is very desirable to eliminate this subjectivity in PnL measurements. Managers do not want to hear each trader say, "I think I made X thousand dollars today." The way this is achieved is through a daily *marking*, or *closing*, process— at the end of the trading day (usually at 3 p.m.), all securities traded by the desk should be *marked to market*. For each security, one trader would be responsible for deciding what its fair market value is at closing time. These *closing marks*, or *closing prices*, are then recorded in the bank's systems and used to calculate the official *closing PnL* of all books; the market value of each security in each book is assumed to be equal to its closing price. As a beginner trader, it is unlikely that we will have the responsibility for closing the 10-year note; most likely it will be closed by a more experienced trader who traditionally trades the 10-year sector. If she decides that the closing price for the 10-year note is 102-01, then our closing PnL becomes what we thought it was ($103,125), and when the head of the desk asks how did we do today, we can modestly say "up a hundred"— not bad for a rookie.[3]

However, imagine a less benign scenario in which we bought $100 million of the 10-year at 101-01 and the market actually went down a bit and is trading around 101-00 at the end of the day. If the closing price is 101-00, our unrealized PnL will be a loss of $31,250—more than enough to erase our initial $3,125 realized gain. On the other hand, if we could only adjust the closing price slightly, to 101-01, then we would close the day up $3,125—not great, but much better than ending our first trading day with a loss.

This illustrates the underlying tension in the closing process: traders have a strong incentive to manipulate the closing marks, perhaps even unconsciously, to make their closing PnL look better. In an illiquid market, where the value of securities is difficult to determine, this manipulation can lead to outright fraud (if we have something in our portfolio that has become utterly worthless, but we keep marking it high to hide the loss). In the Treasury market, where the market value is usually quite transparent, play-

3. In fact, $100,000 a day translates into $25 million a year—that would be a respectable PnL for any institutional trader.

ing with the closing prices cannot hide losses in the long run, but it still can help smooth out the daily ups and downs in *our* book.

The problem with that, and a very serious one, is that we are not the only ones at the bank who have a position in the 10-year note, and everyone will have to use our closing marks. If, for example, the derivatives desk has a $10 billion short position in the 10-year and we mark it a tick higher to make our puny trade look better, the derivatives traders will have to take a $3 million loss in their closing PnL, and they are likely to vigorously contest that by saying that the market actually was 101-00. One of the main responsibilities of the trading management is to avoid these kinds of disputes by making sure that the closing marks are as close as possible to the actual market prices at closing time.

PnL is obviously additive from day to day, which means that our total PnL for the year is the sum of our daily closing PnLs plus today's PnL— and we have some control only over today's PnL, so that is what most traders focus on. To see what makes up the daily PnL, it is useful to split it into different parts (the classification we offer here is quite common, but it is not the only possible one). The first component is *daily carry*. The back office will add all accrued interest and repo charges, plus cash from maturing securities, to our daily PnL every night. This is the number we are given at the beginning of the day, and we have to live with it.

The second component is called *position PnL*. This is the PnL that we would have if we as traders did absolutely nothing all day and simply watched the market value of our positions change. It can be defined as our current positions times changes in their market prices relative to their closing levels (this last quantity is called *price change on day*). Suppose we start the day with our $10 million position in the 10-year note that was closed at 102-01. If the market moves to 102-11, our position PnL will be $10 million times the 10 ticks change in the market price of the 10-year, or $31,250; it will fluctuate during the day and will become our closing PnL when the closing price is set to be the market price.

Finally, there is *trading PnL*; this is the result of today's trading activities and depends on the specific prices at which the trades were done. When, in the beginning of our trading career, we bought the 10-year and then sold it a tick higher, what we got was trading PnL.

Calculating PnL for a book with multiple securities positions and a large number of trades is a tedious task. However, the desire to know our PnL in real time is really more curiosity than a practical need—it is a backward-looking quantity that should not directly affect our next trading action. In a sense, our current PnL is what it is, and our job is to trade in such a way that it does not *change* adversely, so a more practical question that is on most trader's minds is: how will my PnL *change* if the market moves in a certain way? This question is at the heart of the concept of *market risk*.

RISK AND HEDGING

The answer to this question obviously depends on the specific market events we that feel put our PnL at risk, and looking at different sets of events produces different measures of risk. For example, one of the simplest and eminently reasonable questions to ask about risk in a bond trading book is this: what will happen to my PnL if the yield curve moves up or down in parallel, that is, if all yields change by the same amount? We know that for small changes in yields, the price change of any bond is proportional to the yield change, and the proportionality coefficient is called DV01. For a single bond position, the change in PnL from a 1-bp change in yield is then simply the size of the position times its DV01. If we sum up these position-DV01 products for all bonds in our book, we will get a single number representing the sensitivity of our position PnL to a parallel shift in yield; this number is often called the total duration (or total DV01) of the book and is a simple and useful measure of risk. If the total duration is positive, we are *long the market*—if the market rallies and all yields go down in parallel, we make money. If it is negative, we are *short the market*—we will lose money in a parallel yield curve rally.

The importance of this total duration number is that it tells us what to do if we do not want to be exposed to a parallel shift in yields (if we want to be *flat the market*). If we are long the market, we can sell some bonds whose total duration is equal to that of our book, and then we will have a book with potentially many bond positions but zero total duration. The process by which we eliminate certain undesirable risks from our book is called *hedging*, and a useful risk measure should tell us how to hedge against that risk. The total duration does tell us how to hedge, but the risk that it measures is not very realistic, and so its hedging prescription is not very realistic either—from the total duration standpoint, we can hedge any bond portfolio by buying or selling the right DV01-weighted amount of *any* single security; for example, we can hedge a book containing long-end bonds with an appropriately large amount of the two-year note. This hedge will work if 2-year and 30-year yields do in fact move by the same amount, but how often does that happen? A trader would say that this hedge protects us from *duration risk*, but does not protect us from *curve risk*—the risk that the yield curve will do something other than a parallel shift.

As we discussed earlier in this chapter, the Treasury market works as a hub-and-spoke system, where there are five very liquid on-the-run issues and everything else is priced relative to those benchmark issues. Therefore, any yield curve movement we may want to include in our risk assessment is in reality caused by one of the on-the-runs moving relative to another. We can view the prices or yields of the on-the-runs as independent *risk factors* and rephrase our risk question like this: what will happen to the PnL of my book if one of the on-the-runs moves independently of the others—for example, if the 10-year yield moves by 1 bp while the other on-the-runs stay put?

This question is usually answered using the concept of *factor risk*. For every bond on the Treasury curve, we can define *factor sensitivities* that represent how sensitive that bond's yield is to changes in each of our factors (the on-the-run yields). If we can (approximately) represent the yield changes of a given bond as a linear combination of the on-the-run yield changes, then a portfolio of on-the-runs with the weights equal to the coefficients in that linear combination would have the same price change as our bond. If a given bond has 40 percent sensitivity to the 5-year and 60 percent sensitivity to the 10-year, we can replace a $10 million position in this bond with a $4 million position in the 5-year and a $6 million position in the 10-year. If we go through the whole book and do this to all bonds we have a position in, we will end up with a risk-equivalent portfolio containing only the factors of our risk model—the on-the-runs. This factor risk approach can reduce a complex portfolio to a set of five positions that tells us how to eliminate exposure to each of our risk factors; for example, if our book has a total risk weighting in the 5-year on-the-run of $20 million, we can sell $20 million of the 5-year and be perfectly hedged against movements in the 5-year on-the-run within this model.

The factor risk approach recognizes that the price movements of all Treasury securities are very strongly but imperfectly correlated, so that a model based on a limited number of risk factors can describe these movements quite well. There is no single right way to do this—one could use a different number and type of risk factors (on-the-runs are obvious, but not the only possible choice), and use different methods for calculating factor sensitivities. It is important to point out here, however, that no such risk model can provide a perfect hedge. Each Treasury bond has its own identity, and representing its price dynamics as a linear combination of factors is always an approximate procedure. Any portfolio that has been hedged to have zero exposure to the factors of the model will still have so-called *idiosyncratic risk* that cannot be hedged away using only model factors—for example, the price of some off-the-run issue can move because someone is unwinding a large position, even if the on-the-runs do not. The only way to perfectly hedge all risks in a portfolio of securities is to liquidate all positions.

Keeping all risks perfectly hedged at all times is only one of many possible *risk management* strategies, and one that in its pure form is almost never practiced in real life. First, it would be prohibitively expensive— we initiate hedging trades and therefore pay their transaction costs. Second, in many cases we want to have some exposure to market movements; after all, our goal is not so much to keep our PnL from falling as it is to make it grow, which requires taking risks. Therefore, the purpose of hedging is not to eliminate risks, but rather to keep them under control.

Explicit risk limits for every trader are usually handed down by the management—for example, the limits could be no more than $100 million 10-year equivalents in terms of duration risk, and perhaps no more than $50 million in any single maturity sector—and we should be able to (1) measure our levels of risk at all times, and (2) reduce them by hedging when they begin to touch the limits. The best risk management strategy is to keep the risks we want and hedge away the risks we do not want; for example, if we believe that the market is moving up and we are long the market, we may want to keep it this way, whereas if we are short, we may want to hedge. Deciding when and what to hedge is more art than science, and our success depends on our mastery of that art more than on almost anything else.

TRADING MODES AND STRATEGIES

For traders at dealer firms, there are two major modes of trading in terms of sources of PnL. The first is called *flow trading*, or *market making*. This is what happens when traders let customers initiate the trades so that they can collect transaction costs in the form of the bid-offer spread. Again, let us trade the 10-year note to illustrate this process. If a customer requests a bid from us on the 10-year, we quote 101-21+; if someone wants an offer, we quote 23. This act of providing both bid and offer quotes on demand is called *making a market*. Suppose someone does trade with us on the bid side, selling us $10 million 10-year notes at 21+. After a while, another customer wants to buy the tens, and we sell at our offer of 23—we make one-and-a-half ticks of PnL, or $4,687.50, on each $10 million flowing through us (that is why this is also called *flow trading*), and the only risk we took was holding the $10 million long position between the two trades.

If our flows are balanced and the market is not moving much, market making looks like good business: we buy on the bid side, sell on the offered side, make a little money every time, and do not take much risk in the process. However, consider what happens when the market is moving directionally— let us say that the market is falling and everyone wants to sell. As market makers we will be required to buy when everyone is selling, and we will tend to accumulate large long positions when the market is falling. We will first buy at 21+, then at 20, then at 19+, and every time the market ticks down, the value of our accumulated position drops. If the market eventually stabilizes at a much lower level and the customers start buying again, our new offer price will be much lower than the price we bought at, so we will end up with potentially large losses. If the market were to rise dramatically instead of falling, we would be in the same pickle: we would have to sell when everybody wants to buy, and we would accumulate a large short position in a rising market. Financial theory suggests that the bid-ask spread that market makers charge their customers, and their easy profits in quiet times, represent compensation for the potentially disastrous losses a market maker can incur when the market rises or falls rapidly.

To reduce our market-making losses in a directionally moving market, we will want to hedge. Ideally, when a customer sells us something, we immediately try to resell it in the interdealer market, hopefully at a better (or at least the same) price. This is why our bid should always be at or below the bid in the interdealer market, and our offer should always be at or above the interdealer offer. Suppose the market for the 10-year on eSpeed and BrokerTec is 101-22/22+; we can then safely quote 21+/23 to our customers. If we buy from a customer at 21+, we immediately turn around and sell it at the eSpeed bid of 22; if we sell to a customer at 23, we can buy the stuff back from eSpeed at 22+. This is not nearly as lucrative as "pure" market making, where we do not hedge at all, but it is almost completely riskless.

Is there anything to prevent us from charging customers ever-larger bid-offer spreads? Yes, there is, and it is called competition; customers can trade not only with us, but with other dealers as well, and if we increase our spread too much, they will simply stop trading with us and go to other dealers who are willing to be more competitive. Our total market-making PnL is proportional not only to our bid-ask spread, but also to our flow of trades, and that will fall off drastically if we increase our spreads too much. There was a time not so long ago when charging customers an extra tick of bid-offer on the 10-year (as in our example) was common practice; in the Treasury market, those days came to a rather abrupt end with the advent of another electronic trading platform called TradeWeb.

Unlike eSpeed and BrokerTec, TradeWeb is a platform for dealer-to-customer trading. It gives the customer a desktop application that shows real-time *indicative* quotes for all Treasuries (along with many other fixed-income products) that come from multiple dealers. There are about two dozen dealers that submit such real-time prices to TradeWeb. Each customer picks a few favorite dealers, and when the customer wants to buy a 10-year note, she clicks on the indicative price; this sends a *trade inquiry* to the selected dealers. The dealers respond with an offer price for the 10-year that is good for a short period of time (a few seconds) called *on-the-wire time*. During this time, the customer can compare the offers from all selected dealers and pick whichever is better.

The introduction of TradeWeb in 1998 has quickly resulted in a massive transfer of pricing power from the dealers to their customers. Ironically, TradeWeb was formed by a consortium of several dealer firms that were anxious to participate in the online trading boom of the late 1990s. While purely from an investment perspective, the founders of TradeWeb did pretty well (TradeWeb was bought by Thomson for about $500 million in 2004), it is doubtful that the profits on this transaction were enough to compensate the dealers for the erosion of their market-making revenues.

Before TradeWeb, a customer had to call several dealers to get the best price. Few bothered to do it, especially when the market was moving quickly, which allowed the dealers to charge bid-offer spreads that were much wider than those available to the dealers themselves in the inter-dealer market. Once TradeWeb went online, suddenly everybody could see how much each dealer was charging, and the dealers that were willing to reduce their bid-offer spreads saw an instant improvement in the number of trades done through TradeWeb at the expense of other dealers. This competition for trade flow quickly led to the current situation, where the markets quoted to customers are almost exactly the same as the inter-dealer market. This situation can be called *zero-cost market making*: a dealer that buys the 10-year note from a customer can do the trade at the bid price in the interdealer market, so he can (if he is fast enough) immediately sell it on eSpeed for the same price—at no cost, but at no profit either.

The TradeWeb pricing revolution, however, is so far limited to small, low-margin trades. Large trades are still done over the phone and remain a major source of market-making revenue for the dealers. A large trade can be defined as a trade that cannot be easily and instantly executed in the interdealer market; the exact size depends on the security and ranges from anything over $1 billion for the 2-year to anything over $50 million for the 30-year sector. Let us say that a customer asks us to "show (offer) a billion tens," and the 10-year note is trading 100-05/05+ on eSpeed. If we quote 05+ (the same as the offer on eSpeed), sell $1 billion in 10-year notes to the customer, and then mindlessly try to buy it back on eSpeed, we will almost certainly end up moving the market quite a bit—when we buy everything on offer at 05+, the next offer will come in above it at 06, and we will buy all of that as well. This will go on and on until we have bought back the whole $1 billion, which may take perhaps 10 individual trades and move the market a couple of ticks up.

Such clumsy execution would probably cost us several hundred thousand dollars. However, knowing that it would not be trivial to buy back such a large amount, we should have quoted a higher price—perhaps a tick above the eSpeed offer. The customer understands that there has to be some markup, and may not want to go to several dealers at the same time, as they would then know that there is a large buyer in the market and would try to drive up the price. Therefore, the common practice is for a customer who needs to do a large trade to go to a single dealer, usually the one whose judgment and execution skills the customer trusts the most, and discreetly ask to do the trade perhaps a tick or two away from the market (depending on the security, the size, and the market conditions). For the traders at the dealer firm, executing these large trades profitably, without moving the market too much, is a challenge that requires significant skill, but the profit potential is also significant—a single large trade can bring in $500,000 or more. Unfortunately for the dealers, the road to acquiring this most trusted status with an important customer often lies through making very tight markets on TradeWeb for that customer.

Market making used to be the main source of trading revenues for the dealer firms. But the increased competition for customer business is making it progressively harder to make money in this space, so the dealers are turning more and more to the second major trading mode: *proprietary,* or *prop,* trading. Very simply put, prop trading is what happens when we believe that a market will move in a certain way and we bet the firm's capital on that belief by taking the appropriate positions. The simplest proprietary trade is this: we believe that the market will go up, so we take a large long position in the 10-year note. If the market does indeed go up, we make a lot of money; if it does not, we lose.

As we discuss later, most prop trades are somewhat more sophisticated than that, but this simple example allows us to contrast the mindsets of a prop trader and a market maker. For a market maker, the "good" PnL is trading PnL—the goal is to make money without taking much position risk. For a prop trader, the main source of PnL is position PnL. A corollary to that is that a market maker does not (or at least should not) care much about how the market moves, whereas a prop trader's PnL depends exclusively on her ability to correctly anticipate market moves. A market maker makes lots of small trades with a quite small expected PnL for each and lives off small price differences (quarters and half-ticks) over short periods of time (typically minutes), whereas a prop trader usually makes a few large trades and expects to profit from large market moves over longer periods (days or months). Note, however, that there is a growing branch of prop trading (often referred to as *high-frequency trading*) that does attempt to benefit from small mispricings over very short time scales. The defining difference between a market maker and a prop trader in this case would be that the market maker generally does not initiate the trades, but a prop trader generally does.

Finally, there are institutional differences. The traders at a dealer firm can do both prop trading and market making because they have a customer base that they can make markets to, but a buy-side firm can do only prop trading. At dealer firms, the market-making and prop-trading activities are usually separated into different books. The arrangements for who is responsible for these books differ from bank to bank—it could be that each trader on the desk has both a flow book and a prop book, or it could be that some traders do only flow trading and others do only prop trading, or even that there is a dedicated prop trading desk that does prop trades in a wide variety of products (an increasingly common arrangement, essentially mimicking the structure of a hedge fund). Some buy-side institutions, such as hedge funds, see prop trading as their most important, sometimes even their only, activity, while others, such as asset managers, insurance companies, and the like, avoid this term and prefer to see their trading activities as *investing.*

There is indeed a difference between investing and prop trading: most prop trading is *leveraged* (we borrow money to enter into positions), whereas investing is done with *real money*. Investing usually is limited to taking long positions only and holding them for significant periods of time. If we define prop trading as the type of trading where we seek position PnL from market movements, then true fixed-income investing can be defined as the type of trading where the most important source of PnL is carry, or interest income. A classic example of that is when we buy a bond at par and hold it to maturity—we will earn a rate of return (almost) equal to the coupon rate, no matter what happens to market prices during the life of the bond. There are some situations where we are clearly investing for the long term, but we have no carry PnL (such as when we invest in STRIPS). It is important to realize that for a large class of buy-side institutions, carry is almost the only thing they consider when making investment decisions.

The line between prop trading and investment is further blurred by the fact that most prop trades that last for more than one day also have a significant carry component. As we discussed earlier, we will earn a profit on a long position in a bond even if its market price actually drops as long as this drop is less than the carry over the holding period. The way prop traders usually think about the carry component of their PnL is in terms of *forward breakevens*, which are simply forward prices or (more commonly) yields. Forward yields are the yields that we get when we convert the forward price into yield as of the forward settlement date. Usually forward prices are lower than spot prices, so forward yields are higher than spot yields. If we decide to buy a 10-year note at a yield of 4.25 percent and hold it for a month, and the forward yield for a one-month holding term (this is usually called *trade horizon*) is 4.30 percent, then we make money if the yield moves up by less than 5 bp by the end of the month. Our PnL is approximately equal to the difference between the final yield and the breakeven yield times the DV01 of the security.

Many people, however, believe that this simple statement is not the end of the story because of something called *rolldown*. The concept of rolldown is an attempt to capture the quasi-deterministic movement in the bond price as a result of its aging—as we illustrate in Figure 5–14, in a month, our 10-year note will be one month shorter in maturity, and we can expect its yield to decrease as it *rolls down* the yield curve. For a forward horizon of one month, we can then describe our trade by saying that it has 5 bp of carry and 3 bp of rolldown; this means that if nothing happens to the shape of the yield curve, we can expect to earn 5 bp of carry (interest income) and price appreciation equivalent to 3 bp because of this aging effect.

The popularity of the rolldown concept is mainly a result of the fact that it makes many trades look more attractive. Our trade will make money as long as the yields do not move up by more than 5 bp from their current level, rolldown or no rolldown; the rolldown argument is that we should not really use the current yield as our starting point in assessing the trade, but rather should use the "expected" rolled-down yield. From that perspective, the yields would have to rise significantly more (a whole 8 bp) before we would lose money on the trade, which makes the possibility of losses seem more remote.

The concepts of breakeven yields and rolldown become more useful when we consider the next step up in prop trading sophistication, a *curve trade* (simple outright bets on market direction are really frowned upon as undisguised gambling, although they are practiced widely). We have, in fact, considered this type of trade before when we discussed bond swaps in the interdealer market. In the proprietary trading context, a curve trade is a trade where our PnL comes from changes in the slope of the yield curve. The traders, confusingly, often refer to the yield spread between different maturity points on the yield curve as "the curve"—they may say "the 2-30 curve is 250 bp"—so in this terminology, a curve trade is a trade where the PnL comes from changes in that kind of "curve."

The curve slope can change in two ways—it can either steepen or flatten—and there are two types of curve trades to reflect that. A twos-fives *steepener* is a trade where we hope to profit if and only if the curve steepens between the two-year and five-year points. To achieve this, we buy X million of the two-year note and sell the duration-weighted amount of the five-year note; this trade, as we discussed earlier, is insensitive to parallel movements of the yields and is sensitive only to changes in the yield spread, which is what we want, and it will make money if the yield spread *increases*. The opposite of this is called a *flattener*, where we sell shorter-maturity securities and buy the duration-weighted amount of a longer-maturity one.

The PnL of a curve trade is the total duration of either leg (DV01 times position; this is equal but opposite for both legs) times the difference between the *breakeven spread* (the difference between forward yields) and the *spot spread* (the yield spread at which we will exit the trade). Again, people often include the rolldown in this argument; because the yield curve is usually concave, as shown in Figure 5–14, the rolldown on the shorter-maturity leg is almost always higher than that on the longer-maturity leg. The rolldown effect therefore favors a steepener trade and works against a flattener trade.

Interestingly, the carry effect may end up working either way; it all depends on whether we make more carry on our long position than we lose on our short position. Our position in the longer-maturity leg is always smaller because of its larger duration, but it also typically has larger yield—since carry is effectively the product of these two quantities, when the yield curve is sufficiently steep, the carry on the longer-maturity leg can actually be larger than that on the shorter-maturity leg. So if the yield curve is very steep, the carry effect favors a flattener trade (its breakeven spread becomes lower than spot), while the opposite is true in a flat yield curve environment (the breakeven spread is higher than spot).

Yet another step up in sophistication is the *butterfly trade*, which involves trading three securities with different maturities (the two wings

FIGURE 5–14

Economics of holding a long position in a bond for one month. We make money as long as its market yield in that month is less than the forward yield calculated today (the breakeven yield). In a rising interest-rate environment, the forward yields (dashed line) are higher than spot yields (solid line), reflecting positive carry. In addition, we can expect that the yield will roll down the curve as the bond ages; this roll-down effect increases the likelihood that the long position will make money.

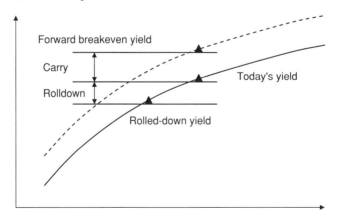

and the body of the butterfly, as shown in Figure 5–15) in an attempt to capture more subtle changes in the shape of the yield curve. For example, a 2-5-10 butterfly is a trade in which we buy 5-year-notes (the body) and sell 2- and 10-year notes (the wings). This trade will make money if the 5-year yield moves closer to the straight line connecting the 2- and 10-year points on the yield curve (if the curve becomes less concave). The total duration of the wings is always the same as that of the body, so the trade is insensitive to parallel shifts in the yield curve, but it has an additional degree of freedom: we can distribute this total duration between the two wings in many different ways. The PnL of the butterfly is proportional to changes in the *butterfly spread*—the difference between the yield of the body and the weighted average of the yields of the wings, with the weights equal to percentages of the total duration that were allocated to each wing.

Unlike outright trades and curve trades, whose rationale is the trader's belief that yields or spreads will move in a certain way (such beliefs are called *views*, as in "I have a curve flattening view"), butterfly trades are typically based on the idea of *mean reversion*. This is, again, a belief that the yield curve has some kind of equilibrium shape, and that the butterfly spread, as one of the measures of curve shape, should therefore fluctuate around some *mean* equilibrium value. According to this view, whenever the butterfly spread observed in the market deviates significantly from this historical equilibrium value, we can expect that it will eventually *revert to the mean*. If the butterfly spread is currently much lower than the mean, we can sell the spread (buy the wings and sell the body) and profit from its expected mean-reverting upward change, and vice versa.

Figure 5–15 illustrates how well this works (or does not work) in practice by showing the history of the 2-5-10 butterfly spread over a period of 2.5 years. There do seem to be periods of time in which the butterfly spread has a well-defined level around which it fluctuates, and during those periods of time, our *mean-reverting* strategy can be quite profitable. The problem is, however, that from time to time this mean level appears to undergo a *regime shift*, during which the butterfly spread moves directionally away from the mean and then stabilizes around a new level. If we follow our mean-reverting strategy through one of these regime shifts, where, for example, the butterfly spread begins to move up quickly, we will buy the spread at the beginning of the shift, assuming that it will revert, but the spread will keep moving against us toward its new equilibrium

FIGURE 5–15

Historical performance of a 2-5-10 Treasury butterfly spread (calculated with the weights 0.45–1–0.55). There are clearly periods of time when the spread fluctuates around a stable mean, and during those periods the mean-reverting trading strategy described in the text would be profitable. Unfortunately, the strategy can also lead to spectacular blowups during regime shifts.

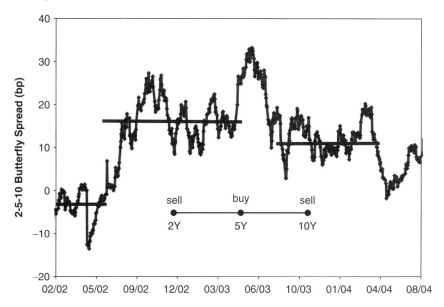

level, and we can incur large losses. This situation is common to all types of mean-reversion strategies, of which butterfly trading is perhaps the simplest example; the art of prop trading is being able to tell when we are in a regime shift situation and changing our views accordingly.

Many traders think about such mean-reverting trades in terms of yet another general trading concept called *relative value*. Whenever the butterfly spread of a 2-5-10 butterfly becomes higher than its historical mean, these traders will say that the 5-year note has become *cheap* relative to 2- and 10-year notes, and whenever the spread goes below the mean, they would say that "fives are *rich* relative to twos and tens." The idea is that if we keep selling things that are unusually rich and buying things that are unusually cheap relative to something else, we will make money over time. The act of analyzing the market in search of securities that have in some sense become rich or cheap is called *rich/cheap analysis* and is a cottage industry within research departments of Wall Street firms; we will spend much of Chapter 17 discussing how this is done.

OTHER BOND MARKETS

Most of the issues we have discussed in this chapter—the issuance process, market making and prop trading in the secondary market, and the mechanics of interdealer and dealer-to-customer trading—work in very similar ways in other government bond markets around the world. As far as the issuance process is concerned, the main difference between the United States and the rest of the world is that in most other countries, the issuance calendar is not as rigid, which generally leads to a larger number of smaller-size government securities being issued. Because of this, there is no real concept of an on-the-run security that concentrates the liquidity to anywhere near the degree seen in the United States (see, however, the story of EUREX futures in Chapter 7).

The execution mechanics in the interdealer bond markets of Europe is increasingly dominated by exchange-style execution on MTS, an Italian company that is becoming as dominant in Europe as eSpeed is in the United States (U.S.-based eSpeed, BrokerTec, and, most notably, TradeWeb are important players in European bond markets as well).

Finally, many governments around the world issue debt in currencies other than their own (often U.S. dollars, but increasingly euro and yen)—something that the U.S. Treasury has never done, at least not yet—and this introduces an interesting FX component into bond trading. Overall, however, my hope is that if you work in the U.K. Gilts market or in Japanese government bonds and all you know about bond trading is from reading this chapter, you will still be well on your way to understanding what is going on around you.

Similarly, the main trading concepts discussed in the second half of this chapter are mostly applicable to other bond markets as well. Several general themes that we touched upon are in fact so universal that they hold no matter what is being traded, and I want to reiterate them here as we leave this chapter so that they will be easier to recognize when they pop up in our discussion of other markets. The first of them is the no-arbitrage (perhaps better called no-free-lunch) principle: if we think that we have found a way to make riskless profits in any market, it simply means that we do not understand the risks we are taking (for example, market making may seem like a sure money pump until we get punished by a large directional move). The second feature of any market is its self-correcting power—its response to any action we take is always to make what we are trying to do either harder or more expensive (for example, if we are trying to buy a large amount of anything, our actions will push the market up and make us pay more). Upon reflection, it is this second principle that is required for market stability. A corollary to this principle is that if we initiate any trading action, we will have to pay for the privilege; this may come in many forms (bid-offer spread, commissions, market impact of your large trades), but the "aggressor pays" principle is quite universal.

Finally, there is a "fastest wins" principle—in any market situation, we win by being the first to do what others are about to do, whether it is right or wrong (we want to buy just before everyone else starts buying, and vice versa). These three simple principles combine to turn the market into an amazing machine that is much smarter than the sum of its individual participants. I continue to be fascinated by how markets work, and I am sure that thousands of my colleagues share this feeling.

To conclude this chapter, let us point out some of the quantitative and technological challenges of the U.S. Treasury market, most of which, again, are common to other bond markets. We have already mentioned the importance of financial analytics, especially that part of it known as *bond math*, to the trading process in bond markets—converting price to yield, calculating durations, and calculating other risk measures is something that traders should be able to do effortlessly, and in Chapter 13 we review the logic behind it. Another imperative of bond trading is the ability to identify and keep track of all securities in the Treasury universe; this is the purview of the *product control* area, whose technological issues we will discuss in Chapter 12, together with the related challenges of maintaining historical data for a large number of securities.

The reader may have noticed that many of the trading activities that we described in this chapter (especially booking of trades, maintaining real-time prices for all Treasuries, and calculating risk and PnL) can and should be automated, and Chapter 15 describes the area of *trading systems* that do all of these things and more. We often referred in this chapter to traders being able to see and interact with market data and other real-time quantities; the technology behind real-time market data is described in Chapter 14.

Last but not least, there is significant scope for quantitative effort in modeling various aspects of the Treasury market. Modeling means not only yield curve (or *term structure*) modeling, which is usually viewed as part of the financial analytics area, but also building models and tools for proprietary trading, analyzing specific trade ideas, and building macroeconomic models of interest rates in general and specific Treasury market issues, such as forecasting Treasury supply, in particular; these issues are usually the responsibility of *market research* areas and are addressed in Chapter 17. In short, the Treasury market keeps a great many Wall Street technical people busy.

Judging by the length of this chapter, it may seem that there is nothing else out there besides the Treasury market. For better or worse, this is not the case. Remember those stocks in your brokerage account? The market where they trade is the equities market, and we tackle it in the next chapter.

CHAPTER 6

Equity Markets

Most of us probably feel that we know everything there is to know about the stock market—after all, we all buy and sell stocks in our personal accounts, and discussing the latest stock market performance is one of the most widespread forms of small talk. However, while we are all familiar with the stock market, this familiarity is usually restricted to the viewpoint of a small individual investor, and that viewpoint is very different from the perspective of the professional Wall Street trading businesses that take the other side of our little trades and that are potential places for employment. In this chapter, we focus on this professional side of the equity market and discuss the main issues that govern institutional equity trading, as well as the technological and quantitative challenges that equity markets face today.

We follow the same approach we took in the previous chapter and start by discussing where equities come from, that is, the *primary market* for equities and the life cycle of equity securities generally, and also briefly go through the principles of *equity valuation*. Most of our time will be spent talking about the *secondary market* for equities, where we recapitulate the role of brokers, dealers, and exchanges; discuss the workings of exchanges in some detail; and review the recent events in the life of the U.S. stock exchanges. The world of equity trading is further along in its transformation to a fully electronic trading model than almost all other markets, and we will spend some time discussing this transition and the problems and opportunities that it creates. The area of *block trading* is a good illustration of the power of technology to change long-standing market practices, and we examine the evolution of block trading and its current state.

Another topic that is relatively unimportant to the individual investor but is absolutely central to institutional equity trading is the concept of an *index*. Here we go through the history of and the rationale behind the main equity indices,[1] briefly talk about *index products*, and explain why indices play such a huge role in today's markets. The discussion of indices and market sectors naturally leads to the concept of risk in equity markets, which we tackle on a qualitative level by discussing its two main pillars: *alpha* and *beta*. Along the way, we also touch upon such topics as program trading, index arbitrage, and how equity trading is organized in a typical sell-side bank.

We have already covered the early history of the stock markets in Chapter 1, and here we focus on more recent events, of which perhaps the most important was the famous stock market crash of 1929. This disaster left a lot of people scratching their heads in dismay, trying to figure out how the roaring stock market could collapse so quickly, and that number included members of the U.S. Congress as well as President Roosevelt, under whose guidance Congress adopted the most sweeping set of market regulations in the world. The consensus was that the root cause of the market collapse was blatant cheating by the issuers of securities and their Wall Street brokers,[2] who were free to issue securities that were fundamentally worthless and then relentlessly plug them to the unsuspecting and unsophisticated public, while enriching themselves personally through the practice of what is now known as *insider trading*. The Securities Act of 1933 and the Securities Exchange Act of 1934 made all of these things illegal and created the *Securities and Exchange Commission* (SEC), which has been enforcing these rules ever since.

The new regulations required issuers to provide complete disclosure of their financial condition in a document called the *prospectus*, prohibited advertising the issue by making claims that were not supported by the prospectus, and provided well-defined restrictions on trading by company insiders. All of these new requirements were backed up by stiff criminal

---

1. Most people actually call them indexes nowadays, but I can't quite bring myself to do it.
2. The 1929 crash also had other causes, to which most of us who lived through the dot-com bust can easily relate, as captured by the following legend about Joseph Kennedy (the father of JFK), one of the greatest stock manipulators of his time (and later the first chairman of the SEC). In the late summer of 1929, he was getting a shoeshine in his Manhattan office and was chatting with the shoeshine boy, who sheepishly admitted that he was also "playing the market" and even asked Mr. Kennedy for investment advice. When the boy left, Joseph Kennedy ordered his secretary to sell all his stock holdings, explaining that there were no more fools left to pour money into the market. A lot of us could have made the same observation in 2000, but, of course, few did.

penalties and generally succeeded in taming the market abuses and restoring public confidence in the market. Similar measures were eventually adopted in most of the developed world. These Depression-era regulations continue to dominate the process of *equity issuance*, by which equity securities are brought into the world. In the next few pages we discuss the issuance process as part of the larger life cycle of equity securities.

THE ISSUANCE OF EQUITY SECURITIES

Equity securities represent shares of ownership in a corporation, so first there has to be a corporation that wishes to sell such shares to the public. Note that as long as the owners of the company want to sell the shares only to their cousins, brothers-in-law, and other relatives and friends, they are free to tell these people anything they want to about the company and do not have to provide any disclosure to market regulators—they have to do that only if they intend to sell the securities to the general public and have those securities trade in the public markets. If they do want to sell their shares to the public (which is the only real way for them to raise a lot of capital), the owners have to go through the process known as an *initial public offering*, or *IPO*, which turns a privately owned corporation into a publicly owned (or simply *public*) company.

The IPO process begins with the company retaining the services of an investment bank, which does several things that are lumped together under the term *underwriting*. First, it helps the company prepare the paperwork required by the SEC and state regulators (which includes the prospectus and the registration forms) and files those documents with the appropriate regulatory agencies. It also provides an analysis of the company's business prospects in an attempt to determine the offering price at which the bank will try to sell the newly created securities to its clients.

While waiting for regulatory approval (which typically takes a few weeks), the investment bank is allowed to talk to its clients about the upcoming offering and collect preliminary indications of interest to see how easy it will be to sell the offering. Depending on this client feedback and on the type and condition of the issuing company, the investment bank will decide whether to conduct the offering on a *best efforts* basis (which means that it promises the company that it will sell as much of the new issue as it can) or on a *firm commitment* basis (which means that it effectively buys the whole issue from the company and assumes responsibility for selling it. The firm commitment is, of course, more expensive—in this case, the underwriting fee that the investment bank charges for the whole process is around 7 percent of the offering amount, which is huge no matter how you look at it[3]—but the bank does take on a lot of risk in this case, and for larger offerings it usually enlists the help of its competitors by forming a *syndicate* with its peers).

Once the regulators approve the offering, the terms of the deal (the offering amount, price, and date, and how much of it goes to which members of the syndicate) are finalized, the stock certificates are printed (unlike government bonds, stocks are in fact pieces of paper, and often very pretty pieces, as we illustrate in Figure 6–1), and the whole IPO machinery is primed for action. The sales forces of the syndicate members go to work; armed with the officially approved prospectus, they get on the phone with their buy-side clients, trying to convince them to *subscribe* to the new issue (agree to purchase some number of newly issued shares). Retail clients usually also have an opportunity to participate in an IPO by placing advance orders with their broker.

On the actual day of the IPO, the shares are distributed to those clients who have subscribed and (unless the issue is *oversubscribed*) to whatever other clients might be interested. When the whole amount has been sold, the syndicate is disbanded and the new stock begins its life. Usually, the underwriter also takes care to *list* the stock on one of the stock exchanges ahead of the IPO so that it can begin trading there right away (this also involves obtaining a CUSIP number from the CUSIP bureau and a *stock ticker symbol* from the listing exchange). Ideally, in a successful IPO, the price at which the stock trades in the *aftermarket* is equal to the offering price—if the secondary-market price ends up much higher, the company could have gotten a lot more money for its shares, but the investors are delighted; if it drops below the offering price, the investors feel stiffed, but the company thinks it has gotten a good deal. In reality, investors have come to expect an initial pop in price right after the IPO, which gives them an opportunity to make a quick profit.

We will return to the issue of IPO pricing in a few pages, but here I want to point out that the IPO is just the starting point in the life of the newborn security; the later events in its life will largely mirror the fortunes of the issuing company. If the company is doing well, then the stock will

---

3. Interestingly, the investment banks refuse to compete on price in this area. One investment bank head compared the IPO process to brain surgery and said that when you are looking for a neurosurgeon, you generally do not haggle about the price.

FIGURE 6-1

A stock certificate. Note the elaborate engraving typical of these documents, the CUSIP number in the upper right, and, most importantly, the signature. Reproduced by permission from Microsoft Corp. Image courtesy of Scripophily.com, The Gift of History (www.scripophily.com).

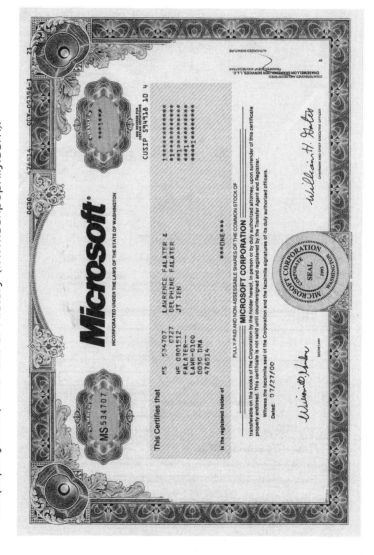

keep paying dividends to its registered holders (each stock certificate is registered to a specific owner, and the registration changes every time it trades). As it grows in price, the company may decide to *split* the stock to keep the price within reach of individual investors; when this happens, each share is replaced by several (two in a *two-for-one split*) new certificates (and the price of each of the shares, of course, is reduced by the same factor, so the total value of the company remains the same). The stock may get listed on additional exchanges.

The company may decide to issue more shares in an *additional*, or *follow-on offering*. Often the existing shareholders get the right to purchase more stock in such additional offerings to keep their ownership share the same (this is called a *rights offering*); if they do not, their ownership gets *diluted*. These *rights* are tradable securities that can be sold to others. Or the company may do the opposite and *buy back* some of the outstanding shares; if it buys back enough shares, the company may go back to being a private entity, and its stock will cease to trade in the public markets. If the company is not doing well, its stock may drop in price to the point where it gets *delisted* from exchanges (to stave this off, the company may do a *reverse split* to combine several shares into one to boost the share price), and if the company goes bankrupt and is liquidated, the stock will become worthless. The company may merge with another company, in which case the stock of the acquired company ceases to exist and (usually) is exchanged for a certain number of shares in the acquiring company.

Things like splits, mergers, rights issues, and so on are collectively referred to as *corporate actions* and make keeping track of the stock a non-trivial exercise. Try plotting the historical price of a stock that has gone through three splits and two mergers, and you will appreciate the pain and hassle that corporate actions introduce into the maintenance of equity products data (we will expand on that topic in Chapter 13).

How do people determine the offering price in an IPO? For that matter, how does one determine the value of any stock? Questions like that belong to the realm of *equity valuation*, which, as we will shortly see, is definitely more of an art than a science. Fundamentally, the value of a stock (or any other security) should be the discounted present value of its future cash flows, which are, of course, the dividend payments. If someone tells us how much the company will pay as dividends at what future dates, we can discount each of those cash flows to the present using the discount function we talked about in the previous chapter, and their total present value will give us the *fair value* of the stock.

The problem is, nobody knows what the dividends will be (unlike the case with bonds, where the coupon payments are known with some certainty). Moreover, some companies do not pay a dividend at all (their stock should thus be worthless, according to this theory). It is a bit more straightforward to estimate the future *earnings* of a company, so another theory has it that the value of a stock is the discounted present value of its future earnings rather than its future dividends. The companies themselves announce their earnings projections for the next few years, and the research analysts at sell-side institutions scrutinize those projections and sometimes make their own earnings forecasts, so there is at least some information about future earnings.

Let us say that this analysis tells us that company XYZ will earn $10 million each year from now on until forever, and there are 10 million shares of this company outstanding, so it is going to earn $1 per share in perpetuity. If we discount all those future earnings back to today using a constant interest rate R, we find that each share should be worth $1/R$ (say, $20 if R is 5 percent). If we invert this calculation, the ratio of *earnings per share* (EPS) to price becomes an effective interest rate, not unlike the yield on a bond (in fact, if we replace earnings with dividends, the ratio of dividends per share to price is officially called the *dividend yield*); if this ratio is high, then the stock is good value, and vice versa. Stock market participants, however, usually invert this ratio when thinking about equity valuations and use the *price/earnings ratio* (or *P/E ratio*) in their analysis. The P/E ratio for an average stock in the S&P 500 is about 17 as of this writing; inverting that would give us an interest rate of 5.88 percent, which compares favorably with the current Treasury bond yields of about 4.5 percent (there is even something called the *Fed model* that does this kind of comparison to determine whether stocks as an asset class are a good value compared to bonds).

The whole concept of P/E ratios as a measure of value was severely tested during the dot-com boom of the late 1990s. Trying to estimate the IPO price of Pets.com, which had no foreseeable earnings, was an exercise in frustration for the investment bankers, who had to invent various replacements for earnings—measures with names like EBITDA (earnings before interest, taxes, depreciation, and amortization)—in order to provide some justification to investors for why they should buy these Internet stocks. Investors, however, really did not need any such justification and were snapping up Internet stocks (it was not uncommon for a stock to go up by a factor of 3 on the day of the IPO) not because of any ratios, but because they believed in their potential for *growth*. Indeed, it is not unreasonable to assume that the earnings of a good company will grow with time instead of staying constant, and if the growth is sufficiently fast, it can make the company quite valuable, even if its P/E ratio is very high. In fact there is a school of thought going back to Peter Lynch that maintains that if the expected rate of earnings growth (in percent) is higher than the P/E ratio, the stock is undervalued, and there is another ratio called PEG (price/earnings to growth) that quantifies this view: a company is undervalued if its PEG is less than 1 (its current average for the S&P 500 is indeed around 1.3).

Other ratios also abound in stock valuation writings; there is the price-to-sales ratio (P/S), also known as the price-to-revenues ratio (P/R), and the most down-to-earth of ratios called the price-to-book-value, or P/B, ratio, which dispenses with attempts to predict the future and simply says that the value of company shares should be at least equal to its "book" value, or the value of its tangible assets, so that the P/B should be greater than 1 (it averages around 3.0 for the current S&P 500). While a lot of effort is being expended in trying to estimate the fair value of equities based on all these ratios, the reality is that a stock is worth exactly as much as people are willing to pay for it in the secondary market, so we leave stock valuation theory behind and move on to discuss the secondary market for equity securities.

TRADING IN EQUITY SECONDARY MARKETS

Who are the participants in the secondary equity markets? Not so long ago, up until the 1950s or so, almost all trading activity in the secondary markets for equities was originated by individuals rather than institutions. Institutions with money to invest—insurance companies, banks, savings and loans, and so on—used to stay away from equities because the then-current perception was that stocks were not a good investment, but rather a speculative device. From a historical perspective, this perception was largely accurate; most of the individuals participating in the stock market were small speculators out to make a quick buck, and the closest equivalent to institutional trading was battles for corporate control, where the leaders of industry and finance of the time (think J. P. Morgan, Cornelius Vanderbilt, and their peers) were effectively doing mergers and acquisitions by buying huge amounts of their rival companies' stock (interestingly, even those big participants almost always acted as individuals rather than in their official capacity as officers or directors of the corporations they led). This was in contrast with the bond market (at least the government bonds part of that market), where institutions such as banks were traditionally the main buyers of government securities (this tradition began in eighteenth-century England, if not earlier).

These bond-trading institutions were few in number and knew their Wall Street trading partners well, so the bond market (as we discussed in the previous chapter) developed as a *dealer market,* where the dealers trade directly with their institutional customers. In the stock market, the number of participants was much larger (as early as the 1790s, when the NYSE was formed, there were thousands of people who traded stocks in the United States), so that the trading system that developed to accommodate them ended up quite different—it is called an *exchange market.* As we discussed in Chapter 2, in an exchange market, the ultimate buyers and sellers generally trade with each other through two intermediaries: they give their orders to a broker, who sends them to an exchange, where these orders meet with other orders and get *executed.* Here we are going to consider this process in more detail; first we will talk about the execution process on an imaginary generic exchange, and then we will apply these generic principles to a few specific exchanges to see how they operate in real life.

I think the best way to understand how exchanges work is to follow the life cycle of an order from its very beginning to its end. It would be nice, a pedant would say, if we defined the concept of an order before plunging into this discussion; we can loosely say that an order is a request to buy or sell a certain quantity of a certain security at a certain price under certain conditions. But if we really want to understand what this means, it is better to go through a specific example first. Therefore, let us try to enter an order into the order entry screen shown in Figure 6–2 and see how far we can get.

The first decision we have to make is whether we want to buy or sell, which means we have to specify the *order side.* The next field is also uncontroversial; we need to specify what we are buying or selling, so we enter some identifier of the security we want to trade (usually something called a *stock ticker symbol,* such as MSFT for Microsoft shares; Figure 6–3 shows the origins of this term). Our next decision is more difficult: should we specify the price? If we do not, our order will be called a *market order—* we will buy our MSFT shares "at market," which means at whatever (best)

FIGURE 6-2

A mock-up of an order entry screen used by an imaginary equity trading system. The display at the bottom shows what happened to our recent orders.

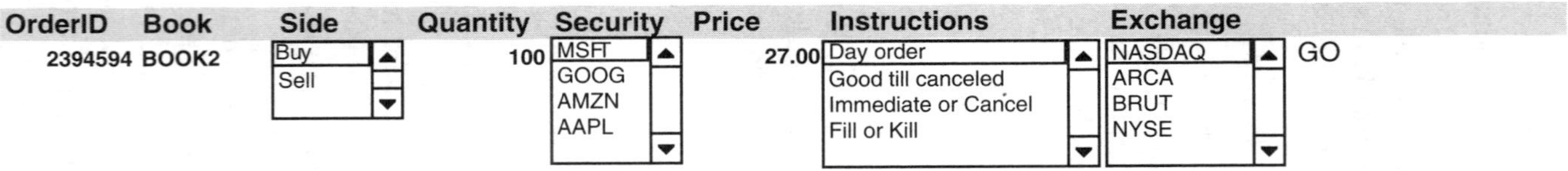

OrderID	Book	Side	Quantity	Security	Price	Instructions	Exchange	
2394594	BOOK2	Buy ▲ ▼ (Sell)	100	MSFT ▲ (GOOG, AMZN, AAPL) ▼	27.00	Day order ▲ (Good till canceled, Immediate or Cancel, Fill or Kill) ▼	NASDAQ ▲ (ARCA, BRUT, NYSE) ▼	GO

OrderID	Book	Side	Quantity	Security	Price	Instructions	Exchange	Status	Time
2394588	BOOK1	buy	1000	MSFT	26.95	Day	NASDAQ	canceled	10:25:02
2394589	BOOK1	buy	700	MSFT	26.98	Day	NASDAQ	accepted	10:26:38
2394590	BOOK1	sell	3000	GOOG	359.02	Day	NASDAQ	accepted	10:33:50
2394591	BOOK1	buy	1200	MSFT	26.99	Day	NASDAQ	filled	10:41:02
2394592	BOOK1	sell	500	AMZN	43.14	Day	NASDAQ	rejected	10:48:14
2394593	BOOK1	sell	800	AAPL	74.76	Day	NASDAQ	submitted	10:55:26
2394594	BOOK2	buy	100	MSFT	27.00	Day	NASDAQ	new	11:02:38

FIGURE 6–3

The term *stock ticker* now refers to a stock symbol like MSFT, but it used to mean the stock ticker machine—Thomas Edison's first invention—that printed out stock symbols and trade prices received by telegraph on a special paper tape (known as ticker tape). This was the first real-time market data system. The machine had a printing head like a type-writer and made a ticking sound as it hit the tape, hence the name. Also shown is the stock transmitter, which was used to send quotes to the stock ticker. Reproduced courtesy of The Stock Ticker Company (www.stocktickercompany.com—it sells working replicas of the stock ticker machine that print stock quotes off the Internet) and Henry Ford Museum & Greenfield Village.

price people are selling it for at that time. If we do specify a price—for example, if we say, "Buy 100 shares of MSFT at 27.00"—our order will be called a *limit order*, and 27.00 will be the *limit price*, or simply the limit. The word *limit* here is in fact appropriate, as the limit price in fact limits the range of prices we will accept—if someone sold the stock to us at 26 instead of 27, we would not complain, so the correct wording of our limit order description should really be "at 27.00 or better," where "better" means lower for buys and higher for sells. Some exchanges support many other kinds of orders (which essentially are spiffed-up market and limit orders that

become active only when certain price-related events occur), but we will
stick with these two major *order types*.

We then have to define the *execution instructions*, which generally
describe how long we want our order to remain valid; the default is usually until the end of the trading day, but we can also choose the order to
be *good till canceled*, in which case it can potentially live forever. On the
other end of the spectrum, we can say that our order should immediately
die if it cannot be instantly executed (this is called *immediate or cancel*).
Sometimes it is also possible to specify which exchange the order should
go to, and even who it should trade with, but we are not going to worry
about such subtleties—we press a submit button and ask, "What's next?"

When we *submit* an order, it gets sent to an exchange (usually as an
electronic message), and the exchange looks it over and performs some
sanity checking on it (such as making sure that the exchange actually
trades the instrument we want, that the price is positive, that it recognizes
the sender of the order, and so on), after which the exchange responds
with an acknowledgment (called an *order ack*) telling us that the order
was accepted. The newly accepted order is then added to the *order book*
that the exchange maintains for each security. This is an important concept that we illustrate in Figure 6–4 by showing a representation of the
MSFT order book on Nasdaq at some (imaginary) moment in time. As
can be seen in Figure 6–4, an order book is a collection of all limit orders
for a security; for each *price point* (we can trade only at a discrete set of
prices), the order book may contain orders submitted by many different market participants. Every time a new order arrives, the exchange compares it
with the orders already in the book using a procedure called either *matching* or *crossing* in an attempt to *execute* the incoming order against one
of the existing orders in the book. To illustrate the execution process, we
will start throwing different orders at the book shown in Figure 6–4 and
see what happens to them.

The highest price at which people are currently willing to buy is the
best bid, and the lowest price at which they are willing to sell is the *best
offer*—26.99 and 27.00, respectively, in Figure 6–4. Let us say our order is
to buy 100 at the (best offer) price of 27.00. The crossing algorithm will
attempt to find a sell order at the price of 27.00 or better to satisfy our buy
order, and in this case it does not have to look very far because the very first
order on the offered side (a sell of 100 at 27.00) is a perfect match to ours.
Both our order and this sell order have reached the climax of their life; the
exchange executes, or *fills*, both of them. Unlike in the case of prisoners,

F I G U R E   6–4

A mock-up of the Nasdaq TotalView representation of an MSFT order book at some imaginary moment in time. The top of the table corresponds to the simple Level I view that shows the last trade price and the best bid and offer (National BBO, or NBBO, is the official term). The order book contains all buy and sell orders, ranked by price and then by time of arrival. MMID (Market Maker ID) identifies the submitter of the order (SIZE means an anonymous submission, usually by a customer of a market maker). Arrows mark orders that would be included in the older Nasdaq Level II display.

	Symbol	MSFT	(Microsoft Corp)		
	Last trade	27.00			
	National BBO	26.99	27.00	6000 × 700	
	BID			OFFER	
MMID	Size	Price	MMID	Size	Price
=> GSCO	2000	26.99	SIZE	100	27.00 <=
=> LEHM	1700	26.99	CINN	500	27.00 <=
=> ARCX	300	26.99	GSCO	200	27.00 <=
=> CINN	1400	26.99	SIZE	200	27.01
=> NITE	600	26.99	BTRD	400	27.01 <=
GSCO	4000	26.98	GSCO	200	27.02 <=
LEHM	6700	26.98	FBCO	1200	27.03 <=
=> UBSW	1200	26.98	SIZE	200	27.03
=> SIZE	1000	26.98	BOFA	3000	27.03 <=
ARCX	200	26.98	TDCM	7000	27.03 <=
=> SCHB	6000	26.98	LEHM	5000	27.04 <=
LEHM	7500	26.98	SIZE	200	27.04
CINN	2000	26.98	SCHB	100	27.04 <=
=> BOFA	4500	26.98	NITE	500	27.04 <=
=> FBCO	2300	26.98	BOFA	14000	27.10
SIZE	2800	26.98	FBCO	1000	27.15 <=
SIZE	1200	26.98	SIZE	4000	27.16
=> BTRD	200	26.97	SCHB	800	27.20
SIZE	35000	26.97	ARCX	10000	27.22 <=
GSCO	5000	26.97	LEHM	500	27.28
UBSW	3000	26.97	SIZE	900	27.28
SCHB	22000	26.97	UBSW	15000	27.30 <=
SIZE	500	26.97	SIZE	5000	27.32

execution of orders is good—every order is created in the hope that it will eventually be executed—and this happens when two mutually agreeable orders find each other. If this sounds like happy matrimony, note this important difference: at least one of the matched orders ceases to exist as a result of the execution process. In fact, in our example, both buy and sell orders cease to exist because not just their prices but also their sizes exactly match.

The exchange will now send an *execution report* to both us and the submitter of the order we executed against. This report will state that we have received a fill of 100 shares at the price of 27.00 (usually it will also contain the time of the execution and, optionally, the counterparty—the owner of the offsetting order). The exchange will also report to all market participants that a trade has occurred for 100 shares at 27.00; this information is disseminated to everybody who *subscribes* to *market data* for MSFT. Depending on the level of their subscription, the recipients of the market data messages receive information about trades, best bids and offers, and the composition of the order book. In real life, the information presented in Figure 6–4 would have come from such market data messages on the highest subscription level, which shows the complete order book, so we would have known that there was an offer at 27.00 before we submitted our buy order. In reality, therefore, we decided to *take* (or lift) the offer we saw in the order book (the opposite act of selling at the best bid price is called *hitting the bid*).

Now, if we submitted a buy order for 200 shares instead of 100 at 27.00, we would have still crossed with that same 100 shares offer, but in this case our buy order would survive the crossing, and its remaining 100 shares would immediately be matched against the next available offer of 500 shares (see Figure 6–4), and we would then cross again for another 100 shares. Our order would get two fills of 100 shares each and cease to exist; the first of the existing sell orders would also perish, and the second would be *partially filled* (for 100 out of the 500 that it wants).

What if we tried to do 2,000 shares? In this case, we would take out all offers at the 27.00 level—we would get three fills for 100, 500, and 200 shares (the sizes of the offers shown in Figure 6–4 for this price level)—after which we would still want 1,200 more shares. Since nobody is willing to sell us more at 27.00 at the moment, our order will stay in the order book as a bid at that price level (thereby becoming the best bid, while the offers at the next price point of 27.01 will become best offers); this is an example of a large order *moving the market*. To get to our full desired size of 2,000 shares, we will now have to wait for someone to come in and hit our bid (by submitting more sell orders at this price).

If we were in a hurry to get the whole 2,000 shares quickly, we should have submitted a market buy order; this type of order does not have a price limit, so first it will cross with the sell orders at 27.00 exactly as described earlier, but then, instead of staying at that price level, it will move on to cross at the next best price of 27.01. In the example of Figure 6–4, we can get 600 more shares at that price, then we will move still higher, to 27.02, where we get another 200 shares, and our order gets its last 400 shares at 27.03. This example of a large market order *sweeping* the book and moving the trade price through several price points in the blink of an eye is a defining trait of exchange-style execution, where all orders are matched instantly (or at least as fast as the exchange can process them), and the liquidity comes from orders sitting at multiple price levels (this is referred to as *market depth*). In contrast, the execution model prevalent in the fixed-income interdealer markets that we discussed in the previous chapter does not allow the trading price to move through multiple price levels instantly; there is a "workup" delay at each price point that allows people to come in from the sidelines and participate in the trade.

When there are multiple orders in the book, how does the exchange decide which to execute first? As we saw in the previous example, the orders in the book have to be ordered in some way (perhaps we should find a different word for ordering of orders; should we say prioritized?), so that when a new order arrives, there is no ambiguity as to which order to match first. This is achieved by using *priority rules*, of which by far the most common is *price-time priority*, which ranks orders based on two things: the order price and the time of arrival. In this ranking, an order with a more aggressive price (higher for bids, lower for offers) goes first (and market orders that do not have a price go in front of any limit order). At the same price level, the order that arrived first goes first. So the sell of 100 at 27.00 that we first crossed against in our example was first in the book because its price was the most aggressive, and it got to the exchange before the other two offers at that price level. This first come, first served approach encourages swiftness; if we want our orders to be executed, we have to be quick in submitting them.

There are other priority rules that prioritize orders based on other criteria, such as order size (some exchanges fill all orders at the same price level simultaneously in proportion to their size; this encourages submitting large orders) or the type of the submitter (on many exchanges, "public" orders go in front of orders submitted by exchange insiders), although price-time priority is by far the most common. In all cases, people trading on any exchange know very well what those rules are and do whatever it takes to try to get their orders in front of everybody else's.

When we trade on an exchange, we can generally do three things with our orders: we can submit them (which is what we have already considered), we can *cancel* them, and we can *update* them. Canceling is another way to end the life of an order; this is done (1) if we change our mind based on some new information and no longer want an order to be executed, or (2) if the market moves so far away from our order's price that it is highly unlikely to be executed. Updating an order usually means changing its size and (on some exchanges) price. From a purely mechanical perspective, when we trade on an exchange, we spend our days (and sometimes nights) submitting, canceling, and updating our orders (this activity is called *order management*), and when the exchange tells us that some of our orders got executed, we keep track of the fills and maintain a record of how much of what we bought and sold at what prices (this task is called *position management*, and the larger task of keeping our PnL under control is called *risk management*). The latter two activities are in fact common to all trading, but the order management part is specific to exchanges and other similar execution platforms that effectively provide a rule-based environment where we can play this trading game using orders as game equipment.

EXCHANGE OPERATION

Let us now move beyond the life of individual orders and consider the life of an exchange, or rather its daily routine. Most exchanges limit their trading hours (in the United States, the major stock exchanges open at 9:30 a.m. and close at 4 p.m. New York time); however, you can often submit orders to them outside those hours. The exchange will typically match the orders that it finds in its order books in the morning during an *opening auction* that establishes an opening price for each stock.

After the opening, people start trading as described previously, and the exchange's job is to make sure that trading goes smoothly. The exchange intervenes in crisis situations when the market moves too much and can halt trading either for individual stocks or for everything across the board. A common situation in which the trading in a particular stock is halted is when there is an important news announcement about a particular company—an unexpected indictment of the CEO for fraud or similar bad news can cause a huge order imbalance in the stock of that company and make orderly trading impossible. If there are no such crises, the exchange just keeps humming along until closing time, at which point the *closing price* for each security is established (it may be the price of the last trade before the close, or it may be determined in a closing auction). After the close, the exchange's clearing and settlement systems go to work, making sure that all trades are properly settled so that the next morning the exchange can move on to the new trading day.

Who are the people trading on exchanges? One cannot just walk off the street into an exchange and start trading stocks—all exchanges limit the privilege of trading on them to their *members*, who have demonstrated their creditworthiness, good moral character, and so on. To become a member of an exchange, not only does one have to have these qualities, but he also has to pay in order to *buy a seat* (it is not the furniture kind of seat, but rather the right to trade on an exchange).

How, then, does the average Joe trade stocks? He does it through one of the exchange members, who acts as a broker that passes on Joe's orders to the exchange and charges Joe a commission for doing so. Even if Joe is an avid day trader who spends his life trading stocks online, the exchanges that his trades are executed on know nothing of his existence—from their perspective, all Joe's orders are in fact submitted by his brokerage firm, which is ultimately responsible for them as an exchange member.

Unlike Joe, most Wall Street banks usually own seats on every exchange, so they can trade commission-free. They do, however, have to pay the so-called *trading fees* and the clearing fees charged by the clearinghouse that settles trades. Those fees are typically much smaller than broker commissions, but if the banks trade a huge volume, the fees do add up, and they are a major source of income for the exchanges (the other sources being the sale of membership seats and the *listing fees* that the issuers pay to get their securities traded on the exchange). We will talk some more about the business model of exchanges in the next chapter when we discuss futures, but essentially exchanges make money by charging their constituents for the services that the exchange provides, which are arranging and settling trades.

Let us now see how these principles work out in real life on various stock exchanges, starting with the *New York Stock Exchange (NYSE)*. The *Big Board*, as it is also called, has been around for more than two hundred years (it was formed in 1792), and, amazingly, it still operates in much the same way as it did from day one. At the center of the NYSE trading model is the *specialist*, a member of the exchange who trades a particular stock. Each stock has one specialist assigned to it, although each specialist may trade several stocks. When I say that the NYSE specialist trades a particular stock, I mean a much stronger statement: the specialist has a monopoly on executing trades in that stock. All orders in that stock are delivered to the specialist's perch at a trading post (this used to be done by floor brokers who worked for brokerage houses representing the order, but it is now done by an electronic order routing system called *SuperDot*) and put in the order book.

The specialist is (or at least was until very recently) the only person who knows the content of the order book, and he plays the role of a crossing engine in our generic exchange by matching up buy and sell orders in the book. The specialist is also allowed (and at times required) to add his own orders to the book, thereby buying and selling for his own account. To ensure orderly price movements, the specialist is expected to step in as a buyer when everyone else wants to sell, and be a seller when everyone wants to buy, so that in addition to their order-crossing responsibilities, the specialists also act as market makers who add liquidity (although, unlike market makers in other venues, they are not required to provide continuous bid and offer quotes at all times—only when the order book is very lopsided). The point of the specialist system is that all liquidity in a stock becomes concentrated in one place and one place only, the specialist's trading post, so that if investors want the best price, this is the only place they can realistically go, which in turn guarantees that they will meet everybody else's orders there and get the best possible execution.

The specialist has a huge (perhaps, critics say, unfair) advantage over other players who try to make markets in (or simply trade) his stock in that he can see the order book and can thus predict the short-term price movements in his stock better than anyone else, which allows him to trade the stock profitably for himself. But in return for this privilege, the specialist undertakes to keep prices stable and the bid-offer spread reasonably narrow (which, as we discussed in the last chapter, can be quite costly for the market maker if the market moves a lot); the proponents of the specialist system claim that this informational advantage is fair compensation for the costs of keeping the market working smoothly for everyone. This subject can be (and is) endlessly debated, but the empirical fact is that the specialist system, with all its quaint notions of human oversight of the trading process, has worked extremely well for all market participants over the last two centuries and is likely to continue to do so.

In recent years, the NYSE has made some concessions to the realities of the electronic trading era: it does now have a system (*NYSEDirect*) that can execute orders without the specialist's participation, but the overwhelming majority of orders still go through a specialist. The exchange has also started to make the order book data available through a system called

OpenBook. As I write this, the NYSE is preparing to merge with one of its all-electronic rivals, Archipelago Exchange, so by the time this book comes out, the Big Board will almost certainly be more electronic than it is today, but the specialist system will probably continue to thrive there.

A distinguishing feature of the NYSE is that it has the most stringent listing requirements of all major U.S. exchanges, so that over the years (centuries, rather), it has ended up listing and trading most of the largest U.S. corporations. To even be considered for listing on the Big Board, a company has to be worth at least $750 million and must also satisfy a host of other criteria in terms of the number of shareholders, revenues, earnings, and so on. Most importantly, the company has to submit to the NYSE corporate governance and disclosure rules. Only about 2,800 companies out of several hundred thousand U.S. businesses are listed on the NYSE. In fact, the term *listed stock* has come to mean a NYSE-listed stock, despite the fact that all other exchanges also have listing requirements.

In the nineteenth century, shares of companies that failed to make it onto the Big Board traded just outside the NYSE building on Broad Street; the trading occurred right there on the sidewalk in what has become known as the *curb market.* It was only in the 1920s that the curb traders moved into their present location a few blocks away and later became the American Stock Exchange, or AMEX. This exchange trades stocks of smaller companies (initially it was focused on oil and mining stocks, but now it lists all kinds of companies) and has also diversified into derivatives products such as stock options (see Chapter 9) and exchange-traded funds. There are also so-called regional exchanges (in Philadelphia, San Francisco, Chicago, Boston, and Cincinnati) that are in a similar situation: way behind the NYSE in terms of volume and looking for additional product lines to bolster their revenues. All the regionals and the AMEX use the specialist system and in this regard are almost indistinguishable from the NYSE. However, the majority of smaller and younger U.S. companies trade on yet another exchange, Nasdaq, which is different from the NYSE in many respects.

When Nasdaq started out in 1971, it was not really a stock exchange; it was one of the world's first large-scale computer networks, created by a defense contractor for the National Association of Securities Dealers (NASD). The NASD had a problem: it had thousands of broker-dealer members all over the country who traded thousands of smaller companies' stocks *over the counter (OTC)*—that is, directly with each other and with the public—and the world of OTC stock trading had become a complete mess by the mid-1960s. If a person wanted to buy the stock of a local brewery or some other small company, he asked his stockbroker to find out what the price was, and the stockbroker had to figure out which security dealers traded that stock, call up several of them to see if they would be willing to sell the stock, and then ask for quotes. The quotes varied widely, and it was often hard to find a dealer that was willing to trade at all (especially if an obscure stock was involved).

The process was cumbersome, transaction costs were huge, and the problem kept getting worse because the investment bankers of the day were aggressively bringing a greater number of smaller companies public, so the secondary OTC market had to do something to accommodate this flood of new entrants. The NASD correctly identified the lack of *price transparency* as the main problem (this fancy term means that nobody knew what prices other people were willing to trade at), and it decided to build an Automated Quotation system for its members (that's what the *aq* in Nasdaq stands for). The idea was that the dealers in each stock (who in this context are called *market makers*) would submit their current bid and offer prices to such a system, and the rest of the NASD members (for example, a local stockbroker) would subscribe to the system and be able to see the bids and offers submitted by every dealer from all over the country, which, in turn, would make it much easier to get a good price. Building such a system was quite a technological feat at that time, but in a country that was racing the Russians to the moon, anything technological seemed possible, and the system was deployed in just a couple of years.

The costs of building the system were recouped by selling subscriptions to the NASD members. These were of three types. The cheapest, a *Level I* subscription, provided a terminal that displayed the best bids and offers for a selection of stocks and identified market makers who were willing to trade at those prices. This information was all that a local stockbroker cared about, but for professional traders at the market-making firms and elsewhere, it was not sufficient—they generally wanted to know more about the composition of the order book. These professionals could subscribe to *Level II* data, which showed the best bid and offer submitted by each market maker, while *Level III* was reserved for the market-making firms themselves—it was Level II plus the ability to submit quotes.

Note carefully that Level II data did not really represent a full view of the order book; if a market maker had more than one bid (or, more importantly, had customer limit buy orders), the Level II display would not show those. In Figure 6–4, we indicate with arrows the orders that would be shown by the Level II display; we can see that in a typical case, about half of the book's content would not show up on such a display. This is not how things are supposed to work on our generic exchange, but then Nasdaq was not really an exchange at this point—the OTC market remained a dealer market, very similar to the government bond market described in the previous chapter, where all trades have a dealer at one end. If one dealer had a customer order that could cross with a customer order that another dealer held, too bad; the dealers were not expected to share their private order books with anyone, and they did not (which is how the government bond market still works). In fact, even if one dealer's bid crossed with another dealer's offer, Nasdaq would not execute a trade—initially, it was just a quote display system, not a trading platform.

This began to change in the early 1980s, when Nasdaq introduced its first electronic trading system, called *SOES* (small order execution system), which automatically executed small customer orders (up to 1,000 shares) against the market-maker quotes displayed by Nasdaq. This was intended as a simple labor-saving device to automate the processing of small orders submitted by lots and lots of individual investors so that the traders at the market-making firms could sit back and focus on bigger and better things, such as orders from their institutional clients, and the SOES system did that. However, some of those individual investors turned out to be much more sophisticated than the creators of SOES expected, and they quickly turned this system into a major pain in the neck for market makers.

Before SOES, market makers had little incentive to keep their quotes current, as they were purely indicative. Suppose there were three market makers in a stock and they all showed the same bid and offer, say 27 to 27¼ (stock prices were quoted in eighths up until 2000, when the market switched to cents in a process known as *decimalization*). If the market went up quickly, the market makers had to adjust their quotes, for example, to 27½ bid to 27¾ offer, and ideally they should have been doing these adjustments more or less simultaneously. In reality, though, it may have taken a minute or more for all of them to move their quotes, so there would be some short periods of time where one market maker would show 27/27¼ and the other two would already show 27½/27¾ On a true-blue exchange, the stale 27¼ offer would have crossed with the 27½ bid, but Nasdaq did not do such crossing, and this created an opportunity for the users of the SOES system—if someone with access to SOES spotted the situation just described in time, that person could buy from the sluggish market maker at 27¼ and immediately sell at the new bid price of 27½, making an instant riskless profit.

Suddenly, the market makers found that being slow in adjusting their quotes was costing them real money. Their first reaction was to complain bitterly, denounce SOES as a stupid invention, denounce the SOES users who picked them off in this way as *SOES bandits*, initiate legal proceedings against the brokers who gave these early day traders direct access to the SOES system, and issue vague threats that if this did not stop, they would be forced to widen their spreads or stop making markets altogether. However, most of the market makers eventually realized that this was not going to go away and invested in upgrading their market-making systems so that they stopped creating easy pickings for the SOES bandits.

Effectively, SOES forced Nasdaq to become a more efficient market, and the SOES controversy died down by the early 1990s, only to be replaced with another. Nasdaq market makers were accused of colluding to keep the bid-offer spreads wide, and these accusations ultimately led to a far-reaching reform of the whole Nasdaq model. In January 1997, the SEC adopted a new set of *order-handling rules* that essentially required the market makers to display their customers' orders alongside their own, and, more importantly, to expose the prices available to them internally on private interdealer networks known as ECNs (electronic communication networks). The first ECN, Instinet, actually preceded Nasdaq by about a year—it started out in 1970 as an interdealer broker that allowed OTC market makers to trade anonymously with each other in exactly the same way that eSpeed and BrokerTec allow bond dealers to trade with each other, as described in the previous chapter.

The new order-handling rules essentially required the market makers to open the ECNs to their customers, who now were supposed to be able to see the orders posted on the ECNs and submit their own orders there. The ECNs saw this as an opportunity to increase their share of the market, and several new ECNs, such as Island, Archipelago, BRUT, and REDIBook, sprung to life after 1997. There were more than a dozen ECNs trading U.S. stocks in 2000, but they went through a bout of consolidation, and there are now only six major ECNs left (Figure 6–5). All ECNs operate very much like the generic exchange we described earlier, with orders being matched automatically and a fully visible limit order book, and both the institutional traders before 1997 and the individual day traders after 1997 liked those features and directed an increasing share of their orders to those electronic platforms, so that by 2000 the ECNs had succeeded in capturing more than a third of the total trading volume in Nasdaq stocks.

Recognizing their importance (and also wishing to make their liquidity available to the general public), the SEC in 1998 adopted further

FIGURE 6-5

ECNs operating in the U.S. equity markets at the end of 2005.

ECN	MMID	Web Site	Trading Hours (EST)	Type	Comment
INET ATS, Inc	CINN	www.inetats.com	7am - 8pm	ATS	Combination of the two original ECNs -- Instinet and Island
Track ECN	TRAC	www.trackecn.com	7:30am - 9pm	Exchange	
Archipelago Exchange (ArcaEx)	ARCA	www.tradearca.com	8am - 8pm	Exchange	Absorbed REDIBook and is now merging with NYSE
Bloomberg Tradebook	BTRD	www.bloombergtradebook.com	24 hours	ATS	
Brut ECN (The Brass Utility)	BRUT	www.ebrut.com	8:30am - 6pm	ATS	Absorbed another ECN, Strike Technologies, in 2000
Attain ECN	ATTN	www.attain.com	8am - 6pm	ATS	
NexTrade	NTRD	www.nextrade.org	24 hours	Exchange	Also wants to be a futures exchange

regulations requiring each Alternative Trading System, or ATS, to decide whether it wanted to be treated as an exchange (which lives off trading fees and is self-regulated) or as a broker-dealer (which lives off commissions and is effectively just another market maker that exposes its order book for everyone to see).

The explosive growth of the ECNs created what is known as *market fragmentation*: while each of the ECNs operated a modern and efficient all-electronic market, the people submitting the orders had to decide which ECN to go to (a problem known as *order routing*). This could have led to the market splitting into several nonintersecting pools of liquidity, but in practice, despite all the talk of market fragmentation, this problem quickly corrected itself, as the ECNs started linking their order books and routing orders among themselves.

Finally, in 2002, Nasdaq itself came out with a new system called SuperMontage that effectively consolidated all orders from its market makers, the retail customers of those market makers, and all the ECNs into a *centralized limit order book*, or CLOB. The display shown in Figure 6–4 corresponds to the SuperMontage replacement of the old Level II data; this product is called TotalView and simply shows everything in the order book, just as we assumed it would in our discussion of how a generic exchange operates. It may be ironic that it took Nasdaq 30 years to get to this point, but it had a long way to go from its beginnings as a quotation system in a dealer market to a modern order-driven exchange.

To summarize, at present all existing U.S. exchanges are converging to our generic exchange execution model: the ECNs were there from day one, Nasdaq is effectively there after the introduction of SuperMontage, and the NYSE and other brick-and-mortar exchanges are holding on to their specialist system but moving in the direction of full automation. At the end of the day, the execution model of all these markets is quickly converging, and the only important difference between them remains the source of liquidity. On the NYSE and other specialist-based markets, the liquidity comes from customer orders and from specialists; on ECNs, it comes from just the customer orders; and on Nasdaq, it comes primarily from the market makers. However, once the order gets into one of those markets, these days it will be handled similarly regardless of its origin, so from a technical perspective, the situation is much simpler now than it was just a few years ago. This execution model convergence is further enhanced by the fact that all major European exchanges—the London Stock Exchange (LSE), Deutsche Borse, and EuroNext (which ate up most of the remaining national exchanges that used to operate in continental Europe)—switched to an all-electronic model long ago.

Therefore, on a certain level, all stock exchanges today have become the same, and their present structure really reflects their origins as markets for very many small individual players. It is great for an individual trader that her order to buy 100 shares of Amazon.com is treated by the exchange with the same respect as a large order from Fidelity, but is it great for Fidelity? Beginning in 1950s, institutional investors flocked to the equity markets in search of enhanced returns that they could not get in their traditional fixed-income space, and by now between 50 and 70 percent of all equities trading is originated by institutions: mutual fund companies, pension funds, hedge funds, corporations buying back their stock, and so on. Some of these organizations control massive amounts of money that they wish to invest in various markets to achieve superior investment returns, and the exchange-based structure of the equities markets does not lend itself easily to absorbing these massive amounts.

To see what the problem is, let us consider a hypothetical example of a mutual fund manager who is in charge of a $1 billion asset allocation fund that invests in various asset classes. The manager woke up in the morning and decided to do a minor readjustment of her portfolio—sell $25 million of Treasuries and invest this money in Microsoft stock. She passes this request to her trading desk, and the traders there begin to work on it. The first part of the request, exiting a $25 million position in the on-the-run 10-year Treasury note, is accomplished with one mouse click (if it was not the on-the-run, it could have taken more mouse clicks, but as we saw in the last chapter, in the Treasury market we do not experience size constraints until we start talking billion-dollar trades).

Now we want to buy $25 million worth of MSFT, which at the last trade price of 27.00 translates into about 900,000 shares. This sounds like an awful lot of shares, but in the grand scheme of things, the trade we want to do is quite small—MSFT is one of the most liquid equity securities on Earth, with daily trading volume of about 70 million shares (out of about 10 billion outstanding shares), so our size is just over 1 percent of the daily volume. We look at the order book display (as shown in Figure 6–4) and immediately see that there is a problem: if we total up all offers at all price levels, we can buy only about 70,000 shares at the moment, and we will have to go up in price to 27.32 (or more than 1 percent) to get the last bits of available liquidity. This effect (a large order moving the market price against itself) is called the *market impact* of the order, and for large orders it is the main component of the transaction costs, far ahead of commissions and even the normal bid-offer spread that everybody has to pay.

How do we avoid market impact? Clearly, submitting a market buy order for 900,000 shares in this environment is not the way to do it, and neither is submitting a limit order for that amount—that would be even worse than a market order, since everyone would then see that there is a large buyer and move their offers higher, and people would start putting in bids just above our limit price to trade ahead of us. Doing such a large trade directly on the exchange would cause a huge market impact and thus would be ruinously expensive. The reality is that our order for 900,000 shares is simply too large to be easily executed on the exchange, and that makes it a *block order*—what are we supposed to do with it?

BLOCK ORDERS

This is such a common problem that the markets have developed special mechanisms to deal with it. The traditional way of executing block orders is to do them off the exchange. We can approach a dealer firm and ask it to simply sell the whole size to us (perhaps at a price of 27.50—clearly the price is going to move up, and this markup gives the dealer some room to buy back those shares and still make a profit), or we can talk to a block broker and ask it to manage the trade execution. A block broker would then contact its institutional clients to see if anyone was interested in selling a large chunk of Microsoft stock, and more often than not would find a few counterparties. In this case, the price may be more tolerable (perhaps 27.25), but we will have to pay the broker a hefty commission.

A more modern way of executing block trades is to turn to one of the *crossing networks*; these are effectively ECNs that specialize in block trades. The most popular crossing networks in the United States are POSIT, Liquidnet, and Pipeline, but more and more competitors are entering this space. What crossing networks do is collect large buy and sell orders from their customers; instead of trying to match them up instantly, as an exchange would do, they attempt to accumulate these orders over time and then periodically (a few times a day, or just once at the market close) conduct a *crossing session*, where all buys are crossed with all sells at a single crossing price. The crossing price is determined elsewhere; it can be the exchange closing price (which is what the NYSE uses during its after-hours crossing session) or some average of exchange bids and offers at some point in time right before the crossing session (which is what POSIT uses).

This way, both buy and sell traders avoid the market impact of their orders, but they have to pay a trading fee to the crossing network, and they run the risk that they will wait a whole day and their orders will not get executed at all.

Another modern approach to block orders is called *algorithmic trading*. Our definition of a block trade says that it is a trade that cannot be easily and instantly executed on the exchange, but it does not say that the trade cannot be executed there at all. In our Microsoft example, over the course of a typical trading day, the exchange will trade almost a hundred times more shares of MSFT than we want. There must be a way for us to tap into that liquidity; we just have to work at it. Instead of trying to execute the whole order in one shot, we can split the block order into many smaller chunks and execute them sequentially, so that each trade we do has little or no market impact. This way, we minimize market impact, but we expose ourselves to *time risk*: since it is going to take us a while to execute all of those chunks, the market can move against us while we are doing that. This basic tension between market impact risk and time risk makes such parceling of block orders a highly nontrivial problem, and many of the best quantitative minds on Wall Street are currently struggling with it because a lot of money is at stake, even by Wall Street standards.

Qualitatively, the problem is easy to understand: if we try to execute the order all at once, we will move the market a lot; if we stretch it out over the whole day, we completely lose control over the execution price, as the market can drift far, far away from where it was when we received the block order. As we begin to split the order into pieces and allow more time for their execution, we will at some point find the sweet spot that makes our *execution strategy* optimal, with not too much market impact, but still completing the order within a reasonable time. Translating this hand-waving argument into an actual execution strategy that has an algorithm for splitting the order and executing each piece of it is what algorithmic trading is all about.

There is no single right way to do this, and algorithmic strategies differ greatly in how they approach the problem, but most of them take into consideration at least some of the following factors: (1) the size of the order relative to the average daily volume and the trading volume observed over the last few hours or so, (2) market conditions (price volatility and directionality of price movements), (3) the instantaneous composition of the order book, in particular, how the book is distributed between the bid and offer sides and how the orders are distributed across different price points, and (4) what is happening to the market as a whole and to similar stocks (we may want to get a tad more aggressive in buying MSFT if Cisco stock just shot up). There is a whole spectrum of different algorithmic strategies that emphasize different pieces of this puzzle and that are appropriate for different market conditions.

Sell-side banks now routinely offer algorithmic trading strategies to their institutional clients as a service that is usually called *AES* (this acronym is much more stable than the underlying name, where the last two letters always stand for execution services, but the first A can mean algorithmic, automatic, or advanced). Clients that use AES are given an order entry screen where they can type in how much and what they are buying or selling, then select from a menu of available AES strategies, hit Go, and watch the strategy execute their order in the market. Typically the clients can also specify some constraints for each execution strategy (for example, do not exceed 30 percent of the total volume and complete the trade in no more than four hours). Developing and selling AES services has become a very lucrative business for the sell-side banks (the clients are charged hefty commissions for the use of these services, but it is much cheaper for the bank to run an algorithmic strategy than to have a human broker do it)—it is growing at a furious pace (over 200 percent in 2005) and attracts a lot of quantitative talent.

The users of AES naturally want to know if they are getting a good deal by executing their orders through this fancy mechanism, and AES systems routinely provide them with some measures of execution quality known as *execution benchmarks*. Measuring the quality of execution is also a nontrivial problem; if a user's order was executed in, say, 200 individual trades at different prices, does she compare the average price she got with the closing price, with the opening price, with the market price at the time she submitted the order, or with something entirely different? Clearly, comparing it with a snapshot of market prices at any particular point in time does not make much sense in this case; one has to use some price measure that is spread out over time in a way similar to the way in which execution is spread out.

A standard benchmark that has emerged in this space is called *VWAP* (volume-weighted average price, pronounced "vee-wap"). A VWAP of a stock over a given time period (usually the whole trading day) is just what the name implies: we take the price of every trade done within the averaging period, multiply it by the size of that trade, total up these products, and then divide by the total size traded. VWAP captures something that even an old-school fund manager can understand: the price at which an average share got executed. If our buy order was executed at a price below VWAP, we got a better deal than an average trader; if it's worse than VWAP, an average trader did better than we did. It is also very easy for market participants to calculate, as the trade data are available to everybody (all exchanges, as well as data providers such as Bloomberg, report VWAP for all actively traded stocks at the close as well as for hourly or even 30-minute periods during the day).

There are, of course, alternative similar measures, such as C-VWAP (competitive VWAP), calculated by Nasdaq (this attempts to exclude small trades), but straight VWAP is the standard; all AES strategies specify how their average price compares to VWAP as part of the execution report provided to the customer. In fact, one of the most popular AES strategies simply guarantees that our order is executed at the VWAP price (and is therefore called a VWAP strategy); this price is, of course, unknown at the beginning of the averaging period, but once the period ends, the AES provider fills our whole order at VWAP. (Providers try to execute the order during the averaging period and, if they are any good, get a better price for themselves, but if the price they got is worse than VWAP, they have to eat the loss.)

STOCK INDICES

So far our discussion has been on the level of an individual stock, but one of the defining features of equity markets is that there are just so many of those stocks—2,800 NYSE-listed stocks, 4,800 Nasdaq stocks, and more than 3,000 stocks on the OTC Bulletin Board (these are the so-called penny stocks that do not qualify for Nasdaq listing) in the United States alone; 2,800 on the LSE; 2,300 on EuroNext; over 5,000 on German exchanges; about 3,000 in Japan; and over 2,000 in the rest of Asia. This introduces a new level of complexity; unlike government bonds, which are on some level all the same, each of these equity securities is as unique as the company it represents.

Keeping track of all of these securities and trying to find attractive investment opportunities among the multitude is absolutely out of reach for an individual investor because of the sheer size of the task. Poring over the data, rumors, and trading history of individual stocks is the job of Wall Street stock analysts. We will take a closer look at their work in Chapter 17, but here we just note that what stock analysts do is taken for granted these days—

we fully expect that someone will have written a well-researched piece about any stock we may consider buying—but it was not always this way.

The man who almost single-handedly created stock research was one Charles Dow, an American journalist, who in 1883 started publishing *Customer's Afternoon Letter* (which was renamed the *Wall Street Journal* six years later). In this brief daily newsletter, Dow started presenting investing information that was impossible for an average investor to come by in those days—not just stock quotations, but also financial data about the companies, analysis of their business prospects, and so on. For nearly half a century, up until the bout of financial regulation following the Great Depression mandated the disclosure of such data, the *Wall Street Journal* remained almost the only source of reliable stock market advice and helped establish the standards for stock research.

While the main focus of Dow's publication was giving investors reliable opinions about individual stocks, he almost immediately felt the need to present his readers with some simple metric that reflected the performance of the stock market (which in those days meant the NYSE) as a whole, so (right after inventing stock research) he came up with another seminal stock market concept: the idea of a *stock index*. He published the world's first stock index (called the Dow Jones Index) in July 1884; this average contained mostly railroad stocks (which were the dot-coms of the day), and it took Dow until 1896 to come up with the *Dow Jones Industrial Average* (DJIA), which is still with us today in a big way. It is incredible that one man could invent not one, not two, but three of the main ideas underpinning financial markets today (Dow is also credited with creating the *Dow theory*, the foundation for *technical analysis*, which we discuss in Chapter 17), not to mention creating a thriving Dow Jones business empire (some people are more talented than others, are they not?). But I digress—back to Mr. Dow's second invention, stock indices.

Dow's first indices were almost comical in their simplicity: he selected 11 stocks for his Dow Jones Index, added up their prices, and divided by 11, so the resulting index value was really a simple price average. It did its job just fine, capturing the overall movement of the market in a simple, easy-to-understand number. From the investment point of view, the Dow Jones Index (and the later Dow Jones Industrial Average, which worked the same way) measured the price performance of a portfolio consisting of one share of each stock in the index. This "average" approach worked for a while, until one of the index components decided to do a stock split—its price went down by a factor of 2, so if Dow had done nothing, the index would have dropped markedly even though the market had not really moved. So he made an adjustment for this: he doubled the weight of this company in the average to bring the index back to where it was before the stock split. This adjustment mirrored what would have happened to our index portfolio with one share of everything—if one of those shares split in two, we would have to count its price twice from that point on.

As time went by, all the index components began to acquire such multipliers as a result of stock splits, stock dividends, and other corporate actions, and the index lost its original simplicity as an average. In 1928 Dow Jones gave up trying to maintain all these multipliers and switched to a new approach to managing the index, or rather restored the old one, but with a twist. In this methodology, the index value went back to being a simple sum of prices divided by a number called a *divisor*, which is exactly the way Charles Dow constructed the index to begin with, except that the divisor was no longer equal to the number of components, but instead started absorbing all the effects of the corporate actions. If one of the companies split its stock, so that its price went down, the divisor would be adjusted downward so that the index value remained the same. If a company was taken out of the index and replaced by another, again the divisor would be adjusted for the difference in their prices in order to keep the index value unchanged. After almost 80 years of such divisor adjustments (which almost always push it downward because of stock splits), the DJIA divisor has gone down from 30 (the number of stocks in the index) to 0.12.[4]

Today, more than a hundred years after its inception, the DJIA remains the best-known stock market index among the general public. Despite its iconic status in the popular imagination, however, the DJIA is not without problems, and some of them were pointed out very early on. The first problem stems from its price-weighted nature: a $1 move in a component stock that costs $100 has the same effect on the index as a $1 move in a component stock that costs $10, even though in the first case it is a 1 percent change and in the second it is a 10 percent change. The second problem is that, because of its divisor methodology, it is not an *investable* index—you cannot easily replicate its performance by constructing a portfolio of stocks.

---

4. The Dow Jones Indexes Web site, www.djindexes.com/mdsidx/index.cfm?event=showAverages, has a table with the DJIA components and the divisors that I highly recommend as an illustration of this discussion (I tried to reproduce it as a figure here, but could not get Dow Jones to give me permission to use it).

In the 1920s, Dow Jones got its first competitor in the index space; the Standard Statistics Bureau, which later became Standard & Poor's, developed an index that addressed these shortcomings of the Dow averages. The new index (which became known as the S&P 90 and had grown to become the *S&P 500* by the 1950s) was not price-weighted, but instead was weighted by the market capitalization of its component stocks; S&P took each stock's price, multiplied it by the number of shares outstanding (the result is market capitalization, effectively the total market value of the company), added up these market capitalizations for all components in the index, and again divided by a divisor (selected in such a way as to make the index value in 1941—the base period—equal to 10) to get the index value. This market-cap weighting procedure takes care of simple corporate actions like stock splits automatically (both the stock price and the number of shares change in a split, but market cap does not) and makes the index investable—its value is a weighted sum of prices where the weights automatically adjust for corporate actions, so if we buy a portfolio of stocks with these weights and hold it, its price performance will track the index value exactly. Of course, the divisor (and the index portfolio) still has to be adjusted if one company in the index replaces another.

This market-cap weighting approach has become the standard for the great number of new indices that have proliferated since the dawn of the computer era. While the early indices could be maintained with little more than pencil and paper, the newer indices tended to be more *broad-based* and included a much larger universe of stocks, and players old (Dow Jones and S&P) and new (Wilshire and Russell) started leveraging computer technology to develop and maintain a snowballing number of equity indices. In the 1970s, Wilshire Associates introduced an index that included almost 5,000 stocks, and this still remains the broadest measure of the performance of the market for all U.S. equities (and if you are interested in the performance of smaller companies, you can use the Wilshire 4500, which is the Wilshire 5000 less the 500 stocks in the S&P 500). There are also indices that select only the middle tier of companies in terms of market capitalization (such as S&P Mid-Cap 400) and, of course, a lot of international indices that aggregate stocks by country and by market cap within a country. There are also indices that separate companies into value stocks (with low P/E ratios; they look like good value) and growth stocks (which have high growth prospects according to some criteria); these are called *style indices* because they correspond to the two textbook investment styles, value investing and growth investing.

Maintaining all these indices is no small task. Index companies have to collect all the prices and the information about outstanding shares for thousands of companies every day to compute the index values, make adjustments to the divisors when necessary, calculate the total return on each index by adding dividend information to the price change information, and then disseminate the index data to interested parties. These index companies do not do this out of love of number crunching; there is robust demand for index data from the community of investment managers.

As the mutual fund industry began to develop in the 1950s, equity indices turned from an investor education tool into something that was absolutely central to this industry's operation. You would think that if someone manages an investment fund and her investment decisions were such that the fund made money this year, then she's been doing a good job this year, and if the fund lost money, then the opposite is true. The fund managers, however, gradually became unwilling to measure their performance by this straightforward yardstick. Their argument was that if they invested in equities and the whole equity market went down 10 percent this year, there's no way their investment picks could make money, and if they managed to lose less than the overall market, say 8 percent, then they were doing a good job.

But who said the overall market went down 10 percent? That's where the equity indices came in very handy: they filled the acutely felt need for independent and objective benchmarks against which fund managers' performance could be measured. At present, a typical equity investment fund declares in its prospectus which index it is trying to outperform: if the fund intends to invest in large U.S. companies, then the appropriate index would perhaps be the S&P 500; if small-cap companies are what the fund wants to invest in, it would pick one of the several available small-cap indices. Furthermore, if the fund wanted to invest in small-cap energy-sector companies or something equally specific and could not find an existing index that mirrored its investment preferences, the index data providers would happily develop an index if there were enough demand—this is how the family of indices grows.

If we are a fund manager who is trying to beat a particular index, we may want to start by *replicating* that index—buying every company in the index in the correct proportion. Once our money is invested this way, we can then begin to exercise our stock-picking prowess by selling the stocks we think are going to do worse than the index average and buying those that we think will do better. How much tweaking we do is up to us, but in aggregate we typically end up investing the bulk of our fund in our benchmark index; that is why it is very important that the index be investable (i.e., that there is a portfolio of stocks whose performance is identical to that of the index).

Some indices are more investable than others; this is the reason for the success of the Russell indices, which in the 1980s introduced an important improvement to the standard market-cap weighting methodology called the *float adjustment*. Let us say that a company has 10 million shares outstanding, but 6 million of those shares are held by the company's insiders or corporate partners (when two companies own a significant chunk of each other's shares, it is called *cross-holding*, and a surprisingly large proportion of equities is held this way), so there are really only 4 million shares available for public investors. Russell argued that it is really this *investable float* of 4 million shares that should be used as the weight in an index, not the full 10 million that would be assigned by the standard market-cap weighting procedure. It constructed all its indices this way, and this methodology (and the Russell indices) got a wide following among fund managers, who found that without this float adjustment, too much money ends up chasing too few shares, whereas investing in a float-adjusted index distributes the transaction costs more realistically (other index providers have also moved toward this method in recent years).

The fact that so much money (the U.S. mutual funds industry has about $7 trillion under management) is effectively invested in index-replicating portfolios of stocks turns *index rebalancing* into a major market event. Take the Russell indices as an example; once a year, in July, Russell updates the composition of its indices by dropping companies whose market caps have declined, adding the new up-and-coming companies, and adjusting the weights of all stocks in the index to reflect the changes in the index composition. This rebalancing process may sound like a trivial housekeeping task, but look at it from the perspective of the mutual fund managers who use one of the Russell indices as a benchmark. If our portfolio tracked the "old" index and now the index composition has changed, we have to do some trading to reflect those changes: buy the stocks that have been added to the index, sell those that have been dropped, and adjust the holdings of everything else. With an index of 2,000 or 3,000 names, that's quite a lot of trading that has to be done, and this makes index rebalancing days quite challenging—the trading volume goes way up, the prices of the affected stocks move dramatically, and the worst thing is that everybody is trying to do the same set of trades, which exacerbates both volatility and execution costs. Or look at it from the perspective of a company that has been dropped from a major index: many if not all of the mutual funds that are holding the company' stock will have to sell it, with a predictably devastating effect on the stock price. Either way, changes in index composition have become a major equity-market driver, and this trend is only getting stronger.

Another factor behind the increasing importance of indices for the equity markets has been the emergence of *index products*, which are financial products (things that we can buy and sell) whose value is tied directly to an equity index. Remember how we described the activities of a typical equity fund manager as first buying the index portfolio and then trying to improve upon it by picking good stocks? It is not unreasonable to ask whether this stock picking actually works, and the answer to this question has been well known since the early 1970s: however devastating this may sound for the fund managers, the average mutual fund fails to outperform its index, so the investors in an average fund would be better off if the manager just bought the index and never touched the resulting portfolio. Interestingly, this is not because the fund managers are not good at picking stocks; it is largely because of the transaction costs of trading in and out of a lot of stocks (the asset management fees charged by the managers themselves also do not improve the returns).

As the evidence of the ultimate futility of trying to beat the market accumulated, the mutual funds industry decided to give investors the option of simply joining it. John C. Bogle, the founder of Vanguard, created the first *index fund* in 1975, which simply replicated the returns of the S&P 500. The market for index funds has grown by leaps and bounds ever since, helped by the much lower fees that these funds charge compared with the more traditional *managed funds* (note that the index funds also require some management to deal with index rebalancing).

The emergence of index funds was a major, if not the main, factor in the growing importance of indices in equity markets. One limitation of index funds was that, like all mutual funds, their shares could be traded only once a day, at the market's close. The next generation of index products that appeared in the 1980s, the *index futures*, removed this constraint. We will deal with index futures in the next chapter; here we just state that these are products traded on an exchange in real time whose dollar value is by construction proportional to the underlying index value. These products became convenient proxies for buying or selling the whole index-replicating portfolios of stocks, and a few of these new-fangled index futures have grown to be some of the most liquid securities anywhere in the space of just a few years.

Why not trade index funds on an exchange? This idea was pioneered by the AMEX and was first implemented in 1993, when the AMEX received SEC approval to trade Standard & Poor's Depositary Receipts (SPDR), which later became known as Spiders. These securities are effectively shares of specially constructed index funds replicating various S&P indices. We can do everything with Spiders that we can do with stocks—buy and sell them on an exchange (AMEX), borrow them and sell them short (they are even exempt from the *uptick rule*, which allows short sales of stocks only when the price moves up)—and we also get all the diversification benefits of an index fund, so these products quickly became very popular, and other such *exchange-traded funds*, or *ETFs*, have literally flooded the market in the last few years. The AMEX still trades most of the ETFs, but they have spread to Nasdaq and the NYSE, and many fund companies (major players are BGI, with its iShares family of funds; Merrill Lynch, with its HOLDR products; State Street, with StreetTRAKs; Vanguard, with VIPERS; and many more) compete with one another by issuing more and more new exchange-traded fund products.

Among the most popular ETFs, along with the Spiders, are the Qubes (an ETF with ticker symbol QQQQ that tracks the Nasdaq 100 index) and the Diamonds (which track the DJIA and have the symbol DIA), but there are over a hundred other ETFs that track almost every index, and the idea of ETFs has already spread beyond equities to fixed-income and commodity funds. ETFs are a big hit with individual investors, they generate a lot of income for the mutual fund companies, the exchanges love them because of the trading fees they bring in, and the sell-side banks and other market makers now generate a lot of revenues by trading ETFs, so everyone is happy,[5] and the future of ETFs looks extremely bright.

The existence of such exchange-traded index products also made something called *index arbitrage* possible. This term refers to a trading strategy in which we keep comparing the real-time price of an index product with the total price at which we can buy an index-replicating portfolio of stocks. Since the index products trade independently of the underlying stocks, their prices do not have to be the same, and if there is a significant difference between an index futures price and the price of a replicating portfolio, we buy one and sell the other, then wait until the prices converge, which guarantees us a profit. Index arbitrage is the mechanism that forces the real-time

5. It must be the individual investors that are actually paying for this bonanza, but the way they do it is not obvious to them—this, more than anything else, makes ETFs a truly brilliant financial innovation.

price of an exchange-traded product to be very closely tied to the underlying stock market. We'll talk about this in more detail in the next chapter; here I just want to point out that to do index arbitrage at all, we have to be able to buy and sell portfolios that contain large number of stocks very quickly, and that led to the emergence of another 1980s stock market innovation: *program trading.*

Initially the term *program trading* referred to a type of trading in which large number of buy and sell orders were generated by a computer program and sent to the exchange simultaneously. In the 1980s, the computers generated order tickets for such multisecurity trades, but those tickets still had to be executed by hand on the exchange floor. The floor brokers and traders viewed these computer-generated orders with great suspicion and were quick to put much of the blame for the October 1987 crash on the proliferation of program trading. This led the NYSE and other exchanges to introduce certain restrictions on such trades and compile statistics about how many such trades are being done (we reproduce an NYSE program trading report in Figure 6–6).

The NYSE defines a program trade as a *basket order* for more than 15 stocks with a total value of more than $1 million, and as we can see in Figure 6–6, today almost 60 percent of all the flow it receives falls into this category. Index arbitrage remains a robust but not dominant source of program trading, but these days people do a lot of basket trades for many other reasons. In general, this term may have outlived its usefulness—almost every trade today is a program trade in the original sense of the word because computers are involved in the generation and submission (and often also the execution) of pretty much every order, so maybe calling these trades basket trades would be more accurate.

EQUITIES TRADING

Figure 6–6 also gives us a handy list of the equity market players that are responsible for the bulk of the trading volume, and of course we recognize these as the large sell-side banks that dominate the Treasury market (and every other market, for that matter). These banks also employ the vast majority of the quantitative and technical people involved in equity markets, so it makes good sense for us to discuss how equities business is organized at these companies.

Equities trading is typically segregated from trading in fixed-income securities and commodities—each of these banks has an *equities division*

FIGURE 6-6

A sample program trading report from NYSE (it issues such a report every week, available from its Web site, www.nyse.com). Reproduced by permission from the NYSE.

PROGRAM TRADING PURCHASES AND SALES

December 12 - December 16, 2005

TRADING ON NYSE (AVERAGE DAILY - MILLIONS)	CURRENT WEEK	PREVIOUS 52 WEEK AVERAGE[1]
TOTAL NYSE VOLUME[+]	1,793.7	1,770.8
TOTAL PROGRAMS	1,175.0	1,169.0
BUY PROGRAMS	604.8	583.4
SELL PROGRAMS	570.2	585.6

PROGRAM TRADING AS % OF TOTAL NYSE VOLUME	65.5% 66.0%

TRADING BY EXECUTING MARKET (PERCENT)	CURRENT WEEK	PREVIOUS 52 WEEK AVERAGE[1]
NYSE	53.5%	59.5%
NON-U.S. MARKETS+	3.3%	3.3%
OTHER DOMESTIC	43.2%	37.3%

QUARTERLY EXPIRATION

+Does not include program trading activity by non-U.S. subsidiaries of NYSE member firms.

TOTAL: AVERAGE DAILY - MILLIONS OF SHARES		
	2,194.8	1,958.9

NYSE PROGRAM TRADING - 15 MOST ACTIVE MEMBER FIRMS
(MILLIONS OF SHARES)

	INDEX ARBITRAGE	OTHER STRATEGIES SUBJECT TO RULE 80A(c)[**]	ALL OTHER STRATEGIES	TOTAL	PRINCIPAL	CUSTOMER FACILITATION	AGENCY
UBS Securities, LLC.	-	-	654.6	654.6	538.4	-	116.3
Goldman, Sachs & Co.	5.9	-	635.6	641.5	218.8	90.6	332.0
Credit Suisse First Boston	133.4	-	504.1	637.5	407.7	9.5	220.4
Morgan Stanley & Co. Inc.	6.3	0.4	628.0	634.7	241.2	5.3	388.2
Deutsche Bank Securities	127.9	-	472.0	599.9	47.1	64.2	488.6
Lehman Brothers, Inc.	39.1	-	466.9	506.0	204.3	5.2	296.5
Banc of America Securities LLC	0.6	-	415.9	416.5	109.1	131.2	176.2
Merrill Lynch, Pierce, Fenner, & Smith, Inc.	-	-	412.9	412.9	145.6	53.6	213.7
RBC Capital Markets Corp.	145.9	-	78.2	224.1	-	-	224.1
Bear Stearns	15.0	-	146.1	161.1	28.5	1.2	131.4
Citigroup Global Markets	-	-	139.6	139.6	35.6	43.2	60.7
Calyon Securities (USA) Inc.	10.9	-	118.7	129.6	1.4	-	128.1
Nomura Securities International Inc.	55.1	-	61.8	116.9	94.0	4.6	18.4
JP Morgan Securities, Inc.	-	-	94.7	94.7	53.7	0.4	40.7
BNP Paribas Brokerage Services Corp	2.0	-	83.6	85.6	2.2	-	83.4
TOTAL FOR 15 MEMBER FIRMS	542.1	0.4	4,912.7	5,455.2	2,127.6	409.0	2,918.7
TOTAL FOR ALL FIRMS REPORTING	621.5	0.4	5,252.9	5,874.8	2,213.7	409.1	3,252.0
% OF TOTAL	10.6%	0.0%	89.4%	100.0%	37.7%	7.0%	55.4%
% - AVERAGE (PREVIOUS 52 WEEKS)[*]	11.5%		88.5%	100.0%	40.5%	8.7%	50.9%

NYSE Research
December 2005

+ Total NYSE official volume, including Crossing Session II
[1] Average is previous 52 week rolling average. For non-expiration weeks this includes 40 non-expiration weeks; for monthly expirations this includes 8 monthly-expiration weeks;
for quarterly expirations this includes only 4 quarterly expiration weeks. Totals may not sum exactly due to rounding.
** See Appendix.

Note 1: NYSE program trading totals include purchases and sales during regular trading hours as well as during Crossing Sessions II and IV.
Note 2: Program Trading Totals in this report were compiled from member submissions through December 21. Subsequent changes to these data may occur.

that focuses on equity markets. This division is further subdivided into broad business lines, such as cash equities and equity derivatives. The cash equities business basically does what we have talked about in this chapter—it trades stocks, both for the firm's own account (this is called the *principal* business because the firm is acting as a principal in a customer-initiated trade) or on behalf of its buy-side customers (this is called either *agency* trading, where the firm is acting as an agent of a customer, executes the trade on an exchange somewhere, and earns commissions, or *customer facilitation*, where the firm helps its customers execute block trades). In addition to these businesses (whose contribution to the total volume is tabulated in Figure 6–6), there are also typically a market-making business, where the firm makes markets in Nasdaq stocks, and a proprietary trading business, where the firm basically uses its own capital to speculate in the equities market (the index arbitrage desk is often a separate business, but it can also be part of this proprietary trading business).

Each of these businesses has one or several trading desks, each with anywhere from a couple to a couple of dozen traders. Each trader usually specializes in a particular market sector, sometimes in just a single actively traded stock, so that staying on top of all the news, rumors, trading patterns, and order flow for all the stocks in the sector is still humanly possible. Armed with all this information, the traders face the flow of orders generated by the firm's sales force and/or electronic trading systems. On some desks, traders have discretion over whether a customer order is executed internally (in which case the resulting trade goes into the firm's books) or externally (in which case the order is routed to an external exchange and the firm earns commissions). Note that proprietary traders, unlike *flow traders*, who have to deal with customer order flow, have the luxury of trading when they want to, so their job is somewhat less grueling, but they have to pay the bid-offer spread for that privilege of initiating transactions.

EQUITY-MARKET RISK

At the end of the day, the job of an equities trader is the same as the job of any other trader: to keep the PnL of his books positive and growing. As we discussed in the previous chapter, a large part of that job is understanding the risks to the book's PnL and being able to hedge them appropriately. To see how people think about risk in the equities trading world, it is helpful to recall our discussion of fixed-income risk in the previous chapter. In the fixed-income world, one can easily define the risk factors: the prices of a handful of very liquid instruments, such as on-the-runs and futures, that drive the price changes of everything else.

The degree of correlation between these risk factors and the prices of individual fixed-income instruments such as Treasury bonds is very high, and so, if we hedge our portfolio by buying and selling the appropriate number of these liquid instruments, we can eliminate most of the price risk. The reason all fixed-income products are so strongly correlated is that they all essentially represent sets of future cash flows and differ only in how these cash flows are spread over time, so there is a lot of inherent similarity between any two Treasury bonds, for example. This is demonstrably not so in the equities world; fundamentally, we would expect that there should be very little in common between the price performance of MSFT and, say, Merck, as the two companies have completely different business models, growth prospects, and financials.

Nevertheless, the main idea of the standard approach to equity-market risk (which is known as the *market model*) is that the prices of both stocks (and, in fact, of all stocks) should to some extent follow the behavior of the market as a whole (as captured, of course, by one of the indices we have talked about so extensively). The market model postulates that the return on every stock can be represented as a linear regression on the returns of the market. We illustrate this approach in Figure 6–7, where we regress the monthly returns of MSFT against the monthly returns of the Nasdaq 100 index.

The straight regression line on this figure is called the Security Market Line, or SML, and the coefficients in its linear equation are the central concepts of any discussion of equity risk. The slope of the SML is called the *beta* of a stock (0.82 in our example); it indicates that, on average, for every 1 percent change in the Nasdaq 100, the price of MSFT will change by 0.82 percent in the same direction. At first blush, beta looks very much like the hedge factors we discussed in the fixed-income context, but it is not; because it is computed in the returns space rather than the price space, one has to adjust for the relative pricing of the stock and the index instrument used for hedging. For example, if we want to sell some QQQ index funds (currently priced at \$40) to hedge the market exposure of MSFT (currently priced at \$27), and we know that the beta is 0.82, a \$1 change in the QQQs will cause $0.82 \times {}^{27}\!/_{40} = 55$ cents change in the price of MSFT, so if we sell 55 shares of QQQ for every 100 shares of MSFT we hold, the resulting portfolio will have no exposure to the market.

FIGURE 6–7

Market model–the regression of MSFT monthly returns since 1990 against the monthly returns on NDS (Nasdaq 100 index). The regression line (known as the security market line in the market model) has a slope that is called beta (0.82 in this example) and an intercept (0.53 percent) that is called alpha. The R squared of the regression is 0.48. Data taken from Yahoo! Finance (finance.yahoo.com).

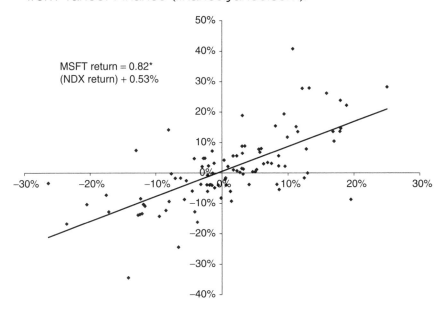

The market model may be good enough for the academics, but, as Figure 6–7 makes clear, it is a very naïve approximation of what is actually going on—the regression in Figure 6–7 captures only about 50 percent of the variability in MSFT returns. Of course, this regression has only one factor (the Nasdaq 100 index), and it is likely that its quality would improve if we introduced more factors. What could these factors be?

We could use more indices that attempt to match what MSFT stands for more closely; for example, Microsoft is both a large company (and thus belongs to the S&P 500 index) and a technology company (and thus can be measured against the Nasdaq indices). If we use a broad market index and a sector index that captures behavior common to the whole industry sector, the regression improves somewhat, and, of course, the more indices we throw in, the better it gets, up to a point. The leading equity risk model from a company called BARRA uses no fewer than 13 market and sector factors to describe the returns of U.S. stocks (moreover, it has 13 more nontradable factors like company size, volatility, earnings growth, and the like that make the regression even better). These full-blown multifactor models can produce hedge factors for a large variety of stocks. However, in practice, each individual trader who trades a fairly small selection of similar stocks often simply relies on their betas against one or at most two appropriately selected indices to hedge her books.

So now we know what betas in the market model regression are used for—what about the other coefficient (0.53 percent in Figure 6–7), which is appropriately called *alpha*? The story of alpha is in many ways even less plausible than that of beta. Where beta measures the sensitivity of our portfolio to market drivers and is thus mostly used for hedging by the flow traders, alpha measures the *excess return* of a portfolio over a market index and is thus of great interest to those who put portfolios together: fund managers at buy-side companies and proprietary traders at sell-side banks and elsewhere. If we are a fund manager and we put together a portfolio with an alpha of 10 percent against our market index, we've done well—we are beating our index by 10 percent.

The actual usage of the alpha concept is in reality quite holistic; nobody believes that he can beat the market by doing lots of linear regressions and picking stocks with high intercepts, but whatever he does to get the excess returns is often expressed in terms of alpha, so the term has acquired an almost mythical status as the holy grail of proprietary trading. When we hear a prop trader talking about "sources of alpha" in his trading strategies, we should know that he is referring to whatever market inefficiencies he is trying to exploit, not to the regression coefficients.

Equity markets have gone through and are continuing to go through a period of unprecedented change, much of it driven by developments in technology, and they continue to attract a large number of quantitative and technical people. Based on our discussion in this chapter, their main areas of activity are electronic trading and related modeling and technological issues such as AES (we review some of the technical challenges in this area in Chapter 15), stock research and valuation methodologies (Chapter 17), and equity risk modeling. Equity markets are also inseparable from the options markets, which we discuss in Chapter 9, and the futures markets, which are the topic of the next chapter. Onward, then, to the futures.

CHAPTER 7

Financial Futures

Futures trading is one of the more colorful areas of the global financial system. It evokes images of pit traders frantically shouting at each other, fortunes being made and lost in a speculative frenzy, shady deals, and smoke-filled rooms. It is also one of the most important and at the same time one of the least understood areas of finance. In this chapter we will focus on financial futures, which underpin almost everything else in capital markets, but in order to tell their story, we will also have to discuss the history, organization, and functioning of the futures markets in general.

DEVELOPMENT OF THE FUTURES MARKETS

Futures (unlike stocks and bonds, which originated in Europe centuries ago) are a distinctly American invention, and a fairly recent one, dating back only to the 1860s. In a certain sense, they were brought to life by the political geography of the United States in the nineteenth century. In 1850, the eastern seaboard contained well over 80 percent of the U.S. population, but most of the agricultural commodities that this population needed were produced elsewhere—in the Midwest (grains and cattle) and the South (cotton). Grain from the midwestern states and territories was first shipped down the Mississippi to New Orleans and from there by sea to the East Coast. In the 1830s, the Erie Canal made it possible to ship grain through the Great Lakes, and the city of Chicago was born on the shores of Lake Michigan as a hub of this grain trade. Soon thereafter, the railroads made the Great Lakes route less important, but Chicago retained its grain hub status.

While grain flowed from the Midwest to the East, money had to flow the other way. Financing the grain trade was a complicated and often quite risky business. Merchants on the East Coast effectively had to advance money to grain dealers in the Midwest to purchase grain months before it was actually grown, harvested, and brought to market. If the harvest was unusually good (or bad), the price of the grain could end up being very different from what had been assumed months ago, and various intermediaries in the process had a very strong incentive to profit from this discrepancy by refusing to honor prior commitments. As the volumes of grain trade grew, the need for a better financing system became increasingly apparent.

One major weakness of the existing system was a lack of standardization, and the first task of the *commodity exchanges* that began to form in the 1840s in the Midwest was to define various types, or grades, of grain to make it *fungible*, so that someone purchasing, say, No. 2 Northern Spring Wheat knew exactly what he was getting, regardless of which individual farmer or grain elevator the wheat came from. One of these early exchanges was the Board of Trade of the City of Chicago, which was formed in 1848 and is now known as the *Chicago Board of Trade* (CBOT or CBT). It began its long and illustrious history by establishing a system for weighing, inspecting, and certifying grain shipments passing through the port of Chicago.

Initially the board was little more than a meeting place where members could discuss matters of local interest, resolve contract disputes, and have lunch (often provided for free to boost attendance), but over time its members became increasingly involved with the actual trading of grain. The trades they did with various grain merchants were known as *forward contracts*; such a contract specifies when, where, what type, and how much grain is to be delivered by the merchant, and how much he would be paid for it upon delivery. These contracts could be bought and sold prior to the delivery date; however, the market was quite thin, as it was difficult to find another trader that needed exactly the same quantity, quality, time, and place of delivery. CBOT began standardizing various aspects of these contracts in the late 1850s, and by 1865 it had developed something pretty close to what is still traded on CBOT today: the wheat *futures* contract. We reproduce today's CBOT wheat contract specification in Figure 7–1.

The contract shown in Figure 7–1 standardizes all aspects of the contract settlement process except one: the price. It describes in rather precise terms the *underlying commodity* that is to be delivered under the contract: the quantity, the quality (by listing specific grades), delivery times (any time

FIGURE 7-1

CBOT wheat futures contract specification from CBOT Web site (www.cbot.com). Reproduced with permission.

Wheat Futures

Contract Size
5,000 bu

Deliverable Grades
No. 1 & No. 2 Soft Red, No. 1 & No. 2 Hard Red Winter, No. 1 & No. 2 Dark Northern Spring, No. 1 Northern Spring at 3 cent/bushel premium and No. 2 Northern Spring at par. Substitutions at differentials established by the exchange.

Tick Size
1/4 cent/bu ($12.50/contract)

Price Quote
Cents and quarter-cents/bu

Contract Months
Jul, Sep, Dec, Mar, May

Last Trading Day
The business day prior to the 15th calendar day of the contract month.

Last Delivery Day
Seventh business day following the last trading day of the delivery month.

Trading Hours
Open Auction: 9:30 a.m. - 1:15 p.m. Central Time, Mon-Fri. Electronic: 7:32 p.m. - 6:00 a.m. Central Time, Sun.-Fri. Trading in expiring contracts closes at noon on the last trading day.

Ticker Symbols
Open Auction: W Electronic: ZW

Daily Price Limit
30 cents/bu ($1,500/contract) above or below the previous day's settlement price. No limit in the spot month (limits are lifted two business days before the spot month begins).

within the *contract month* up until the last delivery day), and delivery locations (which are not shown in Figure 7-1 but are described in the exchange *rulebook*). Equally important, it also regulates all important aspects of the trading process, such as trading hours, the way prices are quoted, minimum price movement (tick size), and maximum daily price shifts that trigger suspension of trading.

Note that the contract offers some leeway in both the time of delivery and the exact type of wheat that can be delivered. This is intentional; the futures contract is designed to appeal to as many traders as possible, so that almost anyone who wishes to trade grain for delivery sometime in, say, July would be likely to prefer to trade July wheat futures instead of negotiating a specific forward contract with another trader (who might or might not be there at settlement time). By forcing large number of traders to transact in a single futures contract instead of a myriad of individually negotiated forward contracts, the exchange makes it quite easy to find both buyers and sellers—the increased liquidity more than makes up for the reduced delivery choices.

Let us look at the life cycle of a futures contract in more detail. Suppose that on June 15, one trader on the floor of the exchange sells another one July wheat futures contract at a price of 90 cents a bushel. Further, assume that neither of the traders had any prior position in that contract; in this case, this transaction creates a new instance of this futures contract on the fly. One trader is now long one contract (he is now *the long*), the other is short one contract (*the short*), and the total number of such contracts in existence (known as the *open interest*) went up by one. Note carefully that at this time, *no money changes hands*.

On July 1 (the first day of the delivery month), the underlying wheat can be bought at 70 cents a bushel. The short can now fulfill his delivery obligation by buying 5,000 bushels of wheat at 70 cents (for a total of $3,500) and delivering it to the long, who will then pay the short 90 cents a bushel under the contract (or a total of $4,500). What is the net economic result of this activity? The long has paid $4,500 for wheat that can be sold only for $3,500, so the long has lost $1,000, while the short has gained the same amount.

Note that if the long has no interest in the actual physical wheat, the two traders can dispense with the delivery process altogether. They can cancel out their mutual obligations as follows: the long pays the short 90 cents a bushel (the original transaction price), while the short pays the long 70 cents a bushel (the offsetting transaction price, equal in this case to the price of the underlying), so the long loses $1,000 and the short gains $1,000, just as if the delivery had taken place. In this *closeout* process, the long and short positions simply annihilate each other; the total number of outstanding futures contracts (the *open interest*) goes down by one, and nobody touches the underlying wheat. It is often said that futures allows you to trade the *price* of a commodity separately from the commodity itself, which is as good a definition of a *financial derivative* as I ever came across. Today, over 99 percent of all futures contracts end by closing out the positions rather than in actual delivery.

In the early days of futures trading, futures contracts were settled between individual exchange members in the manner just described. This model, however, scales poorly with the number of traders and, more importantly, is open to credit risk, as individual traders can default on their obligations. The next major innovation in the history of futures trading, the clearinghouse, largely resolved these settlement issues. Clearinghouses began to develop in the 1880s, but it took a few decades for them to take their modern form (CBOT did not have a mandatory clearing system until 1925).

The first function of the exchange clearinghouse is to act as counterparty to every futures trade—a seller to all buyers and a buyer to all sellers. Every trade done on the exchange floor between Exchange Members A and B is split in two: in one of these trades, Exchange Member A buys X futures contracts from the clearinghouse; in the other, the clearinghouse buys X contracts from Member B at the same price. When it is time for the members to close out their positions, they settle the trades with the clearinghouse (which is always there), not with each other.

Note that by construction the net position of the clearinghouse itself in any futures contract is always zero. This reflects a larger simple but powerful truth: futures trading is a zero-sum game. In capital markets (stocks or bonds), if we add up the long and short positions of all the secondary-market players in a particular security, we will get a positive number equal to the outstanding amount of that security. Moreover, the issuer continues to pay interest (or dividends) on that outstanding amount, so that in aggregate there is a flow of money from the issuers to the participants in the secondary market. In the futures market, there is no external issuer (the contracts are always created in long-short pairs), so that the sum of all long and short positions in any contract is always identically zero, and there are no money inflows from outside the market. Therefore anybody's gain on a futures position is always someone else's loss; we have seen that in the example given here, but this is a global conservation law that holds for any futures contract (and, of course, for the futures market in general, since that market can be seen as the sum of the markets for each listed contract type). In the early settlement system just described, these gains or losses remain unrealized until the positions are closed out or delivery takes place. In a modern clearinghouse-based settlement system, these gains and losses are made real at the end of each trading day by a process known as *mark-to-market settlement*.

The clearinghouse maintains accounts for its members (who are usually also members of one or more associated futures exchanges), where all futures trades are recorded after verification, or *clearing*. At the end of each trading day, the clearinghouse *settles* trades done in each account on that day. The essence of mark-to-market settlement consists of determining the value of every futures position relative to its *end-of-day mark*, or the *settlement price* (the equivalent of the closing price for stocks and bonds), which is determined by the exchange at closing time for every contract and is either equal or reasonably close to the last trade price at closing time (Chicago exchanges close at 2 p.m. Central Time, which is 3 p.m. in New York).

After the settlement prices are determined, the clearinghouse goes through every member's account and determines its daily PnL using an exceedingly simple algorithm: the gain or loss on every trade in a given futures contract is its settlement price less the trade price. So if a member bought wheat futures today at 70 cents and the contract settled at 80 cents, the PnL is 10 cents per contract. After doing this for all futures contracts in a member's account, the clearinghouse immediately credits (or debits) the account with the daily PnL. Effectively, the clearinghouse declares that the value of each contract is its settlement price; if someone paid a different price for it, he gets (or pays) the difference in cash. It is easy to see the beauty of this simple process; for example, if the futures position was established before today, it can be viewed as having a trade price equal to yesterday's settlement price because yesterday all positions were revalued, or marked, to that price. All prior trading history becomes irrelevant after the marking process is complete.

According to our zero-sum-game principle, when the clearinghouse has finished debiting and crediting all member accounts with their daily mark-to-market PnL, it should find that the sum of all credits is equal to the sum of all debits; in fact, it merely redistributes the money among members' accounts. However, the cash balance in each individual member's account can and does change, and to prevent it from going negative, the clearinghouse requires each member to *post margin* (also known as a *performance bond*). The *initial margin* is what a member should deposit in his clearinghouse account before he can place his buy or sell order (the margin requirement is, of course, proportional to the number of contracts the member wishes to trade).

If a member's positions made a profit today and his cash balance increased above the initial margin, he is free to withdraw the difference. If he experienced a trading loss today, his cash balance will decrease, and if it falls below the *variation margin* (also known as the *maintenance margin*), the clearinghouse will demand that he deposit more money (this is known as a *margin call*). If he fails to replenish his account within a specified time (usually by the next morning), his positions are liquidated immediately and the clearinghouse absorbs the loss if it is greater than what the member had in his margin account.

The net result of the margin system for the clearinghouse is that it prevents the accumulation of losses, so that in practice nobody can default on a large scale and the exposure of the clearinghouse is limited to (a fraction of) the daily loss of a defaulting trader. For the traders, the main result is never having to worry about a counterparty's defaulting, but there are also two important side effects. One is that what matters in futures trading is the *difference* between the initial and the final price, not the absolute price level—unlike with bond and stock trading, traders never have to pay the full price of a futures contract; they just need to deposit the initial margin to enter a trade. The other feature is that in futures trading, traders realize their gains or losses every day instead of in a big chunk at the end of the trade (we will return to this point in the next chapter when we discuss convexity adjustments).

The margin requirements for each type of contract are set by the exchange. Maintenance margins reflect the expected daily price volatility of the contract and are therefore typically quite low—around 5 percent of the contract price on average. The initial margin requirement depends on whether one is a *hedger* or a *speculator*; futures exchanges classify all their members into one of these two categories. For hedgers, the initial margin is the same as the maintenance margin, while for speculators it is marked up by 20 to –50 percent to give the clearinghouse more wiggle room to deal with potential losses. These terms—hedger and speculator—have a larger meaning, which we discuss next.

HEDGERS AND SPECULATORS

A hedger is a futures trader who does care about the underlying commodity and generally tries to reduce (hedge) the price risk associated with it. For example, if we are a wheat producer, and we worry that wheat prices will drop, we can sell wheat futures and lock in the price for our grain. Conversely, if we are a miller, and we worry that wheat prices will rise, we can buy wheat futures to lock in the current prices. In both situations, futures trades are backed by the underlying commodity, so the overall financial position of the hedgers is unlikely to deteriorate catastrophically—for example, if we take a ruinous loss on our wheat futures position when wheat prices crash to the ground, we will save about the same amount when we purchase wheat for our mills. Therefore, the risk of default for hedgers is significantly less than that for *speculators*, who, by definition, do not have any interest in the underlying commodity and are just trying to make a buck trading its price movements.

While the actions of hedgers are usually seen as a worthy economic activity, the term *speculator* has negative connotations—in fact, accusations of excessive speculation almost led to an outright ban on futures trading in the late nineteenth century, as we discuss in Chapter 9. However, over time, market participants came to recognize that speculators play an essential role in the market: they assume the price risk that the hedgers are trying to offload. Instead of outlawing speculation, the government settled on regulating it by introducing limits on speculative positions and requirements that positions above a certain size be disclosed.

Given the importance of hedging activities for futures trading, we need to take a closer look at how hedging works. Let us say that we own (are long) the underlying product and want to hedge its price movements, so we sell the appropriate number of futures contracts (however much underlying commodity we have divided by the size of each contract; for example, if we have 50,000 bushels of wheat, we sell 10 wheat futures contracts against it). Now if both wheat and wheat futures go up or down in price by the same amount, we are perfectly hedged. But why should the price movements of the underlying and the futures be exactly the same?

The argument for this is based on the idea of *convergence*. When the futures contracts expire, they become equivalent to the underlying (which can now be immediately delivered to the holders of long futures positions, as in our previous example) and should therefore have the same price— futures prices and cash prices should *converge* at expiration. This, however, does not mean that prior to expiration, the cash price and the futures price should be the same, and in fact they are not. The difference between the cash price and the futures price is called the *basis* of a given futures contract.

The main reason that basis exists is the presence of *storage costs*: futures price should be equal to today's cash price plus what it would cost to store the commodity until the expiration date. If the futures price is higher than that value, the futures are *rich* to the cash product (the basis is too low); we can sell the futures, buy the underlying and store it until delivery time, and profit from the difference. This is called *basis trading*; when we are long the underlying and short futures, we are *long basis* and our PnL is proportional to changes in the basis (we profit when the basis increases). Those who hedge long positions in the underlying by selling futures against it are in fact long basis and are therefore exposed to the risk that the basis will change unexpectedly—the *basis risk*.

For many futures contracts, the storage costs are indeed the main source of basis, so that whenever storage (or *carry*) costs are positive (as we would expect for most storable commodities), the futures price should be higher than the cash price. Moreover, in this situation we can expect the term structure of futures prices (futures prices as a function of expiration month) to be upward-sloping, as storage costs increase with the duration of the storage period (which is time to expiration). Since for most futures there are in fact several expiration months trading simultaneously, the term structure can often be empirically observed and compared to actual storage costs.

What such analysis reveals is that for many types of futures (including all of the financial futures, which will be our focus later in this chapter), storage costs are in fact the only factor explaining both basis and the term structure of futures prices. However, it also shows that there are many situations that cannot be explained this way, such as when the observed term structure of futures prices is downward-sloping; when this happens, the futures are said to be in *backwardation*, whereas in the more normal upward-sloping term structure, they are said to be in *contango* (this word means "premium for deferring payment" and is a synonym for the concept of basis).

Backwardation in commodity futures happens in situations where market participants cannot realistically go *short basis* (i.e., where it is difficult or impossible to short the underlying commodity), so that the arbitrage between cash and futures prices becomes difficult to execute. This frequently occurs with consumable commodities such as crude oil, where people are often willing to pay extra for immediate supply, which can make the cash price higher than the futures price. These situations offer interesting opportunities for both theoretical analysis and trading profits and have attracted such luminaries as John Maynard Keynes, the famous economist, who in the 1930s both traded such futures with spectacular success and produced the first theory of what he called *normal backwardation*. This fascinating topic is, regrettably, beyond the scope of this book.

THE MECHANICS OF FUTURES TRADING

So far we have discussed how exchange members trade futures—how does everybody else trade them? Everybody else has to go through one of those members, who acts as a broker. In the United States this broker is usually a firm and is called a *futures commission merchant* (*FCM*). Futures traders open accounts with one or many such commission merchants, who are members of the exchange and can execute orders on behalf of their customers (and, of course, charge commissions for this service). Commission merchants also provide daily mark-to-market clearing and settlement and maintain margin for their clients' accounts. All big Wall Street banks act as commission merchants and are clearing members of most futures exchanges. Typically there is a futures desk that executes futures trades for both external clients and other trading desks within the firm, often by providing direct electronic connectivity to the exchanges. In many cases, big banks also have their own brokers on the floor of the more important exchanges; their job is to execute large trades and provide intelligence about the market.

Unlike other products, such as bonds and stocks, futures can trade only on the exchange, so there are restrictions on in-house futures trades between different desks and even between different trading books on the same desk (one cannot create an open interest outside the exchange). Exchanges are keen to maintain this rule because it protects their revenues: the exchange charges its members a trading fee on a per-contract basis for every trade, while the clearinghouse collects a clearing fee for clearing and settlement. Both fees are typically very small (less than a dollar per contract), but for large banks they add up to millions of dollars a year, so when exchanges began to compete by listing similar contracts, slashing such fees was a favorite and very effective tactic. Another important source of revenues for the exchanges is the sale of membership rights. In fact, some exchanges maintain a two-sided market for various categories of membership on their Web sites. Membership is open to both organizations and individuals (in both cases, there are requirements as to credit quality and reputation), and a seat on a major exchange can be had for about $1 million. We list some of the more important futures exchanges in Figure 7–2.

Futures were among the first financial products to go electronic. Reuters started distributing futures prices from the exchanges on its market

FIGURE 7-2

Major futures exchanges as of early 2006 (they keep buying each other, so the list may change in the near future).

Full name	Acronym	Nickname	Year founded	Location	Major product lines
Chicago Board of Trade	CBOT	The Board	1848	Chicago	Agricultural, Interest Rate (Treasury and FED futures), Equity Index futures (Dow), Metals
Chicago Mercantile Exchange	CME	The Merc	1898	Chicago	Eurodollar, Equity Index (SP500), Cattle, FX, Inflation and Weather
New York Mercantile Exchange	NYMEX		1882	New York	Oil, Nat. Gas, Gasoline, Electricity, Metals
New York Board of Trade	NYBOT		1870	New York	Cotton, Sugar, Orange Juice
EUREX	EUREX		1996	Frankfurt	German bond futures, stock index futures
Euronext.Liffe (formerly London International Financial Futures Exchange)	LIFFE	Life	1982	London	Euribor, stock index, agricultural
London Metals Exchange	LME		1870	London	Base metals
International Petroleum Exchange	IPE		1980	London	Brent crude oil

data platforms in the mid-1970s. At the time, Reuters developed a system of symbols for futures contracts that largely survives to this day. In this system, a futures contract is uniquely described by a *Reuters Information Code (RIC)*, a sequence of three to six characters illustrated in Figure 7–3. The last character is a digit indicating the expiration year, the letter to the left of it indicates the expiration month (as is seen from Figure 7–3, the month letters are highly nonintuitive, but you would do well to memorize them, or at least the four codes for the standard quarterly cycle: March, June, September, and December), and the leftmost characters are the contract code, indicating what kind of futures it is. According to this system, WZ6 is the wheat (W) futures contract expiring in December (Z) of 2006, while TYU7 is the U.S. Treasury note future (TY) contract expiring in September (U) of 2007. Figure 7–3 lists some of the more common contract codes, which, like the month letters, rarely make any sense. While this symbology clearly hails from the early days of computing, it remains pervasive among traders, who often refer to the futures contracts by their RIC codes instead of by their names, so anyone involved with futures trading should understand this language.

FIGURE 7–3

Reuters symbology for futures. Every future symbol ends with a digit identifying the expiration year, preceded by a letter code identifying the expiration month, preceded by a one- or two-character code identifying the contract. Thus, CLM7 is a crude oil contract expiring in June 2007 (note that this system cannot support more than 10 years worth of contracts).

Month codes:		Contract → CLM7 code		Common futures contracts	
Jan	F				
Feb	G	Month code		CL	Crude oil
Mar	**H**			W	Wheat
Apr	J			ED	EuroDollars
May	K		Year		
June	**M**			TU, FV, TY, US: Treasury futures	
July	N	Special codes:		FF	Fed Funds
Aug	Q				
Sep	**U**	C1	Front contract	SP	SP500
Oct	V	C2	Next contract	DJ	Dow Jones futures
Nov	X				
Dec	**Z**				

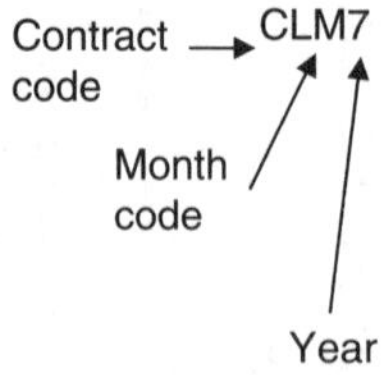

FINANCIAL FUTURES

By the 1970s, futures exchanges around the world had listed contracts for every conceivable agricultural and industrial commodity.[1] Commodity prices were (and are) very volatile, and these commodity futures came to be recognized as useful tools for dealing with this price volatility. The early 1970s unleashed unprecedented volatility in the financial markets area: the collapse of the Bretton Woods exchange-rate system ended the era in which all currencies were rigidly pegged to the dollar, so that the foreign exchange business suddenly had to deal with exchange rates that started moving all over the place. At the same time, the major Western economies began to suffer from significant inflation, exacerbated by the oil shock of 1973, which caused interest rates to become very unstable.

To their credit, the leading futures exchanges quickly recognized that this situation called for the same treatment that they used so successfully in volatile commodity markets, and they began introducing *financial futures* contracts, where the underlying was a financial product rather than a commodity. These early efforts were perhaps the first stirrings of the derivatives revolution that has completely transformed the financial industry over the last three decades.

The first financial futures contracts were listed in 1972, when the Chicago Mercantile Exchange formed a subsidiary called the International Monetary Market (IMM), which began trading foreign exchange futures. The first interest-rate futures contract was the Ginnie Mae futures (since defunct) on CBOT in 1975, where the underlying was a bond issued by GNMA (see Chapter 10). CME took another step in the realm of interest-rate futures by listing a futures contract on Treasury bills in 1976. However, the first truly revolutionary interest-rate futures contract was the U.S. Treasury bond futures contract launched by CBOT in 1977, which remains one of the world's most liquid securities to this day. We reproduce the contract specification for the UST bond contract in Figure 7–4.

As is clear from Figure 7–4, the Treasury bond futures contract works in much the same way as the wheat futures contract, except that the deliverable is a Treasury bond instead of wheat. The specifications cover the same issues: size of the contract ($0.1 million), deliverable grades, price

---

1. Except onions; the regulations of the futures markets in the United States explicitly state that futures on onions are illegal. The onion farmers pushed this through in the 1950s with the help of a young congressman from Michigan named Gerald Ford—the future president of the United States.

FIGURE 7–4

U.S. Treasury bond futures contract specification from CBOT Web site (www.cbot.com). Reproduced with permission.

30 Year U.S. Treasury Bonds

Contract Size
One U.S. Treasury bond having a face value at maturity of $100,000 or multiple thereof.

Deliverable Grades
U.S. Treasury bonds that, if callable, are not callable for at least 15 years from the first day of the delivery month or, if not callable, have a maturity of at least 15 years from the first day of the delivery month. The invoice price equals the futures settlement price times a conversion factor plus accrued interest. The conversion factor is the price of the delivered bond ($1 par value) to yield 6 percent.

Tick Size
Minimum price fluctuations shall be in multiples of one thirty-second (1/32) point per 100 points ($31.25 per contract) except for intermonth spreads, where minimum price fluctuations shall be in multiples of one-fourth of one-thirty-second point per 100 points ($7.8125 per contract). Par shall be on the basis of 100 points. Contracts shall not be made on any other price basis.

Price Quote
Points ($1,000) and thirty-seconds of a point; for example, 80-16 equals 16/32

Contract Months
Mar, Jun, Sep, Dec

Last Trading Day
Seventh business day preceding the last business day of the delivery month.

Last Delivery Day
Last business day of the delivery month.

Trading Hours
Open Auction: 7:20 am - 2:00 pm, Chicago time, Monday - Friday Electronic: 7:00 pm - 4:00 pm, Chicago time, Sunday - Friday Trading in expiring contracts closes at noon, Chicago time, on the last trading day

Ticker Symbols
Open Auction: US Electronic: ZB

Daily Price Limit
None

Margin Information
Find information on margins requirements for the 30 Year U.S. Treasury Bonds.

quotations (in thirty-seconds, just like the underlying bonds), minimum trading increment (1 tick), and delivery period. Treasury bond futures trade on a quarterly cycle, and the contract for the nearest delivery month (the *front contract*) is much more liquid than the *back contracts*. The Reuters contract symbol for this contract is US, so USH7 is a bond futures contract expiring in March 2007.

Later, CBOT also listed similar Treasury futures contracts on other sectors of the Treasury curve—the 10-year note (TY), 5-year note (FV), and 2-year note (TU) futures—that differ only in the maturity of the deliverable Treasury notes (the tick size on these contracts is also smaller, reflecting the smaller price volatility of the shorter-maturity Treasuries). What is genuinely new for all these contracts is the settlement convention based on the concept of the *conversion factor*, which we now proceed to explain.

According to Figure 7–4, any Treasury bond with more than 15 years to maturity can be delivered into the bond futures contract (the discussion of callables in the specification is superfluous, as there are no more callables in that maturity range; see Chapter 5). The 15 years are counted from the first day of the delivery month. If we take the USH5 contract as an example, we count from March 1, 2005, and find that there were 24 bonds ranging in maturity from May 2020 to February 2031 that could be delivered; they form the *deliverable basket* for this contract.

The reason the contract is structured to have more than one bond in the basket is to avoid *delivery squeezes*—situations in which someone acquires most or all of the outstanding deliverable bond (and, optionally, also establishes a huge long position in the corresponding futures contract) and forces the shorts to pay exorbitant prices for the deliverable and/or for the futures contracts. Having more than one bond in a basket makes this strategy much harder to execute (although there have been successful examples of that in note futures, such as the Fenchurch scandal in 1993), but only if the deliverable bonds are more or less interchangeable.

If the futures price were made equal to the underlying bond price at delivery (as is the case for almost all commodity futures), this could never work, and we illustrate why in Figure 7–5a, which shows the *forward* prices of (some of) the bonds in the USH5 deliverable basket as a function of their *spot* yields. Note that it is the forward prices rather than the spot prices that have to be compared to the futures price—as we discussed in Chapter 5, forward bond prices include the cost of carry to the delivery date. In Figure 7–5, the forward prices are calculated for delivery on the last business day of the contract month, assuming that the repo rate is the

F I G U R E   7–5(a)

Forward prices for bonds in the deliverable basket of the USZ4 contract as a function of their yield. (a) The bond with the lowest coupon is obviously the cheapest. To make the delivery basket more homogeneous, the delivery invoice price is made equal to the price of a bond divided by its conversion factor, which is the price that yields 6 percent (i.e., the inter-section point of the price-yield curves in this figure with a vertical 6 percent line). (b) The converted forward prices are much more uniform, but when the yields are much lower than 6 percent, the bond with the lowest duration (slope) becomes the cheapest to deliver, while for yields above 6 percent, the highest-duration bond becomes the cheapest. For any given futures price, we define the implied yield curve as the yields corresponding to the intersection points between the curves in (b) and a horizontal line representing the futures price.

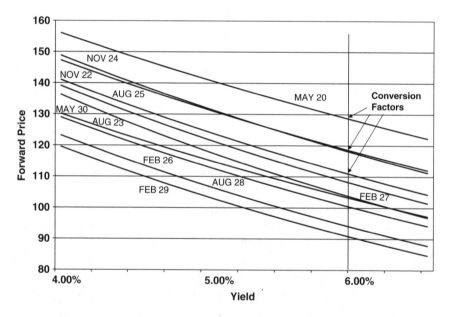

same for all bonds. The bonds in the basket are so different in terms of maturity, coupon, and duration that for any reasonable combination of their yields (which form an almost continuous yield curve as a function of maturity, as we described in Chapter 4), one bond, specifically the one with the lowest coupon, will always be much cheaper than all the others, so everyone would just deliver that one.

F I G U R E   7–5(b)

(*Continued*)

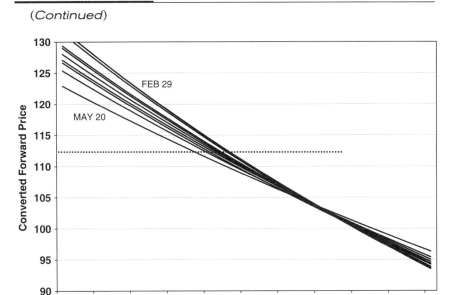

In order to make the bonds in the basket more or less equivalent, the contract specifies a different delivery (also known as *invoice*) price for every bond in the basket; the delivery price is the futures price times that bond's conversion factor. Because of this provision, what we should compare to the futures price are not (forward) bond prices per se, but rather converted forward bond prices (a bond price divided by that bond's conversion factor). The factors are selected in such a way as to make all converted prices more or less the same. Specifically, if we draw a vertical line corresponding to a constant yield of 6 percent, the conversion factor for a given bond will be the price at which its price-yield curve intersects that vertical line (or, as the contract specification in Figure 7–4 puts it, the conversion factor is the price of the bond that yields 6 percent).

We show the relationship between yield and *converted* bond prices in Figure 7–5b. By construction, all converted prices should be equal to par when the yield is equal to 6 percent (in practice, this is only approximately true in Figure 7–5b because it shows forward prices for the last delivery date of the month, while the conversion factors are calculated by rounding the time to maturity to the nearest quarter). Therefore, if the yield curve were flat and all long-end yields were 6 percent, all bonds in the basket would be equivalent from the delivery standpoint. The value of 6 percent is picked by the exchange to approximate the likely level of long-term yields. When the contract was first announced in 1977, this value was set at 8 percent, which was appropriate given the high rates prevailing at the time. In 1999, the CBOT changed this value to 6 percent to reflect the significant drop in rates that had taken place since the mid-1980s (of course, within two years of that, the rates went down another 2 percent or so).

Consider what happens when the yield curve deviates from the constant 6 percent assumption. If we assume that the yield curve is flat, we can determine the fair price for the futures by drawing a vertical line corresponding to that yield value and finding the first (lowest-price) intercept with one of the converted price curves in Figure 7–5b. When the yields are below 6 percent, the first intercept is always with the curve corresponding to the *lowest-duration* bond in the basket (duration is simply the slope of the curves in Figure 7–5b). Therefore, when yields drop far below the 6 percent value, we typically find that the shortest-duration (which almost always means the shortest-maturity) bond in the basket will be much cheaper to deliver than all others. Note that if all yields were to become much larger than 6 percent, the opposite would be the case: the longest-duration bond would be the *cheapest to deliver*, or *CTD*. If the yields are far enough away from 6 percent, the CTD is so much cheaper than the nearest contender that we are effectively back to the single-deliverable model; in this case, the futures price is simply equal to the converted forward price of the CTD.

This simple procedure for determining the CTD breaks down when the yield curve is not flat, because each bond will then have its own yield value, but Figure 7–5b suggests a more general approach: instead of starting with a single yield and trying to find the futures price that corresponds to it, we can start with a futures price and draw the corresponding horizontal line. The intersection points of this horizontal line with the converted price-yield curves give us an *implied yield* curve for the deliverable set (a value of yield for each bond) corresponding to that value of the futures price (more accurately, the implied yield curve corresponds to the constant converted price). If the real yield curve were the same as the implied curve, all bonds in the set would be equally cheap to deliver into the futures contract at that futures price. To examine the relationship between the real and implied yield curves, we start with the five-year note contract because it has fewer deliverable securities.

In Figure 7–6, the solid dots represent the actual spot yields of the Treasury notes in the five-year sector on a day in mid-November 2004 (we show only those that are deliverable into the FVZ4 contract). The open dots represent the implied yield curves for different futures prices. The topmost curve corresponds to the futures price of 108; we can tell that this price is clearly too low relative to where the deliverables are trading because all implied yields are far higher than the actual yields. As we increase the futures price, the implied yields move down, closer to the actual curve, and finally, for the futures price of 110-09+, one of the implied yields touches one of the actual yields.

When this occurs, we know that the note where the intersection occurs is the cheapest to deliver, and its converted price is equal to the futures price. At this futures price, the other bonds in the deliverable basket are much more expensive (their actual yields are much lower than the implied

FIGURE 7–6

Comparison of implied yields for different futures prices for the FVZ4 contract with the actual yields of the notes in its deliverable basket. Because the implied curve is much steeper than the actual curve, the implied curve and the actual curve intersect at just one point, which determines a single cheapest-to-deliver note.

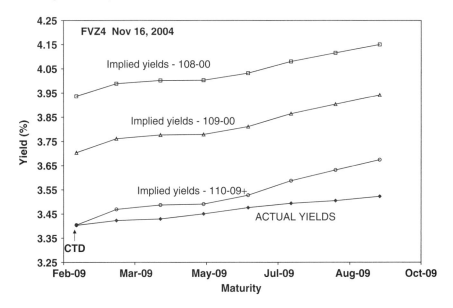

yields corresponding to that futures price), so there is little question about which of them is the cheapest to deliver. This is to be contrasted with Figure 7–7, where we show the same analysis for the USZ4 contract (again, actual yields are from mid-November 2004). In this example, the slope of the actual yield curve is comparable to that of the implied curve, so that, as we increase the futures price, the two yield curves bump into each other almost simultaneously for a large set of bonds, so it is difficult to tell which of them is the CTD. This is how bond futures were meant to behave, and this is where their pricing and trading gets interesting.

Consider how much we should pay for a futures contract in this situation. If there is only one deliverable bond, the price of the futures should be equal to the converted forward price of that bond; otherwise we could make a risk-free profit by buying futures and selling the deliverable bond for forward settlement, or vice versa. Suppose that currently the futures price is somewhat lower than the forward bond price; we buy the futures

FIGURE 7–7

Implied and actual yields for the USZ4 contract. Here, the implied and actual curves have similar slopes, so there is a wide range of bonds where the curves almost touch. The shortest distance between them represents the value of the delivery option.

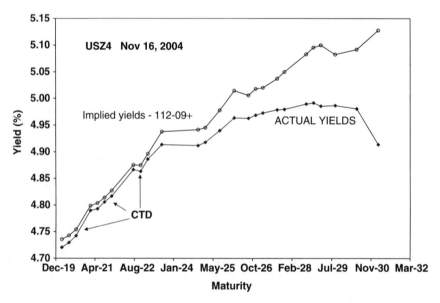

and sell the bond, and watch the two prices converge at expiration: the futures will have to richen up to match the deliverable price, and we will make money on the difference.

However, this sure-fire scheme can go very wrong if there is another bond that can become the CTD. In this case, if we correctly guess which bond will end up being the CTD and we buy futures below its forward converted price, we will make money on the trade, but if we do not guess correctly and "our" bond does not become the CTD, then the futures price does not have to converge to its price and will in fact converge to something cheaper, which means that we may lose money on the trade. Because of this possibility that the futures price may find something cheaper to converge to, the futures price should always be *less* than the converted forward price of any bond in the basket, just as shown in Figure 7–7; the difference is the value of the *delivery option* held by the short. The value of this option depends on the volatility of the yield curve and, most importantly, on the relative position of the implied versus actual yield curves; it ranges from a few ticks (thirty-seconds) in the situation shown in Figure 7–7 to almost nothing (0.01 tick) in the situation of Figure 7–6.

This type of trading—buying bonds and selling futures against them or vice versa—is quite widespread and is known as *bond basis trading*. For bond futures, the basis is defined as the bond price less the futures price times the conversion factor. If we use the current bond price for this calculation, we get the *gross basis*, whereas if we take the forward bond price corresponding to the delivery date, we get the *net basis*, which is also often called the *basis net of carry*. As we discussed in Chapter 5, when the short-term repo (or financing) rate is less than the yield on the bond (i.e., when the yield curve is upward-sloping), the forward bond prices are less than the spot prices, and therefore the net basis is lower than the gross basis.

This is illustrated in Figure 7–8, where we show a snapshot of gross and net basis for long-end Treasuries relative to the nearest bond futures contract for the situation shown in Figure 7–7. The net basis is almost the same for several bonds in the 2021–2023 maturity range (around 3 ticks in this example), reflecting the value of the delivery option. While we can always find one bond with the smallest net basis and call it the cheapest to deliver, in reality this does not mean much, as another bond may easily become CTD by that definition a few minutes or even seconds later. On the other hand, in the situation shown in Figure 7–6, the net basis on the shortest-duration bond is zero and all other notes have a large net basis; in this case, there is no ambiguity about which of them is the CTD, and the delivery option has no value.

FIGURE 7-8

Gross and net basis for the USZ4 deliverables for the situation depicted in Figure 7-7.

	Basis	Net Basis
UST Bond 8.5 Feb 20	28.75	6
UST Bond 8.75 May 20	29+	5.31
UST Bond 8.75 Aug 20	28.12	4.66
UST Bond 7.875 Feb 21	24.12	3.33
UST Bond 8.125 May 21	26.37	4.19
UST Bond 8.125 Aug 21	24.62	3.11
UST Bond 8.0 Nov 21	26	4.23
UST Bond 7.25 Aug 22	22.25	3.4
UST Bond 7.625 Nov 22	25.25	4.68
UST Bond 7.125 Feb 23	22+	4
UST Bond 6.25 Aug 23	25.75	6.44
UST Bond 7.5 Nov 24	34.12	14
UST Bond 7.625 Feb 25	33	13.16
UST Bond 6.875 Aug 25	35.37	17.74
UST Bond 6.0 Feb 26	37.75	22.66
UST Bond 6.75 Aug 26	37.75	20+
UST Bond 6.5 Nov 26	40.37	23.33
UST Bond 6.625 Feb 27	39.62	22.74
UST Bond 6.375 Aug 27	44.12	27.98
UST Bond 6.125 Nov 27	49.12	33.21
UST Bond 5.5 Aug 28 Rg	56.12	42+
UST Bond 5.25 Nov 28	59.87	46+
UST Bond 5.25 Feb 29	64.37	51.47
UST Bond 6.125 Aug 29	62.75	47.36
UST Bond 6.25 May 30	72.75	55.37
UST Bond 5.375 Feb 31	115.75	99.41

In such steep yield curve environments, the trader who is *long basis* (long the bond and short the future) earns interest income every day from her bond position and therefore should generally want to hold this position as long as possible—to the last delivery date, which is the last business day of the delivery month (all our forward price and yield calculations in Figures 7–4 through 7–7 were done under this assumption). However, when the yield curve is inverted, the carry on the bond becomes negative, so that the delivery is likely to occur as soon as possible—on the first business day of the delivery month. The exact time of delivery is another option held by the short, but the value of this *time option* is usually very small.

Some interdealer brokers execute such basis trades as a single trade. Consider the interdealer quotes shown in Figure 5–12; the right side of the page shows basis quotes for Treasuries in the 10-year sector against both December and March (TYZ4 and TYH5) contracts. The quotes are in terms of the gross basis and are expressed in ticks, just like the Treasury prices themselves, except that they remain in ticks when the number goes over 32. For example, the bid of 35 for the Aug 12 means that we can sell this note and buy the TYZ4 contract so that the difference between the note price and the futures price times the conversion factor is 35 ticks = 1.09375. This is another example of trading off-the-run Treasuries relative to something more liquid, which in this case is the futures contract instead of the 10-year on-the-run.

Interestingly, these same Treasury notes are also quoted on the same page relative to the 10-year on-the-run, which may create an arbitrage opportunity if the 10-year note and the note futures move relative to each other (i.e., if the basis of the 10-year note itself changes abruptly). However, a lot of traders watch this relationship very closely and trade to profit from such transient misalignments, and as they put in the corresponding bond swap trades and basis trades, the market moves to eliminate the mispricing.

HOW FUTURES ARE TRADED

At this point we need to spend some time discussing how futures are traded. Currently there are two parallel systems for futures trading; one is *pit trading*, which is done by human brokers and traders on the exchange floor (the pit is a recessed area on the exchange floor where traders in a particular type of futures congregate), and the other is electronic trading on various exchange-specific platforms. Despite its long and storied past, it is unclear at the moment how much longer pit (also known as *open outcry*) trading will survive under the assault of electronic platforms. Some exchanges (most notably main European exchanges such as LIFFE and EUREX) have already gone all-electronic, but the major Chicago exchanges still maintain parallel systems during the official trading hours, with electronic trading available outside those hours. Pit trading is increasingly used only for large orders, which are submitted over the phone in the hope that a floor broker will do a better job of filling them than a computer system will.

Given this state of affairs, we will focus on electronic futures trading in our discussion. The good news is that despite the fairly large number of existing electronic platforms (the major ones are CME's GLOBEX, LIFFE's

CONNECT—also used by CBOT—and EUREX, which itself is an electronic platform), the salient features of futures trading do not depend much on either the platform or the type of contract and essentially follow the order-driven exchange execution model that we spent so much time discussing in the previous chapter.

Just like equities markets, the futures markets have *depth*—a thick stack of orders that is deep enough to accommodate the execution of large orders instantly. This, however, has the potential to cause significant instantaneous price swings when a large order sweeps the whole stack. In contrast, the cash bond markets provide depth not in price space, but rather by extending trades in time through their workup mechanism, which forces the market participants to stop and consider trading at the current trading price. As a result, the bond and note futures trade much more frequently than the underlying cash instruments—a bond futures contract in the United States would trade perhaps every couple of seconds, while its European counterparts would often trade several times a second.

Bond futures in Europe have an interesting history. The first financial futures exchange in Europe was LIFFE (London International Financial Futures Exchange), which opened its doors in 1982 and started trading contracts on short-term interest rates (more on that later in the chapter). But it also wanted to emulate the success of CBOT's Treasury futures, and in 1988 LIFFE listed a contract on German government bonds in the 10-year sector. This contract, known as the Bund futures (after the underlying bonds called *Bundesanleihen*, or "obligations of the German state"), quickly became very popular. Unlike the situation in the United States, where Treasury futures complement an already quite liquid cash bond market, the liquidity of Europe's fragmented bond markets left much to be desired, and the Bund futures offered a very efficient way to trade European interest rates.

By 1994, the Bund contract accounted for more than 30 percent of all volume on LIFFE, where it traded in the open-outcry format. Then the DTB (Deutsche Terminborse), a German exchange, mounted a stiff challenge to LIFFE in this area by listing an identical contract and offering customers various incentives to switch to it. In 1997, DTB formed a joint venture with the Swiss exchange SWX called EUREX, which from day one was built as an all-electronic exchange with faster, more efficient execution. By 1998, almost all Bund futures volume had migrated to EUREX and kept growing at a breakneck pace, overtaking the Treasury bond volume in 2000, after the introduction of the euro. At present, the front Bund futures contract is by far the most liquid security in the world, with over 1 million contracts trading daily.

The Bund and its sister contracts, the Bobl (five years) and the Schatz (two years), are similar in structure to the Treasury futures and trade on the same quarterly cycle. The most important difference is that there is a much narrower range of maturities for the deliverable bonds, which (together with a €2 billion minimum issue size) results in much smaller deliverable baskets. At the time of this writing, only three (almost identical) bonds were deliverable into the Bund contract. Another, less important, structural difference is that for EUREX futures, there is only one delivery date (the tenth of the expiration month), so there is no time option.

The phenomenal success of these futures is largely the result of the fragmentation of European national government bond markets—basically the whole Eurozone, with its 350 million population and a GDP approaching that of the United States, has only these three liquid securities to trade in the long-term interest-rate space, and all other government bond prices are usually linked to these three futures. In the next chapter we will discuss this linkage in a bit more detail.

In Europe as well as in the United States, bond futures give fixed-income traders a set of very liquid instruments that are closely tied to the government bond markets. In a "single-deliverable" situation, the economic benefits and risks of being long a futures contract are almost indistinguishable from those of having a long (forward) position in the underlying bond. Therefore, these futures can be used as more liquid replacements for the underlying bonds in many situations, most notably (1) when one wishes to acquire exposure to (bet on) interest rates, and (2) when one wishes to hedge an existing such exposure. For example, just as we can hedge one bond with another (by taking an opposite duration-weighted position, as described in Chapter 5), we can hedge a bond position with futures contracts.

In the single-deliverable case, a futures contract can be treated as the CTD bond with its DV01 divided by the conversion factor; this simple rule of thumb tells us how many contracts to buy or sell against a given bond position (although we have to be careful with this when the CTD can change). This hedging and risk-taking ability that the bond futures added to the fixed-income markets was and remains the major reason for the success of these products. Bond futures, however, can play this role only for long-term interest rates, while similar needs exist for short-term rates as well. We now turn to another class of interest-rate futures that fulfill those needs in the short-term (or money-market) rates area.

MONEY MARKET FUTURES

The search for a successful money market futures contract started in the United States in the mid-1970s. The first such futures contract, CME's T-bill futures, in fact was listed in 1976, one year before the T-bond contract. That contract worked exactly like the bond futures, except that the deliverable was a three-month Treasury bill. Unlike the Treasury bond contracts, the T-bill contract was only moderately successful (and did not survive to the present day; it is still listed, but it has not traded since September 2003).

We need to recall the market realities of the 1970s to appreciate the challenges that a successful short-term interest-rate futures contract had to overcome. In the United States, the 1970s were the decade of inflation and wage and price controls, and one of those controls was a cap on the interest rates that U.S. banks could pay their depositors. In an attempt to curb the relentless rise in interest rates caused by high inflation, the Fed revived one of the Depression-era rules called Regulation Q, which capped the deposit rates (especially the rates that banks charged each other for interbank deposits)—the theory was that rates were rising because the banks were competing for deposits too aggressively and thus were pushing the rates higher and higher, so the government had to restrain them. Of course, the market quickly found a way to get around those controls—the banks started issuing certificates of deposit[2] that were exempt from the rate cap, and banks and people started buying those CDs, either directly or through the money market mutual funds that sprang up to meet the needs of the investing public.

While the T-bill futures were well received by the Treasury market, the banks and other money market participants cared much more about the rates on these certificates of deposits, which in practice did not follow the T-bill rates too closely, mostly because T-bills were exempt from many regulations that banks were subject to. During the 1970s, the spread between CD rates and comparable-maturity T-bill rates fluctuated between as little as 50 bp and as much as 500 bp, often within a matter of days, so anyone who wanted to use the T-bills and T-bill futures as proxies for the rates prevailing in the private debt market had a very hard time. CBOT tried to address these problems by listing two different contracts on *commercial paper* (short-term discount instruments issued by corporations) in the late 1970s, but they did not work out.

Then, in 1981, both CME and CBOT listed contracts on certificates of deposit issued by a U.S. bank. Those contracts initially did quite well,

---

2. A certificate of deposit, or CD, is just what the name implies: a deposit certificate that can be traded; buying it is exactly like depositing money in the bank at a fixed interest rate.

as they provided a way to replicate the behavior of these very popular products, but they ran into severe problems a year later when the Mexican government defaulted on its debts, leaving many leading U.S. banks with huge loan losses. When the CD futures contracts were designed, they did not distinguish among CDs issued by the major U.S. banks and allowed the delivery of any of those that were in the right maturity range. Now suddenly some of these major banks were in such trouble that their CDs had become practically worthless, and so did the corresponding futures contracts—as we know by now, the price of the futures contract is driven by its cheapest to deliver. Thus the U.S.-based CD futures died an early death, and the story of money market futures acquired a European dimension.

After World War II, the U.S. dollar was the dominant world currency, and a lot of dollars ended up outside the United States, with Europe holding the biggest share. Their owners wanted to be able to do the same things with these dollars that they did with their national currencies, beginning with the ability to deposit them in banks and earn interest on those deposits. In the early 1960s, the European (most notably London) banks started opening such *Eurodollar* deposit accounts for their customers (interestingly, the Soviet Union was one of the major drivers of the development of Eurodollar banking services, as it had a lot of dollars from oil sales but could not deposit them in the United States for political reasons).

When the Regulation Q interest-rate caps began to constrain deposit rates in the United States in the early 1970s, Eurodollar deposits, which were not subject to those caps, suddenly became much more attractive even for U.S. institutions, and the Eurodollar deposit business really took off. Very soon the Eurodollar customers demanded and got other financial services, such as the ability to issue bonds against these Eurodollars. This *Eurobond* business proved extremely lucrative for London banks and was a principal factor in bringing London back as a major financial center. The leading U.S. banks wanted a piece of the action too, and by the end of the 1970s all of them had offices in London, where they quickly became major players in the Eurodollar market. Therefore, by the early 1980s, the rates on Eurodollar deposits were very much relevant to the U.S. banking system, and the futures exchanges tried to develop a product linked to these Eurodollar deposit rates.

The main problem with developing a futures contract reflecting the Eurodollar deposit market was the absence of an obvious deliverable. There were Eurodollar certificates of deposit, but they were not nearly as widespread as in the United States, where certificates of deposit were used mainly to get around the interest-rate caps—a problem that did not exist in the Eurodollar market. Deposit rates themselves could not be used either, because they could not be traded—a time deposit is a nontransferable contract between two parties. In this situation, the CME came up with an idea that proved revolutionary for financial futures: the concept of *cash settlement*, which dispenses with the need for physical delivery of anything. The best way to explain this concept is to describe how the resulting *Eurodollar futures* ended up working.

The Eurodollar futures aim to represent an interest payment on a three-month Eurodollar deposit of $1 million. That payment would be $1 million times the annual deposit rate, which we shall call R, times the length of the deposit period, which is exactly one-quarter of a year. If the deposit rate R changes by 1 bp, this interest payment would change by $25. How would we construct a futures contract whose value changed by the same amount if the underlying rate changed by 1 bp? The way CME solved this problem was to declare that the futures price should depend linearly on R, and that the settlement amount should be one-quarter of the change in price times the $1 million notional.

Specifically, the price of a Eurodollar futures contract is defined as $100 - R$, with R expressed in percent, so that if R is 2 percent, the futures price is 98.00. The price-rate relationship is inverted, so that Eurodollar futures prices would look more like the prices for other interest-rate futures that existed at the time, say, T-bill futures prices, which look like the prices of these discount instruments and are just under 100. Because, as we noted before, only changes in futures prices matter, not the absolute level, the 100 in this definition is irrelevant (if it was 1,000, nothing would change except that the prices would stop looking like T-bill prices). What is relevant is the minus sign (meaning that the futures prices drop as the rate increases, just like the prices of other fixed-income products), and, of course, the exact definition of the reference rate R.

To be able to settle Eurodollar futures, CME needed a well-defined reference rate that reflected conditions in the Eurodollar deposit market. Since every bank can quote its own rate for deposits, CME developed a survey process that worked as follows: Every morning CME asked several leading London banks to quote (offer) a rate for a $1 million Eurodollar deposit for different terms (from overnight to 12 months). The banks responded with their quotes, and the CME, for each such term, then (1) threw away the top and the bottom 25 percent of the responses,[3] (2) averaged the remaining responses, and finally (3) announced the result as the official

---

3. This is done to eliminate the possibility that an individual bank could try to manipulate the survey to its advantage by quoting an off-market rate.

LIBOR (London Interbank Offered Rate) for that term (LIBOR rates apply to deposits beginning in two London business days—on the *spot* date). Since 1997, this survey has been conducted not by CME but by the British Bankers Association, and the results (now called BBA LIBOR) are announced every business day at 11 a.m. London time. Various news and market data organizations then distribute the results to the whole world; most market participants look at them through Moneyline/Telerate page 3750, which we reproduce in Figure 7–9. As you can see in Figure 7–9, LIBOR rates are announced for all the major currencies, not just for U.S. dollars. The mysterious rate *R* against which the CME Eurodollar futures settle is the three-month U.S. dollar LIBOR rate (1.41 percent in Figure 7–9).

Eurodollar futures expire on the third Wednesday of the contract month (which is called the IMM date). LIBOR rates for that date are announced two days earlier, the previous Monday, at 11 a.m., at which point the expiring futures contract stops trading and the final settlement price is calculated as $100 - R$, as explained previously. All expiring contracts are then cash-settled: the clearinghouse closes all long and short positions at the settlement price (effectively buying all outstanding long positions and selling to all outstanding short positions, so that open interest becomes zero). The net effect of this cash settlement process is that the profit or loss of the holders of long and short positions becomes proportional to the difference between this final settlement price and the price at which their positions were established.

FIGURE 7–9

The LIBOR page 3750 on Moneyline/Telerate (now part of Reuters). Reproduced with permission. © Reuters 2006.

| 12/10   18:54 GMT | [BRITISH BANKERS ASSOCIATION LIBOR RATES] | | | | | 3750 |
| 10/12/02 | RATES AT 11:00 LONDON TIME 10/12/2002 | | | | 10/12 11:33 GMT | |
CCY	USD	GBP	CAD	EUR	JPY	EUR 365
O/N	1.29125	4.26875	2.75167	2.90000	SNO.04625	2.94028
1WK	1.32375	4.07188	2.77167	2.86256	0.04625	2.90232
2WK	1.33250	4.01250	2.78167	2.86125	0.04625	2.90099
1MO	1.42125	3.99125	2.79500	2.92500	0.05750	2.96563
2MO	1.41000	3.99625	2.81667	2.91625	0.06000	2.95675
3MO	1.41000	4.00695	2.83500	2.91313	0.06375	2.95359
4MO	1.42000	4.01070	2.85000	2.90481	0.07250	2.94515
5MO	1.42000	4.01500	2.86333	2.89125	0.07563	2.93141
6MO	1.43000	4.01750	2.87500	2.88519	0.07938	2.92526
7MO	1.45000	4.02875	2.89667	2.88063	0.08188	2.92064
8MO	1.47000	4.04125	2.92000	2.88000	0.08313	2.92000
9MO	1.49000	4.05250	2.94333	2.88000	0.08938	2.92000
10MO	1.52125	4.07102	2.97333	2.88000	0.09188	2.92000
11MO	1.55500	4.09297	3.01500	2.88000	0.09438	2.92000
12MO	1.59375	4.11625	3.05167	2.88306	0.09625	2.92310

An attentive reader would notice that this is exactly what happens to the 99 percent of all "normal" futures that end their life by closing out rather than by physical delivery; the cash-settled futures merely remove this 1 percent chance of actual delivery. It is true that the cash-settlement process makes little difference in practice, as most futures are effectively cash-settled anyway, but the concept of a futures contract that is not linked to anything tangible (a pure betting device, if you will) was very controversial for futures regulators. The Commodity Futures Trading Commission (the U.S. futures regulator) took almost two years after CME's original application to establish that the proposed cash-settlement procedure would not lead to excessive speculation and abuses.

The Eurodollar futures finally started trading on CME on December 9, 1981, and the financial futures markets have never looked back. After the collapse of the CD futures the following year, the Eurodollar futures quickly overtook the T-bill contract as the dominant money market futures instrument and went on to become CME's most successful product ever, with 300 million contracts changing hands in 2004. CME started out by listing 12 quarterly contracts (again for the March, June, September, and December quarterly cycle) covering the first three years and gradually extended the Eurodollar *futures strip* to 40 contracts covering ten years. However, the huge liquidity of these products is distributed very unequally among these contracts, with over 90 percent falling within the first three years, as shown in Figure 7–10.

At expiry, the price of each contract will become equal to (100 minus) the three-month LIBOR for the expiration date, but what do we make of Eurodollar futures prices before the expiration? They can be said to represent what the market *thinks* the three-month LIBOR will be at the expiration of each contract. The plot of (100 – the futures price) as a function of contract expiration date is called the implied term structure of forward three-month LIBOR (Figure 7–10); it tells us how the market thinks the rates will evolve. If the traders believe that the three-month LIBOR on some future date will be higher than what is implied by this plot, they will sell the corresponding Eurodollar contract until its price drops to reflect that belief, and vice versa; the Eurodollar futures, by design, allow people to bet directly on the future level of LIBOR rates very easily.

However, the relationship between Eurodollar futures prices and the future LIBOR rates is in fact much stronger than mere market consensus; trading Eurodollar futures today allows people to *lock in* future borrowing or lending rates. To see how this works, consider the following example:

FIGURE 7-10

Daily trading volume for Eurodollar contracts outstanding as of September 16, 2005. Almost all liquidity is concentrated in the first three years of the Eurodollar curve. The line shows the term structure of implied three-month LIBOR based on closing Eurodollar prices for that date. Data from Chicago Mercantile Exchange, www.cme.com.

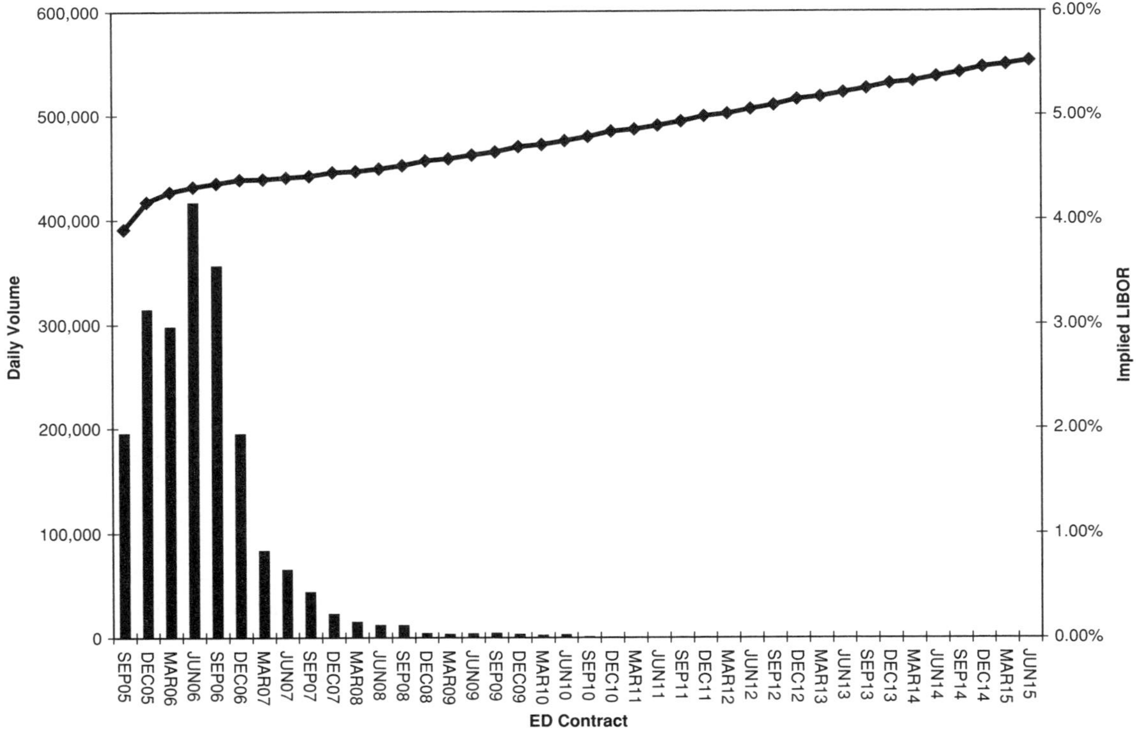

223

suppose that for whatever business reason, you will have to deposit $1 million for three months on March 19, 2008 (the expiration date of the EDH8 contract), at the three-month LIBOR, whatever that will be on that date. This is called a *floating-rate* deposit, and this example represents a very common situation for anyone borrowing or lending at the currently prevailing rate of interest, which of course changes (or *floats*) with time.

Clearly nobody knows what the three-month LIBOR will be on that distant date, and therefore we do not know how much we will earn on that deposit, but if we want to eliminate the uncertainty associated with this obligation, the Eurodollar futures allow us to do just that. Let us buy one EDH8 contract at its current market price of 94.00 (which translates into a LIBOR rate of 6 percent) and just wait until it expires and our floating-rate deposit begins. Suppose the three-month LIBOR on that date comes out to be 7 percent. The amount of money we will earn on our deposit is $1 million times ¼ times 7 percent = $17,500, but the futures price will drop from 94.00 to 93.00, so we will lose $1 million times ¼ times 1 percent (change in price) = $2,500 on our EDH8 position, so overall we will earn only $15,000, as if our effective lending rate were 6 percent instead of the actual 7 percent. Now suppose that, instead of rising to 7 percent, the rates crash to 2 percent by the expiration date of the contract: in this case we will make only $5,000 on our deposit, but our futures position will bring us a $10,000 profit, so overall we still make $15,000 and our effective lending rate is still 6 percent—the *implied LIBOR rate* at which we bought the futures contract.

This is, of course, completely general; the implied rate on the Eurodollar contract is the effective rate that we will receive on that faraway deposit no matter what the rates do in the future if we hedge it by buying the matched-maturity futures contract. Although the implied LIBOR term structure shown in Figure 7–10 does not give us the ability to see what rates will do in the future, it gives us something that in some ways is even better: a way to eliminate the uncertainty of floating-rate borrowing and lending. The fact that Eurodollar futures give people a convenient way to bet on as well as hedge LIBOR rates not only is a major reason for their popularity, but is also largely responsible for the widespread acceptance of LIBOR itself as an interest-rate benchmark.

Eurodollar futures were among the first securities to trade around the world and around the clock. In 1984, CME entered into a mutual offset deal with SIMEX (Singapore International Monetary Exchange) whereby SIMEX listed the same contracts, and trades that were done on one exchange could be offset in the other. LIFFE also listed Eurodollar contracts, but they were in competition with the CME product rather than a complement to it. This made it possible, for the first time, to trade an (almost) identical futures contract in Asia, Europe, and the United States; because of the time differences, this meant that one could trade Eurodollar futures almost around the clock.

In 1987, CME took another step toward globalizing futures trading by announcing the development (jointly with Reuters) of its electronic GLOBEX system, which was meant to give people from all regions round-the-clock access to its products. GLOBEX went live in 1992 and gradually became the dominant platform for Eurodollar futures—at the time of this writing, it accounts for over 70 percent of all CME volume, most of it in Eurodollars. GLOBEX trading continues to coexist with pit trading on CME; the timings of the GLOBEX and pit trading sessions are illustrated in Figure 7–11. There is only one hour downtime in the late U.S. afternoon, when the U.S. markets have already closed and the Asian markets have not yet opened.

We should mention here that while GLOBEX was the first global futures trading platform, it is by no means the only one. EUREX provides similar round-the-clock access to its electronic trading platform, and LIFFE and CBOT use LIFFE's CONNECT platform to trade futures from both exchanges on a similar time frame (the downtime period, however, is different—an hour later than for GLOBEX). The concept of closing time, where the exchange closes for the day and has the whole night to settle trades done during the day, is becoming increasingly quaint in the futures trading world; the only vestige of this that is likely to endure is the daily closing (or settlement) price for all contracts, which is still needed for mark-to-market settlement purposes.

The phenomenal success of Eurodollar futures paved the way for a variety of other financial futures in general and interest-rate futures in particular. In the interest-rate world, we should mention LIFFE's EURIBOR futures, which are the Eurozone's counterparts to Eurodollars (they are using a competing EURIBOR index instead of euro LIBOR), as well as its short Sterling futures, which do the same for the British pound interest-rate markets (LIFFE's long Sterling futures are 10-year Gilts bond futures, which are also very popular in that market). In Japan, the Tokyo International Financial Exchange (TIFFE, now called TFX) trades similar TIBOR futures (CME has an identical Euroyen product). In short, there are now direct equivalents to the Eurodollar futures in every major currency. There are also direct

FIGURE 7–11

GLOBEX and pit trading hours (all times are Chicago time–U.S. Central Time), illustrating the concept of side-by-side pit and electronic trading. From CME Web site, www.cme.com/trading/get/abt/sidebyside4530.html.

EXAMPLE: EURODOLLAR FUTURES

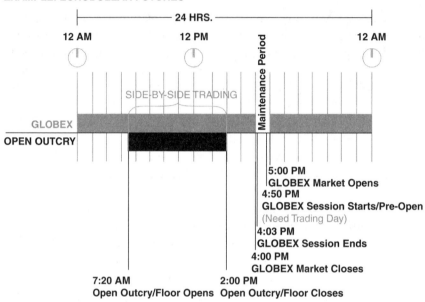

generalizations of that concept; for example, CME has so-called LIBOR futures that settle against one-month LIBOR (and LIFFE has the same for the euro and pound markets).

Two money market futures products—the fed funds futures from CBOT and the EONIA futures from LIFFE (although EUREX also has a competing contract)—are conceptually different from the Eurodollar futures in that the rate they settle against is an overnight rate averaged over the contract month (although the quoting convention is the same: 100 minus the average rate). These *average-rate* futures are designed to mimic the economics of the repo market; a typical securities lending transaction is rolled over every day at the new overnight rate, so that, for example, financing costs for a long position in a bond are in fact proportional to the average overnight rate over the financing period.

CBOT lists 12 monthly fed funds futures (FF) that settle against the average of the closing fed funds rate reported by the Fed every day. The averaging period is from the first day of the month to the end of the month—the futures expiration date. For the front FF contract (for the current month), this introduces an interesting situation in which the current prices of these futures depend on the month-to-date history of the fed funds rate. LIFFE lists nine monthly EONIA futures contracts that settle against the average of the official European Overnight Index reported by the ECB, and the averaging process is a bit more complicated (it is done by pretending that you invest €1 on the first of the month and reinvest it and the interest at the EONIA rate every day, so it includes the effect of compounding, while the procedure used for fed funds futures does not). Both contracts (especially the European version) are doing quite well in the marketplace because they match the huge repo market so well.

STOCK INDEX FUTURES

The concept of cash settlement, which proved so successful for Eurodollars, made it possible to design futures on other "undeliverable" financial quantities. As we saw in the Eurodollars example, all you need to make cash-settled futures work is a reliable settlement value that represents something that people care about and would be willing to trade. CME had to create the LIBOR index for this purpose to make Eurodollar futures work, but many stock indices that were already around in the late 1970s appeared ripe to become the underlying for cash-settled futures.

The idea of stock index futures sounds even simpler than the Eurodollar futures concept—the futures price at expiration could be simply made equal to the value of the underlying stock index as reported by its provider on the expiration day. Such futures would be convenient proxies for the underlying equity markets, just as other types of futures are proxies for their underlying commodities, and with growing trading volumes in the equity markets, the futures exchanges had reason to believe that such futures might become popular. Well, they had no idea just how popular these products would get in just a few years.

Interestingly, the first exchange that thought of creating a futures contract on a stock index was the Kansas City Board of Trade (KCBT), which in 1977 applied to the CFTC (the U.S. futures market regulator) to start trading a futures contract on the Dow Jones Industrial Average.[4] KCBT changed

---

4. Some CBOT members were talking about doing exactly that back in 1968, but at that time the exchange decided that this product would violate existing gambling laws.

its mind a few months later and reapplied for a similar product that would use the Value Line Index (which had a wide following among investment managers at the time) instead of the DJIA. It got permission to do this four(!) years later and started trading the Value Line futures in early 1982. CME was only a couple of months behind with futures on the S&P 500, which has quickly grown to be one of the more liquid securities on the face of the Earth (CME claims in its promotional materials that it was the first *successful* equity index futures contract, which may sound self-serving but in reality is a huge understatement). CME quickly followed up on its initial success by listing contracts on many other indices (most notably the Nasdaq Composite and the Russell family). The futures on the DJIA, which were meant to be the first of them all, had to wait until 1997 (Dow Jones was reluctant to license its index for this speculative purpose), when CBOT started trading the Dow futures.

Despite some institutional differences, all equity index futures work essentially the same way, which we review using CME S&P 500 futures (SP) as an example. The dollar value of the futures contract is tied to the underlying S&P 500 index value using a *multiplier* that defines how many dollars each index point is worth. For SP futures, the multiplier is $250, so that an index value of 1,200 translates into a contract value of $300,000. If this appears a bit steep, we should recall that at the time the contract was designed, the index stood at about one-tenth of what it is today, so the contract value was correspondingly less. However, as we emphasized before, the absolute value of the contract is irrelevant; what matters is the change in price, and the minimum price increment for the SP contract is set to be 0.1 index point, which translates into a much more manageable $25.00 per price tick.

In the late 1990s, CME introduced the so-called E-Mini version of this contract, with a multiplier of $50 and a minimum price tick of 0.25 index point = $12.50; this was designed for electronic trading, but it proved to be much more attractive for individual investors than for institutional players. Within a couple of years, most of the liquidity migrated from the larger SP 500 contract into its E-Mini version (the yearly volumes are 15 million SP versus 200 million E-Mini contracts as of early 2006). The two contracts are freely exchangeable (or, as they say, *fungible*)—one can always ask the exchange to convert five E-Minis into one SP contract, and vice versa. Most other early index futures products have a similar mini version, and even the more recent Dow futures have two versions, with multipliers of $5 and $10. Once these trading parameters have been set, the equity index futures trade just like any other futures contract—pushed up and down by supply and demand—until they are forced to converge to their underlying index at expiration.

Equity futures trade on the March quarterly cycle and expire on the third Friday of the contract month. Originally the final settlement price that was used to cash-settle all outstanding contracts was the closing value of the underlying index on that Friday. Just as with Eurodollars, the cash-settlement process means that the clearinghouse closes out all outstanding long and short futures positions at the final settlement price (e.g., if we buy one SP contract at 1,200 and the final settlement price is 1,202, our account is credited by the difference of 2 index points times the $250 multiplier = $500).

The closing price seemed an obvious choice, but, like many obvious choices, it quickly led to severe unintended consequences as the trading volumes in index futures grew. The problem was that a lot of people started engaging in *index arbitrage*, which we briefly mentioned in the last chapter. Buying an index futures contract allows us to lock in the value of the underlying index at expiration, but this is not the only way to do it—the other way is to simply buy all the stocks in the index in the correct proportion. When we buy the stocks in the index, we have to finance our purchases, but we collect the dividend payments that the stocks may make, so the value of the index we locked in is based not on the spot prices at which we bought the stocks, but rather on their forward prices (spot prices plus the interest charges less the dividends collected—just as with anything else, forward price is spot price plus the cost of carry).

There is no a priori reason why these two ways of replicating an index should cost the same, and it is possible that we can buy the futures at 1,200 when the forward price of the index-replicating stock portfolio is only 1,195; in this case, we sell the futures and buy the stock portfolio, and then simply wait for the futures to expire. Let us say that the final settlement price for the futures (which is also the closing price of our stock portfolio) comes out to be X. We then make $(1,200 - X)$ index points on our short futures position and $(X - 1,195)$ on our index-replicating stock portfolio; no matter what X comes out to be, we make 5 index points. This is as close as we can come to true arbitrage; the only thing we need for this to work is to be able to sell our stock portfolio at X on the expiration day.

Now, if X is based on Friday's closing price of the index components, and if a lot of people play this game, then we would expect that the stock exchanges where the underlying stocks are trading would be flooded with orders to buy and sell the index stocks at the closing level, and that is exactly what started to happen in the mid-1980s as index futures gained in popularity. The stock exchanges, and especially the NYSE specialists, really hated that. Let us imagine we are a specialist on an expiration Friday at 4 p.m.; we are ready to go home, and then we suddenly get a flood of buy orders for our stock at exactly the closing price. How are we going to fill them this late in the day? We may be required to fill these orders out of our own account and go into the weekend with huge open positions, which is, of course, very risky. Certainly we will feel entitled to complain about this rather bitterly, and so the NYSE and other stock exchanges started complaining to CME and then to the Securities and Exchange Commission, and eventually (in 1987) the index futures settlement process was changed.

The solution that the futures exchanges, the stock exchanges, and the index product providers have come up with was to use something called the *Special Opening Quotation*, or SOQ, as the final settlement price for the index futures. SOQ is in some sense the exact opposite of the closing index value; while the closing value is based on the last trade of the day, the SOQ is calculated based on the first opening trade of the day. At opening time, none of the index stocks have traded yet, so the SOQ is equal to the previous day's index close. As the first stock opens, its price in the index is replaced with the price at which this opening trade occurred, and this is repeated for all stocks until they all have traded at least once (if one of them fails to trade at all, the exchange will wait until the end of the trading day and then calculate the SOQ using its previous close). If we think about it, we will see that the SOQ is (close to) the price we would get for the index portfolio if we placed a market order for it at the open; assuming that the first trade on a stock filled our order, the portfolio would be executed at the SOQ.

Usually all stocks in major indices open fairly quickly, certainly within a couple of hours, so the SOQ becomes known quite early in the day and the stock exchanges have much more time to accommodate the flood of orders related to index arbitrage. Index futures expiration Fridays are still some of the busiest trading days (as we can see in Figure 6–6, index arbitrage accounts for a significant fraction of stock trading volume), but the price gyrations that accompanied such expirations in the mid-1980s (when they were called "triple-witching" days) are now largely a thing of the past.

An interesting story from the early days of index arbitrage illustrates the hidden dangers of this seemingly straightforward process. As I mentioned, the very first equity index futures contract was the Value Line contract on the Kansas City Board of Trade. The Value Line Index, on which it was based, is a bit unusual in that it is not really representable as the weighted sum of stock prices; instead, it is constructed as a weighted product of the returns on its constituent stocks. Whatever the theoretical merit of that index construction approach, it proved fatal for the Value Line futures contract, and what killed the contract was clumsily executed index arbitrage.

Most people who tried to arbitrage this index future (which was historically the first and became very popular after its introduction in 1982) ignored the subtleties of the index construction and simply approximated it with a weighted portfolio of stocks. However, Fischer Black (of Black-Scholes fame) pointed out that because the index was in fact a geometric rather than an arithmetic average, it would always underperform the approximating weighted portfolio of stocks, and the degree of underperformance depends on how volatile the constituent stocks are. This led him to a formula for the fair value of the Value Line futures that contained a small but significant volatility correction.

Instead of publishing the formula in an academic journal, he explained it to the equity derivatives traders at Goldman Sachs, where he was spending his sabbatical leave from MIT. The Goldman traders started selling the contract to other would-be arbitrageurs who were willing to pay the naïve higher price for it. Within a year, Goldman made over $100 million using this trading strategy (no doubt ruining some smaller players who traded against it), the Value Line contract lost almost all market share[5] as people became afraid to trade it, and Black left MIT and stayed at Goldman, where he was eventually made partner.

What are the reasons for the enduring popularity of index futures? First, they provide a convenient and cost-effective mechanism for replicating equity indices, which is useful for many things besides index arbitrage, most importantly for hedging price risk in equity portfolios (as we explained in Chapter 6, equity risk is based on the idea of sensitivities, or betas, to a selection of indices). In recent years, the index ETFs have provided some competition to index futures in this space, but as of this writing the futures are still much more liquid and cheaper to trade.

---

5. KCBT tried to revive the contract by switching to the arithmetic average for the underlying index in 1988, but the contract never really recovered. However, to this day KCBT's Web site contains an almost heartfelt explanation of the differences between geometric and arithmetic averaging, complete with formulas and charts—a monument to the adage "what you don't know can hurt you."

Second, they allow people to place large bets on the direction of equities markets with very little money down, and this (especially since the introduction of the mini contracts) has proved very attractive to millions of individual investor/speculators. Like any futures, stock index futures are highly leveraged instruments; we deposit only the initial margin and can control a position 20 times the size of our investment. The explosive growth in trading volumes of equity index futures indicates that they fill an important need in the marketplace, and their future looks bright as they enter their third decade of trading. As a matter of fact, the importance of the leveraged aspect of futures trading has led many exchanges in the last couple of years to introduce futures on individual stocks so that people can speculate on them in a highly leveraged way.

As the futures exchanges continue to innovate, it is probably best for the reader to learn about the current state of affairs directly from the exchanges' Web sites (I provide some pointers in the Recommended Reading section), as any list that could be compiled now will probably be somewhat obsolete by the time the book comes out. However, I cannot resist mentioning the CPI futures listed by CME in 2004; these contracts settle not against an interest rate or anything tradable, but against the *inflation rate* as measured by the U.S. Consumer Price Index. At this point it is not clear how well these new products will fare in the market, but I think they represent an interesting idea to move beyond the capital markets to their economic drivers.

TECHNICAL CHALLENGES OF THE FUTURES MARKETS

Despite their comparatively short history, financial futures have become totally indispensable for the capital markets in general, and I hope that this chapter provides a sufficiently lucid introduction to this interesting market segment. As is our practice, we conclude the chapter by a brief overview of the technical challenges specific to the futures markets. Most futures are fairly simple products that do not require much quantitative analytics—the challenges they present are more in the areas of market data and connectivity. Futures prices often move so fast and there are so many trades that reading their market data and submitting electronic orders to the exchanges are nontrivial, performance-constrained tasks; we discuss some of the issues associated with this in Chapters 14 and 15, while related issues of product data for futures are briefly touched upon in Chapter 12.

Bond futures are an exception to this rule in that they usually do require sophisticated modeling to predict the delivery probabilities for available deliverables, as well as to provide such common risk and return measures as yield and duration. There is no standard model for bond futures, and every firm (and sometimes every trading desk) typically builds its own toolkit for these tasks—this is an interesting area of quantitative analytics that is always in demand. But the importance of futures for the quantitative analytics area lies mainly in their ubiquity; they are used as building blocks for so many types of complicated derivatives that it is imperative that all derivatives systems "get them right."

Armed with our freshly minted knowledge of financial futures, we are now ready to take on interest-rate derivatives in the next chapter.

CHAPTER 8

Interest-Rate Swaps

The markets that we discussed in the previous chapters have one common feature: the financial products traded there are defined and "manufactured" elsewhere. Each bond and stock has a well-defined set of properties that were established when it was issued, the specifications of futures contracts are defined by the exchange where they are listed, and the participants in the secondary market simply accept these definitions. For equities and futures, the trading takes place on centralized exchanges, whereas for bonds it happens *over the counter* (between dealers and customers directly), but in all these cases there is an external definition of what is being traded—investors, securities dealers, and regulators unambiguously agree on what each product is and can settle trades based on simple product identifiers, such as a stock symbol or a CUSIP number. Legally, a bond or a stock is a contract between the investor and the issuer, and a futures (or an exchange-listed option) contract is a contract between the exchange and its members—the issuers and exchanges are the third parties that define and create the products, which change hands in bilateral buy-sell transactions; all that is left for the traders to negotiate is the price.

There is, however, a huge market for products whose properties are negotiated directly between the buyer and the seller. For example, a transaction in which Party A agrees to pay Party B $1 million today, while Party B agrees to pay $1.05 million back in one year (which is what happens when you deposit money in a bank at a fixed rate of 5 percent) is perfectly legal and may make good economic sense for both parties, even though the product being exchanged is unique to this transaction. The same is true of a transaction in which the parties agree to exchange multiple payments (usually called cash flows) in the future, and where the amounts are not fixed, but instead depend on some future events such as interest rates at a particular future date, the level of a stock index, an exchange rate, and the like.

Each such transaction creates a unique financial product called an *OTC (over-the-counter) derivative*. Its uniqueness lies not only in the precise definition and timing of its cash flows, but also in who the counterparties are. For example, if A does a derivative deal with B and then does an identical but opposite deal with C, so that all cash flows cancel out exactly, the deals do not cancel each other out because A still has to get payments from B and pass them on to C on each payment date. This feature of OTC derivatives is very important and sets them apart from the previously discussed markets, where buying a security and then selling it leaves no obligations to anybody.

Entering into such arrangements may seem like something few people would do voluntarily, but before we discuss why people do OTC derivative deals, let us put all doubts to rest here: over the last 25 years or so, OTC derivatives have grown to be the largest market of all and have completely transformed the financial industry. Figure 8–1 shows some statistics about the size of the OTC derivatives market. The numbers are in billions of

FIGURE 8–1

The size of the over-the-counter (OTC) derivatives market as reported by the Bank for International Settlements (www.bis.org).

TABLE 19

AMOUNTS OUTSTANDING OF OVER-THE-COUNTER (OTC) DERIVATIVES
BY RISK CATEGORY AND INSTRUMENT
(In billions of US dollars)

Risk Category/Instrument	Notional amounts					Gross market values				
	2003 June	2003 December	2004 June	2004 December	2005 June	2003 June	2003 December	2004 June	2004 December	2005 June
TOTAL CONTRACTS	169,658	197,167	220,058	251,823	270,100	7,896	6,987	6,395	9,243	10,694
Foreign exchange contracts	22,071	24,475	26,997	29,580	31,075	996	1,301	867	1,546	1,141
Outright forwards and forex swaps	12,332	12,387	13,926	15,242	16,031	476	507	308	643	464
Currency swaps	5,159	6,371	7,033	8,223	8,236	419	567	442	745	549
Options	4,580	5,717	6,038	6,116	6,809	101	136	116	158	129
Interest-rate contracts	121,799	141,991	164,626	190,502	204,393	5,459	4,328	3,951	5,417	6,698
Forward-rate agreements	10,271	10,769	13,144	12,788	13,573	20	19	29	22	29
Interest-rate swaps	94,583	111,209	127,570	150,631	163,749	5,004	3,918	3,562	4,903	6,077
Options	16,946	20,012	23,912	27,082	27,071	434	391	360	492	592
Equity-linked contracts	2,799	3,787	4,521	4,385	5,145	260	274	294	498	717
Forwards and swaps	488	601	691	756	1,176	67	57	63	76	89
Options	2,311	3,186	3,829	3,629	3,968	193	217	231	422	527
Commodity contracts	1,040	1,406	1,270	1,443	1,693	100	128	166	169	271
Gold	304	344	318	369	288	12	39	45	32	24
Other commodities	736	1,062	952	1,074	1,406	88	88	121	137	247
Forwards and swaps	458	420	503	558	738	-	-	-	-	-
Options	279	642	449	516	668	-	-	-	-	-
Other	21,949	25,508	22,644	25,913	27,793	1,081	957	1,116	1,613	1,866
Memorandum item: GROSS CREDIT EXPOSURE	–	–	–	–	–	1,750	1,969	1,478	2,075	1,900

dollars, so the table says that there were over 270 *trillion* dollars worth of such deals outstanding in 2005, and that this number almost doubled between 2003 and 2005. Huge does not begin to describe it—the size of this market, its growth rate, and the profits that financial firms make trading these products all defy comprehension.

In this chapter, I will clarify how the OTC market works and why it has grown so popular, and then I will discuss the related quantitative and technological challenges. The focus will be on a particular type of OTC derivatives called *interest-rate swaps*, which, according to Figure 8–1, are by far the most common species of these animals. Unlike the historical approach of other chapters, I will start by explaining the mechanics of an interest-rate swap as it is known today; only then will I talk about the various economic and noneconomic reasons for the astounding popularity of these products (yes, I will briefly go over the history of this market here). I will then proceed to the concept of a swaps curve, which has become absolutely central for interest-rate markets, and finally finish the chapter with a brief overview of how swaps (and, more generally, OTC derivatives) trading is organized on Wall Street today.

THE MECHANICS OF AN INTEREST-RATE SWAP

So what is an interest-rate swap? It is a contract between two parties, one of whom is usually a dealer firm, while the other can be another dealer firm, an asset manager, a hedge fund, or pretty much any corporation. In that contract, the parties agree to exchange payments in the future. The payments are structured to emulate the interest payments on a certain notional amount, and the two parties differ in how they calculate the interest. One party pays the other a fixed rate of interest (which is called the *swap rate*), while the cash flows going the other way are computed using a *floating* interest rate (usually the three-month LIBOR rate), as shown in Figure 8–2. The timing and periodicity of the payments can be individually negotiated, but there are market conventions that an overwhelming majority of interest-rate swap transactions follow. The following example illustrates the conventions of the U.S. market, where floating payments are quarterly and fixed payments are semiannual.

Let us say that we are swap traders at a dealer bank, and we have just entered into a two-year swap agreement with our friends at another bank at a fixed rate of 5 percent for a $100 million notional amount. We know

FIGURE 8–2

Schematic of a two-year interest-rate swap described in the text. As time goes by, the two parties to the swap exchange payments, represented by vertical bars. The floating-leg payments depend on the value of three-month LIBOR at the beginning of the coupon period and are therefore unknown when the swap is initiated.

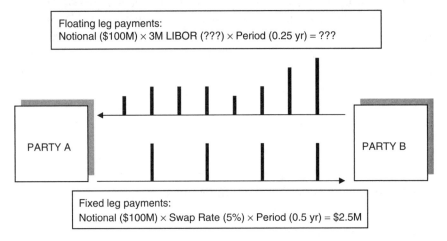

Floating leg payments:
Notional ($100M) × 3M LIBOR (???) × Period (0.25 yr) = ???

PARTY A

PARTY B

Fixed leg payments:
Notional ($100M) × Swap Rate (5%) × Period (0.5 yr) = $2.5M

that today's three-month LIBOR rate is 4.5 percent (as explained in the previous chapter, LIBOR is set daily at 11 a.m. London time). We can then compute the amount of the first floating payment: it is today's LIBOR times the length of the first *coupon period*, which begins at the *spot date* (two business days ahead of today) and ends three months from the spot date. Determining the actual payment date and the length of the coupon period are surprisingly nontrivial tasks because of various holiday adjustments and the like; we will defer the discussion of all these intricacies to Chapter 13, which deals with financial analytics.[1] Here we will simply assume that if today is May 1, then the spot date is May 3 and the first payment day is August 3, and that the length of this period is exactly 0.25 years. Therefore, our first floating payment comes out to be 4.5 percent times 0.25 times the notional amount, which is $1.125 million, and this is what we will pay to our counterparty on August 3.

   The next floating payment will be due in another three months (November 3, again abstracting from business-day adjustment), and the

---

1. This comment will apply to all date examples in this chapter. Apologies to those who know how convoluted these date issues can get.

rate that will apply to that period will also be set *at the beginning* of that period—the three-month LIBOR for August 3 will be announced two days before, and then we will know what the November 3 payment is going to be. Come November, the process is repeated, and on and on it goes until our last payment on May 3 two years from now. Meanwhile, our friends will make semiannual payments to us based on the fixed 5 percent swap rate that we negotiated with them at the outset of the swap; the first will be a $2.5 million payment due November 3, followed by another such payment every six months until the end of the swap.

REASONS FOR INTEREST-RATE SWAPS

What could be the economic purpose of such an exchange of cash flows? To answer that question, we should consider how the value of the swap changes when interest rates move. As we discussed in Chapter 5, the present value of a set of future cash flows can be calculated by discounting each cash flow to the present date. For the fixed leg of a swap, each future cash flow will be worth less if interest rates rise because the cash flows have to be discounted more, so the present value of a fixed leg is inversely related to the level of rates. For the floating leg, rising interest rates would also cause more discounting, but the payments themselves will grow proportionally larger, so that the value of the floating leg in fact increases with rising rates. The overall value of the swap for us (the receivers of the fixed payments) is therefore a decreasing function of LIBOR, as shown in Figure 8–3. As it turns out, the sensitivity of the swap value to a parallel shift in rates is (almost) the same as the duration of a two-year bullet bond with a 5 percent coupon and $100 million principal, or about $30,000 per bp. Entering into this swap therefore gave us exposure to interest rates, and it is this exposure that is the main attraction of swaps to most market players.

The reason that the interest-rate exposure of swaps is so valuable is that it can be used to hedge the existing interest-rate risk that naturally occurs in almost any large business. The existence of interest-rate risk came to the fore in the 1970s, when the rates became very volatile as a result of out-of-control inflation and the measures taken to fight it. As we can see in Figure 4–2, the volatility of short rates has somewhat abated since then, but still in the last 25 years in the United States, there were three 12-month periods in which the fed funds rate changed by more than 5 percent, and six more 12-month periods in which the short rates moved by more than 3 percent.

FIGURE 8–3

Interest-rate risk characteristics of a swap compared to a similar-maturity bond. The value of both a bond and a swap decreases in a similar fashion when the rates (LIBOR rates in the case of swaps) go up; however, the bond value remains positive, while the swap value, which is the difference between the values of the fixed and the floating leg, can be either positive or negative. At inception, the rate on a fixed leg is usually selected in such a way as to make the initial value of the swap equal to zero.

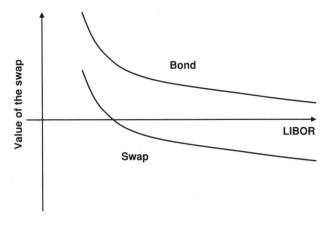

Such sharp swings in rates can have a dramatic impact on many businesses. Consider a retail bank, for example; its business model is to take deposits and make loans. The interest rate it has to pay on deposits rises and falls with changes in short-term rates, while the payments it receives on its long-term loans are much more stable, so when the short rates swing up, the bank is likely to suffer losses. Effectively, a bank is *long duration*: the value of its cash flows drops when rates rise. Many corporations are in a similar situation when they borrow heavily in the commercial paper market to meet their operating expenses; the expenses (and their income) are more or less insensitive to rates, but the borrowing costs will shoot up if the rates rise.

All these entities find it attractive to hedge this interest-rate risk by entering into swaps that allow them to change their interest-rate exposure very easily. There are, of course, other alternatives if one wants to buy or sell duration: one can buy or sell Treasury bonds and notes or other high-grade debt, or a corporation can issue its own bonds. The major disadvantage of buying or selling bonds, however, is that the resulting bond positions have to be reported on the company's balance sheet as assets or liabilities, and this typically requires much red tape. Issuing corporate debt is a still greater hassle; in addition to internal approvals, the company has to go through SEC registration and much else besides (see Chapter 11 for more details). So for most corporations, buying, selling, or issuing $100 million in debt is a very big deal. However, a corporation can enter into a $100 million swap with a simple phone call to a dealer firm (or, increasingly, with a single mouse click) and achieve the same results as far as interest-rate risk is concerned. Since most swaps are structured so that the value of the fixed leg equals that of the floating leg (this can always be done by setting the swap rate of the fixed leg to an appropriate value), entering into a swap does not cost you anything up front,[2] which is another attraction of swaps for many market participants.

These features of swaps have made it much easier for market players to hedge their interest-rate risks, but by the same token, they have also made it easier for many entities to bet on interest rates. A corporate treasurer can now say, "I believe that rates will rise (or fall)" and do a large swap transaction based on this belief (which, as we know, is called "a view" in this context) without having to do much explaining. Giving such speculative ability to people who as a rule were not trained to understand interest-rate risk was sure to lead to trouble, and it did. In the early 1990s, many entities used derivatives (either swaps or something called structured notes, which are similar in spirit) to enhance the return on their investment portfolios by essentially paying a (low) floating rate and receiving a (high) fixed rate. In 1994 the Fed raised rates quickly and unexpectedly, which spelled doom for this simplistic strategy and caused large derivative-related losses in many unexpected places: Orange County, California, lost $1.4 billion and had to declare bankruptcy; Procter & Gamble lost tens of millions; and the victims included Gibson Greetings and some other innocent-sounding names.

This has led to calls for greater regulation of derivatives and in favor of requiring Procter & Gamble to stick to making toilet paper and soap and avoid risky things that it does not understand. Luckily, the financial industry (where many dealer banks also lost hundreds of millions in 1994) developed a much more constructive response to the 1994 disaster by creating a modern risk management infrastructure that has successfully prevented similar blowups since then (at least in the interest-rate area). Nevertheless, you can

---

2. As I discuss later in this chapter, most dealers charge their institutional swaps customers an up-front payment called a credit charge that is designed to reflect their credit standing. The size of this charge is usually quite small (a few basis points).

still hear rants about the nefarious use of derivatives (just Google "derivative losses" and you will see what I mean), with the main argument against them being that they are too complex and require mathematical models that are beyond the cognitive abilities of the author of the rant.

In the early years of the OTC derivatives market development (the early 1980s), there was in fact a certain deviousness to these products, as many of them were intended to circumvent various government-imposed restrictions on the capital markets. The first known swap transaction, a cross-currency swap between the World Bank and IBM (brokered by Salomon Brothers, now part of Citigroup), is a good illustration of the forces driving the market at the time. The World Bank wanted to borrow in Swiss francs, but was prevented from doing so by quotas imposed by its member countries. So it borrowed in dollars and swapped its interest payments with IBM for that company's Swiss franc interest payments—a transaction where both parties effectively pretended to be somebody else in order to get around their borrowing restrictions.

Many corporations at the time faced different borrowing costs in different national markets (or could not borrow in some markets at all), and they took notice of this transaction and started doing the same thing—finding someone who could borrow cheaply in Market A while they could borrow at decent rates in Market B and swapping the interest payments. At the time, there was often little consistency even within a single national market, so that for a given corporate entity, the costs of borrowing at a fixed rate (by issuing bonds) were often out of line with floating-rate borrowing costs, and interest-rate swaps arose from the attempts of corporations to exploit these idiosyncrasies by borrowing in whatever form was cheaper for them and swapping the resulting interest payments for what they really wanted. In most books about derivatives, this *comparative advantage* argument is still presented as the main driver of the swaps market, but in reality it had receded in importance by the early 1990s, when people started turning to the swaps market mostly for speculative and (later) risk management purposes.

In the United States, a major factor in that process has been the parallel explosive growth of the market for mortgages and mortgage-backed securities, which we will briefly discuss in Chapter 10. Mortgages as an asset class are extremely sensitive to interest rates, not just because they are essentially sets of cash flows, but also because of the mortgage holder's ability to refinance when the rates drop. Many organizations, especially mortgage servicers and issuers of mortgage-backed securities, ended up holding truly massive portfolios of residential mortgages worth trillions of dollars. As the sizes of these portfolios kept growing, these organizations found it increasingly difficult to hedge their interest-rate risk with Treasury products, and they started turning to interest-rate swaps for that purpose.

The early 1990s also saw important standardization in the legal framework for swaps transactions. A swap is essentially a legal agreement between two parties, and the need to negotiate the details (such as what happens when one party fails to perform) for every individual transaction was a major drag on the development of this market. In 1992, the International Swap Dealers Association[3] developed something called the ISDA Master Agreement to address this problem. The master agreement is a standard 18-page form covering the main legal angles of a generic derivative transaction, to which the two parties are free to add a schedule containing provisions that they have individually negotiated.

The beauty of the master agreement is that it has to be done only once. After the two parties execute (sign) this master agreement, they are free to do as much derivative business with each other as they like—the confirmation of each individual transaction just gets tacked on to the initial master agreement (which is why for a salesperson, getting a client to sign an ISDA master agreement with your bank is a major coup worthy of putting on a résumé). This development has dramatically reduced the legal risks (and costs) of derivatives business and was a major factor in its rapid growth.

THE SWAPS CURVE

Not only are interest-rate swaps the most widespread type of OTC derivative, but they also play a central role in interest-rate markets in general as a benchmark against which other products are valued and traded. To understand this function of swaps, we need to consider how people determine swap rates. As we mentioned already, the interest rate for the fixed leg of a standard swap is set at a level that makes both parties even—the value of the fixed leg is equal to that of the floating leg. Intuitively, it seems that this requires us to know what the floating-leg payments will be in the future so that we can figure out what the floating leg is worth. While clearly nobody knows what the three-month LIBOR is going to be in three years (or in three months, for that matter), and therefore the dollar value of the future floating payments can only be guessed at, the real question is not

---

3. ISDA was formed in 1985 as the International Swaps Dealers Association and was later renamed the International Swaps and Derivatives Association, keeping the same acronym. Both names are still being used almost interchangeably.

so much what a particular floating payment will be, but rather how much would it cost us today to make sure that we can make that payment no matter what happens to interest rates in the future.

There are two main ways to lock in the value of future interest payments. If we have to pay interest on $1 million on a specific future date, we can enter into a *forward rate agreement* with someone else. A forward rate agreement, or FRA, is itself a popular OTC derivative (see Figure 8–1) and works as follows: when the rate on the future floating-rate payment becomes known (usually at the beginning of the coupon period), we and our counterparty will exchange a payment proportional to the difference between a rate we agree upon today (the FRA rate) and the actual realized value of this rate in the future, to fix our cost of making the floating payment.

Suppose that, as part of a swap agreement, we have to make a three-month LIBOR payment on $100 million principal for a coupon period between May 1 and August 1 next year, and we find a counterparty that does an FRA with us for this period at 4 percent. This means that what we will end up paying on August 1 is going to be 4 percent times 0.25 year times $100 million, or $1.00 million, regardless of what the actual three-month LIBOR rate announced on May 1 will be. If it comes out to be 6 percent, our floating payment will increase to $1.5 million, but our FRA counterparty will pay us $0.5 million, and if the rate comes out to be 2 percent, we'll pay less on our floating payment, but we will have to compensate our FRA counterparty for the difference, so our total cost remains $1 million.

An attentive reader will notice that this is exactly what happens with Eurodollar futures. Owning a Eurodollar futures contract provides a similar hedge for floating payments, as we discussed at the end of the previous chapter: if we have to make a floating payment and we buy the corresponding number of Eurodollar contracts (one contract per $1 million notional), our gains or losses on our futures position exactly offset the changes in the amount of our floating payment. Today's prices for the Eurodollar futures strip therefore tell us almost everything we need to know in order to value a string of floating payments.

As a floating-rate hedge, Eurodollar futures have a big advantage over FRAs because they trade in a very liquid and completely transparent market, so the transaction costs for hedging our floating payments are minimal. Their disadvantage is that, unlike FRAs, which can be tailored to have the exact payment dates we need, Eurodollar futures expire on a predetermined set of dates (the IMM dates), and so in general we have to use certain combinations of them to hedge our specific exposure. For example, if we have the floating payment on a $100 million notional where the rate is set on May 1, we might buy 53 March Eurodollar contracts and 47 June Eurodollar contracts to hedge it. To determine the exact weightings, we need to have some model that will tell us how the rate resetting on May 1 is related to the neighboring Eurodollar rates. More generally, a floating swap leg has a string of floating payments that are hedgeable by a certain combination of Eurodollar futures, and a more practical question is: how many of each Eurodollar contract do we have to buy or sell to eliminate the interest-rate risk on the floating leg?

The concept of a *swaps curve* developed from attempts to provide a systematic way of answering this and similar questions. The idea is to consolidate all available rate information into a single mathematical object in a consistent way. The object of choice is the *discount curve*, which we talked about in Chapter 5 but will quickly describe here. A *discount factor* is a function of time that represents the present value of a $1 payment on a future date. We can relate discount factors to LIBOR deposit rates as follows: if, say, 12-month LIBOR is 5 percent, then we can deposit $1 on the spot date and collect $1.05 in a year, or we can deposit $1/1.05 = $0.9524 today and collect $1 in a year, so the discount factor for the one-year point is 0.9524 if we say that the discount factor for the spot date is 1. In a similar fashion, knowing a deposit rate between any two future dates 1 and 2 [which we shall call $r(12)$] allows us to determine the ratio of discount factors for these two dates: $d(1)/d(2) = 1 + r(12)[t(2) - t(1)]$. The Eurodollar market in fact provides us with such forward rate information: the implied rate on a Eurodollar contract (100 less its price) is a deposit rate for the period beginning on the IMM date when the contract expires and ending three months hence. This information plus the LIBOR fixings allow us to determine a series of discount factors (or, in market parlance, to *build a curve*) using a procedure called *bootstrapping*.

As shown in Figure 8–4, the bootstrapping process starts at the spot date,[4] where the discount factor is known to be 1, and uses a set of known deposit rates to determine the discount factors corresponding to the end dates of those deposits based on the simple formula we referred to in the previous paragraph. Usually the longest deposit rate used at this stage is the three-month LIBOR, as this usually puts us over the nearest IMM date where the first Eurodollar futures contract starts. Then we can determine

---

4. Sometimes the curve construction begins on today's date, and the discount factors for tomorrow and the spot date are determined based on the overnight rate (from today to tomorrow) and the tom-next rate (from tomorrow to the next business day).

FIGURE 8-4

Bootstrapping a swaps curve using Eurodollar futures and a "stub rate." We start out with a discount factor of 1 at $T = 0$. Using a deposit rate (three-month LIBOR), we determine the discount factor for the three-month point. Then we interpolate a discount factor corresponding to the start of the first Eurodollar contract and, using its market price, determine the discount factor for the end of the first IMM period. Then the process can be repeated to get discount factors for other IMM dates.

H5	97.090	2.910
M5	96.810	3.190
U5	96.580	3.420
Z5	96.410	3.590
H6	96.300	3.700
M6	96.200	3.800
U6	96.110	3.890
Z6	96.010	3.990
H7	95.940	4.060
M7	95.850	4.150
U7	95.770	4.230
Z7	95.670	4.330
H8	95.600	4.400
M8	95.520	4.480
U8	95.420	4.580
Z8	95.330	4.670
H9	95.250	4.750
M9	95.170	4.830
U9	95.080	4.920
Z9	94.980	5.020

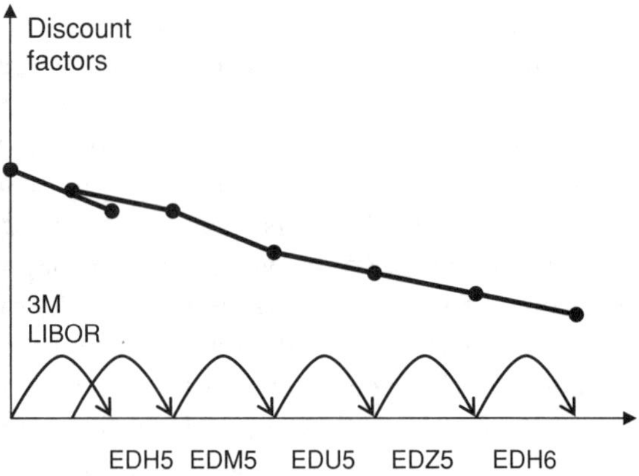

the discount factor corresponding to the first IMM date by interpolating between the already known discount factors. When we know the discount factor for the beginning of the Eurodollar period (from the IMM date to three months hence), we can use the market price of that contract to determine the forward rate for that period and find the discount factor corresponding to its end date, and then we can use the next Eurodollar contract to move another three months out, and on and on, until we run out of Eurodollar futures.

Once we have this discount curve, we can determine a discount factor for any date by interpolation. This allows us to (1) determine the present value of any set of cash flows and (2) determine the forward rate between any two future dates (by taking the ratio of the corresponding discount factors). By construction, if we ask the curve for one of the rates that were inputs to its construction, it will give us the input value back, whereas if we ask for any other rate, it will give us a value that is consistent with all the input rates. Note carefully that this curve has to be rebuilt every time one of the Eurodollar futures trades up or down (which happens every couple of seconds), so the curve is a living, breathing thing that constantly moves to reflect the current market conditions.

Once we have the curve, determining the swaps rate is an easy process: we just need to find the present value of both legs and make them equal. The present value of the fixed leg is simply the swap rate (which we are trying to determine) times the sum of the discount factors for each of the payment dates of that leg. To value the floating leg, we have to calculate the forward rate for each reset date and then discount the resulting payments. As a simple exercise, the reader is invited to do this straightforward calculation and verify that the present value of a floating payment between dates 1 and 2 is the difference of the discount factors for the beginning and end of the period, $d(1) - d(2)$. This makes sense intuitively: this formula suggests that an interest payment is equivalent to taking \$1 at the beginning of the deposit period and giving it back at the end, and thus represents the value of "using" the \$1 over that period.

An interesting corollary to this is that if we have a string of consecutive interest payments (and the floating leg of a swap is really just that),[5] its total value is simply the difference between the first discount factor (1 for a spot-starting swap) and the last discount factor $d(N)$ for the end date of the swap, as all intermediate factors cancel out. Therefore, the value of the floating leg is also easy to determine from the discount curve. The swap rate is then the rate that makes both values equal: $R \times$ [sum of $d(i)$ over the fixed-leg payment dates] $= d(1) - d(N)$ is the governing relationship.

It is worth noting that if we pretend that the notional amount is exchanged at the end of the swap (which means adding $d(N)$ to both sides of this formula), then the floating leg plus that imaginary redemption payment has a value of 1 (i.e., of *par*), while the fixed leg becomes the value of a fixed-rate bond with the coupon rate of R. The value of R that brings the value of that bond to par is therefore usually called the *par swap rate*, as opposed to a swap rate in general, which in theory can be negotiated to be anything for a given swap transaction, whereas the par swap rate is a function of current market conditions and changes with every market tick.

---

5. Because of the vagaries of the business date adjustment process, the end of one floating-payment period does not always coincide with the beginning of the next period, so in practice the valuation of a floating leg is somewhat trickier than what we describe here, but the overall effect of these subtleties is quite small.

This bond equivalence view of swaps is very useful for understanding their interest-rate risk: essentially, the risk is the same as that for a coupon bond with the appropriate coupon rate, since the value of the floating leg is constant in this approach (which provides the justification for why Figure 8–3 looks the way it does).

The swap curve provides a consistent framework for relating the swaps market to the Eurodollar futures market. People noticed early on, however, that there is a small but important inconsistency in using Eurodollars to describe swaps: unlike FRAs, which provide a perfect hedge for each floating payment, the Eurodollar futures have a different timing of payments. An FRA makes one payment when the floating payment itself is due,[6] whereas gains or losses on a futures position accumulate in a margin account over the life of the contract. When the rates rise, we realize losses on the Eurodollar contract right away, whereas the same dollar loss on an equivalent FRA position will be realized only at its expiration, so the two are not exactly equivalent even if their dates match exactly.

An alternative (and more common) way to look at this difference is based on the concept of convexity. The present value of an FRA is a nonlinear and convex function of the underlying rate (it is proportional to $1/\{1 + R \times [t(2) - t(1)]\}$), whereas the payoff of a futures contract is by definition a linear function of the rate, as shown in Figure 8–5. The convexity of an FRA makes it a more attractive product when rates are volatile, since our losses when the rate goes up 10 bp will be somewhat smaller than our gains when the rate goes down by the same amount (as we discussed in Chapter 4, convexity makes the expected value of the price greater than the price corresponding to the expected value of the rate). Because of this *convexity adjustment*, the futures contract should always be somewhat cheaper than an equivalent FRA, and the implied rate from the futures is therefore always somewhat higher than the true forward rate. The difference, as we would expect from Figure 8–5, increases with the width of the rate distribution function at the contract expiration (which is volatility squared times the time to expiration) and can reach 5 to 10 bp for Eurodollar futures that are a few years away. In practice, convexity adjustments are usually calculated overnight using a term structure model (we'll discuss what this is in Chapter 13) and are applied as a rigid shift to live Eurodollar rates.

Eurodollar futures strips technically allow us to build a swaps curve out to 10 years from now because 40 contracts are listed, but in practice the

---

6. In fact, most FRAs pay at the beginning of the coupon period when the rate reset is announced—the amount is discounted to the beginning of the period.

F I G U R E   8–5

Origins of the convexity adjustment. A forward contract is always more valuable than an equivalent futures contract because of its convexity. The more the rate at expiry deviates from the contractual FRA rate, the greater the price difference. The expected value of this difference is called the convexity adjustment; it depends on the distribution of rates at the expiry of the contracts.

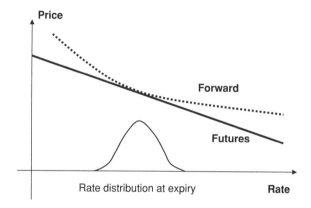

contracts beyond 5 years are rarely used, as the liquidity drops off precipitously for such distant contracts. So what do people do to construct a swaps curve that goes beyond 5 years? They use swaps rates themselves as inputs to extend the bootstrapping procedure beyond the last Eurodollar contract. Suppose we used the first eight Eurodollar futures and built the curve out to 2 years, and someone tells us what the 3-year par swap rate is. We can then try to determine what the discount factor for the 3-year point should be so that a 3-year swap with this known rate prices to par. We determine a schedule of cash flows for that swap and discover that we can price most of them already because we know all the factors up to and including the 2-year point (see Figure 8–6). To price the remaining two cash flows (at 2.5 and 3 years), we introduce another point in the curve, at 3 years, and find the 2.5 years discount factor by interpolation. We then solve for the 3-year discount factor that gives the correct (par) value for the whole 3-year swap. Once we have the 3-year point, we can add the 4-year point, and so on. Most swap curves are extended to 50 years in this way.

Figure 8–7 shows an example of a swaps curve. The discount factors are spaced every three months out to five years (reflecting the periodicity of the Eurodollar futures) and then become yearly. The par swap rates shown in the figure are calculated from those discount factors; beyond five years,

FIGURE   8–6

Bootstrapping a swaps curve using swap rates. In this
example, we have determined discount factors for the first
two years using the first eight Eurodollar contracts. Now
someone tells us the three-year swap rate, and we can
already price the first four of the six cash flows on its fixed
leg. We can then extend the curve by adding a three-year
point in such a way that the present value of all cash flows
(including the last two "unknown" cash flows) is equal to
par. Once the three-year point is known, we can add the
four-year swap rate, and so on.

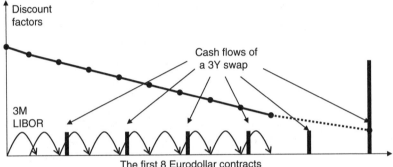

The first 8 Eurodollar contracts

these rates are simply equal to the input swap rates, while below five years
they reflect the Eurodollar prices. We also show three-month forward rates
calculated from the curve (by taking discount factors at time t and $t + 3$
months and dividing one by the other).

Notice that the forward rate curve does not look particularly smooth;
this is the result of the interpolation process required to get the factors
between the known curve points. We will discuss different interpolation
schemes in Chapter 13; here we just note that the whole idea of the swaps
curve is that it can provide a systematic way of determining unknown discount factors based on a finite set of known points, so that the choice of
interpolation method is crucial to the curve construction process. Other
choices during the curve building are how many Eurodollar futures to use
(usually it is either 8 or 20) and which deposit (or *stub*) rates to use at the
very short end of the curve; there is no single "right" way of doing this, and
in fact most trading desks maintain several curves built using different
methodologies.

The swap rates going into the construction of the curve are themselves
tradable things that move every few seconds. There is no centralized market

FIGURE 8-7

A sample swaps curve. The curve is really a vector of date–discount factor pairs, as shown by the bottom curve. The first 20 points in the curve come from Eurodollar futures and are three months apart; the rest of the points come from par swap rates and are one year apart. From these discount factors, one can calculate par swap rates for any maturity (the middle curve); this procedure simply gives the swap rates used as inputs for the curve construction. One can also calculate forward rates between any two dates–the top curve shows a chain of three-month forward rates computed every three months. This forward curve shows a lot of fluctuation, which is mostly the result of the vagaries of interpolation between the few known points.

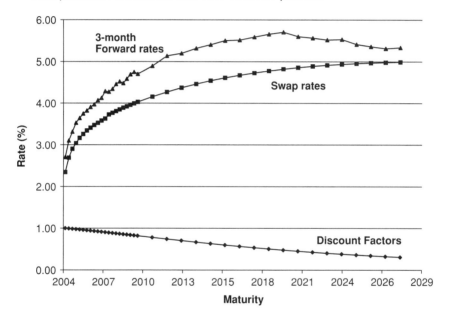

for swaps, so one cannot directly observe how they trade and determine the swap rates accordingly. Instead, swaps are always linked to the most liquid products in the underlying interest-rate market. In the U.S. dollar market, the swap market is driven by the Treasury on-the-runs, and the linkage between these two markets is established through a concept of *swap spreads*. A 10-year swap spread is by definition the difference between the 10-year swap rate and the yield on the current 10-year Treasury. Similar definitions apply to 2-, 3-, 5-, and 30-year swap spreads.

For other swap maturities (which are usually called *tenors*), swap spreads are defined as the difference between the swap rate and the *interpolated Treasury yield*, as shown in Figure 8–8. The interpolation is done in terms of nominal maturity, so the four-year interpolated yield is exactly halfway between the three-year and five-year yields irrespective of the actual maturities of the Treasury benchmarks (which are usually somewhat less than the nominal maturity). The interpolation procedure is structured to be as simple and unambiguous as possible so that everyone can agree on what, say, the seven-year swap spread is.

The idea behind swap spreads is something that is near and dear to any theoretical physicist: separation of time scales. The underlying Treasury yields move every couple of seconds, but the swap spreads are adjusted fairly infrequently (a couple of times an hour). The swap rates then also move with every Treasury tick, while the swap traders focus on maintaining the spreads to reflect conditions in the swaps market. A similar procedure is used in Europe for EURIBOR swaps, where EUREX Bund, Bobl, and Schatz futures are used as liquid points instead of Treasuries and each swap rate is rigidly linked to the theoretical yield of one of those futures, so that as the futures trade up and down, the swaps curve moves with every tick, while the spreads are adjusted much less frequently. The resulting swaps curves in each market reflect up-to-the-second conditions in the underlying

FIGURE 8–8

U.S. dollar swap spreads are by definition the difference between interpolated Treasury yields and the swap rates of the same maturity. The swap spreads are kept constant (or, rather, they are updated infrequently), so that as the benchmark Treasuries trade up and down, the swap rates also move with every Treasury tick.

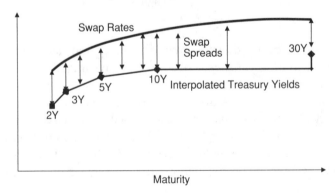

cash (or futures) market and in effect convert the few liquid points in that market into a smooth discount curve that can be used for pricing other fixed-income products. This "benchmark" function of the swaps curves is very important and will be discussed more fully in subsequent chapters.

A major source of information about spreads that every swaps trader in the United States looks at is Telerate 19901, which is often called the most watched data page on Wall Street (Figure 8–9). The spreads shown on this page come from ICAP, which acts as an interdealer broker in the swaps market. Unlike cash market interdealer brokers (such as BrokerTec and Garban, which are now part of ICAP), this page provides only an *indicative* set of swap spreads with a 4-bp bid-offer spread, which is much wider than what most dealers would quote. Despite their indicative status, the 19901 spreads are crucial to price discovery in the swaps market, as everybody tries to keep their spread quotes in line with this page.

What is the economic meaning of swap spreads? They reflect two major market factors: credit risk and the balance between supply and demand. Swaps are indexed to LIBOR, which is a rate for unsecured lending. A LIBOR depositor runs the risk that the bank where the funds are deposited

---

F I G U R E   8–9

Telerate page 19901. For each swaps tenor, the page displays interpolated mid-yield for the Treasuries and bid and offer swap spreads in basis points. The "semi-bond" swap rates (for semiannual fixed-leg payments) are by construction the mid-yields plus the swap spreads. "Annual-money" swaps rates are for swaps where the fixed-leg payments are annual (which is the market standard for shorter-term swaps). © Reuters, 2006. Reproduced with permission.

12/10 20:19 GMT	[MONEYLINE CAPITAL MARKETS:ICAP & BTEC]				19901
TERM TREASURY	YIELD	M-YIELD	SWAP-SPREAD	SEMI-BOND	ANN-MONEY
[2YR 100.07+-076	1.878-874	1.876	37.25-33.25	2.249-209	2.230-190]
3YR	|	| 2.266 |	52.50-48.50	| 2.791-751	| 2.772-732
4YR	|	| 2.656 |	54.00-50.00	| 3.196-156	| 3.178-137
[5YR 99.25 -25+	3.048-044	3.046	47.25-43.25	3.519-479	3.501-461]
6YR	|	| 3.247 |	55.00-51.00	| 3.797-757	| 3.781-740
7YR	|	| 3.448 |	58.75-54.75	| 4.035-995	| 4.020-980
8YR	|	| 3.649 |	57.50-53.50	| 4.224-184	| 4.210-170
9YR	|	| 3.850 |	53.00-49.00	| 4.380-340	| 4.367-327
[10YR 99.18 -19+	4.054-048	4.051	46.75-42.75	4.518-478	4.507-466]
12YR	|	| 4.051 |	70.25-66.25	| 4.753-713	| 4.744-703
15YR	|	| 4.268 |	75.75-71.75	| 5.025-985	| 5.018-978
20YR	|	| 4.484 |	76.50-72.50	| 5.249-209	| 5.245-205
25YR	|	| 4.701 |	60.00-56.00	| 5.301-261	| 5.298-257
[30YR 106.27 -00	4.923-913	4.918	39.75-35.75	5.315-275	5.312-272]
12Y MID-YIELDS USE 10Y MID-YIELDS,ALL OTHERS(EXCEPT ON-THE-RUN) ARE INTERPOLATED					
[BBA LIBOR 1M] 1.42125	[3M] 1.41000	[6M] 1.43000	[12M] 1.59375		

will default over the life of the deposit, and the deposit rate should reflect this risk—it should be higher than a comparable-maturity rate for a Treasury repo, which is unaffected by credit risk. Indeed, historically U.S. dollar LIBOR rates have always been 10 to 100 bp higher than Treasury repo or fed funds rates, and therefore swap rates (which are essentially averaged LIBOR rates) have also been higher than the comparable-maturity Treasury yields. The swap spreads observed at any given time, therefore, reflect the market perception of credit risk, and any event that affects that perception will cause the swap spreads to change. For example, events like the first Gulf war, the Russian debt default and the Long Term Capital Management debacle in 1998, and the corporate scandals of the late 1990s all led to abrupt widening of swap spreads because of fears of bank defaults, followed by a gradual tightening to more normal levels as the impact of these events wore off.

Ultimately, swap spreads reflect the relative desirability of swaps compared to Treasuries, and anything that makes Treasuries more desirable and swaps less desirable will widen swap spreads. The credit events just mentioned widened swap spreads by making swaps appear more risky than Treasuries, but there are other mechanisms that lead to the same result. In early 2000, the U.S. Treasury announced a buyback program aimed at reducing the amount of outstanding Treasury debt. The market interpreted this as a sign that there was not going to be any more supply of long-end Treasuries, which greatly increased the desirability of Treasuries relative to swaps and caused the swap spreads to widen to an all-time high of 160 bp in the 10-year sector. On a micro level, these broad economic forces manifest themselves as changes in supply and demand for swaps and Treasuries: if more people want to receive a fixed rate in swaps, the dealers will gradually reduce the rates they pay by tightening the spreads they quote, while the dealers will widen their spreads when people prefer to meet their demand for duration by buying Treasuries rather than swaps.

THE MECHANICS OF SWAPS TRADING

This brings us to our next topic: how do people actually trade swaps? As is our custom, we look at this process from the perspective of a dealer bank, where there would typically be a dedicated interest-rate swaps desk, either as part of a larger interest-rate business that also includes cash products, as part of the derivatives business, which includes other interest-rate derivatives, or (most often) both. Each trader on the swaps desk trades a certain maturity sector (typically short, intermediate, or long). Whenever a customer of the dealer bank wants to enter into an interest-rate swap, the inquiry will be passed to the appropriate sector traders for pricing. The traders maintain one or more live swap curves that allow them to quickly price both standard swaps (whose rates are themselves inputs into the curve construction) and nonstandard structures (say, a four-year-nine-month swap starting in 10 days). The swaps curve will typically tell the traders what the "fair" swap rate should be, and they will add a bid-offer spread to that depending on the size of the trade and who the customer is. The rate quote[7] is then passed back to the customer, and if the customer accepts the quote, then the trade is instantly executed and the trading desk has yet another swap on its hands.

The new swaps transaction is written to the firm's trade database, usually as a huge record containing all the terms—counterparty, rate, dates of all cash flows, rate reset dates, and so on—and the firm's back office will now manage the obligations resulting from this trade for a long time to come (until the last payment has been made). The traders, however, are mostly concerned with the present value of the swaps they have on their books. The newly done swap has added considerable interest-rate risk to their swaps portfolios, and the main job of the traders is to manage this risk responsibly.

There are several ways of reducing the interest-rate risk of the swaps book. The first, and clearly most desirable, way of offloading risk is to do an identical but opposite swap trade with someone else and earn the bid-offer spread. Let us say we've done a $100 million 10-year swap with Citibank where we pay a 5.00 percent fixed rate, and a few minutes later we do another 10-year swap with British Petroleum where it pays us 5.02 percent fixed on the same $100 million notional. Note that if we cannot find another customer who wants to do an offsetting swap, we can turn to the interdealer brokers such as ICAP or Tullett, which will find us a counterparty for this trade, or we can even go to our competitors (other swaps dealers) directly and do the offsetting trade with them. Either way, if we manage to cleanly offset one trade with another, we have (almost) no interest-rate risk, the floating payments cancel out, and the fixed payments net out to bring us 2.0 bp on the notional over the next 10 years.

Let us compare and contrast this situation with a scenario in which we bought a bond (or a futures contract) on the bid side and immediately

<hr/>

7. In the United States, the market convention used to be to quote the swap spread rather than the rate, but now increasingly the rate is quoted, as has always been the case in Europe and Japan.

resold it on the offered side. In the case of a bond or a future, our PnL is simply the difference between the buy and sell prices times the size of the trade, and once the trades settle, we have no obligation to anyone, so our PnL is really money in the bank. In the case of a similar swap trade (buy on the bid side and resell on the offered side) our PnL is the *present value* of the resulting cash flows. In the example of the previous paragraph, the net result of the two swaps is that we will receive a $10,000 payment every six months for the next 10 years. The present value of that is clearly positive (about $150,000) and actually quite large, but it is not money in the bank, as it will take 10 years to collect all these payments, and their present value will change as interest rates rise and fall.

Perhaps a more revealing example of what happens in swaps (and, generally, derivatives) books is the case where we do an offsetting transaction tomorrow. A 10-year swap tomorrow is not the same thing as the 10-year swap today, as all cash flows will be shifted by one day. The economics of the two trades will be almost the same (we are making about the same amount of money), but now the cash flows do not cancel out, and the firm will have to process 120 payments (40 on the floating leg and 20 on the fixed, for each of the two swaps) over the next 10 years to turn our PnL into cash.

As is clear from the previous example, there is no such thing as a position in the 10-year swap, or a position in any OTC derivative in general; what we have in our book is a spaghetti of cash flows resulting from all previous trades. Large swaps books can contain hundreds of thousands, sometimes millions, of cash flows—how do the traders make sense of them, and, more importantly, how do they make money?

While many of the questions we can ask about a cash products trading book (such as "what is my position in X?") do not make sense for derivatives books, there are some questions that do make sense, and the first of them is, "What is the net present value of all my cash flows?" This number is essentially the PnL that the traders care deeply about. In theory, this question can be answered at any given time by taking the live swaps curve and using it to calculate the present value of all cash flows in the book. In practice, given the huge number of cash flows in a typical book, this kind of full valuation is usually done once a day based on the *closing curve* (the swaps curve built using the closing prices for the Eurodollar futures, on-the-run Treasuries, and the closing swap spreads supplied by the traders).

Another question that makes sense, and is in fact even more important is, "What will happen to my PnL if the 10-year swap rate changes by 1 bp?" More generally, we want to know our *risk exposure* to all liquid instruments that affect our book; typically the set includes Eurodollar futures and standard swap rates. To answer that kind of question, we take the closing curve, "bump" it by changing one of the input rates (say, the three-year swap rate) by 1 bp, and then revalue the whole book using the bumped curve; the difference between the bumped present value and the closing present value represents our risk exposure to the three-year swap rate (it is expressed in dollars per basis point). This calculation has to be repeated for every point on the swaps curve (which means 20 to 40 times), so it is much more expensive than the closing PnL calculation and can be done only once a day, usually overnight.

The results of the end-of-day valuation and risk runs form the basis for the official risk and PnL reports that are submitted to the firm's risk management unit, but for trading purposes it is highly desirable to have intraday (preferably real-time) estimates of PnL and risk. This is no small challenge from a technology perspective and is usually achieved by taking advantage of the fact that the composition of the book(s) changes relatively little during the day (the number of trades done today is small compared to the total number of trades already in the book). If no new trades are done, we can assume that the risk sensitivities do not change when the market moves, and the PnL changes by the scalar product of the risk exposures times the daily moves in all risk factors (again, a physicist would recognize this as a standard linearization procedure). To the extent that new trades are done, the present value and risk exposures of the newly added cash flows can be computed intraday because there are not that many of them.

Figure 8–10 illustrates a typical set of data that a swaps trader will look at during the day. It includes the risk exposures and PnL broken down into various components, which we will now briefly discuss. First, there is something called *hedge PnL*, so we need to discuss hedging. One way to reduce or eliminate interest-rate risk in swaps trading is to buy and sell the appropriate amounts of the underlying liquid products—Eurodollar futures and on-the-run Treasuries (in fact, the risk exposures that we discussed earlier tell us exactly how many futures contracts and Treasuries to buy or sell to eliminate the risk). Hedging swaps with Treasuries and futures is sometimes referred to as swaps *warehousing*—sort of storing them until an offsetting swaps transaction can be done. It is fairly rare (and too expensive) to hedge each individual swap with cash products and futures, so the hedging is done at the level of the whole book. Hedge PnL in Figure 8–10 refers to the PnL of these cash and futures trades; because of the different nature of these products, the PnL and risk properties of hedge positions are usually calculated differently from those of swaps transactions and therefore are reported separately.

Other components of the PnL shown in Figure 8–10 reflect the mechanics of swaps trading. The *amend* PnL shows the impact of today's amendments to the terms of previous trades (such as trade breaks), while the *reset* PnL arises from the difference between the actual three-month LIBOR that is announced every morning and the estimate of that value that was used the night before to compute the closing PnL. These PnL components represent one-time adjustments to the closing PnL and do not change with each market data tick. In contrast to cash products trading, almost all PnL in a derivatives book is unrealized in the sense that only a very small fraction of it is converted into cash each day.

Note that while hedging swaps with Eurodollars is an exact science, hedging with Treasuries (or with EUREX bond futures in Europe) leaves us exposed to *spread risk*—the risk that swap spreads will tighten or widen, so that the PnL of what we thought was a perfect hedge will not exactly offset the PnL of our swaps book. Another type of risk that we do not see displayed in Figure 8–10 is credit risk—the risk that one of our swaps counterparties may default. Different banks make different arrangements to deal with that unpleasant possibility. One solution that is fairly widespread is to require each counterparty to make a (relatively small) payment called a credit charge at the inception of each swap; the amount is calculated by the dealer to reflect the perceived credit risk of a given counterparty. This allows the dealer to assume that the credit risk has already been dealt with, so that whatever happens to the swaps is due only to the movement of rates rather than to changes in the credit standing of a given counterparty.

The daily work of a swaps trader is to watch a display like Figure 8–10 and try to keep the total PnL of her books positive and growing. The first step in this process is to make sure to enter each new trade with a positive PnL, which requires adjusting the swap rate slightly above or below what the curve says is the fair rate corresponding to a zero PnL (effectively, we charge half the bid-offer spread on each trade). Each new trade then adds something to risk exposures, and the art of swaps trading (or any other trading, for that matter) is to manage those risks intelligently, getting rid of exposures we do not want (by hedging with cash products and futures or doing offsetting trades in the interdealer market) and keeping ones we do want. If a swaps trader can control the costs of hedging and avoid bad judgment errors in telling good risks from bad, the initially positive PnL

FIGURE 8-10

A mock risk and PnL display for a set of swaps books.

Risk Instrument	Books IRS001	Books IRS002	Books LONDON08
O/N	$63	($87)	$4,988
1w	$745	($11,478)	$29,628
1m	$9,821	($10,581)	$11,669
2m	$4,778	($12,091)	$19,771
3m	$3,004	($6,918)	$15,162
EDZ5	$19,989	($38,526)	$70,286
EDH6	$7,983	($21,422)	$40,744
EDM6	($1,339)	$1,663	$6,421
EDU6	($14,549)	$22,896	($38,068)
EDZ6	$5,586	($5,678)	$1,430
EDH7	($29,405)	$65,274	($129,917)
EDM7	$40,093	($90,069)	$183,015
EDU7	$33,405	($71,027)	$137,374
SWAP-2Y	$105,004	($215,391)	$438,715
SWAP-3Y	$8,555	($16,984)	$31,704
SWAP-4Y	($21,495)	$48,954	($90,360)
SWAP-5Y	($39,400)	$83,211	($173,175)
SWAP-6Y	($49,540)	$92,724	($195,201)
SWAP-7Y	($19,304)	$44,209	($89,888)
SWAP-8Y	($984)	($5,605)	$8,255
SWAP-9Y	$23,560	($40,470)	$81,470
SWAP-10Y	($12,049)	$21,979	($36,931)
SWAP-11Y	$40,543	($78,870)	$158,625
SWAP-12Y	$6,699	($14,481)	$31,707
SWAP-15Y	($19,239)	$33,919	($64,957)
SWAP-20Y	($44,089)	$87,112	($182,511)
SWAP-25Y	($30,430)	$53,294	($112,462)
SWAP-30Y	($20,495)	$42,151	($94,260)
TOTAL	$7,510	($42,293)	$63,233
PnL:			
Trading	$34,590,434	$590,389	($6,774,098)
Hedge	($23,440,390)	($5,450,033)	$8,394,434
Amend		($45,390)	($13,776)
Reset	$5,049	($945)	($1,443)
TOTAL	$11,155,093	($4,889,462)	$1,539,336

of each trade will remain positive, and the more trades she does, the more money she makes.

As a matter of fact, this sounds remarkably like our description of cash products trading in Chapter 5, but it is much more complicated conceptually and technologically—what motivates people to trade these more complex products? Up until fairly recently, the answer was very simple: this business was very lucrative. The dealers used to charge a 2- to 3-bp bid-offer spread on most swaps, so a swaps trader could easily make $200,000 on a single $100 million trade—a good day's PnL for a typical cash trader. If a swaps desk did just 10 such trades a day, it would bring in half a billion dollars every year. This kind of money more than justified the investment in models and trading systems needed to make derivatives trading possible.

Many other derivatives trading areas still retain this essential feature of doing relatively few but highly profitable trades, but for swaps, these days seem to be gone, or at least are going fast. At the time of this writing, an institutional customer can execute interest-rate swaps electronically on either Bloomberg (which provides several single-dealer swaps trading pages as well as some multidealer ones) or TradeWeb, where the dealers offer two-sided, 0.5-bp-wide markets for up to $100 million notional. Electronic trading in swaps is a relatively recent phenomenon (it started in earnest in 2004), but it is rapidly transforming swaps trading into a low-margin, high-trade-count business, which is exactly what TradeWeb and its brethren did to government bond trading five years earlier. This has greatly expanded the number of institutional customers that trade swaps and is sure to lead to even faster growth in swaps trading volumes.

This process of commoditization, however, is so far limited to the so-called *vanilla* interest-rate swaps: swaps that adhere to standard market conventions in each market and cover only a limited set of tenors. If we enter a new 10-year swap, we are likely to pay about 0.5 bp bid-offer, but if we want to unwind this trade two weeks later, it is likely to be much more expensive because it is now a nonstandard swap with 9 years, 11 months, and 2 weeks to maturity. Most nonvanilla swaps differ only in maturity and/or timing of coupon payments, but there is a larger area of *structured swaps* where the dealers are more than happy to customize the terms of a swaps agreement to meet specific customer needs. Payment dates can be adjusted, the notional value can increase or decrease with time (accreting swaps and amortizing swaps), and the fixed-leg rates can be set either low or high, so that, for example, the customer receives a large up-front payment from the dealer and then compensates for it by paying a higher rate (this is often used as a back-door mechanism to raise funds). There are also a wide variety of swaps that do not follow the "fixed-for-floating" scheme at all and swap different kinds of payments. First, there are *basis swaps*, where people swap interest payments calculated on a different basis—for example, one-month LIBOR payments for three-month LIBOR payments. To make such an exchange fair, the rate on one of the floating legs is adjusted by a constant spread, so a typical basis swap would be swapping one-month LIBOR for three-month LIBOR plus 2.5 bp for 10 years. One of the legs of a basis swap is usually three-month LIBOR, but the other can be based on an entirely different interest-rate index—a Treasury bill rate, prime, a commercial paper index, and so on.

There are also *cross-currency swaps*, which are similar in spirit; in such swaps, the two legs make floating payments in different currencies (for example, one leg pays U.S. dollar three-month LIBOR and the other pays the euro three-month EURIBOR rate). To deal with the exchange-rate risk in such swaps, the parties actually exchange principal amounts at the beginning of the swap at current exchange rate and then again at the end of the swap.

Finally, there are swaps in which at least one leg has nothing to do with interest rates at all; for example, an *equity swap* involves payments of total returns on an equity index (such as the S&P 500) on one of the legs. The swaps market participants demonstrate an almost limitless inventiveness in designing such structures, and I refer those readers who want to familiarize themselves with this area to the Recommended Reading section; here we just note that the swaps market keeps growing rapidly not only in terms of trade volumes, but also in the breadth of coverage.

TECHNOLOGY AND SWAPS TRADING

As should be obvious from our discussion, the swaps market in particular and derivatives markets in general could not have developed to their present prominence (and in fact simply could not exist) without technology in the broad sense, from quantitative models of interest rates to market data feeds to booking and settlement systems. Even if we abstract from the settlement issues, we can trade equities or bonds armed with a phone and an HP12C financial calculator (and people traded these products for centuries without even those technological marvels), but we cannot trade swaps without software that knows how to build the curves, how to compute payment dates and cash flows, and how to calculate the PnL and risk of our positions.

The emergence of the swaps market in the early 1980s was possible only because computer technology had reached a point where such software could be built within Wall Street firms, but it also provided a major impetus for the development of financial analytics in general and resulted in a massive influx of people with quantitative and programming skills into Wall Street trading rooms. As we will discuss in more detail in Chapter 13, the pieces of today's financial analytics toolbox that deal with date manipulation, discount curves, and present value—the core of any financial library—were developed in direct response to the needs of the swaps market. Over the years, the modeling emphasis has shifted from building swaps curves to using them as benchmarks for valuation of all kinds of other financial products, but swaps still provide a lot of technical people on Wall Street with their livelihood, especially if we go beyond financial analytics to trading and settlement systems, which in the case of swaps and other derivatives present huge technological challenges. In recent years, the market has become even more technologically intensive with the advent of electronic trading of swaps, so derivatives technology is likely to remain one of the best places on Wall Street for technical people. After all, that's where the money is.

Interest-rate swaps are almost unique among major derivative products in that they are completely deterministic instruments; as we explained previously, their value is a function of the term structure of interest rates *today* and does not depend on how much those rates will move about in the future. Most derivatives are not like that: their value depends on the future dynamics of financial markets, which is generally referred to as their *volatility*. In the next chapter, we proceed to examine the concept of volatility and the derivatives markets where it plays a central role.

CHAPTER 9

Options Markets

We have gone about halfway through the book without discussing options (the financial instruments that played a central role in the derivatives revolution of the last three decades), and it is time for us to change that in this chapter. Options are of special importance for our narrative because many if not most of the quantitative professionals who migrated to Wall Street during this period saw options as the reason that Wall Street needed their quantitative skills. Options pricing has earned the status of the rocket science of finance, and even though in reality the percentage of Wall Street quants who actually price options for a living is quite small, it remains a matter of professional pride for all the rest of us to be familiar with this subject. This familiarity, however, rarely goes beyond the math, which is a pity, because options have many interesting issues besides pricing.

Our goal in this chapter is to rectify this somewhat by telling the story of options as a financial market. This market is undergoing rapid changes now, and we will attempt to put those changes in perspective by reviewing the history of options trading and the basic facts about how this market operated in the past and how it functions today. Another theme that we will briefly touch upon is the importance of options as fundamental building blocks for other, more complex financial derivatives. I will try to keep the focus away from option valuation issues, but it is impossible to understand this market without at least some qualitative feel for the factors that drive options prices, so we will spend some time trying to develop such options intuition (in keeping with our principle of using no formulas, we will try to do that without ever writing down the Black-Scholes formula!). I hope that after reading this chapter, a novice will know 90 percent of what she actually needs to know about this market, and that much of the remaining 10 percent can be covered by standard pricing software. Enough of these forward declarations, however—let us begin our story.

THE HISTORY OF OPTIONS TRADING

While some people claim that options were described in the Bible, the first serious appearance of options on the world finance stage probably occurred during the Dutch "tulip mania" of 1636. This episode is, however, too crazy to be used as the basis for our scholarly discussion, so we acknowledge the European origin of options and skip forward to a different time and place: Chicago in the late 1860s. This time and place should sound familiar to those who read Chapter 7, and indeed we go to the Chicago Board of Trade, which we discussed in that chapter, as the cradle of the futures markets.

One can argue that CBOT was also the birthplace of organized options markets, although this newborn was kind of unwanted and faced a very difficult infancy. As the CBOT members expanded their futures trading activities (remember, futures were still a fairly fluid concept in 1860s), some of them also began buying and selling what they called "trading privileges"— the rights to buy or sell futures contracts at some later time at prices fixed today. This practice started in the tumultuous Civil War years and was first used by traders as insurance against unprecedented wartime swings in commodity prices. However, it soon became obvious that this "privileged trading" provided huge potential for speculation, and the next three decades saw numerous attempts to banish the practice.

To understand this early options-related controversy (and there will be many more), let us think about what this "privilege" represented. Let us say that a grain futures contract is trading at 30 cents a bushel, and a fellow futures trader approaches us and says that he will sell us the right to buy this contract from him at 30 cents tomorrow. Would we buy this right, and if so, how much should we pay for it?

What the futures trader is selling to us is a *call option*; according to its modern definition, a call option gives us the right, but not the obligation, to buy something in the future at a price that is fixed today (I think that *privilege* is a much better word for the same thing, but unfortunately it has dropped out of the options vocabulary). In Figure 9–1 we show the *payoff* of this call option as a function of the price of the underlying (grains futures contract, in our case). If the futures price drops below the *strike price* of 30 cents tomorrow, say to 25 cents, this option will be worthless. We are not going to *exercise* it; instead, we will buy futures in the open market.

FIGURE 9-1

A call option at expiration is worth the difference between the current price of the underlying (grain futures in our example) and the strike price. If this value is negative, we do not exercise the option, so it is worth nothing. Note that it is the privilege of not exercising the option if it is against our interest (so that its value to us cannot become negative) that makes the option payoff function nonlinear. A put option (the privilege to sell the futures at the strike price) has a similarly nonlinear payoff.

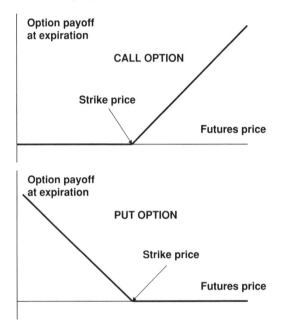

However, if the futures price rises to 35 cents, then we will go to whoever sold us the option and pay him 30 cents for the contract (this is what options exercise means) that we can immediately resell for 35 cents, so in this case the option is worth 5 cents.

Of course, we do not know today what tomorrow will bring, so having such an option is valuable even if it is currently *out of the money* (the current underlying price is less than the strike price), because there is always a chance that the price will go up and the option will become *in the money* before its *expiration* (the remaining case of an option with a current underlying price equal to the strike price is referred to as an *at-the-money*, or *ATM*, option). In our grains futures example, it is clear that the at-the-money option offered to us by our fellow trader is valuable, and if we are concerned that prices may rise by tomorrow, then buying this option makes sense as insurance against the rise in prices. (If we were afraid that prices would fall, we could buy a *put option*, which works exactly the same way except that we get the right to sell at the strike price.) However, the question of exactly how valuable these options were (and how much people would be willing to pay for them) remained unresolved—for the first hundred years of options trading, people relied on their intuition and common sense to decide what options should be worth.

For many people inside and outside CBOT, there was something insidious about such "trade in puts and calls." The so-called agrarian interests representing farmers, who thought that the futures trading itself depressed the prices for their products, seized on options trading as an example of pure, unvarnished speculation that served no discernible economic purpose. The critics were saying that options were much worse than futures because, at least in theory, one buys a futures contract as a proxy for the underlying commodity and delivery can always be made, whereas options did not have a tangible underlying and therefore looked like a pure gambling device.

In fact, part of this hostility to options came from the same source that fuels the opposition to financial derivatives today: the critics were unable to understand why options have value and what drives that value. Admittedly, this is not something that is easy to explain to an average farmer, but the farmers' political leaders did not understand it either, and instead turned to government for help in banning privileged trading as the worst of speculative market abuses. In 1874, the State of Illinois passed a law making privileged trading illegal. CBOT then had to ban options trading from its main trading floor, but the practice simply moved to the many hallways of the building and to the surrounding back alleys. The critics pointed to this shift as evidence that CBOT officials were reluctant to stamp out this sinister activity, and indeed there was something behind these allegations. When CBOT directors decided to hold a trial of a few members accused of illegal trading in privileges, one of the accused made it known that he had evidence that almost every director had actually also participated in the options trade, and the directors quickly dropped the charges.

In practice, not much was done to stamp out options trading aside from an occasional stern pronouncement, and privileged trading hobbled along in this dubious status: it was illegal, the board would not enforce the terms of options contracts (in fact, there were no contracts, just verbal agreements mostly), but everyone was doing it. In 1892, the political opponents of options (a coalition known as the Anti-Option movement) successfully passed a bill in the U.S. Congress known as the Hatch bill that would have made not only options trading but also futures trading and even short selling of anything a federal crime. Luckily for all of us today, after passing both chambers of Congress, the Hatch bill failed on a technicality and never became law. The Anti-Option movement then swiftly dissipated—not because its members had had a change of heart about options, but because in 1895 the prices of agricultural commodities started heading up, reversing a three-decade-long decline that had been the movement's main rallying point.

By the end of the nineteenth century, options trading was alive and well (although still technically illegal) in Chicago, and it had also become widespread in New York and London, where brokers working on the stock exchanges in these financial centers had been trading puts and calls on stocks at least since the 1870s. This stock options trading was transacted on and off the floor of the exchanges, although, as in the case of CBOT, these exchanges also refused to enforce the terms of options contracts. Early in the twentieth century, the participants in the options trade even formed the Call and Put Dealers Association to promote their business.

By the Roaring Twenties (the 1920s, that is), options were routinely used to "incentivize" brokers—company directors gave brokers stock options, whose value increased massively if the brokers succeeded in pushing up the price of the company's stock (a practice known as an *option pool*). Option pools were undoubtedly an important factor in the craziness that went on before the stock market crash in 1929, and in the aftermath of that disaster, options were again held up as the worst of the speculative abuses, so Congress renewed its efforts to ban options trading.

Amazingly, despite being obviously guilty of so many sins, equity options survived the financial regulations of the early Great Depression era, while options on futures (which of course had nothing to do with the stock market crash) were banned. The surviving options brokers and dealers were finally kicked off the floors of organized exchanges, but continued to trade equity options *over the counter* (i.e., off exchange). The over-the-counter equity options market suffered from low liquidity and lack of price transparency—it was hard to find a counterparty to any options trade because agreement had to be reached on so many things (which stock, the strike price, and the expiration date), and even if there were someone who was interested in taking the other side of a particular trade, haggling over price could drag on for weeks, since there was no objective method for determining the value of options.

The idea that propelled options trading into the brave new modern world originated in the late 1960s, again in Chicago. CBOT saw an opportunity to revitalize the equity options market by restructuring it along the lines of its successful futures trading model. To enhance liquidity, CBOT proposed to create *listed options*, sets of contracts similar to futures contracts with a well-defined and limited set of strikes and expirations. The U.S. market regulators refused to allow the listing of such contracts on CBOT itself, but after years of deliberation, they did allow CBOT to create a subsidiary exchange dedicated to options trading. This new exchange was called the Chicago Board Options Exchange (CBOE), and it opened for trading with little fanfare in 1973 (its first trading floor was the former smoking lounge just off the main CBOT floor in the same building).

At first, CBOE listed only call options on 16 stocks (the SEC would not allow trading in put options until 1977). The established dealers in over-the-counter options, mostly based in New York, at first were just amused at how the Chicago "grain traders" were going to encroach on their territory, but their skepticism quickly evaporated as the CBOE's listed options business took off. The existing stock exchanges were more pragmatic and quickly joined CBOE in this game by listing identical contracts: the American Stock Exchange in New York and the Philadelphia Stock Exchange started their options business in 1975, the Pacific Exchange started in 1976, and the NYSE and Nasdaq held off until 1985. All listed options trades were (and still are) cleared by the same entity—the Options Clearing Corporation—that was originally set up by CBOE to clear its trades and that became an important stabilizing force in the options market early on.

By 1982, the daily volume of listed options trading hit half a million contracts a day. Also in 1982, the prohibition against options on futures was finally lifted, and CBOT listed options contracts on its popular Treasury bond futures, which were rapidly joined by listed options on almost every existing futures contract on both CBOT and CME. The next major event in the U.S. options markets was the introduction of options on stock indices in 1983, which have become the most rapidly growing segment of the market. The options markets then continued their explosive growth; as of this writing, about 10 million listed equity options contracts change hands every day.

THE MECHANICS OF OPTIONS TRADING

Let us examine the mechanics of modern-day listed options trading, taking equity options as an example. In Figure 9–2, we show a set of (delayed) real-time quotes for option contracts on Microsoft stock. The stock is currently

FIGURE 9-2

Quotes for listed options on Microsoft stock (from the CBOE Web site, www.cboe.com; reproduced with permission). For each options contract (see the discussion of contract definitions in the text), the table shows the last trade price, the price change since the previous close (or pc; if the price has not changed, this column shows pc), bid and offer prices, number of contracts traded today, and the total open interest.

MSFT   **27.01**   **+0.35**

Nov 07, 2005 @ 23:12 ET (Data 15 Minutes Delayed)   **Bid** 27.00   **Ask** 27.01   **Size** 181x449   **Vol** 77104789

Calls	Last Sale	Net	Bid	Ask	Vol	Open Int	Puts	Last Sale	Net	Bid	Ask	Vol	Open Int
05 Nov 22.50 (MSQ KX)	4.50	+0.30	4.40	4.60	1114	16479	05 Nov 22.50 (MSQ WX)	0.05	pc	0	0.05	0	21488
05 Nov 22.50 (MSQ KX-E)	4.40	+0.40	4.40	4.60	831	16479	05 Nov 22.50 (MSQ WX-E)	0.10	pc	0	0.05	0	21488
05 Nov 22.50 (MSQ KX-A)	4.00	pc	4.40	4.60	0	16479	05 Nov 22.50 (MSQ WX-A)	0.05	pc	0	0.05	0	21488
05 Nov 22.50 (MSQ KX-P)	4.50	+0.60	4.40	4.60	12	16479	05 Nov 22.50 (MSQ WX-P)	0.10	pc	0	0.05	0	21488
05 Nov 22.50 (MSQ KX-X)	4.50	+0.30	4.40	4.60	183	16479	05 Nov 22.50 (MSQ WX-X)	0.05	pc	0	0.05	0	21488
05 Nov 22.50 (MSQ KX-B)	4.50	+0.30	4.40	4.60	80	16479	05 Nov 22.50 (MSQ WX-B)	0.10	pc	0	0.05	0	21488
05 Nov 22.50 (MSQ KX-8)	4.40	+0.30	4.40	4.60	8	16479	05 Nov 22.50 (MSQ WX-8)	0.05	pc	0	0.05	0	21488
05 Nov 25.00 (MSQ KJ)	2.00	+0.35	2.00	2.05	2868	89022	05 Nov 25.00 (MSQ WJ)	0.05	--	0	0.05	114	60657
05 Nov 25.00 (MSQ KJ-E)	2.00	+0.35	2.00	2.10	477	89022	05 Nov 25.00 (MSQ WJ-E)	0.05	--	0	0.05	25	60657
05 Nov 25.00 (MSQ KJ-A)	1.65	pc	2.00	2.10	0	89022	05 Nov 25.00 (MSQ WJ-A)	0.05	pc	0	0.10	0	60657
05 Nov 25.00 (MSQ KJ-P)	2.05	+0.35	2.00	2.10	115	89022	05 Nov 25.00 (MSQ WJ-P)	0.05	pc	0	0.05	0	60657
05 Nov 25.00 (MSQ KJ-X)	2.05	+0.30	2.00	2.10	1026	89022	05 Nov 25.00 (MSQ WJ-X)	0.05	--	0	0.05	84	60657
05 Nov 25.00 (MSQ KJ-B)	2.02	-0.98	2.00	2.10	684	89022	05 Nov 25.00 (MSQ WJ-B)	0.15	pc	0	0.05	0	60657
05 Nov 25.00 (MSQ KJ-8)	2.00	+0.35	2.00	2.05	566	89022	05 Nov 25.00 (MSQ WJ-8)	0.05	--	0	0.05	5	60657
05 Nov 27.50 (MSQ KY)	0.10	--	0.10	0.15	10153	41956	05 Nov 27.50 (MSQ WY)	0.65	-0.30	0.60	0.70	1917	27738
05 Nov 27.50 (MSQ KY-E)	0.15	+0.05	0.10	0.15	2140	41956	05 Nov 27.50 (MSQ WY-E)	0.70	-0.20	0.60	0.70	185	27738
05 Nov 27.50 (MSQ KY-A)	0.10	+0.05	0.10	0.15	12	41956	05 Nov 27.50 (MSQ WY-A)	0.95	pc	0.60	0.70	0	27738
05 Nov 27.50 (MSQ KY-P)	0.10	+0.05	0.10	0.15	232	41956	05 Nov 27.50 (MSQ WY-P)	0.70	-0.45	0.60	0.70	10	27738
05 Nov 27.50 (MSQ KY-X)	0.10	--	0.10	0.15	3172	41956	05 Nov 27.50 (MSQ WY-X)	0.65	-0.30	0.60	0.70	487	27738
05 Nov 27.50 (MSQ KY-B)	0.11	-0.04	0.10	0.15	646	41956	05 Nov 27.50 (MSQ WY-B)	0.66	-0.24	0.60	0.70	155	27738
05 Nov 27.50 (MSQ KY-8)	0.10	--	0.10	0.15	3951	41956	05 Nov 27.50 (MSQ WY-8)	0.60	-0.30	0.60	0.70	1080	27738
05 Nov 30.00 (MSQ KK)	0.05	pc	0	0.05	0	3442	05 Nov 30.00 (MSQ WK)	3.10	-0.20	3.00	3.10	10	4194
05 Nov 30.00 (MSQ KK-E)	0.05	pc	0	0.05	0	3442	05 Nov 30.00 (MSQ WK-E)	5.00	pc	3.00	3.10	0	4194
05 Nov 30.00 (MSQ KK-A)	0.05	pc	0	0.05	0	3442	05 Nov 30.00 (MSQ WK-A)	0	pc	2.90	3.10	0	4194
05 Nov 30.00 (MSQ KK-P)	0.05	pc	0	0.05	0	3442	05 Nov 30.00 (MSQ WK-P)	5.10	pc	3.00	3.10	0	4194
05 Nov 30.00 (MSQ KK-X)	0.05	pc	0	0.05	0	3442	05 Nov 30.00 (MSQ WK-X)	3.00	-0.60	3.00	3.10	5	4194
05 Nov 30.00 (MSQ KK-B)	0.15	pc	0	0.05	0	3442	05 Nov 30.00 (MSQ WK-B)	2.30	pc	3.00	3.10	0	4194
05 Nov 30.00 (MSQ KK-8)	0.05	pc	0	0.05	0	3442	05 Nov 30.00 (MSQ WK-8)	3.10	-1.30	3.00	3.10	5	4194
05 Dec 22.50 (MSQ LX)	4.60	+0.50	4.50	4.60	42	2687	05 Dec 22.50 (MSQ XX)	0.05	pc	0	0.05	0	13037
05 Dec 22.50 (MSQ LX-E)	3.42	pc	4.50	4.60	0	2687	05 Dec 22.50 (MSQ XX-E)	0.05	pc	0	0.05	0	13037
05 Dec 22.50 (MSQ LX-A)	0	pc	4.40	4.60	0	2687	05 Dec 22.50 (MSQ XX-A)	0.05	pc	0	0.10	0	13037
05 Dec 22.50 (MSQ LX-P)	4.00	pc	4.50	4.60	0	2687	05 Dec 22.50 (MSQ XX-P)	0.10	pc	0	0.05	0	13037
05 Dec 22.50 (MSQ LX-X)	4.60	+0.50	4.50	4.60	22	2687	05 Dec 22.50 (MSQ XX-X)	0.05	pc	0	0.05	0	13037
05 Dec 22.50 (MSQ LX-B)	4.50	+0.40	4.50	4.60	20	2687	05 Dec 22.50 (MSQ XX-B)	0.15	pc	0	0.05	0	13037
05 Dec 22.50 (MSQ LX-8)	4.10	pc	4.50	4.60	0	2687	05 Dec 22.50 (MSQ XX-8)	0.05	pc	0	0.05	0	13037
05 Dec 25.00 (MSQ LJ)	2.15	+0.30	2.05	2.15	3786	24265	05 Dec 25.00 (MSQ XJ)	0.10	--	0.05	0.10	75	7009
05 Dec 25.00 (MSQ LJ-E)	2.10	+0.35	2.05	2.15	1964	24265	05 Dec 25.00 (MSQ XJ-E)	0.10	pc	0.05	0.10	0	7009
05 Dec 25.00 (MSQ LJ-A)	1.70	pc	2.05	2.20	0	24265	05 Dec 25.00 (MSQ XJ-A)	0.15	pc	0	0.10	0	7009
05 Dec 25.00 (MSQ LJ-P)	1.85	+0.15	2.05	2.15	250	24265	05 Dec 25.00 (MSQ XJ-P)	0.15	pc	0.05	0.10	0	7009
05 Dec 25.00 (MSQ LJ-X)	2.15	+0.30	2.05	2.15	1253	24265	05 Dec 25.00 (MSQ XJ-X)	0.10	-0.05	0.05	0.10	75	7009
05 Dec 25.00 (MSQ LJ-B)	2.13	+0.43	2.05	2.15	174	24265	05 Dec 25.00 (MSQ XJ-B)	2.50	pc	0.05	0.10	0	7009
05 Dec 25.00 (MSQ LJ-8)	2.10	+0.30	2.05	2.15	145	24265	05 Dec 25.00 (MSQ XJ-8)	0.10	pc	0.05	0.10	0	7009
05 Dec 27.50 (MSQ LY)	0.40	+0.15	0.35	0.40	10451	21324	05 Dec 27.50 (MSQ XY)	0.80	-0.30	0.80	0.85	717	3865
05 Dec 27.50 (MSQ LY-E)	0.40	+0.15	0.30	0.40	1351	21324	05 Dec 27.50 (MSQ XY-E)	0.80	-0.30	0.80	0.85	110	3865
05 Dec 27.50 (MSQ LY-A)	0.35	+0.15	0.30	0.40	450	21324	05 Dec 27.50 (MSQ XY-A)	1.30	pc	0.75	0.85	0	3865
05 Dec 27.50 (MSQ LY-P)	0.35	+0.10	0.30	0.40	44	21324	05 Dec 27.50 (MSQ XY-P)	1.40	pc	0.80	0.90	0	3865
05 Dec 27.50 (MSQ LY-X)	0.40	+0.10	0.35	0.40	1602	21324	05 Dec 27.50 (MSQ XY-X)	0.80	-0.30	0.80	0.85	304	3865
05 Dec 27.50 (MSQ LY-B)	0.36	+0.16	0.30	0.40	858	21324	05 Dec 27.50 (MSQ XY-B)	0.80	-0.30	0.80	0.90	220	3865
05 Dec 27.50 (MSQ LY-8)	0.35	+0.05	0.30	0.40	6146	21324	05 Dec 27.50 (MSQ XY-8)	0.90	-0.20	0.80	0.85	83	3865
05 Dec 30.00 (MSQ LK)	0.05	--	0	0.05	314	185	05 Dec 30.00 (MSQ XK)	3.10	-0.40	3.00	3.10	205	2132
05 Dec 30.00 (MSQ LK-E)	0.05	--	0	0.05	50	185	05 Dec 30.00 (MSQ XK-E)	3.20	-0.30	3.00	3.10	5	2132
05 Dec 30.00 (MSQ LK-A)	0	pc	0	0.10	0	185	05 Dec 30.00 (MSQ XK-A)	3.50	pc	3.00	3.20	0	2132
05 Dec 30.00 (MSQ LK-P)	0	pc	0	0.05	0	185	05 Dec 30.00 (MSQ XK-P)	5.00	pc	3.00	3.10	0	2132
05 Dec 30.00 (MSQ LK-X)	0.05	--	0	0.05	114	185	05 Dec 30.00 (MSQ XK-X)	3.60	pc	3.00	3.10	0	2132
05 Dec 30.00 (MSQ LK-B)	0.02	-0.13	0	0.05	150	185	05 Dec 30.00 (MSQ XK-B)	4.90	pc	3.00	3.10	0	2132
05 Dec 30.00 (MSQ LK-8)	0.05	pc	0	0.05	0	185	05 Dec 30.00 (MSQ XK-8)	3.10	-0.40	3.00	3.10	200	2132

trading at 27.01, and you can see in Figure 9–2 that there are a number of option contracts with strike prices close to this value: 22.50, 25.00, 27.50 and 30.00. The strike prices are set in intervals of 2.50 around the current price (this interval increases to 5 and then to 10 for higher-priced stocks), and if the stock moves outside this predefined range of strikes, new *option series* will be created around the new price.

There are two *expiration months* shown in Figure 9–2, November 2005 and December 2005; in fact, there are four more that did not fit in the table, January 2006, April 2006, January 2007, and January 2008. The options expire on the Saturday following the third Friday of the expiration month (for November 2005, this would be November 19, 2005). The logic behind this set of expiration months is as follows: first, there is the *front month* (which is November 2005 prior to November 19 and would change to December 2005 after that date) and the next month; these two months are always included. The next two contract months are picked from a *quarterly cycle*; all stocks are divided among three quarterly cycles beginning in January, February, or March. Microsoft happens to be in the January cycle (January, April, July, and October), so for the next two listed contracts, we pick the next two months in this series, which gives us January 2006 and April 2006 (this logic provides a range of times to expiration from one to eight months). In 1990, CBOE introduced longer-term options contracts called LEAPS that expire in January of the second and third years; these are the last two contracts (January 2007 and January 2008) in the Microsoft series.

Finally, settlement rules: each contract is for delivery of 100 shares of the underlying stock and can be exercised at any time before the expiration day (for reasons unknown, this is called *American exercise* style, as opposed to *European exercise*, where you can exercise the option only on the expiration day); the stocks will be delivered (and the strike price paid) three business days later. The prices are quoted on a per-share basis, as shown in Figure 9–2 (a bid of 4.00 means you get $400 for one contract). The minimum price tick for an option contract is 5 cents (10 cents for higher-priced stocks).

The whole set of options contracts on Microsoft stock is referred to by Microsoft's *options symbol*, MSQ (more often than not, the options symbol is a truncated version of the stock ticker with a Q thrown in somewhere). As we can see in Figure 9–2, each contract has a letter code, for example MSQKX, which for the initiated means that this is a November call (K) with a strike of 22.5 (X) on Microsoft (MSQ) stock (see Figure 9–3 for the list of other month/strike codes). The last letter in the contract code in Figure 9–2 indicates the exchange from which the quote came; we also list those in Figure 9–3.

FIGURE 9-3

Options symbology-letter codes for expiration months, strike prices, and exchanges. This is valid only for listed equity options, but futures options use an almost identical set of symbols.

Expiration Month Codes

	JAN	FEB	MAR	APR	MAY	JUN	JUL	AUG	SEP	OCT	NOV	DEC
Calls	A	B	C	D	E	F	G	H	I	J	K	L
Puts	M	N	O	P	Q	R	S	T	U	V	W	X

Strike Price Codes*

A	B	C	D	E	F	G	H	I	J	K	L	M
5	10	15	20	25	30	35	40	45	50	55	60	65
105	110	115	120	125	130	135	140	145	150	155	160	165
205	210	215	220	225	230	235	240	245	250	255	260	265
305	310	315	320	325	330	335	340	345	350	355	360	365
405	410	415	420	425	430	435	440	445	450	455	460	465
505	510	515	520	525	530	535	540	545	550	555	560	565
605	610	615	620	625	630	635	640	645	650	655	660	665
705	710	715	720	725	730	735	740	745	750	755	760	765

N	O	P	Q	R	S	T	U	V	W	X	Y	Z
70	75	80	85	90	95	100	$7\frac{1}{2}$	$12\frac{1}{2}$	$17\frac{1}{2}$	$22\frac{1}{2}$	$27\frac{1}{2}$	$32\frac{1}{2}$
170	175	180	185	190	195	200	$37\frac{1}{2}$	$42\frac{1}{2}$	$47\frac{1}{2}$	$52\frac{1}{2}$	$57\frac{1}{2}$	$62\frac{1}{2}$
270	275	280	285	290	295	300	$67\frac{1}{2}$	$72\frac{1}{2}$	$77\frac{1}{2}$	$82\frac{1}{2}$	$87\frac{1}{2}$	$92\frac{1}{2}$
370	375	380	385	390	395	400	$97\frac{1}{2}$	$102\frac{1}{2}$	$107\frac{1}{2}$	$112\frac{1}{2}$	$117\frac{1}{2}$	$122\frac{1}{2}$
470	475	480	485	490	495	500	$127\frac{1}{2}$	$132\frac{1}{2}$	$137\frac{1}{2}$	$142\frac{1}{2}$	$147\frac{1}{2}$	$152\frac{1}{2}$
570	575	580	585	590	595	600	$157\frac{1}{2}$	$162\frac{1}{2}$	$167\frac{1}{2}$	$172\frac{1}{2}$	$177\frac{1}{2}$	$182\frac{1}{2}$
670	675	680	685	690	695	700	$187\frac{1}{2}$	$192\frac{1}{2}$	$197\frac{1}{2}$	$202\frac{1}{2}$	$207\frac{1}{2}$	$212\frac{1}{2}$
770	775	780	785	790	795	800	$217\frac{1}{2}$	$222\frac{1}{2}$	$227\frac{1}{2}$	232	$237\frac{1}{2}$	$242\frac{1}{2}$

Exchange Codes

	E	A	P	X	B	8
Exchange	Chicago Board Options Exch	American Stock Exchange	Pacific Stock Exchange	Philadelphia Stock Exchange	Boston Stock Exchange	International Securities Exchange
Acronym	CBOE	AMEX	PCX	PHLX	BOX	ISE

We will discuss the modern competitive landscape of options exchanges later in this chapter; here we just point out that the open interest for each contract is the same across all exchanges. This is because the options contracts trading on different exchanges can be *mutually offset* (long positions on one exchange can be closed out with short positions on another exchange), since they all use the same clearing agent (the OCC). I should probably have emphasized this earlier: options are exactly like futures (and OTC derivatives, for that matter) in that they are created out of thin air in long-short pairs, and the open interest is simply the number of such pairs in existence.

THE BLACK-SCHOLES FORMULA

As we can see in Figure 9–2, there is significant variability among different exchanges in terms of volume traded, but very little variability in terms of prices. Why is it that everyone agrees that the MSQ Nov05 22.50 call is worth 4.50, but the Nov05 put with the same strike is worth nothing? Again, the answer to these, and in fact all other options valuation questions, was found in Chicago: in 1973 (the same year CBOE opened its doors), two University of Chicago professors, Fischer Black and Myron Scholes, published a paper[1] that forever changed the way people think about the value of options and financial instruments in general. The new options valuation framework was an instant hit with the traders—one can argue that the standing ovation that Black and Scholes received when they visited the CBOT trading floor was a more telling mark of the success of modern options-pricing theory than the Nobel Prize that this research won in 1997.

By 1975, CBOE had adopted Black-Scholes pricing as its official options valuation method, and Texas Instruments started making pocket calculators with the Black-Scholes formula preprogrammed. Since then, whole forests have been felled to print books and papers that explain how and why this formula works, and I list a few of those books in the Recommended Reading section for those who want to understand the details of the derivation. The abundance of these interpretive texts may lead you to think that options pricing is a very complex subject that you should not try at home,

---

1. The story of the Black-Scholes formula is somewhat more complicated than this legend would have it. The work was actually done at MIT in the late 1960s (Black, Scholes, and the other father of options pricing, Robert Merton, all worked at MIT at the time), but no reputable academic journal would accept their papers for several years. When the papers came out in 1973, both Black and Scholes were at the University of Chicago (which allows Chicago to claim the status of the birthplace of options pricing), but Black went back to MIT a year later.

but this is simply not true—the Black-Scholes formula is the mathematical expression of a few basic insights that at their core are in fact very simple and intuitive, and in what follows we discuss those insights rather than the formula itself.

The first of those insights is the realization that the value of an option is the *expected present value* of its terminal payoff (let us focus on European options, which can be exercised only at a single expiration date). As shown in Figure 9–4, a long call position will make money if the price of the underlying ends up above the strike price and will lose money otherwise. We cannot know today which of these two cases we will find on the expiration date, but we can try to estimate the probabilities of different possible outcomes and then calculate the *expected value* of the option payoff averaged over all

F I G U R E   9–4

Option price as an expected value. To calculate the expected value, we average the option payoff over all possible outcomes (underlying prices at expiration) and weight these payoffs by the probability of each outcome. The probabilities are given by a distribution function, which Black and Scholes have postulated to be lognormal. In contrast to the normal distribution, the lognormal distribution does not allow the prices to go negative.

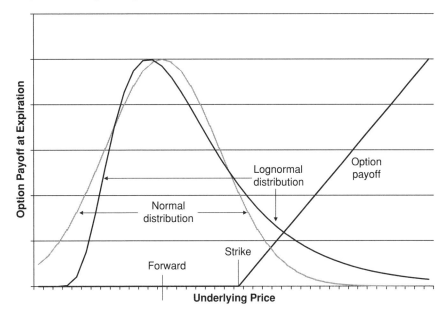

different scenarios (and then calculate its *present value* by discounting that number back to today using an appropriate interest rate).

This is hardly a revolutionary thought in the context of natural sciences (the concept of measurable quantities as expected values pervades physics, from quantum mechanics to thermodynamics), but in the context of finance, the idea of treating prices as random variables that can be analyzed with the powerful apparatus of stochastic calculus was quite new and instantly useful. The first consequence of this approach is that in order to calculate the expected value of any future payoff, you should use the *distribution function* of whatever that payoff depends on. Black and Scholes made an assumption about how the underlying price should be distributed at expiration that (1) was eminently reasonable, and (2) allowed them to calculate the expected value of the option payoff in a closed analytical form.

The first thing we would typically try if we had to guess the distribution function of anything is a *normal distribution* around the expected mean. In the case of a stock price, that mean is the *forward price* of the stock at option expiration (today's price plus financing costs less expected dividends over the term of the option). The value of a call option shown in Figure 9–4 would then (like any expected value) simply be the integral of the product of this distribution function and the option payoff (which is a piecewise-linear function).

There are two problems with this: (1) this integral cannot be taken analytically, and (2) the normal distribution allows the stock prices to go negative, at least in theory (the first of these problems is much more serious than the second). So Black and Scholes tried something different: they said that it is not the prices but the *returns* (relative price changes) that should be normally distributed. The normal distribution assumption means that the price is equally likely to go up $1 or down $1 from its current value, while the Black-Scholes assumption means that the price is equally likely to go up 1 percent or down 1 percent, which means that the resulting distribution function is not normal, but rather lognormal (the logarithm of the price is normally distributed, as shown in Figure 9–4).

The lognormal distribution assumption takes care of both of the problems mentioned previously: the prices cannot go negative (if the price keeps going down by 1 percent, it will never go below zero, whereas if it keeps going down by $1, it eventually will), and the expected value of a call option payoff can be calculated analytically. The second of these statements is a bit less obvious than the first, but it is true nonetheless: as a function of the logarithm of prices, the call option payoff is a piecewise-exponential function, and an exponential times the normal distribution is still a normal distribution around a shifted mean, so that the expected value (the integral of this product over all prices) can be expressed in terms of the cumulative normal distribution function. The Black-Scholes formula for the price of a call (or put) option is easily derived under these assumptions through the following three steps: (1) constructing a lognormal distribution function around the forward price, (2) multiplying that function by the option payoff function and taking the integral over all prices (this is where the cumulative normal distribution functions in the formula come from), and (3) discounting the result back to today using continuous compounding (i.e., by a simple exponential function).

Those readers whose sophomore-year calculus is still fresh in their memories should be able to complete this derivation and write down the actual formula (this is a favorite interview question of many Wall Street quants), but the formula itself will say little to the rest of us, so instead of staring at the formula, let us try to get a qualitative feel for what it means. According to Black-Scholes, the option price is determined by how much overlap there is between the payoff function and the distribution function shown in Figure 9–4, and that overlap depends on a number of factors.

The first of those factors is the relationship between the strike price and the center of the distribution, which represents the forward price.[2] If the forward price goes below the strike price, the overlap diminishes and eventually approaches zero; if it goes sufficiently high above the strike price, the overlap becomes equal to the payoff function itself. We can visualize this by mentally moving the distribution function in Figure 9–4 right and left and estimating the overlap; we should then see why the price of a call option depends on the forward price, as shown in Figure 9–5. We can also observe this pattern in Figure 9–2 (the one with the MSQ options quotes): the call options with strike prices higher than the spot price are worth less and less the higher the strike price gets, whereas for strike prices below the spot price, the call option prices approach the difference between the spot price and the strike price (it really should be forward price less strike price). The put options in Figure 9–2 of course do the exact opposite—their price approaches strike price minus forward price as the strike gets above the forward. In general, put options are equivalent to a combination of the underlying and a call option (e.g., a long put position can be created *synthetically*

---

2. The lognormal distribution is asymmetric, so its peak is below its mean; the difference between the two is represented by the $\sigma^2 t/2$ term in the Black-Scholes formula. Therefore, the actual forward price (which is equal to the mean) is slightly above the peak of the lognormal distribution.

FIGURE   9–5

Black-Scholes prices for a call option as a function of the underlying price, for different volatility levels (from bottom to top, we show prices for $\sigma\sqrt{t} = 0$ percent, 10 percent, 20 percent, 40 percent, and 80 percent). Note how the option prices grow with volatility (approximately linearly for at-the-money options).

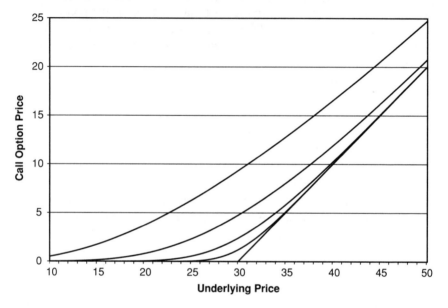

if we go long a call and short the underlying), and because of this *put-call parity*, there is no need to discuss the puts separately.

The other main parameter on which the option price obviously depends is the width of the price distribution function, which brings us to another major contribution of Black-Scholes theory to the modern derivatives markets: the concept of *volatility*. Conceptually, the width of the price distribution function in Figure 9–4 depends on two things: how much the price moves around in a given period of time, and the time to expiration. Volatility is a measure of the former—the intensity of price movements—and (for the lognormal Black-Scholes model) is expressed in percent per year. If the volatility of a stock is 20 percent and the time to expiration is one year, the width of the price distribution function at expiration as measured by the standard deviation parameter σ of the lognormal distribution is 20 percent.

What if the time to expiration is three months? Clearly the distribution function should then be narrower (the price will have less chance to move away from its current value), but by how much? In the approach taken by Black and Scholes, the width of the three-month price distribution is not one-quarter but rather one-half of the yearly volatility. This is because they model the movement of prices by a random walk—the price starts out at its current value and then moves up and down following a Gaussian random process whose variance increases linearly with time. The width of the price distribution function is the square root of that variance and is thus proportional to the *square root* of the time to expiration rather than to the time itself. This is why volatility enters the Black-Scholes formula only in the combination $\sigma\sqrt{t}$—it is the overall width of the distribution that matters. We show how the call option price depends on volatility in Figure 9–5, where we can see that in some sense volatility is what gives any option its value: the option price increases with volatility at any strike price.

How do we know what the volatility of the underlying is? In theory, volatility is a parameter of the stochastic process describing the movements of the underlying price, and it should therefore be possible to estimate it based on the history of price movements. To compute such historical volatility, we take the historical prices of the underlying (say, a year's worth of closing prices), calculate a time series of daily returns (this will give us 252 numbers, one for each business day in a year), and then simply compute their standard deviation. This will give us *daily volatility*, which we convert into the *annual vol* (yes, *vol* is how market participants lovingly refer to volatility) by multiplying it by the square root of 252.

If prices really followed the random process postulated by Black-Scholes, then this historical vol should be independent of the time period over which it was calculated, and this, of course, is patently not true in real life. As we can see in an example shown in Figure 9–6, historically observed (also known as *realized*) volatility does not just vary a little around some stable mean, but in fact can change very significantly over time. The fact that volatility itself is a function of time presents certain theoretical challenges,[3] but it has a very practical consequence for options trading: if we want to price a one-year option today, the volatility we need to put into the Black-Scholes formula is the volatility over the *next* year, which

---

3. This issue has a fancy name, heteroscedasticity, and another options-related Nobel Prize was awarded to Robert Engle in 2003 for research in this area.

F I G U R E   9–6

Volatility of MSFT stock. The dotted line shows realized volatility (annualized standard deviation of daily returns) calculated over the past 30 days, while the solid line represents implied volatility based on observed options prices. Implied volatility data courtesy of IVolatility.com (www.ivolatility.com).

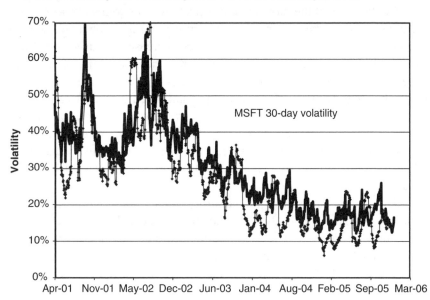

is, of course, unknowable today. In practice, therefore, we cannot really plug a volatility into a Black-Scholes formula and find out what the price of the option is, but we can do the opposite: we can use the observed market price of an option (for example, the $0.80 bid price we see in Figure 9–2 for the MSQ 27.50 Dec 05 put) to determine the volatility that should have been put into the Black-Scholes formula to give the observed option price. This is possible because volatility is the only free parameter in the Black-Scholes formula; everything else that it cares about (current price, strike price, time to expiration, and the discounting interest rate) is unambiguously known.

To find this *implied* volatility, we numerically invert the Black-Scholes formula (there is no analytical inversion); in our Dec 05 MSQ put example, we find that a volatility of 16.784 percent produces the observed price of this option (or, to illustrate the origins of the term, we can say that the price of \$0.80 implies that the volatility should be 16.784 percent).[4] Implied volatility is thus simply another way to express the options price and in no way explains why the price is what it is, but it is an extremely useful concept nonetheless as long as we understand its origins and its limitations.

In Figure 9–6 we compare the implied volatility of MSQ options with the historical (realized) volatility of MSFT stock; we can see that both are in the same ballpark numerically but can differ very significantly at any given time. A convenient way to think about the relationship between realized and implied volatility is to recognize that realized volatility is a backward-looking measure, while implied vol is forward-looking—it represents the market's attempt to guess what the realized vol will be in the future.

Our implied volatility graph in Figure 9–6 is a bit of a cheat because there is in fact no single implied volatility for MSQ options. For example, if we take another option from Figure 9–2 (say, the Dec 05 25.00 call) and calculate implied vol based on its price, we will get 15.879 percent— admittedly pretty close to what we got previously, but not exactly the same. If we keep calculating implied vol for options with different strike prices and then plot the results as a function of the strike price, we will typically find (as we show in Figure 9–7) that (1) implied vol is a convex function of the strike price (a phenomenon known as the *volatility smile*), and (2) it also slopes downward, so that the vol for higher strikes is lower; this is called *volatility skew*. Skew is less universal than the smile (it is almost always there for equity options, but not for other option types). The smile is said to reflect the fact that in reality the probability of large price movements is much higher than what the normal distribution would suggest (in other words, real-world distributions have *fat tails*).

Similar variability of implied volatility exists along the other options-trading dimension, time to expiration. For a given strike price, the dependence of implied volatility on expiration is referred to as the *term structure of volatilities*. If we put both dependences together, we have a *volatility surface*

---

4. The Black-Scholes model technically works only for European options, while all exchange-traded options are American, so in reality people use simple numerical procedures to price these options rather than the Black-Scholes formula itself (the Americanness of real-world options makes them a tiny bit more valuable than what Black-Scholes suggests). Therefore the fact that we have to invert the pricing formula numerically to get the implied volatility is not much of a hindrance in practice, since the vol-to-price conversion is in reality also numerical. In what follows we will ignore these intricacies and talk about Black-Scholes as if this term covers the direct numerical extensions used in practice.

FIGURE 9–7

Schematic illustration of the concepts of volatility smile and skew. The smile refers to the gently parabolic shape of the volatility–strike price dependence, which is often observed for FX and interest-rate options. Stock options usually also exhibit the skew, a systematic decrease of implied volatility with increasing strike price.

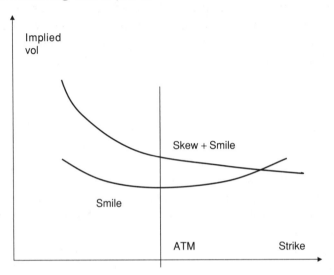

that represents implied volatility as a function of both strike price and time to expiration. The presence of smiles, skews, and vol term structures shows that the real options-trading world is more complex than the Black-Scholes model, where a single volatility number should be good for all options; but the fact that relatively minor adjustments to the constant-volatility model can easily account for these real-world complications means that the Black-Scholes approach captures the essence of options pricing quite effectively— a constant-vol assumption is really not that bad an approximation of what we see in Figure 9–7.

RISK FACTORS AFFECTING OPTIONS

Like all other pricing models, the Black-Scholes model and its numerical extensions really shine when we move beyond the simple pricing questions and start looking at *price risk*, that is, at how much the price of an option can change. Options are risky instruments whose value can drop to nothing or increase many times over very quickly. Understanding the factors that can affect the value of options positions (and consequently being able to control them) is a prerequisite for successful options trading. The Black-Scholes theory tells you in no uncertain terms what those factors are; as we have seen, they include (1) the price of the underlying, (2) the volatility of that price, and (3) time to expiration (the interest rate and the dividend yield are also in the formula, but they are far less important).

Ever since the early papers of Black-Scholes and especially Merton, people have traditionally referred to those risk factors and their numerical measures by the Greek letters that were assigned to the derivatives of the options price with respect to these three things (they are collectively known as *the Greeks* and have become synonymous with options risk). The first of the Greeks is the delta (Δ), which represents the derivative of the options price with respect to the price of the underlying. This quantity is shown in Figure 9–8. Some of us will recognize it as the cumulative normal distribution function, but whether we recognize it or not, we need a qualitative understanding of why it is what it is, and the best way to get that is not to derive a formula for it but rather to look at Figure 9–5, where the options price is plotted versus the underlying price. As is clear from Figure 9–5, delta should be 0 for deep out-of-the money options, it should be 1 for deep in-the-money options, and it should gradually switch from 0 to 1 as we move across the strike price (for at-the-money options, delta should be 0.5); all of this is seen in Figure 9–8.

The usefulness of delta is that it tells us how to *hedge* our options position against changes in the price of the underlying. Delta tells us how many units of the underlying to sell in order to make our position delta-neutral, or insensitive to (small) changes in the underlying price. Let us dispel a frequent misconception here: we did say that delta varies between 0 and 1, but this is true only for a single option contract. Delta (and the other Greeks as well) is additive; if we are long 40 calls with delta of 0.5 each, our total delta is 20, and we should sell 20 units of the underlying (which would be 2,000 shares of the underlying stock) if we want to eliminate the exposure of this position to the movements in the underlying stock price.

This kind of hedging (called *delta hedging*) is really exactly the same as the hedging that is done in other markets (such as hedging futures with cash products, or hedging bond positions with on-the-runs), with one very important difference: unlike most other instruments, options are strongly nonlinear, so their price sensitivities are likely to change significantly as the underlying prices move about. If we hedge a bond portfolio with other bonds or futures to eliminate, say, duration risk, we normally never have to touch that hedge again. With options positions, however, what was a perfect hedge yesterday (or even just a few minutes ago) can become significantly mismatched because the delta itself varies a lot with changes in the underlying price. If the 40 calls that we hedged with 2,000 shares of stock move slightly into the money (if the underlying price goes up a bit), their delta may increase to 0.6, and overall we will no longer be perfectly hedged—our total delta will be equivalent to being long 400 shares.

The sensitivity of delta to the underlying price is called *gamma* (Γ), which is also shown in Figure 9–8 (again, some of us will recognize our old friend the lognormal distribution in this gamma plot). If the overall gamma of our options position is positive, we are *long gamma*, and being long gamma is generally what we want to be. In our 40-call example, we are long the calls and therefore long gamma, and the practical consequence of this is that as the prices rise, our total delta grows larger, whereas if

FIGURE 9–8

Price risk measures for a call option. Delta is the first derivative of the option price (see Figure 9–5) with respect to the underlying price; gamma is the second derivative. Delta ranges from 0 to 1. Since the prices in Figure 9–5 are convex functions of the underlying price, gamma is always positive.

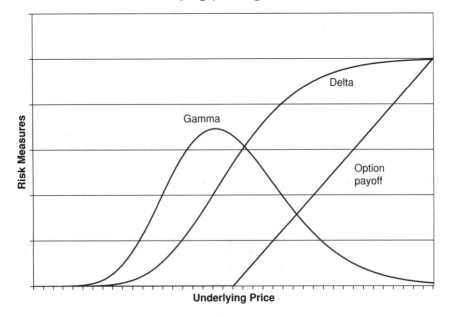

the prices were to fall, our overall delta would shrink. This looks and feels as if someone is giving us more stock as the prices rise, and vice versa in a falling market. So no matter where the prices are heading, if they move sufficiently far away from the starting point where we established our delta neutrality, we make money on a long gamma position. Once the prices have moved sufficiently, we can take profits—buy or sell some underlying to reestablish our delta neutrality, and then wait for the next price move. Keep doing this and people will call you a gamma trader (and the activity itself is called *gamma trading*).

The sensitivity of options prices to their other major driver, volatility, is referred to as either vega,[5] or, among older people and in older texts, kappa (κ). Vega is positive for a long position in any option, reflecting the fact that volatility is what gives options their value. It is highest for at-the-money options and drops off as the forward price moves either up or down, away from the strike price. In fact, the dependence of vega on the forward price looks exactly the same as that of gamma, shown in Figure 9–8 (the lognormal distribution strikes again), so we have not plotted it again. In general, if we are long gamma, we are also long vega, or *long volatility*: if the (implied) volatility increases, the PnL of a long vol position also increases. This vega risk, however, has to be watched closely, as volatility has the potential for changing very dramatically in a blink of an eye (just look at Figure 9–6).

Finally, there is another Greek called *theta* (Θ) that describes how options prices decrease with the passage of time. Unlike the other Greeks, theta is not a genuine market risk, but rather represents a deterministic drift in the option value as it approaches expiration. The reason that options lose value as expiration gets closer is that the terminal distribution function becomes progressively more narrow, which is in fact the exact opposite of the vega risk (where the distribution function gets wider as the volatility increases). Therefore, any position with positive vega (and gamma) has a negative theta: if nothing happens in the markets, the value of our long volatility portfolio will drop every day.

What's worse, unlike the other source of deterministic price drifts in the markets (the carry costs), the drop-off in the value of a long vol options portfolio accelerates dramatically as options approach expiration and the terminal distribution function collapses into a sharp peak around the forward price. In fact, trading options that have just a couple of days to expiration is a grueling job because their risk characteristics can change dramatically with

---

5. Ironically, vega is not even a Greek letter, although the symbol ν used to represent it is a Greek letter *nu*

very small price movements—for example, delta can go from 0 to 1 if the price moves just a few cents over the strike price—so the delta hedges require constant adjustments, which (if enough people do this) can, in turn, cause the underlying price to move even more. Because of this, the price action on options expiration days can often be erratic. This effect is at its worst on so-called *triple-witching* days (the third Fridays of March, June, September, and December), when not just options but also index futures expire.

THE STRUCTURE OF OPTIONS MARKETS

Options trading and risk management are both fascinating topics that are, unfortunately, outside the scope of this book, so here we abandon our brief foray into options valuation and return to our primary focus, which is how options markets are organized. Who are the main participants in modern options markets? We have already mentioned exchanges, but obviously there are also people and organizations who submit orders to those exchanges—who are they? Interestingly, options markets are (or at least were until the last few years) unlike most other financial markets in that most of the order flow is generated by individuals rather than institutions, although this is now changing rather rapidly.

Individuals cannot go directly to the options exchanges, and so they end up submitting their orders to brokers (typically the same brokers that handle their cash trading accounts), and the brokers forward these orders to the options exchanges. Buy-side institutions that trade options go to their sell-side partners to execute their options trades. Inside the sell-side banks, there are typically dedicated trading desks that deal in options of each type (for example, an *equity derivatives* desk would deal with stock and stock index options and futures). When a customer wishes to execute an options trade, this trading desk can either route the order to an exchange (acting as an agent of the customer) or take the other side of the trade (acting as a principal).

This is all very similar to the cash equity trading described in Chapter 6 except for one twist: customers often want to trade options that are not listed on exchanges, with either strike prices, expiration date, or perhaps some other parameters being customized. The derivatives desk has to take the other side of such an over-the-counter trade, and it has to come up with some way of (1) pricing such trades and (2) managing the risk of the options positions that it accumulates in the course of such *principal trading*. In order to price OTC options, the desk uses its knowledge of the state of the market in listed options; typically, the traders use software systems that read in live exchange prices for listed options on the same underlying, build a volatility surface corresponding to these live prices, and then interpolate between the closest points on the options grid (a set of exchange-traded strike prices and expirations) to produce the "right" implied vol for the option that the customer wants to trade.

At the end of each trading day, the traders provide closing volatility surfaces for all underlying stocks of interest, and these closing values are then used to calculate the PnL and risk measures of their trading books. The risk measures include (but are not limited to) the set of Greeks that we discussed previously, at least some of which (delta especially) are often also computed several times intraday (or even constantly updated in real time). This pricing and risk management technology, of course, applies not just to OTC but also to listed options and thus allows the traders to know where a particular contract that perhaps has not traded for a while should be trading. From there, it is only a short step to a business decision to make markets on options exchanges, and in the next few paragraphs we will examine the changing face of modern options market making.

Up until 1998 or so, liquidity on options exchanges was provided mainly by floor-based market makers (also called specialists), who spent their days in the pits on the exchange floor (a pit is a recessed area where people can stand on different levels and see one another easily). The floor brokers representing brokerage houses would bring in orders from the public and ask the crowd of market makers for quotes on a particular contract, the market makers would quote bids and offers, and the floor broker could either hit one of those bids or take one of the offers, or let the order sit in the order book until one of the market makers changed his quotes so that the order could be executed at a better price. The trading crowd developed a colorful system of hand signs for communicating order information, which helped make pit trading an activity that was very lively and fun to watch.

As trading volumes continued to grow, however, it became increasingly apparent that this system was not very efficient, and in the late 1990s the options exchanges started developing electronic order-crossing systems modeled on those that were already in place on stock exchanges in order to take the load off the trading crowd by executing small orders electronically. Again, CBOE initially led the way with its RAES (retail automatic execution) system, but other options exchanges quickly followed. Because of regulatory pressures, options exchanges were forced to open the way for multiple listings, where the same contracts traded on different exchanges, in the late 1990s, and this also required electronic linkage between exchanges to prevent cross-exchange arbitrage.

The exchange members viewed these newfangled electronic things as encroachments on their pit-based livelihood and did whatever they could to slow down the march of electronic trading, but this became impossible after 2000, when a new, completely electronic options exchange, the ISE (International Securities Exchange), started its operations. Within two years its electronic trading model had captured about 30 percent of the market and forced the more traditional pit-based exchanges to introduce competing electronic platforms (another all-electronic player known as BOX, or Boston Options Exchange, joined the fray in 2004).

The liquidity model of these new all-electronic exchanges was completely different; these exchanges signed up external financial institutions to act as designated electronic market makers that were obligated to provide continuous real-time two-sided markets for a set of option series. These external market makers were often based around an equity derivatives desk at a sell-side bank that already had the pricing and risk management technology to support the market-making function, but many other players that had experience making electronic markets in cash equities (Citadel is a good example; Knight Trading is another) also entered this business. The older exchanges quickly followed suit and introduced their own designated market maker schemes (which, however, they tried to make compatible with their pit-based trading model). At present, options market making is a big growth area for many financial institutions, and consequently the focus of options-trading technology is shifting rapidly from the relatively mature pricing and risk management area to a new set of issues related to electronic connectivity, execution models, and order management, topics that we will discuss in Chapter 14.

FIXED-INCOME OPTIONS

On the fixed-income side, listed options (such as options on Treasury and Bund futures) are actively traded, but there are also important OTC options specific to fixed-income markets. In the 1980s, OTC options on Treasury bonds were a popular product—they worked exactly the same way as equity options, but the underlying was a bond price rather than a stock price. Since the early 1990s, however, bond options have been gradually displaced by their LIBOR-based equivalents, called *swaptions*.

A swaption is an option on a swap rate; it gives us the right to enter into a swap at a predefined rate at some point in the future. For example, a 1x5 receiver swaption struck at 5.00 percent confers the right to enter into a five-year swap a year from now, where we would receive a fixed rate of 5 percent. The payoff of this swaption as a function of the five-year swap rate at expiration is (almost) exactly the same as that of a put option: the swaption will be exercised if the rate drops below 5 percent, and the benefit of being able to enter into this swap at an off-market rate of 5 percent is approximately proportional to the difference between the market rate and the strike rate. Most swaptions are cash-settled, with the option holders receiving the net present value of the underlying swap, but physical settlement, where they actually enter into that swap, is also fairly common.

With the market for swaps becoming very liquid and transparent, it has become much easier and cheaper to place (and hedge) bets on interest rates using swaptions rather than bond options, and at the time of this writing, the size of the swaptions market was estimated at about $30 trillion (in terms of notional principal). The market for swaptions is an OTC dealer market in which most trades are done between the sell-side dealers and their buy-side customers, but there are also interdealer brokers that arrange swaption trades between dealers for standard maturities and option terms. This market structure is identical to that of the underlying swaps market, where there is a dealer on one side of every trade, and in fact inside the sell-side banks, swaptions and other interest-rate option products (most notably *caps* and *floors*, which are options on LIBOR rates) are handled by the same interest-rate derivatives desk that trades swaps.

In both the dealer-to-customer and the interdealer market, swaptions are typically quoted in terms of their Black-Scholes volatility rather than their price (which in this case is called the *swaption premium* and is expressed in basis points as a percentage of the notional amount). Given that everyone agrees on a set of expiration dates and swap terms, as well as on what the forward swap rates are, the conversion of premiums to volatilities using the Black-Scholes formula is completely unambiguous (it is not unlike price-to-yield conversion in this regard). In Figure 9–9 we show an example of the *swaptions grid*, a table of at-the-money swaption volatilities for a standard set of option terms and swap tenors. As is clear from this example, in the case of swaptions (and other interest-rate options), the constant-volatility assumption that works reasonably well for equity options would be very far off the mark.

FIGURE 9–9

A swaptions grid from a Reuters information page. © Reuters 2006 (reproduced with permission).

```
21:47 22NOV05   ICAP                           UK69580                    VCAP21
                USD ATM Swaption Straddles - Implied Volatilities
                Please call +44 (0)20 7532 3050 for further details
```

	1Y	2Y	3Y	4Y	5Y	6Y	7Y	8Y	9Y	10Y	15Y	20Y	25Y	30Y
1M Opt	12.2	14.8	16.4	17.3	18.1	17.9	17.8	17.6	17.5	17.3	16.8	16.4	16.2	16.0
3M Opt	13.7	16.9	17.4	18.0	18.6	18.4	18.2	18.0	17.8	17.6	16.9	16.6	16.4	16.2
6M Opt	16.5	18.9	19.0	19.3	19.6	19.4	19.2	19.0	18.8	18.7	17.8	17.4	17.1	16.8
1Y Opt	19.3	20.6	20.4	20.8	20.4	20.2	20.0	19.8	19.6	19.3	18.1	17.4	17.1	16.8
2Y Opt	20.9	21.4	21.0	20.8	20.8	20.3	20.0	19.7	19.5	19.3	16.9	16.6	16.6	16.3
3Y Opt	21.4	21.2	20.8	20.5	20.2	19.9	19.7	19.4	19.1	18.9	17.2	16.3	16.1	15.9
4Y Opt	21.0	20.7	20.4	20.0	19.6	19.3	19.0	18.8	18.5	18.3	16.6	15.7	15.5	15.2
5Y Opt	20.6	20.2	19.8	19.4	18.9	18.7	18.4	18.1	17.9	17.6	16.0	15.1	14.8	14.6
7Y Opt	19.1	18.8	18.3	17.9	18.5	17.5	17.0	16.7	16.5	16.3	14.7	14.0	13.9	13.7
10Y Opt	17.0	16.6	16.3	15.9	15.6	15.3	15.1	14.9	14.7	14.5	13.1	12.5	12.4	12.3
15Y Opt	14.5	14.2	14.0	13.7	13.5	13.3	13.2	13.0	12.9	12.7	11.6	11.1	11.1	11.0
20Y Opt	13.3	13.2	12.9	12.7	12.4	12.3	12.1	12.0	11.8	11.7	10.6	10.1	10.1	10.1
25Y Opt	12.5	12.2	12.0	11.8	11.6	11.4	11.3	11.2	11.1	10.9	10.1	9.6	9.6	6.9
30Y Opt														

```
Options Index <VCAP>                         RIC Index Pages      <ICAPREJ>
ICAP Global Index <ICAP>                     Forthcoming changes  <ICAPCHANGE>
```

The main reason for this is that interest rates, unlike the prices of stocks and futures, have a tendency to *revert to the mean* rather than move aimlessly without any bound. Under the simple Black-Scholes distributional assumption, a stock that now has a price of 10 can drift up to 100 if given enough time (since the width of the price distribution function keeps growing with time). In contrast, the width of the distribution function for interest rates remains limited as time goes by, so that the rates stay within a fairly narrow range. The volatility quotes in Figure 9–9 reflect this bounded nature of the rates distribution—the vols for longer option terms are much lower, so that the width of the rates distribution, $\sigma\sqrt{t}$ (as well as the swaption prices), remains approximately constant as time to expiration increases.

A pricing model for swaptions and other interest-rate options needs to take into account this mean-reverting nature of interest rates. It also needs to account for the fact that there is not just one interest rate but many strongly correlated rates, so that whatever assumptions the model makes about the random process for the rates need to apply to the whole term structure. A number of such generalizations of the Black-Scholes approach, called *term structure models*, were developed in the late 1980s and early 1990s; when we hear names like *Hull-White, Black-Karasinski*, or *Black-Derman-Toy*, or acronyms like HJM or BGM, we should know that all of those refer to different term structure models that are now widely used by interest-rate derivatives businesses to price and manage the risk of interest-rate options. Again, there is a vast literature on the mathematics of such models (we give some references in the Recommended Reading section), so we do not go into that here.

The need for term structure models in the fixed-income world is also driven by the fact that many bonds have optionlike features. Most prominent among those are *callable bonds*, which can be redeemed by the issuer prior to the maturity date (usually on coupon dates) if the price goes above a certain threshold (usually par). A long position in a callable bond is equivalent to a long position in a bullet bond (with a fixed maturity date) and a short position in a call option on the bond price struck at par; if the price goes up and the option becomes in the money, the issuer exercises it and you have to sell the bond at par.

While callable bonds have been around for many centuries (up until the early twentieth century, practically all bonds were callable), accurate pricing and risk management of these products became possible only with the advent of modern options-pricing theory. Callable bonds became popular again when interest rates in the United States dropped to very low levels in 2001, and this time around they spawned a boomlet in interest-rate derivatives that were specially tailored to match the risk profile of callable bonds. A derivatives counterpart of a callable bond is a *cancelable swap*, a combination of going long a swap and going short a swaption to enter into an offsetting swap in the future. However, to match the callable bond structure, where the call option can be exercised only on coupon dates, the swaption in the cancelable swap should also be exercisable on a fixed set of dates. Such swaptions are called *Bermudan swaptions* (which is halfway between American and European), and they have become very popular in the last few years.

This role of options as building blocks for other, potentially much more complex financial products was and remains a primary reason for the enduring attention that options pricing enjoys in the larger financial analytics realm. The availability of options-pricing models in general and term structure models in particular was a major driver for the boom in *structured products* in the early 1990s. These products were effectively combinations of traditional bondlike financing and increasingly complex options. At first these options were relatively simple puts and calls on interest rates, but within a few years structured products began to incorporate options with much more complex payoff profiles. Examples of such *exotic options* include *binary options* (which pay $1 if the underlying goes above a strike level and nothing otherwise), *barrier options* (which kick in if the underlying ever reaches a certain barrier level), and *quanto options* (which pay in a different currency), and there are many more. Exotic options also exist as stand-alone products, especially in equities and FX, and despite fairly modest trade volumes play an important role as the leading edge of financial innovation—this is one of the increasingly rare businesses where having a better pricing model still provides a competitive advantage.

Finally, we should mention the emergence of other *volatility products* that are similar to options in that they derive their value from volatility, but that do this in a nontraditional way. For example, there are now futures that settle against *volatility indices* that are compiled by exchanges like CBOE or EUREX and represent observed levels of implied volatility in certain sectors of the options markets. Pricing and risk management of such products presents interesting theoretical and practical challenges that take traditional options pricing to the new horizons.

TECHNOLOGY AND OPTIONS TRADING

In this chapter, we have briefly reviewed the colorful history and the contemporary state of the options markets, and in conclusion I want to point out the main areas in which options markets require the services of quantitative and technology professionals. Options pricing, understood broadly as the development, implementation, and maintenance of options-pricing models, is just one of those areas, and perhaps the most mature one. As we discuss in our financial analytics chapter, in the financial analytics library of almost any large Wall Street firm, there are implementations of every options-pricing model imaginable, so at present the challenges in this area are not so much in model development as in applying these existing models to various business areas, such as structured derivatives, and integrating them with other technology, such as trading and risk systems. For example, trading systems that support different options-trading strategies and identify the relative value of different classes of options combine options analytics with the ability to execute complex sets of option trades and risk-manage the resulting positions.

The rapid and often painful transition of many options markets into the electronic trading world also presents both challenges and opportunities from the quantitative and technological points of view; the development and perfection of electronic market-making strategies, exchange connectivity, and autoexecution capabilities are keeping a lot of technical people busy. And, last but not least, options play an important educational and conceptual role in modern quantitative finance, not unlike that of calculus in the larger discipline of mathematics: the ideas that led to modern options-pricing theory permeate so many other areas that almost no matter where you end up working, some familiarity with options as a market and as a theoretical construct that facilitates thinking about many other types of financial products is going to be very helpful.

I hope that this chapter serves as a good introduction that will allow you to explore the fascinating world of options and other derivatives on your own (perhaps using the Recommended Reading section as a starting point). We must, however, move on. Our next topic takes us back to the world of fixed income—more specifically, to mortgage markets.

CHAPTER 10

Mortgages and Agencies

We are all familiar with the concept of a mortgage in a personal finance context. Most people in developed countries now have easy access to mortgage financing, and a great majority of those who use this economic staple never ask where the money they borrow to purchase their houses actually comes from. This is a pity, because the answer to this question is quite interesting on many levels. As we will discuss in this chapter, modern mortgage finance would not be possible without capital markets that connect investors (the ultimate source of funds) to the individual mortgage borrowers.

Half of our story will be about the role that capital markets now play in housing finance. As the mortgage-related capital markets evolved over the last half-century, they became very important for the larger financial industry (Figure 10–1), and this will be the second half of our story; we will discuss how mortgage markets are organized, how they are related to other markets that we already know about, and what makes these markets interesting and challenging for the quantitatively inclined. As is our custom, we start with a historical interlude.

THE HISTORY OF MORTGAGES

As I mentioned in Chapter 1, a mortgage is not a new concept. The idea of pledging land for loans is mentioned in the Bible and was used from ancient Babylon to Rome. By the early Middle Ages, it was widely accepted throughout Europe. The word *mortgage* originated in twelfth-century England. Then as now, it referred to a specific type of borrowing in which the borrower *pledges* (the word *gage* means "pledge") some identifiable real estate (a

FIGURE 10–1

Composition of the U.S. fixed-income markets by type of securities at the end of the first quarter of 2005. (Federal Reserve Flow of Funds data from www.federalreserve.gov/releases/z1/current/default.htm). The mortgage markets overtook corporate bonds in the 1990s and now easily dwarf everything else in the fixed-income universe.

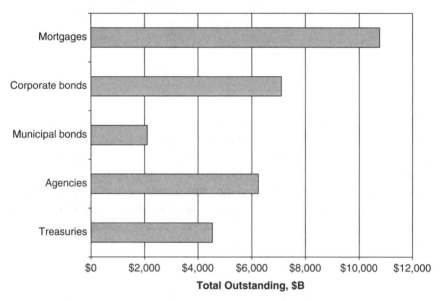

Total Outstanding, $B

house, a farm, a castle, or in some cases a whole village) as a collateral against default.

To translate this into human language, let us consider an example. Suppose we are a feudal knight; we have land and peasants working it, but we have little actual money, and we need money to, say, buy some new armor for the upcoming crusade. What do we do? Highway robbery was one popular solution, but as the Middle Ages progressed, many people opted for a mortgage instead. In that approach, we find a lender (typically a wealthy merchant in a nearby city) and strike the following deal with him: (1) the lender gives us money, and we agree to make periodic (usually annual) interest payments; (2) the lender identifies a piece of our property (say, a nice meadow, or perhaps a house) whose value is comparable to the amount of money borrowed; (3) we agree that if we fail to make an interest payment, the lender can take that piece of property away from us (which is what a pledge of property means); (4) this arrangement continues either forever (in which case it is called a mortgage, or dead pledge), or for some finite period of time (that would be a live gage),[1] at the end of which we repay the lender and the deal terminates. For us, this deal confers the ability to convert our real estate into liquid wealth. For the lender, it is an opportunity to invest his funds with much lower risk than in a loan supported by just our word of honor (which is why the interest rate on mortgages was much lower than that for unsecured loans).

As this example makes clear, originally a mortgage was a way to lose an existing piece of property rather than acquire a new one. Mortgaging property was (correctly) viewed as a sign of fiscal profligacy, and the negative connotations of the word persist in today's language (as in "mortgaging our country's future"). However, by the early nineteenth century, mortgages were increasingly being used much as they are today: as a way to acquire a property that costs more than we can readily pay. A mortgage-assisted property transaction has come to work as follows: (1) we (the buyer) find a property we want and agree with the seller on the price, (2) we commit to paying some fraction of the price out of our own funds, (3) a lender provides a loan for the remaining part of the purchase price, and (4) we pledge (mortgage) our newly acquired property to the lender. While the final relationship between us and the lender would be the same as in our medieval knight example, this more modern usage of a mortgage addressed a basic economic need of the growing middle class, which led to a reduction in the social stigma of mortgages. (However, even well into the twentieth century, having a mortgage on your home was generally viewed negatively.)

In the United States, the movement to make everyone a homeowner started in the early nineteenth century, and by the 1930s about 40 percent of the population owned their homes; however, many people actually bought their homes for cash, and the use of mortgages was limited to lower-income homeowners. The mortgage terms available at that time were, by today's standards, startlingly tough: lenders (typically local banks) required at least a 50 percent down payment, and the length of the mortgage contract was five to seven years. Most importantly, as in medieval times, the borrower made interest payments only, so that at the end of the loan term, the whole

---

1. Some sources suggest that the term "live gage" could also mean an arrangement where the interest is paid not in money, but in the agricultural output of the pledged land (livestock, crops, and so on), which is an even more direct way of converting land holdings into money.

borrowed amount came due and had to be either paid off or refinanced by taking out a new mortgage.

This system did not survive the onset of the Great Depression. The sudden and widespread unemployment caused many people to default on their payments; banks collapsed by the thousands and nobody had any money to lend, so people whose mortgages came due could not refinance their loans and defaulted as well. By 1934, millions of people had lost their homes to foreclosure, and the housing industry was dead—housing starts had plunged 95 percent, and two million workers in the housing construction industry were unemployed, while the parallel collapse of the banking industry meant that funds for housing were nowhere to be found.

At this point, the federal government stepped in and actually did something useful. First, it organized Federal Home Loan Banks (FHLB), a group of banks whose purpose it was to provide funds for mortgage lending. The governing board of FHLB analyzed the problems with the existing mortgage finance system and quickly figured out that a major weakness of it was that the mortgages were not amortizing—the whole loan amount suddenly came due, and it was difficult for borrowers to repay it all at once.

The solution it developed was the home mortgage as we know it today (Figure 10–2): the borrower pays a fixed amount monthly (instead of the traditional every six months), and this amount includes a principal repayment part and an interest part. The principal repayment part reduces (amortizes) the outstanding amount every month. The interest part is equal to the monthly interest on the outstanding amount; since the latter goes down every month, so does the interest payment, and to keep the total constant, the principal repayment amount grows every month. This leads to progressively faster amortization of the loan as it ages—the monthly payment is almost all interest at the beginning of the loan but becomes almost all principal toward the end of it. This arrangement is called a *fully amortized fixed-rate mortgage*, and it is a rare example of a government invention that completely revolutionized an important area of the economy.

Another New Deal government agency that played a key role in restoring sanity to the residential home mortgage business was the Federal Housing Administration, or FHA. Established in 1934, it did two important things: (1) it set minimum standards for home construction, so that the properties being financed could reasonably be expected to outlast the term of the loan (which had become much longer—20 to 30 years), and (2) for those properties that satisfied its standards, the FHA *insured* the lender against the risk

FIGURE 10-2

Monthly payments on an 8 percent fixed-rate fully amortizing 30-year mortgage, per $1,000 borrowed amount. The total payment of $7.34 remains constant over the life of the loan, but its decomposition into interest and principal components changes. Initially the interest component heavily dominates, while principal repayments begin to dominate toward the end of the loan. The interest payment is always proportional to the remaining loan balance, so we can also see how the loan amortizes by following the interest payments line on this chart.

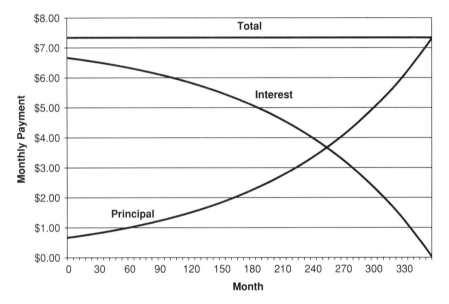

of default for a fee of a few basis points. The result was that lenders became much more willing to commit funds to mortgage lending (even apart from the greatly improved quality of new houses built under the FHA guidelines). This revived mortgage lending in the United States, and the home construction industry rebounded as a result (this also made a good dent in unemployment, which, as some people suspected at the time, was what the government really cared about when it introduced these housing reforms).

However, within a few years the lenders (typically savings and loan depository institutions) simply ran out of funds; they had converted most of their deposit base into mortgages and had no more money to lend. In 1938, the federal government came up with yet another agency to help with this problem; this one was called the Federal National Mortgage Association (FNMA or, as most people call it, *Fannie Mae*), and it is here that our story begins to intersect with the capital markets theme.

Fannie Mae was created to spur the *secondary market* for mortgages (which admittedly existed before Fannie Mae, but on a much smaller scale). Fannie Mae's business was to buy whole slews of mortgages from the depository institutions that had originally created them. These institutions made a quick buck on the sale of mortgages and ended up with money that they could put into mortgage lending all over again, while Fannie Mae essentially invested money in good-quality debt obligations that were insured against default by the FHA, so everyone seemed to benefit. Fannie Mae freed up a lot of capital for mortgage lending and, just as importantly, made mortgage lending truly national in scope, since it could easily shift its purchases to those areas of the country that needed capital the most.

The FHA and Fannie Mae were the only two government agencies that actually earned a profit on their activities and thus required no taxpayer support. Fannie Mae was in fact so profitable that in 1968 it was reorganized and became a public company, with only a small piece of it, now called Ginnie Mae (GNMA, or Government National Mortgage Association), remaining in the federal government as part of the newly established Department of Housing and Urban Development. It was Ginnie Mae that in 1971 introduced another innovation in mortgage finance that greatly increased the attractiveness of mortgages to institutional investors and thus made huge quantities of capital available for mortgage lending. The idea later became known as *securitization* of mortgages: you take a pool of individual mortgages and convert them into a bondlike security that can be sold to investors and has a liquid secondary market. Let us consider how this works using one type of such *mortgage-backed security (MBS)* called a Ginnie Mae pass-through. First, however, we need to introduce a few mortgage market concepts.

MORTGAGES AND
THE MORTGAGE MARKET

A new mortgage is a transaction between two parties, one of which is the individual homeowner. The other party—the one that actually provides the money to the borrower and handles all the necessary paperwork—is called a *mortgage originator*, and there are several different types of those. It could be a *thrift institution*, a pure depository institution whose only source of funds is its customers' deposits. Or it could be a *commercial bank* like Chase, which can get the money for a mortgage loan from its many other lines of business. Finally, it can be a *mortgage bank* like Countrywide, whose only purpose in life is to originate new mortgages; these banks do not take deposits, but instead fund their mortgage origination activities by borrowing money from commercial banks (this has become the most common type of mortgage origination). Mortgage originators charge a fee for their activities (typically about 2 *points*; this means 2 percent of the amount of the loan). You can think of mortgage origination as the *primary market* for mortgages.

Once a mortgage has been originated, it has to be *serviced*—someone has to collect the payments from the borrower and forward them to the lender, keep track of the principal balance, send out the payment notices, maintain escrow accounts for taxes and insurance premiums, and also deal with less pleasant aspects of the mortgage, such as delinquencies, defaults, and foreclosures. Some mortgage originators (especially smaller institutions) retain the responsibility for servicing the mortgages they originate, but it is clear that all these activities have little to do with banking. They are much more like payroll services, and, just like payrolls, they can be outsourced to a third party called a *mortgage servicer*. Mortgage originators can sell servicing rights to their mortgages to such servicers, who will take a servicing fee (typically about 40 bp) out of every payment they handle before forwarding it on.

Even more importantly, the originators can sell the right to receive the mortgage payments to someone else. When an originating bank sells a mortgage to, say, Fannie Mae, the servicer simply forwards the monthly payments to Fannie Mae instead of to the originating bank. As a result of such *secondary-market* trading of mortgages, a typical mortgage today is originated by one bank, serviced by another, and *owned* by someone else again. In fact, you may very well own a (small) part of the mortgage on your own home if you invest in certain mutual funds or participate in a pension plan.

However, secondary-market trading of mortgages is obviously hampered by the fact that individual mortgages are (1) small and (2) unique, so that a pension fund looking to invest $100 million would have a hard time assembling a pool of hundreds if not thousands of individual mortgages worth that amount of money. While it would be a good idea for a pension fund to invest in mortgages—they are safe investments (especially those insured by the FHA and other federal agencies), and they yield more than government debt—something had to happen before such investments could be practically implemented. Mortgage securitization is all about making such transactions possible.

MORTGAGE SECURITIZATION

The goal of securitization is to combine individual mortgages into some-thing larger and standardized—a security with a large issued amount and well-defined properties that could be bought and sold easily. As we men-tioned, the first securitization program was organized by GNMA in 1970, and it works as follows. First, a mortgage originator (typically a bank or a thrift) selects mortgages from its portfolio that (1) are insured by the FHA or other similar agencies, (2) have exactly the same mortgage rate, and (3) are no more than a year old. The originator then combines these mortgages into a *mortgage pool* with a minimum size of $1 million. GNMA inspects this pool to make sure it meets these conditions, and then authorizes the originator to issue a *pass-through* security *backed* by this mortgage pool.

The term *pass-through* simply means that the issuer (or, rather, the servicer) of these mortgages passes all payments made by the underlying mortgages through to the holders of that security in proportion to the size of their holdings (for example, if the total pool size is $10 million and we hold $1 million of this pass-through, we receive 10 percent of every pay-ment), less a servicing fee of 44 bp and a 6-bp fee charged by GNMA for *guaranteeing* the performance of these mortgages, so overall the interest rate paid by this security is 0.5 percent less than the mortgage rate on the underlying mortgages. The Ginnie Mae guarantee means that this mort-gage-backed security is of the same credit quality as U.S. Treasury debt, and our pension fund can now buy it without having to worry about all those messy issues related to servicing and the possibility of default.

GNMA was quickly joined in the issuance of mortgage-backed securities by *Freddie Mac* (FHLMC, or the Federal Home Loan Mortgage Corporation, created by Congress in 1970 to assist the member thrifts of the Federal Home Loan system) in 1971, by Fannie Mae in 1984, and, espe-cially in recent years, by a whole army of banks that issue so-called private-label MBSs (often backed by mortgages that the two federal agencies refuse to touch because they are either too large or of too low credit quality). While their MBS programs are different in some respects, we will focus on their many common features when we consider Figure 10–3, which shows stan-dard information about one of the FNMA mortgage-backed securities.

Let us make sure that we understand everything in Figure 10–3 before we proceed to mortgage valuation issues. First, security informa-tion: we see that the security is identified by a pool number, the prefix

Information about one mortgage pool backing a pass-through security from Fannie Mae. (Source: PoolTalk, www.fanniemae.com/mbs/tools/pooltalk.jhtml; reproduced with permission.)

Common Pool Information

Security Information		Month	Current Factor	Pool Level PTR	Weighted Average (WA) Information	
Pool Number	803673	September	0.94782195	5.00000	WA Original Coupon	5.5000
Pool Prefix	CL	August	0.96386328	5.00000	WA Current Coupon	5.5000
CUSIP	31405Y2E0	July	0.97277820	5.00000	WA Original Maturity	359
Suppress Code	0 - Active	June	0.97421863	5.00000	WA Current Maturity	348
Pool Issue Date	12/01/2004	May	0.97561411	5.00000	WA Credit Score	751
Maturity Date	11/01/2034	April	0.97710518	5.00000	WA Loan To Value	52
Original Balance	$22,567,620.00	March	0.98080449	5.00000	WA Loan Age	10
Pool Loan Count	113				WA Original Loan Term	360

(CL) identifies this pool as a pool of conventional 30-year single-family mortgages,[2] and there are 113 individual mortgages in this pool, with a total outstanding balance of $22,567,620. The security has a maturity date of November 1, 2034, which is the due date of the longest mortgage in the pool, and it carries a coupon of 5 percent. The "weighted average" numbers are just what the name implies: various characteristics of the underlying mortgages, such as maturity and interest rate (coupon), averaged by weighting them by the principal amount of each constituent mortgage loan. You can see that the weighted-average coupon (WAC) is 5.5 percent, which is 50 bp higher than what the security pays; the difference is called the *servicing spread*, which is taken out by the servicer and by Fannie Mae for its guarantee.

The *factors* shown in Figure 10–3 represent the remaining principal balance at the end of each month as a percentage of the original principal. The principal is reduced each month because of the scheduled amortization of each loan, but this is only part of the story—in most countries, the mortgage holder has the right to *prepay* some or all of the outstanding balance, so that the principal amount of the pool always drops off somewhat faster than you would expect based on the scheduled amortization. This seemingly mundane detail turns out to be absolutely crucial for determining the value of mortgage-backed securities, and we will now consider this *prepayment option* in more detail.

To understand why the prepayment option matters, let us begin by comparing two extreme scenarios: (1) we buy a newly issued mortgage-backed security, and it pays us a fixed cash flow every month for the next 30 years (there are no prepayments whatsoever), and (2) we buy that same security and all the mortgages in the pool immediately prepay all the outstanding principal, so we get a single payment equal to the outstanding principal balance. Which of these two scenarios is better for us?

The answer mostly depends on the level of interest rates: if the current rate for 30-year mortgages is higher than the WAC of the pool, then we are better off getting all the principal back at once and reinvesting it at a higher

---

2. There are, of course, many other kinds; the types of mortgage pools reflect the variety of mortgage products available in the market, and include fixed-rate pools of different maturities, adjustable-rate mortgage (ARM) pools of different maturities, balloon pools (for mortgages where some of the principal amount becomes due at the end of the loan term), and some others. The pools are further subdivided by whether the mortgages are single-family or multifamily and by some other criteria, so that at the end of the day, there are several dozen such prefixes that define the specific type of mortgage pool.

rate, whereas if the current rate is lower than the WAC, then we are better off keeping our principal invested at an above-market rate. The problem is that we do not get to choose; it is the mortgage borrowers who have the option of choosing between these scenarios, and on average they will pick the scenario that is good for them and bad for us: if interest rates shoot up, the mortgagors will sit tight with their below-market-rate mortgages and will not prepay anything, whereas if the rates drop, the borrowers will *refinance* their loans (obtain new loans at a lower rate) and use the proceeds to pay off the principal on the old higher-rate loans. We see that the prepayment option is very valuable to the borrower, and therefore reduces the value of mortgage-backed securities from the investor's point of view.

The interesting thing about prepayments is that they are not driven solely by economic considerations such as the level of interest rates, but also reflect the larger realities of life. People prepay their mortgages when they sell their houses for any reason: a job-related move, a divorce, a desire to upgrade, and so on. The mortgage on a house also gets prepaid if the house burns down or is destroyed by a hurricane or another natural disaster; homeowner's insurance takes care of the mortgage balance in such cases. Finally, if a homeowner defaults on his mortgage, the house gets taken away from him, and mortgage insurance pays off the outstanding balance. The level of interest rates is thus just one of many factors driving mortgage prepayment decisions, and that makes prepayments very difficult to predict; even the task of describing the observed prepayment behavior quantitatively is a nontrivial one.

A useful concept in this area was introduced by the Public Securities Association (PSA) in the early 1980s in order to describe changes in prepayments during the life of a mortgage loan. The standard PSA prepayment model simply assumes that all mortgages older than 30 months prepay their balance at a constant annual rate of 6 percent, while for newly created mortgages, the prepayment rate is zero (because few people pay off a mortgage right after taking it out) and increases linearly to 6 percent as the loan age increases to 30 months. This default behavior is meant to reflect the normal housing turnover and can be used as a yardstick for measuring the actual prepayment rate of mortgage pools: if we have a 40-month-old pool that is prepaying at an annual rate of 9 percent, we say that it is prepaying at 150 percent PSA, or that its *prepayment speed* is 150 percent. Historically, the observed prepayment speeds have been as high as 1000 percent and as low as 10 percent, mostly dependent on the changes in interest rates.

In Figure 10–4, we compare the projected cash flows of a 30-year mortgage pool assuming different PSA prepayment speeds. Clearly, even modest prepayment speeds turn the expected cash flows of a mortgage pool into something entirely different from the steady monthly payment that we might naively expect. Despite the obvious dependence of mortgage cash flows on the prepayment assumptions, mortgage market participants still cling to familiar bond market concepts such as yield and its derivatives, duration and convexity.

The yield of a mortgage-backed security is defined as the constant discount rate that makes the present value of its projected cash flows equal to its observed price, which is exactly the same definition as for any bond with fixed cash flows. Unfortunately, this yield is also a function of the prepayment assumptions, so it is difficult to use it as a measure of relative value for different mortgage-backed securities. This is even more true of

FIGURE 10–4

The projected cash flows of a pool of 8 percent 30-year mortgages under different prepayment assumptions in the PSA model. Note the "PSA ramp": the ramping up of the prepayments during the first 30 months of the loan assumed by the PSA model. Most prepayment models have a more graduated description of the ramp period, but they all have to include this concept.

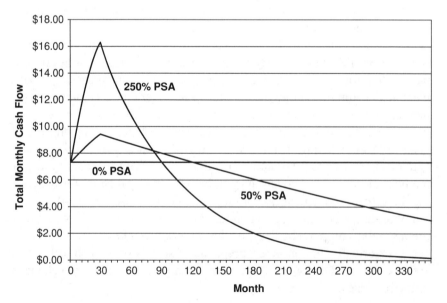

duration and convexity for these securities; taking derivatives with respect to yield should take account of the fact that the prepayment rate (and therefore the security cash flows) is also a function of the yield. When we decrease the yield, the present value of all cash flows increases because there is less discounting, but the cash flows also shift to shorter maturities because of the corresponding increase in prepayment speed.

In fact, the interplay between these two competing effects leads to *negative convexity* of mortgage pass-through securities, an important phenomenon that we illustrate schematically in Figure 10–5. Unlike a "normal" fixed-income security, whose present value can increase way above par when rates drop below its coupon rate, in the case of a mortgage pool, people will simply refinance all of their loans when the rate drops significantly below the WAC of the pool, so that its price levels off and tends to par instead of shooting upward at very low rates, which is what gives the price-yield curve in Figure 10–5 its distinct concave shape.

This negative convexity effect has very important implications for the stability of the mortgage market as a whole. Suppose we are long a portfolio of mortgages and we wish to hedge away its interest-rate risk by selling enough Treasuries to get our total duration down to zero (something

F I G U R E   10–5

Negative convexity of mortgages. When the interest rates drop below the coupon rate of a mortgage pool, the price of the pool approaches par from below instead of increasing rapidly as in the case of a fixed-coupon bond. As a result, the second derivative of the price versus rate (the convexity) of a mortgage pool is negative unless the rates are significantly above the coupon rate.

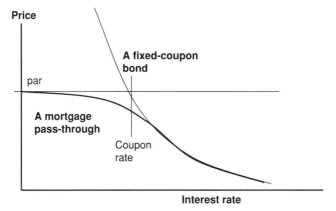

that many mortgage traders do every day). When interest rates drop, our hedge stops being perfect because the duration of our Treasuries increases when rates go down (this is what positive convexity means), whereas the duration of our mortgages goes down according to what is shown in Figure 10–5. To make the hedge perfect again, we have to buy some Treasuries to reduce our short position. The problem is that if the size of our portfolio is sufficiently large, this may cause the whole market to become unstable— if we have to buy lots of Treasuries when the rates go down, this forced buying may push the rates even lower, so we'll have to buy even more to maintain our hedge, which pushes the rates still lower, and on and on. Fortunately, nobody knows how big the mortgage positions have to be in order to cause the underlying interest-rate markets to come unstuck in this way, but the possibility is there.

Hopefully these examples have convinced you that you cannot properly value even simple mortgage pass-throughs without a decent quantitative model of prepayment behavior, and every investment bank that trades mortgage-backed securities does in fact have such a model, often more than one. While their details are proprietary, the general structure of such models is fairly standard. The prepayment speed of a mortgage pool is modeled as a (linear) combination of several explanatory factors; the term structure of interest rates is perhaps the most important ingredient, but other parameters such as the length and shape of the "ramp" period as a function of the age of the pool, seasonal factors, and the type of the underlying mortgages also play an important role. Once the functional form of these factors has been defined, their relative weights are determined by regression analysis of historical prepayment data for a large number of mortgage pools. The resulting regression coefficients can be used to predict what will happen to a given issue of mortgage-backed securities if the factors evolve in a certain way in the future.

The development of such prepayment models in the 1980s made it possible to compare the relative value of different mortgage-backed securities; since the traditional fixed-income measures of value such as yield or yield spread to Treasuries are not very meaningful for MBSs, it is hard to say that Security A is a better investment than Security B because its yield is higher. To make such comparisons, one really has to analyze what will happen to both securities under different interest-rate scenarios, and in the late 1980s Salomon Brothers, a leading mortgage market dealer, introduced a very popular methodology for doing this that became known as *OAS analysis*. OAS stands for *option-adjusted spread*; it is in fact a spread to the Treasury curve (or, more often these days, the LIBOR swaps curve) that is meant to incorporate the effect of the prepayment option and can therefore be used to measure the relative value of a given MBS with respect to the whole Treasury or swaps curve.

The OAS method addressed the central problem of mortgage valuation: since MBSs do not really have a well-defined maturity, calculating a spread to a particular maturity point on another yield curve makes little sense. The OAS approach instead takes the whole reference curve (Treasuries or swaps) and shifts it up (or, in the case of the LIBOR curve, down) by a constant amount until the expected present value of the cash flows of an MBS matches its observed market price. The larger the OAS, the cheaper the security is relative to the reference curve, and the difference in OAS between two securities is a good measure of their relative value.

The hard part of an OAS calculation is determining the expected value of the cash flows of an MBS. This requires a Monte Carlo simulation, where one generates a large number of interest-rate scenarios (which should be consistent with today's yield curve), and then applies a prepayment model to each path to predict what the cash flows would be under that particular scenario. The present value averaged over a large number of scenarios is then compared with the observed price of the security, and the yield curve is shifted and the simulation repeated until these two quantities become the same. In the late 1980s, evaluating an OAS for a new issue of a mortgage-backed security took several hours on a mainframe computer (the investment banks that traded these securities raced to complete the calculations so that they could be the first to tell their customers). Those days are long gone, but mortgage analytics remains one of the heavier parts of quantitative finance.

THE MECHANICS OF MORTGAGE TRADING

How and why did Wall Street get involved with mortgage-backed securities? If you flip back a few pages and take another look at Figure 10–1, you will see part of the answer: the mortgage market is simply huge, and the Wall Street dealer banks are eager to make money in it, mostly as market makers. Many, although not all, sell-side banks have large mortgage trading desks, whose revenues rival and often exceed those of the more traditional interest-rate businesses such as interest-rate derivatives or government bond trading.

In the United States, mortgage trading has a lot of similarities with the Treasury market, beginning with the fact that the prices are quoted in thirty-seconds, as shown in Figure 10–6. Another similarity is that the liquidity is heavily concentrated in the new issues of mortgage pass-throughs.

FIGURE 10-6

A Reuters information screen, <30YRMBS>, showing indicative prices for new production 30-year MBSs for different coupons and four settlement months. The prices for the front month (October) are on the left, and the prices for the forward months (on the right) are obtained by applying the drops (shown under the "Nov/Dec/Jan" heading) to the front month prices. © Reuters 2006; reproduced with permission.

```
08:47 13SEP05        US MBS TBA PRICES - 30 YEAR              US35624              30YRMBS
GNMA 30YR  Oct      CHG   BEY      Nov/Dec/Jan     F   GNMA      Nov      Dec      Jan
04.0  93.19-21      -08   5.045%   08/11/09        O   04.0      93.11    93.00    92.23
04.5  97.04-06      -07   4.973%   08/11/09        R   04.5      96.28    96.17    96.08
05.0  99.18-20      -06   5.093%   08/10/10        W   05.0      99.10    99.00    98.22
05.5  101.12-14     -05   5.219%   09/08/09        A   05.5      101.03   100.27   100.18
06.0  102.28-30     -01   5.019%   07/08/08        R   06.0      102.21   102.13   102.05
06.5  104.06-08     -01   4.709%   07/07/07        D   06.5      103.31   103.24   103.17
FNMA 30YR  Oct      CHG   BEY      Nov/Dec/Jan         FNMA      Nov      Dec      Jan
04.0  92.25-27      -09   5.190%   09/09/09        M   04.0      92.16    92.07    91.30
04.5  96.06-08      -07   5.087%   09/09/09        O   04.5      95.29    95.20    95.11
05.0  98.19-21      -06   5.237%   08/09/09        N   05.0      98.11    98.02    97.25
05.5  100.16-18     -05   5.371%   09/08/08        T   05.5      100.07   99.31    99.23
06.0  102.02-04     -01   5.217%   09/09/09        H   06.0      101.25   101.16   101.07
06.5  103.05-07     -01   5.125%   07/05/06            06.5      102.30   102.25   102.19
GOLD 30YR  Oct      CHG   BEY      Nov/Dec/Jan         GOLD      Nov      Dec      Jan
04.0  92.25-27      -09   5.213%   08/09/09        P   04.0      92.17    92.08    91.31
04.5  96.00-02      -08   5.139%   08/09/09        R   04.5      95.24    95.15    95.06
05.0  98.17-18      -07   5.275%   08/08/08        I   05.0      98.09    98.01    97.25
05.5  100.16-18     -05   5.400%   08/08/08        C   05.5      100.08   100.00   99.24
06.0  102.01-03     -02   5.248%   09/08/11        I   06.0      101.24   101.16   101.05
06.5  103.02-04     -01   5.190%   07/06/06        N   06.5      102.27   102.21   102.15
                                                   G
SEE <MBS/INFO>**********COMMENTS CALL (800) 272-8373****************************
<30YRPREM> <USMBS> <GN30YLDS> <FN30YLDS><FR30YLDS><15YRMBS><BALLOONS>
<GNMA/ARMS> <COFI/ARMS> <GNMA/MPOOLS>  <MSSETTLE1>       Index.....<US/MTG1>
```

The three major types of MBS that are most actively traded are GNMA pass-throughs, Fannie Maes, and Freddie Mac Gold PCs (participation certificates); Figure 10–6 shows quotations for these securities as they would be displayed on a Reuters information screen for the 30-year sector (there are, of course, many other fairly liquid sectors: 15-year, balloons, and especially adjustable-rate mortgages, or ARMs).

Unlike the Treasury market, where there is only one on-the-run security in each sector, in the mortgage market the liquidity is spread over a few dozen securities, which differ in terms of their guarantor (GNMA, FNMA, or FHLMC) and their coupon—since at any given time mortgage rates for different borrowers vary widely, the "new production" MBS can be issued with several different coupon levels at any given time (as illustrated by the bottom rows in Figure 10–6). Despite this wider selection of liquid securities, the bid-ask spreads are fairly tight: usually just a plus (half of $\frac{1}{32}$), just as for on-the-run Treasuries.

MBS are on a monthly issuance cycle; an issuance calendar for every month is published by the Bond Market Association (BMA), formerly known as the PSA (see Figure 10–7 for an example). Again unlike the Treasury market, where the coupon is set at the auction, in the mortgage market the current production coupons are known ahead of time. This enables the market participants to trade these securities before they are actually issued—since all their cash flow parameters (maturity, coupon, and the details specific to each guarantor program) are known, one can calculate their prices and/or present values. This is similar to when-issued trading of Treasuries, but in the mortgage market this is called *to-be-announced*, or *TBA*, trading.

What needs to be announced before a mortgage trade can settle is which specific pool or pools of mortgages will be used for each trade. The "notification date" shown in Figure 10–7 is the day on which the seller has to inform the buyer which specific pools he intends to use to settle the trade. The settlement itself happens on the settlement date, two business days after the notification date.

As we can see in Figure 10–7, there is only one notification date and one settlement date per month for each type of security, so we cannot really choose a settlement date for a TBA trade. However, we can choose the month, within reason: four front months are open for TBA trading, as shown in Figure 10–6. In the right half of that figure, we can see *drops*, or the price differences between quotes for different settlement months, which show how much the price drops when we move from one month to the next. In fact, much of the activity in the TBA market consists of

BMA settlement calendar for MBSs, from Reuters page
MBSSETTLE. © Reuters 2006; reproduced with permission.

```
BMA MORTGAGE BACKED SECURITIES SETTLEMENT CALENDAR
MBSSETTLE8
OCTOBER 2005
    Class A    |    Class B    |    Class C    |    Class D
-------------------------------------------------------------------
    30 Year    |    15 Year    |    30 Year    |    BALLOONS
-------------------------------------------------------------------
 Freddie Mac   |  Freddie Mac  |  Ginnie Mae   |  Freddie Mac

                                                  Fannie Mae
 Fannie Mae    |  Fannie Mae   |               |-----------------
                                                  All ARMs/VRMs/
               |  Ginnie Mae   |                  Multifamily/GPMs/
                                                  Mobile Homes
                                               |-----------------
                                                  Freddie Mac

                                                  Fannie Mae

                                                  Ginnie Mae
 Notification Date
  TUESDAY 11  |   FRIDAY 14   |  TUESDAY 18   |  THURSDAY 20  |
-------------------------------------------------------------------
 Settlement Date
  THURSDAY 13 |  TUESDAY 18   |  THURSDAY 20  |  MONDAY 24    |
```

selling one delivery month and buying another; such switch trades are called
"dollar rolls" (because they are quoted in price, not yield spread), and they
can be executed in one go, much like bond swaps in the Treasury market.

While the overwhelming majority of mortgage trading is done on a
TBA basis, there is also a secondary market for MBSs that have already been
issued. These do not require any pretrade notification, since their characteristics (CUSIP and pool numbers) are already known, so such trades settle
on what is called a "specified" basis (where the buyer and the seller agree on
the specific CUSIP of the security being traded), which is, of course, how
most other markets operate. Again there is a certain similarity here to the trading of Treasury off-the-runs, but in the case of mortgages, the secondary-
market liquidity is spread over a much larger universe of securities.

To conclude our brief overview of mortgage trading, we should mention
that mortgage pass-throughs are only the tip of the iceberg in terms of complexity. By definition, in a pass-through security, all cash flows from the
underlying mortgage pool are passed through to the investor without any
modification. It does not have to be that way, and there is a wider class
of mortgage-backed products in which the cash flows are instead sliced

and diced in creative ways before being delivered to the investors. Such securities are called *CMOs* (*collateralized mortgage obligations*, also known as *REMICs*, which stands for *real estate mortgage investment conduits*). In very broad strokes, these securities separate the cash flows of the underlying pools into *tranches* according to a formal set of rules, and each such tranche is sold as a separate security. For example, Tranche A may receive only scheduled amortization principal payments plus interest, while Tranche B receives all prepayments, so that Tranche A does not have any prepayment risk, while Tranche B has a lot of it. This makes it possible to create securities with vastly different risk characteristics, including some that are very risky and that can become worthless after a relatively modest yield curve move. In fact, such risky tranches nearly did in the nascent REMICs market in 1994; a lot of investors loaded up on them and did not realize that the sharp rise in interest rates that year would lead to the obliteration of their positions. A major outcry followed, and it took the CMO market several years to recover. Today these securities are again respectable and in a certain sense play the role of derivatives in the mortgage market—much less liquid than the more pedestrian pass-throughs, but also far more difficult to model (and to understand) and therefore far more lucrative.

AGENCIES MARKET

You may have noticed in Figure 10–6 that GNMA pass-throughs are more expensive than either FNMA or FHLMC securities, which are priced almost identically—why is that? To answer this question, we need to review the business model of these organizations. As we briefly mentioned, both Fannie Mae and Freddie Mac were created by Congress, but they are *not* government agencies; the official line is that they are private companies serving a public mission (making housing more affordable, or, as the Fannie Mae slogan puts it, building the American dream). As such, they are subject to oversight by the federal government, and in return enjoy certain advantages, which we will discuss shortly. This arrangement makes both of them *government-sponsored enterprises*, or *GSEs*.

There is a host of other, smaller entities in this category, such as Sallie Mae (which makes student loans), Federal Farm Credit Funding Corporation, and some others, but Fannie Mae and Freddie Mac are by far the biggest GSEs, and we will limit our discussion to them. The "public mission" that both of them serve is to make more funds available for mortgage lending, and they pursue this goal by buying newly originated mortgages from the originating lenders. This process is now almost fully automated: a lender fills out a Web form on eFannieMae.com, and the newly made loan disappears from the lender's books and is entered into Fannie Mae's system (and similarly for Freddie Mac); the lender is now free to make another loan, which the GSEs also stand ready to absorb.

Where do the GSEs get the money to pay for these purchases? They get their funding from two main sources. The first we have already discussed: it is the issuance of mortgage-backed securities. As Freddie Mac started doing in the early 1970s, an originating bank can put together a pool of mortgages and hand it over to Freddie Mac, and Freddie Mac will then issue a security backed by these very same mortgages and give it back to the originating bank. At first sight, this seems to be an almost meaningless activity; the cash flows that the originating bank would get from the MBS are almost the same as those it would have gotten without going to this trouble. In practice, however, there is a major difference: it is far easier for a bank to sell this MBS, which is guaranteed by Freddie Mac, to outside investors than it would be to sell the underlying mortgages individually.

Let us take a closer look at the economics of this arrangement. Once the originator has sold the MBS to outside investors, the underlying mortgages are well and truly gone from its books, and the proceeds from the sale of the MBS can be used to make more loans. From the perspective of an institutional investor (think a pension fund or an insurance company), the buyer gets a safe, income-generating security, with interest and scheduled principal repayments guaranteed by Freddie Mac (meaning that if the pool does not generate enough interest or principal payments, Freddie Mac will cover the shortfall from its own sources). From Freddie Mac's perspective, it gets to keep 30 to 40 bp out of every payment as an "insurance premium" that should in theory cover the costs of the guarantee. Fannie Mae does much the same thing (except that it typically simply buys the underlying mortgages from the originating banks and does the pooling itself).

To summarize, roughly half of what the mortgage GSEs do is insert themselves between the mortgage originators and mortgage investors and, for a fee, make the underlying mortgages more attractive to end-user investors. In their MBS issuance programs, the GSEs act as intermediaries—they just pass the underlying mortgages' cash flows through to investors and collect the guarantee fees. This is very similar to what Ginnie Mae does: it guarantees mortgages under its MBS program, but it never owns them. When investors choose between different MBS securities backed by similar mortgage pools, the only real difference is the perceived quality of the agency guarantee. Since both Fannie Mae and Freddie Mac are private companies that could conceivably fail, their guarantee is less strong than that of Ginnie Mae, which carries the full faith and credit of the U.S. government. This is the main reason why the Ginnie Mae securities in Figure 10–6 are quoted about 1 full point higher than either the Fannie Mae or the Freddie Mac securities.

The second major way in which the GSEs finance their mortgage purchases is by borrowing in the capital markets. Here, the GSEs act as principals; they purchase mortgages for their *retained portfolio* and keep the cash flows. To the extent that the cash flows from the retained mortgage portfolio are greater than what the GSEs have to pay on the funds that they borrowed, the GSEs make money. To make this business profitable, the GSEs have to make sure that they can borrow cheaply, and in the remainder of this chapter we discuss how they achieve this goal.

The amount of money that the GSEs borrow is truly astronomical, so they cannot rely on loans from commercial banks. Instead, they issue their own debt securities and sell them to capital market investors. As you can see in Figure 10–1, the amount of GSE debt outstanding currently exceeds the amount of U.S. government obligations (Treasury securities) by almost $1,800 billion. GSE debt securities in and of themselves are a huge segment of the fixed-income market that is usually referred to as the *agencies* market. What exactly are the debt securities just mentioned?

First, the GSEs issue short-term, commercial-paper-type debt called *agency discount notes*. These notes are the direct equivalent of commercial paper issued by other corporations: non-interest-bearing notes that are sold to investors at a discount. The GSEs issue these notes every day through the intermediation of their Wall Street sell-side partners. The sell-side banks talk to their clients who might be interested in purchasing these discount notes (and there is no shortage of such clients—anyone who needs to invest cash for a short period would be interested) and communicate the investor interest to the GSEs. The GSEs then issue new discount notes, which the banks distribute to their clients the same day.

A similar program exists for the longer-term coupon-bearing securities called *agency notes*. These are created by GSEs on a daily basis and pushed through to investors by syndicates of Wall Street banks, which buy these securities from GSEs and quickly (usually during the same day) distribute them to their client base. These types of securities are held by investors to maturity and never trade in the secondary market. This syndication business is quite lucrative for the Wall Street banks (they keep an underwriting fee of a few basis points), and the GSEs raise roughly half of their funds this way.

However, all the parties involved in this process (the GSEs, the investors, and the Wall Street banks) are interested in having a liquid secondary market for agency securities, and to this end the GSEs have instituted issuance programs that largely resemble the way the U.S. Treasury market operates. The securities issued under these programs are called *benchmark securities* by Fannie Mae and *reference securities* by Freddie Mac; these are large issues that are brought to market in periodic auctions. As we can see in Figure 10–8, which shows the Fannie Mae issuance calendar, Fannie Mae issues 3-, 6-, and 12-month benchmark bills and 2-, 3-, 5-, and 10-year[3] benchmark notes, with a minimum size of $3 billion for the notes and $1 billion for the bills (in practice, the size of these issues is often much higher, in the neighborhood of $10 billion for the notes).

Each such benchmark security is announced on the announcement date (when the size of the upcoming issue becomes known), then it is actually sold to the Wall Street dealers through an auction on the *pricing date* (when the coupon on the new issue is determined), and these transactions settle on the *settlement date*. This is perfectly analogous to the issuance process that is in place for the Treasury market (see Chapter 5), except that the agencies are not obligated to issue all maturities every month; they announce what they want to do on the announcement date, and they often skip issues or reopen existing ones, their goal being to concentrate liquidity in a few very large issues. Unlike the U.S. Treasury, GSEs also have an active program of issuing callable benchmark notes, and they also issue debt denominated in other currencies (such as Fannie Mae's global benchmark notes).

The result of these issuance programs is a curve similar to the Treasury curve that we discussed in Chapter 5 that can be called the agency curve: a set of several hundred large securities maturing every few months that these programs have generated over the years. They have a liquid secondary market, facilitated by interdealer brokers such as Garban/ICAP and Cantor Fitzgerald, where current (most recently issued) benchmarks play the role of Treasury on-the-runs. The bid-offer spreads in this market are often ½ tick or less, rivaling those in the Treasury market.

---

3. There used to be a 30-year issuance program at both GSEs, but they have not issued 30-year securities since the early 2000s.

FIGURE 10-8

Fannie Mae benchmark securities issuance calendar (reproduced with permission from FNMA), www.fanniemae.com/markets/debt/pdf/debt_calendar_2005.pdf.

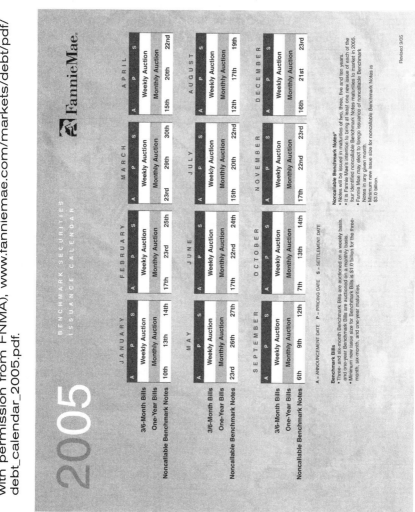

This secondary agency market is closely related to the other major interest-rate markets—not just the Treasury market, but also the interest-rate swaps market. Indeed, if we compare a 10-year agency note with a 10-year Treasury, we find that the products are essentially the same (both promise the investors a set of fixed coupon payments and the principal repayment on the maturity date), the only real difference being that the Treasury is somewhat more likely to keep this promise than a GSE is, so the Treasury note should be somewhat more expensive. Alternatively, we can say that investors demand a somewhat higher rate of interest on their agency investments compared to Treasuries—a fact that is illustrated by Figure 10–9, which provides a comparison of rate curves between the Treasury, agency and swaps markets. We see that the yield spreads between agencies and Treasuries are in reality quite small (typically 20 to 50 basis points) and in fact are smaller than the swap spreads, so the agency curve

FIGURE 10–9

Comparison of the constant-maturity yields for the Fannie Mae agency curve with Treasury yields and swap rates. The spreads between agency and Treasury yields (lower right) are actually smaller than the swap spreads, indicating that the market considers these securities safer than swaps. (Source: www.eFannieMae.com for the Fannie Mae rates; Federal Reserve interest-rate statistics from www.federalreserve.gov/Releases/H15.)

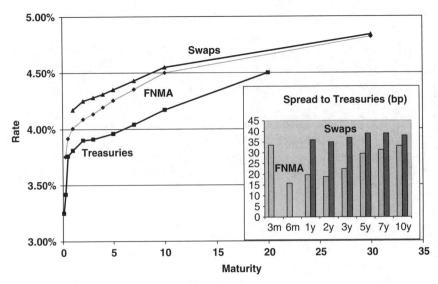

lies between the Treasury curve and the swaps curve. This means that the market thinks the GSEs are less likely to default than the major Wall Street banks that are the counterparties on most interest-rate swaps.

The concept of spread (to either Treasuries or swaps) is central to the agencies market. Agencies are even called *spread products*, which means that they usually trade relative to Treasuries (as duration-neutral bond swaps, so that the PnL of such a trade is a function only of the yield spread of the agency relative to the Treasury bond) or to swaps (as asset swaps), and the quotes for agencies on most interdealer broker platforms are in terms of such spreads.

Such spread trading creates tight integration between the agency, Treasury, and swaps markets. In fact, the agency trading desks in most investment banks are parts of the same rates business as Treasuries and swaps. Fannie Mae and Freddie Mac securities are not the only products that are traded by the agency desks (they also trade securities issued by the smaller GSEs, such as Sallie Mae, and increasingly products issued by the so-called *supra-sovereign* entities such as the World Bank), but these two issuers heavily dominate all aspects of the agency trading business. Moreover, both Fannie Mae and (especially) Freddie Mac are avid consumers of interest-rate derivatives, which they use to hedge the interest-rate risk of their mortgage portfolios (and, of course, they use Treasuries for that purpose also), so they do a lot of business with the mortgage-trading desk.

As a result, Fannie Mae and Freddie Mac are by far the most important customers of any Wall Street fixed-income trading division, and some people have long wondered whether this situation, where these two companies can get Wall Street to do pretty much anything for them, is either desirable or sustainable. While the major GSEs are widely credited with making mortgage markets in the United States the envy of the world and bringing down mortgage rates (by 25 to 50 bp by some estimates), they have a growing group of critics who have pointed out several uncomfortable features of the two GSEs' business model, which has created the so-called *GSE controversy.*

The critics argue that the agencies enjoy an unfair advantage over their competitors in the mortgage finance area: because the agency spreads are so low, the agencies can borrow at significantly lower rates than any of their competitors, and as a result they are much more profitable. And the agency spreads are low, critics argue, because the market thinks that the GSEs have implicit government backing in the sense that should something happen to either Fannie or Freddie, the federal government would step in and bail the agency out one way or another. While both the GSEs and the federal government keep telling anyone who will listen that such backing does not in fact exist, the market seems to believe that it does and keeps the spreads low. The investors are not irrational—despite their public denials, it is hard to see how the politicians would be able to avoid coming to the rescue if one of these two giants (which between the two of them financed three-quarters(!) of all residential mortgages in the United States in the last three years) were to get into trouble.

Thus, because of the perception that Fannie and Freddie are too big to fail, the market keeps giving them more and more easy money and making them bigger still, and some U.S. lawmakers have become seriously uncomfortable with this situation, especially in the wake of accounting scandals at both companies in the last few years. As a result of this growing criticism, it is likely that something in the legal status and market positioning of the GSEs will change in the coming years. Although nobody knows what will happen, the participants of both mortgage and agency markets are awaiting these developments rather anxiously.

TECHNOLOGY IN THE MORTGAGE MARKET

To conclude this chapter, let us review the factors that make mortgage and, to a lesser extent, agency markets some of the more interesting places to be for quantitative and technology professionals. A first, and rather obvious, factor is the unparalleled complexity of modeling mortgage-related products. Before a bank can have a mortgage-trading business, the tools for valuation and risk management of mortgage portfolios have to be in place, and in fact a lot of other things also need to happen on the technology side—for example, the reference data systems suddenly have to support hundreds of thousands of records representing mortgage pools and related MBSs and CMOs. This means that the proportion of trading revenues going into modeling efforts and technology in general is much higher for a mortgage-trading business than for other markets.

For the banks, this creates a significant barrier to entry into this market (which helps to explain why some major banks do not have a mortgage desk). For modelers and technologists, however, this means that their contribution to the business is valued much more highly than elsewhere. Furthermore, unlike most other areas of financial analytics, the mortgage models themselves are actively evolving—the existing OAS-based approaches have major issues, especially in the risk management area, and this creates unique opportunities for quantitative people.

In recent years, mortgage and agency markets have developed unique needs in the area of electronic trading. Both Freddie Mac and Fannie Mae are working hard to automate their issuance process (both the auction-based benchmark programs and the day-to-day issuance) and have made impressive advances in this regard, which the Wall Street banks are just beginning to take advantage of, so there is an increased demand there for electronic trading technology experts. Last but not least, the complex interplay between the mortgage market and other interest-rate markets, together with the sheer size of the mortgage market, puts a premium on any models that can provide quantitative insights into how mortgage developments affect other markets, and vice versa. This makes market research jobs in the mortgage-related areas more interesting than most.

Overall, there are very few other areas of Wall Street research and technology that are more dynamic than this one. The only area that is widely considered even hotter is credit derivatives, one of the subjects of our next chapter.

CHAPTER 11

Credit Markets

The fixed-income markets that we have discussed up to this point in the book (those for government bonds, interest-rate swaps and LIBOR-based derivatives, and mortgage-backed securities) have one important thing in common: they are all driven by macroeconomic factors and rise and fall with the economy as a whole. Equity markets, on the other hand, are about individual companies—the price of each stock is much more sensitive to what happens to that particular company than to things like the unemployment rate. The market for corporate debt, which we discuss in this chapter, straddles this divide: corporate bonds are very much like all other bonds as far as their cash flow structure is concerned, but they are very much like equities in that their price is very sensitive to the fortunes of the issuer corporation, and particularly to its *credit* standing—its perceived ability to pay its debt.

From the perspective of a Wall Street dealer bank that trades all kinds of financial products, corporate bonds are usually treated as something different from both equities and the rest of the fixed-income universe. Trading of corporate debt and related derivatives is usually organized as a separate business unit within the fixed-income division that is called the *credit* business. As the name implies, what the credit business trades is in fact the credit quality of the corporate bond issuers, whereas the rest of the fixed-income universe primarily trades *interest rates* and is therefore organized under the umbrella of the *rates* business. Rates and credit are the two main components of fixed-income trading, although mortgages are sometimes treated as a third area, equal in stature to these two. In this chapter we explore how a credit business operates, examine the mechanics of credit trading, and introduce the main concepts and factors that are in play in this interesting area.

Unlike the mortgage markets that we discussed in the previous chapter, credit markets are (almost) as old as the hills. Corporations issued debt in the form of bonds and notes as early as the seventeenth century. Ever since then, corporations have had to compete for investors' funds with the other main category of debt issuers: governments at various levels, from small municipalities to the emerging national governments.

As I mentioned before, in the early days of capital markets, the debt of governments was just as risky as, if not more risky than, that of private corporations—even national governments frequently defaulted on their debt, leaving investors in the dust. After the formation of strong nation-states in most of Europe in the eighteenth and nineteenth centuries, the debt markets began their current split into rates and credit. Investors started to perceive the debt obligations of national governments as much safer investments than the obligations of corporations and the smaller governments of individual cities and regions. This was (and is) justified by the fact that the last national government default in England was in 1672, the U.S. government has never defaulted on its debt, and even France, Spain, and Germany have done this only a few times in the last three centuries.

On the other hand, individual corporations have defaulted on their debt right and left (and so have many city governments). Investors of course knew this and did not want to get burned, so corporations had to do something to make their offerings more attractive than the debt of the national governments, and they achieved this by offering higher coupon rates. For example, in the mid-nineteenth century, the rates on the debt of the British government were close to 2 percent, while some railroad companies offered bonds with a 15 percent coupon to get the attention of investors; the extra 13 percent of income from a railroad bond would now be called its *government spread* (this term did not, however, come into use until the early twentieth century) and represented compensation for the very real risk that the railroad company would cease to exist in the near future.

Using this tactic, corporations were able to successfully compete with governments for investors' funds, and they continue to do so to the present day. As you can see in the flow-of-funds chart that we used in the previous chapter (Figure 10–1), the current amount of corporate debt outstanding is huge and easily exceeds government debt. The municipal debt also shown in this chart is in many ways similar to corporate debt; if we add the two categories together they would rival even the runaway size of the mortgage market.

ISSUANCE OF CORPORATE DEBT

Let us first review the process by which corporate bonds come into being: the *primary market* for corporate debt. Unlike U.S. Treasury and agency securities, corporate bonds are *nonexempt securities*, which means that the issuer has to prepare a prospectus for each issue, register it with the SEC, distribute it to investors, and so on (see Chapter 6 for more details). As with equities, the investment banks step in and help issuers arrange all this paperwork.[1] After the SEC gives the go-ahead for the new issue, the investment banks distribute the issue to their clients and earn a fee for doing so.

This is all very similar to what happens with equities issuance, but there are several important differences that are worth mentioning. First, corporations turn to borrowing a lot more frequently than they use equity financing, and, again unlike equities, every time they borrow, they issue a new security with its own identity (e.g., CUSIP number) and cash flow structure (maturity date and coupon). Because of this, many corporations have dozens (some have hundreds) of outstanding corporate bonds, while they have only one stock symbol. Second, for a variety of reasons, these bonds are often issued not by the corporation as a whole, but by its individual business units. For example, all automakers, such as General Motors, have a subsidiary that makes car loans, and bonds issued by such a subsidiary are usually assumed to have much higher credit quality than those issued by the manufacturing arm of the automaker. In general, the securities issued by different subsidiaries of the same parent company are often treated very differently.

To summarize these first two differences between the equity and corporate bond universes, imagine a single equity ticker like GM. For purposes of debt issuance, this ticker is split into several legal subentities that can issue bonds, and then each of those subentities issues dozens of different securities. Where we have one security on the equity side, we will end up having a large (and growing) set of debt instruments linked to the same corporate name.

---

1. Municipal and state governments issue their debt obligations (known as municipal bonds, or simply *munis*) in essentially the same way that corporations do. Almost everything I say in this chapter about corporate bonds applies to munis as well. Their main difference from corporate securities is that in the United States, the interest on municipal securities is tax-deductible on the federal level, which allows them to pay lower coupons.

This multiplicity is further compounded by the large variety of different cash flow structures that corporate debt instruments can have. Most corporate bonds are *bullet bonds*, which pay a fixed coupon and return the principal at a fixed maturity date, but there are many other popular structures. *Callable bonds* can be called by the issuer at a predefined call price (usually at par) after some period of time (*puttable bonds* that can be returned to the issuer by the investor also exist, but are less common). Corporations often issue *floating-rate notes* (FRN), where coupon payments are linked to some interest-rate index such as LIBOR or the prime rate (for example, a *prime floater* might pay 150 bp over the prime rate). There are also *structured notes* that have customized schedules for interest and principal payments, which can be driven by other market-specific events (taken to an extreme, this can produce an *inverse floater* that pays 7 percent minus three-month LIBOR on a principal that is linked to the three-year swap rate, and many real structures are even more convoluted than that). Finally, there are hybrid products called *convertible bonds*, which are issued as debt instruments but can be converted into an equity position if the price of the company's stock does well and exceeds a certain threshold. Interestingly, convertible bonds are often traded by the equity divisions of Wall Street banks rather than by their fixed-income credit businesses because of this equity linkage (as are some similar *equity-linked* types of debt products).

Designing and implementing these structures is a lucrative business for investment banks, and offers corporations a way around restrictions on the use of OTC derivatives, since most of these structured notes are in fact complex derivatives products disguised as securities. Much of the progress in financial analytics in the early 1990s was driven by the explosive growth of the structured products business, and this business remains an important area of financial innovation (although some of the bloom has been taken off by the brutal collapse of this market in 1994). The rationale for this astounding variety of product structures is twofold: to make the new issues more attractive to investors and easier to pay off for the issuer. Structured or not, each new issue is still simply a way for the issuing corporation to borrow money (and a way for the investment banks that sell it to investors to earn a fee).

Inside investment banks, each new debt issue is called a *deal*, and the act of actually distributing the new security to investors is called *pricing a deal* (because that is when either the price or the coupon rate of the new issue is determined). Bringing each such deal to market requires coordinated effort by the investment banking division (which convinces the clients to do the deal), *product structurers* from the credit business (who design the cash flow structure of the new security), and the corporate bond trading desk (which actually distributes the new security to investors and later makes a secondary market in it when appropriate).

Most new corporate bond issues these days are accompanied by an interest-rate derivatives transaction that allows the issuer to change the risk profile of the new security. For example, an issuer that sells a fixed-coupon bond to investors can simultaneously enter into an interest-rate swap in which it pays a floating rate and receives a fixed rate; the fixed swap payments cancel out the bond coupons, which effectively converts the issuer's obligations from fixed-rate to floating-rate (and thus reduces the issuer's interest-rate exposure). These transactions are collectively known as *swapping out* the new issue, and they are typically done with the interest-rate derivatives desk of the same investment bank that sells the new securities, so the rates business also gets a piece of the action.

Bringing new deals to market is an essential, bread-and-butter activity for the investment banks, and underwriting debt transactions is more like bread than butter—the underwriting fees are much lower than for equity underwriting (1 to 2 percent, as opposed to 7 percent for equities, although the fees for structured products can be substantially higher), but the debt deals are much more numerous.

CREDIT RISK

Let us now switch to the point of view of an investor in corporate debt obligations and consider the factors affecting the investment performance of corporate bonds. In this book, we leave the structured products aside (they are well covered elsewhere, as we discuss in our Recommended Reading section) and focus on the mainstays of corporate debt: the bullet bonds. On the face of it, a corporate bullet bond looks exactly the same as, say, a Treasury bond or any other kind of bond; it is a set of future cash flows whose present value should be equal to today's price of the bond. As interest rates rise, the price (or present value) should fall, and vice versa, so the interest-rate risk associated with holding a position in a corporate bond is very similar to that of holding any other bond with similar cash flow properties (coupon and maturity). In fact, all the traditional interest-rate measures that we discussed for Treasuries (yield, various types of duration, and convexity) work exactly the same way for corporate bonds as for Treasuries (although the corporate bond market uses slightly different conventions for calculating yields and related quantities).

While it is comforting to know that corporate bonds carry interest-rate risk in exactly the same way as Treasuries do, there is a profound difference between corporates and pure "rates" products such as Treasuries. Interest rates are not the only (and often even not the main) factor that determines the value of corporate debt obligations; this value also obviously depends on the good fortunes of the issuing company. If the financial condition of the company takes a turn for the worse, it may become unable to pay off its bonds, and these bonds may become worthless. This is a risk that all corporate bond investors take, and there is an established way of thinking about and quantifying this risk. And, of course, there is a name for it: *credit risk*.

A natural measure of credit risk would be the *probability of default* by an issuer. Unfortunately, this quantity is not directly measurable; companies do not issue press releases saying, "We have a 10 percent probability of default over the next year." Let us, however, assume for a moment that we know that there is a 10 percent chance that a particular company will default over the next year. How would we price that company's debt obligations?

Consider the simplest form of corporate debt, a discount bill that promises to pay $100 in one year. How much should we pay for that bill today if an identical Treasury bill sells for, say, $97 (which corresponds to a discount rate of 3 percent)? Clearly a corporate bill should cost less than that, and to determine how much less, let us imagine that we buy the corporate bill and sell an otherwise identical Treasury bill. Because the Treasury is more expensive, we will end up with a positive sum of money, which we will call X.

At the end of the year, two outcomes are possible: (1) the company does not default and pays us $100, which we use to pay off the Treasury bill, so we have no net cash flow; (2) the company does default and does not pay anything, so we have to make a $100 payment to cover our short position in the maturing Treasury bill. The money we got on our transaction, X, should be equal to the discounted present value of the cash flows that we get under these two scenarios. In the first, we do not have to pay anything, and in the second, we pay $100, so X is $100 times the probability of default (discounted back at 3 percent, but let's ignore that for a moment) and is therefore simply equal to that default probability. So if the probability of default per year (*default intensity* is the term for that) is 10 percent, the corporate bill price should be $10 less than the Treasury price. Thus, the discount rate on the corporate should be 10 percent greater than the Treasury rate—13 percent versus 3 percent in our example. We see that the yield *spread* between the corporate and the Treasury is, to a good approximation, simply equal to the yearly default intensity.[2]

In practice, this argument is usually inverted; we do not know the default probability, but the *spread* between a given corporate bond and a comparable Treasury can be determined much more directly by observing the prices at which the bond trades (although this, as we will explain, is easier said than done). So if we see our corporate bill move up in price to yield 12 percent, we can conclude that the *implied* default intensity for our company went down to 9 percent per year. Many large companies have a lot of different bonds outstanding covering a large range of maturities (see Figure 11–1), so that instead of a single default intensity number, one can get a whole *term structure* of implied default probabilities by analyzing the spreads on those bonds (although this analysis is usually somewhat more rigorous than our simple example).

Once the default probabilities are known over a wide range of dates, we can value almost any financial instrument that is exposed to this company's credit risk. As we illustrate in Figure 11–1, how to calculate the spreads to Treasuries is often not entirely obvious, given that the maturities of corporate bonds and of the on-the-run Treasuries are all different. This is one of many reasons why the most common way of establishing corporate spreads has become spreading against the swaps curve instead of the Treasury curve. These are called *LIBOR spreads* (as opposed to Treasury, or, more generally, *government spreads*). The difference between the two spread measures is that the LIBOR spreads are smaller by (roughly) the size of the *swap spread* (see Chapter 8) for the appropriate range of maturities. By the way, we can now say that the swap spreads themselves reflect the credit risk of entering into transactions with a typical swaps dealer bank, and that their historical range of 10 to 100 bp corresponds to an implied default intensity of 0.1 to 1 percent a year for those banks.

Note that we have related the spreads to the default probabilities by assuming that, after the risk of default is taken into account, the effective rate of return on corporates should be the same as that on risk-free Treasuries (and on anything else, for that matter). This "risk-neutral" assumption is

---

2. This is really just an order-of-magnitude estimate (the experts on credit analytics will probably laugh at me for this), but it is intuitive and fundamentally correct, so do not be afraid to think of corporate spreads in this simple way.

FIGURE 11–1

Comparison of a corporate curve with the Treasury curve (closing curves on December 30, 2005). A corporate curve is a yield-versus-maturity plot for a representative set of bonds issued by the same corporation. In this example, we use General Electric Capital (a lending subsidiary of General Electric); it has over a hundred outstanding bonds, so only a few of them are displayed here. The corporate yields are always higher than Treasury yields, and the distance between the two curves is the Treasury spread, as discussed in the text. Corporate bond data from NASD BondInfo (www.bondinfo.com), used with permission; Treasury data from U.S. Treasury Interest Rate Statistics. NASD TRACE data. © 2006 National Association of Securities Dealers, Inc. (NASD). Reprinted with permission from NASD.

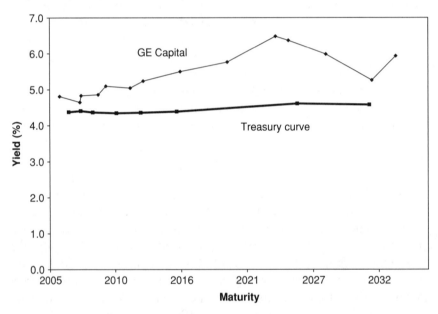

required to make the valuation procedures consistent, but it tends to over-estimate the default probabilities when compared with historically observed rates of default. In the real world, an investor looking at our example would not pay $87 for a security with a 10 percent chance of default if he could buy an absolutely safe Treasury with the same expected return. Perhaps he would pay $80 for taking this risk (and the $7 difference, as we recall from Chapter 4, is called the *risk premium*). If we were to observe our corporate bill trading at this 20 percent yield level (i.e., at a Treasury spread of

17 percent), we would conclude that the default probability is about 17 percent a year, which is significantly higher than what the investor thought
it was. Put another way, in practice, the extra return that investors get on
corporate debt is only partially offset by the risk of default. We will, over
time, earn more by investing in corporates than in Treasuries, and this is
what attracts people to those products in the first place.

Spreads are quantitative measures of credit risk, but often they are not
easy to obtain because of the relative opaqueness of the secondary market
for corporate bonds, so in many situations people turn to the more traditional
qualitative measures of credit quality: the *credit ratings*. A credit rating is
a character code like AA that is assigned to each company by one or more
rating agencies and is meant to indicate how likely the company is to meet
its debt service obligations. The ratings are based not on secondary-market
data (like spreads), but rather on the rating agency's analysis of the company's assets, liabilities, business prospects, and current debt structure.

A company that wishes to be rated as an issuer of debt applies to the
rating agencies to obtain an *issuer rating*; it pays the rating agency for
the service, and the agency then does its thing and produces a rating that
investors can use to decide whether they want to buy the company's debt.
For large bond issues, the company can also ask the rating agencies to rate
a specific issue; this is called an *issue rating*. Both types of ratings are periodically reviewed by the rating agencies, and these reviews can result in
either a *ratings downgrade* (when the agency decides that the financials of
the company have worsened to the point that it has to move the company
to a different notch on its scale), or an *upgrade* when the opposite happens.

We show the ratings scales of the five U.S. ratings agencies recognized by the SEC (these are called *nationally recognized statistical rating
organizations*, or *NRSROs*) in Figure 11–2. Ratings above the thick line
are called *investment-grade* ratings, whereas those below are called non-
investment-grade or, more colloquially, *junk* ratings. Many institutional
investors, such as banks, pension funds, and insurance companies, are prohibited from investing in junk-rated debt obligations (*junk bonds* are also
politely called *high-yield bonds*) because of their extreme riskiness, so a
downgrade to junk status is a catastrophic event for a company: investors
who were holding its debt are forced to sell their positions, which drives
the company that much farther into the hole.

Ratings are not really meant to correspond to any numerical measure like default probability, and there is little historical correlation between
ratings and observed default probabilities. Rather, ratings are a ranking

FIGURE 11-2

Credit ratings by major U.S. rating agencies.

Credit quality		S&P	Moody's	Fitch	A.M. Best	Dominion
Investment grade						
	Highest	AAA	Aaa	AAA	aaa	AAA
	Very high	AA	Aa	AA	aa	AA
	High	A	A	A	a	A
	Medium	BBB	Baa	BBB	bbb	BBB
Non-investment grade						
	Questionable	BB	Ba	BB	bb	BB
	Speculative	B	B	B	b	B
	Highly speculative	CCC	Caa	CCC	ccc	CCC
	Danger of default	CC	Ca	CC	cc	CC
	Imminent default	C+, C, C-	C	C+, C, C-	c	C
	In default	D	No rating	D	d	D

tool that allows you to compare different companies' creditworthiness. You can be reasonably certain that a company that is rated AA is better able to pay its debt than a company that is rated BB (even if it is the same company at a different time in its life), but you cannot say that a rating of AA corresponds to a default intensity of 0.5 percent per year.

Despite their qualitative nature, ratings are an extremely important factor in credit markets, especially on the buy side, where there is a great body of regulations and tradition that revolves around credit ratings. In practice, every issuer has to have a rating or nobody will buy its bonds, so obtaining a rating is not really a matter of choice. The analysts working for the rating agencies effectively do the same thing that stock analysts do on the equities side (Chapter 17): they examine all the available information about the companies they follow and let the investment community know what they think.

Compared with their counterparts in the sell-side banks (which, of course, also employ credit analysts), the analysts inside the ratings agencies seem to be in a better position to provide investors with objective advice, since they are being paid explicitly for their research and not for how much investment banking or trading business they bring in. However, many people think that the ratings agencies create conflicts of interest of their own, since they are ultimately paid by the companies that are seeking the ratings, and of course every company wants its ratings to be good. Another criticism of ratings agencies that has been raised in recent years is that the three main agencies (Standard & Poor's, Moody's, and Fitch) have become too entrenched in this lucrative business; this criticism has been largely answered by the SEC's giving the NRSRO designation to two more rating agencies (A.M. Best and Dominion) in 2003.

There are other similarities between the investment properties of corporate bonds and those of equities beyond the parallelism between credit and equity research. The degree of correlation between the price performance of similarly structured bonds of different issuers is much lower than that for pure interest-rate products, but is typical of what is seen in the equity markets. If one issuer is doing well and another is doing badly, the prices of their bonds will move in opposite directions, just as the prices of their stocks would, despite the common interest-rate component that affects all bonds. People who invest in or trade corporate bonds do the same thing as equity investors: they try to buy the debt of companies that are likely to do well and try to sell the debt of those that are likely to disappoint, which is essentially stock picking, but using bonds instead of stocks.

In fact, the price of a company's stock is a good predictor of the value of its debt. Here the key insight was introduced by Robert Merton, who pointed out in 1976 that in a certain sense, equity is a call option on the assets of the company. Since equity holders have a claim on the assets only after all debt has been paid, Merton argued that the total value of a company's debt should be viewed as the strike price for this option: if the value of the company's assets drops below its outstanding debt, the equity holders will get nothing when the debt comes due and the company is unable to cover it and goes bankrupt. However, if the debt does not have to be repaid for some time, then equity has some time value, as there is a chance that the value of a company's assets will increase enough to cover the debt, just as an out-of-the-money call option on any asset has time value.

The model that Merton introduced to describe the relationship between debt and equity pricing is a version of the Black-Scholes-Merton formula that treats the value of the company's assets as the underlying random variable, the amount of outstanding debt as the strike price, and the observed price of the company's stock as the call option value. Given the strike price and the option price, the model inverts the option price formula and produces the current value of the company's assets and its volatility. From there, we can construct the distribution function for the value of the assets and calculate the probability that this value will go below the strike price (the total outstanding debt) and thus cause the company to default on its debt, which is exactly the default probability that we were discussing earlier. In practice, the Merton model is usually generalized to cover the more realistic case in which not all debt comes due at the same time, but his central idea that equity prices can be used as important inputs into credit valuation models is widely used in credit market practice.

THE SECONDARY MARKET FOR CORPORATE BONDS

Let us now briefly comment on the organization of the secondary market for corporate bonds. Here we need to keep in mind that most corporate bonds never trade in the secondary market; they are bought by investors at the time of issuance and held to maturity. Even for large companies, there are typically just a couple of issues that trade more or less regularly, so that despite the huge amount of corporate debt outstanding overall, each individual debt issue is much less liquid than, say, the stock of the same company.

The corporate bond market is a dealer market in which Wall Street sell-side firms act as market makers for their institutional investor clients. Even for large institutional clients, the bid-offer spreads on any but the most liquid corporate bonds are measured in percentage points, not in ticks, so that getting in and out of corporate bond positions is very expensive. This is not a good market for day traders, and it is geared overwhelmingly toward long-term institutional investors. Despite the low liquidity, trading corporate bonds is a profitable business for the sell-side banks, and corporate bond trading desks (often called *credit desks*) are usually staffed by dozens of traders who specialize in individual industry sectors. The credit traders typically prefer to hedge away the interest-rate risk inherent in corporate bonds and keep only the equitylike credit component, and they achieve that by offloading their interest-rate risk in the Treasury and swaps markets.

In the interdealer market (there are a few interdealer brokers that make a living in the corporate bond market, as well as several electronic marketplaces that trade corporates, although their volumes are relatively low), corporates are typically quoted in terms of spreads to Treasuries, and most interdealer trades are usually done as spread trades (buying or selling a corporate together with selling or buying a duration-weighted amount of a similar-maturity on-the-run Treasury). Increasingly, market participants hedge their corporate bond positions by doing a similar thing in the interest-rate swaps space, which is known as an *asset swap*. In an asset swap, the holder of the bond swaps its cash flows for a stream of floating payments of, say, three-month LIBOR plus X basis points, where the asset swap spread X is roughly the yield on the bond less a comparable-maturity LIBOR swap rate. The actual calculation of the asset swap spreads takes into account both the observed shape of the swaps curve and whatever special cash flow features the bond may have, but to a good approximation we can think of an asset swap position as a combination of the bond and an interest-rate swap, where the fixed swap payments cancel out the bond coupons and the spread over LIBOR we receive in return is our compensation for accepting the credit risk of the bond.

Just as in a standard spread trade, where one bond is swapped for another, the PnL of an asset swap position is proportional to the change in the spread, so that the asset swap structure effectively eliminates the interest-rate risk of the bond and allows the bond owner to participate in any up or down credit-related price movements. As the liquidity in the interest-rate swaps market has grown exponentially, more and more corporate bond positions are being hedged this way. However, many institutional investors simply buy (or sell) corporate bonds *outright*, without any hedging.

The corporate bond market traditionally was very nontransparent in the sense that it was very difficult for anyone but the dealers to know the prices or spreads at which these bonds actually trade, as the overwhelming majority of corporate bond trades are done directly between dealers and customers and never show up on any interdealer screens. This situation has changed dramatically for the better in the last few years, since the NASD introduced mandatory trade reporting requirements for its member dealers in 2002. The dealers are now required to report every corporate bond trade they do to the NASD's Trade Reporting and Compliance Engine, which is known by its acronym *TRACE*, within 15 minutes of the actual trade time. The TRACE system provides a Web interface where anyone can see a summary of the previous day's trading (Figure 11–3), and a history of trades in any given bond (Figure 11–4). In addition to the publicly disseminated data shown in these two figures, TRACE also provides more detailed views of these data, as well as a real-time feed, to fee-paying clients. As we see in these two figures, the total traded volume in the corporate bond market is significant (about 5 percent of the Treasury market volume), but it is spread over such a huge number of bonds that even the most liquid issues trade at best once every few minutes, as opposed to every few seconds for on-the-run Treasuries and milliseconds for the more liquid stocks.

FIGURE 11-3

End-of-day report on the corporate bond market from NASD TRACE (apps.nasd.com/regulatory%5Fsystems/ traceaggregates/). © 2006 National Association of Securities Dealers, Inc. (NASD). Reprinted with permission from NASD.

Last Updated: 10/20/2005

NASD TRACE Corporate Bond Data

Market Breadth

	All Issues	Investment Grade	High Yield	Convertibles
Total Issues Traded	5,119	3,091	1,746	282
Advances	2,353	1,387	845	121
Declines	2,193	1,378	685	130
Unchanged	154	62	85	7
52 Week High	38	18	14	6
52 Week Low	311	245	62	4
Dollar Volume *	17,715	8,665	6,903	2,146

About This Information:
End of Day data. Activity as reported to NASD TRACE (Trade Reporting and Compliance Engine). The Market breadth information represents activity in all TRACE eligible publicly traded securities. The most active information represent the most active fixed-coupon bonds (ranked by par value traded). Inclusion in Investment Grade or High Yield tables based on TRACE dissemination criteria. "C" indicates yield is unavailable because of issue's call criteria.

* Par value in millions.

Most Active Investment Grade Bonds

Issuer Name	Symbol	Coupon	Maturity	Rating Moody's/S&P	High	Low	Last	Change	Yield %
FORD MOTOR CREDIT	F.GAA	7.000%	Oct 2013	Baa3/BB+	96.250	92.912	94.688	−1.125	7.913
CREDIT SUISSE FIRST BOSTON (USA)	CSR.OL	5.125%	Aug 2015	Aa3/A+	100.364	98.009	98.750	0.405	5.289
FORD MOTOR CREDIT	F.IT	7.250%	Oct 2011	Baa3/BB+	97.000	93.254	95.000	−1.188	8.325
BHP FINANCE (USA)	BHP.GH	4.800%	Apr 2013	A1/A+	98.752	98.617	98.666	0.080	5.016
CITIGROUP	C.OH	5.000%	Mar 2007	Aa1/AA-	100.965	100.000	100.671	0.671	4.483
COX COMM	COX.HN	5.450%	Dec 2014	Baa3/BBB-	98.131	97.813	97.813	0.001	5.760
NEXTEL COMM	NXTL.GU	6.875%	Oct 2013	--/A-	106.250	105.000	105.000	−1.500	5.845
VERIZON GLOBAL FUNDING	VZ.MS	7.250%	Dec 2010	A2/A+	109.823	108.500	109.115	−0.025	5.191
MARSH & MCLENNAN	MMC.GM	5.750%	Sep 2015	Baa2/BBB	99.965	98.228	98.492	0.190	5.953
BELLSOUTH	BLS.HW	6.000%	Nov 2034	A2/--	100.625	97.068	100.000	−0.500	6.000

Most Active High Yield Bonds

Issuer Name	Symbol	Coupon	Maturity	Rating Moody's/S&P	High	Low	Last	Change	Yield %
GENERAL MOTORS ACCEPTANCE	GMA.IMW	6.750%	Dec 2014	Ba1/BB	97.752	94.180	96.781	−0.281	7.238
GENERAL MOTORS	GMA.HF	8.000%	Nov 2031	Ba1/BB	105.933	98.000	103.813	3.813	7.660

FIGURE 11–3

(*Continued*)

				Rating Moody's/S&P	High	Low	Last	Change	Yield
ACCEPTANCE FORD MOTOR	F.GY	7.450%	Jul 2031	Ba1/BB+	76.400	71.900	74.938	−0.063	10.223
GENERAL MOTORS ACCEPTANCE	GMA.HE	6.875%	Sep 2011	Ba1/BB	101.094	96.000	96.150	−0.787	7.698
GENERAL MOTORS	GM.HB	8.375%	Jul 2033	Ba2/BB-	76.375	71.500	73.750	−0.750	11.543
TXU CORP	TXU.KI	4.800%	Nov 2009	Ba1/BB+	95.625	94.999	94.999	−0.154	6.213
DANA	DCN.GC	6.500%	Mar 2009	Ba2/BB+	92.000	86.938	87.500	2.500	11.060
FORD MOTOR	F.GW	6.625%	Oct 2028	Ba1/BB+	71.625	67.458	69.875	1.975	9.995
REFCO FINANCE HLDS	RFXC.GB	9.000%	Aug 2012	Ca/D	54.000	47.000	49.250	−5.250	N/A
DELPHI AUTOMOTIVE SYSTEMS	DPHIQ.GB	6.500%	May 2009	Ca/D	67.000	64.500	66.250	0.250	N/A

Most Active Convertible Bonds

Issuer Name	Symbol	Coupon	Maturity	Rating Moody's/S&P	High	Low	Last	Change	Yield %
IVAX	IVX.GJ	1.875%	Dec 2024	--/--	133.301	131.671	132.771	−0.217	−3.722
HALLIBURTON	HAL.GO	3.125%	Jul 2023	Baa2/BBB	165.756	160.150	162.745	−2.364	14.752
IVAX	IVX.GI	1.500%	Mar 2024	--/--	114.488	114.071	114.250	1.917	N/A
APRIA HEALTHCARE GP	AHG.GB	3.375%	Sep 2033	--/BB+	96.499	93.081	96.499	0.812	4.700
SCHLUMBERGER	SLB.GF	1.500%	Jun 2023	A1/A+	121.175	116.500	118.500	−2.125	N/A
CYPRESS SEMICONDUCTOR	CY.GD	1.250%	Jun 2008	--/B-	111.930	102.000	109.540	1.167	N/A
MEDTRONIC	MDT.GC	1.250%	Sep 2021	A1/AA-	102.000	99.000	101.827	−0.201	0.101
RED HAT	RHAT.GB	0.500%	Jan 2024	--/B	101.500	100.000	100.248	−1.002	N/A
MIRANT	MIR.GB	2.500%	Jun 2021	--/--	103.000	100.500	100.938	−1.563	N/A
TYCO INTL GP SA	TYC.OH	3.125%	Jan 2023	Baa3/BBB+	125.900	123.625	125.711	−0.914	−6.505

Source: NASD TRACE data. Reference information from Reuters DataScope Data. Credit ratings from Moody's® and Standard & Poor's.

CREDIT DERIVATIVES

One consequence of the relative illiquidity of corporate bonds is that it is generally very difficult to short a corporate bond. It is hard to find a counterparty that is willing to lend a given issue, and the financing terms for such borrowing are often quite onerous. There are, however, many market participants that are interested in doing just that in order to reduce their credit exposure to a given corporate name. For example, think of a bank that has made a large loan to a corporation. It may want to establish a large

FIGURE 11-4

NASD time and sales report for a BellSouth bond (from the second table in Figure 11-3) from the NASD BondInfo system (www.nasdbondinfo.com/asp/bond_search.asp). This bond was the tenth most active on October 20, 2005, but traded only 14 times on that day. NASD TRACE data. © 2006 National Association of Securities Dealers, Inc. (NASD). Reprinted with permission from NASD.

Time & Sales Search Results: Detail Trades   Time & Sales Search

Issue: **BLS.HW   BLS 6.000 11/15/34**

Execution Date	Time	Status	Quantity	Price	Yield	Comm.	Modifier	2nd Mod.	Special	As Of
10/20/2005	14:07:23:00	T	3000000	97.409	6.192999					
10/20/2005	10:58:38:00	T	3000000	97.3437	6.197955					
10/20/2005	10:54:51:00	T	3000000	97.3037	6.201004					
10/20/2005	10:43:35:00	T	3000000	97.068	6.219013					
10/20/2005	10:43:00:00	T	5MM+	97.448	6.190013					
10/20/2005	10:33:58:00	T	3000000	97.3169	6.199998					
10/20/2005	10:25:00:00	T	3000000	97.3794	6.195235					
10/20/2005	10:23:00:00	T	5MM+	97.382	6.195037					
10/20/2005	09:22:46:00	T	5MM+	97.317	6.20					
10/20/2005	09:15:01:00	T	3965000	97.3138	6.200234					
10/20/2005	09:14:40:00	T	5000000	97.1704	6.211181					
10/20/2005	09:11:47:00	T	4000000	97.2513	6.205002					
10/20/2005	09:10:59:00	T	5000000	97.1204	6.215003					
10/19/2005	12:17:54:00	T	2000000	97.3985	6.193759					Y
10/19/2005	12:17:54:00	T	2000000	97.3985	6.193759					R
10/19/2005	12:17:54:00	W	2000000	97.3985	6.193759					
10/19/2005	12:17:54:00	T	2000000	97.3985	6.193759					
10/19/2005	11:43:00:00	T	2000000	97.461	6.189					
10/19/2005	11:19:04:00	T	1500000	97.719	6.169417					
10/19/2005	11:15:16:00	T	1500000	97.719	6.169417					
10/19/2005	11:14:40:00	T	2500000	97.6985	6.17097					
10/19/2005	11:13:35:00	T	4000000	97.6585	6.174003					

short position in the bonds of that corporation, so that if the corporation were to default, its losses on the loan would be offset by gains on the short bond position. Until the mid-1990s, it was very difficult to offload credit risk in the capital markets. But, when there is a need, there is a way: in response to the widespread need for transferring credit risk, a new class of derivatives has sprung up, which have become known as *credit derivatives.*

Rather than trying to give a general definition of what credit derivatives are, let us consider perhaps the most ubiquitous of them: a *credit default swap*, or *CDS*. A CDS is an over-the-counter derivative transaction in which one party (typically a dealer bank) buys or sells *credit protection* to another party (typically a buy-side firm or hedge fund, but dealer-to-dealer CDSs are also very common). Credit protection for a given bond (called the reference asset) means that if its issuer defaults on the bond, the protection seller will either (1) buy the defaulted bond from the protection buyer at par or (2) pay the protection buyer the difference between par and the *recovery value* of the bond. In both cases (the first is called *physical settlement*, and the second *cash settlement*, for obvious reasons), the party that bought credit protection effectively transfers all credit risk of the reference asset to the protection seller.

The protection buyer pays for this protection by making periodic payments to the protection seller, much like any insurance premiums. These "premiums" are calculated as a percentage of the par value of the reference bond and are typically expressed in basis points. The payments continue until the end of the CDS term or until default occurs, at which point the contract ceases to exist. In some CDS contracts, termination is triggered not by the actual default, but by another *credit event*, such as a ratings downgrade. Either way, the protection seller is swapping credit risk for a stream of fixed payments (which is why this structure is called a swap).

The bank in our example that finds itself overexposed to a particular name can now easily swap out this credit risk simply by buying protection through a CDS transaction, and banks have started doing that on a massive scale. However, this ability to transfer credit risk is only part of the reason why these products have become so popular (as of this writing, the total size of the CDS market in terms of notional amount has passed the $10 trillion mark and has been roughly doubling every year since 2000). Credit default swaps capture credit risk in its purest form, with no extraneous interest-rate component. The CDS premiums are similar in spirit to (and are in fact roughly the same size as) the yield spread over Treasuries, which, as we have seen, represents compensation for the possibility of default. However, it is much more convenient to put on a CDS than to hold a position in the corporate bond and an offsetting Treasury position, where we have to finance both legs of the trade (and, most importantly, show them on our balance sheet) to achieve the same result. Most importantly, we do not even have to own the reference bond to buy CDS credit protection for it, which makes it possible for a lot of players (most notably hedge funds) to make credit bets with little or no initial capital commitment.

Finally, a major strength of CDSs is that to a large extent they do not care which specific bond will be used for settlement in the event of a default (they all would be in the same position when a default occurs), so a single CDS structure can provide protection for all bonds by the same issuer that the protection buyer has. In reality, there are some maturity restrictions on the deliverable bonds, and accrued interest would be different for different issues, but overall the ability of a CDS to collapse the whole collection of debts of a corporate name into a single structure is very attractive and has contributed greatly to the growth of this market.

As the CDS market has grown, it has developed standard structures similar to the standardization that we observed in the interest-rate swaps market—there are standard terms (5 years is by far the most popular, with 2- and 10-year CDSs rapidly catching up, but almost any integer-year term can be traded), standard dates (most CDSs start and end on IMM dates, which improves liquidity), and standard provisions for dealing with the details, such as what to do if a corporation ceases to exist in a restructuring or a merger.

There are other interesting types of credit derivatives (*total return swaps*, *credit default options*, and especially *collateralized debt obligations*) that transfer ideas from options and the mortgages market into the credit derivative realm and are also growing very quickly. We cannot discuss these products here in any detail; instead, we just mention that the explosive growth of the credit derivatives market in the last few years has created a steady demand for quantitative people who understand these products and can build and maintain the technology required to price, structure, and risk-manage credit derivatives. This problem is especially acute on the buy side; a typical buy-side firm, especially in the hedge funds space, at present is unable to independently price and risk-manage all those wonderful CDO tranches and other exotic credit derivatives that it happily buys from the sell side (a situation very reminiscent of what was happening with the mortgage versions of these securities in the run-up to 1994).

Even on the sell side, the pricing and risk management methodology commonly used for credit derivatives is in obvious need of improvement. Credit derivatives are among the very few remaining areas of quantitative finance where having a better pricing model still allows you to make more money, and a growing number of quantitative people who a decade ago would have been working on interest-rate derivatives now labor in the credit derivatives area. I am sure that in another decade there will be something else for them to work on, and on this cheerful note we end our journey through today's financial markets and move on to consider their technological underpinnings.

PART 3

Technology Areas

CHAPTER 12

Reference Data

Wall Street technology is a craft, and just like any other craft, it requires a certain craftsmanship from its practitioners. Knowledge of the underlying business issues (which we tried to develop earlier in the book) and general programming and quantitative skills (which I hope you have mastered elsewhere) are very important, but they are not the only parts of that. In their daily work, Wall Street technologists operate in the context of already existing technology areas; they use services provided by some of those areas and provide services to others. The technology layout differs somewhat among firms, but there are certain areas that are present everywhere and that will affect you regardless of what you do. Being able to recognize these areas, knowing how to use their resources for your purposes, and understanding what they can and cannot provide is an extremely important part of the craft and will largely determine your ability to get things done.

Usually these skills are gained only through experience. The purpose of this part of the book, however, is to assist you in acquiring that experience by providing an overview of these common technical areas. This chapter begins this process with a discussion of product data (*reference data* is a more modern term for it), which is one area that affects almost everything in the Wall Street technology world. What are product data? And what are the products of which we are speaking here?

EXTERNAL PRODUCT IDENTIFIERS

A product is a synonym for a security or an instrument. Generally it is some identifiable thing that a financial firm can buy or sell. The key word for our discussion here is *identifiable*. Let us say that one firm buys a

Treasury bond from another. How do the two firms identify exactly which bond is involved? The first task of product data technology is to make sure that there is no ambiguity about what is being traded by providing an identification system for all securities. The second task is to link this identification system to the properties of the securities. In our bond trade example, the buyer has to pay the seller the accrued interest, and both sides need to agree on the exact amount, so they have to be able to determine what the coupon rate and coupon dates are for the bond being traded. They will ask their respective product data systems to look up this information, using the security identifier.

At first sight, giving identifiers to, say, all Treasury bonds, and then storing the parameters, such as coupons and maturities, in some database does not appear particularly hard. Consider, however, the scale of the task: there are perhaps only a few hundred Treasuries, but there are tens of thousands of stocks, hundreds of thousands of agency securities, and literally millions of corporate bonds and mortgage pools out there, and this is just for the United States (and we aren't even mentioning things like futures and exchange-listed options). Storing such massive amounts of data is a nontrivial task, as is keeping this information reasonably complete and up-to-date.

The need for some securities identification system became apparent fairly early in the computer era. In 1964 the American Bankers Association created a Committee on Uniform Security Identification Procedures (the *CUSIP* committee), which issued its recommendations for a securities numbering system in 1967. The system it recommended reflected the realities of the paleocomputing age: every security was to be identified by a nine-character code, of which the first six characters identified the issuer, the next two characters identified a particular security of that issuer, and the remaining character was a check digit (Figure 12–1).

The issuer numbers were assigned alphabetically to all corporate and government issuers. Of course, some issuers, such as the U.S. Treasury, had many more securities than could be accommodated by a two-digit suffix, so such issuers got more than one issuer number. The two-character security suffix for equity securities contains only numbers from 10 through 88, whereas for debt securities, at least one of the two characters has to be alphabetical (AA, B1, and 1C are all OK). The rightmost digit in any CUSIP code is calculated from the first eight characters by a simple addition technique, so that the systems that use CUSIP numbers for security identification can detect whether any of the characters had been corrupted during the (often nonelectronic) transmission process.

FIGURE 12–1

Structure of CUSIP numbers. The first six digits are a
numerical code assigned to the issuer, the next two identify
an issue, and the last one is a check digit computed from
the other eight.

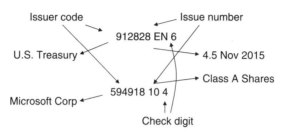

The CUSIP Board of Trustees controls this numbering system, but
the actual administration of it is performed by Standard & Poor's CUSIP
Service Bureau, which (for a hefty fee) assigns the CUSIP numbers for newly
issued securities. By the end of the 1980s, similar national numbering agencies had sprung up in most Western countries to administer their national
securities identification systems. In the United Kingdom, the London
Stock Exchange administers its *SEDOL* system (which has just run out
of numbers in its seven-digit codes and will now start using letters); in
Switzerland, Telekurs assigns *Valorennummern* (which means security
codes). Overall, there are now about 60 such numbering agencies, from
Argentina to Ukraine.

There is also an international standard administered by ISO that
endeavors to assign a unique 12-character ID called *ISIN* (International
Security Identification Number) to every security in the world. This is done
by prepending a two-character country code to a national security ID and
adding another check digit at the end; for example, a U.S. CUSIP 912828DJ6
becomes an ISIN US912828DJ69 (although many countries, such as France
and Germany, assign ISINs to their securities directly). There is also a CINS
number (CUSIP for international securities) that is assigned by the U.S.
CUSIP bureau to non-U.S. securities; this is done mostly because many
computer systems in the United States were designed in the 1970s to use
9-digit CUSIPs and could not accommodate the 12-digit ISIN codes.

Bloomberg and Reuters assign IDs to securities as well; for example,
the futures symbols we discussed in Chapter 7 are internal Reuters IDs (their
importance for futures is enhanced by the fact that futures do not get either
ISINs or CUSIPs). As a result of all these numbering efforts, almost every

security has not just one ID but several: a national ID such as CUSIP or
SEDOL, an ISIN, and perhaps also a Reuters and/or Bloomberg symbol.

The numbering saga does not end with these *external* IDs. Every bank
has its own database of securities, in which each security is given an ID
all over again. That ID is *internal* to the bank (meaning that it cannot be
used for settlement with outside counterparties). In fact, many firms have
several product data systems with different database schemas (mostly for
historical reasons), so a security may very well have more than one internal ID on top of the many external ones. The assignment of these internal
IDs is almost unavoidable, as storing almost anything in a reasonably normalized relational database requires giving every row an ID number, which
has to be unique from the point of view of that database. The external IDs,
sadly, are often not unique. For example, the U.S. Treasury recycles CUSIP
numbers from its securities that matured long ago; Reuters RIC EDH5 can
be a Eurodollar future expiring in March 2005 or 1995 or 2015; stocks that
are listed on more than one exchange have the same ISIN numbers, but for
settlement purposes, you want to have separate securities for each exchange—
the list goes on and on, and maintaining internal securities identification
systems makes sense in this context, as it allows the banks to deal with
each of these quirks in their own way.

INTERNAL SECURITIES DATABASES

What kind of information is stored in these internal securities databases?
First, there are all these IDs, both internal and external, as well as more
human-readable descriptions of the type of security (equity or bond or note
or option or whatever), the issuer, and the particular issue (credit ratings
from major rating agencies can also be viewed as part of these descriptions
and are also stored where appropriate). Then there is a set of dates: issue
date; auction dates; maturity date; sometimes even individual coupon dates;
dividend or ex-dividend dates for stocks; expiration dates for futures and
options; call dates for callable bonds. And, of course, there are numbers:
coupon rates, outstanding amounts, tick sizes for price quotations, and so
on. Finally, many institutional details specific to the firm are often stored
there as well: which desk and which trader trades this security, who created
the record and when, when it was last updated, and the like. Add up all
of that information and you easily end up with several kilobytes worth of
data for every security (I tried to present a sample record as a table and could

not make it fit on one page). The main problem with storing these data is not so much their size, however, but rather their structure.

Designing a database to store products of a single type (I will stick with government bonds as a representative example) is a fairly straightforward task. This is not a book on database design, so I will not go into the five principles of database normalization, but as a practical matter, we would probably have a table listing all government issuers (and giving an internal issuer ID for each), another table for all different types of bonds (say notes and bonds and zero-coupon bonds, again with a type ID for each), and finally one or several product tables that have a unique primary ID for each bond and a column for each of the relevant properties: maturity date, issue date, coupon rate, and the like.

If we build this database and populate it with data, people in the firm will start using it, and pretty soon they will decide that, instead of building a brand new database of agency securities for a new business line that is being created at the firm, it makes sense to store data about those securities in our database, which people already know and love. But many of the agency securities are callable, and our database design did not anticipate that. We end up extending our product tables to accommodate call schedules for callable agencies, but the new call date and call type columns are now blank (or, rather, contain NULLs) for almost everything in the table except a few callables.

The next thing we know, we have to store futures data in our database; they also require a few new columns, but, what is worse, almost all the columns that make sense for bonds do not make any sense for the futures. At this point, we decide that it is better to actually have an entirely separate table for the futures that has only futures-specific columns, and a link table that classifies a given ID as either a bond or a future. This will go on for many years; some new products will be accommodated by extending existing tables and some by creating new dedicated tables, and after a while we will have a database with hundreds of tables, some of which will have hundreds of columns; 90 percent of the data in this database will be NULLs; and the whole thing would make very little sense to an outside observer. But its redeeming quality will be that every software system in the firm will be using it, quirks and all, and dropping this database and switching to another, perhaps more sensible system would be an almost impossible task.

Designing a database schema that can accommodate many different product types is often so hard that a common alternative is *flat instrument storage*; this means that we have a single table with hundreds of columns that can accommodate any product, but most of these columns make sense for only a small subset of products. The major advantage of this design is its simplicity and the unified interface that it presents to the outside world (this is called a *fat interface* in object-oriented design), and many in-house systems opt for this alternative over a more structured normalized database approach.

POPULATING THE DATABASE WITH DATA

Let us assume that we are past the design stage. Our firm already has a product database, and it works—how does it get populated? The answer depends on the type of product and, of course, on the firm. Some products are entered by the back office, or operations; those are typically limited to things like government debt instruments, which are issued fairly infrequently. For example, when an auction announcement is released, back office personnel would use a specially designed application to enter the pertinent parameters of the new security (maturity, issue date, CUSIP, and so on) into the product database. After the auction, the coupon becomes known, and the same people will update the coupon rate in the database.

This is a fairly labor-intensive process that scales poorly with the number of products; it is still feasible to do it manually for some subset of agency securities and for major equity new issues, but with corporate debt and equity securities, this process generally becomes unmanageable. The solution is to use external vendors that provide data feeds for new securities, as well as for so-called corporate action data—information about stock splits and mergers that necessitate changes in the securities issued by the affected corporations. Companies that provide such reference data feeds include FT Interactive Data (the market leader), EJV (which is part of Reuters), Telekurs Financial, and Bloomberg; in 2001, these companies collectively earned about $500 million from reference data services.

Each of those vendor feeds, however, requires some kind of interface with the internal product databases—something that can read the data off the vendor feed and insert them into the internal systems. Development and maintenance of such internal *feed handlers* is an expensive and often frustrating task for the technological organizations of Wall Street firms, as it requires constant communication with the vendors to keep the feed handlers in sync with changes they make to the feeds. This increases the attractiveness of outsourcing the whole product database to a third-party, which would design and install the database in a client firm and be responsible for maintaining all the data feeds.

Companies like Asset Control, FTI, Cicada, SunGuard, and a few others provide such *reference data management* systems, and this is a growing business. If we are building an investment bank from scratch, buying such a system from one of these vendors instead of building our own will certainly save much blood and treasure, and it is also a good solution for large hedge funds (large because these systems are not cheap, and a small operation cannot realistically afford one). For an existing firm that already has extensive product data systems of its own, buying such a product initially results in a duplication of effort as the in-house systems coexist with the shiny new data management solution, as well as with each other, although it still may make good sense in the long run.

Using the plural for in-house product data systems is intentional; there is almost always more than one, and we need to understand how they are related to one another. Typically, there will be a *master* product database in which all new information is entered. However, this database is rarely used for retrieval of securities data; instead, there will be several replicas of this master database that provide read-only access to reference data for a variety of in-house clients. The replicas can be just what the name implies, direct one-to-one copies of the master database, or they can be different databases (or other data repositories) with different data models, often containing just some pertinent subset of the master data. In the case of direct replicas, synchronization with the master is usually done using standard database replication technology (replication across geographical regions is usually done this way): database triggers copy all updates from the master to the replicas. Systems with different data models are kept up-to-date by internal data feeds—processes that read master data, convert them into the format understood by the target system, and copy them there.

At this point, we still may not be convinced that product data maintenance is a big job. It would then be instructive to consider the life cycle of a typical securities record. The security record begins its life some (short) time prior to the security issuance—typically at or before the announcement preceding the actual sale (or auction). At this time, the bulk of the securities record is entered into the product master: the description and type of the new security, its maturity date, its issue date, and whatever other dates are needed, as well as all external IDs (CUSIP, ISIN, and so on) if those have already been assigned by the numbering agencies. This record is then updated after the actual sale (for example, the coupon rate for auctioned securities becomes known only after the sale, as does the actual amount sold).

At first glance, it would seem that this record will never have to be touched again, but this is unfortunately wrong. First, a security may at some point be reissued, there could be stock splits, and so on—all these events have to be reflected in the reference data record. More importantly, the state of the security may change over time. Consider a callable bond; the data record contains the first call date, on which the bond may or may not be called. Clearly it is important to reflect in the data record whether the bond was in fact called on that day; this is often achieved by having a state flag on the record that can take values like "active," "matured," or "called."

Speaking of maturity, what should happen to a bond's reference data record after the bond matures (or is called)? It is tempting to just delete the record, but this would make it impossible to do any kind of historical analysis on it (and may cause more immediate problems if, for example, the firm's trading systems contain records of trades done in this bond that reference its ID in the product data system). So after maturity, the bond is likely to be put into an inactive or matured state but remain in the reference data system.

In addition to such state-changing events, there are other things that necessitate frequent updates to securities records: for floating-rate notes, one has to enter the values of the floating rate at payment points; for inflation-linked securities, the inflation index has to be updated every month, and so on. Finally, sometimes there is a need to create records that do not correspond to any actual securities at all; for example, one may want to create a record for an upcoming issue before the actual announcement, to create an imaginary security to facilitate booking of some derivative trades, and so on. Almost every product data repository is replete with examples of such synthetic securities, which, hopefully, are clearly identified as fakes.

USES OF REFERENCE DATA

Who uses reference data? The short answer is pretty much everybody. Literally any software that does anything with securities (which covers 99 percent of the software used in financial institutions outside of human resources departments) will use one or more of the reference data systems available at the firm. The original purpose of these systems was to reduce errors in the settlement process, but in the last two decades their uses have grown far beyond the back office, to analytics, trading systems, risk management, and research.

Essentially, any software that wants to do any operation with a security will begin by obtaining an ID for that security and looking it up in the reference data system to determine what security it is. This lookup is rarely done by direct SQLing in the product database; there is usually a programming interface to reference data systems that client programs can use. These interfaces often follow the flat instrument storage model mentioned previously; the question that they are designed to answer is: "Here's an ID for my security; give me (some or all of) its parameters." Note that, while this simplifies many common operations, it often makes more structured queries impossible. For example, we can easily ask questions like, "Give me all the securities issued by this issuer between today and 10 years ago with coupon greater than 5 percent" if we query the database directly, but most in-house reference data interfaces lose this kind of flexibility, mostly because the people designing them cannot imagine why these more structured queries are needed (for an answer, go back to Chapter 5 and look at Figures 5–2 and 5–4, which show the maturity and issue date breakdown of the Treasury market—doing this kind of analysis is impossible without at least some of the original relational database capabilities). However, in most cases, finding securities by their IDs is quite enough and deserves a closer look.

Let us say that our software system needs to convert a price for the 10-year on-the-run Treasury into yield. We know that to do the conversion, we need a few pieces of data about the security (coupon and maturity for something simple like a Treasury note). An academic way of doing this calculation would be to find out what these parameters are and plug them into a formula that will provide the result. The "object-oriented" way used by most real software systems goes like this: we want to create a program object that behaves like a Treasury note and knows how to convert its price into yield as well as how to do all other bond math calculations, and then ask that object to do the price-yield conversion for us.

Overwhelmingly, these software objects representing securities are created based on the reference data record: given a security ID, a specially designed part of the system (often called a security loader, bond builder, or something else like that) reads the reference data record for that security, figures out what type of object should represent that security, and fills out the internal data structures of this object. While most such security builders can build these financial objects from a set of parameters as well, in reality the creation of such objects by loading data from the reference data systems is perhaps the most common financial software operation. I would even say this: if you start working at a new Wall Street firm (and your job description mentions the words *securities* and *programming* in the same paragraph), the first thing you should learn is how this is done at your new place of employment: what security IDs you should use, where you should look for these IDs, and what functions you call to build financial objects.

HISTORICAL DATA

So far our discussion of reference data has been limited to what are called *static data*—the properties of securities that seldom, if ever, change (again, think coupon and maturity). However, there are a lot more data that can be usefully attached to a security—things like prices, yields, and spreads—that change every day and can be stored historically for each security. Such *historical data* are very important for both housekeeping tasks (analyzing past trades, resolving settlement disputes) and research (econometric modeling, historical regression, and so on), so most securities firms store such historical information in their reference data systems. The information being stored typically includes closing prices, yields, rates, and spreads, and sometimes whole closing curves, and it can come from either internal sources (for example, a trading desk in the firm would provide closing prices for the securities it trades) or external sources such as Bloomberg, Reuters, or DataStream. The amount (or rather historical depth) of data varies among firms and systems. Typically we can expect to find almost any data that matter after 1995 or so; the data for the early 1990s would be sparser; and beyond somewhere around 1980 there would be just a few select series going deeper into the past.

As with the static data repositories, we may very well find more than one such historical data system in a typical bank. Some of them may have grown out of internal trade databases that also stored closing prices, while others could have been built specifically for the purpose of storing *time series* of prices or other such information. Again, the time-series view of such historical data usually means in practice that we can ask these systems questions like, "Give me a history of closing yields between now and 10 years ago for this security ID," but not questions like, "Give me closing yields of all securities satisfying certain criteria (say all outstanding Treasuries) on May 1, 1997" (this question, by the way, illustrates what a closing prices database is: it is the thing designed to answer such questions). Many third-party reference data management systems such as Asset Control actually combine the static data repository with storage of such historical data from multiple sources, which makes these more structured queries easier.

Relating these historical data to securities is straightforward if we are interested in the closing prices for IBM stock, but what if we want to see the history of the 10-year U.S. dollar swap rate (or the U.S. dollar three-month LIBOR)? Since questions of this kind are in fact very common, the historical data systems usually accommodate them by pretending that swap rates, deposit rates, FX rates, volatilities, and other such factors are all securities and assigning security IDs to all such things. Another example of such pseudo-securities would be a *rolling series* of, say, 10-year Treasury yields; whenever a 10-year Treasury rolls and is replaced by a new on-the-run, the yields in this series would jump from the old security to the new one, so that they no longer apply to any specific security ID; instead, the series will be given a security ID of its own (sometimes more than one, as there is more than one way to build such rolling series). In the same spirit, people often create time series of *constant-maturity Treasuries* (or *CMTs*) containing the yields of imaginary Treasuries whose time to maturity is kept constant (instead of shrinking every day as it does for "real" bonds). This is done by building some kind of smooth Treasury curve based on the closing yields of actual bonds and notes every day, and then interpolating yields for points with an integer number of years to maturity. If we see a security description that says "15-year CM Treasury," it would correspond to one of those constant-maturity time series.

Historical time-series data can typically be accessed either by the security ID or by a *symbol*, which is nothing more than a text-based ID (for example, a dollar-yen exchange rate will probably have some kind of integer ID in the system, but it is much more convenient to be able to use a symbol like "JPY" to call up the historical data). Unlike static data repositories, the historical data are almost never accessed by querying the underlying database directly (in fact, in many cases, historical data are not stored in a relational database at all). Instead, the historical data systems provide a programming interface that allows a client to retrieve data by ID or symbol within a given range of dates. This allows the client to pull the historical data into her C++ program or into an Excel spreadsheet, but some systems go beyond that by providing dedicated GUI applications that can not only retrieve the time series, but also plot and analyze them in various ways.

Support for common time-series operations is also often provided as part of these interfaces; for example, if we want to see the spread between the 5-year and 10-year swap rates, we can sometimes simply request a series of (swap10y – swap5y), and the software will retrieve both time series, subtract the values for each day, and show the time series of the difference. Other operations that are usually supported include calculating moving averages and other statistics, as well as *data filtering* operations (eliminating missing and/or obviously wrong data points).

Most historical data systems contain daily, weekly, or monthly data, but there are a growing number of systems that store real-time data for actively traded products (these are sometimes called *tick databases*). This is definitely the bleeding edge at the time of this writing, as storing and retrieving such intraday data poses significant challenges. First, consider the storage capacity issues: for an actively traded product (a bond future, or perhaps an FX rate), there can easily be a new data point every second, so over the course of a trading day, we will accumulate tens of thousand of data points, and storing a year's worth of data would involve about 10 million points. Estimating storage size for each point at 1 kilobyte, we get 10 gigabytes of storage per year for every actively traded security— even with today's cheap disk storage, this presents something of a challenge. In the interest-rate world, where the number of active instruments is fairly low (perhaps a few dozen), this may still be feasible, but in the equities area, where there are tens of thousands of actively traded stocks, one has to limit the coverage to a few dozen of the most important ones.

Retrieval of such data also presents interesting problems. Most standard time-series analysis tools are built for evenly spaced (daily) data, while the tick data points come at random intervals, so that even simple things like calculating moving averages suddenly require redesign. Finally, the tick databases have to be integrated with the market data systems that carry the underlying real-time data. This area is definitely a work in progress at this time, but it is certain to become more important and widespread in the near future.

I hope that this brief overview has had the effect of impressing upon the reader the importance of reference data technology. It would not be an exaggeration to say that it represents the foundation for all other industry technologies, and we will see numerous examples of that in this part of the book—specifically, when we talk about financial analytics in the next chapter and trading systems in Chapter 14. Chapter 17, on research and strategy, provides some real-life examples of how historical data are used. Regardless of the specific area, reference data are as essential to Wall Street technology as words like *bread* and *mother* are to the English language.

Now that we have covered the fundamentals of this basic securities industry lexicon, we are ready to move on to more interesting things. The next chapter introduces financial analytics.

CHAPTER 13

Financial Analytics and Modeling

There are very few areas of human endeavor outside of fundamental science that require quantitative models for their day-to-day operation. Over the last three decades, the financial industry has become a leading consumer of quantitative models and analytical tools, overtaking more traditionally model-intensive areas such as the aerospace and weapons industries. Despite the stunning growth of financial modeling, it largely remains a mystery to the outside world. Someone who has been trained in hard sciences or engineering can probably figure out fairly easily what kinds of models are needed to design and build an airplane or a ballistic missile, but most quantitative people have only a very vague idea of the models and analytics used in finance. Of course, if you have plowed through this book all the way to this chapter, you should be significantly better off in this regard, as our discussion of financial markets has consistently emphasized the quantitative issues and challenges specific to each area. This chapter consolidates these prior allusions into an overview of the main categories of financial models and analytical tools. We will also discuss how these quantitative tools are developed and used in practice, and what role they play in the larger landscape of financial industry technology.

TYPES OF FINANCIAL ANALYTICS

First off, I have to point out that not everything that addresses a quantitative challenge in the markets will qualify as financial modeling and analytics. There is already a certain body of tradition in these areas, and according to that tradition, "models and analytics" are quantitative tools that are independent of the specific market situation and are generally intended to describe what is going on now rather than to predict and influence what is going to happen in the future. This definition excludes relatively modern quantitative areas such as proprietary trading models, market making, and, more generally, market microstructure models, as well as almost everything based on historical data analysis.

So what is included in "traditional" modeling and analytics? The first, and by far the oldest, branch of this field is usually called *fixed-income mathematics*, or simply *bond math*; it takes care of interest payment calculations, converting bond prices into yields, and computing various other bond characteristics, such as duration and convexity. The second area is more recent and is the best known by far; its subject matter is pricing of financial derivatives in general, but it is often colloquially referred to as *options pricing*. The art and science of *curve building* is usually considered part of derivatives pricing, although it has nothing to do with options. Options pricing is a particular case of *instrument pricing*, which deals with determining the value of various financial instruments given the current state of the markets.

Modeling the market and credit risk of financial instruments and portfolios thereof is the purview of *risk analytics*, whereas things that are specific to such portfolios are usually referred to as *portfolio analytics*. A large area, rivaling derivatives pricing in size and complexity and in fact closely related to it, is *term structure modeling*—yet another concept that is specific to interest-rate markets. Other fixed-income markets require their own specific models; for example, mortgage markets need prepayment models, while credit markets need credit default models. As this brief enumeration makes clear, the traditional quantitative modeling area is heavily tilted toward the fixed-income markets.

These models and tools exist not as theoretical abstractions, but rather as functioning software. When a derivatives trader needs to price a swaption, she does not pull a book from the shelf to find out how to do it; she simply enters a few things into her spreadsheet or trading system, and the modeling software figures out the answer. In this book, we look at models and analytics as a technology area, and the questions that we need to ask from this point of view are not so much about the quantitative content of the models as about more mundane issues, such as how this software is created, distributed, and used. Let us start with the usage question.

DEVELOPMENT OF FINANCIAL ANALYTICS

In real life, financial analytics almost always lives inside other software applications that serve specific business purposes—trading systems, pricing spreadsheets, risk reporting systems, and so on—which perform the calculations not out of theoretical interest, but rather in order to do something meaningful with their results. There is no screen on my desktop that I can bring up and say, "And this is our financial analytics suite," but almost any piece of software used in and around Wall Street trading businesses has some financial analytics components.

From the software development perspective, this means that financial analytics is generally implemented not as stand-alone applications, but rather as libraries that other applications can use. In the early days, financial calculations were often coded directly into specific applications that required them—a trader would program Black-Scholes into his pricing spreadsheet, while the developer of a trade entry screen for the same options desk would program Black-Scholes yet again into that screen, and at the same time the people who were responsible for computing the end-of-day PnL for that same desk would do the same thing all over again inside their software. This was no great issue in the case of the relatively simple Black-Scholes formula, but as people started implementing more and more complex financial models inside different systems, problems began to arise; aside from the obvious duplication of effort, the analytics built into different systems often produced slightly different answers to the same questions.

To address these issues, most financial industry organizations have moved to centralize the development of financial analytics software. At present, a big sell-side firm typically has a single group of developers that is responsible for all financial analytics libraries across the whole organization, in sharp contrast to the situation just a few years ago, when such software was created by dozens of quants spread all over the place. This centralized group maintains and updates the code implementing the models, builds the analytics libraries, and distributes them to all users in the firm. The corporate vision behind this is that when a derivatives trader in New York, an interest-rate products salesperson in London, and a risk officer in Tokyo want to know what yield corresponds to a price of 99.01 for the 10-year Treasury, they should all get the same result, regardless of what specific software system they used to do the calculation.

In the case of price-to-yield conversion, this actually works as intended: everybody gets exactly the same model, and that model gives the exact same results to everyone. But when we start looking at more complex or less commoditized models, the picture becomes less clear-cut. These models often keep evolving, and different systems in the firm may end up using different versions of the libraries that implement these models. Since the business users that want the new models never like to wait until the central modeling group gets around to making the improvements they want, the traders and desk quants often create their own versions of the models that they care about, and those versions then slowly propagate back to the centralized modeling group. On the whole, however, the centralization of financial analytics development on Wall Street has made great strides in the last few years and has firmly become the standard.

Another development of the last few years is that, despite the fact that every major bank has a dedicated modeling group that over the years has implemented every imaginable model, there are third-party vendors of financial analytics software that are increasingly successful in selling their products to financial industry firms. While much of the growth of such third-party financial analytics vendors is driven by the hedge fund industry (a typical hedge fund does not have enough technology resources to support the internal development of standard financial analytics), many traders in big firms are also finding the third-party products more powerful, intuitive, and flexible than the offerings of their own modeling groups. Because of the growing popularity of such products, a lot of people that develop financial analytics now work in the financial software industry rather than in the modeling groups of the major Wall Street firms.

USERS OF FINANCIAL ANALYTICS

We have already mentioned some of the major consumers of financial analytics products. Within the trading businesses, there are two main categories of systems that use financial analytics libraries. The first of these are the trading systems (the subject of Chapter 15); these are internally developed software systems that automate and facilitate various aspects of trading, such as trade entry, pricing, and inventory management. These systems use only in-house analytics, and this usage is tightly controlled in terms of which versions of the libraries are used for what parts of the trading systems. The second major front-office usage mode is much more freewheeling. Traders, salespeople, and research analysts always have a lot of spreadsheets where they play with various aspects of their markets, and such spreadsheets use all kinds of financial models and analytics. The technology organizations of the big banks (and their financial modeling groups) are forever trying to limit the proliferation of trader spreadsheets, but it is a losing battle; as a practical matter, any financial analytics package has to have an Excel interface (either as an add-in or as a COM dll), or no one in the front office will use it.

Beyond the front office, the next category of users of financial analytics products is risk management systems. These typically are written in high-level languages, use the approved in-house analytics libraries, and often really put those libraries through their paces. The tasks that these applications typically perform are computationally heavy (for example, calculating PnL and risk for derivatives books with hundreds of thousands of trades), so it is here that the computational efficiency (or, more often, inefficiency) of the models is of critical importance.

Finally, a growing area of financial analytics usage consists of client-facing applications. The larger sell-side firms these days usually offer their buy-side clients some form of access to their financial analytics tools as well as historical market data; this is done mostly just to keep those clients happy and willing to trade with the firm, but sometimes a modest fee is charged (especially in the case of hedge fund clients). The clients typically get a Web site where they can call up various screens that perform certain standardized financial analytics tasks—curve building, forwards, trade analysis, and the like—as well as regression analysis of almost any historical time-series data. These screens rarely do anything on their own, but simply route the client request to the sell-side firm, where the request is processed on its servers, with the results displayed to the clients. These areas are, of course, full of Web developers, but there are also people who handle the financial and computational content of the requests. They rarely develop financial models per se, but they need to be very well versed in what the firm's official financial analytics libraries can and cannot do, and they often interact with the modeling groups very closely. An interesting specific of this area is the integration of analytics with historical data analysis, which is almost never done by the more traditional financial analytics consumers.

CONTENT OF FINANCIAL ANALYTICS LIBRARIES

Now that we have discussed how financial analytics is used, perhaps it is (finally) time for us to talk about exactly what is in those libraries. This book is not meant to be a financial analytics book (as we discuss in the Recommended Reading section, there are many excellent books that are solely focused on this subject), but we will devote the next few pages to a high-level overview of the main pieces of which the financial analytics libraries are made. This will not teach you financial analytics, but it will give you an idea of what kinds of problems and tasks it is meant to handle.

There is no better place to begin this overview than with the *date library*, which is the heart of any financial analytics system. The date library handles the mundane but surprisingly nontrivial tasks of date manipulation, which is used literally everywhere in financial calculations. What can possibly be nontrivial about date manipulation? Well, as a warm-up exercise, let us consider the *year fraction calculation* issues. Interest rates are always expressed as annual percentages, and this implies that if we need to calculate the actual amount of an interest payment for borrowing between two given dates, we take that interest rate times the number of years that have passed between the two dates; generally this will not be a whole number of years, so this length of time is usually called the year fraction.

Most people would agree that the year fraction between January 1, 2005, and January 1, 2006, is exactly one year, but let us try different sets of dates and see if everything remains as simple and straightforward. Next example: how many years are there between January 1, 2005, and February 1, 2005? We can argue that this is exactly 1 month and there are 12 months in a year, so we would get a year fraction of exactly $\frac{1}{12}$. Or we can argue that there are 31 days between these two dates, and there are 365 days in a year (except that some years have 366), so the year fraction calculated this way comes out to be $\frac{1}{11.774}$. A physicist would dismiss this slight difference as completely irrelevant, but if we multiply these year fractions by a $100 million notional amount and, say, a 5 percent interest rate, we get payment amounts that differ by about $8,000—certainly not something that a physicist would ignore. And then there are month-end effects: what is the year fraction between March 31 and April 30? Is it exactly $\frac{1}{12}$? And the leap-year effects: how many years passed between February 28, 1996, and February 29, 2000? Is it four years or four years and one day? Again, lest we dismiss this as nit-picking, one day of interest on a $100 million notional amount at 5 percent is worth about $14,000.

Incidentally, I remember that as late as February 1999, not all Wall Street systems even knew that there was going to be a February 29, 2000 at all (some of them erroneously assumed that the year 2000 was not a leap year), and so when the one-year swap was supposed to end one year from February 28, 1999, some banks thought that the end date was going to be February 28, 2000, and others thought that it was February 29, 2000. As a result, for most of that day, people could not agree on what the one-year swap rate was, and the whole interest-rate swaps market was essentially shut down as a result.

This anecdote illustrates another set of tasks that would be handled by the date library: *adding terms to dates*. This issue arises every time we need to determine payment dates for almost any interest-rate contract, as most such contracts are negotiated using *terms* like three months, one year, and so on. If we add one year to January 1, we get January 1 next year, right? Not necessarily; January 1 is a holiday, and if we actually expect a payment at the end of our contract period, we will need the period to end on a business day. So how would we perform this business-day adjustment in the case of January 1? Would we adjust forward to January 2 or backward to December 31?

As with the year fraction calculations, there is no single right answer to these kinds of questions, but there is a rather pressing need to make sure that both parties to any transaction agree on the answers without a trace of ambiguity; otherwise almost every trade in interest-rate and derivatives markets would not be able to settle. This need has led to the creation of various *conventions* that resolve such date manipulation ambiguities. The year fraction calculations use the so-called *day count conventions,* which are sometimes referred to as the *basis* for interest calculations. There are no fewer than six different day count conventions. One of the most widely used is called *actual/360* (also called the *money market basis* because most money markets use it); with this convention, we take the actual number of days between two dates and divide by 360 (which is an approximation of the number of days in a year). This and other conventions based on the actual number of days give different year fractions for different monthly periods, while for many purposes it is desirable to have one month always equal to $\frac{1}{12}$ of a year, and there are several day count conventions called *30/360* that attempt to achieve this result by forcing each month to have 30 days (this requires some fiddling with the thirty-first day of those months that have one, which can be done in three different ways).

Another group of date-handling conventions are business-day conventions, which tell us what to do if a payment date falls on a day that is not a business day. The most commonly used is called *modified following*, which says that we should move to the next business day unless this puts us into the next month, in which case we should move back to the previous business day. There are several other conventions similar to this that are actively used in various markets. The main challenge here is not so much the conventions themselves, but rather figuring out whether a given date is a business day, which brings us to the thorny subject of holidays.

We might think that all we have to do is have a list of holidays for a given country (this is usually called a *holiday table* or *holiday schedule*) and check that a date is not Saturday or Sunday or in this list. The first problem with this is generating the holiday table for many years ahead (which is what we have to do when we compute payment dates for a 50-year swap), as many holidays do not fall on a fixed date (e.g., Thanksgiving in the United States is the last Thursday of November). Easter is notorious in this regard, as the rules determining when Easter occurs in a given year involve the first full moon after the vernal equinox—something that a financial library has no easy way of knowing.

Actually, Easter also provides a good illustration of another problem with our holiday table idea: Good Friday (the Friday before Easter Sunday) is in fact a holiday in the U.S. bond markets, but the stock exchanges are open, so whether we should consider it a business day depends on the specific market (there are several other "partial" holidays like this). So we need not just one holiday table but several, one for each market, and sometimes even two for each market, since there are both trading holidays (where there is no trading) and settlement holidays (when the Fed and the banks are closed and we cannot settle trades). For example, Columbus Day in the United States is a bond market holiday but not a settlement holiday. Add all this up, and we find that a good financial library will have upwards of 20 holiday tables for the United States alone and perhaps 200 such tables worldwide, and this information has to be kept up-to-date because holidays can and do change. Then there are one-time holidays—think September 12 and 13, 2001, in all U.S. markets (no trading and no settlement, although it did not feel like a holiday at all) or June 11, 2004, which was suddenly declared a holiday in honor of Reagan's funeral. In such cases, the people who maintain financial libraries have to scramble rather urgently to update the holiday tables.

A date library has to deal with all these issues in a manner that is both precise and efficient. For reasons of efficiency and convenience, most financial libraries represent dates as integers (Julian date) rather than as day-month-year structures (so Y2K was never an issue for financial libraries, as the year is not stored explicitly). A Julian date simply shows how many days have passed since a starting date, for example, since January 1, 1960, in some systems, although a far more common choice is making January 1, 1900, equal to 1 (then, say, January 1, 2000, comes out equal to 36,526); Excel uses this date representation, and it is best for a financial library to respect that fact.

The library contains functions that calculate year fractions between dates (and maintains a set of day count conventions used as inputs to such functions) and functions that add terms to dates that use business-day conventions and holiday tables. These latter functions are often generalized to generate *date sequences*, for example, the whole set of payment dates for an interest-rate swap. These computations are often optimized for speed, since they are done over and over inside many financial models. In general, though, in a date library, the emphasis is on accuracy rather than speed; there is no room for error in date manipulation, since it is used for settlement, and everyone needs to agree on the payment dates and interest amounts. The quality of a financial library is largely determined by its ability to get all the intricacies of date handling exactly right. Modeling sophistication does not help much if one of the payment dates for the security we are pricing is off by a day.

A similar emphasis on accuracy is present in *bond analytics* libraries. Their main task is performing price-to-yield conversion, and since yields (and their cousins, spreads) are very often used for quoting, the parties to yield-based trades have to agree on the price to a very high accuracy. The underlying mathematics of yield calculations stays firmly within high school algebra: the bond price P is expressed as a function of its yield y by an explicit formula that says that (1) the price is the sum of the discounted values of each coupon plus the discounted value of the principal paid at maturity; (2) each of these *cash flows* is discounted using a constant interest rate equal to the yield, for example, the nth coupon of a bond that pays annual coupons is assumed to have a discounted value of $C/(1 + y)^n$. Essentially, the bond price ends up being a polynomial in the period discount factor, $1/(1 + y)$, and therefore calculating price given the yield is trivial and can be done on a pocket calculator (in fact, being able to do this on a vintage HP12C calculator distributed to trader trainees in many banks until very recently used to be an important rite of passage for fixed-income traders).

The price-yield relationship cannot be inverted analytically, so there is no explicit formula that determines yield given the price. This calculation has to be done numerically, by solving a nonlinear equation $p(y) = P$. The function $p(y)$ is very well behaved (see Figure 4–4), there is always a unique solution, and the derivatives $p'(y)$ and so on are known analytically, so that the standard Newton-Raphson root-finding method generally does a superb job of it. While for many bond market professionals Newton-Raphson, let alone more complex numerical methods, sounds like pure black magic (and many fixed-income books treat it this way), the mathematics of bond calculations is not the main hurdle that bond analytics libraries have to overcome.

The real challenges that bond analytics libraries face are twofold. The first set of problems is very similar (and often identical) to the date manipulation issues discussed earlier. Should each coupon period be assumed to have the same length? If not, how that length is to be calculated? Should we adjust the coupon dates if they fall on a nonbusiness day? Most importantly, how do we count days for the purposes of accrued interest calculation? There are many such details that need to be resolved to determine the payment dates and the year fractions for all time periods that go into the yield calculation, and there are important further details that are specific to yield calculations. How do we treat the *stub* (the time period between the settlement date and the first coupon), which is generally shorter than the regular coupon period? What do we do if a bond has a nonregular coupon period at the beginning or at the end (the long/short first/last coupon)? In practice, an overwhelming majority of problems with yield calculations are traceable to some of these details being treated incorrectly rather than to any numerical calculation issues.

As with date calculations, the answers to all these questions are codified into a market convention, which is referred to as the *yield calculation convention*. As a representative example, here's the convention for calculating yield for U.S. Treasuries: (1) all coupon periods are assumed to have the same length, ½ year; (2) all cash flows are discounted to the first coupon date, and then from that date to the settlement date using the stub discount factor of $1/(1 + yt_s)$, where t_s is the year fraction between the settlement date and the first coupon date; (3) the stub year fraction is calculated using the actual/actual day count convention (the actual number of days in a period over the actual number of days in the current coupon period); (4) accrued interest is also determined using the actual/actual basis.

Since each of these four calculations can in theory be done in several different ways, the potential number of possible yield calculation conventions is fairly large. Thankfully, only about a dozen are actually used in various bond markets around the world, but a good bond analytics library has to support all of them. For each market, there is typically a default yield calculation convention, but people should be able to calculate yield using other conventions. For example, in the U.S. Treasury market, people often use *true yield* (where payment dates are adjusted for holidays), or *money market yield* (where the stub coupon period but not the accrued interest is computed using the actual/360 basis), and the analytics library should allow users to switch conventions easily.

The second set of issues that bond analytics libraries have to deal with is related to the properties of the bonds themselves. To compute the yield on a bond, a user needs to know its maturity date, the coupon rate, all coupon dates, sometimes an issue date (or, rather, something called the *dated date*, from which the coupon interest begins to accrue), and any nonstandard features such as a long or short first coupon period. It is impractical to make all these parameters inputs to the yield calculation, since setting them explicitly would impose a huge data entry burden on the user. In fact, the user would probably have to go to the firm's reference data repository to find out all these details about the bond in order to enter them into the yield calculation function.

Most bond analytics libraries are willing to automate this step: they are integrated with the reference data systems and can determine all the relevant details of a bond based on an identifier such as CUSIP. A typical setup for a yield calculation is as follows: (1) the user specifies which bond she is interested in by giving a bond identifier to a bond construction function provided by the bond analytics library itself; (2) the library accesses the firm's reference data repository and retrieves all the pertinent data for that bond; and (3) it stores all these details in a data structure called a *bond object*. Once a bond object has been constructed, the user can do any calculations on it without regenerating the static data, such as cash flow dates and amounts. Not only is this a labor-saving device that cuts down on data entry, but the caching of the cash flow structures also greatly improves the speed of price-yield conversions.

The idea of representing a financial instrument as a software object that mimics the properties of the instrument and stores all relevant details about it is in fact central to financial analytics software development, and we will encounter it over and over again as we move on. An extension of this bond object idea is to have a *results object* for the results of the yield calculations. Yield is not the only thing that can be calculated for a bond—there are also various types of durations (derivatives of price with respect to yield), as well as convexity (the second derivative), all of which can be calculated very easily once the yield is known. To take advantage of this, many bond analytics libraries calculate all these things (often called *bond measures*) any time the user asks for any one of them—since most of the computational time in a price-yield conversion is taken up by the iterative process to find the right yield, we might as well calculate as many derived things as possible once the yield is found. Putting all these bond measures in a results object allows the analytics library to cover the very frequent case in which the user wants not just yield but also duration, DV01, and convexity for a given price. In summary, reference data integration and the design of objects used by the library are much harder to get right than the simple numerical issues of yield calculations.

A *curve library* is a software implementation of the net present value concept that plays a crucial role in interest-rate markets. The net present value (or *NPV*) is a scalar product of the cash flows of a given financial instrument and the discount factors corresponding to the cash flow dates; the curve library deals with the generation, storage, and manipulation of the discount factors, while the cash flow generation is generally the job of the date library. The curve library is built around *curve objects*; these are containers for the discount factors whose purpose in life is to be able to return a discount factor for a given date. If we can get that, then we can easily calculate net present value and other interesting things such as forward rates (which, as we recall from Chapter 8, are effectively ratios of discount factors for different dates).

Again, creating a function that returns a double (discount factor) given a date may appear trivial until we consider the underlying logic of *curve construction*. A discount curve object never stores discount factors for all dates; instead, it has a number of date points (or *nodes*) where the discount factor is known (typically corresponding to the maturity of whatever instruments were used to build the curve, as we will discuss later). If it is asked for discount factors corresponding to its nodes, the curve simply returns the stored values, but for all other dates, it has to *interpolate* between the nodes.

This seemingly innocuous complication makes the whole net present value analysis qualitatively different from the parts of financial analytics we have discussed so far. Since there are many different ways to interpolate, there is no unique net present value of anything, and therefore NPV is almost never used for settlement. You can calculate NPV for a bond in five different ways, but what matters for settlement is the price at which you can buy or sell it in the market, which may or may not be close to the theoretical NPV values. From the software design point of view, this makes a huge difference: your calculation no longer has to agree with everybody else's to the ninth significant digit, so you are free to come up with any reasonable way to solve your problems.

For curve libraries, this freedom begins with the choice of interpolation method. The "goodness" of the interpolation method is typically evaluated based on how smooth the curves (and their derived quantities, such as forward rates) look when plotted as a function of time. Since for constant interest rates, the discount factors decrease exponentially with time, *exponential* interpolation between neighboring points is the most commonly used method, but there are other similar methods based on interpolating forward rates rather than discount factors. Spline interpolation methods are also often used, although that leads to issues with curve construction methods, which we discuss next.

As mentioned in Chapter 8, discount curves are constructed from the observed prices of a set of *input instruments*; in the (by far the most common) case of swaps curves, these instruments are Eurodollar futures and par swaps. These instruments are added to the curve one by one, in maturity order, and each additional instrument is used to determine another node (discount factor/date pair) in the curve in such a way that the curve *prices* that instrument exactly, which means that its NPV calculated from the curve is equal to its input price. This *bootstrapping* process is dependent on the chosen interpolation method because adding a new instrument often introduces more than one cash flow beyond the range of dates for which the factors are already known; the discount factors for all such intermediate points are determined by interpolation between the last known point and the unknown node point corresponding to the maturity of the instrument. This explains why splines and other nonlocal interpolation methods complicate the curve construction process: since touching one point in a spline interpolation affects the interpolated values everywhere, adding a new instrument to a spline-interpolated curve generally requires recalculating all previously determined discount factors, that is, going back to the beginning of the bootstrapping process.

Another, more subtle reason why bootstrapping a curve can end up being an iterative process instead of a simple one-off calculation lies in the nature of floating legs in swaps. For reasons discussed in Chapter 8, the value of the floating leg is often assumed to be equal to par; it is quite insensitive to interest-rate movements because, for example, the increase in value resulting from larger payments in a rising rate environment is canceled out by the decrease in future discount factors. In fact, this is true to a very good approximation, but it is an approximation nonetheless—it ignores certain date-handling subtleties.

For example, when the payment dates are determined for a floating leg, the convention is to start from the maturity date and go backward: subtracting three months, adjusting for holidays, and subtracting again until we get to the beginning of the swap. As a result, we get a date sequence in which some neighboring dates may end up being closer or farther apart than three months because of weekend and holiday adjustments. On the other hand, when we determine forward three-month LIBOR, we take one of those payment dates and move three months *forward*; most of the time we will get the next payment date in our sequence, but sometimes we will not (we may end up on the other side of a weekend). In those cases, we determine the payment amount (the forward rate) using one set of dates, but we do the discounting using a slightly different set of dates, so the value of this payment is slightly different from par and, what is worse from the computational point of view, this difference is a function of the discount factors.

This matters because if we do not automatically assume that the floating leg of a swap is valued at par, then we have to calculate its value during the bootstrapping process to ensure self-consistency, which makes curve construction an iterative process. Every time a new swap is added to extend the curve, we first assume that floating leg is valued at par, then we determine the new node discount factor, reprice the floating leg and discover that its NPV is slightly different from par, set the fixed-leg value equal to that new value, and repeat the process until we achieve convergence. This is a good example of how the attention to detail that is characteristic of financial analytics can turn a seemingly straightforward task into a complicated and numerically expensive process. In practice, the value of this floating-leg effect is at most a couple of hundred dollars on a $100 million swap, but it is a very popular interview question, which is another reason that we mention it here.

Moving on to the "rocket science" of financial analytics—options pricing—we discover significant variety in the structure of the libraries that deal with this area. The design that I find the most convenient actually spreads options pricing all over the financial library by making it part of the more general *product libraries* that deal with different kinds of financial products. This approach recognizes that optionality is just another property of many financial instruments that needs to be taken into account when these instruments are priced. For example, options themselves are a class of financial products (think equity options, FX options, options on futures, and so on; see Chapter 9 for more detail).

The financial library should provide a way to construct an object representing an option that contains all its relevant properties, such as expiration and strike price. This instrument object should then have a pricing function that can take volatility information as an input and produce a price for the option. A more convoluted option product, such as an interest-rate swaption, will need more inputs into its pricing function (such as, at a minimum, a swaps curve). A callable bond (see Chapter 9) can be represented as a combination of a "normal" bullet bond and a swaption, but a financial library typically does this decomposition for you: a bond object will be constructed based on reference data information, and the library should see from the reference data that the bond is callable and then make sure that it is priced accordingly. All products with optionality require some kind of volatility input for their pricing; this can be as simple as a single volatility number, or as complicated as a full-blown two-dimensional volatility surface. The financial library will typically have a section (similar to the curve library) dedicated to representing volatility objects and will provide functions to construct volatility surfaces from market data (similar to curve bootstrapping functions).

The instrument-pricing functions, of course, ultimately need to use the underlying rocket science, which is best isolated in one or several *model libraries*. The model libraries provide support for the mathematics of options pricing—something that, as we have emphasized many times, is beyond the scope of this book. The traditional approach to options pricing is based on stochastic differential equations that, on a very simplistic level, attempt to model the random path that the price of the underlying will take. Any financial library will support several models that are rooted in this approach.

First, there is the Black-Scholes formula and its extensions; this model covers the cases in which the underlying equations can be solved analytically. Note that in many options markets, volatility quotes are by definition converted into prices using Black-Scholes, whether this makes modeling sense or not. In this regard, volatility-to-price conversion is similar to price-yield conversion for bonds: because it can be used for settlement, there is no room for creativity here, and our results should be the same as everyone else's. In most cases, however, Black-Scholes is not enough, and the underlying stochastic differential equations have to be solved numerically.

The most popular numerical methods used in an options-pricing context were developed specifically for that purpose: they make use of the idea of a *pricing tree*, such as the one shown in Figure 13–1. For someone trained in numerical analysis, these trees look mildly amusing, but they have an advantage over the more scientifically sound methods in that they are very intuitive (read "correspond to the way a typical trader thinks about options"), and therefore business users are quite comfortable with tree-based options pricing. This cannot be said of the standard numerical methods that were used in physics and engineering for decades prior to Black-Scholes: stochastic

FIGURE 13–1

A binomial tree representing a popular numerical method for derivatives-pricing problems. The underlying price or rate can go either up or down at each tree node, with the probabilities of up or down movements selected in such a way as to reproduce the desired drift and diffusion. A forward pass through the tree begins with the current underlying price at $T = 0$ and ends with its terminal distribution function at expiration. The option price is then found by going back through the tree and discounting the payoffs at each node of the tree.

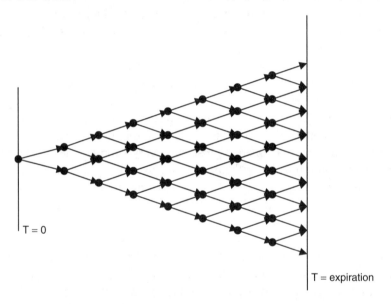

T = 0

T = expiration

calculus is largely equivalent to partial differential (PDF) equations, which describe everything from fluid flow to nuclear explosions.

The numerical methods developed for such PDF equations (diffusion equations in particular) can be used for options pricing and are generally much more robust and efficient than the homegrown tree-based methods. Their usage is typically restricted to "hard" cases that the trees have trouble handling, but most financial libraries implement these methods (called either *lattice* or *PDF* pricers). Another popular and very powerful numerical method used for options pricing is *Monte Carlo*, which simulates the underlying price by generating a large set of random paths and using those paths rather than a regular lattice for numerical integration; this is especially useful for multifactor problems, where the lattice methods (or their tree counterparts) are too numerically expensive.

The *term structure* models for interest rates are based on the same kind of stochastic math and numerical methods used for pricing traditional options, but they are usually much more difficult to implement, maintain, and use; one can argue that this area is the most mathematically and numerically complex part of financial analytics. The task of a term structure model is to describe future distributions of interest rates for the purposes of pricing various interest-rate derivatives. Since interest rates for different maturities are closely related to one another, term structure models have to describe the whole term structure (interest rate as a function of maturity) simultaneously.

Many term structure models attempt to do that by describing the dynamics of an imaginary *short rate* (an interest rate for an infinitely short period) with a random-walk stochastic differential equation; each future path of the short rate allows one to calculate the interest rate to any maturity by simple compounding, and these rates are then averaged over all interest-rate paths. Such models differ in how they specify parameters and the functional form of the equations that describe the path of the short rate. There are perhaps a half-dozen standard term structure models that every financial library implements (in addition, every bank will have one or several home-grown models, usually minor variations of the standard-issue ones).

For a surprisingly large class of such models, there are analytical solutions not only for interest rates themselves (or rather for the discount factors, or, as financial theorists prefer to call them, zero-coupon bond prices), but also for the prices of many simple options such as caps and floors. Needless to say, if one takes some arbitrary values for the model parameters, the model will generate a term structure that bears no resemblance whatsoever to the one actually observed in the market, so in practice the most important part of term structure modeling is determining these parameters in such a way that the model results are consistent with the observed yield curves (and with the prices and volatilities of the actively traded interest-rate options). This process is known as *fitting* term structure models to the market, and any serious financial library provides fitting routines, which are often more numerically complex than the models themselves.

The typical usage cycle for a term structure model goes like this: we pick a model whose properties are adequate for the instruments we are pricing, then decide how we are going to fit the model—to the complete swaps curve or perhaps just to certain benchmark points, whether any volatility data should be included in the fit, and so on. The number and type of the fitting inputs are usually fixed for a given type of model, but the choice of actual maturity and volatility points is left to us, so in practice there are often many different ways in which the fitting can be done. Then follows the actual fitting, which is often a highly numerically intensive process that can easily take from a few seconds to a few minutes for more complex models.

The outputs of the fitting procedure are the parameters of the term structure model, and once they are known, the final stage—using the model with these hard-won parameter values to determine the prices of the instruments we are interested in—is usually a piece of cake compared to the fitting process. Therefore, all financial libraries separate model fitting from the actual pricing by providing object representations of the models. These *model objects* store the fitted parameters, which are calculated once (usually based on closing market prices for the previous day) and then can be reused for pricing large sets of instruments. It is common to see instrument-pricing routines that take such model objects as inputs instead of discount curves and volatility structures—the market information contained in the rate curves and volatility surfaces is passed to the model object during the fitting process.

USE OF FINANCIAL ANALYTICS FOR RISK MANAGEMENT

There are other fairly complex models used for specific fixed-income markets, such as mortgages (prepayment models) and credit (default models). Their implementation usually follows the same object-oriented approach, and their main usage mode is also similar to what we have just described. These models are very interesting and, unlike the more standard term structure models, are still evolving, but describing them would take us too far afield. Instead, we will briefly discuss how financial models are used beyond instrument-pricing tasks, specifically, their use for *risk management* purposes.

While we devote the whole of Chapter 16 to risk management technology, our account of financial analytics would be grossly incomplete without mentioning its risk management applications. In broad strokes, risk management analytics is what happens when we take the standard pricing analytics and use it to answer what-if questions, such as what will happen to the price of this or that instrument if something changes. Upon closer inspection, we will find two major kinds of risk analytics, which I will loosely call front-office risk and back-office risk. Front-office risk analytics answers a trader's need to hedge his books, and the main questions it answers are centered around this hedging problem. An equities trader who is long U.S. equities may want to sell some SP index futures to eliminate his exposure to "the market"; a bond trader who is short the 10-year sector may need to buy some 10-year notes—the financial library allows these traders to quantify exactly how much of what they should buy or sell to hedge their market risk. Back-office risk management tools take a broader view of the risk; they are focused on larger questions like how much money the bank as a whole can lose if the markets turn against its positions.

Front-office risk analytics is a direct outgrowth of pricing analytics. The models used to price financial instruments always use some measure of current market conditions as inputs. For example, the price of an option is a function of the price of the underlying, and the value of an interest-rate swap depends on the Eurodollar futures prices. In their simplest form, risk calculations simply take a derivative of the instrument price with respect to one of these input market levels. This derivative tells us directly how much of the "reference instrument" we have to buy or sell to eliminate the sensitivity of our positions to that instrument. For example, as we discussed in Chapter 9, the delta of an option is nothing but the derivative of its price with respect to the price of the underlying, and it is a direct measure of how much of the underlying we need if we want to hedge away our price risk. Similarly, if we have an interest-rate product whose value depends on, among many other things, the price of the tenth Eurodollar futures, we can find out how many of that futures contract we need to buy or sell to eliminate our exposure to that particular futures contract by taking a derivative.

In the case of simple options, the derivatives (the "greeks") are known analytically and are usually calculated together with the prices, but for the great majority of real-life financial instruments, this has to be done numerically. Most financial libraries provide systematic ways of calculating such derivatives, which are usually based on the idea of "bumping" the discount curves used for pricing. For example, if we price a product using the "real" closing swaps curve, then construct another swaps curve that uses all the same inputs except that the tenth Eurodollar contract price is "bumped" by 1 bp and repeat the pricing procedure, the difference between these two prices is the numerical derivative we are looking for. A typical risk library would cycle through all instruments in the curve, bump each of them, and return the resulting sensitivities to each input instrument.

The front-office risk functions work fine for single instruments or small portfolios, but they are generally unsuitable for large trading books, let alone for the aggregated positions of business units, which is what risk managers are concerned about on the firmwide level. These back-office risk calculations extend the basic price sensitivities idea in two important directions. First, it is wastefully inefficient to calculate the risk of a large portfolio on an instrument-by-instrument or trade-by-trade basis; a financial library typically provides ways of aggregating those positions and/or trades into larger chunks before their price sensitivities are calculated.

More importantly, the portfolio-level risk models recognize the obvious and very strong correlation between many market inputs. For example, there are typically some 40 or so interest rates that go into the construction of a swaps curve, and a front-office risk model would give us sensitivities to each of those 40 inputs as if they were totally independent. This answers the question of how to hedge the portfolio, but it does not answer the question of how much money we stand to lose (or gain) if we leave those positions unhedged. Let us say that our price sensitivity to each of the 40 points comes out to be $10,000 per basis point, and the daily rate volatility of all maturity points is 10 bp/day. If the rate movements at each point were totally independent random variables, we would expect that as some rates move up and others move down, the standard deviation of our PnL would be $10,000 times 10 bp/day times the square root of 40, or about $0.63 million per day. If, on the other hand, the rates are perfectly correlated and the whole curve moves up 10 bp, we stand to lose $4 million instead.

So correlation of market inputs obviously matters a lot, and financial libraries provide tools for dealing with these correlations, which we will discuss in more detail in Chapter 16. These tools are integrated with the so-called value-at-risk calculations (which tell risk managers the standard deviation of the PnL of various bank portfolios over different time horizons). A somewhat independent part of risk analytics libraries deals with *scenario analysis*, where we specify a scenario for future market behavior and the library tells us what will happen to a given portfolio of instruments under this scenario. Overall, the risk management area of financial analytics exhibits large variability in its implementation and its level of integration with the pricing libraries, so that when we compare risk analytics libraries between two major banks, we often find very little in common in their structure.

MAINTENANCE OF FINANCIAL ANALYTICS LIBRARIES

This latter comment applies to some extent to all financial libraries; in some places all financial analytics are integrated into a single huge library, whereas in others the same functionality is spread over three dozen individual libraries. There are pros and cons to each approach. A single library (or a modest number of well-separated libraries) has the advantage of consistency (any low-level changes are automatically applied to the whole thing), whereas if we have 40 little libraries and we have to fix a date-handling bug, we may find that making sure that all 40 continue to work is a nontrivial task. On the other hand, the task of change management is significantly easier in the "many small libraries" environment, where we can change a library that is used in one area of the firm without affecting anyone else—something that presents a big challenge in a single-library environment, where that single library affects absolutely everything and where any changes require a major testing effort to make sure that they do not break anything.

Given that every financial model we read about in financial analytics books is already implemented within the financial libraries at any major Wall Street firm, why change these libraries at all? Or rather, what do the people in charge of those libraries do all day? In reality, financial modeling efforts continue, but the activity has slowed down significantly over the last 10 years. The main drivers of financial modeling at present are the credit and energy derivatives businesses, where models are much less standardized than in the more traditional interest-rate derivatives and term structure modeling areas, but even there the actual development efforts are typically focused on extending the existing models to new product classes rather than on innovations in financial theory. There is also always an ongoing effort to make the calculations more efficient, especially in the risk management area.

Another source of change in the financial libraries is attempts to reverse-engineer models used by competitors. A good example here is the OAS calculation for callable bonds used by Bloomberg, which has become a de facto standard among traders in agency bonds. The trades are agreed upon in terms of Bloomberg OAS because that is what the traders and their customers see on their Bloomberg screens; but then the trades have to be entered into the firm's trading systems, and these systems typically do not know how to convert Bloomberg OAS into price. The firm's financial libraries will typically offer several different ways of doing an OAS calculation, many of which will be much more theoretically sound than the Bloomberg methodology, but this is of little help in a situation in which the two counterparties have to do this calculation in exactly the same way.

As we mentioned, this situation exists in almost all bond markets on the level of yield calculations, which are simple enough for everyone on Wall Street to agree on how to perform them. When a similar requirement is applied to more complex financial products, everyone has to use the same model, whose internals are unknown, and everyone then tries to figure out how the

Bloomberg standard works internally and reproduce it in-house. These efforts usually meet with little success, but they keep the financial engineers busy churning out successive approximations to what Bloomberg does.

Interestingly, rather than share its analytics, Bloomberg now offers its customers access to its servers; when a person or a computer system within the firm needs to do a financial calculation, it can now do that calculation on a Bloomberg server instead of calling the in-house library. This application service provider model is perhaps the biggest threat to financial analytics development on Wall Street, because at the end of the day it is difficult to justify the huge expense of developing and maintaining all these tools and models in-house, and most business users of financial analytics would happily let Bloomberg handle their computational needs.

Financial analytics as a discipline is now entering its fourth decade, and it has matured to the point where most of the contents of a financial library are essentially the same everywhere. This rocket science is rapidly becoming commoditized (which is exactly what happened with rockets before the rocket scientists started deserting that field for the greener pastures of Wall Street), and for the overwhelming majority of today's quantitative population on Wall Street, financial analytics is something they use rather than something they develop. In this regard, it has become much closer to calculus, or perhaps the numerical methods: a valuable tool whose use is required knowledge, but whose proprietary content is minimal.

However, financial analytics is used so widely that no matter where you work inside Wall Street, as long as it has anything to do with trading, you will do yourself a favor if you spend some time figuring out how your area is using it. This effort will involve some reading about the actual models used, and it will also involve understanding the specifics of how the models are implemented at your firm. At a minimum, you want to know where to find the financial libraries, how to figure out which models live where, and how to load these libraries into your spreadsheets or other applications; these local details may take as much effort to master as the analytical content of the models themselves.

I would like to conclude this chapter with this advice for the financial engineers entering the industry: before you start thinking of creating and implementing models of your own, spend some time poking around in your firm's financial libraries. The chances are good that what you are thinking of is there already.

CHAPTER 14

Market Data

One feature of almost any trading floor that never fails to impress a first-time visitor is the enormous amount of data being absorbed by the people working there. These days, a typical trader will have between two and six flat-screen monitors filled with all kinds of flickering numbers and charts. The flickering is of a kind that is seldom seen on a home PC; the numbers move on their own! Whenever a futures trade happens in a CBOT trading pit in Chicago, within milliseconds (well, maybe hundreds of milliseconds), the new trade price is splashed on thousands of trading screens the world over. Foreign exchange and stock index quotes keep flashing several times a second; news headlines scroll down, sometimes highlighted in bright colors. These market displays are often a sight to behold and add considerably to the excitement on the trading floor. We used bits and pieces of these screens in Part 2 of the book to illustrate various market concepts, so hopefully the reader should be able to figure out what at least some of these flashing numbers actually represent. In this chapter, we address the technological mysteries behind them.

A technologically literate observer who is seeing these screens for the first time will probably ask herself at least some of the following questions: How exactly does this work? What makes the numbers and charts on the screens move on their own? Where do all these numbers come from? How does every trader manage to lay all this data out in his own unique way? Does it ever break? Clearly, the generation, handling, and worldwide distribution of live market data is a remarkable technological feat, and anyone working in the industry should have at least a rudimentary understanding of how that feat is accomplished.

In this chapter, we will explore the fundamentals of market data technology. We will start with a functional description of a "generic" market data platform, briefly touch upon the history of such platforms, and then describe how live data are published, distributed, and used. We will then spend some time on the "Does it ever break?" question by discussing common market data problems and typical solutions to those problems, which form an important part of any market data system. We will conclude the chapter by describing how this technology fits into the larger scheme of things in a typical Wall Street firm, and what technical roles people can fill in this space.

OPERATION OF A TYPICAL MARKET DATA SYSTEM

From the technology perspective, we should talk about *real-time* data systems rather than market data systems, as the data that are shuffled around by such systems do not have to be market-related. In fact, many software vendors refer to these systems as "real-time messaging" or even "enterprise integration" systems and try to emphasize that they can be used for much more than market data proper, but in practice most real-time data remain related to markets and trading. However, for the purposes of explaining how a typical such system operates, it is indeed convenient to abstract from the data content, and in the following discussion we should think of "data" in the original dictionary sense—as pieces of any information.

It is instructive to think of a typical real-time data platform as a cross between a network and a database. The constituent parts of the system are computer programs that run on machines connected by a normal Ethernet network. However, the way these components talk to each other follows the database concept of storing and retrieving pieces of data based on some search criteria rather than on the network concept of sending packets from one device to another. The mechanism for making a network function like a database can be called the *publish-subscribe paradigm*. Let us say that we have two programs on a network, and one wants to send some data to the other. The "network" way of doing that is for the two programs to establish a connection and then send whatever data they like back and forth. In this situation, the content and format of the data do not much matter, but the network location of each program matters a great deal, as the programs have to be able to find each other.

The "database" way of doing the same thing is to focus on the data by giving them a name. For example, the first program can send futures prices to the second, and this stream of data can be given a string label, often called a *subject* or a *topic*, such as "FUTURES_PRICE." The data stored under this subject can, for example, be another string, such as "Price = 101.5." The first program (the *publisher*) would then update (publish) the data stored under this subject whenever it has a new futures price, so the subject would remain "FUTURES_PRICE," but the value stored under it would keep changing; for example, it may become "Price = 101.49" at the next update. The second program (the *subscriber*) would subscribe to this subject, which means that it will receive a callback anytime the subject has new data stored under it. This way, the two programs need to agree only on the subject and on the format of the data; their network locations become completely irrelevant. Note that this is in many ways analogous to subscribing to a newspaper—every day the name of the newspaper (the subject name) is still the *New York Times*, but the content keeps changing.

The publish-subscribe mechanism needs an intermediary between subscribers and publishers—something that can remember all valid subjects and know where to send the updates, as illustrated in Figure 14–1. This intermediary is known by different names in different real-time data systems. For the purposes of our discussion, we will call it the data manager. Each

FIGURE 14–1

A market data platform organizes traffic between computers on a network into a set of subjects that are published by some processes and subscribed to by others. The central data manager program keeps track of all subscribers and publishers and redirects the messages between them.

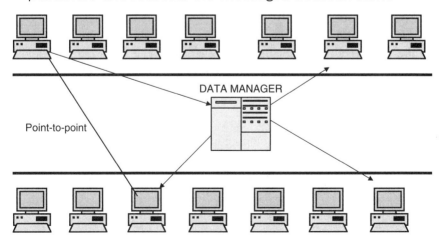

publisher tells the data manager what subjects it wants to publish and sends updates for all those subjects to the data manager. Each subscriber tells the data manager what subjects it is interested in, and the data manager forwards the updates it receives from the publishers only to the interested subscribers.

As is clear from Figure 14–1, the data manager acts largely as a network switch, redirecting network traffic from publishers to subscribers. In fact, when the first such systems were created in the 1980s, hardware network switches (which today can perform a similar function) did not exist and the networks' capacity was much lower than today, so in those days this switching function of the data manager was crucial for reducing the load on the network. But even more importantly, the data manager is responsible for maintaining the logical database structure. It keeps the list of all subjects that anyone wants to publish and/or subscribe to, and it often enforces subject naming conventions by rejecting names that do not conform to those conventions. For each subject, it maintains a list of publishers (some systems allow only one publisher per subject) and a list of subscribers. Usually one publisher services many subscribers.

Another attribute of a subject that the data manager optionally maintains is its *latest value*. When a new subscriber comes online and tells the data manager that it is interested in the subject called "FUTURES_PRICE," the data manager can simply begin forwarding the futures price updates to that subscriber (acting just like a network switch would). However, it can also provide the last value that was published before the subscriber connected, which may come in very handy in those cases where the data are updated fairly infrequently. This requires the data manager to *cache* (store) the last published value for every subject,[1] which is something that a network switch cannot do.

The market data platforms installed at financial institutions are provided by third-party vendors (although, as with everything else, there may be banks that build their own). The pioneer in this field was TIBCO, which developed its TIB (The Information Bus) software in the late 1980s. Reuters came out with a competing platform called TRIARCH (Trading Room Information ARCHitecture) just a couple of years later. Eventually (in 1996) Reuters bought TIBCO and started developing next-generation platforms that combined features of both TIB and TRIARCH, such as Rendezvous and, later, RMDS (Reuters Market Data Solutions). Afterwards, TIBCO again became

---

1. In some systems, the data caching function is performed by a separate program that works closely with the data manager.

F I G U R E   14–2

Common market data platforms.

Name	Vendor	Data Mgr	Subjects
TRIARCH TRading Information ARCHitecture	Reuters	Sink Distributor	RICs
TIB (The Information Bus)	TIBCO	TIC	RICs/Subjects
RendezVous	TIBCO	RV Server	Subjects
Talarian	Talarian/TIBCO	RT Server	Topics

a separate company (still partly owned by Reuters) and recently acquired another competitor with a popular product called Talarian.

Each of these software vendors will of course say that its offering is unlike any other, but in reality all these systems have a lot in common with one another as well as with the generic "data manager" product discussed previously. In Figure 14–2, we show what the data manager program is called in each of those platforms and list the platforms' most important distinguishing features. All these products cost millions of dollars and represent a huge commitment for the client institution, since it is very difficult to migrate from one such platform to another. The vendors typically provide the executables and supporting libraries for the data manager and related components, an API consisting of libraries with header files allowing the client to develop its own subscribers and publishers, as well as some standard subscribers and publishers.

SOURCES OF MARKET DATA

A very common type of vendor-supplied publisher is a *data feed*. This is a program that connects to an external data vendor (often a broker or an exchange), reads quotes using a vendor-provided interface, and publishes them to the data manager so that multiple users inside the organization can see and use these quotes. A variation of that type of publisher is a *news feed*, where the data being distributed are news pages rather than market quotes. To make our "FUTURES_PRICE" example more realistic, consider a data feed that publishes the real-time prices for CBOT Treasury futures described in Chapter 7. Rather than calling the subject "FUTURES_PRICE," we will make the subject name contain the futures contract symbol so that it is clear which product the prices are for.

Another compelling candidate for inclusion in the subject name is the name of the data feed itself, since this makes it possible to determine where the subject comes from just by looking at the name. The different parts of the name are joined together by a separator character that depends on the system (a dot for TIB, an exclamation mark for TRIARCH, a slash for Talarian); ours shall be the vertical bar. So the subject that our futures data feed is publishing would be something like TYZ7|CBOT_FEED1 (instrument name|source name). Note how this naming convention allows us to have more than one data feed for the same instrument; for example, TYZ7|REUTERS_IDN would contain futures prices for the same instrument coming from another feed.

Typical content of a futures price subject is shown in Figure 14–3. There is, of course, a lot more there than just price—there is little reason to skimp on the amount of data. This is an example of *elemental* data, where the information is split into its constituent elements. Every interesting bit of data in this record has a (hopefully descriptive) name and a value, so that all a user who is interested in, say, trade price has to do is to search through this text looking for the name "trade price," and the value will be right next to it. In this example, both field names and values are stored as text, but obviously it is possible (and somewhat more efficient) to store values in a binary form. In that case, each field has a name, a type (double or integer or text or whatever), and a value.

One can also expand the concept of elemental data in another direction by keeping the data in text form but making them more structured by using a more sophisticated markup language such as XML instead of the somewhat pedestrian name-value pairs. It is also a good practice to have the publisher name and the instrument name as fields in the elemental data record, even though they are also available as part of the subject name; this makes the life of a subscriber somewhat easier by keeping all relevant information in the same place.

Elemental feeds are a relative novelty. Initially, most of the market data were (and some still are) provided in the form of *pages*, such as those shown in the Treasury market chapter (e.g., Figure 5–12). A page is still a subject in the market data system, with a name like PAGE26|GARBAN, but its value is simply a blob of text. This is a natural way to publish news articles, but for pages containing quotes for a large number of instruments, as is the case in Figure 5–12, it is somewhat lacking in detail.

This structure worked perfectly fine as long as all one wanted to do with the pages was simply look at them—a human brain usually has no trouble figuring out which price goes with what security shown on the page. However, if these data are to be used by other computer programs, the information on these pages needs to be broken down into elemental records on the level of

FIGURE 14–3

Sample content of a market data message for a Treasury futures contract. This example shows a subset of fields from the Reuters TRIARCH system. © Reuters 2006; reproduced by permission.

RIC_NAME	USH6
SEQ_NO	18448
DISPLAY_NAME	US T BONDS MAR6
IDN EXCHANGE ID	CBT
TIME OF UPDATE	12:55
CURRENCY	USD
TRDPRC 1	114.09375
TRDPRC 2	114.09375
TRDPRC 3	114.09375
TRDPRC 4	114.09375
TRDPRC 5	114.09375
HIGH_1	114.3125
LOW_1	113.90625
BID	114.0625
ASK	114.09375
BIDSIZE	576
ASKSIZE	241
BID_2	114.0625
ASK_2	114.09375
ACCUM VOLUME	27220
TRADE DATE	10-Jan-06
TRADE TIME	12:55
OPEN INTEREST	591841
LOTSIZE	100000
PRIM ACT 1	114.09375
PRIM ACT 2	114.09375
PRIM ACT 3	114.09375
PRIM ACT 4	114.09375
PRIM ACT 5	114.09375

individual securities. This process is known as *data shredding*, or parsing. A page shredder subscribes to a page subject and parses the text on the page line by line according to some configuration rules, trying to decipher the security, bid and ask prices, and sizes, along with perhaps some benchmark information. If a line is parsed successfully, the shredder publishes the results as an elemental record on another subject, something along the lines of 3_125_AUG_08IGARBAN26IGARBAN_SHREDDER; the name of that subject should identify the security, the source page, and the name of the shredder that publishes the data. Needless to say, this process is often very error-prone and is quickly being displaced by *digital feeds* that read elementized quotes directly from an electronic system provided by the broker or exchange.

The availability of elementized market data has led to the emergence of internally developed (*in-house*) programs that subscribe to elemental feeds for securities, process the data, and republish them in some processed form. For example, a program can subscribe to all available market quotes for a given bond, find the best bid and best ask, and publish a different subject containing such "best market" information. From the point of view of the data manager, such a program is both a subscriber and a publisher; it subscribes to one set of subjects and publishes on another (generally a single program cannot subscribe to and publish on the same subject). This type of program can provide real-time prices for many securities, as we will discuss in the next chapter. Another example of an in-house publisher would be a program that reads book positions from a database and publishes those positions to the market data platform. Yet another program can then subscribe to both prices and positions and calculate real-time PnL, which again can be published on the market data platform, and on and on. Typically the subjects published by such internal systems greatly outnumber the raw market data subjects coming in from external data feeds.

All data vendors want money for their services, and they are rarely content with simply charging a flat fee per organization; they want to be paid for every user that looks at or otherwise uses their data. This introduces another layer of complexity into market data systems, called *permissioning* or *entitlements*. The data manager needs to know if a specific subscriber has permission (i.e., has paid) to look at a specific bit of data. Typically this is implemented as a separate part of the system; let us call it the entitlement server. The entitlement server maintains a list of users and, for each user, a list of subjects (or perhaps something more general, such as a string pattern) that the user is allowed to look at. Note that this information does not have to be real-time, as it rarely changes and is usually stored in a normal relational database.

When a new subscriber connects to the data manager, the latter identifies the user by the login information (sometimes the workstation IP address is also used as part of the credentials), and then asks the entitlements server whether this user is allowed to see whatever subject she is trying to subscribe to; if not, the subscription fails, and the subscriber gets an error message instead of the data. Sometimes the permissioning is even more restrictive and the data manager simply refuses all connections from subscribers and publishers unless their users are registered in the permissioning database. Finally, note that outputs of in-house systems (prices, positions, and so on) are also often subjected to permissioning restrictions even though the users would not have to pay for such data; this is mostly driven by traders being uncomfortable with the idea that anyone can see their positions and PnL.

WAYS OF DISPLAYING DATA

The last few pages were a long answer to one of our original questions: where do market data come from? Now we know that they come from internal and external data publishers. Let us address another question raised at the beginning of the chapter, how people manage to display market data on their screens in a wide variety of ways. The vendors of market data systems understand that if the typical end user cannot see the data in a convenient form, their platforms have little value, so they have developed many GUI products to address the market data display needs. TIBCO's display software for its TIB platform is called MarketSheet; Reuters has several generations of such products currently in use, most notably RTW (Reuters Trader Workstation) and Kobra 3000Xtra. These products can now do much more than just display market data, but at their heart they are glorified spreadsheets; they give the user a window that can be split into multiple areas, and for each area the user can specify which market data subject she wishes to see, and in what form. The software then subscribes to the desired subjects and begins to receive updates just like any other subscriber.

It is in the area of displaying the data they receive that these programs really shine. The spreadsheet comparison is meant as a compliment, because these programs are very flexible and endlessly configurable in a way that is reminiscent of Excel (with which they are often tightly integrated). They can show price quotes in many different ways (and we can make them do things like turn the price green if the bid size is greater than the ask size, or control the logic used for flashing and other visual cues), display charts by integrating live data with historical data, show cross-referenced news pages, and so on; an example is shown in Figure 14–4, but it really helps to see it live to appreciate the power of these interfaces. The flip side of this flexibility and visual pizzazz is that these front ends are anything but thin clients and consume a lot of resources on the trader's workstation.

FIGURE 14-4

A screen shot of Reuters Kobra market data display application. © Reuters 2006; reproduced by permission.

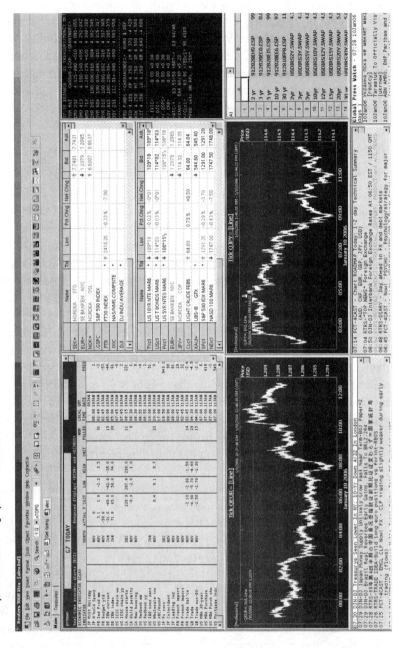

As we would expect, Excel spreadsheets are also major consumers of market data. Almost all market data platforms have Excel interfaces developed for them, so that a spreadsheet can subscribe and even publish market data (although the latter is really frowned upon from the production control perspective). There are add-ins and libraries that provide Excel functions that, for example, take as arguments the name of the market data subject and the field name in the data record and return the current value of that field, so that it is fairly easy to pull things like market quotes and positions into spreadsheets. One disadvantage of Excel is that the spreadsheet has to be refreshed periodically to see the latest updates, as its dependency mechanism is not event-driven, but this can easily be automated (this issue has in fact been resolved in the more recent versions of Excel through something called RTD server). While the vendor-provided GUIs like MarketSheet are more convenient than Excel if all we want to do is look at data that are prettily arranged on the screen, Excel really has no competition when we need to do some calculations based on the live data. MarketSheet and Kobra support simple calculations like adding two bits of data, but they are primitive compared to what Excel can do. Traders and quants often build very elaborate models in Excel, using both live market data and the quantitative analytics libraries that we discussed in the previous chapter.

There are also internally developed GUI programs designed to display data produced by the in-house publishers mentioned earlier. They are often very tightly integrated with the in-house publishers in terms of subject names and data format. We will discuss such programs in more detail in Chapter 15. Here we just mention that they function along the same lines as the other market data display programs but are infinitely less configurable.

Market data platforms live on networks, and there are interesting networking aspects to their operation. A very common network-related issue is the situation in which market data are being published on one network segment and need to be used in another segment, say, in another building or in another geographical location. The standard answer to this need is *bridging*, or routing, the data between segments. This is accomplished by a program (typically a part of the standard distribution package for the market data platform, but sometimes a third-party application) that subscribes to data in the source segment, routes the messages to the target segment, and passes them on to the data manager that is running there so that the users on the target segment can see these data. These "bridges" are usually highly configurable; we can specify which subjects to include in the routing process, and sometimes it is possible to change the subject names to something different in the target network segment.

Similar bridging can be performed between two different market data platforms if the organization has more than one platform deployed, so, for example, it is possible to bridge data over from TIB to TRIARCH and the other way around. This bridging across different systems is usually more difficult, as the message formats in the two systems can differ substantially, so that the bridge often has to restructure the messages in nontrivial ways. Finally, we note that data bridging can cause network stability problems when there are multiple bridges going in opposite directions—if a subject is bridged from Place A to Place B and then, perhaps inadvertently, from Place B to Place A, the link between the two places can be completely overwhelmed by the resulting loop. For this and other similar reasons, bridging is typically used in a tightly controlled manner.

To complete our overview of market data–enabled software, we need to mention another class of programs that are mostly used for development and testing purposes: record and playback software. A market data recorder is a program that subscribes to a given set of subjects and records all updates in a database or, more often, in a file. A playback program reads data from this database or file and publishes them to the market data platform, preserving the values and the timing of the recorded data. This functionality is necessary for in-house development of market data–enabled software, which is often deployed and tested after hours or on weekends, when all markets are closed and therefore there are no live market data. Many such systems cannot even run without some critical data being available, and the playback programs can provide a simulated environment in which such software can be tested and debugged. This functionality should be used judiciously, with the common danger being that some of the canned data played back in this manner can linger on the network until the markets open and can be mistaken for live values.

COMMON MARKET DATA PROBLEMS AND SOLUTIONS

This latter point leads us into a discussion of common market data problems. Let us imagine that we are a trader looking at our market data display and seeing a very attractive price for something; we send a market order to buy that something, and we buy it, but at a much higher price because what we saw on our screen was wrong—for example, it was published by a playback program from a three-day-old recording. This kind of mistake can completely ruin our trading day, and therefore one of the main requirements for any market data platform is that there should be some assurance that the data it disseminates are current and valid.

Data can become stale or invalid if their publisher goes down or if they were published by something other than their "official" publisher. The example with the playback program falls into the latter category, but the former is far more common. In general, it is impossible to guarantee that a data feed will never go down—both the data feed software and the server it runs on can malfunction or crash. The purpose of data quality assurance (DQA) in a market data system is not so much to prevent these malfunctions as to make them obvious so that the users of the data will know that the data are invalid.

One common approach to DQA relies on the fact that the data manager program knows which publisher is supposed to publish a given subject, and consequently knows all subjects published by a given publisher, so that it is in a position to take some action if it is told that a particular publisher is dead. Often every publisher is required to have an independent connection to either the data manager itself or another closely associated program that checks the health of the publisher every few seconds (usually by exchanging small *heartbeat* messages). If the heartbeats from the publisher stop coming, the data manager declares all data that are supposed to come from that publisher invalid; usually all subscribers to any of the affected subjects will get an error message instead of the next update.

The invalidation of messages from publishers that appear to be dead is a good first step in the quest for data quality assurance, but it does not provide an absolute guarantee of data quality. The publisher can be in a bad state but continue to send heartbeats, or the problem may be upstream from the publisher; for example, a data feed that is reading data from an exchange will happily pass on bad data if the exchange itself is having problems with its systems. A more common example would be an in-house publisher that relies on external data feeds to produce some in-house data; if these external feeds go down, and the data manager properly detects this and invalidates the raw data, what should happen to the outputs of the in-house publisher?

The developers of the in-house publisher should handle this error condition explicitly; they can either decide to kill the publisher if there are problems with the input data and rely on the data manager to invalidate its outputs (rarely a very good choice), or they can make sure that the outputs are invalidated in some other way. For example, the output prices or yields can be set to zero or another obviously invalid value (note that for many financial quantities, such as spreads or even yields, zero is in fact a perfectly valid value), or the outputs can be made to contain a field that explicitly indicates whether the data are valid or invalid. In the latter case especially, this approach relies on the ability of the consumers of the data to handle these invalidated outputs correctly, and the consumers rely on the ability of the publishers to handle data errors correctly; needless to say, this does not happen with 100 percent reliability, particularly in large systems.

A complementary approach to ensuring data quality is trying to prevent failures of the system components in the first place. This is often achieved by *redundancy*, or *fault tolerance*, which aims to make sure that the overall system can survive a loss of any (or even many) components without noticeable degradation. In a market data system, this can be achieved by having backups for important publishers. The purpose of a backup publisher is to take over if the primary publisher fails for any reason. For example, we can have more than one data feed connecting to the same external source. At any given time, only one of these feeds will actually publish data to the data manager (this will be the *primary* feed), while one or more *secondary* feeds will do everything that the primary does (connect to the exchange, process incoming updates, and so on), except that they will not publish the resulting data.

The data manager will be told which of the feeds is the primary feed and which are backups. If the primary feed goes down, the data manager will find out about it within a couple of seconds through the heartbeating mechanism and will assign one of the backups to be primary publisher. In this approach (often called *hot backups*), the newly minted primary publisher will start publishing immediately, as it was already up and running and connected, so that the users of the data lose them for only a couple of seconds—the time between the loss of the primary and when the data manager finds out about it. Another approach, which is less robust but far easier to implement, relies on *cold backups*, which are started only when the primary publisher fails. Typically any publisher, especially a data feed, needs a few tens of seconds to fully come up, as it needs to connect to several places, so in a system with cold backups, a loss of the primary feed results in an outage that can last a couple of minutes.

While the approaches just described greatly reduce the likelihood of trading on stale quotes, they do not entirely eliminate bad data, and therefore all users of market data, both humans and computer programs, need to have some mechanisms for detecting and rejecting dubious data. Generally these involve checking the incoming data against some other pieces of information and rejecting those updates that do not pass the check. This process is often referred to as *market data filtering*.

Any filtering logic requires some reference, a known good alternative for the data in question. The most common approach is to have multiple sources for the same piece of data. For example, futures prices can be read directly from the exchange or from an alternative data vendor such as Reuters. When there is more than one source of data, it is possible to perform sanity checks on the incoming data based on both the data values and the timing of the updates. The timing check is fairly obvious: if you have two sources for the same data and one of them stops updating while the other continues to tick away, you are almost always better off trusting the second source and rejecting the first as stale. This is easy for a human trader looking at a screen to do, and computer programs generally follow the same logic. Note that this requires the programs to remember at least the last update time and often also calculate something like an average time between updates, so that implementing the timing checks is not an entirely trivial exercise.

The same can be said about checks involving data values. Any incoming price update can be checked against prices from other sources or against remembered past values such as the last trade price or perhaps the closing price for the security, and can be rejected if it stands out too much. In cases where there are multiple data sources, the filtering logic can use a "voting mechanism" in which the correct value is derived by a preponderance of evidence from all available sources and perhaps cached previous data; for example, if two of three available sources have the same price and the third is off, rejecting the third seems the right thing to do.

Value-based checks have the potential to go beyond simply rejecting incoming data and attempt to correct some common errors. As an example, consider so-called *handle* errors. A handle is the integer part of the price; for example, 101-31 has a 101 handle, and the fractional part is 31 ticks. If the price moves up 2 ticks, it should become 102-01; but brokers often forget to change the handle when this happens, as everyone is focused on the fractional part, so the feed may very well report that the price has gone to 101-01. If an application sees 101-01 from one source and 102-01 from two others and the last trade was at 102-00, then it can determine that 101-01 is a handle error and correct it. However, many data errors cannot be corrected in any reasonable way, most notably shredding errors resulting from incorrect parsing of broker pages, as described previously.

Experience shows that sloppily implemented data filters are more dangerous than no filters at all. An overreliance on past values can cause the program to reject valid prices when the market *gaps* (moves by a lot—for example, after an economic number announcement). When closing prices are used for filtering, the program can end up rejecting all market data on days with big market moves. To avoid these and other similar pitfalls, the filtering logic has to be adaptive and should be able to handle many different scenarios, which often makes it a very big part of market data–enabled applications.

Filtering logic should be part of a more general error-handling strategy in market data applications. Other common errors include failure to subscribe to the desired topic, missing data fields in the expected data record, and/or other data format changes. One group of errors that is both very common and very difficult to recover from involves the loss of quasi-static data such as closing prices, instrument identifiers, settlement dates, and the like. Most market data systems are designed for data that are updated very frequently, so that the loss of a single update rarely causes problems. However, in the case of data that are published rarely (once a day for the previous examples), often all we have is one update, and if this is lost (or rather is not cached properly), the data become unavailable. The loss of quasi-static data may mean that the whole subject becomes unavailable, or just that certain fields in a data record lose their values, depending on the platform and on the sophistication of the caching logic used by it.

The data elements in the previous example are almost always critical for the subscribing application (it is difficult to price or determine PnL for an instrument whose ID is unknown), so whenever these errors occur, the result is often a complete loss of functionality for the subscribing application, and the recovery is not trivial. The first step in recovery typically involves republishing the static data, which is usually difficult to accomplish without restarting the publisher. The second step in recovery is making sure that the subscribing application sees the newly republished data, which often does not happen because many in-house market data processors are written to handle such static data only at start-up. Many major outages have been known to originate from the loss of a single closing price and the resulting application restarts that did not go smoothly.

The lessons of such disasters can be summarized in two bits of wisdom. First, any market data publisher should have a way of republishing everything it knows internally without restarting (for example, in response to a control message), and this functionality should override any and all internal checks on whether a particular bit of data has changed since last publication. Second, putting the handling of quasi-static data exclusively into the initialization logic for a market data subscriber is inviting trouble; there should always be an alternative way of getting such data into a running program, such as forced repeat of some initialization steps, or perhaps reading such data from an alternative source such as a file or a database.

Another frequent source of problems is related to naming conventions for the market data subjects of interest. There are two major approaches to naming the subjects. One can be called the "first principles" approach, where any subject name is constructed from known elements, such as the instrument name, publisher name, broker name, and so on, according to some predefined rules. If this approach is followed and both subscribers and publishers adhere to the same set of rules, each subscriber can construct all the subjects it needs from first principles, such as the instruments and sources it is interested in. Our previous futures price example follows this approach: the subject name TYZ7|CBOT_FEED1 is made up of two elements known in advance, the instrument name and the data feed name.

The advantage of the first principles approach to subject naming is conceptual clarity and readability, but it is not without problems. The first problem is the need for close coordination between subscribers and publishers, as both have to agree on naming conventions. The second problem is the proliferation of subscription subjects. If a certain instrument is traded by three brokers, and they can show quotes for it on two different pages each, a subscriber who wants to see all available quotes will have to construct at least six different subject names to prepare for all a priori possibilities. In reality, only one or two of those will have some data at any given time, so the rest of the subjects will be simply deadweight, and in systems following this approach, these deadweight subjects often greatly outnumber the "real" ones.

Finally, the presence of instrument names in the subject names is a disadvantage when the instruments change as a result of an on-the-run or futures roll. For example, if TYZ7 is the front future today, but tomorrow the front contract becomes TYH8, everything that needs to know the front contract price will have to start subscribing to a new subject name. This widespread problem is often addressed by goading the data feeds into publishing futures and on-the-run prices using a logical name such as TY_FRONT or 10Y_OTR instead of the actual instrument name, but that usually requires nontrivial enhancements to the data feed logic.

Because of these considerations, the second approach to naming, which can be called "inquiry-based," is now gaining ground. In an inquiry-based approach, the subscribers have a way of asking the publishers about the subject names for particular bits of data they are interested in. The publishers can then name the subjects anything they want, following any naming convention (which they do not have to share with anyone), and send the resulting names in response to a query by a subscriber. In this naming approach, the TYZ7 prices could be published on a subject called 3895Z44_03, and that subject name will be internally associated with TYZ7. A subscriber asking for TYZ7 prices will be given this subject name, but if someone asks for front contract prices (and this happens to be the front contract), the same name will be returned. While the subject names in this approach are often completely undecipherable (which sometimes complicates maintenance and support), they are guaranteed to be consistent between subscribers and publishers, and subscribers need far fewer of them.

Another set of issues that often complicate the operation of market data systems is performance-related. It is fairly obvious that a poorly written subscriber can be overloaded by incoming market data messages. What is perhaps less obvious is that the presence of the data manager as a centralized dispatcher of messages can amplify the problems of a single client into a systemwide outage. When a client becomes CPU-bound, it is no longer able to process all market data updates coming its way, and in many systems the data manager takes it upon itself to store these updates in a buffer until the client recovers and is able to process them. If, however, the client never recovers, this buffer can grow without bounds and impair the performance of the data manager itself, affecting all other users of the market data platform.

The usual way of dealing with this "slow consumer" problem is continuous monitoring of data manager buffers or queues and forcible disconnection of the offending slow consumers. The developers of market data applications need to keep in mind that their code has the potential of bringing down the entire market data platform, even if it looks completely innocuous (sometimes stopping your program in the debugger can have interesting side-effects in a real-time system).

The opposite of a slow consumer is an overactive publisher. If a publisher suddenly goes berserk and begins to publish some subjects very frequently, the data manager can be overwhelmed, and all other publishers and subscribers can be affected. An especially dangerous scenario is when the outputs of the berserk publisher are used by other publishers; their publishing rate also increases dramatically, resulting in a "market data storm" that again has the potential for bringing down the entire platform.

The solution to market data storms is, again, continuous monitoring of the health of the data manager and the whole market data network. Typically there is a dedicated market data group within the technology organization whose job it is to perform such monitoring and other necessary maintenance of the market data infrastructure—deploying and configuring market data software, and periodic restarting of the data manager, data feeds, and other components. Their other functions may include maintaining relationships with data vendors and responding to user problems.

People working in such market data groups need a thorough understanding of the system's complex technology, as well as a reasonably good grasp of the kinds of data published on their system. These groups usually do little software development themselves (what they do is mostly limited to adapting vendor software to the needs of their firm), but they often play an important support role to the community of developers from other areas that use market data in their applications, especially at the design stage. They also are playing an increasingly important role in applications support as more and more of the in-house software becomes market data–enabled.

In general, the growing importance of market data technology for financial institutions is largely following the same path as database technology in the late 1980s; at that time, much of the disparate internal data was moved en masse into relational databases, while today we are witnessing the process of moving a lot of those same data to real-time data platforms. This trend is likely to continue, and anyone working in the industry is increasingly likely to become either a user of real-time data or a "processor" of it in a development or modeling role. The next chapter, on trading systems, illustrates this trend by showing how a market data platform can become a mechanism for integrating disparate applications.

CHAPTER 15

Trading Systems

You may have noticed that many of the trading activities that we described in the second part of the book are repetitive tasks that invite automation, and indeed much of Wall Street technology is directed at making the trading process less labor-intensive and less error-prone, as well as more profitable (and more enjoyable). The technology created to facilitate trading (which is our catchall definition of *trading systems*)[1] is very diverse. It evolved from pencil-and-notepad-based approaches to modern algorithmic trading systems in little more than 20 years, and this adolescent growth spurt is continuing unabated. Unlike other branches of Wall Street technology, the trading systems area has experienced very little standardization up to now, so parts of it that are a single system in one place can be three separate systems in another, and newcomers to this field are often overwhelmed by the sheer number of (and nonobvious relationships among) such systems. This chapter intends to shed some light on this complex but very interesting area.

In order to make some sense of the bewildering variety of trading systems, let us begin by reviewing the life cycle of a trade. This life cycle in fact begins before the trade is made, with the idea of a trade forming in someone's mind. From the perspective of a broker-dealer, this can be called the *trade solicitation* stage, and it is very important; trade ideas are often planted in the minds of buy-side customers by sell-side salespeople, but giving customers attractive technology tools that make them want to trade can play the same role. The solicitation stage ends when the customer makes a trade

---

1. In some books for the day trader market, the term *trading system* has come to mean what Wall Street traders refer to as a "trading strategy": a set of rules that tell what to buy or sell and when. At the risk of disappointing some of my readers, I must state up front that this chapter is not about such trading strategies (although we will briefly discuss one).

inquiry, and this triggers the next stage in the trade life cycle: that of *pricing* the proposed trade. Many trade ideas end right there because the customer does not like the price, but many other trades turn from ideas into actual trades when the customer accepts the dealer's offer and the trade is *executed*. The newborn trade enters the conveyor belt that ultimately turns trade tickets into money. First the trade needs to be booked, which generally means entered into the firm's trade databases and recorded in one of the trading books.

After this *booking stage*, the trade's life begins to evolve in two directions. One of them leads to the settlement of the trade: it has to be communicated to the back office and entered into the settlement and payment systems, which will then make the agreed-upon payments and initiate delivery of the securities involved. Note that for derivatives trades such as swaps, years will pass before they are fully settled, so settlement is a process and not a one-shot action. Settlement and the related processes (netting and clearing) deserve a chapter if not a book of their own (and we will point out some in the Recommended Reading section), but in this book we will mostly focus on the other aspect of the trade's life, which remains within the front office. The trade has an impact on the traders' positions and on their risk, so from their point of view, after the trade is made, it enters the stage of *position and risk management*, where in a certain sense it remains forever. To recap, a trade goes from solicitation to pricing to execution to booking to risk management, and all trading systems can be categorized by the stages in this trade life cycle in which these systems are involved.

Armed with this simple methodology, let us now go through the typical trading systems that are in a broker-dealer firm and discuss what each of them does. In this process, we will use Figure 15–1 as our road map (I will refer to this figure constantly throughout the chapter, so you may want to copy it and have it in front of you as you go through the text). First, a quick recap of the broker-dealer business model (you may turn to Chapters 2 and 3 for more detail): a broker-dealer firm is like Janus, with two faces, one directed at its buy-side customers (the left side of Figure 15–1), and the other turned to exchanges and interdealer brokers (shown on the right side of that figure).

In its broker capacity (mostly in equity and futures markets), a broker-dealer takes orders from buy-side customers and executes them on external exchanges; we can visualize this by imagining an order originating on the left in Figure 15–1, flying through the broker-dealer layer (between the two thick vertical bars), and hitting the exchanges on the right (note that there

FIGURE   15–1

Typical trading systems in a broker-dealer firm.

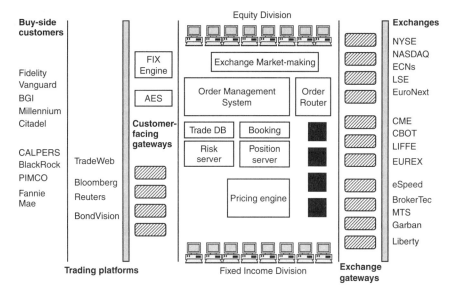

is also information flow in the other direction as the execution results are reported back to the originating customer). In its dealer capacity (in most fixed-income and FX markets), the broker-dealer takes the other side of customer trades; the trades still originate on the left, but they never cross the right vertical bar in Figure 15–1, which represents the boundary between the firm and its exchange/broker partners. The firm can also initiate trades on exchanges on its own, so orders may cross the right boundary here even if nothing comes in from the left side.

TRADE SOLICITATION SYSTEMS

We are now ready to start our review of trading systems, beginning with those that help with the trade solicitation stage; these are generally known as *customer connectivity* systems. The traditional approach to trade solicitation is twofold: one-half of it is salespeople calling up customers and plugging various trade ideas, while the other half is establishing a good relationship with customers so that whenever they want to trade for their own reasons, they turn to the salesperson who takes good care of them rather than to his competitors. The first approach tends to produce infrequent but large and juicy trades that are often somewhat complex and difficult to automate. The second, however, results in frequent small and simple trades, which, in the old scheme of things, the salesperson still had to handle. Whenever a customer needed to adjust her hedge, she would call up a salesperson and ask for a quote on $10 million five years; the salesperson then had to ask the traders for the price, book the trade, and so on, and this would happen 35 times a day—a perfect example of a repetitive task that was amenable to automation.

Since the early 1990s, every dealer firm has attempted to automate this kind of trading by giving customers the option of executing these run-of-the-mill trades electronically. This is generally done by giving the buy-side customers some desktop software that (1) allows them to see real-time prices for the products they care about, and (2) allows them to execute trades at those prices without the salesperson's involvement. On the dealer's side, this software connects to a dedicated server program, which is usually called a *gateway*; its job is to handle message traffic between the customer and the dealer, as well as to take care of housekeeping tasks such as customer authentication (in Figure 15–1, these are represented by boxes in the "customer-facing gateways" column).

The client-side part of the trading software allows clients to log onto the gateway, load a list of securities that they are interested in, and, for each of those securities, see the live bid and offer prices submitted by the dealer or routed from exchanges. Clicking on a security in such a trading screen opens up a trade ticket, where the customer can fill in the order (i.e., specify buy or sell and the size) and click a submit button; this will send an order to the dealer's gateway. Once the order is received by the gateway, it is passed on to other parts of the trading systems universe, which can execute it, and the results of the execution (like how much was filled, at what time, and what price) are sent back to the gateway, which in turn forwards them to the originating customer.

In the early days, each dealer had its own such system talking its own language, so that a typical buy-side trader had to run a different trading application for each dealer he wanted to trade with, and this quickly became unmanageable. In the equity markets, this quandary was solved by getting all such systems to speak the same language; that language is known as the *FIX* (Financial Information eXchange) protocol. FIX standardizes the format of the messages that fly back and forth between various parts of trading systems. A FIX message is a set of name-value pairs representing various pieces of a trading order, such as size and price, but instead of using human-readable strings for names, it uses integer codes called FIX *tags*. For example, instead of saying "Price = 100" and "Total Size = 5," a FIX message would say "44 = 100" and "38 = 5" (Figure 15–2 presents some of the more ubiquitous FIX tags and a few sample FIX messages).

FIX started out in 1993 as a communication protocol used by Fidelity to send orders to Salomon Brothers, and over the next few years it became

F I G U R E   15–2

The FIX protocol uses numerical tags for common fields in order-related messages, and for some of these fields enumerates their possible values. The field-value pairs are held together in a message either by a separator (# is used in this example, but it does not have to be; in fact, ^ is more common) or by more elaborate means, such as XML tags (there is an XML version of FIX called FIXML).

FIX Tag	Meaning	Values	
1	Account	T3191	
11	Client order ID		2897393
35	Message Type	A = LOGON	
		D = NEW ORDER	
		3 = REJECT	
		8 = EXECUTION REPORT	
		W = MARKET DATA	
38	Order Size		200
39	Order Status	0 = NEW	
		1 = PARTIALLY FILLED	
		2 = FILLED	
40	Order Type	1 = Market	
		2 = Limit	
44	Price		27.01
54	Order Side	1 = buy; 2 = sell	
55	Symbol	MSFT	‑

New order: buy 200 shares of MSFT at 27.01
1#T3191#11#2897393#35#D#38#200#39#0#40#2#44#27.01#54#2#55#MSFT

Order Acknowledged
1#T3191#11#2897393#35#8#38#200#39#0#40#2#44#27.01#54#2#55#MSFT

Order Filled
1#T3191#11#2897393#35#8#38#200#39#2#40#2#44#27.01#54#2#55#MSFT

so widely adopted by both buy-side and sell-side firms that at present almost all equity order flow between dealers and customers is FIX-based. This allows buy-side clients to have a single order entry screen that can send order messages to any dealer, and it allows the dealers to handle all incoming order flow through a single gateway, which is usually called the *FIX engine*. As the FIX protocol grows and expands, more and more order types are being handled this way (for example, FIX version 4.4, the latest as of this writing, added a lot of features for fixed-income and derivatives markets), so its future looks bright and secure. However, there are still cases in which buy-side clients use a dedicated non-FIX application to trade with the dealer, of which the most common are various AES (advanced execution services; see Chapter 6) order entry systems.

Interestingly, the fixed-income markets (which generally are a few years behind equities as far as electronic trading systems are concerned) found a completely different solution to this same problem of a single customer wanting to trade with multiple dealers through a single application. That solution came in the form of TradeWeb, a company formed in 1998 that inserted itself between the dealers and their customers as a *trading platform*, which is a set of servers hosted by TradeWeb to which both customers and dealers can connect and through which they can trade (see Chapter 5 for more details about TradeWeb's business model). TradeWeb offered buy-side customers a single application for trading with multiple dealers, effectively achieving the same result as FIX did in the equity space, and it quickly destroyed the various proprietary single-dealer trading systems that existed at the time. A company called BondVision offers similar services in Europe, and in the last couple of years Bloomberg has also entered this business (leveraging the fact that everybody runs its desktop application anyway, so they might as well trade through it).

TRADE PRICING SYSTEMS

All these trading platforms provide their users with software through which they can connect to the platform's servers and see live quotes submitted by the dealers for various fixed-income instruments (the list today includes U.S. Treasuries, euro governments, U.S. and European agency securities, mortgage-backed securities, and even OTC derivatives such as interest-rate swaps). Generally, if a buy-side client wants to trade on one of these quotes, all she has to do is click on that quote and a trade ticket will open. What happens after that depends on whether the quotes are *firm* or *indicative*.

Firm prices mean that the trade request is automatically executed at the price seen in the trade ticket if the size is within agreed-upon limits—the dealer cannot reject the trade or change the price. Indicative prices mean that when the client hits the submit button, a *request for quote* (called RFQ) is sent to the dealer (or dealers in the case of multidealer platforms like TradeWeb). The dealer responds with a quote, which may differ from the indicative price depending on the size of the proposed trade (as well as on who the customer is). The software that handles these RFQs on the dealer side can either determine the quoted price automatically (for small trades) or route the request to a trader if the size is large or if the request is unusual in other ways (for example, a nonregular settlement date). The trader can then adjust the price accordingly or reject the query altogether.

The responses from the dealer(s) are then sent back to the customer and displayed on her trading screen, and she has a few seconds (called *on-the-wire time*) to select between competing responses (if any) and decide whether to accept the trade at all (note that this gives the customer a valuable time option, which is a source of concern for many dealers). Once the customer clicks accept, the trade is final. The RFQ-based (or *inquiry-based*) systems are generally more popular with both dealers and customers for a number of reasons, such as the possibility of manual intervention in large trades, but they involve more back-and-forth communication and require more complex logic on the systems side.

While buy-side clients generally are happy to use the trading screens provided by TradeWeb and its brethren, for the dealers the task of interfacing with the trading platforms is significantly more complex. The dealers have to submit real-time quotes for all instruments they wish to trade, which generally requires them to maintain some kind of real-time pricing system that determines the levels at which they are willing to buy and sell at any given moment and publishes these prices on the firm's internal market data network. To get these quotes to an external trading platform, the dealer needs a gateway that on one end connects to the firm's market data network and reads the firm's real-time prices, while on the other end it connects to the trading platform and submits buy and sell quotes based on these prices. The gateways therefore have to interface with the trading platform's software in order to submit quotes and track their status, and to that end the trading platforms provide application programming interfaces (APIs) that allow the dealer's gateway processes to do all these things.

Because all these APIs are different, the dealers have to write different pieces of software to create gateways for each of their trading partners, which can easily number in the dozens (especially in Europe), and keep this software in sync with the changes made by these trading platforms. This translates into a massive development effort on the dealer's side. To reduce this development and maintenance burden, a European company named ION provides consolidation services; it takes on the burden of interfacing with each individual trading platform in the fixed-income area and gives the dealers a single API for their software (MarketView), through which they can trade on any of the ION-supported platforms. MarketView is now a de facto standard for gateway development in the fixed-income area.

A customer-facing gateway often encapsulates some fairly complex business logic that goes far beyond forwarding price updates. First, it needs to determine which prices to send to what customers. When it responds to an RFQ from a specific customer, it takes prices from the internal market data network and adjusts them by applying a customer-specific bid-offer spread, which may also depend on other factors, such as market volatility. Another type of price manipulation that often happens on the gateway level is pricing of spread, butterfly, and other combination trades. The gateway finds prices for each security involved in such trades and calculates the quoted value (yield spread, for example), again applying some customer-specific adjustments.

However, the gateway's main task is to handle the flow of outgoing quotes and incoming orders, and this task is often highly nontrivial in its own right. For RFQ-based systems, each trade inquiry can go back and forth several times, and the gateway needs to keep track of the many versions that are coming through it. At any given time, it can have several queries for the same instrument on its hands—for example, one for a small size that is being negotiated automatically, another for a much larger size that is being manually handled, and yet another perhaps as part of a spread trade—all with different prices and at different stages of the negotiation process, and managing all of them can quickly get quite complex.

For firm quote–based system, the order-handling logic is even more convoluted; for these types of quotes, one has to enumerate all the quotes that have been sent out to the trading platform and keep track of each order's *state*. When the gateway submits an order, the platform acknowledges receipt of the order, and the state goes from submitted to accepted. The order can then be canceled by the platform, canceled by the submitter, filled, partially filled, updated with a new price or new size, combined with another order, and on and on. The logic that the gateway follows in order to manage order state is typically implemented as a *state machine*—effectively a huge if-then-else statement that says that *if* the order is in state X, *then* here is a list of things we can do with it. This kind of code is a nightmare to debug and maintain, which helps explain why gateway development is such a labor-intensive process.

In the equity world, where the order management logic is much more standardized, there is a tendency to take this logic out of the gateways and place it in a centralized *order management system* (or OMS), as shown in Figure 15–1. In this approach, the gateways merely forward the order messages to and from this central order processing facility and thus become stateless and therefore much simpler. The flip side of streamlining the gateways is that the central order management system becomes very large and complex. A large broker-dealer processes hundreds of thousands, perhaps several millions, of equity orders every day, and it may be handling tens of thousands of orders at any given instant—although many of them do not result in trades, they still need to be shepherded through all the stages in the order's life, from submission to acknowledgment to potential modification, cancellation, or execution, so the central order management system has a big job to do and often is the logical center of all trading technology in an equity trading shop.

Incoming orders have to be stored in the system's internal data structures (and usually also persisted externally in case the system crashes), and for every incoming order message, the system has to quickly find the corresponding order and update its state. Last but not least, orders that are done (i.e., that have been either executed or canceled) have to be removed from the system. The order messages generally come at the system from three directions: in Figure 15–1, these would be right, left, and top. The messages coming from the left are client messages; clients can submit, modify, and cancel their orders. Messages coming from the top are from the firm's traders and salespeople, who may execute customer orders or submit their own. Finally, messages coming from the right are from the *exchange gateways* that connect the firm with the stock and futures exchanges (and with interdealer brokers in the fixed-income world). These gateways usually work the same way as the customer-facing gateways we have already discussed; they send the order flow to the external execution platforms, which reply with order messages reflecting the state of those orders. The actual connection to the exchange may either be FIX-based or use a proprietary API, and the gateways may or may not perform some order management functions.

In the equities world, where a single stock is usually traded on multiple exchanges, an additional system called the *order router* often is inserted between these gateways and the order management system; it tries to route the outbound orders to the exchange that appears to offer the best price at that moment. Interestingly, the order router is almost always called a smart order router, or SOR; this does not imply the existence of stupid order routers (which could use the same acronym), but rather refers to the increasingly complicated logic that these routers employ in trying to find the best execution conditions.

One task that is unique to exchange-facing gateways is the provision of market data, which are essentially information about orders submitted by others. The electronic platforms of the exchanges allow their users to subscribe to a list of instruments and receive very detailed market data messages about those instruments, often containing not just the best bids, offers, and trade information, but also order book information with varying degree of completeness. The exchange gateway on the dealer side reads this information and republishes it on the firm's own internal market data network. This kind of market data is often called a *direct feed*, as opposed to the more traditional way of obtaining market data, where a third party such as Reuters deals with the exchange to collect market data from it and then distributes those data to its Wall Street customers, who pay (hefty) market data fees for this service. Third-party market data are almost always significantly slower (and often less detailed) than what is provided by such direct feeds, so this market data distribution function of the exchange gateways is very valuable to the firm—so valuable, in fact, that in many cases the firm runs two exchange gateways, one for the order flow and another *view-only* version that does not trade but only receives and distributes market data.

TRADE BOOKING SYSTEMS

The orders moving through all these gateways and systems ultimately want to become trades. If a trade is executed outside the firm on an external exchange, the firm simply forwards an execution report to the customer (and collects a commission). If, however, one of the traders inside the firm takes the other side of a customer order (or trades on an exchange), the trade needs to be entered into the *books and records of the firm* (this is an official term from a compliance perspective), and this is the task of booking systems, which are also shown in Figure 15–1.

Booking systems predate electronic trading by at least a decade and played a seminal role in the trading systems area in general. Many first-generation trading systems started out as *trade blotters*, which initially were just what the name implies: electronic replacements for the paper blotters on which trades were recorded in the olden days (until the mid-1980s generally). A trade blotter presents a trader with a screen on which she can enter, one trade per row, the details of each trade she does, and where she can see the list of trades done today. The trade details to be entered include the ID of the security, the book to put the trade in, the type of trade (buy or sell), the settlement date, the counterparty, and, of course, size and price. This presents a significant data entry burden, so many trade blotter systems attempt to simplify this process by using standard GUI means such as drag-and-drop, picklists, context-sensitive defaults, and the like.

As trade blotters evolved to make entering trades easier, they often acquired rudimentary real-time pricing capabilities as well—it is very convenient for the trader to have the system come up with an approximate price once a security is entered so that he can adjust the price if necessary instead of having to figure out what the price should be. Thus trade entry systems often graduated from mere data entry to being the main pricing tool for the desk. From there, position and risk management features often followed, and the lowly trade blotter evolved into a full-fledged trading system integrated into a single application.

In the early days, the trade blotter usually was the only way in which a trade could be entered into the firm's *trade database*. After the trade details were entered, the blotter performed some basic data validation and wrote the trade into the database (the database assigned the newly entered trade a trade ID, which the blotter also usually displayed). In modern trading systems, the trades done electronically are also booked electronically as part of straight-through processing (STP), which is a catchall term for technologies used to integrate the trade messages with the back-office systems. Usually the booking system (or booking engine), as shown in Figure 15–1, becomes a server process that talks to the execution systems such as gateways and/or the order management system and puts all electronic trades into the appropriate books (there should always be something in the order message that allows the booking system to figure out where to book the trade: the book either is explicitly specified or can be inferred from the trader/desk name). In this server-based booking scheme, the trade blotter on a trader's desktop can still be used to enter trades manually, but mostly it is used as an electronic window into the trade database that shows the trader the list of trades (both voice and electronic) done in her book(s). We will discuss trade databases and related issues in a bit more detail at the end of this chapter.

As we mentioned, early trading systems often had rudimentary real-time pricing capabilities integrated into a booking application that ran on each trader's desktop. A later trend has been toward server-based pricing systems that generate and publish real-time prices for everything that a trading desk is interested in. Unlike the old arrangement, where each trader maintained his own set of prices, server-based systems provide real-time prices that are shared by everybody over the market data network. Such pricing systems in fact go way beyond just prices and typically also calculate all kinds of derived quantities (yields, durations, asset swap spreads and in fact all types of spreads imaginable, theoretical prices from various models, and so on), so the data record published at every price tick often contains dozens if not hundreds of numbers. The users—traders, salespeople, and other front-office folk—can see all these data, displayed either in special GUI applications designed to work with the pricing system or in spreadsheets that subscribe to the market data network. These same prices are used by trading gateways to trade on the external electronic markets, as well as for calculating real-time PnL and risk. How do such pricing systems work? This is an interesting question; we will address it using fixed-income markets as an example, but the systems used for market making in options (and cash equities) follow a similar logic.

As we discussed in Part 2 of the book, a defining characteristic of the fixed-income markets is a two-tiered structure in which we have, on the one hand, a relatively small number of extremely liquid and frequently traded securities and, on the other hand, a large number of securities and derivative products that are much less liquid and trade relative to the first-tier liquid products. The core of each fixed-income pricing system therefore consists of some mechanism for pricing the liquid products (which are often called *actives* in this context): Treasury and German bond futures, Eurodollar futures, and the Treasury on-the-runs.

On one level, pricing a liquid product such as Treasury futures is easy; we can simply look at where it is trading on CBOT (by looking at the market data feed from the exchange) and say that we are willing to make the same market that we see on the exchange (which means that our bid is equal to the CBOT bid and our offer is equal to its offer). The rationale for this is the idea that if someone buys the futures contract from us at our bid price, we can turn around and hit the CBOT bid to buy that contract there at the same price (this is "at-cost" market making). Typically, in addition to the bid-offer prices, we also want some measure of a mid, or fair price (mostly for PnL purposes). The typical choices for the mid price are either the midpoint between the observed bid and offer or the last trade price. So as a first approximation, a system that simply reads live market data for all liquid products and (after minimal processing to add a mid price) passes them through to the firm's internal network would largely do the job. This is a very good example of the rule that in almost any project, the first 10 percent of the effort gives us 90 percent of the benefit—to improve upon this simplistic market data–driven pricing system for liquid products, we have to work hard and be really creative.

It is not obvious why this system needs improvement until we actually begin to trade on the prices produced by the system. Then we quickly discover that no-cost market making is harder to pull off than it seems. Since our first-approximation pricing system follows the exchange or broker markets, it is by construction always a bit behind them; the amount of the lag between a market move and the time we update our quotes in the external electronic markets can vary from a few tens to a few hundred milliseconds (or even a few seconds in some of the less nimble systems). It is surprising how often people will trade with us on prices that we can no longer hedge because the source market has moved away.

This lag, plus the occasional market data problem, almost guarantees that we will lose money trading on these prices (although probably not a lot of it). One approach to solving this problem is to make our system faster, which is a good thing in any market (we will talk some more about this later on). The other approach, which is specific to fixed-income markets, attempts to get the pricing system to lead the market instead of following it by recognizing and exploiting the fact that everything in the fixed-income world is very highly correlated. In its simplest form, this approach can be illustrated by the following example.

Suppose we are making a market in two securities: an on-the-run 10-year Treasury and the Treasury note futures contract. Any trader will tell us that these two securities usually move together, so if we observe the futures trading up, we may want to take that into account in our pricing of the 10-year note—we may want to raise our offer and/or improve our bid in anticipation that the next price tick on the 10-year will also be up. Converting this example into a working algorithm, however, is not trivial. As usual, the devil is in the details: how to quantify the correlations between price movements, when to use this correlation-based information to adjust prices, how much to adjust them by, and exactly how to adjust them.

The answers to all these issues need to be thought through, resolved, implemented, tested, and maintained. This is where the other 90 percent of the effort goes in developing pricing systems for liquid securities, and the success of this effort very often makes the difference between the P and the L in the trading PnL of electronic trading. Because of this, a lot of resources are now being devoted to this area, from fundamental market microstructure studies to the magic of technical analysis (or pattern recognition). As you can imagine, predicting the next market move is not easy.

Let us assume for now that we have mastered the pricing of the liquid products—what about pricing the rest of the fixed-income universe? There are several choices for pricing fixed-income products that fall in this second liquidity tier. All of them involve using the live prices for at least some of the actives, but they differ in what additional inputs are used to get at the final prices. The first and simplest of them is what I will call a trader-driven model, which means that the only additional information used by the model is inputs from the traders. The most common example of that would be pricing a corporate bond or an agency as a spread to a Treasury on-the-run: the trader types the spread into some kind of pricing GUI (typically a spreadsheet or a spreadsheetlike application that is used to view and control the live prices); the pricing system reads this input spread, adds it to the live on-the-run yield, and gets the live yield for the target instrument, which is then converted into price. Usually the traders also specify the bid-offer spread to be applied to that final price, so this mechanism provides a very simple but consistent algorithm for calculating a set of tradable prices or yields for almost anything that can be rigidly linked to a liquid product or a set of products.

Note that live pricing of swaps also falls into this category. In the United States, swap rates are by definition the on-the-run Treasury yields plus swap spreads, which change fairly infrequently, so the traders simply maintain a set of swap spreads that they believe reflect the market conditions, and the pricing system recalculates live swap rates by adding these spreads to the interpolated Treasury yields every time the Treasuries move. In Europe, people use German bond futures as active instruments that drive the swaps curve; the set of inputs maintained in this case varies but generally is equivalent to maintaining a constant spread between each integer-maturity euro swap rate and the equivalent yield on one of the three futures. The short end of the swaps curve is priced using live prices for the relevant short-term interest-rate futures chain (Eurodollars for the U.S. dollar; EURIBOR for euro curves). Note that even in this case, the convexity adjustments subtracted from the live Eurodollar rates are usually put in by the users rather than calculated, so that effectively the short end is also priced as a spread to Eurodollar rates.

The live swap curves produced in this way can themselves be used for spread pricing—for example, we can calculate live prices for almost any bond by maintaining a constant spread to swaps (either a matched-maturity swap spread or an asset swap spread; we discussed these in Chapter 11). Using swap curves rather than on-the-run Treasuries as the pricing benchmark has the big advantage of eliminating the maturity mismatch between a product and its benchmark.

Consider this example: suppose we are pricing a Treasury note with 7 years to maturity, and we can specify a spread to either the 5-year or the 10-year on-the-run. As long as the 5- and 10-year yields move in parallel, the choice of benchmark does not matter, as the yield on our security will move by the same amount as both benchmark yields. But suppose the yield curve steepens, so that the 5-year yield moves up by less than the 10-year yield (let us say they move up by 5 and 10 bp, respectively); given its position on the yield curve, our 7-year note should then move by about 7 bp, but our spreading methodology would move it by either 5 bp or 10 bp, depending on which benchmark we used. We therefore have to keep adjusting our spreads for changes in the curve slope, and this sometimes makes spread pricing a very labor-intensive task. In contrast to this, asset swap spreads do not suffer from this problem, as they automatically incorporate the shape of the swaps curve, so maintaining asset swap spreads is somewhat easier, especially in markets like agencies and corporates, where much of the actual trading is done as asset swap trades.

How do the traders know what the spreads should be? The answer greatly depends on the market. For securities that trade infrequently, there are two components to it: (1) where did this security trade historically (if the trader bought a corporate bond from a customer a couple of days ago at 350 bp over the 10-year, she may be willing to sell it at 340 bp), and (2) what happens to more liquid but similar securities (if the spreads on an actively traded recent corporate issue have widened as a result of credit concerns, the trader may want to widen her spreads on all bonds of that issuer by a similar amount). However, there are securities that trade in the interdealer market, and the spreads observed in the interdealer market are major inputs into the pricing of such securities. This group includes off-the-run Treasuries, some T-strips, European government bonds, U.S. benchmark agencies, and similar issues. In this case, there is a strong temptation to use the interdealer market data to automate the pricing of these securities and reduce the burden of manual pricing. This leads to a second major group of fixed-income pricing models, which I will refer to as market data–driven.

These models take live market data from the interdealer markets and attempt to produce internal prices that are consistent with where these securities trade in the interdealer market.

This usually requires some preprocessing of the market data, as they are almost always relative to an active security, which may be different for different brokers: for example, an agency note can be quoted at 5 bp bid over the 10-year Treasury on Garban and at 55 bp over the 5-year on Liberty, a Treasury note can have a swap box market relative to the 10-year note and a basis market versus the Treasury note future, and so on. To determine whether these quotes are consistent with each other and to establish the best available bid and offer, the market data preprocessor converts all these quotes into *equivalent cash quotes* (the "absolute" prices given the quoted spreads, basis, and other such information and given where the reference active securities are trading right now).

Unlike the quoted spreads, the resulting cash prices move with every movement of the actives, and every time they change, the preprocessor needs to reevaluate all such quotes for all affected securities. For each security, it needs to look at the equivalent cash levels from all available brokers and determine the best bid and best offer for each security. If the best bid is higher than the best offer from another broker, the system should indicate to the traders that the market for this security is *inverted*; this is either an arbitrage opportunity or (more often) a sign of problems with the market data.

The best markets coming out of this preprocessing are then used as one of the inputs in pricing of the corresponding market sectors. Unlike the pricing of actives, where market data are by far the most important factor in pricing, for the less actively traded sectors, relying on market data exclusively is rarely a good idea. First, these data may or may not even be present for any given security, so the pricing logic should be able to price a security even if it is not trading in the interdealer market at the moment. Second, even if the security is trading, it is typically for small size, and if the trader is pricing a large trade, the existence of a puny $1 million bid in the broker market does not necessarily mean much. Third, there may be errors or problems with market data; unlike the situation with actives, where such things are evident immediately, market data problems involving less actively traded issues can sit undetected for hours. Therefore, a critically important piece of market data–driven pricing models is the ability to price a security even if the market data for it are not there or are wrong.

To do that, the model needs to look not just at one individual security, but at its sector as a whole and make use of the *pricing relationships* between securities in the sector. These relationships are typically established on the basis of historical analysis of closing yields and/or spreads and/or their daily changes; for example, we can establish that two neighboring securities have always traded 1.5 bp apart for the last 30 days, so if we see a good tight market on one of them, we can also determine where the other should trade by adding the 1.5-bp historical spread. It is, of course, rarely as simple as this; typically the model establishes some kind of correlation matrix between the relevant securities and uses these historical relationships to fill the gaps in market data inputs. The trader inputs are also used to override the model if it ends up doing something wrong. Overall, these market data–driven models generate prices that are by construction consistent with the interdealer market and make pricing a much less burdensome task for the traders.

Finally, the last major type of pricing models can be loosely called *factor models*. These are based on the idea that almost everything in the fixed-income universe is very strongly correlated, so the movements of any set of securities can be related to changes in a relatively small number of driving factors. More often than not, these factors are identified with the active securities. For example, the movements of the Treasury curve can be to a good approximation related to movements in the five on-the-runs—specifically, yield changes on the day for any Treasury can be represented as a linear combination of changes on the day for the on-the-runs.

The coefficients of this linear combination are called risk factors for each security and can be determined on the basis of either a yield curve model or historical correlations (or a combination of both). Once these factors are known, the factor model can determine the changes on the day (and therefore the live yields and prices) for any security given the market data–driven changes in the active factors. The results of factor models can be used either directly, as official live prices (perhaps after some trader-entered adjustments), or as inputs into market data–driven models to provide a theoretical price that can be used to accept or reject market data inputs (if market data prices are far away from a factor model price, it is almost certainly the market data that are wrong). The main usage of such factor models is not so much for pricing as for risk and PnL attribution, which is why they are present in some form in almost all trading systems.

All these pricing models have a similar data flow, which follows a cascading scheme in which any changes in the prices of actives lead to recalculation of every price that is linked to them. An uptick in the two-year Treasury causes price recalculation for all Treasury notes that are directly linked to the two-year and for all the factor model prices for all sectors in which the two-year is one of the factors; most importantly, the U.S. dollar swaps curve will be rebuilt with the new two-year rate, and then everything that is linked to the swaps curve (potentially hundreds of agency, mortgage, and corporate issues) needs to be repriced as well.

This data flow is naturally represented as a *pricing graph*, a directed graph where nodes correspond to pricing calculations to be performed, while edges are linked to the inputs to and outputs of such calculations. The software implementation of pricing systems is therefore usually built around a *graph execution engine*, a generic piece of software that understands the concept of a graph, keeps track of all nodes and edges, and works as follows. Whenever some of the input data change, this triggers the calculation of all the nodes where the changed data are inputs. If the outputs of some of those nodes have changed as a result of this calculation, and they are used as inputs to other calculation nodes, those dependent nodes are then also triggered, and if their outputs have changed, then their child nodes are triggered, and this goes on until there are no more nodes whose inputs have changed.

This execution engine is also linked with the market data platform so that some of the edges can be associated with records on the market data network; this association implies that the engine will subscribe to those market data subjects that are used as input edges in the graph and will publish the subjects that contain the resulting calculated prices and other quantities. This graph executor can also be thought of as a digital filter that performs a complex transformation of incoming market data messages into another set of market data messages containing prices for the relevant securities.

For a pricing system that handles a large number of securities, the pricing graph is huge—it typically has a half-dozen calculator nodes for each priced security, so the total number of nodes sometimes reaches 10,000. This is usually too much for a single graph execution engine to handle, so the graph is split into several subgraphs (usually by security type or sector, so that agencies will be in one graph, corporates in another, and so on), which are given to several instances of the graph execution engine running on different servers in the pricing server farm. This graph distribution requires another software piece that can be called the graph manager; this is the part of the pricing system that knows about the whole graph, knows how many graph engines are running, and sends an appropriate chunk of the graph to each of those engines. The graph manager program also performs an important data quality assurance function; since it is the only part of the system that is in a position to know which security is priced by what graph engine, it can invalidate prices for all securities priced by a given engine if it goes down or otherwise disconnects from the graph manager.

Generally the pricing graph changes from day to day, and keeping it up to date is not a trivial task. Bonds mature, they move between sectors as a result of aging, new securities are issued, futures roll, and so on—the composition of the pricing securities universe keeps changing. When a bond matures, the nodes and edges that were involved in pricing it have to be taken out of the pricing graph; when new securities are added, the corresponding nodes and edges have to be constructed and added to the graph. These kinds of changes can in theory be done intraday by asking the graph manager to modify the graph and change the affected subgraphs executed by the respective graph engines, but in practice any significant graph modifications usually require restarting the pricing farm.

Because it is difficult to construct the graph dynamically, it is usually prepared through an overnight process that is given a set of rules about which securities are to be priced and what models should be used. This process then generates the entire pricing graph according to these rules and stores it in some kind of persistent storage—more often than not in a flat file or in a specially designed database. At start-up, the graph manager program reads the graph from the persistent storage and goes from there.

The main challenge for this graph generation process is determining the securities universe. This is trivial for governments and swaps, of which there are only a relatively small number, but for things like agencies (of which there are hundreds of thousands) and corporates (which number in the millions), some additional selection rules have to be applied. Usually those rules simply say that if our desk has a position in Security X, we need to price Security X, which requires the graph generator to go to position and/or trade databases to figure out what to include in the graph.

This server-based architecture leads to pricing systems that are huge in scope, often including dozens of graph execution engines running on large server farms, even though 90 percent of what they end up doing is adding a spread to the reference yields. There is also a supporting infrastructure— market data, networks in general, reference data, trade and position providers, various GUIs for the traders to interact with the system, and so on—all aimed at performing the task that the first-generation blotter-based pricing systems used to perform with far less effort.

Aside from their complexity and the associated stability glitches (any issue within any of the numerous supporting areas, such as static data, has the potential to knock out the whole pricing system), the server-based pricing systems suffer from two other problems. The first is a direct result of their design requirement to provide a single set of prices for everybody. Sometimes we do want multiple sets of prices—for example, when we want to perform a *what-if analysis* (*what* will happen to the prices in my sector *if* the 10-year Treasury goes up 1 bp?). This can be trivially done in a spreadsheet or generally in a desktop-based pricing system, but for a server-based pricing system, providing such trader-specific data is an almost insurmountable challenge.

The second issue is performance and speed: because of the modular design of such systems, the processing chain involves several "hops" over the market data network. From the gateway that sees an update to a futures price, the price update hops to the graph execution engine, which calculates the new price and publishes it to the market data platform again, so it takes another hop back to the exchange gateway. Because of all that hopping plus processing delays inside the graph engines, by the time the firm's order is updated on the exchange, it is from several hundred milliseconds to several seconds old. This is generally OK for the purposes of real-time PnL and other internal uses, as well as for trading with relatively unsophisticated customers, but for actively traded securities, this kind of delay makes profitable electronic trading against other dealers all but impossible.

ALGORITHMIC TRADING

Trading systems that are designed for trading in the interdealer markets or on the exchanges simply have to be more nimble, and this argues for a more integrated design in which all stages of decision making, from market data acquisition to order state handling to strategy decisions to submitting orders, are integrated within a single application or a set of applications that communicate through shared memory space or other similarly fast mechanisms. The purpose of such *algorithmic trading* (sometimes also called *statistical arbitrage*, or *statarb*) systems is overwhelmingly proprietary trading rather than customer-driven flow trading, and therefore they generally attempt to make profits by executing a *trading strategy*, a set of rules that define what to buy and sell under which market conditions. I have to be even more vague in this area than in most other places in the book, because the details of such trading strategies (at least the profitable ones) are a closely guarded secret (for this reason, such systems are also commonly called *black-box* systems, and this is how they are shown in Figure 15–1), but there are certain commonalities that we can mention without adversely affecting anyone.

In Chapter 5 we briefly discussed a mean-reverting trading strategy based on the idea that a certain tradable quantity (a butterfly spread in that example) has a stable long-term mean and that any significant deviations from it tend to reverse themselves. Figure 15–3 illustrates the expected behavior of the butterfly spread. To turn this market view into a trading strategy that can be automatically executed, it needs to be presented as an algorithm, and we can illustrate the essential features of such algorithms using a mean-reverting strategy as an example.

The main ingredients of a trading strategy are *entry and exit rules*, which in our case can be formulated as follows. The entry rule: if we have no position, and the current value of the butterfly spread is more than X above or below its mean value M, we are going to buy/sell Z units of the butterfly spread. The exit rule: if we have a position of Z or fewer units of the butterfly spread, and the current value of that spread falls below $Y < X$ on the other side of the mean (see Figure 15–3), we are going to liquidate this position. If all that the spread does is fall below $M - X$ (at which point we buy Z units of it) and then rise above $M + Y$ (at which point we sell those Z units), then these entry and exit rules are sufficient for the system

FIGURE 15–3

How a black-box trading strategy works. We watch the thing we are trading (in this example, it is a 2-5-10 Treasury butterfly), and whenever our entry condition is satisfied (the spread drops below $M - X$ or rises above $M + X$), we attempt to put on a position, which we then attempt to unwind when the exit condition is triggered (the spread rises above $M + Y$ or falls below $M - Y$).

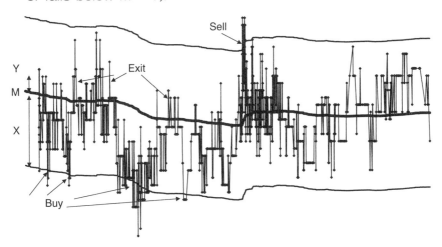

to operate, and it can be expected to produce profits proportional to $(X + Y) \times Z$ on every such trade.

There are two reasons why this money pump may fail to work as expected. One is that the spread may decide not to mean-revert; let us say that it went above $M + X$ and we sold our Z units, and then it just keeps moving against us, away from the mean—what are we supposed to do in this case? The rules that handle such undesirable scenarios are usually called *stop-loss rules*. In our example, this rule may say that if we have a position and the spread moves against us by more than $3 \times X$, we liquidate the position at a loss. While entry and exit rules cover desirable market behavior, the stop-loss rules should cover all other possibilities, so that the system knows what to do no matter what happens (for example, one of the stop-loss rules may simply be that if a position has been held for more than T hours, we liquidate it—an easy way to ensure the completeness of our set of rules).

The parameters of this trading strategy can be fine-tuned using a process called *back testing*, which, exactly as its name implies, consists of checking how a strategy would have performed in the past. We need good-quality historical data for such back testing (in fact, this is one of the main reasons why trading firms spend so much money and effort on maintaining a decent set of historical data), as well as some type of simulator to apply the strategy rules to historical spreads and collect statistics on how the strategy would have performed. Such simulations are then run for different values of strategy parameters (the most important are entry, exit, and stop-loss thresholds) to see which combinations work (produce positive PnL) and which do not.

Back testing is an important sanity check for a trading strategy, but even if something seems to work during back testing, it may still fail in real life. Part of the reason for this is, as any mutual fund TV commercial tells you in small type at the corner of the screen, that past performance is not a guarantee of future results; but the factor that we will focus on, execution quality, is usually far more important and is often decisive in the ultimate performance of algorithmic trading systems.

When the trading algorithm decides to buy something at a price X where it thinks that something is currently trading, the system will issue a set of orders for the trading platforms it is connected to (if what we are trading is a spread of some sort, these orders generally involve buying and selling more than one security). Ideally, these orders are instantly and fully executed, and our cost of establishing the desired position is in fact equal to X, just as we planned, but in reality we will almost always pay more, for two reasons: First, the market may have moved away between the time we saw the data that caused us to make our trading decision and the time our orders actually reached the trading platform. Second, we may not be able to execute the whole amount we want at the current price. The first problem can be somewhat mitigated by making our system as fast as possible (that is why, as we mentioned, these systems are typically optimized for speed), but the second requires significant creative effort. An algorithmic trading system has to be prepared for imperfect execution and deal with it in an intelligent manner depending on the market conditions.

The following example can illustrate the problems that arise in this area. Suppose we are trying to buy a spread between two securities, which involves buying a certain amount of one and simultaneously selling a weighted amount of the other, and the market is falling rapidly. We will probably be able to buy the thing we want fairly easily, but selling into a falling market can be difficult, and we may fail to execute the sell leg of our trade at the price we wanted, so we end up having a long position in the first security and no position in the second. The system has to decide whether to just let the situation be (which is likely to lead to a loss on the long position in a falling market), try to sell the second security more aggressively (which is likely to lead to a loss by selling lower than we wanted to originally), or try to get rid of the long position in the first security that we just bought. Finding a good cost-effective solution to situations like that usually requires more programming and intellectual effort than the entry/exit logic of the underlying trading strategy, but it is essential for the ultimate profitability of the trading system.

Because of the relative complexity of the execution layer that deals with imperfect execution issues, it often make sense to use this layer to run more than one trading strategy; for example, the same execution layer can be shared by a strategy that trades butterfly spreads between 2-, 5-, and 10-year Treasuries and strategies that make markets in each of those three securities. An interesting dimension in such multistrategy systems is the possibility that they may want to trade with each other—for example, the butterfly strategy may want to buy the 5-year at the same time that the market-making strategy wants to sell it. In theory, the execution layer can then *cross* these trades internally, without sending the orders to an outside trading platform. This would make the execution faster and also save the commission and trading charges that you would have to pay on external platforms.

The next step in using an algorithmic execution layer for internal crossing is to show other traders in the firm what the system wants to do in the hope that they may want to take the other side of some of these trades. We can also give those traders a GUI application that would allow them to submit the orders they want to do to this *internal crossing engine*, whose job becomes to try to match the orders submitted by both human traders and automated trading strategies; those that do match are then executed in-house, while the rest are passed through to the appropriate external platforms. By some estimates, between 10 and 20 percent of all trading flows inside a major trading firm can be internalized in this way, so these internal crossing systems (which are sometimes called *internal brokerages*) are becoming increasingly popular. This is an example of how technologies developed for proprietary trading find usages outside that area.

TRADE AND POSITION MANAGEMENT SYSTEMS

We have spent most of our time in this chapter talking about pricing and execution systems: those parts of the trading systems universe that are designed to generate new trades. There are equally important parts of that universe, however, that focus on managing trades that have already been done, and we will briefly touch upon these systems in the remainder of this chapter, beginning with trade databases.

Trade databases are among the most critical pieces of the firm's infrastructure, as they are the source of all the information required by the back office to settle trades. While the implementation and data models used by such databases vary widely, the trade data themselves are always handled with utmost care and backed up often, replicated across locations, and otherwise safeguarded from accidental loss and/or corruption. One way in which the trade databases protect their integrity is through the use of a specially designed software layer that all client applications have to use to communicate with them (direct SQLing into trade databases is rarely allowed). This software layer plays the role of an API that supports trade entry and trade retrieval and is usually called a *trade management* system or something similar.

Another software system that works closely with the trade management system usually performs *position management*. Since the trade database contains the full list of trades done in each book, it is in theory possible to recalculate positions at any time based on those trade records, but that would be wastefully inefficient; instead, the position management layer keeps track of the positions on an ongoing basis (this process is often referred to as *aggregation service*) and stores them separately from the trade records (although the positions and trades are usually reconciled periodically). This, of course, makes sense only for things such as stocks, bonds, and other identifiable securities, where you can always combine trades done at different points in time into a single position in that security; as we discussed in Chapter 8, trades in swaps and most other derivatives (except exchange-listed futures and options) cannot be aggregated.

Aside from the trade entry systems and electronic posttrade feeds that we have discussed already, whose job it is to record the newly executed trades, the trade and position management systems have another important set of clients that work in the other direction: front-office systems that calculate risk and PnL for each trading book and display the results to the traders. As we discussed in Chapter 5, the risk profile of a trading book should tell the trader what will happen to the PnL of that book if each of the risk drivers changes. A trader should be able to define the risk drivers (a set of actively trading securities that are used to hedge the book) and then see how much risk she has in each of those drivers in a display similar to what we showed in Figure 8–10.

The traders spend much of their day watching these risk numbers because, unlike everything else they see on their displays, the risk numbers tell them what to do next—they tell them what to buy or sell to eliminate the risks they do not want. Risk changes with each new trade, but it also somewhat depends on the price movements (because the relationship between prices and rates or yields is generally nonlinear), so it may change slightly even if no new trades come in. If we neglect this weak price dependence, calculating the risk numbers will not require real-time prices.

Risk calculations ideally should be performed in real time. This is fairly easy to do for trading books that contain only cash products, where all trades can be consolidated into positions; in this case, one can determine the risk factors (the sensitivities to changes in the drivers) for each security ahead of time (usually overnight), so that all that has to be done in real time is to multiply the real-time positions provided by the position management system by these risk factors. All that is really needed to perform this calculation in real time is position information, and here "real time" can mean different things—typically most booking systems have a delay of up to a few seconds between the time the trade execution is confirmed and the time it is actually booked into all the proper databases and picked up by the position management service. This delay between committed positions and booked positions is a source of much difficulty for systems that use position or risk information to make trading decisions, and therefore some systems try to tally up positions themselves based on execution messages that come before the actual booking, making their risk as real-time as possible.

For derivatives books, the risk calculations are much heavier; they involve building discount curves using the "bumped" values of the risk drivers and repricing all cash flows in a book using these bumped curves (and, where appropriate, doing a similar perturbation analysis on the volatility structures required to price the book). Given that large books can contain hundreds of thousands of individual cash flows and a similarly large number of individual option positions, these risk calculations often require hours of number crunching, which is impossible to do in real time. This work is instead done overnight by batch jobs that calculate risk and PnL for derivatives books given the closing prices of the previous business day and produce official risk and PnL reports.

Real-time risk systems usually only process today's trades in real-time and add their risk to the risk of all previous trades, which has been laboriously calculated overnight. Real-time PnL calculations generally follow the same principle; they start out with the results of overnight PnL processing and add the PnL of today's trades to that. Note that if the risk of the book is known, calculating PnL is easy, as it is simply a scalar product of the risk weights in each driver times the change on day of the drivers. This approach is, of course, based on linearization of the book valuation problem, so PnL calculated in this way is approximate; the full book valuation is performed overnight and may produce slightly different results from the real-time calculation based on the previous day's risk factors. Note that unlike risk calculations, intraday real-time PnL depends on the availability of both real-time and closing prices, so a single missing closing mark can completely mess up the PnL of every book that has a position in that security.

THE IDEAL INTEGRATED SYSTEM

In the next chapter, we will return to the discussion of risk from a somewhat different viewpoint. To conclude this chapter, however, we step back and ask the following questions: Is it possible to have a single trading system that would cover all trading needs, from trade entry to electronic trading to risk management to automated strategy execution? Why do traders have to run a half-dozen different applications: one for trade entry, many specialized GUIs for trading with each broker and exchange, one to view and control prices, one for risk and PnL, plus perhaps a couple of spreadsheets that run their pet pricing models or build the curves in their own special way?

The reason for the industry-standard hodgepodge of disparate trading systems is, as with almost everything else, historical: different pieces of the trading systems puzzle were built by different people at different times. It is rare for business users to want to replace all parts of their trading infrastructure at the same time, so typically they will identify, say, trade entry and say, "This is our weakest area, so we want to have a more modern replacement built for that." Two years later, they replace the risk system, and so on. Keeping all these disparate pieces working together is a major challenge for in-house technology developers, and once the level of complexity of the existing arrangement increases beyond a certain limit, people start thinking seriously of replacing the whole mess with a single system, or perhaps a suite of systems that can seamlessly talk to one another.

There are three main things that are needed to make this integrated ideal work. The first of them is a common data model. Different parts of the trading system should think of a trade, or a bond, or a price, in the same way, using the same software objects to represent common trading objects throughout the system. Part of that common data model is a shared database for storing trades and related objects whose design reflects the data model used by the software pieces. Since existing trade databases or reference data systems rarely conform to the new design, it often becomes necessary to make a local copy of static data and/or trade records, and this copying should continue on an ongoing basis. The second requirement is not strictly necessary, but is extremely helpful from the user's point of view: all user-facing applications (pricing and trade blotters, risk displays, and so on) should have the same look and feel and the same basic set of controls.

Finally, the communication between different parts of the system should be standardized—the objects passed over the messaging platform should reflect the internal data model. This makes the resulting system easily extensible and makes it possible to construct it in stages, which is usually the only way an integrated system can become reality. At the first stage of its deployment, the new integrated system will replace one piece of the existing infrastructure, for example, trade entry. Once all the issues related to the decommissioning of the old trade entry system have been shaken out, the integrated system can take over another function. The whole process can take a couple of years or more and can be painful at times, but this is the way of the future.

In conclusion, I realize that this introduction to the trading systems area has been very superficial. It is very difficult to do better than this in a field that is so diverse and fluid and growing so rapidly. This rapid growth, however, guarantees that many of my readers either are working on trading systems or will be at some point in their careers. Given how little else has been written about the issues and challenges of this area, I have reason to hope that our discussion was useful to those who are considering moving into this field, and that it may have clarified a few things for those who are already working there. Whether it worked as intended or not, we simply have no more time to spend on this topic, and we move on to the next chapter, on risk management.

CHAPTER 16

Risk Management

Risk management is one of the most overused terms in the English language; in today's usage, it can mean anything from nuclear nonproliferation to birth control. In this chapter, we will talk about the meaning of this term in the context of the financial industry, where it is (thankfully) somewhat more specific: the risk that is being managed is *financial risk*, or, in plain language, the risk that the organization will lose money.

Figuring out how much money a large financial organization can potentially lose is not an easy task, and it requires a great deal of both technology and quantitative talent. A large percentage of the Wall Street quantitative workforce is employed in various risk management–related pursuits, and there is so much buzz about risk management in the financial press that in the minds of many people both inside and outside the industry, this term has begun to represent the whole of financial technology—a point of view that we shall attempt to dispel in this chapter. We will argue that, despite the avalanche of books, articles, and Internet resources devoted to risk management, it remains part of a larger whole—an important and growing part, but not, as yet, an utterly dominant part.

To prove this point, and, more generally, to educate the reader about this field, we will focus on explaining what risk management is and, just as importantly, what it is not. Our plan is to go through common risk management activities from the perspective of a dealer bank and discuss their business purposes and technological challenges. This discussion will be directed primarily at technical readers who are new to the industry and want to get a feel for what people working in risk management actually do, although I hope that the latter group would also find it useful (or at least would enjoy a few historical tidbits, which I am about to provide).

THE HISTORY OF RISK MANAGEMENT IN THE FINANCIAL INDUSTRY

Prior to the 1970s, risk management meant buying insurance and taking other similarly prudent measures to safeguard property (fire safety rules were thus viewed as a risk management tool). The financial industry did not really have a good understanding of the risks associated with either commercial banking or the securities business. This began to change in the 1970s, and, interestingly, the change originated on the commercial banking side, which had not previously been known as a fount of innovation. During that period, violent swings in interest rates brought some banks in the United States to the brink of collapse; the management of those banks could not understand what had hit them, but at least some people in the banking community started asking questions like, "What would happen to our financial results if the Fed raised rates by another 1 percent?"

The commercial banks faced the very practical question of how much money they needed to set aside for reserves to ensure that those reserves would be large enough to cover possible losses, and the first stirrings of modern risk management were in this area. In 1974, following an unpleasant incident with a German bank called Herstatt,[1] a group of bankers and banking regulators formed the so-called Basel Committee on Banking Supervision, which for the first time attempted to quantify the risks faced by commercial banks and to provide recommendations for dealing with those risks. It took the Basel Committee until 1988 to actually issue such recommendations, which became known as the Basel Accord. This set of regulations, now called *Basel I*, dealt mostly with how to allocate regulatory capital (we'll explain what this is later in the chapter), but it did require banks to set up some organizational structures that would look over the financial position of the bank as a whole and monitor its exposures. These entities were the seeds of modern risk management organizations.

Meanwhile, on the broker-dealer side of the industry, a derivatives revolution was taking place. As we discussed in Chapter 8, early derivatives were often designed as ways to circumvent government controls and

---

1. The German banking regulators closed down Herstatt in June 1974. On the morning of the day it was closed, the bank received large deutsche mark payments from several New York banks as settlement for the foreign exchange trades done a day earlier, but by the end of the day the bank was officially insolvent, so it never delivered the offsetting U.S. dollar payments to the New York banks. As a result, those banks did not have the funds to pay some of their counterparties, who then failed on some of their trades; this chain reaction went on for several days and seriously spooked both the banks and their regulators.

other regulations. Few people in the 1980s understood (or cared about) the risks associated with financial derivatives, but as their volumes grew into the trillion-dollar range by the early 1990s, some people (most notably the Fed in the United States) started to worry about these risks. It was at this time that the term *risk management* really entered the financial industry vocabulary—conferences were held on the topic, promotional pens were distributed, and so on.

Despite the fact that most of the theoretical work underpinning modern risk management practices was done during this period (the late 1980s into the early 1990s), largely by the research departments of major Wall Street banks, few big banks understood the need to put this theory into practice. This changed rather abruptly in 1994, when an unexpected upswing in interest rates led to huge losses for most Wall Street banks; as this disaster was unfolding, risk management proponents had every right to say, "We told you so," and the top Wall Street management largely got their message. Some banks, such as J. P. Morgan, actually were using fairly systematic risk management procedures already, and, under pressure from its customers, in late 1994 J. P. Morgan released a service called *RiskMetrics* that allowed its clients (and just about anybody else) to use its internal risk management methodology and data. RiskMetrics was a huge public relations success for J. P. Morgan, and the timing could not have been better, coming as it did right before Wall Street announced its disastrous 1994 results and almost at the same time as the famous Orange County bankruptcy (see Chapter 8). Because of this, RiskMetrics and its underlying value-at-risk methodology played an important role in the development of the risk management field.

However, the imperative to limit losses was just one of the reasons why Wall Street warmly embraced the idea of risk management post-1994. After a series of highly publicized financial failures linked to derivatives, Wall Street realized that it had to do something to address its image as the purveyor of snake-oil-type shady derivatives deals, or the whole derivatives business—a major profit center for the industry—would wither and die.

The response of the industry was nothing short of brilliant: Wall Street relabeled derivatives as risk management tools. The argument was that, yes, these products are risky, but if used correctly, they can offset other risks that their clients have. A lot of derivatives salespeople started calling themselves risk managers; their job now became helping clients analyze their risks and suggesting appropriate risk management products to offset those risks. This approach has done wonders to improve the industry's image—and, by the way, the derivatives business *really* took off after that. The increased prominence of risk management has at least as much to do with this marketing tactic as with a genuine desire to understand and limit the risks inherent in the banking and securities business. We will, however, focus on the latter.

THE FUNCTIONS OF RISK MANAGEMENT

What are the problems that modern risk management organizations are trying to solve? As we discussed in Part 2, the traders in the front office typically think of risk in terms of "What will happen to my PnL if the market moves in a particular way?" In many ways, managing such risks is what traders do all day, but each trader sees only a small part of the overall picture. In contrast, the mandate of the risk management organization is to aggregate risk across business units and, ultimately, the whole bank, and to express it in simple terms that senior management can understand. The managers of each business unit need to know how much risk their traders are taking (and how much money they are making), while the people at higher levels in the organization need to make sure that the bank as a whole has enough capital on hand to withstand any reasonable market adversity. Senior managers also may want to make sure that the amounts of money their business units are making are commensurate with the risks those units are taking. Risk management is a catchall term for activities that make it possible to see this kind of big picture.

There are two major components of risk management. One can be called *risk measurement*; its subject matter is calculating risk measures based on current positions across the whole bank according to some agreed-upon methodology. The other is *risk enforcement*; this involves setting some limits on how much risk can be taken by the bank as a whole, by each division, by each business unit, and on down to the level of the individual trader, and then making sure that those limits are not exceeded.

Risk measurement is, in essence, a back-office technology function; its tools are software and database systems that crunch the daily numbers and produce risk reports for the enforcing side. Risk enforcement is a business function; setting risk limits, monitoring compliance with those limits, and dealing with instances of noncompliance requires a completely different set of skills from what is needed on the risk measurement side. The organizational structure varies among banks, but typically there is a risk management group (or sometimes even a full-blown division) of perhaps a few hundred people, headed by a *risk committee* and a *chief risk officer*. For each *risk-*

taking unit in the bank (meaning a trading desk and various conglomerations thereof up to the trading division level), there is a *risk manager* whose job it is to make sure that her risk takers do not get out of line. The risk management technology organization works for those risk managers in the same sense as the front-office technology organization works for the traders. Sometimes there is also a thin layer of risk analysts who act as intermediaries between risk managers and their technology units. Risk analysts help risk managers understand the risk reports and the methodology used to produce them, and help the technology units understand and implement this methodology. There is an increasing tendency to absorb this advisory function into the technology side of risk management.

Another function that is often absorbed into the risk management structure is *operations and product control*. This area is what used to be called the back office; its job is to make sure that trades get settled, trade breaks are investigated and reported, new products are set up in the reference data systems, the trade support hotline is manned, and so on. These activities, of course, long predate the emergence of modern risk management organizations, and the current tendency to incorporate these back-office functions into the larger risk management framework is due to the growing awareness of the importance of *operational risk*, which can be defined as the risk of screwing up the operational issues involved in settling trades (failing to receive payments or securities in exchange for payments).

There is a more sinister side to operational risk; this term covers losses from the unauthorized trading activities of *rogue traders*, which, as we know from the Barings debacle,[2] can bring down even a large bank. The new version of the Basel Accord (Basel II) explicitly calls for banks to quantify their operational risk (and set aside capital to cover it), and in response many banks have changed their organizational arrangements to make operations part of the overall risk management framework. The importance of this for our narrative is mostly that a lot of back-office systems that used to be outside of risk management technology now are being absorbed into it. Operational risk joins the more traditional risk categories that the risk

---

2. Barings, one of the oldest British banks, had to declare bankruptcy in early 1995 after its head of futures trading in Singapore, Nick Leeson, accumulated an almost £1 billion loss on his unauthorized trades. Leeson was able to hide his unauthorized trading losses for years because he was also in charge of the back office in Barings Singapore. He was betting that the Nikkei stock index would rise and had accumulated a huge long position in Nikkei futures. Instead, he got the Kobe earthquake—the Nikkei index plunged, and he got margin calls for hundreds of millions of pounds that the bank could not meet. This story has been used as justification for expanding risk management organizations ever since.

management organizations are dealing with: *market risk* (the risk that market movements will adversely affect the value of the bank's positions) and *credit risk* (the risk that one of a bank's trading counterparties defaults).

THE RISK MANAGEMENT PROCESS

The job of risk managers begins when the traders' job ends. Once the traders have closed their books and gone home for the day, the risk management process takes the end-of-day positions as inputs and processes them into various risk measures, which are then distributed to relevant people, analyzed, and perhaps acted upon. The first step in this process is to produce *daily PnL reports* for each trading book. Generating such PnL reports is perhaps the oldest part of the financial technology: it was there not just before risk management, but even before personal computers (and in fact is still done on mainframes in a lot of places).

For cash trading books, the process is relatively straightforward; the software generating the report reads all security positions in the book from the positions system, reads all closing prices for those securities from whatever system is used to store them, reads a list of all trades done in this book from yet another system (the trade database), and calculates the mark-to-market value of the book as a scalar product of closing prices times positions. The change in the book value less what was paid for each trade is the daily PnL. Note that doing all of this is still quite convoluted technologically (access to several different systems is required), but it is trivial from the computational point of view.

This cannot be said of the derivatives books; these are typically valued by calculating the net present value of each trade, given the closing values for the underlying securities and some volatility information. First, there are often a lot of trades—large books can contain tens of thousands of deals, and determining the value of each requires some valuation model (hopefully, but not necessarily, the same for all deals in the book), which can be as simple as Black-Scholes for equity options and as complex as Monte Carlo–based term structure models for interest-rate derivatives books.

These daily valuation runs, where position and trade databases meet valuation models, amount to a lot of repetitive number crunching, and it is no small challenge to complete those runs on a timely basis. Traditionally, the target time was the next morning, but since the next layers of the risk management process may require the results of those book-level valuation runs, the time requirements for daily book valuation have now been compressed to perhaps a couple of hours after the close. It is a sign of true valor for the technology organization to be able to generate so-called *T + 0 PnL reports* that are ready within an hour or so of the closing time, as opposed to the more traditional reports, which are distributed the next morning (and are called T + 1 PnL reports in this context; they also show the overnight interest, or *carry*, and are therefore different from the T + 0 reports).

This is one area in which performance optimization is crucial, and a lot of effort goes into optimizing the valuation models, but there are also interesting technological approaches that can be usefully applied to speed up the daily valuation grind. Since these calculations are easily parallelized, a popular solution is to distribute these runs across a large number of computers; some banks maintain large server farms just for this purpose, while some other systems cleverly take advantage of the fact that most desktop workstations in the bank sit idle at night and distribute these calculations across people's workstations.

No matter how they are optimized, these daily valuation runs are by far the largest computational job done in a financial organization on a daily basis, and it would be a shame if their only output was a single PnL number for every book. Usually it isn't; even the most antiquated mainframe systems produce a breakdown of PnL into trading PnL, position PnL, and carry, and the more modern systems tend to generate a host of other numbers and display them in a *PnL attribution report*. Such reports attempt to explain the PnL in terms of the contribution of various market movements to the overall PnL number. In Figure 16–1 we show a mock-up of a PnL attribution report for an interest-rate swaps book that shows that for the IRS_1 book, out of the daily PnL of −$49,000, $79,000 was due to the trades done that day, and the rest was due to market movements: −$155,000 was due to the changes in swap rates, $28,000 was due to the movement in the Eurodollar futures, and so on.

Actual reports can be much more elaborate and break down the PnL by a host of other factors (by counterparty, by country or currency, and so on), but their common feature is that they generally require calculating not just the PnL, but also its *sensitivities* to various market factors, which are determined by repeating the valuation many times with different values of the input market data and then taking the difference of the results. Calculating these sensitivities is sometimes delegated to a separate process that runs either in parallel with or after the valuation run proper and is sometimes referred to as the *risk run*.

FIGURE 16–1

Sample PnL attribution report, which breaks down the daily PnL of each book into explanatory components.

Business unit:		Interest-rate derivatives		
Date:		1/31/2006		
Currency:	USD			

Books	IRS_1	IRS_2	IRS_3	SWPTN
Daily PnL	**−$49,045.68**	**$74,115.24**	**$7,569.13**	**−$16,513.03**
Market moves:				
Eurodollars	$28,339.87	$3,288.12	−$92,300.00	$8,344.78
Swap rates	−$155,663.09	$45,576.87	$18,823.15	−$20,387.90
FX changes	$0.00	$25,990.23	$0.00	$0.00
Vol changes	−$3,398.88	−$739.98	$2,833.56	$43,229.32
Rate resets	$2,546.13	$0.00	$4,358.58	$0.00
Trading	$79,551.17	$0.00	$73,881.17	−$53,405.17
Amend	−$493.00	$0.00	$0.00	$5,477.90
TOTALS:				
Explained	−$49,117.80	$74,115.24	$7,596.46	−$16,741.07
Unexplained	$72.12	$0.00	−$27.33	$228.04

These sensitivities (for example, deltas of an equity derivative book) are often more valuable for downstream risk management systems than the PnL numbers themselves, and it makes good sense to store them somewhere so that these downstream systems can get at them. Therefore, most daily valuation systems write the results of their computations into another database (often called the risk database). In fact, the primary driver for saving the results into a database is the desire to separate the calculations from the actual generation, printing, and distribution of the resulting reports; the report generation process can simply read data from the database and does not have to calculate anything. The book-level risk reports are usually distributed to each trader in paper form, but increasingly this is being replaced with a Web-based distribution where reports are often generated on the fly and can be endlessly customized.

RISK-BASED PERFORMANCE MEASUREMENT

Book-level risk reporting really serves traders more than risk managers, and its overall focus is on, "How much money are we making?" Higher up the risk management pyramid, the focus shifts to "How much do we stand to lose?"—rather than wanting to know the sensitivity to each risk factor, management wants to know how much money its trading units can realistically lose tomorrow or this week (note that the focus shifts not only from optimism to pessimism, but also from past to future). A related but subtly different question is, "How much capital do we have to have on hand to survive any reasonable adverse event in the markets?" Comparing the answers to these questions for each business unit with the PnL of those units is called *risk-based performance measurement*; the idea is that the best performers make a lot of money per unit of risk, so if some unit begins to make 10 times more money but takes 100 times more risk, this is not a desirable development. Over the last 30 years, the financial industry has developed well-established procedures to answer these kinds of questions, and we proceed to review them in the next few pages.

The most common measure for estimating likely losses is the *value-at-risk* method, widely known by its cool acronym *VaR*. The term *value-at-risk* was first used in the 1993 Group of 30 report on financial derivatives, but the concept itself has been used since the mid-1980s in a number of large U.S. banks, most notably Bankers Trust (now part of Deutsche Bank) and J. P. Morgan for almost a decade prior to that (J. P. Morgan's RiskMetrics service did much to popularize the VaR approach).

VaR is a very simple and powerful concept. To understand it, let us first assume that we have a portfolio consisting of a single security (say, IBM stock). We know the current price of IBM and its volatility, and therefore we can construct a distribution function for the stock price at any forward horizon. For short time horizons (the typical VaR horizon is either 1 day or 2 weeks, which is 10 business days), we can neglect the difference between the normal and lognormal distributions and simply say that the price will be normally distributed around its current value with a standard deviation equal to daily price volatility times the square root of the number of days in our period (Figure 16–2); let us say that this standard deviation comes out to be $1. If someone now asks us what is the probability that we will lose less than $1 by the end of our period, we can recall our college statistics and say that it is 84 percent (the value of the cumulative normal distribution at one standard deviation below the mean)—for any given dollar amount of losses, we can read the percentage chances that we will lose less than that amount of money right off the normal distribution function.

VaR asks a slightly different question: what is the loss that we will not exceed with the probability X? The answer is simply the inverse of the nor-

FIGURE 16–2

Value at risk: Using the distribution function for the value of
your portfolio at some forward horizon (for example, 10 days
from now), you go down the value axis until you find the
point where the probability that your portfolio is going to be
worth more than that is equal to a specified number (say,
95 percent). Value at risk, or VaR, is the difference between
that worst-case limit and the current portfolio value.

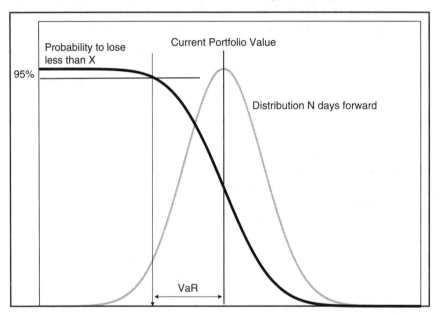

mal distribution function: for the commonly used 95 percent probability, VaR
is 1.645 standard deviations (or $1.65 in our example), and the 99 percent
VaR is $2.33 (of course, if our distribution function is not normal, these
numbers have to change). To summarize, we specify (1) a portfolio of securities, (2) the time horizon, and (3) the probability quantile, and, once we
have established the distribution function for the value of our portfolio at the
end of our period, VaR is the dollar amount of losses that we will not exceed
with the given probability. For example, if the 99 percent 10-day VaR of a
portfolio is $1 million, our loss over the next 10 days should exceed $1
million only on one out of 100 trading days.

For more complicated portfolios, such as realistic trading books, the
only thing that changes in this VaR recipe is how to get the forward distribution function for portfolio values. For cash products such as stocks, this

is fairly straightforward if we know the variance of each stock in the portfolio and the covariances between all these stocks. Since many financial products are very highly correlated, the covariances are very important—where do we get them? We can estimate the covariances based on historical price movements, or we can buy covariance matrices from third parties that compile such data (BARRA is a popular provider).

Even when the covariances are all known, for a portfolio of 10,000 stocks, we are looking at a covariance matrix with 50 million elements that we have to sum over—a nontrivial amount of work even for modern computers. To simplify such portfolio distribution calculations, people often *factorize* the correlation matrix. In most markets, we can find just a few factors that explain most of the observed behavior of all assets in the market (for example, three factors, level, slope, and curvature, typically capture over 95 percent of what a yield curve can do), and by expressing the price of each asset as a function of these few factors, we can evaluate the variance of the portfolio using just the covariance matrix between the factors. This trick dramatically reduces the computational complexity of VaR estimates with very small loss of accuracy and is therefore widely used.

Another common approach is to take historical prices for each stock and calculate the value of a given portfolio on each day in the last X years; this operation is only linear in the number of stocks and gives us a good-quality empirical distribution function for the portfolio value, which is exactly what we need for VaR. Another version that is kind of in between these two tricks is to use a Monte Carlo simulation of prices with a given covariance matrix, which also produces an empirical distribution function much more efficiently than the full-blown covariance analysis. Either way, in the case of "linear" portfolios, all we get out of these computations is, effectively, a normal distribution that is fully described by its standard deviation, and any VaR measure is simply that times a coefficient like 2.33.

The situation is a bit more complex for derivatives portfolios. The value of many derivatives contracts is highly nonlinear in the price of the underlying, so that even if the underlying prices are normally distributed, the derivatives book can have a weird distribution function, often highly asymmetrical. Since VaR is really about the tails of the distribution, approximating such nonstandard distribution with Gaussians is generally not a good idea. People do it anyway, because doing a full-blown VaR simulation for a large derivatives portfolio is just not feasible computationally. Instead, the derivatives are replaced with their deltas (this is where the deltas calculated during daily valuation runs come in very handy), and in this linearized version, calculating the VaR of a derivatives book is exactly the same as the VaR calculation previously described for cash products.

Sometimes the calculation includes not just deltas, but also gammas (second derivatives); this quadratic approximation is known as the delta-gamma VaR model. Nevertheless, conceptually VaR works for derivatives just as well as for simple products, and it allows risk managers to compare the riskiness of vastly different businesses objectively—nothing is more objective than a dollar amount of the possible losses.

There are many reasons why VaR has become so popular: unlike many other risk measures, such as position limits or stop-loss limits, it is a forward-looking measure that also accounts for the common practice of hedging. A well-hedged book has a small VaR even if the nominal positions are very large because of anticorrelation between the positions and the hedges. If we mishedge our book, the VaR will be unusually large, and we will spot it immediately, hopefully before we incur large losses. And, of course, the conceptual simplicity of VaR is an asset: when the risk committee tells the CEO that our 10-day 99 percent VaR is $120 million, most CEOs can understand that this is how much money the company can lose if something bad happens, even if they do not understand the underlying methodology.

VaR has conceptual drawbacks; it tends to overestimate the benefits of diversification. It will always say that the risk of a large portfolio is much smaller than the sum of the risks of its components because they are not perfectly correlated and thus will partially offset each other. This may very well be true under historically normal market conditions, but in reality, when market crashes happen, everything seems to move the same way—the correlations may suddenly become almost perfect, and we may end up losing several times as much as we expected based on VaR calculations. People understand that, and try to come up with other measures that represent the impact of an extreme adverse event. For example, we can say that it is very comforting that the VaR of our equities division is only $70 million, but how much would we actually lose if *all* U.S. equities drop by 20 percent tomorrow? What if the whole Treasury curve rallies by 100 bp over the next week? What if the dollar/yen exchange rate goes up by 20 percent?

The art of asking and answering such questions is called *scenario analysis*, or sometimes *stress testing*. Conceptually, answering such questions is fairly easy; all we have to do is revalue the portfolios we care about using the hypothetical "scenario" market data instead of the actual closing levels. However, putting together a software system that allows people to specify a wide variety of scenarios and test them against different parts of the bank's portfolio is a highly nontrivial task. Compared to the VaR calculations, there is much less standardization in this area, so there are few common approaches that we can discuss here; suffice it to say that scenario analysis capabilities are an important part of any serious risk management approach.

CAPITAL ALLOCATION

Another risk management concept that is widely used, especially on the commercial banking side, is *capital allocation*. Very simplistically, if our assets can fluctuate in value, we may want to keep a certain percentage of their value around in a highly liquid form (cash in the vault, for example, or, more realistically, in an account with a Federal Reserve bank)[3] to cover the losses if the value of our assets does go down.

Generally, the riskier the assets, the more capital we want to put aside—how do we determine exactly how much? This is what capital allocation rules are about. Various banking regulators have created many such rules over the years; for example, Basel I rules recommend putting aside 8 percent of the notional value of all corporate bonds in your portfolio, 1.6 percent of the value of the bank loans, and 0 percent of the value of the government bonds to cover our credit risk, plus an amount roughly equal to the 10-day 95 percent VaR of our *trading book* to cover the market risk. U.S. securities firms are covered by another set of rules called UNCR, which specify complex formulas for the required amount of regulatory capital that are similar in spirit to the simple Basel I rules.

Many banks object to such rules on the grounds that their internal risk management systems provide better measures of risk than the rules promoted by regulators, and currently the regulations permit banks to calculate regulatory capital requirements based on their own methods for evaluating market risk *and* credit risk. The banks, therefore, have to perform these capital allocation calculations for their whole portfolio, and they generally have found it useful to extend such calculations to various parts of the overall portfolio, often down to the level of the individual trading book. As a result, in addition to a VaR number for every business unit, there is also another, similar number (typically called *economic risk capital*) that represents the part of the overall capital requirement that is

---

3. The concept of "capital" for capital allocation is a thorny subject (in most cases, banks can put aside liquid securities in lieu of cash), which we will wisely leave out of this introductory discussion.

allocated to that particular business unit. It is this second number (the capital charges) rather than VaR that is used for internal performance measurements: if the activities of our business unit require the bank to put aside $100 million and we make $20 million a year, our *risk-adjusted return on capital* is 20 percent, and we can be compared with other business units using this metric. Calculating these capital charges is one of the main activities of the risk management organization.

TECHNOLOGY AND RISK MANAGEMENT

Let us now turn to the technology aspects of risk management, or rather measurement. Here's a challenge: our bank has 2,000 trading books, 200 trading desks, and 70 different lines of business that trade every imaginable security and derivative product, and we need to calculate VaR and capital charges for each of those books/desks/businesses every night—how would we go about it?

First, we obviously need not just some methodology for calculating these risk measures, but also a software implementation of that methodology. We also must have supporting data: correlations or historical time series of relevant prices, which can easily number in the tens of thousands, and all of which have to be updated periodically (preferably daily). Then, we need valuation models for every type of product our bank trades (and there are dozens of different types), and these should be not only accurate and widely accepted, but also designed to work with our VaR system (and many of them have to be calibrated every night). While putting all of this together is a huge job, this is the easy part of risk management technology (although from reading the literature about risk management, we may conclude that it's the only part). All of these "quantitative" things are fairly standard across banks, and many if not most of them (especially valuation models) are really outside of the risk management purview; they just need to be adapted for use with risk models.

No, the hard part of risk management technology is not in the valuation methodology—it is in how to get the positions and trade information to which these models have to be applied. No two business units will use the same system for storing their trades and positions: some of them will use multiple systems, the books will close at different times, the same products traded by different desks will go to different position repositories—risk management systems have to sort through this tangled mess, and it is here that most of the time is spent and most of the problems occur.

It is almost impossible to get the risk management analytics to understand the hodgepodge of inventory systems; instead, the position and trade information is usually copied to a centralized risk database in some normalized way that the risk analytics can work with. For each of the several dozen inventory systems, there would be a dedicated *risk feed*, a process that on one end knows the specifics of the source position or trade system, and on the other end knows the data model of the risk database and can convert the information about new trades and positions into this common form.

This is also where corners are often cut to reduce the number of trades and positions that the risk calculations have to deal with. This is done mostly by *aggregating positions* in similar securities (for example, combining all bonds in some maturity sector into one position) and by *bucketing cash flows* of interest-rate derivatives (adding up cash flows from different trades that are due within a certain range of dates, called a *maturity bucket*). The VaR calculations are then performed against this centralized repository, which also usually stores the results. Again, this is a good place to reuse some of the results of the daily valuation runs, especially portfolio deltas, so this process has to be configured to run after the valuation runs have been completed.

The results of this laborious process are then used to produce the risk reports that the risk managers look at. Increasingly, this is done not via paper, but through another layer of technology called a *risk reporting system*. Such a system would have a user interface that allows the user to specify what subset of books, business units, and/or security types she wishes to analyze. It then runs a set of queries against the risk database to retrieve the results and performs *risk aggregation* across the requested business units. Since the VaRs of different portfolios cannot simply be added up because of correlations between the portfolios, the system that populates the risk database has to generate some cross-correlation information as part of its nightly routine to make such risk aggregation possible. It then presents the results to the user in a configurable format (although such systems almost always also support the generation of preconfigured reports).

Risk aggregation, or *collation* (which means the same thing), is the focus of *credit risk* systems. In contrast to market risk systems, which try to measure risk resulting from market price movements, credit risk systems try to measure risk related to default by a counterparty. Credit risk is a much less trivial problem on the level of the whole bank than on the level of a single trading book. A typical investment bank can have a variety of exposures to a single large counterparty, such as GM or Ford: its corporate bonds desk can have a $100 million long position in GM bonds, its repo desk may have a $500 million short-term loan to GM, various derivatives desks may have swaps and structured derivatives with GM, and, most importantly, the bank may be in the middle of settling various security and derivatives trades with GM. All these interactions present varying degrees of financial risk in the event of GM's default: the bonds will probably lose most of their remaining value, but the repo loan will be fine because it has collateral posted by GM, and some derivatives positions may actually come out ahead as a result of the default (and hopefully the pending trades all settle as *delivery-versus-payment*, so there is no danger of delivering securities and never getting paid for them).

The task of credit risk management is to know how much is at stake: for every one of the thousands of counterparties, credit risk systems have to compute some measure of the overall *exposure* (that would be credit risk measurement), and the enforcement side would have to establish some limits on such exposure per counterparty per business unit and work with those units to make sure that the limits are not exceeded. Suffice it to say that measuring such credit exposure is a task that is even messier than measuring market risk because it involves two new components: everything has to be sorted by counterparty, and some trades may be collateralized, which reduces if not eliminates credit risk on those trades.

Credit risk enforcement is also a more contentious process than that for market risk. Typically, all new derivatives trades have to receive pre-clearance from the credit risk system, which has to make sure that this new trade will not cause credit limits to be exceeded (note that this requires credit systems to be able to do this kind of what-if analysis). Historically, credit exposure limits and credit risk in general were set separately from market risk limits, and this practice mostly continues to this day; but there is a movement toward consolidating every kind of risk management—market, credit, and operational risk—under the same umbrella, at least organizationally.

This concludes our review of the risk management area, and many of you (especially those who have been exposed to risk management literature) are surely asking at this point if there is more to risk management than this. Yes, there is—there is a lot more detail that we did not even try to touch upon, but functionally the picture presented in this chapter is reasonably close to reality, even if it is far less glamorous than you might expect. Most technical people working in risk management do not manage any risks; they build and maintain a complex infrastructure that makes it possible to measure organization-level financial risks. Some of this work requires a great deal of quantitative modeling, but there is also a great deal of drudgery on the level of systems integration issues. This is one of the messier areas of financial technology, often a patchwork of legacy systems that has to be held together—which, by the way, is why many banks opt for third-party risk management (and, more generally, back-office) systems, and several large software vendors, such as Sunguard, Summit, BARRA, and Imagine, make a comfortable living in this space.

Even the risk managers who are business-side consumers of this technology rarely manage risk—ultimately, the risks are taken and managed by the risk takers in the front office.

The role of the official risk managers in this process is advisory at best and adversarial at worst; their interaction with the risk-taking side is mostly along the lines of "you have exceeded this or that limit" rather than along the more constructive lines of "our models suggest that shifting some of your rates exposure to that sector will position you better while reducing overall risk." This, however, is slowly changing for the better, which will make risk management a far more rewarding occupation. As it is, risk management is an important and growing area of employment for technically minded people, and I hope that our discussion has given you a flavor of what kind of issues you will have to deal with if you end up working in this area.

In our next chapter we move on to another area with a very high quantitative and analytical component, that of research and strategy.

CHAPTER 17

Research and Strategy

Back in Chapter 3, when we discussed the various job roles available to quantitatively inclined people on Wall Street, I mentioned research as a possible career choice. In this chapter we look at research not so much as a career choice, but rather as a technology area. Most people working in research would probably object to this designation, but it is valid nonetheless: the inputs and outputs of the research process, just like those of the risk management process that we just finished discussing, are quite technology-intensive, and research practitioners need to understand the technological underpinnings of their craft in order to be effective. This chapter presents an overview of the main quantitative and technological issues you may encounter while working in a research role, but before we delve into the discussion of those issues, let us briefly go over the business rationale and drivers of research.

THE GOALS OF RESEARCH

The terms *research* and *strategy* both mean something different in common usage from what they mean in a Wall Street context. Wall Street research is not really research understood as an abstract pursuit of new knowledge, and Wall Street strategy is not really what most people understand as strategy. When I first heard clients call me a strategist, I almost turned around to see if perhaps von Clausewitz was behind me on a horse. So what is meant by research on Wall Street? Rather than trying to define it as an activity, let us focus on understanding its goals.

The main goal of the research produced by a Wall Street sell-side firm is to convince the firm's buy-side clients to trade with it by offering these clients some interesting commentary and analysis of market trends and events, coupled with specific trade recommendations. The term *strategy*, or *investment strategy*, sometimes refers to the trade recommendation part of the research output, but there is a growing tendency to use it interchangeably with research (probably because a strategist sounds more dignified than a researcher).

When a sell-side strategist recommends that clients buy Treasuries and sell corporate bonds, it is understood that his firm stands ready to take the other side of the recommended trade, and that may seem like a suspicious contradiction—after all, if a firm believes this is such a great trade idea, why is it willing to put on its exact opposite? This is not as sinister as it looks; the firm is willing to put on this trade, or its opposite (or any other trade, for that matter), because it generally does not care how these trades will perform in the long term; it will usually unwind them a few minutes or even seconds later and make a small profit on the bid-ask spread and/or commissions. Because of this difference of time horizons, it is entirely possible that the client who follows the strategist's advice makes money and so does the strategist's firm.

The advice that the firm's research organization gives to its clients does not even have to be in the form of direct trade recommendations; as long as a firm's research helps the clients make sense of the markets and the economic and political events affecting them, the clients will be inclined to give their business to that firm. At least, that's the theory, and we should note that it works in other ventures. For example, a cabaret singer attracts more customers to a nightclub, and those who are already attracted order more beer as she sings and dances—she does not sell any beer herself, but she is undeniably useful to her establishment. Yes, there is the highly publicized potential for conflicts of interest between the research's stated goal of providing objective advice and the likely impact of that advice on the trading or investment banking revenues of the firm; this interesting topic has been well covered elsewhere, and rather than spending time on it, let us take a look at the mechanics of the research organization.

THE RESEARCH ORGANIZATION

There are three main research areas in a sell-side bank that are usually organizationally independent of one another: *equity research, fixed-income research*, and *economic research*. Equity research is what we hear about on CNBC. The people working there are called stock analysts; each follows a group of companies or maybe larger industries, and their job is to pore over the financial statements and other things that affect the companies they cover and provide equity trading recommendations (all those notorious "strong buy" ratings) and other insights to the buy-side clients and sometimes the media. The area of *credit research* (mostly present at credit rating agencies, but some investment banks have it as well) does exactly the same thing for corporate bonds; it is almost identical to equity research in the content of the analyst's work, but it is directed at institutional rather than retail clients.

The fixed-income research area is much more macro-oriented; it is focused on things like rates, spreads, and supply and demand for interest-rate products, and the people working there try to make sense of the movements of interest rates and various segments of the fixed-income markets, and again give investment advice to their buy-side clients based on their understanding of the market situation. Finally, economic research probably comes closest to the academic definition of research. Investment banks find it useful to maintain their own teams of economists, who analyze the economic situation, make economic forecasts based on this analysis, and generally make sure that the firm knows everything relevant about the economic forces affecting it (I think the fact that such economic research groups exist and the banks gladly pay for their upkeep tells us all not to rely too much on the free economic statistics from the government agencies). Each research area is split into smaller groups (usually by product area or by industry sector, and, of course, by region), which work closely with the salespeople covering this area on the trading side.

I will mostly focus on fixed-income research—this is where the demand for quantitative skills is the highest (and also where I have some firsthand experience)—but much of what I am going to say also applies to the other two areas. For example, all research areas are similar in that, unlike almost all other areas in the firm, their output is not money, but rather information and ideas; when those are put in writing, we get documents that can be distributed to clients, and there are several different kinds of documents.

The most common type of research document is known as a *weekly*; it is a real paper publication that is printed every week, usually on Fridays, and distributed to clients by Monday morning. Each of the several groups working inside, say, fixed-income research contributes what is called a *piece*; this is a document in which the group describes any developments of interest in its area during the current week, complete with charts, tables, and other illustrative materials, and is usually 5 to 10 pages in length. The pieces are submitted to the editors (yes, you can be an editor and work at an investment bank), who copyedit, correct grammar, and so on, and then send the pieces back to their authors for revisions. Once the pieces are OK'd by the editors, they are also reviewed by the compliance people to make sure that the pieces do not say anything untoward, after which they are sent to a production group (or sometimes an outside printer), where all the pieces are put together, printed, and distributed to the clients (the distribution is increasingly being done by e-mailing the PDF version of the weekly).

The weeklies are also distributed on trading floors and are put in conference rooms and reception areas (in the hope that a client coming in for a meeting will pick one up and read it). If you work in a sell-side bank, reading one of these freely available weeklies is one of the best ways to get a feeling for what research output looks like, and doing this on a regular basis can be a great educational resource: the pieces are usually well written, often interesting and informative, and heavy on market jargon (after all, they are directed at buy-side professionals), which can confer a feeling of being in the midst of the market action while also providing a chance to learn the market terminology.

In addition to the weeklies, there are often also *dailies*, which usually take the form of an end-of-day e-mail describing the trading action and other noteworthy events of the day, perhaps with some mention of tomorrow's events and the related prognostications. Dailies are much less polished and official-looking than the weeklies, and in some areas are written by traders rather than research people. The economics research team typically sends out analytical pieces right after the release of important economic numbers to provide its take on the just-released reports, along with some context and advice. The economics research team often also goes in the other direction in terms of publication frequency and releases a quarterly publication containing a set of its forecasts for all important economic series, such as GDP, unemployment, CPI, federal budget balance, and so on.

Important market events such as auctions, IPOs, and large moves often elicit commentary from the research people covering the affected area. Such comments are typically one to two pages in length, in either e-mail or PDF format; they are edited and compliance-reviewed, so they feel more dignified than the spur-of-the-moment dailies. And then there are pieces describing trade ideas; these are short and have a sense of urgency about them, saying that in view of recent market developments, we believe it is time to sell the corporate bonds in the automotive sector (please see the table at the end of this document showing the quotes for some such bonds from our corporate traders), and replace them in your portfolio with seasoned

Fannie Mae mortgages (again see the table with quotes from our mortgage desk in the back). Add to this the automated reports that some of the models used in research generate at the end of each day, and we get the picture of a steady stream of research pieces emanating from any research group; the quantity and quality of these documents is an important, if a bit mechanistic, measure of the group's performance. If you are considering working in research, what this means is that you will have to do some writing, and quite possibly a lot, so you'd better be reasonably good at it.

THE QUANTITATIVE BASIS FOR RESEARCH

All these writings, however, are expected to have some basis in fact, and this is where quantitative modeling comes in. When a research piece says that we believe that something or other is likely to happen, there should be a "because" clause that explains why we believe that, and that clause more often than not makes a reference to some kind of quantitative analysis of data pertaining to the subject of the piece. In the simplest example, an equity research piece may say, "We believe that Company X is overvalued because we went to the trouble of comparing its P/E ratio to that of every other company in its sector, and it is 210 percent higher than the sector's average"; if we were writing that, we should, at a minimum, be able to (1) find all companies in a given industry sector, probably in our firm's reference data system, (2) determine the companies' current prices from a closing prices database, (3) obtain data about the earnings of these companies, probably from an external vendor like DataStream, (4) divide the prices by the earnings per share, calculate statistics across the sector, and maybe even prepare a histogram of P/E ratios, and (5) write a research piece around this analysis.

In this example, the actual math involved in producing the piece is trivial, but the supporting infrastructure is not—we need access to reference data, closing prices data, and earnings information, all of which the firm makes available to us. As a research analyst, we need to know where to look for the information we need, but we do have a huge advantage over most buy-side clients (and private investors) because we have access to all kinds of data that the firm collects from internal sources and outside vendors (often at great expense). In fact, most of the time it is not analytical prowess but rather the availability of hard-to-find data that gives the research groups inside sell-side banks an edge over their counterparts in other places and allows them to produce a steady stream of interesting and informative pieces that their clients simply cannot produce themselves.

The informational advantage of sell-side research organizations is greatest in the area of historical data: because these banks trade every imaginable financial product, they naturally retain a long history of closing (and sometimes even real-time) prices for just about any financial instrument. This is a great resource for the research organization, and it would not be an exaggeration to say that almost every research piece uses at least some historical data to justify its conclusions and recommendations. How exactly do we use historical data to justify anything? This question is at the ideological center of the whole research enterprise, and we will spend the next few pages answering it.

ANALYSIS OF HISTORICAL DATA

The mathematical toolbox that people use to work with historical data is somewhat grandly called *historical time-series analysis*. Thick books have been written about it (see the Recommended Reading section), but we will review only a couple of ideas out of that toolbox. The first of them is (surprise, surprise) simple *linear regression* used to establish a relationship between two or more time series. Ever since the dawn of modern portfolio theory in the 1950s, academic researchers have used linear regression to relate returns on a stock to returns on the market as a whole; we discussed this in Chapter 6, and I recommend that you go back there and take a look at Figure 6–7, which we will use to illustrate the mechanics of this process.

Hopefully most of you know how regression works, but I'll remind you anyway: you have a vector of numbers y_i that you are trying to explain, and you have one or more other, explanatory vectors (let's stick with one) called x_i that you think y_i depends on—in the "market model" example, the x's are daily returns on the index and the y's are daily returns on the stock. You postulate that there is a linear relationship between the x's and the y's, so that $x = a + by + e$, where e is the error term, also known as the *residual* of the regression. You then determine the values of the regression coefficients a and b in such a way as to minimize the norm of the error vector e (in a least-squares regression, the norm is the sum of the errors squared). Basically, as you can see in Figure 6–7, you plot y as a function of x and try to find the straight line that best approximates the observed cloud of points. This problem is guaranteed to have a solution, and the degree to which the solution makes sense is measured by a quantity called R *squared* (which happens to be the square of the correlation coefficient R between x and y); it shows what percentage of the variability in y is explained by x.

If R squared is 100 percent, y is a straight linear function of x with no errors; if it is zero, using x to explain y simply does not work. The time series of returns to which the regression is traditionally applied has the important property of being a *stationary* time series, which means that it fluctuates around a stable mean (zero in the case of returns), unlike the time series of prices themselves, which is liable to bounce around without any clear bounds. Does it make any sense to apply regression to such nonstationary series? Not in traditional statistics, but the consensus established since the late 1980s among financial market researchers[1] holds that, yes, we can apply regression to nonstationary series provided that the residual of the resulting regression comes out to be a stationary series that fluctuates around zero; if this property holds, the two series are said to be *co-integrated* (and the act of regressing the various financial quantities themselves—prices, yields, economic indicators—rather than their first differences, or returns, is referred to as *co-integration*).

Consider the following example of a Treasury butterfly spread: we take the time series of the yields on the 2-year, 5-year, and 10-year Treasuries, all of which vary all over the place and are therefore nonstationary. However, they move in a very similar way, so that it is possible to form a linear combination of these series that behaves like a stationary series. In Figure 17–1 we show what happens if you take the 5-year yield series and subtract from it 0.46 of the 2-year series and 0.54 of the 10-year series; the resulting combination fluctuates around a stable mean and looks like a stationary series (there are statistical tests that we can run on a time series to see whether it is stationary or not, and what we see in Figure 17–1 passes those tests).

How did we find the coefficients of this co-integrated combination? By regression, of course—I simply regressed the five-year series on the other two series exactly as described earlier. Note that linear regression is a very robust procedure; we can pick any number of arbitrary time series and regress one of them on the others, and it will work in the sense that you will get valid regression coefficients. However, if you do this for randomly picked time series, the residual of the regression will generally not be a stationary process, so the co-integration property is not a given. Why, then, do the Treasury yields in this example seem to be co-integrated?

The residual of our butterfly regression is also a tradable quantity (the butterfly spread) that you can buy and sell by buying and selling the

---

1. Clive Granger and Robert Engle, the recipients of the 2003 Nobel Prize in Economics, started this process in 1987.

FIGURE 17–1

This butterfly spread is a linear combination of the time series of yields on the 2-year, 5-year, and 10-year Treasuries with the weights shown in the table. It is also a tradable quantity; we can set up a position whose PnL will track the butterfly spread (buy the 2-year, sell the 5-year, and buy the 10-year using the weights from the table). The butterfly spread is expected to quickly revert to its mean, so buying it when its value has dropped far below the mean is likely to be profitable.

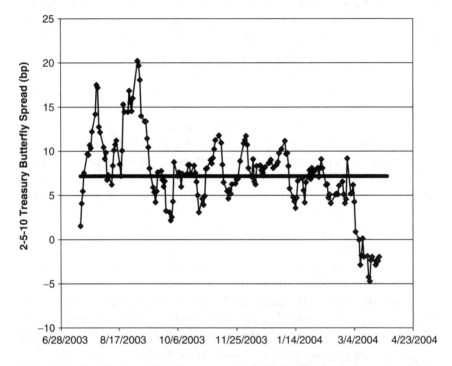

		Spot		1 M Forward	Weights	
	Security	Yield	Price	Yield	Duration-wt	Par Amount
buy 2Y	T 1.625 Feb 06	1.848	99–187	1.880	0.46	1.10
sell 5Y	T 3.250 Jan 09	3.177	100–103	3.199	−1	−1.00
buy 10Y	T 4.250 Nov 13	4.217	100–082	4.234	0.54	0.29
		Spot		Forward	Target	
	Butterfly spread (bp)	−5.0		−4.8	5.2	

body and wings of the butterfly in the correct proportions. Whenever the spread deviates far from its mean, people will start putting on such butterfly positions in order to profit from the spread's expected return to the mean, and in the process of doing so, they will tend to eliminate the deviation. The mathematical fact that the yield series are co-integrated has its basis in this trading behavior, and other examples of co-integrated financial series usually can also be traced to similar behavioral mechanisms. What the sell-side research analysts are often trying to do is to invert this process: by spotting interesting co-integrated relationships, they can try to infer what the market will do and make trade recommendations to their customers based on such predictions. For example, an analyst looking at Figure 17–1 will probably be tempted to write a trade recommendation piece that goes something like this:

> Over the last seven months, the 2-5-10 Treasury butterfly spread has been remarkably stable. Now, however, it has moved sharply below its mean, and we believe that the spread will quickly revert to its long-run average. Therefore we recommend that you put on a position detailed in the accompanying table in order to profit from the expected reversal. For the securities we chose to implement this trade (again, see table), the long-run value of the butterfly spread is +5.2 bp, while the spread currently stands at −5.0 bp (−4.8 bp on a one-month forward basis), and we expect the spread to rally 10 bp to our +5.2-bp target, at which point we recommend exiting the trade. Set a protective stop at negative 8 bp. We will continue to monitor this trade in the coming days.

In reality, the piece would be longer and more polished, but it would contain two essential elements: a chart whose role is to present convincing evidence that the proposed trade makes sense, and a table showing the customers exactly what to do in order to implement the trade. It will not contain any mathematical mumbo-jumbo about co-integration, regression coefficient stability, the sources of data for the analysis, or any other such information, which does not mean that these issues are not important—the customers trust the analyst to get all of these things right, and doing so consistently is a central part of the analyst's craft and a foundation for his professional reputation. Despite the fact that regression and co-integration do not really explain why the trade should go as the piece suggests, for a surprisingly large proportion of the buy-side clients, the arguments that our hypothetical piece employs to make its point meet their burden of proof, and they would be inclined to follow the piece's recommendation and put on the proposed trade (and in this particular case they would have done quite well—the spread did in fact mean-revert within a week, exactly as the piece said it would).

The historical correlation arguments that research pieces deploy do not have to be quite as explicit as they were in this example. Consider Figure 17–2, where we simply plot together the euro/U.S. dollar exchange rate and the 10-year U.S. dollar swap rate. For the period of time covered by this chart, the two series do seem to follow each other closely, and if we did regress one series on the other, the residual would look much like Figure 17–1, but the chart as it stands would be sufficient for an analyst to argue that we are observing an unusual degree of correlation between the foreign exchange and the fixed-income markets in the United States. She may even offer a theory for what is going on, something along the lines of people selling euro-denominated assets (which brings the euro/U.S. dollar line down) and investing the proceeds in U.S. fixed-income assets (which would drive their prices up and rates down), and some clients may find these arguments interesting and perhaps even convincing enough to put on a trade (buy euro and sell swaps) to exploit the gap between the two curves that is opening at the right edge of the chart (which would have performed disastrously; the two lines sharply diverged thereafter). Other clients might consider this argument rather flimsy and would not trade on it, but would still read the piece for its entertainment value—as this example illustrates, many of the daily conversations between buy-side clients and sell-side salespeople and strategists revolve around these kinds of vaguely regression-based observations, which both sides sift through in search of profit opportunities.

Is there anything in time-series analysis beyond linear regression? One interesting tool is known as *GARCH*; it is used to analyze time-dependent volatility. As we have seen in Chapter 9, the volatility of returns on stocks (and almost anything else) is not constant over time (see Figure 9–6). A closer look at the patterns of volatility changes reveals that typically high-volatility periods are more likely to be followed by more high volatility, and vice versa; mathematically, this means that the time series of volatilities (or rather squared returns, which are one-day volatilities) is *autocorrelated* (the next value depends on what the previous values were).

One can easily generate time series that have this autocorrelated property; for example, if we say that the next value of whatever we are trying to model (volatility in our case, or rather its square σ^2) is a linear

FIGURE   17–2

Sample chart from a research piece showing a relationship
between two markets.

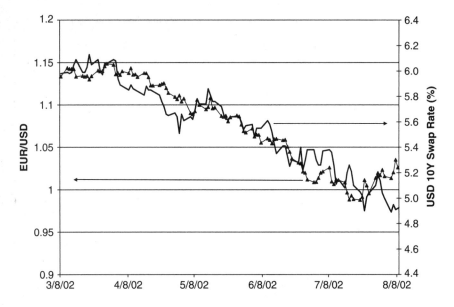

function of our previous value plus a random term ($\sigma_{n+1}^2 = a + b\sigma_n^2 + e_n$),
then the next values would clearly be correlated with the previous ones (this
procedure is called *autoregression*, since the equation linking the next value
with the previous one looks like a linear regression equation, so we are regressing the thing on itself). Now, if instead of a random error term, we take a
series of observed squared returns on a stock (times another coefficient c,
i.e., $e_n = cr_n^2$) and we generate a time series of such autoregressed volatilities, then they will come out to be high during the periods of large market
movements (where squared returns are high) and will decay gradually afterward, which is exactly what we see empirically in Figure 9–6.

   To estimate the autoregression coefficients that best match the
observed series of returns, we use a maximum likelihood estimate: at any
time point, we can ask how likely it is that the observed return r_n^2 would
be produced by a process with the volatility σ_n^2; the likelihood of the whole
time series of returns is the sum of the likelihoods (logarithms of probabilities) of all the points, and we try to maximize that total likelihood by trying
different coefficients a, b, and c until we find their optimum values (many

FIGURE   17–3

GARCH volatility estimate for Microsoft (MSFT). The vertical
bars are annualized daily returns on MSFT stock (absolute
values), and the thick line is GARCH volatility σ_n calculated
with a = 10.5, b = 0.8, and c = 0.15 as described in the text.
The volatility estimate rises when the stock moves around a
lot and falls when it does not. The GARCH line extends
beyond the last data point, providing a forecast for volatility
(it simply decays exponentially to its long-run value).

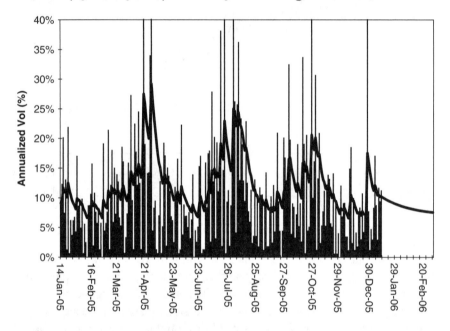

software packages such as Mathematica will happily do this). After this
brief explanation of how GARCH works, we can finally disclose what this
acronym stands for, beginning from the right: CH is for "conditional heteroscedastic," which in English means "something whose volatility changes with
time"; AR is autoregressive; and G is for "generalized" (which does not mean
much of anything), so we get "Generalized Autoregressive Conditional
Heteroscedastic" (model?)—a truly grand name. Figure 17–3 illustrates the
main concepts of GARCH.

I mention GARCH mostly because academic researchers are very
excited about it (Robert Engle even won the Nobel Prize in Economics
for his early research on GARCH); its actual usage in financial markets
practice remains fairly limited (one obvious constraint on its adoption by

sell-side research organizations is that the clients who are able to understand what it is are few and far between). GARCH is used for two things:
it allows us to make volatility forecasts (which are not particularly spectacular, as we can see in Figure 17–3), and it gives us a measure of realized
volatility that makes much more sense than the mindless moving average
of returns shown in Figure 9–6. For day-to-day trading of options and related
derivatives, realized volatility is almost irrelevant, but for longer-horizon
option trades, people routinely compare the observed implied volatility with
realized vol to determine whether they should go long or short. If the implied
volatility is significantly higher than the realized, people will say that
the volatility is rich and that it (options) should be sold, whereas if the
implied vol is much below the realized, they will say that vol is cheap and
would buy options. Having a better measure of realized vol obviously helps
this specific kind of *rich-cheap analysis.*

Rich-cheap analysis, also known as *relative value modeling*, is the second pillar of market research, alongside regression. In our options example,
it was based on historical arguments, but in most cases rich-cheap analysis
is cross-sectional in nature: we take a snapshot of where the market is and
look across the securities universe in search of things that are rich and things
that are cheap. The prerequisite for being able to find these things is the
ability to define what is *fair value* for each security under given market conditions, and this is exactly what relative value models do: they provide a
theory for what each security should be worth. This concept is probably
easier to grasp in the fixed-income markets, where, as we have discussed in
Chapter 8, the theoretical net present value of many securities can be calculated in a consistent way using discount curves.

If we want to treat such net present values as fair values to which the
real prices of our securities should converge, we need a discount curve that
is itself "fair" in some sense—how can we get that? There is no single right
way to do it, but there are certain guidelines that these models generally
follow. The fair curve has to fit the market, but not too closely. For example, a standard swaps curve fits the swaps market perfectly by construction,
so all swaps are fairly valued (their rates from the curve match the observed
rates)—this is great for many purposes, but not for relative value analysis,
where we want to see some deviations from theoretical values. If we take
the swaps curve methodology and fit the curve to the observed swap rates
only at certain maturity points (say, 3 months, 2 years, and 10 years), then
these points will be priced fairly, but all others generally will not lie on
the curve—to determine the rate on a 5-year swap, our curve will have to

interpolate between the known 2-year and 10-year nodes, and this inter-polated rate will generally not be equal to the market 5-year rate. In this case, some swap rates will be higher than what our curve predicts (i.e., cheap to the curve) and some will be lower (rich to the curve), so any such loose fitting procedure can be used to spot deviations from fair value. But why would anyone expect the interpolated rate to be the fair value to which the observed rate should return?

This of course depends on how we interpolate. If we just draw a straight line between the nodes, it is unlikely to give us convincing fair values. But if instead we use a term structure model that describes the evolution of interest rates more or less from first principles, and then fit (find the parameters of) this model so that it correctly prices our benchmark maturity points, then we may say that this model does not just interpolate between the nodes, but rather represents the way interest rates should behave. If our interpolated curve has this larger meaning, then any deviations between what the market currently does and the model's predictions should be fleeting, and we can thus expect that things that are rich to the model will drop in price and vice versa. Despite the fact that this reasoning does not tell us when the convergence to fair value will occur in any given case, it sounds convincing enough for many buy-side money managers (as well as for many proprietary traders inside the sell-side banks themselves), and so these rich-cheap arguments and the models that produce them are used very widely in sell-side research. Figure 17–4 shows a typical relative value plot that we may see in a research piece.

Relative value models are popular to the extent that every bank will generally have at least one such model (some have several) for every major market. Some of these are pure term structure models, some are equilib-rium models (where the model parameters have some larger econometric meaning, such as risk premium or long-term interest rate), and some are based on historical regression of prices, volatilities, or economic time series such as inflation, budget balance, debt supply, and the like. None of these models are really in the public domain, so we cannot discuss them here in any detail, but we can ask why they are widely perceived to have predictive power—there must be a behavioral mechanism that causes the market to follow the relative value arguments, and that mechanism works roughly as follows. If every market participant were using the same relative value model (for example, the hypothetical one from Figure 17–4), it would then act a self-fulfilling prophecy: if a security became rich to such a "unified" model, everyone would start selling it, and its price would quickly drop until the model stopped flagging it as rich.

F I G U R E   17–4

An example of rich-cheap analysis for long-end Treasuries, whose closing yields (black dots) are compared with their theoretical values (the solid line) coming from a relative value model (which is wholly made up to produce this figure). The dots falling below the curve represent securities that are rich; those that are above the fair value are cheap.

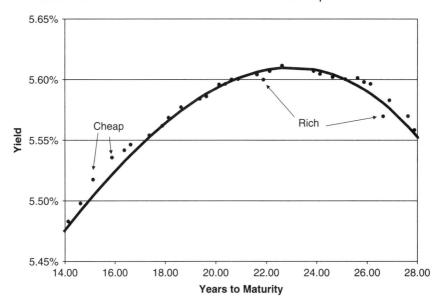

In reality, people use different models that approximate fair value differently, so something that is rich in one model can be fairly priced in another. But all of the models effectively interpolate between observed prices, and there is only so much leeway in doing that; if we take a security in Figure 17–4 and move its yield downward by, say, 5 bp, any relative value model would flag it as rich (and those that would not are not worthy of the name), so for large deviations from fair value, any model will correctly predict that such deviations will quickly revert back to fair value. Different models, however, will differ in how soon they spot these deviations, and the best models will not be the first to do so, but rather will act like our "unified" model: they will call the security rich just before everyone comes to the same conclusion and starts selling it. The models also differ significantly in how easy they are to use and maintain, so there is room for a healthy variety of such relative value models, all of which have their strengths and weaknesses, but overall provide a useful way of looking at the markets.

TECHNICAL ANALYSIS

The final area within research that we are going to mention is known as *technical analysis*. Technical analysis can be defined as an attempt to predict market behavior based on the past history of prices. Technical analysts plot the past history of prices on charts (which is why technical analysis is often called *charting*, and its practitioners are called *chartists*) and then try to find certain patterns in those charts that they think indicate that the market is about to move up or down. We can identify a technical analysis research piece by its terminology, which includes terms like *support* and *resistance* (the magical price levels that prices are supposed to bounce off of), *trend lines* (straight lines drawn through the tops and bottoms of the price charts), *trading channels* (areas between trend lines), upside and downside *breakouts* (prices going outside these channels), moving averages, *Bollinger bands*, *head-and-shoulders* tops, oscillators, engulfing patterns, and dozens more equally mysterious things that I have neither the time nor the qualifications to explain (in fact, you have to be a Certified Financial Technician—an imprimatur conferred by the International Federation of Technical Analysts—to interpret the secrets of this craft).

The whole idea of technical analysis flies in the face of the efficient market hypothesis, which maintains that we cannot predict what the market will do, period, and believers in efficient markets theory tend to view technical analysis as a form of superstition that over time will be eradicated by better educational efforts. In practice, there is little evidence that this eradication will ever occur, or, more generally, that the efficient markets people are winning their argument against technical analysis. There was a period of time (between 1960 and roughly 1985) when playing with technical analysis charts at work could get a person fired from almost any financial institution, but today technical analysts work openly in both buy-side and sell-side research organizations and distribute their recommendations to customers just as other analysts do (which is why we mention this area here). If there is any stigma still attached to being a technical analyst, there is very little of it on today's Wall Street, although in academia it is still a big no-no.

For better or worse, most quantitative people are thoroughly indoctrinated in efficient markets theory when they come to Wall Street, so they tend to look at technical analysis with disdain, and few of them end up working in this field (which is my main excuse for not explaining technical analysis in more detail). However, my personal experience (shared by many of my former physicist colleagues) suggests that this may change. The first crack in the armor of an efficient markets believer usually appears when he notices that the most ardent defenders of the credo are those who know the least about the markets: 100 percent of first-year financial engineering students believe in efficient markets, while almost none of the experienced traders share that pure worldview.

After observing market behavior for a time, it becomes clear that at least some of the technical analysis terms make good practical sense; for example, moving averages and moving volatilities (from which Bollinger bands are constructed) are useful reference points for gauging whether current prices are rich or cheap and effectively do the same thing as the more academically respectable relative value models. Even the concepts of support and resistance, which seem like complete nonsense to a believer in efficient markets, tend to work in practice; for example, if a lot of people place their stop-loss orders at a particular price point, then as prices fall, they will certainly at least pause at that level, if not bounce off it, and a technical analyst has a decent chance of figuring out where that support level is (right below the previous low is one common technical rule for finding support levels).

Unlike the more mechanical quantitative models that we discussed previously, many technical analysis concepts are explicitly rooted in psychology and the thought processes of market participants. Charles Dow, considered the father of technical analysis and whom we met in Chapter 6, had a theory that there is a group of better-informed market players (often called *smart money*) who largely determine which way the market will go, and he viewed technical analysis as a way for an ordinary investor to uncover the tracks left by the smart money and to follow them—a goal that makes very good sense, even if some of the technical analysis tools seem a bit silly. Finance professors may laugh at technical analysis and tell funny stories about it,[2] but they do not move the market, while the people who do (investment managers and sell-side traders) usually take technical analysis predictions seriously and thus help turn them into reality (if an influential technical analyst declares that a stock is poised for an upside breakout, the managers and traders will all rush to buy it, and this will cause the breakout). To sum it up, as a practical matter, it is almost always useful to know

---

2. One such story is about a finance professor who had his students flip a coin every day and plot the results on a chart; he later showed the chart to a technical analyst, who did his analysis and declared that this stock was poised for an upside breakout.

what the technical analysts are saying about the market, even if we view these prognostications with a good dose of skepticism; this attitude is shared by most buy-side clients and explains why the sell-side research organizations make sure that they have technical analysts to cover that need.

As things stand today, if you have a quantitative/hard sciences background and you come to work in a sell-side research area, it is highly unlikely that you will be asked to write technical analysis pieces, but you will work alongside people who do, and I think that trying to understand what these people do is more constructive than the usual outright dismissal of their work as some kind of voodoo. So pick up a good book about technical analysis (again, see the Recommended Reading section) and at least learn what all these technical terms actually mean—even if you do not believe in them, they will be useful in conversation with clients and traders. And then, who knows, maybe you'll become interested in the field and start using these tools—after all, the technological foundation of technical analysis is almost the same as that of the time-series analysis we discussed at the beginning of this chapter.

As you may have noticed, the quantitative methods used in research have a different flavor from those employed by the more traditional financial analytics—they are less precise and more speculative, but also more fun—and this difference largely explains the traditionally somewhat tense relationship between the research and financial analytics groups. People working in financial analytics tend to view themselves as paragons of rigor and objectivity, and see their research counterparts as freeloaders who have no claim to the noble quantitative mantle, but still use it to produce glitzy output based on shaky foundations. People working in research view themselves as repositories of profound market knowledge, which their quantitative analytics counterparts are sadly lacking.

Both sides have a point, but the relationship need not be confrontational; both areas do useful work, and in practice they usually cooperate smoothly. The differences between their approaches can be traced to different underlying mathematical concepts. Traditional quantitative analytics is based on the idea of *interpolation* more than on anything else—all derivatives pricing, curve and model fitting, and the like are on some level nothing but glorified interpolation schemes that tell what this derivative should be worth if its neighbors are observed to have such and such prices. Research is based on the idea of *regression*; it tries to relate market concepts through empirical studies of their past history and make predictions about their future based on such studies.

The interpolation approach is much more rigorous, but it is cross-sectional in nature (it looks at a snapshot of the market and has no sense of history) and is best suited for the problems related to short-term flow trading (and flow traders are, unsurprisingly, the main customers of quantitative analytics). The regression approach has a timeline; it progresses from what was happening up until today to what might happen in the future, and its predictive power, limited as it is, makes it useful to buy-side investment managers and sell-side salespeople, who have much longer time horizons. Both interpolation and regression are simple and powerful concepts, and it is best to have both in your quantitative arsenal.

This concludes our review of research as the client-facing side of quantitative finance. It is an interesting place to work, with unique challenges, and I hope that this chapter helped you form an idea of what it is about. This latter comment, as a matter of fact, applies not just to research, but also to the whole financial technology realm, which we have reviewed in this part of the book. There are many other areas that are very much worthy of discussion, but we have to stop somewhere. In this part of the book, the focus of our narrative has been on describing what is available out there. Now we are ready to move on to the last part of the book, where we talk about how it all is actually used in practice.

PART 4

Technology Practices

CHAPTER 18

Production Cycle

In this part of the book, we will discuss how the various pieces of Wall Street technology introduced in the last few chapters are actually used in real life. We will focus on common practices used to develop, deploy, operate, and support these software systems. Most newcomers to financial industry technology do not realize that this subject even exists, while many experienced Wall Street technologists can be forgiven for thinking that perhaps this is the only subject that matters because it often dominates their daily professional life. Our goal here, as in the rest of the book, is to help the reader understand what is going on by describing common problems, solutions, terminology, and motivations of the main players, and I hope that the following three chapters will prove useful to newcomers and "old hands" alike.

Of the three verbs we just mentioned—develop, operate, and support—we begin with "operate." In this chapter, we assume that we are part of a technical group that is responsible for a financial software system that has already been developed and deployed, and that never breaks, so there is no need for support; thus, we concentrate on the issues related to its normal operation. Of course, "software system" is a very generic term (a spreadsheet run by a trader is also a financial software system), so, more specifically, we will consider a major trading system that covers a large number of securities and serves many business users. We will call this "our system" for the rest of the chapter. For the purpose of our discussion here, the details of what our system is supposed to do are much less important than its size and complexity—we want a large, complex system that is server-based and that uses other systems, such as product databases, market data, historical data, analytics libraries, and so on. During business hours, our system's users (traders, salespeople, research, and support staff) interact with it and hopefully get what they want out of it. This is, however, only part of the story; let us consider what happens to this system when nobody is using it.

SHUTTING DOWN AND RESTARTING THE SYSTEM

One would expect that the system would in some sense be switched off at the end of the day and turned back on before people return to work the next morning. The first group of issues that we are going to discuss in this chapter stems from the fact that shutting down and bringing up a complex software system like ours is often a highly nontrivial task. The system usually contains many processes, perhaps dozens, running on multiple servers. Turning the system off therefore requires someone or something to access all these servers, find these processes, and cause them to exit. Similarly, turning our system on involves making all these processes start on their various servers. Before we discuss how this is usually done, it is reasonable to ask why we have to do this at all. Why not just let the system run forever, if restarting it sounds like too much trouble?

Running forever has its problems, too. Almost everything (including the servers that these processes run on) has to shut down periodically for maintenance, and the reality of most large financial software systems is that some maintenance is required daily and is performed every night. The most common reasons for these daily updates are that (1) there are a lot of data that are calculated and updated only once a day, such as closing prices, rates, curves, risk factors, baselines for PnL, and so on, and these data are typically read in only when the system starts up; (2) the universe of securities that the system is dealing with can change every day as some instruments mature and new instruments are issued; and (3) changing the date used by the system and its components to do financial calculations and for display purposes may be nontrivial, as it is often determined only once, at start-up.

Of course, each of these updates can in theory be performed dynamically (without restarting the system), and most systems are able to perform some of them without a restart. However, conceptually, it is much easier to have a system that simply wakes up every morning and reads all the quasi-static data that it needs without worrying about what those data were yesterday. Because of this desire to keep the design simple (or because of the inability to execute a complex design), the vast majority of financial software systems require a daily restart to pick up quasi-static data changes. This is fine as long as the system works as intended, but it becomes very problematic when the quasi-static data prove not so static—for example, if some closing prices were wrong, loading the corrected prices would require restarting the system during business hours, which often causes aggravation to the users. We will address possible problems in Chapter 20; in this chapter, we live in a perfect world where nothing ever breaks.

So in practice, most large-scale financial systems are restarted (or, in trade parlance, *bounced*) every night. There are typically three stages to this process. First, the system is shut down by terminating all or most of its server processes. Then the data it needs for the next day are prepared by a series of automated steps, usually referred to as the *overnight batch* process. Note that it is often not strictly necessary to stop the system before its data are updated, so the second and third stages sometimes overlap in time or even switch places. Finally, the system is started up anew before the start of business the next morning. Let us consider the first and the third stages first.

A large software system usually consists of multiple server-side processes, often constantly communicating with one another, that produce some data (prices, risk, PnL) that are displayed by client applications running on every user's desktop. Shutting down this system requires finding all the server-side and client-side processes and terminating each of them. One of the simplest ways to do this is to program all these processes to exit at a particular time, say at midnight. This is often done for the client-side processes (they shut themselves down overnight, and the user restarts them when she comes in the next day) because they typically affect only a single user, and no great harm is done if an application hangs and fails to exit.

For server processes, the shutdown mechanism is usually more elaborate and flexible. A common approach to restarting server processes is based on the concept of a *configuration table*, which, for each server, lists the components of the system that are configured to run on that server by specifying the names and locations of the executables to run, together with their parameters (usually passed in as command-line arguments). When the system is brought down, a shutdown script is executed on each server. The script looks in the configuration table (typically stored in some central repository, such as a database) for the list of processes expected to be running on that server and brings those processes down by either sending a shutdown message (for those components that support such messaging) or killing the process on the operating system level. When the system is brought up, a start-up script is executed; it goes to the same configuration table, reads the list of processes to be started and their arguments, and starts them one by one (perhaps after checking that they are not running already).

Most readers will know what a script is, but let us define it for those who don't: a script is a computer program written in one of the many scripting languages (Perl, UNIX and Windows shell command languages, and JavaScript probably cover 90 percent of the scripts used in the financial industry; the rest are written in proprietary scripting languages developed in-house, believe it or not). Unlike true *binaries*, or *executables*, which are built from code in high-level languages like C++ or Java, scripts are just human-readable text files that can be executed by running them through a command interpreter program. They are the weapon of choice for simple chores—reading data from a database and writing them to a file, copying files, creating reports, starting and stopping bigger programs—that do not require much interactivity or continuous operation. They are typically small and easy to understand and maintain (although I've seen 6,000-line-long Perl scripts). You want to be proficient in at least one of those languages if you work in financial technology. But back to our system and its overnight restart.

Two factors often complicate the shutdown/restart sequence. One is that at least some components of the system communicate with one another, and this often creates dependencies between them, so that Component X will not be able to do any useful work until it gets some data from Component Y, and so on. Because of this, the components usually need to be shut down and started up in a particular order, which can also be specified in the same configuration table.

Another subtler issue is related to preserving (*persisting* is the proper term) the system's *state*. For example, let us say that a trader has entered a spread for a bond he is pricing into the system's client GUI, and that spread was passed on to the server components for use in their computations. When the trader comes back to work tomorrow, he usually expects the system to still know the spread that he entered the day before. From the system's perspective, this spread and other user inputs are part of its internal state, which may also include the results of some internal computations that remember prior data (a moving average of prices is a good example of that). In a running system, such data are stored inside the memory space of certain system components and will be irretrievably lost when those processes are terminated unless something is done to preserve them. With user inputs, this persistence is often achieved by recording every user input to a database table dedicated to that purpose and by having the system read the last known values of all the inputs from that database during start-up.

Note that when a market data platform is used for passing user inputs between the client side and the server side of the system, its caching capability provides a natural way of persisting user inputs: the input topics will stay in the market data platform's cache until the next day (unless, of course, the market data cache itself is restarted). However, sometimes the component that is using these inputs is itself responsible for persisting them, in which case we cannot just kill the process; we have to issue a more gentle shutdown request that gives it a chance to save its data into persistent storage (database or flat file) so that they can be read in during the system's start-up.

THE OVERNIGHT BATCH STAGE

The overnight batch stage that in most cases falls chronologically between the shutdown and the restart is where some real work is done. The most typical example of what is actually done during this stage involves processing derivatives books. Determining their mark-to-market value and risk factors is often not feasible intraday because of computational complexity; instead, it is done overnight based on the new closing values for liquid market instruments: futures, on-the-run Treasuries, and swap curves. These calculations often take many hours for large books. They are, however, easily parallelized, and the state of the art is to distribute them to multiple computers (whole *server farms* are maintained for this purpose) and then collect the results and store them in a form such that our trading system can use them the next day.

Computational complexity, however, is not the only or even the main reason to relegate certain tasks to the overnight batch; in fact, anything that depends only on closing prices and positions and/or has to be done once a day usually ends up as part of the overnight processing. Examples include generating end-of-day PnL and position reports, fitting term structure models to closing curves and generating risk factors, and even simply moving closing data from other systems into "our" databases and data files so that our system can quickly read them at start-up.

Updating the security universe that the system deals with—removing matured or expired instruments, adding newly issued ones, and rolling the futures and on-the-runs when necessary—is also an important part of overnight processing. The last of these tasks is an example of a process that does not depend on closing prices and is entirely driven by the change in the business date. Note that many tasks in the overnight process inherently depend on one another: for example, first we process closing prices and make sure they are there; if that is successfully completed, then we can do valuation and risk; only then can we generate risk and PnL reports; and so on. The actual dependency graphs for such overnight processing can quickly get very complex for large systems, and organizing and scheduling all the different components of the overnight batch is a task that is both nontrivial and business-critical.

The operating system tools for task scheduling are generally inadequate for large-scale overnight batches. UNIX has *cron* and *at* commands; Windows has scheduled tasks—all of these are fine for managing a single workstation, but they have three main problems when it comes to organizing batch jobs in multiserver systems. The first problem is that there is no central location where we can see the status of jobs scheduled to run on different servers; we have to go through each server to see all jobs. The second problem is that it is well nigh impossible to make a task scheduled on one server dependent on the success of another task on another server, which is what we need to be able to do in a multiserver environment. Finally, all these scheduled tasks, being computer processes, can and do fail, and the only way to check whether they have succeeded or failed is to go through each server and look.

These shortcomings have led to the development of dedicated software products called *job management* systems, which provide a centralized way of setting up, executing, and monitoring repetitive tasks in multiserver environments. As with everything else, some banks develop such systems in-house, but one third-party product, AutoSys from Computer Associates, has gained wide acceptance in the industry, and in the next few paragraphs we undertake a brief description of how it works.

AutoSys is organized around a database server called Event Server that stores all information about scheduled tasks across the whole company (or at least a sizable part of it). For each such task (called an *AutoSys job*), the database stores many pieces of information, such as the name of the machine on which the job is to be run; the command to be executed, including the full path binary name and all command-line arguments; the conditions that need to be satisfied for the job to run (e.g., the time); the owner (the user whose account will be used to run the job); where the log files go; and so on. Each job has a unique ID in AutoSys, and is given a unique and hopefully descriptive name. AutoSys provides a "job information language," or *JIL*, that makes it possible to define jobs by specifying all these pieces of information in a text file, which is then run through a JIL interpreter that writes it into the database. It also provides a GUI and a Web interface that allow us to see a list of all jobs whose name fits a pattern. So for our system, we will make sure that all our jobs start with the same string (our_system_job% will be our pattern).

Each server that AutoSys works with runs a daemon process that talks to the central AutoSys server process, called the Event Processor. This central server scans the database looking for jobs to execute. When the conditions for running a particular job are met, the AutoSys server sends that job to the daemon running on the target server for execution. The daemon attempts to execute the command and reports the state of the job back to the server.

Job state is a central concept in AutoSys that we need to understand in more detail, which we will attempt to do by following a typical path of job execution. The job begins its life in an INACTIVE state. When the conditions specified in its definition are met (e.g., the time is 1:00 a.m.), it goes into a STARTING state, which means that it is put onto an execution queue. When it is successfully submitted to the AutoSys daemon on the target server and the daemon kicks it off, it goes into the RUNNING state. If it successfully completes, its state becomes SUCCESS; if it fails (which means that its return value is greater than some parameter, usually zero), its state becomes FAILURE.

Each state change generates an AutoSys *event* that can be used to trigger execution of other jobs. The most common example of this is making one job run when another is successful; for example, we can define our_system_job2 to run when our_system_job1 is successful, and this in turn is configured to run at 10 p.m. every day. At 10 p.m., AutoSys will kick off our_system_job1 on the server we told it to run on. When this job completes successfully, AutoSys will check in the database whether any other jobs should be triggered by this SUCCESS event; it will find our_system_job2 and proceed to execute it, since that job's only start condition is now met. We can be more demanding and say that our_system_job2 should run at 10:15 if the previous job is successful; in this case, if our_system_job1 completes before 10:15, AutoSys will wait until that time to make sure that both the time condition and the dependency condition for our_system_job2 are satisfied before kicking it off. Whether these two jobs are running on the same server or not is completely irrelevant for AutoSys.

The dependency mechanism driven by these job states is quite powerful and allows for the creation of very elaborate chains of interdependent batch jobs. In large and complex batches, the jobs are often organized in *boxes*, which can be thought of as folders, or directories, for AutoSys jobs. An AutoSys box is a type of job that does nothing except trigger the execution of "normal" jobs that are put in that box. For example, suppose we have seven servers where our system's processes should be running, and we want to start the system up on all of them at a certain time if some or perhaps all jobs that form our overnight data processing successfully complete. We have to create a separate job to start the system on each of the seven servers; let us call these jobs our_system_job_start-up_1 through our_system_job_start-up_7.

Instead of specifying the start conditions for each such job, we can instead put these seven jobs in a box called our_system_job_start-up_box (to put a job in a box, we simply specify the box name in a special field in its configuration record) and make that box dependent on the success of previous jobs and also run at a particular time. This way, when its start conditions are met, it will go into the RUNNING state, and this will kick off all the start-up jobs contained in it; once all of them successfully complete, the box itself will go into the SUCCESS state (and if any single one fails, the whole box will be marked as FAILURE). Using boxes, the overnight job sequence for our system can be organized into a shutdown box, one or more data processing boxes, and a start-up box, which makes it easier to manage.

We promised to keep this chapter limited to an ideal world in which nothing ever breaks, but our description of the overnight batch in AutoSys begs the question: what happens if one of these jobs fails? Wouldn't the jobs that are dependent on the one that's failed just stop in their tracks so that our system would not come up in the morning? Yes, they would stop in their tracks until the failed job is rerun and becomes a success, and this is exactly what we want to have happen. There is usually little point in bringing up the system if some of the initial data that it needs are unavailable or wrong, as we will end up having to fix the problem and restart the system later anyway when the problem is discovered.

To make sure that the system does come up in the morning even if some of its overnight jobs fail, these failures need to be addressed quickly, and the first step in doing that is making sure that the people who can fix these problems are notified immediately. AutoSys helps with that too; jobs can be configured to *raise an alarm* if they either fail or get stuck (run for longer that some configurable length of time). This alarm (think of it as a message describing the failed job) goes to an organizational unit that we will call the *technology operations center*, which is staffed 24/7.

When the operations center people receive an alarm about an AutoSys job failure, they proceed to track down someone from a list of people called a *support rota*, which is associated with each AutoSys batch. If we are at the top of that rotating list, the operations center will call us soon after the job fails (yes, that means that it will wake us up in the middle of the night, and if it can't wake us up, it will call the next person on the rota), and we will be expected to find out what was wrong with the failed job, fix it, rerun the job, and tell the operations center that all is well. We will describe how all of that works in more detail in Chapter 20 (we are clearly wandering out of our ideal world here), but this built-in support for different levels of failure notification is a central feature of AutoSys and is one of the main reasons for its wide adoption in the industry.

DAILY SYSTEM OPERATION

Other than this overnight processing, what else happens in the daily life cycle of our system? It is increasingly becoming standard practice across Wall Street to have the technical group responsible for the system perform a *start-of-day check* after the system has restarted in the early morning, but before the users start working with it. During the check, someone from our group will positively verify that the system did in fact come up and is in a good, usable state. Performing this check before the start of the trading day makes it possible to address problems that may have slipped past the AutoSys defenses and restart the system if necessary without causing an outage during the day. I consider this an extremely useful practice, although it does entail some human cost because someone will have to come in quite early every day.

The check is performed by going through a start-of-day *checklist* and usually involves checking the state of the AutoSys batch; checking the log files of the major system components for errors, or rather the absence thereof; bringing up and playing with client-side components of the system; and perhaps other steps, limited only by the imagination and experience of the people who developed the checklist. Parts of these checks, such as the log file scan, are often automated. After the check is complete, the person who did the check is often expected to write a start-of-day, or *SOD*, report, which usually is an e-mail that goes to our technical group plus the business users of the system (sometimes it is restricted to their management). The SOD report should say that the system has been checked and should list major and minor problems that took place overnight and/or were discovered during the check and/or were reported by the users; in our ideal world, this report would be a one-liner saying that everything is fine with the system and it is ready for a new day. On the business side, there is often a start-of-day message as well; it would typically be written by someone in trading or research and would be devoted to a review of the day ahead. It usually briefly goes over economic releases, security auctions, and other events scheduled for today, and discusses our expectations for them.

The start-of-day report marks the official start of the normal operation phase in the system's life cycle. During this phase, the system does what it was programmed to do; our system is a trading system, so it would process trades, analyze risk and PnL, help the users price new derivative deals, and so on. Its ability to do all these wonderful things, however, is contingent on the continuing health of its supporting infrastructure, and it is a good and widely followed practice to proactively monitor that health during the normal operation phase. The specific things that are monitored vary from system to system, but we can list some common indicators here: disk space and CPU utilization on the system's servers, market data and general network traffic in its network neighborhood, the status of internal and external connections that the system makes, scanning log files for errors, and the general responsiveness of the system, measured by some statistics such as how long it takes to process a user input or to book a trade.

This monitoring is almost always automated and is at least partly done through the technology operations center, which will alert the relevant people if, say, one of the servers is about to run out of disk space. Having such monitoring in place is especially important during bursts of market activity (triggered, for example, by releases of economic reports, as described in Chapter 4); its results make it possible to address overload problems in an intelligent way, which is hard to do without knowing exactly what parts of the system are overloaded. The system monitoring can involve so many things that sometimes its results are displayed using a dedicated application called a *digital dashboard*, which has a set of warning lights for each thing being monitored (of course, in our ideal world, all these warning lights are solid green all the time).

An important event in the daily life of almost any software system on Wall Street is the daily marking of the books. Contrary to what we may expect, this usually happens a couple of hours before the end of the trading day (in the U.S. fixed-income markets, the books are closed at 3 p.m. New York time, when the futures exchanges close). In fact, for many derivatives systems, this is where their day in fact starts: once they get a new set of closing prices for the underlying products, they can begin the often arduous work of valuing and risking derivatives portfolios.

Let us assume here that it is our system that is responsible for the marking process. It will then offer the users a mechanism for loading live prices (or their snapshot taken at closing time) for all the securities they need to mark into some kind of GUI, review those prices for accuracy, correct them if necessary, and finally enter them into the official repository for the closing marks. Almost universally, in a big bank, there will be multiple databases where the closing prices are stored, so after our system enters the marks into one database, other systems will start a flurry of activity copying these data into their databases. As users across the firm begin loading today's marks into their systems, problems like missing or incorrect closing prices are often found and reported back to the desks that generate the marks. They are resolved by the business users reviewing and reentering the contested marks, which on the systems level will require our system to stand ready to perform such revisions for some period after the official marking time.

As the day draws to a close, the systems side may send out an end-of-day (*EOD*) report listing the results of the day, perhaps with some statistics on the system's performance during the day, which can also mention any problematic issues that occurred. The business side almost always issues end-of-day market commentaries from individual desks discussing the market action during the day and possible factors behind it; the audiences for those are mostly the firm's clients and salespeople. There are also official risk and PnL reports for each desk and each trader, which are part of the risk management process and are not widely distributed, at least not to the technology side, although our system may play a part in generating such reports. The day grows old, and everyone goes home—which begins the new production cycle.

FOLLOW-THE-SUN TRADING

I have purposely avoided the question of when the business day actually starts and ends, because to answer it properly, we need to go global and discuss when the day starts and ends in different regions, and this discussion is going to occupy us for most of the remainder of this chapter. Every

big investment bank has offices all over the globe, but most of them are
sales offices that have little to do with technology—the main locations
for the technology infrastructure and workforce are New York, London,
and Tokyo (and increasingly Singapore, but we will leave that out). In
equity markets, the hours are dictated by the stock exchanges in each location and are 9:30 a.m. to 4 p.m. in New York, 8 a.m. to 16:30 p.m. GMT
in London, and 9 a.m. to 3 p.m. in Tokyo (with a generous lunch break
from 11 to 12:30).

Interest-rate markets do not have official opening and closing times
in any of these locations, but the prevailing practice is as follows. In New
York, traders usually come into the office between 7 and 7:30 a.m. and
leave between 5 and 5:30 p.m. The semiofficial start of trading is 8 a.m.,
and trading ends at around 5 p.m., but if a customer calls at 5:15 p.m. and
asks to do a trade, it is executed with no questions asked, so instead of
there being sharp start and end times, the trading activity gradually picks
up between 7:30 and 8 a.m. and dies down between 5 and 5:30 p.m. London
follows much the same schedule, while Tokyo starts later (around 9:30 a.m.)
and ends earlier (around 4 p.m.), again with a lunch break for an hour around
noon when the market activity in the JGB market stops. The fun begins
when we try to figure out how these business hours in each location line
up with each other; their relationship is shown in Figure 18–1, which, I
think, offers ample food for thought (try to schedule a teleconference
involving people from all three offices and you'll quickly see what I mean).

The first thing that is evident from Figure 18–1 is that a major investment bank is akin to the British Empire of old in that the sun (almost) never
sets on it. As New York goes home, the trading day in Tokyo begins, and
it continues into the early morning hours in London, when Europe begins
trading. The London trading session continues into the New York morning
(because of a smaller time difference, the London and New York sessions
significantly overlap), and the New York trading session reaches the early
morning hours in Tokyo, and the cycle begins again. This is often called
follow-the-sun trading. A closer look at Figure 18–1 reveals that there is
a brief gap in this follow-the-sun sequence when none of the three offices
are trading—between about 5:30 and 7 p.m. New York time (7:30 to 9
a.m. in Tokyo, very late evening in London)—whose significance we will
discuss shortly.

Many interest-rate products are traded out of one office only (JGBs
out of Tokyo only, Eurogovernments out of London only), but an increasing number of product classes are traded in all three (U.S. Treasuries and

FIGURE 18-1

Timing of the trading sessions in the major offices of a large trading firm. The boxes correspond to the time when a particular location is open for trading (small boxes at the sides of larger boxes depict the ramp-up and ramp-down periods at the beginning and end of a trading day). The only gap between the trading sessions is between 6 and 7 p.m. New York time.

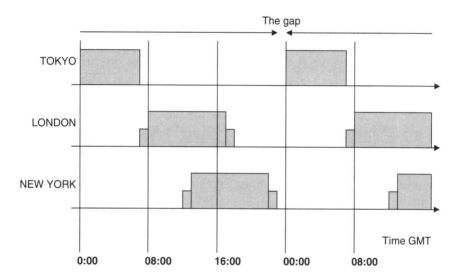

U.S. dollar swaps and derivatives in particular), and then there are some, depending on the bank, that trade out of New York and London but not Tokyo (U.S. agencies and mortgages often fall into that category). Eurodollar futures also trade round the clock on CME's Globex system, and so do the Treasury futures on CBOT's (or rather LIFFE's) electronic platform, again with a brief gap in the New York evening hours.

For products trading in multiple locations, the usual business-side arrangement is that the desks trading them are part of a single global business unit, with the same traders often rotating among the different offices. Being a single business unit involves having a common PnL from trading a common set of books, which is often done by having a single global book that is passed from location to location. Trades done in Tokyo are booked in the global book until the end of the trading day there, at which time the book is passed on to the desk's London traders. The act of passing on trading responsibilities for the book is often called the *handover* process.

On the business side, this simply involves the traders sort of shaking hands over the phone, discussing whatever trades were done, market events, and customer interactions that occurred during Tokyo trading; once the London traders are fully aware of what is going on, they take over the ownership of the book or books and Tokyo goes home.

A similar process is followed during the London-to-New York hand-over; however, because the London afternoon largely overlaps with the New York morning, the global books may be handed over to New York at 8:30 a.m., but the London traders will typically continue trading with the firm's European clients using another book, which will be handed over at the end of the London day.

Another business issue that follow-the-sun trading raises, and one where there is significant variability among the banks, is that of closing prices: does each region mark the global products at the end of its day, or should this be done in one "main" office only? You may see it done either way, and even when every, say, U.S. Treasury has a London closing price and a New York closing price and (far less often) a Tokyo close for the same business day, the official PnL reports could still be based on only one set of marks (New York for U.S. Treasuries).

The handover issues on the systems side are significantly more complex. Let us start with the concept of global books. A trading book is ultimately a set of records in a database that has to be hosted somewhere, so having a set of global books that can be easily and transparently passed from location to location usually requires each region to maintain its own copy of the trade database and have a replication system in place that keeps these three databases in sync at all times. But the books are almost never accessed directly. Traders usually interact with a trading system like ours to book the trades—how should such server-based systems be organized in a global environment? Let us consider some alternatives.

The obvious alternative is for each location to run its own copy of the system. The advantage of that is simplicity, but this is usually greatly outweighed by the disadvantages. First, it is wastefully expensive to maintain three sets of servers, external connections, and especially support and development people, but that alone never stopped anyone on Wall Street. The second drawback is more serious: if each copy is locally controlled, it is difficult to get these system copies to exchange information so that each sees the same set of trades and uses the same set of prices. There are known cases where an adroit hedge fund would buy something from one office of a global bank and immediately sell it at a profit to another office of the same bank—having three disjoint systems in the three locations creates an opportunity for such regional arbitrage. Finally, the handover of book ownership, connections to external parties, and primary trading and pricing responsibilities is difficult to accomplish, as the regional systems do not really talk to each other. So a more common situation is for the server side of the system to be hosted in one region and for users from other regions to access the system remotely. This arrangement makes sure that everyone is looking at and trading from the same set of data, but it raises a long list of issues of its own.

The best case for such global systems is for users in all regions to run the system's client applications and have them directly connect to the servers in the hosting office as if their geographical location did not matter. This, however, is possible only for systems where the amount of data exchanged between the clients and the server applications is relatively small. In systems using live market data, this arrangement is not feasible in its pure form because the regional offices are on different network segments; the data have to be routed back and forth across the firm's wide area network (see the discussion on market data routing in Chapter 14). The WAN has much lower capacity than the local area network and can easily be overwhelmed by the massive amount of market data that our system will try to pump through it. This problem can be papered over by routing only a subset of more critical and perhaps less frequently changing data, but this reduces the users in the nonhosting regions to second-class status.

Another solution for remote access to the system's servers is to have users from faraway offices log onto workstations in the hosting region using terminal emulators such as Citrix or PCDuo that allow, say, a user in London to have a window on her London workstation that contains a connection to a remote workstation in New York; this arrangement effectively pretends that our user is physically located in New York without transporting her there in person. In fact, it is an electronic improvement over an earlier state-of-the-art that involved people in New York coming to work at London hours (at 2 a.m. New York time) to trade global products with European clients of the firm (or even at Tokyo hours to trade with Asian clients): the misery of these overnight traders is now being relieved by technology. This "remote login" option also entails sending data back and forth over the WAN, but the amounts are much more manageable; only keystrokes and mouse clicks go one way, and only screen image updates go the other.

One argument that is frequently raised against such remote login solutions is that if we were to lose WAN connectivity while Tokyo traders were driving the London-hosted system, the system might end up with no users controlling it and might continue auto-quoting and doing trades without human supervision and perhaps at disastrously wrong prices. To address these concerns, many global systems include a feature that can be called a *dead man's switch*; its job is to turn off the system if the connectivity to the users that remotely control it is lost. This is much easier said than done, and inordinate amounts of effort are sometimes spent on developing such features, even though in most cases a simple phone call to the operations center will work just as well.

The real technological challenge of follow-the-sun trading lies not so much in how users interact with the remote system, but rather in the simple fact that globalization of trading leaves little or no time for overnight processing and system downtime in general. A system that is run locally in New York can be brought down after the close of business (say around 6 p.m.), and restarted before the traders get in (say around 6 a.m.), which leaves 12 hours or so for overnight processing. In contrast, a system that is shared between New York and London has to be up by London morning (2 a.m. in New York), which cuts the available downtime to 8 hours or so. Adding Tokyo to this picture cuts the acceptable downtime to just a couple of hours (between 5:30 and 7:30 p.m. in New York), and for many systems it is simply impossible to complete all of the necessary processing in such a short time window.

Including Tokyo also has an interesting side effect in that the system will have to start in the New York evening hours but use the next day as the business day because it will already be tomorrow in Tokyo. If the system were properly designed to always use a configurable and externally specifiable date as the business date in all financial calculations, as well as for display purposes, all we would have to do is make sure that this logical business date is advanced around 6 p.m. New York time instead of at midnight. The unfortunate reality, however, is that the code is often littered with calls to now(), getDate(), and other such functions that get the date from the operating system; these calls are completely harmless as long as you start the system after midnight, but in order to advance the date earlier, all such calls need to be found, reviewed, and replaced with something that uses the logical business date. This is vaguely reminiscent of the Y2K problem, which taught us that this is not a trivial task in a large system with millions of lines of code. Usually these date issues are by far the most nettlesome and costly problem in making the systems ready for global operation.

The only real solution to this is to move away from the concept that the system has to be restarted to pick up the initial static data, which, as I pointed out earlier, is how most existing systems operate. Ideally, systems like ours should be run 24/7 (or rather, as it is often said, 24/5½—the only downtime should be after the Friday close of business in New York and before Monday morning in Tokyo, which is Sunday afternoon in New York), with overnight processing streamlined as much as possible and data being fed to the running system as they become available. Most Wall Street systems are not there yet at the time of this writing, and they and the people who operate them continue to struggle with the issues we touched on in this chapter. Solving the global puzzle remains very much a work in progress.

In this chapter, we have walked through a day in the life of a typical large financial software system and discussed some of the many difficult questions that need to be addressed in order to operate such complex systems. I hope the reader will begin to appreciate the fact that these systems do not just happen—they require continuous monitoring and configuration effort to stay healthy and productive. Given that complexity, our main assumption of this chapter—that these systems never break—should by now really strain the reader's credulity, and rightly so; we will devote all of Chapter 20 to the question of what happens when the software does develop problems. However, a discerning reader of this chapter may have started asking another set of questions: Where do these systems come from? How are they created, and who creates them and monitors them and fixes problems with them? We will tackle these questions first; in the next chapter, we enter the kitchen of Wall Street software development.

CHAPTER 19

Development Cycle

Wall Street rivals Silicon Valley in its quantity of raw software output, but this output does not go to computer stores; instead, it is used inside Wall Street firms to support their business processes. One can reasonably ask why the securities industry has ended up venturing so far outside its core competency of financial intermediation into the realm of high-powered programming—after all, if Wall Street companies do not generate their own electricity and do not build their own buildings, why would they write their own software? The short answer is that they want to be in control of critical pieces of their infrastructure (and, as a matter of fact, for that same reason, they sometimes do generate their own electricity[1] and build their own buildings; witness Goldman Sachs's tower in Jersey City, which seems to be visible from every point in New Jersey no matter which way you look, or much of Canary Wharf, for that matter).

Wall Street software development has a 20-year-long history, which we touched on briefly in Chapter 3, and we can see a snapshot of that history when we look at the portfolio of systems in almost any major bank. Some systems are cutting-edge, some are aging, and I have heard of banks that still run some of their stuff on VAX computers from the early 1980s (because that software would not run on anything else). Much if not most of the software development effort in any given firm is directed at decommissioning older systems and replacing them with shiny new ones. Of course, by the time the new ones are finally built and broken in, they are no longer all that

---

1. During the Northeast blackout in August 2003, an overwhelming majority of Wall Street firms in New York continued to work without interruption, even as all other important things like traffic lights went dark across the region; they had emergency generators, and the generators kicked in seamlessly.

new, and the next generation of managers decides to make its name by replacing those systems with something yet more modern, and on and on it goes.

The point I am trying to make is that software development does not have an identifiable end, where all needed software has been built and everyone can go home. Replacing older systems with new ones that meet the rapidly changing business requirements is an ongoing process, a cycle in fact, or perhaps even a series of cycles. The big cycles may last for years and consist of a generational change of systems, whereas small cycles last for weeks or months and consist of ongoing improvements, enhancements, and maintenance of existing actively used systems such as the one we discussed in the previous chapter. In this chapter, we examine the mechanics of the software development cycle and review the activities of the people who make it happen.

As I explained in Chapter 3, software development on Wall Street is done by development groups organized at various levels in the firm. Each group will have from a couple to a couple of dozen developers plus perhaps a few managers (who usually, but not always, also do some of the development work). A viable development group will have a mix of junior and more experienced people, at least some of whom have a good grasp of the business needs of the areas served by the group. While there is some specialization within the group, its members will typically work quite closely together. What do they do all day?

THE HARDWARE INFRASTRUCTURE

They write code, then build it, then test it, and then deploy it; we will go through all these stages one by one in just a minute, but first I need to address a long-neglected issue. Before we can develop any software, we have to have some hardware to do it on, so let us briefly review the typical hardware *infrastructure* of a Wall Street firm. When people come to work in such a place, they have several computers on their desks; these are called *workstations* and usually are late-model Windows PCs, but many people also have either a Linux or a Solaris box as a second workstation. These are the machines for reading e-mail, running trading screens and market data displays, and, for developers, for doing development work.

However, most of the important software, either third-party or in-house, runs not on those workstations but on *servers*. Servers differ from workstations in that they are held to a much higher performance and availability standard—we can flip the power switch on our workstation at any time, but servers are isolated in a special location called the *data center*, where they sit on racks in electronically locked air-conditioned server rooms and are monitored 24/7. There is a dedicated *server team*, and the people on this team are the only people who are allowed to physically touch the servers and are responsible for their continued health and well-being; it is important to know who these people are and to work with them in order to do something with a server-based software system. Similarly, there is a *network team* that looks over the network hardware connecting all these machines and much else besides, and a *database team* (also known as database administrators, or DBAs); these infrastructure support groups are indispensable partners to the development teams and help shape the firm's hardware environment to meet the business needs.

The concept of a hardware *environment* is actually very important to our narrative, and we will return to it many times later in this chapter. We can think of it as a self-contained set of servers, network connections, and databases that can run a single copy of a particular system or systems in such a way that it does not interfere with other existing copies of these systems. The most important of these environments is commonly called the *production environment*. In the production environment, also often referred to as the *live* environment, everything that the system does is for real: real traders use it to make real trading decisions where real money, often a lot of it, is at stake. The first principle of Wall Street software development is respect for the production environment. Development means change, so ultimately some changes are applied to the systems in production, but given how complex most such systems are, these changes need to be carefully controlled and planned. Allowing people to make random changes to live systems has an easily realized potential for breaking or damaging those systems, which can lead to large losses for the business users. Much of the development work is driven by the desire to avoid or at least minimize such expensive mistakes.

WRITING CODE

After this stern admonition, we are ready to go back to discussing the first software development activity, which is the writing of code. First, what is code? Most people use this term for programs written in high-level languages such as C++ or Java; such code needs to be compiled and built to turn it into a binary (an executable file that we can actually run and that will actually do things). However, most software systems also include code written in various scripting languages, such as Perl, Unix shell, or JavaScript; this type of code exists as human-readable files that can be given to the corresponding command interpreter to do things. Either way, code physically consists of a set of text files, and writing code is therefore the act of creating, editing, and storing such files. Other things that are important for the operation of almost any software system, such as configuration files or databases, autosys jobs that are used to run the system, environment variables, Windows registry settings, and so on, should also be thought of as code and treated in a similar way.

Ultimately, then, the code for any software system is nothing but a bunch of text files. Each developer could, in theory, simply store these files on a hard drive on his workstation, but this would make it hard for several people to work on the code at the same time. In practice, the code is always stored in a *source control system*, which can be thought of as a centralized database for text (and other types of) files. The most widespread systems of this type are Microsoft SourceSafe, Clearcase (made by Rational, now part of IBM), and CVS (which is part of most standard Unix distributions).

All source control systems support several basic operations. First, we can retrieve files from the system and put them on our own hard drive. When we ask the source control system to do that, it will put the files on our drive in a read-only mode, so we will not be able to change anything. If we do want to change something in a file, we *check out* the file from the source control system; this gives us a writable copy of the file and tells the source control system that someone is working on that file. If another person wants to work on that same file while we have it checked out, one of two things can happen, depending on the specific source control system we have: either it will refuse to let the second person check the file out, or it will warn her that we already have it checked out and then give that person a writable copy. When we are done with our changes, we *check in* the file; this puts our changes into the source control database and makes them available to others. If more than one person had the file checked out (where this is allowed at all), the changes made by the different people need to be *merged* into a single version, and the source control system usually provides some tools for that.

In most cases, the database stores only differences between one checkout and the next, so if all we did was add one line, only this line would be physically added to the storage. This system makes it possible to have access not only to the latest version of each file (called the *head of the code*), but also to all previous versions. This is critically important in a multiuser environment, as it allows people (1) to see who changed what and at what time, and (2) to *revert* to one of the previous versions of the file if the latest version has problems.

While some source control systems have much additional functionality (sometimes bordering on the ridiculous in its complexity), the basic cycle of working with a source control system is fairly straightforward. We begin by getting the code we need from the source control system to our machine. Source control systems are typically used by the whole bank or a significant chunk thereof, so they contain millions of lines of code organized into hundreds of *projects* (directories); we have to pick only the projects we need, but we should get everything that is required for our projects to build. Then we check out the files we want to modify and edit them to our satisfaction. For code written in the compiled languages, we would typically use an integrated development environment such as Visual C++ or Sun's Workshop (for Solaris) to do the editing as well as the compiling and building. Once we are happy with our changes, we check the files in, and they become part of the shared code base.

One of the basic rules of conduct in a shared development environment is never to check in anything that does not compile and build without errors. If we do this, we impair other developers who get the latest version of the shared code and try to build it on their computers. Most of the time, if the project we are working on does not build because someone else has introduced an error, we cannot continue our work and we are forced to either ask the offender to fix the error or check out the offending file and fix it ourselves. Note that it is often impossible to guarantee that no errors have been introduced—for example, suppose that we and a colleague are working on two unrelated files from the same project; each of us introduces a global variable, and we just happen to give these variables the same name. In this case, the code happily builds for each of us until we both check in our changes, at which point it stops building for everybody. Because no individual developer can make sure that the head of the code in source control always builds, there is almost always a *system build* (often done on a dedicated machine called the *build box*) where the group periodically runs a build script that gets the latest version of the relevant code and tries to build it; any breaks in the system build are usually promptly investigated and resolved.

TESTING THE CODE

Of course, just because the code builds fine does not mean that it also works fine; once we have made our changes, we need to test that the resulting binaries actually work as we intended. This, unfortunately, is not an easy task. Very few programs developed on Wall Street are stand-alone, self-contained executables that we can just run and see what happens; almost everything will use some services from the outside world: product databases, market data, various configuration parameters, and the like. Therefore, before we can test our changes, we have to create a *local development environment* for our binaries to make sure that they can connect to wherever they are supposed to go and perhaps run other programs that our binary needs to connect to (this can be quite a chore, so people usually develop scripts to automate this).

The second problem with local testing is that if our program actually does something to the places it connects to (let us say that it writes trades to a trade database and/or publishes something to the market data network), we want to make sure that our local environment does not affect the *production* system or systems that are currently being used by the business users—we do not want the traders to respond to a sudden avalanche of bogus trades generated by the program we are testing or see some funny prices in their market data displays. To deal with this problem, we want a development (or test) version of the trade database as well as another instance of the market data network and another instance of whatever other systems our program may affect—the problem of creating a local test environment usually goes much further than just configuring our box a certain way. Having a second copy of every system that our program uses is clearly expensive and difficult to maintain, so people often take shortcuts in this area; but in general it is almost impossible to test the changes to the system without a development environment, which represents a recognizable replica of whatever is used in real life. This environment, of course, will be shared by other members of our development group and perhaps other groups.

Suppose we went through all the trouble of setting up this local test environment, we ran our program on our workstation, and it did what we wanted it to do (perhaps after a few tweaks here and there); this still does not mean that it is ready to go. There is a whole branch of computer science that deals with testing and "quality assurance" issues, and its term for what we just did is *unit test*: we have tested an isolated piece of the system after changing it. It is, however, entirely possible that there are other pieces of the system that communicate with our piece, and that the changes we made to our piece will break something in those other pieces. The only way to make sure stuff like that does not happen is to do a *system test*, where all pieces of the system are tested at the same time. Since the whole system typically involves a lot of different binaries that are designed to run on different servers, what is required for a system test is a whole set of development servers plus all the services, such as test databases and so on, that we talked about before.

Once all members of our group say that the pieces they have been working on are ready for such a test, we do the following: (1) all of us check in our changes to the code, (2) we do a system build that picks up all these changes and creates a complete set of new binaries, and (3) we *deploy* all those new binaries and whatever configuration changes are supposed to go with them on the development servers. Finally, (4) we run a set of batch jobs similar to the one that starts up the system in production, but configured for this development environment, and (5) we see if the system comes up and works as intended. Often this process is repeated yet another time in yet another test environment called the *user acceptance testing* (UAT) environment, which works just as we previously described, but takes more care to reproduce the production environment as faithfully as possible; its primary purpose is to give the end users a chance to play with the system and make sure that whatever new features they wanted actually work as intended before it is officially released to them.

Once the components of the system are deployed to the test environments, they usually spend a few days there so that everyone can test the system thoroughly. You may wonder why this testing should take so long—isn't it just a matter of checking that the new functionality we just added works as intended? Unfortunately, it is not that simple. Checking that the new functionality is working is the easy part. The hard part is making sure that the new features did not break any of the old functionality; since there is usually so much of it, positively verifying that everything continues to work is exponentially more difficult than simply checking a couple of new features. Much of that old functionality kicks in only under specific conditions that may not be present during the test period, so that most of the code that handles special cases, unusual date conditions such as end-of-month and end-of-year, and the like is not really tested during a garden-variety system test. This is my favorite example, taken from real life: suppose we want to format the current date as 02/02/2002, and we know the month and the day; we just have to append a zero in front of them if they are less than 10. By mistake, we say in our code "if(month ≤ 10) append the zero." This works just fine 11 months of the year and breaks only in October, so if we are writing this code in November, we can test the system until we are blue in the face and we'll never find this problem, but it will blow up on October 1 next year. It is easy to imagine generalizations and extensions of this simple example, so the message is: no matter how much you test, you are never going to find all the bugs.

This, however, does not stop people from trying, and that makes good sense. Given that systems problems can (and do) lead to serious financial losses for the business side, the development groups usually put up a valiant, if ultimately futile, testing effort to prevent those problems. Let us briefly review the various types of tests that can be performed. We have mentioned one already: a *functionality test* checks that the system responds to users the way it is supposed to. An *accuracy test* consists of reproducing the result of some calculations that the system performs and demonstrating that the results are correct within a reasonable accuracy. A *performance test* and its extreme version, a *stress test*, put the system under some simulated load to make sure that it remains responsive and reasonable under stress. But the crown jewel of the testing realm is the *regression test*.

A regression test is what happens when we try to compare what the system is doing against *known good results*. As an example, consider a regression test of a financial analytics library where we are about to modify some date logic that can affect absolutely everything. The first stage of the regression test is the preparation of known good results; to do that, we make a list of all the calculations that the library does, all products that it can price, and all special date conditions that it handles (end-of-month and so on), and then we run all these calculations and record their inputs, outputs, *and* some performance measures, such as how long these calculations took, which, needless to say, amounts to a lot of work. Most of it needs to be done once and then periodically updated as the library improves and expands, so let us imagine that someone has done it already and that we have known good results available. Let us also assume that another component of the regression test (sometimes called the *test engine*), a script or a similar program that reads in the list of test cases and puts our financial library through its paces for each case, is also available. Then we should pick a time when the library is in a good state (we will discuss how to pick such a time a bit later), run the test engine, and store its output, which will now serve as a known good results set. After we have made our changes to the date logic (plus whatever other changes other people working on our library have made in the meantime), we run the test engine again and get another set of results, which we then compare to the known good results.

The best-case result of a regression test is for the new results and the known good results to be exactly the same (which proves that the library still does everything it did before in exactly the same way). Of course, this hardly ever happens (if, after all the work people have done on a system, it continues to do everything the same way, one can begin to question the value of that work), so there will usually be differences, and the hard part of regression testing is explaining those differences. The differences come in two flavors: expected differences (which are intended consequences of our code changes) and unexpected differences (which are what the regression test is designed to catch). The challenge is to tell the difference between these differences: is the 0.1-bp change in some obscure swap rate reasonable given our changes to the date logic, or is it due to something else?

You can see how going through the test results and explaining away the differences can be a lot of work, even in our financial library case, which is reasonably straightforward. Now consider how much more complicated such a test would be for a system that uses real-time market data or involves multithreaded components whose output can depend on the processor load of the machine. For such real-time systems, the best regression test one can often hope for is running the new version of the system from a test environment alongside the production system and simply eyeballing their differences. There is an almost unlimited variety of regression tests that one can design for a specific system, but all of them share a common feature: they all require a significant up-front investment in designing the tests, followed by an ongoing maintenance effort to keep them current as the system grows. Because of this, many actual Wall Street systems do without regression testing and pay the price in reduced quality and reliability.

What is the outcome of all these testing efforts? It is usually and officially called the *go/no-go decision*.[2] Ultimately, it is about whether the new version of the system is good enough to be put into the production environment. This decision is taken by (the managers of) the development group based on the preponderance of the evidence collected during testing. As we emphasized earlier, if testing did not uncover any problems with the software, this does not necessarily mean there are no problems. However, it usually does uncover problems, and the go/no-go decision focuses on these known problems; each problem can be either fixed or pulled (the problematic change can be rolled back). Unless some of these problems are so severe that the system is pretty much unusable, after fixing up the known issues, the management declares that it's a go, and the next stage of the cycle begins: the *production rollout* (or *release*).

---

2. This must be a Pidgin English term.

THE PRODUCTION ROLLOUT

The production rollout consists of replacing the copy of the system that is actually used by the end users with the new copy that was being tested. An important step of each rollout is *deployment* of the system components to the production environment, which means copying the new binaries, scripts, and so on to their proper locations on the production servers. This stage is usually automated by using install scripts that distribute the software from a central location (often the build box) to all servers. It would be far easier, of course, to have all this software on a network drive and just mount that drive onto the production servers, but that is a big no-no: network mounts are considered unreliable because the mounting process can hang and take the whole server out of commission. The deployment is accompanied by coordinated configuration changes to the environmental variables, database tables, and the like to make sure that the system operates correctly in the production environment. Note that this is essentially the same process that is used to put the system into test environments, so its steps can be (and are) tested during test environment deployments.

The main difference between the production rollout and deployment to a test environment is that the production rollout is for real—the live system usually has to be shut down for the rollout, and any problems during the rollout process are likely to affect the system's stability afterward. Because of these high stakes, production rollouts require management sign-off on both the technology side and the business side. Usually production rollouts are scheduled in advance so that everyone can plan their development and testing activities and the business side knows what to expect. However, it is sometimes necessary to do an unscheduled, or emergency, rollout to fix problems that slipped past the prerollout tests, or when dictated by some external events (a good example of this is Reagan Friday: when President Reagan died in 2004, all U.S. financial markets decided to shut down for the funeral on June 11, which required everyone to change the systems to mark that day as a holiday).

Rollouts are usually done after the markets close and the production system can be safely shut down. After the system is deployed, either everyone can go home and let the system come up on its own during its normal overnight start-up sequence, or the system can be brought up in order to test that everything is working properly. While the desire to be thorough is commendable, it is often difficult or impossible to test the system when all markets are closed and there are no live data or trades feeding through, so the value of postrelease testing is often dubious. However, it does uncover problems sometimes (and other times there are problems with the deployment process itself or with configuring the system during the roll-out), so any rollout involves the possibility of a *rollback*, in which the production system is either fully or partially restored to what it was before the rollout started. Because any rollout can go wrong, it is imperative that all the binaries, configuration information, and other data for the live system be backed up before attempting the rollout; otherwise the rollout becomes irreversible.

The morning after the rollout, the development team verifies that the system is in a good state and that all new features work as intended, and tells the business users about these new features (which sometimes involves training in how to use them). Hopefully this will conclude the release cycle, and the users will start enjoying the new features while the developers go back to their battle stations to prepare for the next rollout. In reality, however, there are always some problems with both new and old features introduced by the rollout. As the reports of these problems come in, the development group deals with them in several possible ways. Some bugs may be severe enough to require an emergency rollout to fix them. Some may be less damaging, and the users may be able to live with them for a while; these are put on the *bug list* and will be addressed in the next rollout. Finally, some problems may be the results of configuration or user input errors and can be fixed at run time.

After the system stabilizes, one useful thing that is highly recommended but not always performed is to *label the code*—take a snapshot of the code in the source control system that corresponds to the system that was rolled out (perhaps with a few postrelease fixes). These release labels greatly simplify the task of finding differences between versions of the system. The immediate aftermath of a release is also a good time to perform whatever regression tests the group supports in order to get a new set of good results. Another postrelease action that is highly recommended but rarely performed is to *document* the release: update or expand the documentation for the system to reflect the new features and changes introduced during this release. After these postrelease chores are taken care of, we go back to the beginning of the cycle (although, as philosophers would say, on a higher level, as the system is now hopefully better than it was at the beginning of the previous cycle).

THE CREATIVE SIDE OF SOFTWARE DEVELOPMENT

Our description of the development cycle may bring to mind the legendary comment made by Ernest Rutherford to an especially hard-working student in his lab: "When do you think?" So far, we have focused on the mechanics of the development process and have neglected to discuss the "thinking" side of it. The creative process that drives software development is more difficult to break into stages, but in a certain sense it follows a cycle of its own. The beginning of that cycle occurs when the business users realize that some problem that they face when doing their business requires a technological solution—perhaps they want to break into a new market, or to serve their customers faster or better, or to reduce the amount of time they have to spend on simple chores.

There is usually an ongoing dialogue between the business users and their technology counterparts, and ideally the first stirrings of a new system or a new set of features come to life as part of that dialogue, where the traders will say, "Here's what we are trying to do, and this is why it's so hard—can you give us some tools to deal with it?" The technology folks discuss the challenges with the business-side people and among themselves and come back with ideas about how to build a technological solution to the original problem. It is at this stage that it is extremely important that the technology people understand how the business works; once these ideas solidify into design specifications, it is usually too late to change anything important.

To produce a good design, the technical people need a combination of three skills. First, they need to be technically competent (since management often is involved at this stage, technical competence is not a given), which here means that they need to know what technological solutions are possible and how much work is involved in each. Second, they need to have business competence. At least some members of the team need to understand not just what the users are saying, but also what is left unsaid: the context of the problem, its relationships with the other things the business does, and the likelihood that the system will eventually be used for other similar things. Finally, they need to understand the local context—not only do they need to know how things should be done in theory, but they need to know how things are done here, in this firm, with its particular mix of systems and businesses.

The process of turning the vague initial desires of the business folks into workable plans that can accommodate the current and future needs of the business and do so in a technically sound way and within the existing infrastructure is an exciting and creative journey that can take weeks or even months. It usually culminates in the creation of a prototype (often called a *straw man*), which is a working piece of software that does some of the main things that the final system will do and demonstrates that the proposed solution is workable. If the prototype is successful, the next stage is the creation of a *development plan* that details the steps to the final product.

Like any complex project, the new system is not created in one go, but rather progresses through a series of intermediate *milestones* where some parts of it become operational. There could be many rollout cycles between these milestones, during which smaller pieces of the system (called *deliverables* in this context) are gradually delivered to the business users. The work the developers are doing during this *implementation phase* is often of a higher-level than the demands of the rollout cycle would seem to require; building and validating new models, creating new software frameworks, or bringing new trading platforms into the fold can take many months of work, and this often leads to tension between the long-term nature of such projects and the immediacy of the build and release cycle. In fact, in many groups, the division of labor between members often reflects this dichotomy, with some people specializing in longer-term, more theoretical things, while others tend to deal with the daily demands of the development process.

I hope that this description of what Wall Street software developers do has given you some understanding of how technology is created. However, you should realize that the reality is usually messier than the orderly sequence of stages that we just went through. In some places, the development, testing, and deployment stages are all mixed together in a rapid-fire sequence, where something developed this morning ends up in production by early afternoon. In other places, the rollout cycles become more like eons, with every little change being documented, tested to death by specially hired teams of quality assurance people (yes, QA can mean that too), and put through three test environments, with a sign-off by five managers being required before it is released to the users (who then have to wait months for simple fixes). In practice, it is hard to say which approach works best; pell-mell unstructured development does lead to more production problems but can be seen by the business side as more responsive than a heavily structured process where every step is regulated by rigid procedures enforced by many management layers. In practice, as with everything else, the ultimate success of the software development enterprise is much more a function of the quality, competence, and experience of the people doing it than of the procedures put in place to guide and restrain them.

CHAPTER 20

Production Support and Problem Management

After reading the previous chapter, where we discussed at length how much effort and care goes into developing and testing the software used by Wall Street firms, you may expect that once this software is released to the users and begins its productive life, it just chugs along happily without any problems. Unfortunately, this is not the case—as we tried to emphasize, no amount of testing can find all possible problems; all that testing can do is reduce the frequency and severity of systems issues. It is therefore an unfortunate reality of life that production systems do break, and once they break, someone has to deal with their failings.

Resolving systems problems is in fact one of the most important tasks that Wall Street technical folks have to perform. Sadly, it is also a task for which most of us are at first completely unprepared, and this lack of preparation and training significantly adds to the stress and frustration of those who have to handle these situations. In this chapter, I intend to outline some general principles that, in my experience, make production support less of a challenge and can simplify life for those who are called to perform these tasks. As in the previous chapter, I hope that this information will be useful both for newcomers to financial technology, who will get a flavor of what to expect in such problem management situations, and for "old hands," who may find here some ideas that they can use in their daily work.

WHY IS PROBLEM MANAGEMENT IMPORTANT, AND WHO SHOULD DO IT?

The first question we need to address in this area is, why am I making it sound as if systems problem management is such a big deal? It is a big deal because the stakes are often quite high. When trading software goes bad, it always costs the traders money, and it can be quite serious money. A single trade on a bad price can cost the firm tens of thousands, while trades done based on wrong risk information can easily wipe out a couple of days' worth of PnL. The worst possibility, however, is a situation in which the users cannot trade at all because of systems problems; aside from significant opportunity costs (an hour of downtime on a desk that makes $1 billion a year means that it is $0.5 million behind), this aggravates customers and presents very real risks to a firm's reputation. If a customer calls with a large trade and is told that the firm cannot do it because its systems are down, she will do this trade elsewhere and will think twice before turning to the firm again.

An analogy that I find helpful in developing the right attitude toward financial software problems is, again, automotive in nature: whenever the phone rings and traders report a problem, in many areas of financial technology, it is a safe bet that the losses incurred are greater than the property damage in an average traffic accident. The right attitude, therefore, is that whenever you hear the dreaded words *production problem*, you should drop whatever you are doing and start dealing with it.

Who should deal with systems problems? There are two common organizational arrangements in this area. The first is that there is a dedicated production support group that takes the first report of a problem: there is a support hotline that the users call if they think something is not right with their systems. The members of this support group are trained to recognize common system issues, and in some cases they can resolve these issues on their own. However, the list of typical issues is usually quite short (if a system keeps breaking in the same way, changes will be made to it to prevent that particular failure), so more often than not the support group is unable to do anything meaningful about the problem. The best it can usually do is determine which of the many systems is affected and pass on the issue to those who can deal with it—the developers who built the affected system.

Since in the great majority of cases, the system issues are transferred to the individual developers anyway, in many firms there is no support group at all (which is the second of the common organizational arrangements); instead, the business users contact individual developers directly rather than call a common support hotline. This second arrangement requires the business users to know who to call for what kind of problem, and it may take them a while to figure that out, but it generally results in faster resolution of the problems. Either way, with or without the support group standing between the developers and the users, if you are a developer who understands how a particular system is put together, at some point your phone will ring and bring news of a systems failure, together with demands that you fix it right away. Let us now discuss the basic principles for handling such calls.

HOW TO HANDLE PROBLEM REPORTS

The main thing to do during these problem report calls is to separate information from noise. The person who is calling for help is not going to tell you everything you need to know unless you guide him into giving you all the relevant details. He is calling because he is frustrated and angry, and probably has just lost some money because of a systems issue, so the initial report may sound like, "The . . . system sucks, I just sold $50 million of . . . four cents off the . . . market; who is going to write a . . . check to cover this loss," and so on (expletives deleted).

It is in fact very typical for these problem reports to be loaded with emotion rather than information. While you would be well advised to empathize with your user's feelings and show some repentance right away, you need to calm the caller down so that she can provide the information you need. And, in fact, you need quite a lot of it: when the problem happened, how the caller noticed it, the ID of the bad trade/bad security, and so on. As you ask these questions and (this is important) record the answers on a piece of paper, you should remember that your first priority is to determine the extent of the problem. So you should also ask questions like, "Is it just you, or are others around you complaining of similar things?" "Is it just the 10-year, or do you see wrong prices in other sectors?" and, most importantly, "Is it still wrong, or do you think it (prices, risk, whatever was wrong) is OK now?"

The first decision you have to make, based on these answers and perhaps on your own observations, is about how to prevent any further harm from the problem you are trying to diagnose. If you feel that the issue (bad trade, lost trades, wrong risk, or whatever it is) is not a minor glitch that you fully understand and know how to fix, you should assume that it is likely to recur. You should then tell the users about it right away and get them to stop quoting in external markets or to stop trading altogether—it is hard to admit that the system is broken, but it is much harder to explain afterward why you decided to go on trading with a broken system.

At this stage, it is often helpful to get some input from the management on both the business side and the technology side; you should tell them what you have been able to determine about the state of the system and the likelihood of its doing something bad in the immediate future, and help them decide whether to stop using the system entirely or to continue using it in a limited way. Generally, at this initial stage, nobody has all the information, so any decision to take or not take defensive action is likely to be based on intuition and experience rather than hard facts (and can, of course, turn out to be wrong afterward).

After this initial damage assessment, the next step is *not* to fix the problem, but rather to notify all the people who either are affected by it or can help you fix it. The most common way to do that is to send out a notification e-mail to these people (all of whom should be put on a special mailing list ahead of time); it should be short, should explain what the problem is (or at least what the symptoms are) and what you are going to do about it based on your current understanding of the situation, and, whenever possible, should contain an *ETA* (estimated time of arrival, which in this case means time when the problem will be resolved). This e-mail serves several purposes. For the business users, it provides evidence that the systems people are aware of the problem (so that they do not have to report it over and over again) and that someone is working on it. For your technical colleagues, it serves as a call for help; it is implied in these notification e-mails that if any recipient knows something that could explain what is going on, she will let you know. Finally, for the management, the notification e-mail (and the whole e-mail chain that is usually started by it) serves as a record of the problem and who did what to resolve it.

This problem-tracking function is often formalized in various in-house problem-management systems. These usually provide an intranet Web site where you (the person dealing with a problem) are required to open a *problem ticket* and fill out an often lengthy form with information such as which technology areas are affected, the severity of the problem, your name and staff ID, and the like. These systems are designed to give top management a bird's-eye view of the health of its technological realm—managers can see how many problems of what severity there are at any given time in each area, and this is meant to increase the quality of their decision making. This information is sometimes integrated into *digital dashboard* applications, which have warning lights for each technology area that light up in yellow or red if an area has more than a certain number of problems. I am not sure how useful all of this is to top management, but from the point of view of a front-line developer, these systems are rarely helpful in resolving problems—filling out forms instead of dealing with the actual problem at hand is not the most efficient way to resolve anything.[1] In practice, therefore, the front-line support people tend to either ignore or bypass the official problem-management systems, and my advice is to delegate dealing with these systems to a secretary if one is available or to your management whenever possible.

DIAGNOSING THE PROBLEM

Once we are past the notification stage, we enter the diagnosis stage, which means that it is time to figure out what the problem is. This task requires both technical and people skills, with the latter being more important (as always). There are several different technical approaches to finding out what is wrong with the production system, and we will discuss them momentarily, but the first priority is to make sure that you get adequate help from your colleagues. There are always a few people in your group who are knowledgeable enough about the system to participate in the investigation, and they normally will be willing to help (and you should not be shy about asking for such help). What you want to do with these offers of help is to prevent duplication of effort and meaningless running around, and you do that by asking people to do different parts of the puzzle solving instead of all trying to do the same thing. If your colleagues are not sitting right next to you, open a conference call with them, so that if someone finds the cause of the problem, the rest of you know immediately.

Diagnosing a systems problem is not unlike diagnosing a medical problem in that the patient (your system) is still alive and running and is typically only partially impaired, and you want to discover what is wrong with it without shutting it down. There are many ways to peek inside a running program, and you may have to try several of them before you find what you are looking for. The most common way of looking at what a process is doing is to examine its *log file*. Almost all in-house software components write some information about their state into a plain-text log file (and those that do not should be immediately redesigned to start doing that).

---

1. The following true story largely formed my attitude toward digital dashboards and all that goes with them: during the Y2K scare, a team of consultants in a major investment bank developed (at great expense) a digital dashboard that was supposed to monitor how the bank's systems coped with the turn of the century. It had the distinction of being the only application in the bank that did in fact break completely at the stroke of midnight on January 1, 2000—everything else worked just fine.

This is how a log file ought to work (consider this my wish list). First, it is written to a standard location on a shared drive so that you can look at it without logging on to the server where the program runs. Its name contains the name of the program that creates it (and also perhaps its process ID), as well as both the date and time when the log file was opened (so that if the program runs twice, the old log file is not overwritten). Every line in the log file begins with a time stamp, and the very first line is the complete command line that started the program, with the full path and name of the binary and all command-line arguments. During initialization, some programs read configuration information from a database, or perhaps from environmental variables, and all such configuration parameters should be echoed into the log file.

After the initialization stage, the program should log only errors, or perhaps warnings about problematic conditions that it encounters during execution, plus a heartbeat message every minute or so to indicate that the program is alive. Error and warning messages should be informative and should contain all the information you will need to resolve these error conditions: source code location (filename and line number) generating the message; any and all IDs (of the affected securities, trades, and so on), together with human-readable description of those objects; plus an accurate description of what the program thinks is wrong with them (this last requirement may seem obvious, but it is the one that, in real life, is violated the most). I wish that all log files I have seen were like that, but at least you can gauge the quality of a particular log file by how close it is to these principles.

When you look at a log file of a problematic process, you can usually quickly verify that the program was started with the correct arguments, and then look (grep or regular expression search) for error messages that contain some pattern related to the problem at hand (for example, an ID of one of the securities or trades that users are complaining about). A lot of problem investigations end right there; if the log file clearly says that this or that is wrong with the object of your investigation, you are done with diagnosing the problem (and the log file, or rather the person who designed it, should get a congratulatory pat on the back). Often, however, the problem is with something that the program creators did not consider worthy of a log file error message, in which case the log file has no mention of the problem, and you need to use other tools to find out what is wrong.

One of the more powerful ways to do that is to send a *debugging message* to the program. The purpose of a debugging message is to force the program to dump all details of its state related to a particular calculation into the log file (or perhaps publish them to the market data network). Clearly the program has to be designed to recognize debugging messages (which are typically sent either over a market data network or through a point-to-point connection), and code has to be in place to collect and dump the relevant program variables and structures, so (alas) not every program supports this kind of diagnostics tool. It is especially appropriate for systems that handle large numbers of securities in a parallel way, as this tool makes it possible to isolate the state of calculations for an individual security (or trade, or customer, and so on).

The debugging message is a powerful tool, but it usually results in truly massive amounts of output, which may be a bit difficult to process (and care should be taken to dump the state only once; otherwise the program will spew out megabytes of identical text every second, which not only fills up the file system, but also slows down the program to the point where it may become completely unusable). At a minimum, this debugging output should contain inputs and outputs of whatever calculations are being performed. Note that even if the debugging facility is not available, you can often access inputs and outputs directly if they are read from and published to the market data network; checking the inputs and outputs wherever possible should be one of the first diagnostic steps and may very well reveal the problem.

If all these tools have been tried and the problem still has not been resolved, it may be necessary to reproduce the problem in one of the development environments. As we discussed in the previous chapter, development environments should contain a copy of the system that is being prepared for the next release, so in general the system in such an environment is not the same as the one that is running in production, but it is still worth checking whether the problem exists in one of the development environments anyway. If it is in fact present there, this means that the changes made to the system since the last production rollout are unrelated to the problem at hand. If the problem is not present in the development copy, it usually means that either one of the latest changes has solved the problem, or the problem has to do with the way the system was started, which usually helps in narrowing down the problem.

Sometimes it becomes necessary to roll back the software in a development environment to the production version in order to reproduce the problem. In a development environment, you have much more power not only to diagnose the problem, but also to test possible fixes, since that environment as a whole and its various components can be restarted at will, and you also have complete freedom to change user inputs and environmental parameters. This possibility of using a development environment to resolve production problems is why you generally want to keep at least one such environment in a fully working state at any given time. If the problem can be reproduced locally (when you run the affected program on your workstation), you can then run that program in a debugger, which gives you all manner of access to the program's internals and should allow you to disentangle almost any issue.

Despite this variety of diagnostic tools, diagnosing systems problems is not easy and usually requires a great deal of experience and critical thinking. It is often hard to figure out where to look and what to look for. What should guide your thinking in such situations is Rule 1 of applications support: *determine what has changed.* The problem you are looking at almost certainly did not exist yesterday (or people would have complained about it yesterday), so it has been triggered, directly or indirectly, by something that changed between yesterday and today. What could that be?

In the simplest case, there was a change in the code that explains the newly bad behavior of the system. Since software changes in the production environment are almost always tightly controlled, as explained in the previous chapter, it is relatively easy to rule this possibility in or out. If your group did a software release yesterday and something does not work today, looking at the *changes* in the code that handles the affected area is very likely to explain what is going wrong. If there was no official rollout, but you see that the affected binary has a recent time stamp, someone must have violated the change management rules; let management deal with the violation, but make sure that you find out who made the change and why it was made. If there was a code change and today's problem is sufficiently serious, the best thing to do is usually to roll back the changes and restart the system, and then figure out what was wrong with the changes, as the figuring out part is often very time-consuming. The code in this context means not just the high-level code of the compiled languages, but most definitely includes any configuration files or databases; if anything has changed in that area of the code, it is highly likely those changes are related to the problem that cropped up today.

Another area where changes may have been made is hardware—new servers, new network configurations, operating system upgrades, and the like should be immediately suspect. Fortunately, these kinds of changes are controlled as tightly as code changes, so it is fairly easy to find out if anything was recently done to the hardware. Of course, hardware can also develop problems of its own despite the lack of management permission: servers can crash, databases can hang, network switches can fail, and so on. Hardware failures are usually sufficiently obvious, and whenever they occur, the challenge is not so much to diagnose why the system is not working as it is to determine how to bring it back up with a different hardware configuration (there should be a plan for doing that, as we discuss later in this chapter).

After code and hardware changes, the next culprit is usually very fundamental: the passage of time, or, more specifically, the change of date. A system that performs any kind of financial calculations has the potential to behave differently on different dates, especially under special date conditions such as the end of a month or a year, February 28/29, and IMM dates (third Wednesdays of the month); if either today, the spot date (two business days ahead), or the default settlement date for a given market hits one of those special cases, long-dormant bugs in the date logic can suddenly be activated and either produce incorrect results of some calculations or cause complex calculations such as curve generation to fail completely.

The change of date also has an indirect effect on the securities universe that the system is dealing with; some securities may have matured or been called today, some may have been issued yesterday, or some of the on-the-runs or the important futures may have rolled. For example, a newly issued security that was not in the system yesterday may have its static data set up incorrectly and cause some calculations to fail today. It often makes sense to review the differences between the composition of the securities universe between yesterday and today (and if your system does not make such comparisons easy, you should add such functionality as soon as practical); if you see some weird securities going into the system or some perfectly legitimate securities being deleted, you are almost certainly on to something that is relevant to your problem.

Changes in the securities universe illustrate a larger issue: even if nothing has changed in your system, there may have been changes in "partner" systems that provide yours with reference data, trade data, positions, market data, closing prices, and heaven knows what else. A system that you read closing prices from may have had an issue last night, one of the market data feeds may have changed the format of its messages, a trade database may have performance issues, and so on—unlike the case of your own system, where you at least know about all changes and out-standing problems, you will not necessarily be aware of every problem with each of those supporting systems.

The owners of many middleware systems that provide services to other technology groups usually make some (rather half-hearted) efforts to notify downstream systems of any issues that they have, but most people ignore these notifications, as 99 percent of the time they are completely irrelevant to your area. Therefore, as a practical matter, the interfaces with other systems in the bank are very frequent causes of trouble. If every sys-tem in the bank has a 5 percent chance of developing a problem on any given day, and you use services provided by 10 such systems, your system is likely to get in trouble every other day—the overreliance of financial industry systems on in-house services is perhaps the main reason why so much time is spent on production support.

Understanding the interdependencies between various systems in your bank is critical to your ability to resolve issues with your system, as is maintaining good relationships with the people who own the systems on which you depend. It is one thing to just send an e-mail to the reference data group saying that your system has problems with some changes that the group introduced last night, and it is quite another to be able to call (or maybe walk over to) your friends in that group and ask them to help you with your problem—they will give you much better and quicker assis-tance if you ask for it informally, and if they know that you can be trusted not to make a big fuss even if they made a mistake.

Establishing such an informal network of contacts with your col-leagues in other groups is a long process, and its success is based on mutual respect: your willingness and ability to reciprocate and help them with their problems are usually much more important than mere socializing at lunch or after work. This actually applies also to your relationships with people within your group and with your business users; instead of figuring every-thing out on your own, it is almost always better to have a good relation-ship with someone who knows more than you do about a specific part of your system and ask that person for help if you suspect that that area is playing a part in the problem you are looking at. In fact, I would call this Rule 2 of application support: if you do not understand something outside your area of expertise, do not try to figure it out (there is usually no time for that), but rather find someone who knows the problem area well and get him to help you. Here I can speak from experience; problem management does require technical skills, but ultimately it is a social process.

FIXING THE PROBLEM

Suppose now that, whether by applying your technical prowess, your social skills, or both, you have finally found out what is wrong with your system, and, moreover, that you know how to fix the problem. Depending on the complexity and severity of the problem, you will reach this stage anywhere from a couple of minutes to a couple of hours after the original problem report. The fix always requires some intervention into the production system, and at this stage the challenge is to make sure that this intervention will not cause more problems than it is intended to resolve.

In some cases, all that is required to fix the problem is a small change to a user input or perhaps some configuration parameter that can be read in dynamically; in that situation, you can just go ahead and do it, and then tell the users (and your management) that the problem is solved. Usually, however, the required fix is more intrusive; since most software processes configuration information only at start-up, at least some of the system components may have to be restarted to pick up configuration changes. If the problem is with the code itself rather than the configuration, you may have to perform an emergency release—repair the code, build an updated binary, and put it out into the production environment—which almost always requires stopping the process running the existing (broken) binary and restarting it with the new one. If you do have to restart some or all of the system to fix the original problem, the system will be wholly or partially unavailable for some period of time. If the original problem was fairly minor, the ultimate wisdom of such an intraday fix is not obvious; yes, the system is somewhat impaired, but people may still be able to use most of its functionality, and if you bring it down to apply your fix, it will become completely unusable for a while.

Resolving this trade-off is ultimately a business decision, and you should discuss it with your management and the management of the business unit. Since you have just spent time and effort figuring out how to fix the problem that your users have complained so bitterly about, you are probably eager to go ahead and restart the system in order to get it fixed. However, in all but the most severe cases (when the system is completely unusable or is down already), an intraday restart carries a lot of risks. Restarting a large system is a fairly elaborate process that is usually taken care of by a well-tested sequence of overnight jobs that is designed to bring the system up reliably, but not necessarily in the fastest way possible. During intraday restarts, people often try to cut corners and skip or speed up some of the steps in the normal restart process. This works some percentage of the time, but it also invites errors, so it is not unusual to get the system halfway up and then remember that some essential step has not been performed, so you have to start all over. Similar quandaries often arise when you try to restart only certain parts of the system; surprisingly often, what appeared to be a fairly straightforward shortcut that you just dreamed up in a flash of inspiration hits totally unexpected snags and makes the overall situation much worse.

Intraday system restarts therefore have a lot of potential for turning a small glitch into a major system outage, and painful experience suggests that they should be avoided if at all possible. If the users are unable to live with the problem for the rest of the day and you are forced to restart, the restart should be performed only through a well-tested procedure, preferably by rerunning the full sequence of overnight jobs. The only exception to that rule is if your group has developed an accelerated start-up sequence to be used specifically for emergencies (or procedures for a partial restart of only certain components), and these procedures have been extensively tested in development environments.

Needless to say, before you go for a system restart or another highly disruptive intervention, you should notify the users and your management. You should tell them (e-mail is the best way to do it) what you are planning to do and how long you think it will be before the system becomes available again, and give them a few minutes to respond to your notification—the desk may be in the middle of pricing a deal or waiting for an economic number, and they may ask you to wait for a better time.

A lot of real-life systems problems are, thankfully, of a less serious variety and require only minor adjustments (sometimes simply telling the users how to do what they are trying to do), so the major systems outages that we have been focusing on are generally fairly rare. When they do occur, however, it is common practice to follow up with a *postmortem*. In the problem management context, this rather morose term means analysis of the causes of the outage and of the steps taken to ensure that it will never happen again.

Postmortems can take different forms, from a brief e-mail to a series of meetings followed by a long report, but their essential components are fairly common. A postmortem report should contain the timeline of how the problem happened, including any events in other areas that were later found to have contributed to the problem, a detailed description of the steps taken to identify and resolve the problem, and a proposal for what needs to be done to prevent the outage from happening again. In many cases, the business side also makes an estimate of the losses the firm incurred as a result of the outage (this is known as a *business impact statement*); while these estimates are often subjective (and often inflated), they are useful in that they do tend to focus the minds of the technology-side management. System issues have been known to cause multimillion-dollar losses, and in such extreme cases the banks do take administrative steps—from firing people to putting management bonuses in jeopardy—to make sure that the pain is distributed appropriately.

PREVENTING SYSTEM FAILURES

The potential for harsh consequences of major system failures is a major driver of technology initiatives aimed at preventing system outages and improving the reliability of various pieces of technology in general. The main themes of such initiatives are identifying single points of failure (where a failure of one component makes a large system completely unusable), developing redundancy schemes such as hot and cold backups for major components, tightening the screws on unauthorized code changes, and beefing up prerelease testing efforts.

In the post-9/11 world, these system stability efforts are often intertwined with corporate initiatives aimed at ensuring business continuity in the event of a disaster. Almost all financial-sector companies now have *disaster recovery* (DR) sites, where, in particular, all their systems are meant to be replicated so that business can be fully resumed from the emergency location in case their main office is taken out. In practice, most such disaster recovery sites are far from complete from a systems perspective, and even where replicas of all important systems do exist, they often run in a scaled-down hardware configuration and are not monitored nearly as closely as the real thing. The existence of such replicas, however, opens up interesting possibilities for resolving systems issues in the main production systems: the disaster recovery replicas can often be used as replacements for the main production systems when these are hit by major outages. Since everything is on a network, the fact that the DR systems are geographically far away is usually irrelevant, and users can be switched to those systems fairly easily.

Another approach to disaster recovery is to take advantage of the already existing geographic diversification of major financial companies, almost all of which have major centers in New York, London, and Tokyo. It is fairly easy to imagine a disaster that would take out New York *and* its suburbs, where all U.S. disaster recovery sites are located (the Northeast blackout of 2003, which affected the whole region, is one real-life example, but if a major hurricane were to strike the New York area, it would amount to the same thing), but it makes little sense to seriously plan for a disaster that takes out New York, London, and Tokyo at the same time (if that should happen, we will all have other things to worry about besides business continuity).

In fact, there is already a significant body of experience with these regions helping one another out in both a business and a technological sense. In the days after 9/11, many U.S. clients of major investment banks could still trade through the banks' London offices (where the traders stayed late to support the U.S. customers). Cantor Fitzgerald, whose New York offices were obliterated in the attack, resumed trading for its U.S. clients out of London in just a couple of days. On the technology front, cross-regional cooperation is a part of daily life for these global companies, and one of its main dimensions is the area of systems support. End-of-day systems issues in London (problems with the closing prices and risk and PnL reports, as well as certain back-office issues with netting and settlement) are routinely handed over to New York so that people in London can go home, and New York can sometimes hand such issues over to Tokyo or Singapore (although there is a gap of a couple of hours in this case between end of day in New York and start of day in Asia), and of course Asia can pass its unresolved issues on to London.

This westward, follow-the-sun movement of unresolved systems problems is benign and improves the quality of life of the technology folks in all regions. Unfortunately, these things flow in the other direction as well; as we discussed in Chapter 18, many "global" systems are in fact run from a single region, and the problems that users of such systems experience in other regions often are passed on to the developers in their home area, despite the awkwardness of the time differences. For example, if a New York–based system is being used in London and exhibits a problem in the London morning hours that the local support people cannot resolve, the New York developers will get called in the middle of their night to deal with the issue. Similarly, Tokyo morning problems may be propagated to London (where it is the dead of night) or New York (where it is still early evening).

OVERNIGHT SUPPORT

These cross-region support calls have a lot in common with the more established overnight support routine, which was originally designed to deal with issues arising during overnight batches within a single region and typically works as follows. Each technology group designates one person to be on overnight support duty every night, and the lucky guy is rotated every day or perhaps every week. The schedule that indicates who is on support on what nights is called a *support rota*, and it is given to the operations center that oversees the overnight batches. If a batch job belonging to this group fails or gets stuck, the operations center calls the person in the rota (and if the center can't reach her, it moves on to the next person on the list); typically the person gets awakened in the middle of the night and told which job failed, after which it becomes her responsibility to resolve the issue. The global twist on that routine is that nowadays these calls in the dead of night are as likely to come from your colleagues or perhaps the business users in other geographical regions. What do you do if you find yourself in this situation?

The first thing you do is establish a remote connection to your office. All financial institutions provide some mechanism by which their employees can connect to their systems from home. In recent years, this is almost always done by a virtual private network (VPN) established over your own broadband connection (which you are assumed to have at home). Your employer will usually provide a computer from which you can establish such a connection; since a VPN connection effectively makes your computer part of your employer's corporate intranet, your employer generally wants to control what is installed on that computer, and therefore finds it safer to give people computers that are configured according to its standards (and where you do not have admin rights, so you generally cannot install stuff yourself). Another option that is less convenient but more portable is a so-called SSL (secure socket layer) connection that you can establish from a Web browser on almost any computer. In this arrangement, your browser window displays your office desktop through a terminal server connection and gives you access to e-mail and your network drives, but not much else.

In both cases, you need something called SecurID to establish a connection. SecurID is a credit-card-sized electronic gadget made by a company called RSA. It has a little LCD window displaying a six-digit number that changes every minute or so; this number becomes part of the password you need to enter when you log in remotely, so you need to physically hold the thing in your hand to be able to connect to the office. Once you connect, you are more or less in the same position as if you were at the office as far as what you can do to fix system problems is concerned; the speed of a broadband connection is typically more than adequate, but you will usually have less screen space.

The main difference between doing production support from home in the middle of the night and doing it in the office is that at home, you are on your own—you cannot just walk over to your colleagues and/or managers to ask for help. It is also often possible that someone half a world away is also looking at the same problem, and that you will start stepping on each other's toes in trying to resolve it. Therefore, the first thing you do in such situations is check your e-mail to see if there are any messages about the problem and if anyone is already on the case, and the second thing you do is send an e-mail to your group and perhaps to your colleagues in other locations stating that you have received this problem report and you are going to look at this. Be sure to include your phone number so that people can call you, or ask another office where people are in at this hour to set up a conference call about the problem and dial into that (all banks provide a toll-free number through which you can access the internal phone system).

Then you start looking at the problem. If you can quickly and comfortably resolve it on your own, do so, and then send out a notification e-mail saying that you took care of everything, after which you can go back to bed. If, however, you find that your investigation leads you into an unfamiliar area and it will take you a while to figure out what is wrong, immediately apply Rule 2 and call (and wake up) the person who you think can help you in this area—this does inconvenience people, but it will always result in much quicker resolution (it is a good idea to keep handy a list of the home phone numbers of those of your colleagues whom you are likely to bother in such situations). You can generally put off lengthy postmortems until you come into the office later in the morning, but before you go back to bed, you, or maybe other people that you brought into the investigation, should send out an all-clear e-mail once the problem has been resolved (or you all agree that the resolution can wait until normal office hours).

At this point, you may think that resolving systems issues is not a lot of fun. It is true that it is often stressful and somewhat frustrating (and overnight support is just downright hard even in the physical sense), but systems support has certain redeeming qualities, which I want to highlight in order to conclude this chapter. Nothing raises your credibility with your colleagues and your business users faster and higher than the ability to deal with emergencies calmly, professionally, and efficiently. As I have tried to emphasize, this requires a great deal of both technical and people skills, and those who end up doing it well are highly valued by all stakeholders—peers, management, and business clients—which usually extends into the compensation area as well.

Ironically, it is often better for you professionally if your system keeps developing problems that you then resolve in a highly visible and classy way, rather than if you build your software so well that it never breaks (in which case nobody will ever have to ask you for help, and people will soon forget your name); call this snatching victory from the jaws of defeat. The downside for good problem solvers is called the support trap: if you are good at support, you may end up doing it all the time, and you should definitely try to avoid this situation (the best way to do that is to train others to do support instead of you). That being said, few things in your professional life will be as satisfying as leaning back after you and your comrades-in-arms have slain another dragon that was threatening your software castle—you do not want to slay dragons all day, but even an occasional battle gives you a chance to enjoy the feeling of being on the right side in the perennial struggle of good versus evil.

Conclusions

Well, this has been a long book, and you managed to read it all the way through to reach this point, so I think you deserve a proper good-bye and some parting words of advice on what to do with your newly acquired knowledge of financial markets and their technology. This is what this brief concluding section is about.

On one level, answering the question of what to do with what you have learned from the book is quite simple: you should recognize that your newfound knowledge is limited and incomplete and that you should start using it as a platform to find out more about things that matter to you. In any given area, there is a wealth of resources, both in book form and on the Web, that in most cases make it amazingly easy to find the answers to your specific questions (I list some of them in the Recommended Reading section, but Google and Amazon searches will easily give you more). In this book, I tried to show you what kind of questions you should ask when you are studying financial markets, and I hope that the book has given you an organizing framework for processing the information you will find in your quest for answers.

As far as technology-related questions are concerned, the task of finding out how different financial companies approach their technical and quantitative challenges is difficult, if not impossible, if you are outside the industry. However, if you are already working in the industry, your corporate intranet can be a great resource. The best resource of all, of course, is people who know the things you are interested in. It is perfectly appropriate for you to approach people working in an area that you have questions about and ask those questions—most people are happy to talk about their work and will gladly satisfy your curiosity (at least, this is how I found out most of what I know). Do this for a few years, and you will know all that is worth knowing about your area of specialization, and, most importantly, you will know how to find out what you do not yet know so that you can keep up-to-date with new developments.

This latter point about keeping up-to-date is very important. The pace of change in the modern financial industry is astoundingly fast, and any knowledge you have will age pretty quickly. This unfortunately also applies to what you have learned from this book. I am writing this in February 2006, and I started working on the book in midsummer 2004 (not quite two years ago), which, of course, is but a blink of an eye in the centuries-long history of the financial world. Nevertheless, in this brief period, major futures exchanges (CME and CBOT) abandoned their membership structure and became public companies, the NYSE is merging with ArcaEx (one of its all-electronic rivals), the U.S. Treasury is bringing back the long bond, the trading volumes in listed options and in credit derivatives have both doubled, and the list goes on and on.

By the time you read this, many other similarly important changes will have taken place. This book gives you a snapshot of what the industry looked like circa 2005, but what you really want to know when you are thinking about your career is what it will be like in a few years. I can argue that knowledge of the past (especially the recent past, which is what this book has tried to reflect) is a prerequisite for understanding what the future holds, but it is reasonable for you to try to extrapolate some of the themes you may have spotted in this book and ask if these trends are likely to hold.

TRENDS IN FINANCIAL TECHNOLOGY

All I can really add to this divination effort is to list the trends that I have witnessed in my time and offer my opinion as to whether these trends are likely to continue, with the standard disclaimer that predicting the future is an inexact science. At the end of the day, your guess is as good as mine. The most visible of those trends, and one that bodes well for financial technology, is that the financial industry has become inseparable from that technology—the likelihood that it will ever go back to its old pencil-and-paper ways is zero. Much of this transformation happened before I joined the industry in the mid-1990s and was related to the growth of derivatives businesses, which require the quantitative ability to model the markets they operate in, coupled with the technological ability to crunch the numbers that these models need in an exact but efficient way.

This first phase of the Wall Street technological revolution was fairly painless for Wall Street businesspeople. The newfangled derivatives desks did not encroach on anyone's existing territory; instead, they brought in boatloads of new revenues in the classic high-margin, low-volume way that Wall Street really excels in. In contrast, the second phase of the revolution, which I witnessed personally, was and continues to be a lot more controversial from the business perspective. The advent of electronic markets has had the tendency to transform these high-margin, low-volume operations into low-margin, high-volume affairs, and this has brought about a lot of real pain for many traditional Wall Street businesses.

The brutal reality of this brave new world is that if a computer can do what you are doing better and cheaper, you will not be doing it for very much longer. In this way, people who used to work at interdealer brokerages have been largely displaced by electronic trading platforms, pit traders on most European exchanges have met the same fate (although U.S. exchanges are still fighting this tide), cash equity desks in many Wall Street banks have already disappeared (and the rest will disappear soon), and, much as it pains me to admit it, my personal favorite—government bond trading, which used to be such a major profit center—is probably heading down the same path. I think it is likely that this process will continue; after conquering the cash trading areas, the electronic trading revolution will move on to derivatives and attempt to convert them into the low-margin, high-volume format that is its trademark. This has already happened with equity options, it is happening now with interest-rate swaps, and even more modern areas such as credit default swaps are at risk.

The practical consequences of this for technical and quantitative people are twofold. First, the demand for technical talent in this space is likely to continue unabated. On some level, computerization of trading leads to a net job transfer from business areas to technology areas—a cash equity desk once had upward of 30 people; they are now replaceable by a trading system that may require 5 to 10 people to operate, but these will be different people who are much more likely to be in the target audience of this book. Second, if you are working (or considering working) for one of the areas that are at risk of being taken over by the electronic trading wave, you should either join the tide and learn something about electronic trading or try to find another area that is not at risk in this sense.

The problem that many of the old-school traders, salespeople, and brokers have with this whole electronic trading revolution is that it presents them with two almost equally unpleasant choices: if they fight the adoption of electronic trading in their area, they will lose their customers to their more tech-savvy competitors, while if they surrender to the electronic trading onslaught, they may eventually lose their jobs in the new business model. You can forgive them for being less than ecstatic about this, and this has made business-technology relations in this area much more adversarial than in the more traditional derivatives technology. This, however, is changing rather rapidly for the better; the next generation of business managers (people in their thirties who grew up playing early Nintendo games) tends to view this controversy in much more pragmatic terms. People in this generation accept the inevitability of change in their trading model and are much more interested in finding new ways to make the new high-volume trading model profitable. This is another trend that I believe will continue, if only because the businesspeople really have no choice in the matter.

You may ask at this point whether there are any trends that I have observed that I do not mindlessly extend into the future. Yes, there are (I just put the ones that I believe will keep going first), and one such trend is the explosive growth of financial technology. The story of financial technology so far has been that of uninterrupted upward movement. It has grown tremendously since I joined the industry (by a factor of at least 3 in terms of headcount), and if its present rate of expansion is mindlessly prolonged into the future, in another 10 years most Wall Street institutions will change from being trading businesses with small technology appendages to being technology companies with small trading businesses on the side. I just do not believe that Wall Street businesspeople will allow this to happen (besides, this would not be sustainable economically, but that is a secondary issue).

Like any story of unbroken ascent, this situation leads to hubris and waste. The leaders of Wall Street IT have gained significant power in their firms and do not see any serious threats to their position. The technology organizations that they run are protected from external competition by a strong institutional bias against third-party systems of any kind. As in all areas of human endeavor, this lack of competition often results in poor-quality and very expensive products.

The rationale for internal software development originally was that we can put a system together faster than we can find a third party to do it and thus can reap a competitive advantage in our trading until our competition catches up. Once everyone got the same systems, the rationale shifted to our systems being in some (often intangible) way superior to those of our competitors (a claim that is impossible to confirm or refute because no firm will tell its competitors how its systems are put together). Nevertheless, it soon became apparent to the business users that many models and systems, especially in the more mature areas such as derivatives pricing, are in fact exactly the same everywhere (only the bugs are in different places, and thus can be considered proprietary content), and then the rationale shifted again to our superior knowledge of our own systems so that we can support them better and fix them faster when they break. As I described in Chapter 3, the Wall Street firms eventually moved to streamline their software development effort so that at least the more commoditized software is developed in only one place within the bank instead of there being five different groups working for five different desks. But industrywide this multiplication of effort continues unabated, with every bank writing the same, say, financial analytics libraries on its own.

The only force that holds this system together is tradition. In the early days of financial technology, the trading businesses paid for their technology expenses the same way they paid for dinners with clients: as a small cost of doing business with no questions asked. As the technology organizations grew, so did the technology expenses, but the early in-house relationships survived the exponential growth in technology costs and turned into a textbook single-supplier situation. When the business side decides that it needs some new technology, its own technology organization gets this job by default—potential providers of similar systems are not even invited to compete with the in-house teams. In rare cases, a cost-conscious business may want to take a look at what's available externally, but overwhelmingly such businesses turn to the in-house technology groups for help in evaluating the external alternatives, and this evaluation predictably results in the conclusion that it is best to build it ourselves.

As a result, a lot of stuff that should have been bought has ended up being built in-house; among the systems developed internally by financial firms (presumably because the commercially available alternatives were not up to their exacting standards), I have seen programming languages, C compilers, database drivers, job control systems, and, perhaps most ridiculous of all, e-mail clients, spreadsheets, and word processors.[1] The technology organization correctly figures that the more such systems it develops, the more people it will need to support them, and the organization will grow ever larger and more powerful. The single-supplier system is the core mechanism that has allowed the technology organizations to grow by leaps and bounds without fear of external competition or consolidation.

As long as the clients of the single suppliers (which in this case means the Wall Street trading businesses) continue to not care about how

---

1. I originally wanted to write that we develop everything but word processors, but then someone showed me an internally developed word processor.

much the technology costs, this system can grow and prosper, and so it has done quite spectacularly during the time I observed it. Is this because the system is so perfect, or is it because Wall Street really has not had a down year since 1994? I do not know, but I strongly suspect the latter, and I often ask myself what would happen if a severe downturn forced the Wall Street businesses to rethink their approach to technology spending. They cannot abandon their technological toys, but they could turn to different, more cost-effective suppliers of these toys, which to me means that the financial software industry would come out a big winner in any readjustment of this kind, at the expense of the internal technology organizations. Of course, a lot of people made the same prediction five years ago and went on to found software companies in anticipation of the big windfall, and by and large they are still waiting. The status quo may well continue; I just do not see how it can continue indefinitely.

What this means on a practical level for Wall Street's technical workforce is that you may want to consider working for a financial software company rather than a big bank. The financial software industry is already doing much better and has made big inroads into the traditional Wall Street technology turf, especially in the areas of risk management, back-office processing, and financial analytics, and I think there is a good chance that over time it will take over most of the development tasks that are now performed by the Wall Street technology units. This may happen in a big and brutal readjustment or, more likely, as a gradual shift, but if it does, I think the economics and the headcounts of financial technology would be much better balanced than they are today.

Back to the trends that I think will continue: regarding the barriers to entry into financial technology and quantitative finance, I think it is getting more difficult to enter this occupation directly from a hard sciences or engineering background without demonstrating at least some educational credentials reflecting your interest in the industry. Ten years ago, a Wall Street firm would routinely hire a physics Ph.D. with no prior industry experience and no formal education in finance (that is how I got here), but this was largely because it was almost impossible to acquire educational credentials in financial technology in those days, as the educational system really did not have anything like that to offer. Over the last 10 years, this has changed; many universities now have programs geared toward the financial industry, and the Wall Street firms have started to expect a job candidate to have taken at least some classes that are related to finance (Economics 101 is what most people actually end up taking).

The currently available educational offerings include a growing number of financial engineering programs as well as stand-alone classes on various aspects of finance that you can take as part of your coursework at many U.S. universities. The response of the American educational system to the practical needs of the financial industry reminds me of the adage about how the generals are always fighting the last war instead of preparing for the next: the content of the financial engineering programs that I am aware of is overwhelmingly focused on derivatives and risk management, which were hot topics on Wall Street 5 to 10 years ago. However, going through such a program will be undeniably useful no matter what you end up doing in the financial industry, so it is definitely worth considering for those who are thinking of a Wall Street job. I have reasons to hope that this book will be useful in bridging the gaps between what you can learn in these programs and the reality on the ground.

The future of the financial technology profession may have its ups and downs, but what gives me reason for long-term optimism about its prospects is the remarkable resilience and history of innovation of the financial industry itself. The lure of profits in the market brings out the creativity of the market participants like nothing else, and they will always try to gain an edge through creative applications of technology. As early as 1815, Nathan Rothschild used carrier pigeons to be the first to learn about Wellington's victory over Napoleon, and he made a killing buying British government bonds on the London Stock Exchange when everyone else thought the British army was doing badly. Market players have tried to use every major technological milestone since then (railroads, the telegraph, the telephone, and many, many others) to gain an informational advantage over others in the market game, and my impression from observing them in action is that they will always try to do that—it is the very nature of the game.

If you are good at technology and you understand the markets, there will always be things for you to do in this space. Some markets may disappear, but the trading crowd will move on and create other markets; some strategies may become unprofitable and will be replaced with others; the organizational structures of the markets will change; but the overriding constant in all of this is that people will always come up with something new and interesting in their attempts to win the market game. They can't stop; there's simply too much money in the game, and this hustle and bustle was, is, and always will be a source of opportunities to turn your brainpower into profits.

May you have a good time doing that.

Recommended Reading

CHAPTER 1, "FINANCIAL MARKETS"

There is no shortage of books covering the generalities of financial markets, although they are typically written for a "business-side" audience. In this group, I like Andrew Chisholm's *Introduction to Capital Markets* [1]; it is well written and reasonably short, and while it is European in origin, it does not focus on Europe. A similar but U.S.-centric book is Fabozzi and Modigliani [2]; however, it is much longer and somewhat denser stylistically. A well-written nontechnical guide [3] is part of the *Economist* series and has good coverage of international markets. I should also mention a popular textbook by Van Horne [4] that focuses on interest-rate markets. There are also much more expansive tomes, such as the famous *Investments* textbook [5] which is used in MBA programs everywhere.

All the books in this group share two disadvantages. The first is that they are far too detailed for a quantitatively literate reader—roughly half the space is taken up by relatively trivial examples, so someone who can add without a calculator can be bored easily. Second, they lack historical depth, which I think is very unfortunate, as it is much easier (and much more fun) to figure out how the markets operate today from a historical perspective. Luckily, we have the towering figure of Sidney Homer to take care of that problem. His book with Richard Sylla [6] about the history of interest rates is one of the best nonfiction books I have ever read. It combines an astounding depth of research with a wonderfully clear and readable style. The authors start at prehistoric times and cover everything from ancient Greece to twentieth-century Latin America, so the size of the book is a bit intimidating, but this should not put you off. Reading this book will be a considerable investment of your time, but it will pay off handsomely in amazing insights into human economic behavior, the drivers of financial markets, and that most elusive of qualities: a sense of history.

If you care more about equity markets, read B. Mark Smith's very accessible work [7] which covers the history of stock markets around the world. A recent coffee-table book called *The Origins of Value* [8] contains a collection of interesting and lavishly illustrated articles about early financial markets and is worth every penny of its surprisingly modest price tag for the illustrations alone. Two more books provide interesting historical accounts that are relevant for the capital markets. Charles Kindleberger's *Financial History of Western Europe* [9] is written from a monetarist perspective and discusses the evolution of money and the ways people think about money. Larry Neal's *The Rise of Financial Capitalism* [10] focuses more narrowly on the English and Dutch financial markets of the seventeenth and eighteenth centuries, and rightly so—most of today's financial markets and their fundamental instruments and institutions were either invented or perfected during that period. I would, however, recommend reading these two books after you become more familiar with today's capital markets.

I am not aware of any Web resources that provide a broad overview of the financial markets area. However, Investopedia.com [11] offers a useful glossary of financial terms, and Wikipedia [12] has a surprisingly good collection of articles about financial markets (as well as almost everything else).

[1] Andrew Chisholm, *An Introduction to Capital Markets: Products, Strategies, Participants* (Wiley, 2002).

[2] Frank J. Fabozzi and Franco Modigliani, *Capital Markets: Institutions and Instruments* (Prentice Hall, 2002).

[3] Mark Levinson, *Guide to Financial Markets* (Bloomberg Press, 2003).

[4] James C. Van Horne, *Financial Market Rates and Flows* (Prentice Hall, 2000).

[5] Zvi Bodie, Alex Kane, and Alan J. Marcus, *Investments* (McGraw-Hill, 2004).

[6] Sidney Homer and Richard Sylla, *A History of Interest Rates* (Rutgers University Press, 1996).

[7] B. Mark Smith, *Equity Culture: A History of the Global Stock Market from Ancient Rome to Silicon Valley* (University of Chicago Press, 2004).

[8] William N. Goetzmann and K. Geert Rouwenhorst (eds.), *The Origins of Value: the Financial Innovations That Created Modern Capital Markets* (Oxford University Press, 2005).

[9] Charles P. Kindleberger, *A Financial History of Western Europe* (Oxford University Press, 1993).

[10] Larry Neal, *The Rise of Financial Capitalism: International Capital Markets in the Age of Reason* (Cambridge University Press, 1993).

[11] www.investopedia.com/.

[12] en.wikipedia.org/wiki/Main_Page.

CHAPTER 2, "MARKET PARTICIPANTS"

There are other books in addition to the already mentioned [1] through [4] that cover the general topics of this chapter in varying amount of detail. I will mention first a thankfully short book by Richard Roberts (also part of the *Economist* series) [13]: it focuses a bit too much on various financial scandals of recent years, but it is quite useful nonetheless. The classic text in this area is Thomas Liaw's *The Business of Investment Banking* [14] (be sure to pick the latest 2005 edition), which, as the title suggests, is mostly concerned with the sell side of Wall Street. Another well-known textbook by Herbert Mayo [15] (I hear that the new, ninth edition is in the works) is more broad in coverage, but I like Liaw's book better. I also like Stuart McCrary's lucid *Hedge Fund Course* [16] which explains everything I ever wanted to know about the hedge fund industry. In general, these books are useful as references if you have questions beyond what we covered in this chapter, but actually reading them from cover to cover would probably be a bit too much if all you want is a general understanding of the financial industry.

As far as Web resources go, I am sorry to report that, as a rule, the public Web sites of Wall Street firms are full of utterly meaningless marketing blubber about synergies and other such topics and are therefore completely useless for the purposes of figuring out what the company does, how many people work there, and other similarly down-to-earth bits of information. Of course, if you are interested in a particular company, by all means go and look at its Web site; just do not expect to find much information. In contrast, market regulators such as the SEC [17] and NASD [18] in the United States, and especially FSA [19] in the United Kingdom, maintain very useful Web sites where you can easily find what they do in the markets they regulate, get a lot of information about the markets themselves, and access a treasure trove of documents.

[13] Richard Roberts, *Wall Street: The Markets, Mechanisms, and Players* (Bloomberg Press, 2003).

[14] Thomas K. Liaw, *The Business of Investment Banking: A Comprehensive Overview* (Wiley, 2005).

[15] Herbert B. Mayo, *Financial Institutions, Investments, and Management: An Introduction* (South-Western College Publishing, 2003).

[16] Stuart A. McCrary, *Hedge Fund Course* (Wiley Finance, 2005).

[17] www.sec.gov/.

[18] www.nasd.com/.

[19] www.fsa.gov.uk/.

CHAPTER 3, "FINANCIAL FIRMS AND THEIR PEOPLE"

One book that everyone even remotely connected to Wall Street should read is *Liar's Poker* [20]; it is an extremely well-written novel about Salomon Brothers in the mid-1980s that captures many cultural traits of the Wall Street environment (although much has changed since then and many of the behaviors that Lewis describes are much harder to find these days in their pure form). A somewhat less dramatic but very thoughtful account of the migration from physics to finance is written by one of the most prominent participants in that process: Emanuel Derman's *My Life as a Quant* [21] abounds with interesting observations, thoughts, and useful information that is especially relevant for quantitative and technical readers. On a more practical note, a company called Vault Inc. [22] has developed a number of what it calls Career Guides to various parts of Wall Street; it sells these guides on its Web site, but you can also get them on Amazon and probably other places. I highly recommend them, especially for those of you who have no industry experience. Finally, for the job seekers among you, I mention the Web sites of two reputable headhunter agencies, [23] and [24] (this is not to say that all others are disreputable, although some are; it's just that I know that these two are good).

[20] Michael Lewis, *Liar's Poker: Rising through the Wreckage on Wall Street* (Penguin, 1990).

[21] Emanuel Derman, *My Life as a Quant: Reflections on Physics and Finance* (Wiley Finance, 2004).

[22] www.vault.com/.

[23] www.analyticrecruiting.com/.

[25] www.smithhanley.com/.

CHAPTER 4, "MARKETS AND THE ECONOMY"

There are many economics textbooks that you may want to at least look through to see what kind of science economics is, such as Mankiw's *Principles of Economics* [25]. A number of shorter books focus on interpreting economic news and its market impact; *By the Numbers* by Carnes and Slifer [26] is a classic, and I also like the more recent book by Yamarone [27] as well as the somewhat older but also very good *Handbook* by Rogers [28].

Most agencies that provide economic data maintain user-friendly Web sites where you can find current releases and historical data, discussions of their methodology, and so on; the Web sites of the Bureau of Labor Statistics [29] (CPI, unemployment, and a variety of other interesting stuff about the U.S. labor force) and the Bureau of Economic Analysis [30] (GDP and its components) are good examples. My discussion of the pre–Federal Reserve U.S. banking system is largely based on a nice article [31] by Jon Moen that I found on EH.net, which itself is a very useful Web resource for those interested in economic history. The Federal Reserve maintains a number of Web sites with current and historical economic data (I think [32] is the official one, but the Fred system maintained by the St. Louis Fed [33] is more convenient and has more data). Finally, the New York Fed has a very informative and easy-to-use Web site [34] with cool stuff such as a virtual visit to its gold vault.

For those who are fascinated with the concept of yield that we encountered in this chapter and would like to understand its math, there is no better resource than the new edition of the classic *Inside the Yield Book* [35]. It is worth the purchase price just for the foreword by Sidney Homer and Martin Liebowitz's introductory chapter. The math is, as you will find, fairly trivial, but if you want to understand how bond traders think about it, you should read this book. Another excellent book in this space is Marcia Stigum's *Money Market Calculations* [36], a no-nonsense guide to the welter of day count and yield calculation conventions that make the interest calculations surprisingly nontrivial. This book, unfortunately, is very hard to get (it has been out of print for many years, and no one seems willing to sell it used, which does not surprise me). I will mention more mainstream sources for bond math when we get to financial analytics (Chapter 13).

As I mentioned in the main text, there is a strain of libertarian thought that maintains that central banks are evil and should be abolished. Murray Rothbard's book on this subject [37] is the best example of this genre that I'm aware of (despite its unconventional subject matter, it is a surprisingly good read).

[25] Gregory N. Mankiw, *Principles of Economics* (South-Western College Publishing, 2003).

[26] Stansbury W. Carnes and Stephen D. Slifer, *By the Numbers: A Survival Guide to Economic Indicators* (Gilmour Drummond Publishing, 1996).

[27] Richard Yamarone, *The Trader's Guide to Key Economic Indicators* (Bloomberg Press, 2004).

[28] Mark R. Rogers, *Handbook of Key Economic Indicators* (McGraw-Hill, 1998).

[29] www.bls.gov/.

[30] www.bea.gov/.

[31] Jon Moen, "The Panic of 1907," www.eh.net/encyclopedia/?article=moen.panic.1907.

[32] www.federalreserve.gov/releases/.

[33] research.stlouisfed.org/fred2/.

[34] www.ny.frb.org/.

[35] Martin L. Liebowitz, *Inside the Yield Book: The Classic That Created the Science of Bond Analysis* (Bloomberg Press, 2004).

[36] Marcia Stigum, *Money Market Calculations* (Irwin Professional Publishing, 1991).

[37] Murray N. Rothbard, *The Case against the Fed* (Ludwig Von Mises Institute, 1994).

CHAPTER 5, "THE U.S. TREASURY MARKET"

The best all-around book about the Treasury market that is reasonably current is Bruce Tuckman's *Fixed Income Securities* [38]. Fabozzi's mammoth

Handbook of Fixed Income Securities [39] is a useful reference that adorns many desks, although I cannot imagine anyone actually reading through its 1,500 pages. Christina Ray's excellent book [40] takes a trader's perspective, but unfortunately it is very hard to get these days (and is getting a bit dated)—you may use Tamara Mast Henderson's book [41] instead; it is more recent, but also more entry-level.

For general trading concepts, I warmly recommend Alexander Elder's latest book [42]. Like his previous books, it is honest and insightful, and it captures the issues that any trader struggles with every day (although it has nothing to do with Treasuries). There are many other books for the individual trader market, but I cannot recommend any of them—read at your own risk.

There are good books that cover the gaps in this chapter's coverage of the government bond markets. Two books by Batten and Fetherston are excellent sources for the European fixed-income landscape [43] (they cover the massive changes brought about by the introduction of the euro) and Asian fixed-income markets [44]. The high-growth area of inflation-linked securities that I left out of the chapter is to some extent covered in [45] and [46].

As far as Web resources go, it turns out that the U.S. Treasury maintains an excellent Web site [47] that explains and documents the thought process behind its funding decisions. Information about security auctions, outstanding securities, and the history of public debt can be found on an equally good but separate Web site maintained by the Bureau of Public Debt [48]. It is a better source for this kind of information than any in-house reference data system that I have ever come across. The Bond Market Association's Web site [49] is where everybody goes to find out about market holidays and early closes, but it has a wealth of other useful information as well.

[38] Bruce Tuckman, *Fixed Income Securities: Tools for Today's Markets* (Wiley, 2002).

[39] Frank Fabozzi, *The Handbook of Fixed Income Securities* (McGraw-Hill, 2005).

[40] Christina I. Ray, *The Bond Market: Trading and Risk Management* (McGraw-Hill, 1992).

[41] Tamara Mast Henderson, *Fixed Income Strategy: A Practitioner's Guide to Riding the Curve* (Wiley Finance, 2003).

[42] Alexander Elder, *Come into My Trading Room: A Complete Guide to Trading* (Wiley, 2002).

[43] Jonathan A. Batten, Thomas A. Fetherston, and Peter G. Szilagyi (eds.), *European Fixed Income Markets: Money, Bond, and Interest Rate Derivatives* (Wiley Finance, 2004).

[44] Jonathan A. Batten and Thomas A. Fetherston, *Asia-Pacific Fixed Income Markets: An Analysis of the Money, Bond, and Interest Derivative Markets of the Region* (Wiley Finance, 2002).

[45] Brice Benaben (ed.), *Inflation-Linked Products: A Guide for Investors and Asset and Liability Managers* (Risk Books, 2005).

[46] Mark Deacon, Andrew Derry, and Dariush Mirfendereski, *Inflation-Indexed Securities: Bonds, Swaps, and Other Derivatives* (Wiley Finance, 2004).

[47] www.ustreas.gov/offices/domestic-finance/debt-management/.

[48] www.publicdebt.treas.gov/sec/sec.htm.

[49] www.bondmarkets.com/.

CHAPTER 6, "EQUITY MARKETS"

Equity markets are well covered in the introductory books [1] through [3], as well as in the *Investments* tome [5]. If you want a more entry-level text, try Dalton [50]. An interesting book by Larry Harris [51] covers the organization of exchange markets and the details of the order execution process in much detail; this book is a favorite of my equity technology colleagues, although it is a bit too academic from my perspective (just who are those "informed traders" that he keeps talking about?). For those who like to have a historical perspective, Charles Geisst's history of Wall Street [52] is largely confined to U.S. equity markets history, and I especially like two books ([53] and [54]) about the history of the main U.S. stock exchanges. These exchanges maintain useful Web sites ([55], [56]), and so do many U.S.-based ECNs.

Larry Harris's book [51] has good coverage of block trading issues, but those who are interested in the actual nitty-gritty of algorithmic trading should read *Optimal Trading Strategies* by Kissell and Glantz [57]. This recent book presents the execution issues in all their complexity, but remains accessible to a casual reader.

Unlike data on the bond markets, data on equity markets (current and historical prices) are available from any number of Web sites (I use Yahoo! Finance). Equity index providers—Dow Jones [58], Russell [59], and S&P [60]—have a lot of interesting data on their Web sites, including index construction methodology and historical values. We will talk more about index futures in the next section, and as far as the ETFs go, I find the ETF Guide Web site [61] very useful. Finally, the issues of equity risk are explained in adequate detail in the *Investments* textbook [5], as well as on BARRA's Web site [62].

[50] John M. Dalton, *How the Stock Market Works* (Prentice Hall, 2001).

[51] Larry Harris, *Trading and Exchanges: Market Microstructure for Practitioners* (Oxford University Press, 2002).

[52] Charles R. Geisst, *Wall Street: A History: From Its Beginnings to the Fall of Enron* (Oxford University Press, 2004).

[53] Mark Ingebretsen, *Nasdaq: A History of the Market That Changed the World* (Prima Lifestyles, 2002).

[54] Robert Sobel, *The Big Board: A History of the New York Stock Market* (Beard Books, 2000).

[55] www.nyse.com/.

[56] www.nasdaq.com/.

[57] Robert Kissell and Morton Glantz, *Optimal Trading Strategies: Quantitative Approaches for Managing Market Impact and Trading Risk* (American Management Association, 2003).

[58] www.djindexes.com.

[59] www.russell.com/US/indexes/us/default.asp.

[60] www.standardandpoor.com.

[61] www.etfguide.com/index.htm.

[62] www.barra.com/.

CHAPTER 7, "FINANCIAL FUTURES"

Those who want to learn more about the history of financial futures should read an excellent article by Susan Gidel in *Futures Industry Magazine* [63] (the magazine's Web site is itself a great resource for issues affecting futures markets). Another Web article [64] (from the Economic History

Web site) goes even deeper into the past. A fascinating account of CBOT's early years can be found in Lurie [65].

For any area of knowledge, it is usually quite difficult to decide which book is the best, but in the case of interest-rate futures, there is no such problem: *The Treasury Bond Basis* by Galen Burghardt and Terry Belton [66] is the only book you need if you want to know how bond futures work and what you can do with them. Similarly, Galen Burghardt's book about Eurodollar futures [67] is far and away the best source for that area. For simple nonfinancial futures, there are a lot of books describing these products from an individual investor's (or rather amateur trader's) perspective; George Kleinman's book [68] is one of the better ones. I owe the story about the demise of the Value Line Index futures to Larry Harris [51]. I had heard it before as part of Goldman's oral tradition, but Harris has a good explanation of what happened, and, in fact, of many other issues relevant to futures exchanges.

And, at long last, we get to the book that should have been number one in this list: John Hull's *Options, Futures, and Other Derivatives* [69]. This text, now in its sixth edition, is the closest thing to a Bible for Wall Street quants—it is widely believed to have all the answers to any quantitative question about any derivative product. When my younger colleagues ask me what book they should read about quantitative finance, I always say "Hull" (and then they ask to borrow my copy and never return it; I have bought four copies during my Wall Street career, and the latest one is lost again). Hull focuses on quantitative issues related to derivatives and treats them with amazing clarity and elegance; you can probably skip the rest of this bibliography if you decide to get this book. I waited until this section to tell you about it because futures are our first derivative products, and Hull has several chapters devoted to futures that cover everything from fundamentals to the fairly complex math that some of these products require.

A very good Web resource for anything related to futures (and commodities) exchanges is the Exchange Handbook Web site [70]. The information offered there ranges from the directory of these exchanges to a wide selection of articles about many relevant topics (I quote a few of those in what follows). Many futures exchanges, most notably CBOT [71], CME [72], and EUREX [73], maintain their own excellent Web sites, where you can find everything from contract specifications to delivery rules to market data to trading volume information. Finally, a popular futures-related Web destination is the CFTC Web site and more specifically the "commitment of traders" report [74], which, according to some people, contains valuable insights about what the futures markets will do next.

[63] Susan Abbott Gidel, "100 Years of Futures Trading: From Domestic Agricultural to World Financial," *Futures Industry Magazine*, December/January 2000, www.futuresindustry.org/fimagazi-1929.asp?iss=93&a=607.

[64] Joseph Santos, "A History of Futures Trading in the United States," www.eh.net/encyclopedia/?article=Santos.futures.

[65] Jonathan Lurie, *The Chicago Board of Trade 1859–1905: The Dynamics of Self-Regulation* (University of Illinois Press, 1979).

[66] Galen Burghardt and Terry Belton, *The Treasury Bond Basis* (McGraw-Hill, 2005).

[67] Galen Burghardt, *The Eurodollar Futures and Options Handbook* (McGraw-Hill, 2003).

[68] George Kleinman, *Trading Commodities and Financial Futures: A Step by Step Guide to Mastering the Markets* (Financial Times/Prentice Hall, 2004).

[69] John C. Hull, *Options, Futures, and Other Derivatives* (Prentice Hall, 2005).

[70] www.exchange-handbook.co.uk/index.cfm.

[71] www.cbot.com.

[72] www.cme.com.

[73] www.eurexchange.com/index.html.

[74] www.cftc.gov/cftc/cftccotreports.htm.

CHAPTER 8, "INTEREST-RATE SWAPS"

I think that you can get a good overview of the interest-rate swaps market from general-purpose books such as [1], and of course Hull [69] has a lucid treatment of the subject. There are, however, many books dedicated to the swaps market, ranging from the relatively short and entry-level Flavell [75] to a four-volume, 5,000-page treatise by Das [76] (which covers other derivatives also). An early work by Marshall and Kapner [77] has interesting tidbits about the origins of swaps and derivative markets. The early shenanigans of the OTC derivative markets are sermonized against in Philippe Jorion's book [78], written right after the Orange County debacle.

Among the Web resources that are relevant for swap markets, I should mention the Web site of the Bank for International Settlements (BIS) [79]. BIS collects a lot of interesting statistics about derivatives markets and a host of other things, and its Web site offers those, together with research reports on a number of related subjects. The ISDA Web site [80] focuses on market organization issues and is quite useful as well.

[75] Richard Flavell, *Swaps and Other Derivatives* (Wiley Finance, 2002).

[76] Satyajit Das, *Swaps and Financial Derivatives: Products, Pricing, Applications and Risk Management* (Wiley Finance, 2004).

[77] John F. Marshall and Kenneth R. Kapner, *Understanding Swaps* (Wiley, 1993).

[78] Philippe Jorion, *Big Bets Gone Bad: Derivatives and Bankruptcy in Orange County. The Largest Municipal Failure in U.S. History* (Academic Press, 1995).

[79] www.bis.org/.

[80] www.isda.org/.

CHAPTER 9, "OPTIONS MARKETS"

Again, Hull [69] is a very good source for understanding options, especially the quantitative issues surrounding these products. The CBOE Options Institute publishes a guide to options markets [81] (last updated in 1999) that goes through a lot of institutional details of how the markets are organized, and I have found it quite useful. From the individual investor's perspective, McMillan's classic *Options as a Strategic Investment* [82] is unquestionably the best source. There are dozens of books that deal with options pricing, of which Natenberg [83] is among the most popular (I also liked Neil Chriss's book [84]). An interesting (and wonderfully short) book by Baird [85] describes options trading from the perspective of a market maker; this really should be a hot topic now, given how important options market making is to Wall Street these days, but amazingly this 1992 book seems to be the only thing written about the subject.

There is no shortage of Web resources for those interested in options. The OCC Web site [86] is among the better ones, offering a lot of interesting market statistics and information about market mechanics. It used to have a lot of educational materials about options in general, but that has been moved to a new Web site [87] maintained by the Options Industry Council, which is where you should go for answers to basic options-related questions. Finally, CBOE [88] and especially ISE [89] have extremely informative Web sites, offering lots of statistics and market data, explanations of options symbology and terminology, and a lot more.

[81] Options Institute, *Options: Essential Concepts* (McGraw-Hill, 1999).

[82] Lawrence G. McMillan, *Options as a Strategic Investment* (Prentice Hall, 2001).

[83] Sheldon Natenberg, *Option Volatility and Pricing: Advanced Trading Strategies and Techniques* (McGraw-Hill, 1994).

[84] Neil A. Chriss, *Black-Scholes and Beyond: Option Pricing Models* (McGraw-Hill, 1996).

[85] Allen Jan Baird, *Option Market Making: Trading and Risk Analysis for the Financial and Commodity Option Markets* (Wiley Finance, 1992).

[86] www.theocc.com/.

[87] www.888options.com/.

[88] www.cboe.com/.

[89] www.iseoptions.com/.

CHAPTER 10, "MORTGAGES AND AGENCIES"

To gain a more detailed understanding of the mortgage markets in the United States, you can turn to Joseph Hu's *Basics of Mortgage-Backed Securities* [90]. It has a remarkably clear overview of the market and, despite being quite short, covers most of the issues that our chapter has left out. Fabozzi's *Handbook of Mortgage-Backed Securities* [91] is much more readable than many of his other books and is a widely accepted reference text in this area. A collection of articles [92] from Salomon (a pioneer in this field) is also a useful source.

A book by Stanton [93] has an interesting discussion of government-sponsored enterprises that provides some much-needed perspective on the current debate about Fannie and Freddie. Both of these companies maintain good, informative Web sites ([94] and [95]); if you get past the main section, which touts how these companies help homeowners, and move on to the investors section, you will find descriptions of their issuance programs, data about outstanding debt issues and mortgage-backed securities, information about mortgage pools, and a lot more interesting stuff.

I was always puzzled by how the United States got to be so hooked on the idea of homeownership—those of you who wonder about how the country got into its current state of addiction will greatly enjoy Jackson's *Crabgrass Frontier* [96].

[90] Joseph Hu, *Basics of Mortgage-Backed Securities* (Wiley, 2001).

[91] Frank J. Fabozzi, *Handbook of Mortgage-Backed Securities* (McGraw-Hill, 2001).

[92] Lakhbir Hayre (ed.), *Salomon Smith Barney Guide to Mortgage-Backed and Asset-Backed Securities* (Wiley, 2001).

[93] Thomas H. Stanton, *Government-Sponsored Enterprises: Mercantilist Companies in the Modern World* (American Enterprise Institute Press, 2002).

[94] www.fanniemae.com/index.jhtml.

[95] www.freddiemac.com/.

[96] Kenneth T. Jackson, *Crabgrass Frontier: The Suburbanization of the United States* (Oxford University Press, 1987).

CHAPTER 11, "CREDIT MARKETS"

Despite the huge size of the corporate bond market, not much is written about it—Moorad Choudhry's book [97] is just about the only one I'm aware of—but there is a good reference source [98] about municipal bonds. The thought process behind credit ratings is well illustrated in Ganguin and Bilardello [99], while the more general quantitative issues of credit risk are covered in a great number of books, of which I recommend Bluhm, Overbeck, and Wagner [100], if you have to pick one. The NASD TRACE system, which made the credit markets so much more transparent, is accessible on the Web; the daily aggregates can be seen at [101], while the BondInfo system [102] provides information about trading patterns for any individual corporate issue.

Unlike the corporate bond market, the credit derivative market, being a hot new thing, is the subject of a large number of recent books, of which I selected three for this guide ([103] through [105]); you can easily expand this list by doing a search on Amazon.

[97] Moorad Choudhry, *Corporate Bond Markets: Instruments and Applications* (Wiley Finance, 2005).

[98] Bond Market Association, *The Fundamentals of Municipal Bonds* (Wiley, 2001).

[99] Blaise Ganguin and John Bilardello, *Standard & Poor's Fundamentals of Corporate Credit Analysis* (McGraw-Hill, 2004).

[100] Christian Bluhm, Ludger Overbeck, and Christoph Wagner, *An Introduction to Credit Risk Modeling* (Chapman & Hall, 2004).

[101] apps.nasd.com/regulatory%5Fsystems/traceaggregates/.

[102] www.nasdbondinfo.com.

[103] Gunter Meissner, *Credit Derivatives: Application, Pricing, and Risk Management* (Blackwell Publishers, 2005).

[104] Geoff Chaplin, *Credit Derivatives: Risk Management, Trading and Investing* (Wiley, 2005).

[105] Janet M. Tavakoli, *Credit Derivatives and Synthetic Structures: A Guide to Instruments and Applications* (Wiley Finance, 2001).

CHAPTER 12, "REFERENCE DATA"

Selling reference data products is a $500 million a year business, but you can't tell that by doing a literature search—there is barely anything at all in print. There is stuff on the Web, however, in particular a very well-written and informative article from the Exchange Handbook Web site by Angela Wilbraham [106] which anyone who wants to know more about this area should read. Beyond that, there is the Web site of the Association of National Numbering Agencies [107], as well as the sites of its individual members, of which the U.S. CUSIP bureau [108] and U.K. Sedol Masterfile [109] are probably the most visited.

[106] Angela Wilbraham, "Reference Data 101" (Exchange Handbook, 2004), www.exchange-handbook.co.uk/ articles_story.cfm?id=47684&search=1.

[107] www.anna-web.com/.

[108] www.cusip.com/.

[109] www.londonstockexchange.com/en-gb/products/
       membershiptrading/techlib/sedolmf.

CHAPTER 13, "FINANCIAL ANALYTICS AND MODELING"

There is no shortage of books about financial analytics; if anything, the challenge is finding good ones among the many dozens, perhaps hundreds, of titles published over the last two decades. Let us begin with the fundamentals. Surprisingly, stochastic calculus is not normally part of the standard math curriculum for most hard sciences, a problem that Oksendal's book [110] solves elegantly and completely. Similarly, Monte Carlo methods are often not included in numerical analysis courses, and Paul Glasserman [111] takes care of that. And, of course, anyone involved in quantitative programming in any field should have a copy of the *Numerical Recipes* [112].

I continue to believe that Hull [69] covers more than 90 percent of what most quants need to know about financial analytics, but there are other books that focus more narrowly on the computational aspects, most notably Lyuu [113]. I have already mentioned a couple of books that cover fixed-income math and date manipulation ([35] and [36]), but the ultimate reference source for this is Fabozzi's *Fixed Income Mathematics* [114]. The general problematics of derivatives pricing are well illustrated in Clewlow and Strickland [115] and the more recent Baz and Chacko [116]. In the term structure modeling realm, I like Brigo and Mercurio [117] and the more down-to-earth James and Webber [118], as well as a more abstract text [119] by Musiela (he is the M in HJM and BJM) and Rutkowski. A recent book by Jan Dash [120] attempts to emphasize the parallels between physics and quantitative finance; I don't quite know what to make of it.

Among the multitude of Web resources related to financial analytics, I will mention two. The first is the Web site of the International Association of Financial Engineers [121], and the second [122] is maintained by Paul Wilmott, himself a prolific writer in this area. Both sites attempt to unite financial engineers and their fellow travelers worldwide into a community—a worthwhile goal from my perspective.

[110] Bernt K. Oksendal, *Stochastic Differential Equations* (Springer, 2002).

[111] Paul Glasserman, *Monte Carlo Methods in Financial Engineering* (Springer, 2003).

[112] William H. Press, Brian P. Flannery, Saul A. Teukolsky, and William T. Vetterling, *Numerical Recipes in C: The Art of Scientific Computing* (Cambridge University Press, 1992).

[113] Yuh-Dauh Lyuu, *Financial Engineering and Computation: Principles, Mathematics, and Algorithms* (Cambridge University Press, 2001).

[114] Frank J. Fabozzi, *Fixed Income Mathematics* (McGraw-Hill, 1996).

[115] Les Clewlow and Chris Strickland, *Implementing Derivative Models* (Wiley, 1998).

[116] Jamil Baz and George Chacko, *Financial Derivatives: Pricing, Applications, and Mathematics* (Cambridge University Press, 2004).

[117] Damiano Brigo and Fabio Mercurio, *Interest Rate Models: Theory and Practice* (Springer, 2001).

[118] Jessica James and Nick Webber, *Interest Rate Modelling: Financial Engineering* (Wiley, 2000).

[119] Marek Musiela and Marek Rutkowski, *Martingale Methods in Financial Modelling* (Springer, 2002).

[120] Jan W. Dash, *Quantitative Finance and Risk Management: A Physicist's Approach* (World Scientific, 2004).

[121] www.iafe.org/home.php.

[122] www.wilmott.com/.

CHAPTER 14, "MARKET DATA"

Given how widely market data technology is used these days, it is disappointing that so little has been written about it. An interesting article from the Exchange Handbook Web site [123] focuses on the organizational issues in the market for market data (yes, there is such a thing, again a multibillion-dollar business that is completely ignored by the trade literature). TIBCO's Web site [124] seems to be the lone outpost of any information about this huge field. Maybe this will change.

[123] Andrew P. Delaney, "The End of the Age of the Big Vendors?" (Exchange Handbook, 2004), www.exchange-handbook.co.uk/articles_story.cfm?id=47671&search=1.

[124] www.tibco.com/.

CHAPTER 15, "TRADING SYSTEMS"

Again, despite the billions spent by financial industry firms on their trading systems, there is almost nothing in print from which you can learn about this area. There is a book about electronic trading [125], but it is rather sloppily written. The FIX protocol is described in a book by Courtney Doyle [126], and at least in the case of FIX there is an official Web site [127] with documentation, protocol specifications, and so on. There are a few good books ([128], [129], and [130]) about the back-office side of trading infrastructure, which is partly why I left this area completely out of this chapter. Beyond that, I can only suggest that you start reading periodicals such as *Waters* magazine [131] and *Wall Street and Technology* [132], which are full of articles about how people do trading systems, but of course never define what those systems are and what they do.

[125] David James Norman, *Professional Electronic Trading* (Wiley, 2002).

[126] Courtney Doyle, *The FIX Guide: Implementing the FIX Protocol* (Xlibris Corporation, 2005).

[127] www.fixprotocol.org/.

[128] David Weiss, *After the Trade Is Made: Processing Securities Transactions* (Prentice Hall, 1993).

[129] Michael Simmons, *Securities Operations: A Guide to Trade and Position Management* (Wiley, 2002).

[130] Hal McIntyre, *How the U.S. Securities Industry Works* (Summit Group Press, 2004).

[131] www.watersonline.com/.

[132] www.wallstreetandtech.com/.

CHAPTER 16, "RISK MANAGEMENT"

Unlike other areas of financial technology, there is such an abundance of books about risk management that I can only scratch the surface in this brief overview. Crouhy, Mark, and Galai [133] is a good all-around text, while Dorfman's textbook [134] takes a more expansive view of risk management together with insurance. Marrison's book [135] recognizes that there is such a thing as risk measurement and focuses on the nitty-gritty of it. Steve Allen's book [136] is one of the more popular treatments of risk management in the financial markets, whereas the latest book by Deventer, Imai, and Mesler [137] (they have written several similar-sized books in the past) attempts to include commercial banking and has many interesting insights about current practices and the culture of risk management.

For a description of the mainstream financial risk methodologies, I recommend Jorion's classic [138], which has done much to popularize the VaR concept, and Gallati's book [139], which has a good description of capital allocation. A really great source on VaR and much else besides is Glyn Holton's *Value-at-Risk* [140]. Not only is it fairly recent, but it is also a very thoughtful and well-written book. In fact, Holton maintains a number of extremely useful Web sites about risk management through his Contingency Analysis consultancy [141]. In particular, I found his Risk Glossary [142] very handy in the preparation of this chapter. He also has an extensive bibliography of risk-related books [143], complete with his own reviews, which I highly recommend if you want to go beyond my simplistic list.

There is a great periodical about risk management and, more generally, financial engineering issues: *Risk Magazine*. Unlike other financial technology periodicals that I have mentioned, its Web site [144] does not provide free access to the magazine's content, but it is very interesting nonetheless.

[133] Michel Crouhy, Robert Mark, and Dan Galai, *Risk Management* (McGraw-Hill, 2000).

[134] Mark S. Dorfman, *Introduction to Risk Management and Insurance* (Prentice Hall, 2001).

[135] Christopher Marrison, *The Fundamentals of Risk Measurement* (McGraw-Hill, 2002).

[136] Steve L. Allen, *Financial Risk Management: A Practitioner's Guide to Managing Market and Credit Risk* (Wiley, 2003).

[137] Donald R. Van Deventer, Kenji Imai, and Mark Mesler, *Advanced Financial Risk Management: Tools and Techniques for Integrated Credit Risk and Interest Rate Risk Managements* (Wiley, 2004).

[138] Philippe Jorion, *Value at Risk: The New Benchmark for Managing Financial Risk* (McGraw-Hill, 2000).

[139] Reto Gallati, *Risk Management and Capital Adequacy* (McGraw-Hill, 2003).

[140] Glyn A. Holton, *Value-at-Risk: Theory and Practice* (Academic Press, 2003).

[141] www.contingencyanalysis.com/.

[142] www.riskglossary.com/.

[143] www.riskbook.com/.

[144] www.risk.net/.

CHAPTER 17, "RESEARCH AND STRATEGY"

Hamilton's *Time Series Analysis* [145] is a great textbook that is a Bible to all those working with time series, inside and outside the financial markets. Another good textbook by Greene [146] explains the main concepts of econometrics. One econometrics book by Campbell, Lo, and MacKinlay [147] is quite popular among financial market researchers (for reasons that completely elude me). Carol Alexander's *Market Models* [148] has become a standard reference text among the same constituency; it covers all the standard tools in the research toolbox in adequate detail.

I promised to mention a few books about technical analysis. The seminal work here is John Magee's classic tome [149] (now in its eighth edition), and another book with a very wide following is John Murphy's [150]. These two books probably outsell everything else on my bibliography list taken together (with the possible exception of *Liar's Poker*) by a factor of 10. And there are many, many others—just take a look at the Web site of Traders Press [151].

The greatest example of independent market research is *Gartman's Letter*, which Dennis Gartman distributes by e-mail to paid subscribers. My impression is that every trader reads it, and if you have any trader friends, you can ask them for a sample copy; this newsletter is a perfect example of what people look for in research publications (besides, it has an excellent track record of calling market turns in everything from gold to stocks to hard red winter wheat). If you do not have trader friends, you can try to subscribe through the Alberdon Web site [152] (which, however, explicitly warns that this is not for individual investors).

[145] James Douglas Hamilton, *Time Series Analysis* (Princeton University Press, 1994).

[146] William H. Greene, *Econometric Analysis* (Prentice Hall, 2002).

[147] John Y. Campbell, Andrew W. Lo, and A. Craig MacKinlay, *The Econometrics of Financial Markets* (Princeton University Press, 1996).

[148] Carol Alexander, *Market Models: A Guide to Financial Data Analysis* (Wiley, 2001).

[149] Robert D. Edwards and John Magee, *Technical Analysis of Stock Trends* (CRC, 2001).

[150] John J. Murphy, *Technical Analysis of the Financial Markets: A Comprehensive Guide to Trading Methods and Applications* (Prentice Hall, 1999).

[151] www.traderspress.org/categories/technical_analysis.asp.

[152] www.alberdon.demon.co.uk/introducingtgl.htm.

CHAPTER 18, "PRODUCTION CYCLE"

There is really not much written about the subject matter of this chapter, and generally the whole Technology Practices part of the book. Some issues related to client/server systems are discussed in [153]. Information about Autosys can be found on the Computer Associates Web site [154]. There is also a book that discusses general IT production services [155], but to me it is too generic to be of much use in the financial software development context.

[153] David Ruble, *Practical Analysis and Design for Client/Server and GUI Systems* (Prentice Hall, 1997).

[154] www3.ca.com/solutions/Product.aspx?ID=253.

[155] Harris Kern, *Rich Schiesser, and Mayra Muniz, IT Production Services* (Prentice Hall, 2004).

CHAPTER 19, "DEVELOPMENT CYCLE"

A good article in Wikipedia [156] explains the principles of source control and, more generally, software configuration management. There are also two books ([157] and [158]) that cover this subject, as well as software testing and release cycle issues.

[156] en.wikipedia.org/wiki/Software_Configuration_Management.

[157] Stephen P. Berczuk and Brad Appleton, *Software Configuration Management Patterns: Effective Teamwork, Practical Integration* (Addison-Wesley Professional, 2002).

[158] Michael E. Bays, *Software Release Methodology* (Prentice Hall, 1999).

CHAPTER 20, "PRODUCTION SUPPORT AND PROBLEM MANAGEMENT"

I found one book about problem management [159], but I had a hard time reading it—your experience may be different.

[159] Gary Walker, *IT Problem Management* (Prentice Hall, 2001).

INDEX

Page numbers with *n* indicate a note

Accrued interest, 129–130
Accuracy test, system code, 488
Activities, pricing models, 406–408, 410
Additional offering, 156
AES, 178–179
Agencies, mortgage, 298–302, 309–319
Alarm, job management, 470–471
Algorithmic trading systems, 177–178, 414–418
Alpha, 152, 192
American Stock Exchange (AMEX), 169, 186, 268
AMEX (American Stock Exchange), 169, 186, 268
Analysis of data, 446–455
   (*See also* Financial analytics and modeling)
Antwerp, Belgium, 6, 40, 41
APIs (application programming interfaces), 401–402
Application programming interfaces (APIs), 401–402
Arbitrage
   index arbitrage, 186–187, 229
   no-arbitrage principle, 148–149
   statistical, 177–178, 414–418
   uses of, 18
ArcaEx, 514
Asia, 41, 224–225, 473–479, 507–508
Asset management companies, 28, 39, 52–53
Auctions, 104–112, 166
AutoSys, 468–471

Back contracts, 207
Back office, 47
Back-office risk, 371–373, 426–427
Back testing, 416
Backups, 388
Backwardation, 201–202
Bank of England, 72, 76
Banks
   central banks, 9, 35, 70–77
   commercial banks, 39
   Federal Reserve, 70–87, 104–105, 226–227
   investment banks, 24–26, 38–39, 153
Basel Accords, 424, 427
Basis risk, 201
Basket order, 187
Benchmark securities, 314
Benefits, jobs, 61–64
Best bid/best offer, 162–163
Beta, 152, 190–192

Bid price, 26
Black, Fischer, 231, 272
Black-box systems, 414–416
Black-Scholes formula, 20, 231–332, 272–281, 289, 367
Block orders, 151, 176–179
Bloomberg, 32–33, 54, 88, 260, 343–344, 346, 348, 373
BLS (Bureau of Labor Statistics), 87–88
BMA (Bond Market Association), 309
Bogle, John C., 185
Bond analytics libraries, 361–364
Bond basis trading, 213–215
Bond Market Association (BMA), 309
Bond math, 96, 149, 354
   (*See also* Yield curves)
Bond swap, 122–123
Bond switch, 120–122
Bonds, 10, 100
   (*See also* Treasury markets and securities)
Book-level risk, 428–430
Books (*See* Trade books)
Boom-and-bust, business cycle, 69–70
Bootstrapping, 245, 250, 365
Breakevens, 143–145
Bridging, market data, 385–386
Broken system (*See* Problem management)
Broker-dealer firms, 30, 38, 40, 43–47, 53, 396–397
Brokers, 29–36, 54
BrokerTec, 113–120, 140
Budget deficit, public debt, 98–101
Bug list, 491
Bullet bonds, 10, 324
Bureau of Labor Statistics (BLS), 87–88
Business cycles, 68–70
Business impact statement, 507
Butterfly spreads, 408, 415, 417, 447–449
Butterfly trades, 145–148
Buy back, 156
Buy-side firms, 27–29, 37–39, 42, 395–397

Calendar (*See* Dates)
Call options, 264–268, 272–277, 281–282
Callable bonds, 10, 102–103, 289–290, 324
Cancel orders, 165–166
Cancelable swap, 290
Cantor Fitzgerald, 32, 113, 121, 314, 508
Capital allocation and charges, 435–437
Capital market development, 5–15
   (*See also specific types of markets*)

Careers in financial firms, 55–64, 492–493, 497, 515–519
Cash flows (*See* Interest-rate swaps)
CBOE (Chicago Board Options Exchange), 268
CBOT (*See* Chicago Board of Trade [CBOT])
CD (certificate of deposit) futures, 218–219
CDS (credit default swap), 336–338
Census (debt), 6–7
Central banks, 9, 35, 70–77
Certificate of deposit (CD) futures, 218–219
Changes in code, and diagnosis, 502–504
Charting, 456–459
Cheapest to deliver (CTD), 209–215
Checklist, start-of-day, 471–472
Chicago Board of Trade (CBOT)
  financial futures, 194–195, 205–207, 210, 216–219, 226–227, 475
  options, 264, 266–268, 272
Chicago Board Options Exchange (CBOE), 268
Chicago Mercantile Exchange (CME), 205, 218–225, 228, 230
Clearing and settlement services
  derivatives, 336–337
  and exchanges, 167
  explained, 33–35
  financial futures, 229
  futures, 197–199
  mortgage-backed securities, 309–310, 314
  netting, 34–35, 47
  options, 268, 270
Clearing yield, 108
CLOB (centralized limit order book), 174
Closing curve, 256
Closing price, 166–167, 229–231
CME (Chicago Mercantile Exchange), 205, 218–225, 228, 230
CMO (collateralized mortgage obligations), 311
CMTs (constant-maturity treasuries), 351
Collateralized mortgage obligations (CMO), 311
Commercial banks, 39
Commercial paper, 16, 218
Commodity exchanges, 194–199
Commodity futures, 18–19, 194–199
Common data model, 421
Compensation, jobs, 61–64
Compliance division, 37
Configuration table, 465–466
Constant-maturity treasuries (CMTs), 351
Consumer price index (CPI), 68, 91
Contraction, business cycle, 69
Contracts, futures, 194–199
Convergence, 200
Conversion factors, 207–210

Convertible bonds, 324
Convexity, 82, 85–86, 248–249, 305–306
Corporate actions, 156
Corporate debt (*See* Credit markets)
Cost of carry, 131
Coupon payments
  agency notes, 313–314
  corporate debt, 324
  interest-rate swap, 238
  Treasury securities, 11, 80–82
  WAC, 302–303, 305
  (*See also* Interest rates)
CPI (consumer price index), 68, 91
CPI futures, 232
Creativity, software development, 492–494
Credit default swap (CDS), 336–338
Credit derivatives, 335–338
Credit markets, 321–338
  CDS, 336–338
  credit derivatives, 335–338
  credit risk, 325–332, 435, 437–439
  development of, 322
  issuance of corporate debt, 323–325
  vs. other capital markets, 321–323
  primary market, 323–325
  recommended reading, 534–535
  secondary market, 332–335
Credit ratings, 329
Credit research, 443
Crossing sessions, 176–177
CTD (cheapest to deliver), 209–215
Currency markets, 17
Curve building, 354
Curve libraries, 364–366
Curve trades, 144–148
CUSIP, 106–107, 126, 154, 342, 344, 363
Customer connectivity, 397–398

Dailies, 428–430, 444
Daily system operation, 471–473
Data center, 483
Data manager programs, 377–379, 382, 383, 385, 387–388, 392–393
Data quality assurance (DQA), 387
Data shredding, 381
Databases (*See* Market data; Reference data)
DataStream, 350
Dates
  library of, 358–361
  system code, 464, 468, 478, 487–489
Dead man's switch, 478
Deal, corporate debt, 324–325
Dealer banks, 24–26, 38–39, 153

Debt markets, 5–12, 97–104
Debugging message, 500–501
Deliverables
  futures, 19, 194–196, 207–209, 216–217
  system code, 493
Delivery options, 213
Delta, 281–282
Demutualization, 31
Deployment, 490
Depository Trust Company (DTC), 34
Derivative markets
  credit derivatives, 335–338
  development of, 19–20
  duration, 81–82
  explained, 19–20
  futures contracts as, 197
  OTC, 235, 236–237, 244
  pricing, 354
  and risk management, 425–426, 428
  technology, 48
  VaR, 433–434
  volatility, 262
  (*See also* Options markets)
Desk quant jobs, 57–58, 59
Development plan, system code, 493
Diagnosis of technical problems, 499–504
Diamonds, 186
Digital dashboard, 472, 498–499
Direct feed, 404
Disaster recovery (DR) sites, 507
Discount, 16
Discount curve, 127–128, 245
Discount factor, 245–246
Discount rate, 16
Display (*See* GUI display)
Distribution, option values, 274–279
Dividends, 14–15
Divisions, sell-side firm, 44–45
DJIA (Dow Jones Industrial Average), 180–181,
  227–228
DJIA futures, 227–228
Dow, Charles, 180, 181, 457
Dow Jones Industrial Average (DJIA), 180–181,
  227–228
DQA (data quality assurance), 387
DR (disaster recovery) sites, 507
DTC (Depository Trust Company), 34
Duration, 81–82
Dutch East India Company, 13
Dutch Republic, 8–9, 13

E-Minis, 228–229
Earnings, IPO, 157

Earnings per share, 92
ECB (European Central Bank), 76–77
ECN (electronic communication networks),
  172–174
Economics and the market, 67–96
  business cycles, 68–70
  central bank role, 70–77
  economic research, 442, 443–444
  interest rate setting, 77–87
  recommended reading, 525–526
  yield curve, 87–96
Education, financial jobs, 61, 518–519
Efficient market hypothesis, 456
Electronic communication networks (ECN),
  172–174
Elemental data, 380, 382
Emotions, and problem reports, 497
Employment reports, yield curve, 87–91
End-of-day report, 473
Entitlements, data vendors, 382
Entry and exit rules, 415–416
Environments, production, 483
EONIA, 226–227
Equity markets, 151–192
  block orders, 151, 176–179
  development of, 13–15, 152–153
  equities trading, 187–189
  equity-market risk, 189–192
  equity valuation, 151, 156–158
  exchanges, operation of, 166–176
  indices and index products, 152, 179–187
  issuance of securities, 151, 153–158
  mechanism for, 14–15
  orders, 159–166
  primary markets, 151, 153–158
  recommended reading, 528–529
  research, 442
  secondary markets, 151, 158–166
  valuation of, 151, 156–158
Errors, code, 485, 491, 500
eSpeed, 113–120, 140–141
ETFs (exchange-traded funds), 186
EUREX, 216–217, 252
EURIBOR, 252
Eurobond, 219–225
Eurodollar futures, 244–254
Europe
  bond issuance, 148
  central banks, 76–77
  Eurobond, 219
  futures, 216–225, 244–254
  ID systems, 343
  interest-rate swaps, 252–253

Europe (*Cont.*):
  market development in, 5–10, 40–42
  as options origins, 264
  risk management, 424
European Central Bank (ECB), 76–77
Excel spreadsheet, 356, 383–385
Exchange market, 159
Exchange-traded funds (ETFs), 186
Exchanges
  commodity, 194–199
  development of, 13–14
  equity market, 159–166
  explained, 30
  financial futures, 215–217
  firms and people, 54
  follow-the-sun trading, 473–479, 507–508
  futures, 194–199, 202
  IPOs, 154, 156
  market participants, 29–33
  operation of, 166–176
  options, 267–268, 270–272, 272, 284–286
  OTC, 169–170, 235–237, 242, 284–288
  regulators in, 36–37
  trading systems, 395–397
Execution, 151, 162–165, 176–179, 396–397, 412
Exercise of options, 264–265
Expansion, business cycle, 68–69
Expected value, options, 273–275
Expiration, options, 265–266, 268, 270–285, 287, 289
External ID number, 341–344

Factor models, pricing, 411
Factor risk, 137–139
Fair value, 156, 453
Fannie Mae (FNMA), 298–302, 309–319
Fault tolerance, 388
FCM (futures commission merchant), 202
Federal budget deficit, 98–101
Federal funds rate, 74–77
Federal Home Loan Banks (FHLB), 296
Federal Home Loan Mortgage Corporation (FHLMC), 300, 309–314, 317–318, 319
Federal Housing Administration (FHA), 296–297, 300
Federal National Mortgage Association (FNMA), 298–302, 309–319
Federal Open Markets Committee (FOMC), 73–74
Federal Reserve, 70–87, 104–105, 226–227
Feeds, data, 379–382
Fees, exchanges, 167

FHA (Federal Housing Administration), 296–297, 300
FHLB (Federal Home Loan Banks), 296
FHLMC (Freddie Mac), 300, 309–314, 317–318, 319
FICC (Fixed Income Clearing Corporation), 34
Filtering, market data, 389–390
Financial analytics and modeling, 353–374
  bond analytics libraries, 361–364
  contents of library, 357–372
  curve libraries, 364–366
  date library, 358–361
  defined, 96
  development of, 354–356
  interpolation approach, 246, 249–252, 364–365, 458–459
  maintenance of library, 372–374
  model libraries, 367–370
  product libraries, 366–367
  quantitative modeling, 20–21, 48–52, 445–446
  recommended reading, 536–537
  risk management uses, 370–372
  types of, 353–354
  users of, 356–357
  (*See also* Yield curves)
Financial firms and people, 43–64
  asset managers, 52–53
  brokers, 54
  compensation and benefits, 61–64
  exchanges, 54
  hedge funds, 53–54
  jobs, business and technology, 55–64
  recommended reading, 524–525
  risk management, quantitative, 51–52
  sell-side firm structure, 44–47
  technological impact, 47–55, 59–60
Financial futures, 193–233
  development of, 193–204, 205, 218
  FX, 17–18
  hedgers, 199–202
  index futures, 185–186
  mechanics for trading, 202–204, 215–217
  money market futures, 218–227
  popularity of, 231–232
  reasons for, 205
  recommended reading, 529–531
  speculators, 199–202
  stock index futures, 227–232
  technology impact on, 232–233
  Treasury securities, 205–215, 218
Financial Information eXchange (FIX), 398–400

Financial markets, development of, 3–21
  capital markets, 5–15
  commodity futures, 18–19, 194–199
  debt market, 5–12
  derivatives, 19–20
  equity markets, 13–15, 152–153
  financial futures, 193–204, 205
  futures markets, 18–20
  FX, 17–18
  money markets, 15–18
  mortgage-related markets, 293–298
  options markets, 20, 264–268
  purpose of, 24
  quantitative modeling, 20–21
  reasons for, 4
  recommended reading, 521–523
Financial markets, participants in, 23–42
  brokers, 29–33
  clearing and settlement services, 33–35
  exchanges, 29–33
  geography of, 40–42, 58
  institutional view, 37–40
  investment banking, 24–26
  making money, 40
  recommended reading, 523–524
  regulators, 35–37
  structure of market, 26–29
  technology impact on, 31–33
Financial technology (*See* Technology)
Firm quotes, 400–401, 402–403
Fitting procedures, 369–370
FIX (Financial Information eXchange), 398–400
Fixed Income Cleaning Corporation (FICC), 34
Fixed-income investments
  mathematics, 354
  mechanism for, 15
  options, 286–290
  pricing models, 406–412
  research, 442, 443
  (*See also specific markets*)
Fixing technical problem, 505–507
Flat instrument storage, 345–346, 349
Float
  corporate debt, 324
  indices, 184
  interest-rate swap, 237–239, 243–244
  Treasury securities, 10–11
Flow trading, 138–139
FNMA (Fannie Mae), 298–302, 309–319
Follow-on offering, 156
Follow-the-sun trading, 473–479, 507–508
FOMC (Federal Open Markets Committee),
  73–74

Foreign exchange (FX), 17–18
Forward contracts, 194, 207–209, 366
Forward price, options, 275
Forward rate agreement (FRA), 244–254
FRA (forward rate agreement), 244–254
Freddie Mac (FHLMC), 300, 309–314,
  317–318, 319
Front office, 47, 48, 59, 356
Front-office risk, 370–372
Fully amortized fixed-rate mortgage, 296
Functionality test, system code, 488
Future value, STRIPS, 127
Futures commission merchant (FCM), 202
Futures markets, development of, 18–20
  (*See also* Financial futures)
FX (foreign exchange), 17–18

Gamma, 282–283
GARCH, 450–453
Gateways, 397–398, 400–406, 414
GDP (gross domestic product), 68, 76, 77, 87
Geography of financial markets, 40–42, 58
Germany, 216–217, 424
Ginnie Mae (GNMA), 298, 300, 310, 312–313
Globalization, follow-the-sun trading, 473–479,
  507–508
GLOBEX, 225–226
GNMA (Ginnie Mae), 298, 300, 310, 312–313
Go/no-go decision, 489
Goals of research, 441–442
Government bonds (*See* Treasury markets and
  securities)
Government National Mortgage Association
  (GNMA), 298, 300, 310, 312–313
Government-sponsored enterprises (GSEs),
  311–318
Government spreads, 327
Greeks, options, 281–284
Gross domestic product (GDP), 68, 76, 77, 87
Growth, P/E ratio, 157–158
GSEs (government-sponsored enterprises),
  311–318
GUI display
  market data, 383–386
  reference data, 331
  technology practices, 466, 469, 473
  Treasury data, 113, 114, 118

Hammurabi, laws of, 5
Handle errors, 389–390
Handover process, 475–476
Hardware infrastructure, 481, 482–483
Head of the code, 484–485

Hedge PnL, 257
Hedging
    defined, 136
    financial futures, 199–202
    hedge funds, 28, 53–54
    interest-rate swap, 239–241, 244–245
    market risk, 136–148
    mortgage-backed securities, 305–306
    options, 281–282
    Treasury markets, 136–138
Heinz, Augustus, 71
Historical data, 350–352
Holidays, 360, 490

ICAP, 32, 121, 253, 314
Ideal integrated trading systems, 420–422
Identification system, 342–344, 349, 405
IMM (International Money Market), 205,
    245–246
Implementation of system code, 493
Index arbitrage, 229
Index products, 152, 185
Indicative quotes, 400–401
Indices, stock, 152, 179–187
Inflation, 68, 76, 84–85, 232
Infrastructure, hardware, 481, 482–483
Initial public offering (IPO), 153–158
Initialization, problem reports, 498–500
Insider trading, 152
Institutional investors
    defined, 27–28
    financial market participants, 37–40
    investment banks, 24–26, 38–39, 153
    market impact of orders, 175–176
    market vs. proprietary trading, 141–143
    technical analysis, 456–459
    Treasury security auctions, 107
Instrument pricing, 354, 367
Interdealer market
    explained, 30
    mortgage-backed securities, 314, 317
    Treasury securities, 107, 112–113, 118–124,
        128, 133, 139–141
Interest-rate swaps, 235–262
    commoditization of, 260–261
    credit derivatives, 336
    development of, 242
    mechanics of, 237–239, 254–261
    options on, 286–288
    OTC derivatives, 236–237
    pricing, 408–409
    reasons for, 239–243
    recommended reading, 531–532

Interest-rate swaps (*Cont.*):
    spread, 251–252
    spreads, 327
    swaptions, 286–288
    swaps curve, 243–254, 243–255
    technology, 260–262
    warehousing, 257
Interest rates
    accrued interest, 129–130
    credit vs. fixed-income markets, 321–322
    Federal Reserve involvement, 74–78
    interest-rate risk, 239–240, 241
    setting, 77–87
    swap vs. floating, 237
    (*See also* Coupon payments; Mortgage-
        related securities; Yield curves)
Internal ID number, 344
Internal securities databases, 344–346
International Money Market (IMM), 205,
    245–246
International Securities Exchange (ISE), 286
International Security Identification Number
    (ISIN), 343
International Swap Dealers Association (ISDA),
    243
Interpolation approach, 246, 249–252, 364–365,
    458–459
Intraday restart, 505–506
Investing vs. proprietary trading, 142–144
Investment banks, 24–26, 38–39, 153
Investment strategy, defined, 442
IPO (initial public offering), 153–158
ISDA (International Swap Dealers Association),
    243
ISE (International Securities Exchange), 286
ISIN (International Security Identification
    Number), 343
Issuance of new securities
    corporate debt, 323–325
    data maintenance, 347–348
    equity securities, 151, 153–158
    explained, 24–25
    IPO, 153–158
    mortgage-backed securities, 309–310, 315
    ratings of, 329
    Treasury securities, 10–11, 78–80,
        99–112

Job management systems, 468–471
Job state, 469
Jobs in financial firms, 55–64, 492–493, 497,
    515–519
J.P. Morgan, 428

Kansas City Board of Trade (KCBT), 227–228, 231
KCBT (Kansas City Board of Trade), 227–228, 231
Kennedy, Joseph, 152n2
Keynes, John Maynard, 201–202
Known good results, systems code, 488

Latest value, 378
LIBOR (*See* London Interbank Offered Rate [LIBOR])
Libraries, financial analytics, 357–377
LIFFE (London International Financial Futures Exchange), 216, 225–227
Limit losses (*See* Risk management)
Limit order, 161–162
Liquidity, 29
Listed options, 268
Live pricing models, 406, 408–409
Local code, 486
Log file, problem diagnosis, 499–500
London, England
  central banks, 76
  Eurobond, 219
  financial market development in, 9, 40–42
  follow-the-sun trading, 473–479, 507–508
  ID systems, 343
  LIFFE, 216, 225–227
London Interbank Offered Rate (LIBOR)
  corporate debt, 327, 333
  financial futures, 221–225, 227
  interest-rate swaps, 237, 238, 245–246, 253–254, 261
  mortgage securities, 306–307
Long basis, futures, 201, 214
Long position, futures, 196, 197

Macroeconomics (*See* Economics and the market)
Margins in futures, 198–199
Market data, 375–393
  common problems and solutions, 386–393
  direct feed, 404
  display of, 383–386
  economic, and yield curves, 87–91
  enabled software, 386
  market data system, 376
  recommended reading, 537
  research jobs, 58
  sources of, 379–383
  system operation, 376–379, 388
  technology and, 50
Market fragmentation, 174

Market impact of orders, 175–176
Market makers, 139, 142
Market making, 138–142
Market model, 190
Market orders, 159, 161–162
Market risk, 136–148, 428, 435
Markets (*See under* Financial markets; *specific topics*)
Matching engine, 54
Maturity, 80–81, 84–85, 99–100, 102–104
MBS (mortgage-backed security), 298, 300–301, 306–310, 312
Mean reversion strategy, 146–147
Mechanics of trading
  financial futures, 202–204, 215–217
  interest-rate swaps, 237–239, 254–261
  mortgage instruments, 307–311
  options, 268–272
Medieval and Middle Ages, 6–9, 17
Membership, exchange, 167
Merton, Robert, 20, 331
Middle office, 47
Middleware systems, 59
Model libraries, 367–370
Models and analytics, 353–354
Monetary policy, 9, 72–77
Money markets, 15–18, 218–227
Monte Carlo model, 307, 368, 428, 433
Morgan, J.P., 71–72
Mortgage, as term, 6, 293–294
Mortgage-backed securities (MBSs), 298, 300–301, 306–310, 312
Mortgage originators, 298–299
Mortgage pools, 300–307
Mortgage-related securities, 293–319
  agencies for, 298–302, 309–319
  vs. credit markets, 321–322
  development of, 293–299
  GSEs, 311–318
  interest-rate sensitivity, 242–243
  issuance of new securities, 309–310, 315
  MBSs, 298, 300–301, 306–310, 312
  mechanics of mortgage trading, 307–311
  mortgage market, 298–299
  mortgage securitization, 300–307
  recommended reading, 533–534
  technology impact, 318–319
Municipal bonds (munis), 323n1
Mutual funds, 38, 183–186

Naming conventions, market data, 391–392
NASD (National Association of Securities Dealers), 36, 169–171, 333–334, 336

NASD TRACE, 333–334
Nasdaq, 169–172, 174, 268
National Association of Securities Dealers
   (NASD), 36, 169–171, 333–334, 336
National central banks (NCB), 77
National Securities Clearing Corporation
   (NSCC), 34, 35
NCB (national central banks), 77
Net present value (NPV), 364, 453–454
Netting, 34–35, 47
Network, market data system, 376, 385
New York, NY, 40–41, 42, 473–479, 507–508
New York Clearinghouse, 71
New York Stock Exchange (NYSE), 14,
   167–169, 174, 268
No-arbitrage principle, 148–149
Notes, 100
Notification, problem reports, 497–499
NPV (net present value), 364, 453–454
NRSRO ("nationally recognized statistical
   rating organization"), 329, 330, 331
NSCC (National Securities Clearing
   Corporation), 34, 35
NYSE (New York Stock Exchange), 14,
   167–169, 174, 268

OAS (Option-adjusted spread) analysis, 306, 373
OCC (Options Clearing Corporation), 268, 272
Offer price, 26
OMS (order management system), 403
Open-market operations, Fed, 73
Operational risk, 427–428
Option-adjusted spread analysis (OAS), 306, 373
Option symbol, 270
Options Clearing Corporation (OCC), 268, 272
Options markets, 263–291
   Black-Scholes formula, 272–281, 289
   development of, 20, 264–268
   fixed-income options, 286–290
   mechanics of trading, 268–272
   opposition to, 266–267
   pricing, 354
   recommended reading, 532–533
   risk factors, 280–284
   structure of, 284–286
   technology impact on, 285–286, 290–291
   (*See also* Derivative markets)
Options pricing, 367–368
Order management system (OMS), 403
Orders
   books for, 162, 166, 168, 170–171
   ECN, 172, 174
   equity market, 159–166

Orders (*Cont.*):
   execution of, 166–176
   market impact of, 175–176
   routers for, 397, 403–404
Organization of research, 442–445
Organizational chart of sell-side firm,
   44–47
OTC (over the counter), 169–170, 235–237,
   242, 284–288
Over the counter (OTC), 169–170, 235–237,
   242, 284–288
Overnight batch, 465, 467–471
Overnight production support, 508–511

P/E (price/earnings) ratio, 157–158
Panics, 69–72, 152
Par swap rate, 247–248
Pass-throughs, 300, 309
Performance, risk-based, 430–435
Performance test, system code, 488
Permissioning, data vendors, 382
Pieces, 443–444
Pit trading, 215
PnL (profit and loss)
   components of, 135–136
   equity-market risk, 189–190
   explained, 133
   futures contracts, 198, 201
   interest-rate swaps, 256–261
   market risk, 136–148
   real-time calculations, 420
   reporting, 428–430
   risk management, 429–430
   as trader's work, 46–47
   Treasury markets, 132–148
Populating reference database, 346–348
Portfolio analytics, 354
Portfolio managers, 52
Position management, 396, 418–420
Postmortem, system code repair, 506
Premiums, CDS, 337
Prepayment of mortgages, 302–304, 306
Present value, 127, 273
Prestiti, 7–8
Prevention of technical problems, 507–508
Price discovery, futures, 19
Price/earnings ratio (P/E), 157–158
Price risk, 26–27, 280–281
Price-to-yield curve (*See* Yield curves)
Pricing, models of, 406–412
Pricing graph, 412–413
Pricing in trade life cycle, 396, 397
Pricing tree, 367, 368

Primary markets, 24–25, 104–112, 151,
  153–158, 323–325
Priority rules, 165
Problem management, 495–511
  diagnosis of the problem, 499–504
  fixing the problem, 505–507
  importance of, 495–497
  overnight production support, 508–511
  person to handle, 496–497
  recommended reading, 542
  report handling, 497–499
  system failure prevention, 507–508
Problem ticket, 498
Product data (*See* Reference data)
Product libraries, 366–367
Production cycle, 463–479
  daily system operation, 471–473
  global trading, 473–479
  overnight batch, 467–471
  overnight support, 508–511
  production environment, 483
  recommended reading, 541
  rollout, 489–491
  shut down/restart, 464–467, 505–507
  support for, 496, 508–511
  (*See also* Problem management; Technology)
Profit and loss (*See* PnL [profit and loss])
Program trading, 187
Proprietary trading ("prop"), 141–148
Prospectus, 152–153
PSA (Public Securities Association), 303–304
Public debt, 97–104
  (*See also* Treasury markets and securities)
Public Securities Association (PSA), 303–304
Publish-subscribe paradigm, 376–379
Put option, 265, 266, 275–276

Quant-trader jobs, 56–57, 492–493, 497, 515–519
Quantitative modeling, 20–21, 48–52, 445–446
  (*See also* Financial analytics and modeling)
Qubes, 186

RAES (retail automatic execution), 285
Rates businesses, 321
Rating agencies, 329–331
Real-time data systems, 376
Recession, business cycle, 69
Recommended readings, 521–542
Recovery, business cycle, 69
Redundancy, 388
Reference data, 341–352
  database design considerations, 344–346
  external product identifiers, 341–344

Reference data (*Cont.*):
  historical data, 350–352
  internal securities databases, 344–346
  management systems, 347
  populating database with, 346–348
  pricing models, 411–414
  recommended reading, 535–536
  trade databases, 418–420
  uses of, 348–350
Reference securities, 314
Regression approach, 446–447, 449–451,
  453–454, 458–459
Regression test, 488–489, 491
Regulation Q, 218–219
Regulations, 35–37, 152–158, 218–219
Relative value models, 454
Release, system code, 489–491
Remote connection, problem management,
  509–510
Rentes (debt), 6–7, 11
Repairs of technological problem (*See* Problem
  management)
Reports, technical problems, 497–499
Repurchase agreement ("repo"), 130–132
Request for quotes (RFQ), 401, 402
Research and strategy, 441–459
  analysis of historical data, 446–455
  goals of, 441–442
  jobs in, 58–59
  organization of, 442–445
  quantitive basis of, 445–446
  recommended reading, 540–541
  regression approach, 446–447, 449–451,
    453–454, 458–459
  technical analysis, 456–459
  technology and, 49–50
Restart system, production cycle, 464–467,
  505–507
Retail automatic execution (RAES), 285
Returns, 80, 274
Reuters, 32–33, 54, 88, 202–204, 343–344, 350,
  378–379, 381, 383, 384
RFQ (request for quotes), 401, 402
Rich-cheap analysis, 453–455, 457
Risk
  back-office, 371–373, 426–427
  basis, 201
  book-level, 428–430
  credit, 325–332, 435, 437–439
  equity-market, 189–192
  factor, 137–139
  front-office, 370–372
  interest rate, 239–240, 241

Risk (*Cont.*):
  in interest-rate swaps, 257
  market, 136–148, 428, 435
  operational, 427–428
  in options markets, 280–284
  price, 26–27
  real-time, 419–420
  spread, 258
  in Treasury markets, 136–138
  VaR (value-at-risk), 431–434, 436, 437
Risk aggregation, 437
Risk analytics, 354
Risk-based performance measurements, 431
Risk enforcement, 426
Risk feed, 437
Risk management, 423–439
  capital allocation, 435–436
  exchange operations, 166
  financial analytics, 370–372
  firms and people, 51–52
  functions of, 426–428
  history of, 424–426
  performance measurement, 430–435
  process of, 428–430
  quantitative, 51–52
  recommended reading, 538–540
  system for, 357, 370
  technology, 436–439
  trade life cycle, 396
Risk premiums, 84–87, 328–329
Risk reporting system, 437
Risk run, 429
RiskMetrics, 425
Rockefeller, John D., 71
Rogue traders, 427
Rollback, 491
Rolldowns, 143–145
Rolling series view, 351
Rollout, production, 489–491
Rome, ancient, 5–6
Roosevelt, Franklin D., 152
Routing, market data, 385–386
Rulebook, exchange, 195
Rules for codesharing conduct, 485
Russell indices, 182, 184

Salaries, jobs, 61–64
Sales jobs, 55–56
Sales research jobs, 58, 59
Scenario analysis, 372, 434–435
Scholes, Myron, 272
SEC (Securities and Exchange Commission),
    35–36, 152, 172, 186, 268, 329

Secondary markets
  credit markets, 332–335
  equity markets, 151, 158–166
  explained, 25–26, 38–39
  Fannie Mae, 298–302, 309–319
  Freddie Mac, 300, 309–314, 317–318, 319
  IPOs, 154
  mortgage-backed securities, 298–302,
    309–319
  Treasury securities, 112–123
Securities and Exchange Commission (SEC),
    35–36, 152, 172, 186, 268, 329
Security Market Line (SML), 190–192
Security sector, pricing relationships, 410–411
Self-correcting markets, 149
Sell-side firms
  equities trading, 187–189
  explained, 38–39
  geographic diversity, 40–42, 58
  investment banks, 24–26, 38–39, 153
  structure of, 26–27, 44–47
  (*See also* Financial firms and people;
    Research and strategy)
Sensitivities, 429–430
Series 7 exam, 36–37
Servers, 482–483
Servicer, mortgage, 299
Settlement services (*See* Clearing and
    settlement services)
Short basis, futures contracts, 201–202
Short position, futures, 196, 197
Short rate, 369
Short trading, 108–109, 123–124
Shut down system, production cycle, 464–467
Shutdown script, 465–466
SIMEX (Singapore International Monetary
    Exchange), 224–225
Singapore International Monetary Exchange
    (SIMEX), 224–225
Skills for quant jobs, 55–64, 492–493, 497
Slope of yield curve, 81–87
"Slow consumers," market data, 392
Small order execution system (SOES), 171–172
Smart money, 457–458
SML (Security Market Line), 190–192
Social skills, problem reports, 497
SOES (small order execution system), 171–172
Software developer jobs, 59–60, 492–493, 497
Software system development cycle, 481–494
  creative side of, 492–494
  financial analytics, 355, 356
  growth of, 47–52
  hardware infrastructure, 481, 482–483

Software system development cycle (*Cont.*):
  importance of, 54–55
  recommended reading, 541
  rollout, 489–491
  standardization of, 517
  testing code, 485–489
  trends in, 516–519
  writing code, 483–485
  (*See also* Production cycle; Technology)
Solicitation, trade, 46, 395, 396, 397–400
SOQ (Special Opening Quotation), 230
Source code control system, 484
Sources of market data, 379–383
S&P 500 futures, 228–229
S&P (Standard & Poor's) indices, 182, 185, 186, 228–229
Special Opening Quotation (SOQ), 230
Specialists, NYSE, 167–168, 285
Speculators, 28, 199–202, 241
Spiders, 186
Splits, stock, 156
Spot rates
  futures contracts, 207, 211, 213, 221, 229
  FX, 17–18
  Treasury securities, 131–132, 143–145
Spread products, 317
Spread risk, 258
Spread trade, 121
Spreads, 26–27, 251–252, 322, 327, 409–410
Standard & Poor's indices (S&P), 182, 185, 186, 228–229
Start-of-day report, 471–472
Static data, 350
Stock analysts, 442
Stock certificates, 154, 155
Stock index futures, 227–232
Stock indices and index products, 152, 179–187, 227–232
Stock market (*See* Equity markets)
Stop-loss rules, 416
Storage costs, futures price, 200–201
STP (straight-through processing), 35, 405
Straight-through processing (STP), 35, 405
Strategy, defined, 442
Straw man, 493
Stress test, system code, 488
Strike price, 264, 265, 275
STRIPS, 125–128
Structured products, options, 290
Style indices, 182–183, 185
Supply and demand, yield curves, 93–94
Swaptions, 286–288
Swaps (*See* Interest-rate swaps)

Symbol, security, 351
System build, 482
System test, 486–487
Systems (*See* Technology)

Talarian, 33, 379, 380
TBA (to-be-announced) trading, 309
Technology
  data manager programs, 377–379, 382, 383, 385, 387–388, 392–393
  ECN, 172–173
  electronic trading, 113–123
  exchange operations, 168–176
  financial futures, 215–217, 232–233
  firms and people, 47–52, 54–55, 59–60
  futures contracts, 202–204
  interest-rate swaps, 260–262
  jobs in financial firms, 55–64, 492–493, 497, 515–519
  market development and participants, 21, 31–33
  mortgage-related markets, 318–319
  operations center, 471
  options, 285–286, 290–291
  portfolio management, 52
  production cycle, 463–479
  risk management, 436–439
  software system development cycle, 481–494
  trends in, 514–519
  (*See also* Market data; Reference data; Trading systems)
Telerate 19901 page, 253
Term structure modeling, 354
Testing, system code, 486–489
Testing code, 485–489
Theta, 283
Thinking-side of software development, 492–494
TIBCO, 35, 378–379, 383, 537
Tick databases, 352
Ticker symbol, 159, 161
Time option, 214–215
Time-series analysis, 446–448, 450–452
Time series view, 350
TIPS (Treasury Inflation-Protected Securities), 100
To-be-announced trading (TBA), 309
Tokyo, Japan, 41, 42, 473–479, 507–508
Trade blotters, 404–405
Trade books
  book-level risk, 428–430
  order books, 162, 166, 168, 170–171
  production cycle, 472–479
  trading system, 396, 397, 404–414, 419–420

Trade database, 405
Trade management trading systems, 418
Trade pricing trading systems, 400–404
Trader, as job, 56–57
TradeWeb, 140–141, 260, 400, 401
Trading, 30–31, 113–123
  (*See also specific topics*)
Trading book, 46, 125–126, 129, 428–430, 435
Trading divisions, sell-side firm, 44–45
Trading floor, 45–46
Trading platforms, 400
Trading strategy, 414
Trading systems, 395–422
  algorithmic trading, 414–418
  defined, 395
  development of, 421
  ideal integrated, 420–422
  life cycle of, 395–397
  position management, 418–420
  recommended reading, 538
  solicitation systems, 397–400
  technology and, 50
  trade books, 396, 397, 404–414
  trade management, 418
  trade pricing, 400–404
Treasury bills, 123–124
Treasury Inflation-Protected Securities (TIPS),
  100
Treasury markets and securities, 97–150
  auctions of, 104–112
  BrokerTec, 113–120
  as commercial paper, 16–17
  credit risk, 327–328
  eSpeed, 113–120
  Federal Reserve System, 70–87, 104–105,
    226–227
  financial futures, 205–215, 218
  government spreads, 327
  interest-rate setting, 78–80
  interest-rate swaps, 254, 257–258
  issuance of securities, 10–11, 78–80, 99–112
  mechanism for, 10–12, 128–132
  vs. mortgage trading, 306–307, 314, 316–317
  panic response, 71–72
  primary market, 104–112
  PnL, 132–148
  public debt structure, 97–104
  recommended reading, 526–528
  reference data, 342, 343, 344, 349, 351
  risk and hedging, 136–138
  secondary market, 112–123
  securities switch and swap, 120–123

Treasury markets and securities (*Cont.*):
  STRIPS, 125–128
  TradeWeb, 140–141
  trading modes and strategies, 138–148
Trends in financial technology, 514–519
Triple-witching days, 284

UAT (user acceptance testing), 487
Unemployment, 68
Unit code test, 486
Updated orders, 165–166
Updates, production cycle, 464–465, 471
User acceptance testing (UAT), 487
Users (*See* Software system development cycle)

Valuation, 151, 156–157, 273–280, 429
Value-at-risk (VaR), 431–434, 436, 437
Value Line Index, 228, 231
Vanguard, 185
VaR (value-at-risk), 431–434, 436, 437
Vega, 283
Vendors, financial data, 346–348, 379–383
Volatility, 262, 276–280, 290, 450
VWAP, 178–179

WAC (weighted-average coupon), 302–303, 305
Wall Street Journal, 180
WAN (wide area networks), 477–478
Warning messages, system code, 500
Weeklies, 443
Weighted-average coupon (WAC), 302–303,
  305
Wide area networks (WAN), 477–478
Wilshire indices, 182
Workstations, 482
Writing code, software, 483–485

Yield, 7–8, 79, 80, 304–305
Yield curves, 78–96
  bond analytics libraries, 361–364
  defined, 78–80
  features of, 80–84
  futures conversion factors, 207–211
  inflation, 84–87
  interest-rate markets, 94–96
  macroeconomic influences, 87–91
  proprietary trading ("prop"), 141–148
  risk premiums, 84–87
  supply and demand, 93–94
  Treasury, 78–87

Zero-coupon bonds, 125

ABOUT THE AUTHOR

Alex Kuznetsov, Ph.D., is a theoretical physicist by training, but since 1997 he has pursued a career in the financial industry. He worked at several Wall Street firms, including Goldman Sachs and Barclays Capital, before joining Credit Suisse, where he currently is a director in proprietary trading technology. Alex's professional interests include algorithmic trading, electronic market making, econometric modeling, and interest-rate derivatives. He has a long-standing interest in educating his technical colleagues about the fundamentals of Wall Street business and technology, and to that end he has developed and taught training courses for that audience. This book is outgrowth of those efforts.

Alex was born in Kiev, Ukraine, and studied in Moscow, Russia, before coming to the United States in 1991. He and his family now live in New Jersey.